SAILING THE SEAS

A VOYAGER'S GUIDE TO OCEANIC GETAWAYS

EXPLORED BY DAYYAN ARMSTRONG & ROSS BEANE

gestalten

SAILING COLLECTIVE

CONTENT

THE ART OF VOYAGING, P. 4
THE SAILING COLLECTIVE STORY, P. 6
1   GULF OF NAPLES, ITALY, P. 8
2   PONTINE ISLANDS, ITALY, P. 20
3   COASTAL SICILY, ITALY, P. 32
4   AEOLIAN ARCHIPELAGO, ITALY, P. 44
5   SARDINIA, ITALY, P. 56
6   MAJORCA, SPAIN, P. 66
7   STRAIT OF BONIFACIO, FRANCE, P. 78
8   COTE D'AZUR, FRANCE, P. 90
9   DODECANESE ISLANDS, GREECE, P. 100
10 SARONIC ISLANDS, GREECE, P. 110

11 GULF OF FETHIYE, TURKEY, P. 122	**17** BRITISH VIRGIN ISLANDS, P. 190
12 ŠIBENIK ARCHIPELAGO, CROATIA, P. 132	**18** DOMINICA & MARTINIQUE, P. 204
13 DALMATIANS ISLANDS, CROATIA, P. 144	**19** GRENADA & THE GRENADINES, P. 214
14 PENOBSCOT BAY, USA, P. 156	**20** PHANG NGA BAY, THAILAND, P. 226
15 SAN JUAN ISLANDS, USA, P. 168	**21** NOSY BE, MADAGASCAR, P. 238
16 SANTA CATALINA ISLAND, USA, P. 180	**22** LEEWARD ISLANDS, FRENCH POLYNESIA, P. 250

THE ART OF VOYAGING

Sailing connects us with our ancestors. At one point in time, someone stood at a shoreline looking out towards a vast horizon wondering what lies beyond. Their curiosity drove them to harness the wind. Each of the many cultures that invented sailing did it differently and with varying motives, but always underpinned by that same thirst to chase the horizon.

Today, it's this very curiosity of our ancestral roots that binds our affinity with the sea. We experience our world differently when we set sail, the tranquility and solitude while we slowly glide upon the water is balanced by the very real risks and joys of being a sailor.

Arriving at new ports, we are welcomed by a new culture. From island to island, sea to sea, we observe and learn the beautiful diversity of each community living by the coast. Aboard the vessel, a crew creates its own community, living and working together in motion with the common goal: to see the world in all of its life-changing magnificence.

Over the course of almost a decade, Sailing Collective has accumulated nearly six years at sea, exploring coastal regions from Madagascar to French Polynesia, Maine to Grenada, Majorca to Turkey. The information included here is a sweeping survey that covers a small slice of sailing itineraries as they have been experienced during a 10-year period of Sailing Collective voyages. This book seeks to understand human and natural history as seen from a mariner's perspective sailing these coastlines and island regions. The better a sailor understands the natural elements, cultural history, customs, and traditions, the more meaningful their voyage will be. Serving less as a technical guide, this book was created to inspire.

There's an art to voyaging and each sailor will express it differently. This book is not intended to be a traditional step-by-step manual but is rather aimed to stimulate the imagination and incite adventure. It goes without saying that there is more to see and do in every destination than we've outlined in these pages.

Equally, efforts have been made to include harder-to-find and more adventurous routes in each location, but, in order to ensure this book doesn't become encyclopedic in length, certain details were left out. For example, we trust that if you sail the British Virgin Islands you won't fail to notice the popular, third-largest island of Virgin Gorda, but our chapter on BVI doesn't include it. The thousands of sailors who anchor along its shoreline will have their own recommendations to share. The intention of this book is to build your own curiosity to hear the stories of those who have sailed there and better yet, experience it for yourself. The same goes for each chapter: locations listed are to paint a picture of the tenor of the itinerary and not provide an exhaustive list.

Any adventure at sea, whether it is circumnavigating Tortola or completing a transatlantic passage, will be made safer by preparedness. Mariners collect a library of books, maps, and charts in preparation for an expedition. Good skippers spend their time thinking about the potential obstacles ahead whereas a novice may only be focused on the nice breeze and calm waters. Be prepared for the wind to pick up and swell to build at any moment, for visibility to get worse, for equipment to fail and rigging to break. Proper preparation is not worrying about the future, it is anticipating the unknowns and it will serve you well when matters get serious.

Where charts and navigation instruction in this book have been provided, they are for reference and orientation. If a harbor approach is mentioned, it is to paint the picture for you and not a set of instructions on how to approach, which should always be done with your charts out and your wits about you. Incredible pilot guides have been written about most of these locations and we highly recommend that you set to sea with them in your ship's library.

For mariners who have the opportunity to sail an itinerary and become familiar with those waters, a deep-rooted bond is created. The more we learn about a place—be it weather forecasting, cultural traditions, or local cuisine—the better we understand it, and the more we enjoy the experience. But sailing is not just for sailors. Approaching a new place slowly by sea is an experience unmatched by many. There is a thrill of looking over charts and planning a course. Lifting anchor, setting sail, and navigating towards the next safe harbor requires focus and keeps our curiosity peaked. As you slowly make your approach, the island might feel familiar after pouring over charts, studying every detail and mark. When you arrive at the harbor, moor your boat after the passage and there you are, safely anchored in a new port of call.

Our memories are defined by our experiences. Our goal is to get you behind the helm of a boat on your own adventure. We sincerely hope that you replace each chapter of this book with the pages of your own logbook penned on the margins of a salt-stained chart. Your version will have pages that ours doesn't, and those will be the most meaningful ones. The discoveries made, the unexpected moments, the trials and hardships overcome, those are the prizes of life. We believe our ancestors would agree: there is no better place to find them than the deck of a boat under sail.

THE SAILING COLLECTIVE STORY

Sailing the Seas is co-written by Dayyan Armstrong and Ross Beane, the founders of Sailing Collective. The Collective was conceived in 2011 while we were in our mid-20's, fueled by our ambition to share knowledge and experiences. We set out with a team of mariners to create sailing experiences for the travel community by crafting itineraries around the world. The team of captains created a collective pool of information that was shared amongst us, in keeping with the mariners' tradition of swapping stories for better navigation.

Our early voyages were quite basic, with only one captain and a small group of adventurers. Everyone on board helped sail the ship and participate with the planning of the voyage ahead. In time, the philosophy of the organization shifted towards hospitality and we added a culinary program with on-board chefs, elevating the experience by marrying exploration and bespoke hospitality.

The aim was—and still is—to explore the world. Where there is a body of water, we'll find a sailboat and create an itinerary. Since our foundation, we have designed journeys through more than 40 archipelagos and coastlines worldwide.

Our work is underpinned by our sense of discovery. For instance, Sailing Collective captains do not typically scout locations before embarking with the community. This is deliberate. For a non-mariner, the opportunity to sail with a captain during their maiden voyage illuminates the spirit of exploration we strive to create. No matter how much time is put into advance planning, the subtleties of a location, from its culture to currents, will never fully be what was expected. We create itineraries but are not beholden to following them. If we sail past an island and we notice an unnamed cove on the charts, we'll drop our sails and see what there is to experience.

We came at sailing sideways, not through the local yacht club or being from a sailing family, but rather through our own curiosity. We were born in the mid-1980s and became brothers through the marriage of our respective parents at age 7. Growing up along the Gulf of Maine, old-timers taught us how to read charts and we'd sail along the Maine coast using dead reckoning. For us, sailing was a romance with the sea and a way to adventure beyond the shore. Hard learned lessons were imprinted on us from our successes and failures while we cruised home waters during our formative years.

The Gulf of Maine was our backyard, a difficult coastline to navigate as teenagers aboard our 24' sloop. We sailed along thousands of islands and numerous archipelagos in an area known for its jagged ridgeline and large tidal drop. The Gulf of Maine can go from a blue-skied afternoon to a foggy maze with hardly a moment's notice. These voyages created our understanding of what makes an expedition meaningful.

Our upbringing instilled in us a craving for knowledge and adventure. At age fourteen, Dayyan accompanied his mother in Bolivia during a semester-long research trip living among remote indigenous villages in the Andes. At age fifteen, Ross traveled with his father from southern Chile to Costa Rica, climbing some of South America's tallest mountains along the way. These events would become pinnacle experiences that shaped the future to come. Since then, we have spent a collective 30-plus years on and around sailboats, traveling worldwide.

But the journey isn't just about us, it's about the community that has formed around the Sailing Collective. Whether we are creating a new itinerary or writing a book about them, the Sailing Collective is the summation of our team's collective experience. So thank you to everyone who has been part of creating this history, to each captain, chef, photographer, and traveler who has joined our adventures, the thousands of wide-eyed explorers, each of whom has in one way or another shaped the information offered here. And for that, we are grateful.

DAYYAN & ROSS

ITALIAN CHARM IN THE GULF OF NAPLES

THIS BAY IS THE FABLED HOME OF THE SIRENS, THE MYTHICAL CREATURES WHO LURED ILL-FATED SAILORS ONTO THE ROCKS WITH THEIR ENCHANTING SONG. IN REALITY, THIS GRAND GULF IS AWASH WITH HISTORY.

Naples is a vibrant southern Italian city; home to indulgent cuisine, it is the birthplace of dried pasta and, yes, pizza. The region is also famous for being the site of the ancient city of Pompeii. This major port city is the jumping-off point for sailing the Sorrentine Peninsula and the Campanian Archipelago, including the seductive island of Capri. South of Sorrento, you'll find yourself along the coast of the Gulf of Salerno, where the famed towns of Amalfi and Positano sit tucked under formidable cliffs. Heading west from here, you can sail to the intoxicatingly wonderful Phlegraean Islands: Ischia, Procida, Vivara, and Nisida. Capri sits off the Sorrentine Peninsula between two gulfs, of Naples and Salerno, and has an international reputation as a retreat for artists, writers, and celebrities.

Homer's epic poem, the *Odyssey* (800 BC), depicts a voyage through this region, and several of the islands are described in recognizable detail, although the names have changed. Local residents don't doubt the existence of the fabled sirens, who lured Greek sailors onto the rocks, even if they have never heard them sing. Life at sea is the backbone of their society and its dangers are respected just as the merits are celebrated by local residents and visitors alike; as a sailor, you arrive at a welcome understanding of what it means to journey on the sea.

To understand sailing the Gulf of Naples, you must understand the city of Naples itself, with all its illustrious culture, family sentiment, organized chaos, and unique and beautiful magnetism. A look into Naples's past will help you understand the present. Cars have replaced the horse-drawn carts and fashion might have shifted, but, other than that, the streets look about the same as they have since the days of the Roman Empire. Out on the islands there are ripples of Neopolitan city life, mostly arriving on the daily ferries and going home again as the sun sets.

Italians come to the islands to fall into the groove of oceanic living. Families usually arrive during the summer months from the mainland to relax and offer their children

the delights of a childhood on the seashore that their grandparents experienced in much the same way before them. On a sunny day, when the wind is light, swimmers of all ages venture out from the rocks into the sea with all of the freedom of a school of dolphins, but when dark clouds linger in the sky and the sea turns dark and violent, children and adults alike stay inside, listening to the rain drive sideways onto their wooden shutters. On a sailboat you are even more tied to the rhythm of the sea. Get your quiet night at anchor in wilderness cove when the weather allows; take refuge in the safe harbor of a close-by seafaring town when it doesn't.

PROCIDA

Procida is the smallest island in the region and one that should not go unnoticed. It is perhaps the most untrammeled island, with the fewest visitors during the summer months, and a recommended first destination after leaving the busy ports of Naples under sail. Sandwiched between Ischia and Capri, this secret of an island is modest and wears its charm quietly, appearing like a forgotten land as you sail towards its shore. Home to two main harbors, one on either side of the island, and plenty of anchorages around them, access by boat is easy.

On the northeast coast lies Marina di Sancio Cattolico. The protected harbor here will provide great shelter in any inclement weather conditions. Ferries to Ischia and the mainland cycle on and off the docks all day, just outside the seawall of the marina. To the south you will find Corricella, the commercial fishing harbor used by both small local fishing boats and bigger trawlers; it has no space for visiting yachts. In settled weather you can anchor just off the seawall or further southwest along the beach. Buildings line the hill in disorganized rows of brightly painted yellows, pinks, blues, and reds, with houses built cascading down onto one another. Stairs wind their way through the alleyways of the steep neighborhood. Sat atop the settlement is a domed yellow church and, next to it, the Palazzo d'Avalos—a 16th century palace-turned-prison that sits majestically at the peak of the island, overlooking the bay.

Leading up to Corricella along the bay is a dramatic black sand beach, popular with the Neopolitan city dwellers who enjoy it on the weekend days during the hot summer months. Dinghy or swim ashore and you'll find yourself enjoying a refreshing beverage and a *granita al limone*—a shaved ice snack made with fresh local lemons, sold to you by an Italian working one of the beachside café stands. This beach is a long walk from town and often overlooked by the few tourists who show up on the island's shores. Luckily for sailors, you can drop anchor in the bay and arrive in style.

ISCHIA

Sitting just six nautical miles from Procida is the renowned island of Ischia—the largest of the Phlegraean Islands. Its volcanic origins left Ischia with an imposing mountain peak and the famed natural thermal baths that sit along the ocean's edge. Even when the island is busy, in the summer months, it is a quiet retreat compared to Naples; sailing by, you see its lush greenery and brightly colored flowers from afar. Vineyards and groves of olive trees sit on terraced farmland, high above the water. It is home to four safe marinas and some less

---

LOCAL SPECIALTY

The dish that symbolizes the local cuisine of Ischia is coniglio all'Ischitana, *an Ischian-style rabbit stew, which has been made for centuries because of the abundance of wild rabbits on the island (said to have been brought over by the Romans two millennia ago). There is dispute, however, regarding the proper way to prepare the dish. One side of Ischia prepares it with tomatoes, and the other side without.*

well-protected anchorages, including many secluded coves, accessible only by boat.

Anchoring at the foot of a castle is not an everyday activity, even for the most experienced sailors. The medieval castle, named Aragonese, sits imposingly high above the anchorage on the eastern coast of Ischia. The sea is deep, clear blue and the rocks have small trees clinging to their sheer faces below the ancient fortifications. On the horizon is Mount Vesuvius, and on the opposite shore is a charming village with streets along the water's edge that connect, via a long causeway, to the castle gates. Other travelers are braving the hot sun to explore; you cruise past them and tie off the dinghy to the seawall with your sailboat just a stone's throw away.

Even though the anchorage here is seductive enough, and it is possible to spend a lazy afternoon on deck just taking it all in, Aragonese Castle, is worth a few hours of exploration. It was originally built in 474 BC by Hiero I of Syracuse and has been a pinnacle of military infrastructure ever since. This imposing fortification served as a lookout, its dramatic site atop sheer sea cliffs making it remarkably effective; inhabitants could spot invading forces hoping to strike and take control of the island's resources. Most of the castle is intact and open to the public until sunset. The abundance of beautiful spaces now serves multiple functions, housing art-restoration seminars, a café, more than one museum, and a church. Grapevines grow on the steep terraces inside the castle walls and wine made from their fruit can be ordered at the café.

Baia di Sorgeto, located along the southern coast of the island, is a rocky and steep cove, home to a small restaurant and a natural thermal bath. Steaming hot freshwater flows from the island into the cove and, when it hits the salty ocean water, it creates a natural thermal bath in the rocky water along the beach. Local residents have created various pools among the rocks, where you can lounge in shallow waters enjoying a drink or a snack from the on-site restaurant. People do arrive by car, but Sorgeto is truly best seen by sailboat. In front of the cove is deep water, where you can anchor and then swim to shore to enjoy this natural wonderland. The restaurant serves simple yet delicious food and is a perfect option for lunch.

NEAPOLITAN FOOD

The first pizzeria in Italy and the entire world is Antica Pizzeria Port'Alba, opened in Naples in 1830 and is still open today.
The classic Margherita pizza, native to Naples, was named after Queen Margherita Maria Teresa Giovanna of Savoy after her visit to Naples in the 1800s.

CAPRI

From the watchtowers of Ischia's castle, Capri appears in the heat of the summer haze, 15 nautical miles away. The island sits off the coast of the Sorrentine Peninsula and is perhaps the most famous island in the Mediterranean. Sheer cliffs rise hundres of meters from the ocean along most of Capri's shoreline. Only a single marina on the north, and a small, fair-weather landing on the south, grant you access to all that waits onshore. Since its earliest times, the island has had a prestige that draws interesting and high-profile visitors. Emperors had their summer palaces built here, to enjoy the engaging vistas of Mount Vesuvius and the Bay of Naples. Aristocrats and rulers have called Capri home during the summer months throughout the ages. Artists, writers, and painters have immortalized it during their stays on the island.

Sailing, nautical mile after nautical mile, the scale of the island unfolds until you are in the shadow of the cliffs and realize how truly grand it all is. Warm orange sunlight shining on its western cliff during the late afternoon looks unreal, like a painted backdrop behind

a movie set. The Punta Carena Lighthouse, at the southwest tip of the island, sits high above the water. In 2019, the last of the lighthouse keepers left their post on the cliff peak, putting to rest 152 years of active duty.

On the eastern shore is the Blue Grotto—a cave that is famous for its stunning blue hue in the afternoon, as the sun shines through underwater passes to illuminate it. It is too deep to anchor at the entrance to the grotto and the only access is by local tour boat, one of which will pick you up from your boat and take you around the cave on a short tour for a per-person fee. The experience of waiting in line to enter detracts from the majesty of the cave itself to the extent that this is not a "must see" stop, despite its international fame.

The town of Capri runs through the notch between two peaks on the island's spine. The waterfront on both sides is lined with mega yachts at anchor, in a "who's who" of the ultra-wealthy. Marina Grande is often packed and is very expensive but there is no suitable anchorage in rough weather for small boats, so it may be your only viable option. In settled weather you can sail past the lighthouse and anchor on the south side of the island at Piccola; the anchorage can be rolly even on fairly calm days but the holding is good, in deep sand. The famed rock archway on Faraglione di Mezzo, big enough to take a small boat through, is on the east side of the anchorage. Once situated, dinghy ashore to dine at any number of quintessentially Italian restaurants that zig-zag up the windy steep roads connecting to the port on the other side of the island.

AMALFI

On the sail from Capri to Amalfi you pass Licosa, San Pietro, and La Galetta, three small islands that were the home of the sirens in Homer's *Odyssey*. Half woman, half bird, the sirens would sing beautiful songs to lure sailors onto the rocks and are largely regarded today as symbolic of the dangers of the sea in Greek mythology. Sirens or not, you can venture a brief stop to swim on these rocky islands, but best not to spend the night, as the anchorages are poorly protected and you might fall prey to the siren song and end up on the rocks if your anchor drags.

The town of Amalfi itself sits in a dramatic valley, cut into a steep coastline that is famous for its combination of rugged terrain and beautiful architecture. The cliffs that dwarf the cathedral in town only serve to make its grandiose steps and Italian Gothic facade more impressive. A very nice marina with floating docks sits in the inner harbor and municipal tie-ups are available along the inner seawall. A short walk to the Piazza del Duomo in the center of town brings you to lively cafés and a very nice bakery. Venture up alleyways that lead off from the square to explore the winding routes that locals stroll every day on their way to the market by the water.

Amalfi is a striking place to sail to and has a long history of seafaring, from the mythical to the more recent. The inventor of the maritime compass as we know it today, with a magnetic needle floating under glass, was born in Amalfi around 1,000 years ago. Even before that, Amalfi was the capital of the maritime republic known as the Duchy of Amalfi, an independent state whose merchants dominated Mediterranean and Italian trade during the 10th and 11th centuries.

~

The Gulf of Naples is a very enchanting itinerary that takes mariners across seas that have been sailed for millennia. By the period of time in which Homer's heroes sailed the Tyrrhenian Sea, these islands were already being developed by great civilizations and the ongoing legacy can be observed while sailing here. While some sailing areas do highlight nature or great sailing, the Gulf of Naples itinerary throws the focus onto idyllic Italian architecture, and a unique and thriving culture.

COLORFUL LOCAL HOUSES AND BEACH LIFE (ABOVE). A FISHERMAN PREPARING NETS IN PROCIDA (BELOW, RIGHT).

CAPTAIN'S NOTES *GULF OF NAPLES*

RECOMMENDED ITINERARY

Corricella, Procida
40° 45'25"N, 14° 1'35"E
Anchor along the northeast side of the bay, outside the breakwater. Proceed with care along the east and middle passage, as there are shallow areas along the shoal. Anchor and take a stern line to the breakwater, though only during calm seas, as the anchorage is exposed to the north, east, and south. During inclement weather, sail to the north marina: there are 490 berths with good shelter from the prevailing westerly winds.

Aragonese Castle, Ischia
40° 43'44"N, 13° 57'40"E
Anchor in 8–13 meters on the south or north side of the castle. Holding is better in the south, with easier dinghy access to shore. Do not anchor inside the moorings but close. Be sure when dropping anchor that, if the wind swings south during the night, you have plenty of swing room so as not to collide with the fishing boats on moorings. Anchoring closer to the castle is fine. Be cautious of a large rock indicated on Navionics in the anchorage closer to the shoreline. There is a water taxi stand that will do pick ups and drop offs for 2 euros, per person.

Sant'Angelo, Ischia
40°41'45"N, 13° 53'45"E
Anchor in 6–10 meters of very good sand, with excellent holding and plenty of room. Anchor further away from the beach or closer to town, but do not block the entrance (anchoring is also not advised in strong southerly winds). In peak season, there is an anchorage fee with a charge of 10 euros per bag of trash. Dinghy in and tie up anywhere safe. The marina is very nice, with quality services, but reservations are required and we recommend calling a day in advance. It is protected from all but strong easterly wind. Radio in when arriving and be prepared for a stern-to tie.

Porto di Amalfi Marina Coppola, Amalfi
40° 37'51"N, 14° 36'6"E
Anchoring off Amalfi is difficult because the coast is very exposed, and should be done in a calm season only. Select moorings are available, but be sure to check with the local mariners, as many moorings are for fishermen only. Berth along the quay using the bowlines provided by the marina.

RECOMMENDED ANCHORAGES

Aragonese Castle, Ischia
Sant'Angelo, Ischia
Sorrento
Marina de Coricella, Procida
Marina Piccola, Capri

ITINERARY DURATION

8 days, including Pontine Islands
5 days, including Amalfi Coast

PREVAILING WINDS

Wind patterns in this part of the Tyrrhenian Sea are variable, with no major prevailing winds. In inclement weather, safe anchorages and marinas must be chosen wisely to avoid rough, and unsafe anchorages. Because the islands are exposed, without shoreline protection, the seas easily pick up and become agitated, which can make for uncomfortable passage-making. When seas are calm, the wind tends to be light in the morning and switches to a light westerly in the afternoon. Checking the weather daily is important and asking harbor workers for their prediction is recommended.

SEASON

May through to October

FOOD

The Campanian region is known for its wine, tomatoes, dried pasta, and seafood, and the best provisioning is found at small, family-run stores selling specialty items. Fish stands work with select fishing fleets and markets offer fresh vegetables produced by small regional farms. The Piennolo del Vesuvio tomato is a DOP product grown at the base of Mount Vesuvius and is sweet, with a unique teardrop shape; it is commonly found in the local provisioning markets.

GOOD TO KNOW

Magnetic variance
Magnetic Declination: +3° (EAST)

ITALY
N
W
E
S
PHLEGRAEAN ISLANDS
PROCIDA
ISCHIA
MARINA DE CORICELLA
ARAGONESE
CASTLE
SANT'ANGELO
NAPLES
GULF OF NAPLES
SORRENTO
AMALFI
AMALFI COAST
CAPRI
MARINA PICCOLA
TYRRHENIAN SEA
0
10
NAUTICAL MILES
NOT FOR NAVIGATION

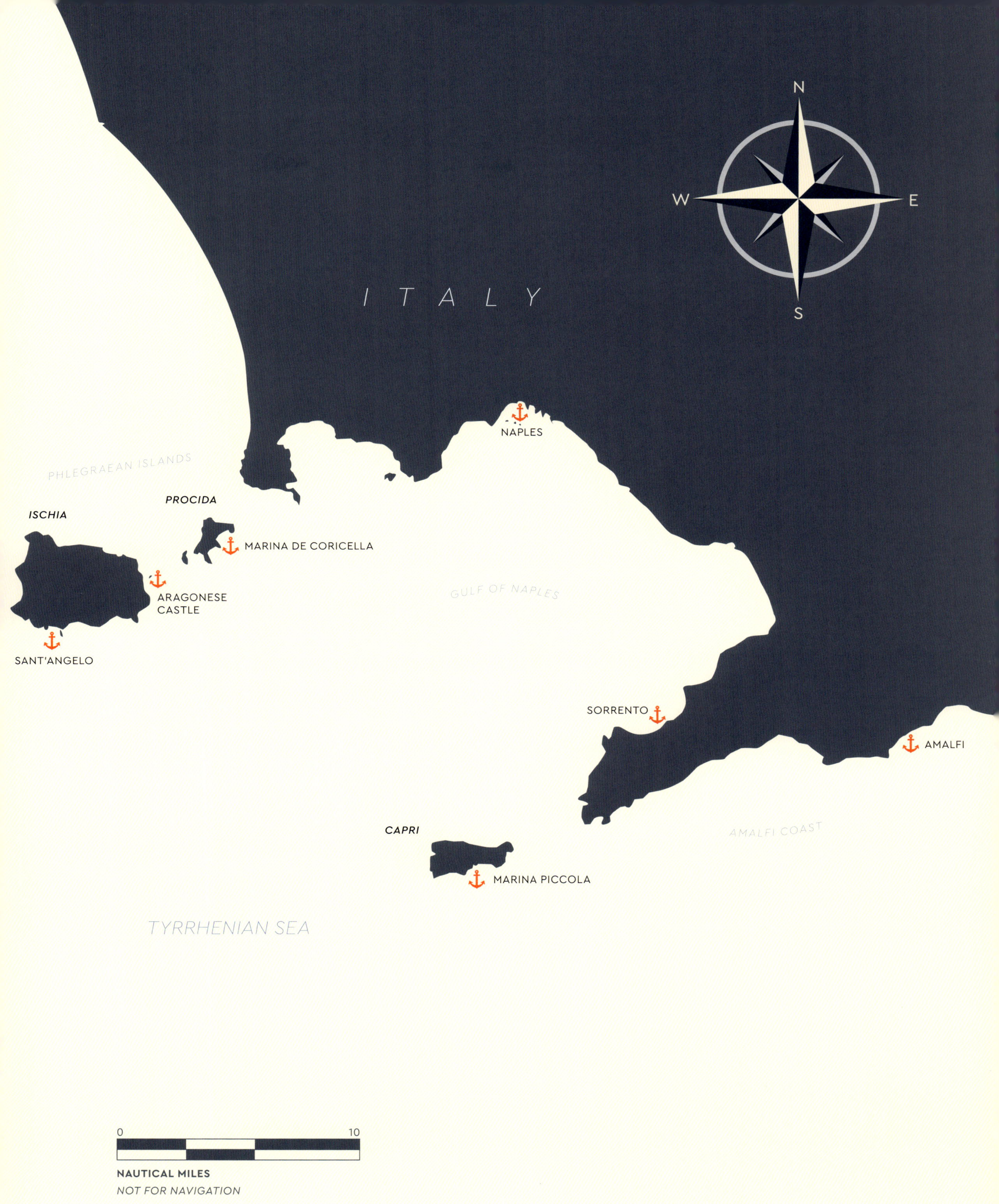

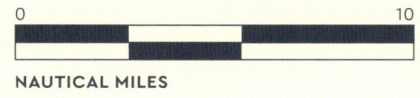

PEARLS OF THE MEDITERRANEAN

THIS MYSTERIOUS ARCHIPELAGO OFF THE COAST OF ITALY FEELS LIKE ITS OWN UNIVERSE, SEPARATE FROM THE MAINLAND. THE PONTINE ISLANDS FASCINATE VISITORS WITH THEIR ALLURING BEAUTY, BOTH ABOVE AND BELOW THE SEA'S SURFACE.

Known for clear, fluorescent-seeming waters, strikingly beautiful natural scenery, idyllic vertical towns, and incredible seafood, these islands have been dubbed the "Pearls of the Mediterranean." A voyage to the Pontine Islands is a journey to a lesser-known way of life that moves at its own pace—each harbor home to idyllic Italian island culture and natural splendor.

Sailors setting out to explore the Pontine begin their voyage in the Gulf of Naples and sail about 60 nautical miles westward, departing from one of several available ports—including Procida, Sorrento, Castellammare di Stabia, and Naples itself—and passing the islands of Capri and Ischia on the way. As stunning as the Amalfi Coast, Capri and other famed seaside villages may be, the opportunity to sail these lesser-explored islands and coves is not to be missed. This sailor's paradise is located further out into the Tyrrhenian Sea than other islands in the region; leaving safe-harbor may feel like sailing into the open ocean. Yet, in time, you see the cliffs of Ponza from afar. It is a long journey, but one that comes with many rewards.

Le Isole Ponziane, as they are known in Italian, are a cluster of six islands including Ponza—the largest in the archipelago—Palmarola, Gavi, Zannone, Ventotene, and Santo Stefano. Ponza and Ventotene are the only two inhabited islands in the group, with just one small restaurant on Palmarola. Both Ponza and Ventotene have medium-sized towns that are home to islanders and vacationing Italians, mostly from Naples or Rome, who spend their summers enjoying the delightful blue waters and bountiful landscapes along the islands' shorelines. International tourism is not so prevalent on these islands, compared to nearby Capri or Ischia. These islands, whose culture and traditions have their roots in the days of the Roman Empire, served as a retreat for wealthy citizens in ancient times, and sometimes as an escape for prominent exiles. Today, the summer residents are escaping from a very different Rome, aiming to relax and enjoy a pace of life unlike that found in the busy cities.

The Pontine Islands offer not only great conditions for sailing, but also numerous accessible harbors; picturesque seaside villages have local charm and laid-back attitude in abundance. It is a destination that will make you want to stay awhile once you have

PONTINE ISLANDS
ITALY

21

made the voyage to its shores. Filled with hard-to-access grottos, gorgeously desolate pebble beaches, and remote and dramatic cliff formations, the Pontine Islands are a true playground for mariners and are best seen from the deck of a boat under sail.

VENTOTENE

Ventotene is the closest to the Gulf of Naples and often the first port of call when sailing to the Pontine Islands. Like the rest of the nearby islands, Ventotene was established during the Roman Empire. Emperor Augustus constructed a grand villa on the island as a site on which to celebrate holidays and as an escape from the politics of Rome. On this little island lived Augustus' daughter, Julia the Elder, banished from Rome following an adultery scandal and under watch in her palace for the rest of her days. Only a long day's sail from the edges of Rome, Ventotene was convenient for the elite Romans who needed an escape from the capital, for reasons both good and bad.

Over the last 2,000 years, the island has not lost its charm and the traditional and beautifully idyllic village of the same name has changed only a little. The population is currently 300 yearly residents, the population jumping to about 700 Italians during the summer months. During peak season, harbors are full with transient sailors on their Pontine Islands itinerary. Stepping off your boat and onto the island is like going back in time: children swim in the ancient grottos lined with ancient carved steps that lead into the sea, while grandparents enjoy conversations in the island's town square with the stresses of modern life nowhere felt.

Cala Rossano and Porto Vecchio (the Roman port) are the two harbors in Ventotene accommodating transient sailors. Porto Vecchio is the more beautiful of the two, with its history immediately observable. It lies in a man-made basin excavated by the Romans, its reinforced harbor walls built using ancient concrete. The construction sits strong and protects this town from the violent Tyrrhenian Sea during the fierce and abrasive storms that pass by throughout the year. The first sign of civilization when approaching from the east is a white lighthouse standing at the entrance to the port. To the north of the lighthouse is the town center, which sailors reach via a famed yellow zig-zag pedestrian walkway.

Local fishing boats are very active in the harbor. Directly past the transient slips for sailboats, fishermen prep their nets and sort their fish after a long day at sea. The fleet of fishing boats is colorful and the fishermen's appearance traditional, even as

> A voyage to the Pontine Islands is a journey to a lesser-known way of life that moves at its own pace.

fishing practices have modernized. An astute visitor can detect a unique Ventotene dialect of Italian, particular to the island, when listening to the fishermen and locals talk among themselves. Along the port are ancient Roman caves originally used by fishermen and mariners for storage. These spaces have recently been converted into restaurants and a wine shop that sells local varieties; an island-made Amaro that's crafted from the wild arugula cultivated only here on Ventotene is worth seeking out.

PONZA

Ponza is the largest island in the archipelago and also the most popular. The small island is 24 nautical miles west from Ventotene and arguably one of the most celebrated in the Tyrrhenian Sea for its wild beauty and idyllic island lifestyle. Compared to Elba or Ischia, two other nearby islands, Ponza isn't that large, but once you reach the island, you could easily enjoy weeks sailing around the cliff-lined coastline.

The eastern face is known for its steep limestone cliffs that drop dramatically into the emerald sea below. When making the approach to Ponza, sailing west from Ventotene, the first thing you'll notice is these jagged outcrops, brightly illuminated by the sun. The anchorages are lined by chalk-colored white-and-beige rocks, with lush greenery in the layered landscape above. The anchorage is busy during the summer months with boats of all sizes lining the coast, from mega yachts to dinghys. Swimming off the boat, looking up at the dramatic rocks above, is a highlight; the air is fresh and pure and you can see octopuses and other local fish along the sandy seafloor.

The safe anchorages scattered around the island draw sailors to seek refuge from multifarious winds that blow from all directions from the main harbor. These shelters located on the east side of Ponza are referred to by locals as "porto." Eight mini-marinas along the bay are available for sailors to dock alongside while exploring the town. The finger piers extend from the shoreline and can accommodate roughly ten boats at a time, and reservations for these spots should be made in advance. Lining "porto" is a seawall that protects the center of town. Local fishing boats and visiting sailors can dock along stern-to depending on the available space.

The main town of Ponza is situated in a small bay protected from westerly winds. The port has one of the most spectacular harbor entrances across all of the Mediterranean, and entering by boat is a truly unique experience. The colorful town of Ponza is equal parts charming and sophisticated—the type of island town that inspires sailors to dock and explore, pretending they're locals if only for an afternoon. There are cascading, colorful houses connected by winding walkways and small roads. Restaurants, gelaterias, and fish markets line the streets.

Standing in town looking out, your eyes run along the limestone cliffs of the eastern coast and out to sea. Take a break from boat life and venture into town for the celebrated tradition of aperitivo—a time during the early evening hours to enjoy Italian snacks and a cocktail such as a Negroni or a Campari soda with friends. Numerous restaurants on the island offer menus showcasing produce from the island and seafood from its waters.

PALMAROLA

Palmarola is a small island located eight nautical miles from Ponza and a day's sail from the main port. The island is characterized by its sheer beauty and the dramatic size of the sheer cliffs along the eastern coast. There are a variety of anchorages on Palmarola—ideal locations in which to spend the afternoon swimming from your sailboat through various grottos and beaches. The anchorage off a small island called Fornina is positively lunar: the cliff face and the island itself are cratered like the surface of the moon.

One restaurant is open during the summer season to serve sailors and the boats shuttling travelers from nearby Ponza. The restaurant serves local pasta dishes and fish that has been freshly caught by Ponza's fishermen. It is located on a west-facing pebble beach with gorgeous and rewarding sunset views. Most sailors decide to depart Palmarola and sail towards Ponza to drop anchor in soft sand along the eastern coast.

WINE PRODUCTION

Antiche Cantine Migliaccio is the local wine from Ponza. Emanuele Vittorio and Luciana Sabino went into production in 2000 after preserving the ancient wine producing traditions while adding modern techniques. Four varieties are produced with Biancolella blended with Forastera the most popular. Annually, only 8,500 bottles are produced.

~

The Pontine Islands make up one of the most unique archipelagos in all the Tyrrhenian Sea and they are widely celebrated among sailors because of their extraordinary beauty and unique characteristics. Their isolation is in perfect contrast to the bustling hubs of Rome and Naples. Exploring the history, natural beauty, and intriguing Italian island culture is an experience that's highly recommended for sailors and all curious travelers alike. The Pontine Islands are among Italy's finest and most romantic islands to sail.

PENSIONE SILVIA ON PONZA

Pensione Silvia is a small restaurant and local pension run by Paula Silvia, third generation to operate the establishment. Located in the bay of Santa Maria, Silvia offers authentic Pontine dishes that showcase the ingredients of the island and serving local wine from the island. The restaurant sits along a pebble beach with views of town, which eliminate at sunset. The outdoor seating area is covered by bamboo siding setting the scene for a non-assuming but spectacular dining experience. The house special is simple pasta dish: Paccheri with swordfish served with a fish-based sauce and rossed with spicy arugula.

PONTINE ISLANDS | ITALY

CAPTAIN'S NOTES *PONTINE ISLANDS*

RECOMMENDED ITINERARY

Ventotene
40° 47'49"N, 13° 26'2"E
Berth in Porto Vecchio. Go bow-to the quay on the west side of the harbor. This is good shelter, though there is a surge with the northwest wind. Laid moorings are available at most berths.

Ponza
40° 53'48"N, 12° 57'39"E
24 nautical miles from Ventotene is Ponza, where you can berth in Ponza Harbor. There are several marinas in the bay; go stern-to or dock alongside the pontoon dock as directed. The harbor is protected in all weather except east-northeast wind. During inclement weather, the dockmaster may not allow boats to dock. Pontoons are numerous, and reservations should be made in advance during the high season.

Cala del Porto, Isola Palmarola
40° 56'28"N, 12° 51'15"E
Anchor in 5 meters of sand in Cala del Porto, located on the northwest side of the island. The anchorage is open to the west and caution is recommended during strong westerly wind.

RECOMMENDED ANCHORAGES

Cala Frontone, Ponza
Cala Gaetano, Ponza
Cala Chiaia di Luna, Ponza
Cala Feola, Ponza
Faraglione di Mezzogiorno, Palmarola
Cala del Porto, Palmarola
Cala Rossano, Ventotene

ITINERARY DURATION

4 days, recommended sailing the Pontine Islands

9 days if extending itinerary to the Gulf of Naples

PREVAILING WIND

Prevailing winds blow from northwest to southwest, and pick up in the late afternoon. In summer, the *Sirocco* wind can blow up from the Sahara, bringing humid weather. The *Libeccio* wind blows from the southwest, and the *Tramontana* is a strong north-northeast wind that blows from the Alps, often at gale force. When the *Libeccio* blows, the seas become rough and passage between Ventotene and Ponza is not advised.

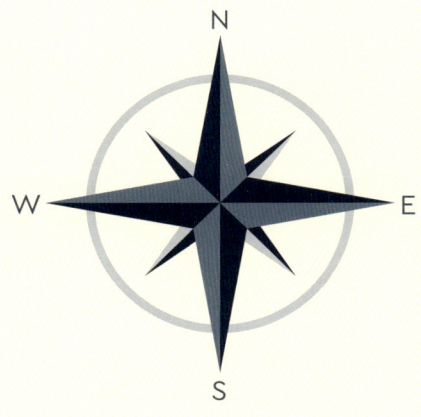

TYRRHENIAN SEA

CALA PARATA GRANDE   PORT VECCHIO

ISOLA DI SANTO STEFANO

ISOLA DI VENTOTENE

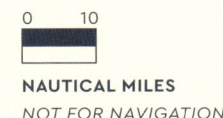

NAUTICAL MILES
NOT FOR NAVIGATION

SEASON

Sailing is best between late May through to the middle of October. Harbors are closed during the winter season and the winds are quite unpredictable.

FOOD

Try local delicacies such as *Zuppa di Lenticcie di Ventotene* (Ventotene lentil soup with octopus), with the local tipple—*Amaro alla Rughetta di Ventotene*, made from island wild rocket. Visit the Antiche Cantine Migliaccio, in the region of Lazio, to sample local wines.

GOOD TO KNOW

Swimming
The largest of the Pontine Islands offers a range of unique experiences. Anchor off Arco del Parroco in Cala d'Inferno and swim through the archway located off the shoreline. Good, enjoyable swimming can also be had on Cala Fonte and in the bay of Cala Gaetano, where the shoreline is made up of dramatic volcanic rock formations. It is possible to rent a vintage Citroen Méhari and circumnavigate the island by car if you are looking for adventure on land.

Ventotene
Walk from the port in Ventotene for gelato at Zi'Amalia and dine at Ristorante Da Benito. Shops located inside Roman caves are located along Via Porto Romano and you can round out your day with a swim in the bay of Scoglitiello.

Magnetic variance
Magnetic Declination: +3° (EAST)

ANCIENT CULTURE AND RUGGED BEAUTY

THIS GRAND ISLAND HAS WELCOMED VISITORS VOYAGING ACROSS THE MEDITERRANEAN IN ITS FAMED PORTS FOR MILLENNIA. SAILING ALONG THE COAST OF SICILY IS A JOURNEY THROUGH LAYERS OF HISTORY.

There is no single way to describe Sicily. Its multifaceted layers of landscape and culture defy classification. The island rises up proudly and powerfully from the depths of the Mediterranean Sea and has a cultural history that spans thousands of years. The beauty and bounty found here have long been praised by its early discoverers, by seafaring empires and pirates alike—from the Greeks to the Byzantines, Spaniards, Arabs, and Normans. Its history is rich and varied, with waves of invaders having left their influence on the culture, and new traditions being assimilated and passed down through the generations. Modern Sicily is the benefactor of its storied past. Culture and tradition here are worldly and unique, as Sicilians have gleaned the best of each passing empire and shaped it all into what, today, is distinctly their own.

Sicily has been at the crossroads of maritime activity since the earliest of Mediterranean civilizations. With only 78 nautical miles between western Sicily and Tunisia, this island sits in the central passageway for many mariners and the island simply cannot be avoided when navigating this region, even though most sailors choose to cruise the Aeolian Islands or simply sail by during a longer passage across the Mediterranean. The island is big, the southern coast can be rough, and safe harbors are not always abundant.

Sailing the northern or southern route around the island offers two very different experiences. Sailing north through the Strait of Messina, which divides Sicily from Calabria, conveniently leads you round towards the port town of Milazzo, where you can make the jump to the Aeolian Islands. Continuing westward, a 45-nautical-mile sail will take you to Cefalù, and Palermo is just an afternoon's voyage from there. The other option is a southern voyage, bypassing the major ports of Sicily altogether and heading towards Malta or Pantelleria; this may be the best route if your end destination is Majorca or the Atlantic Ocean.

On land and at sea, Sicily has known hardship: earthquakes, plague, and a multitude of volcanic eruptions, as well as thieves, pirates, and raiders, have all left their mark on the island over the decades. From monarchical swindling during the 200-year Spanish rule to the Ottoman ransacking of cities, tumult

is a distinctive part of Sicily's complex history. Each invasion brought about new voices and visions, however, and the evolving culture of the island found its voice among the merging influences brought in from afar. So, during your sailing voyage, explore this great island's fascinating landscape and dynamic culture.

PALERMO

Nearly all sailors cruising the north coast of the island will sail towards Palermo, the largest city in Sicily and home to the largest port, at the center of Sicily's maritime way of life. The marina is crowded with sailboats and those walking towards the waterfront from the city's edge see masts peek out from behind the buildings. Palermo is home to charter bases for sailors headed east towards the Aeolian Islands or west towards the Aegadian Islands, including Favignana. The harbor also attracts sailors making longer passages eastward or westward across the sea. With numerous small harbors and coves on either side of the city, set your waypoint towards the port to explore this captivating cityscape.

> **Palermo is a place of contrasts: old-world beauty and decadence meets with a hovering sense of decay and a persevering culture.**

The municipality is situated at the heart of the vast Conca d'Oro ("Golden Shell") bay. Oscar Wilde wrote in a letter to his lover, Robbie Ross: "It is beautiful, the most beautifully situated in the world—it dreams away its life in the Gold Conca, the exquisite valley that lies between two seas." When wandering from the docks into the historical center of Palermo, it is easy to be overwhelmed by both the magnificence and mess of this city. The center itself has a rich history and many architectural gems. Founded by the Phoenicians, Palermo was once an important Carthaginian stronghold until it was conquered by the Romans in 254 BC.

The city's wealth has come and gone, creating layers of splendor and destruction that can be seen within its bustling streets. For every baroque-style aristocratic palace with bougainvillea-lined gardens, you'll find a century-old damaged building that is boarded up and lies crumbling, covered in graffiti. It is an intriguing place of contrasts: old-world beauty and decadence meets with a hovering sense of decay and a persevering culture.

Hidden urban passageways, exquisite cathedrals, beach access, and statement-making cuisine make Palermo the perfect home base and entry point to kick-off a Sicilian adventure. Sail here to eat spaghetti tossed with buttery sea urchins, to wander the enchanting streets at night, to experience the chaos and beauty that covers every street, to simply get lost in it all.

CEFALÙ

Across the hundreds of nautical miles of coastline, there are endless itinerary possibilities. The harbors on the island that historically became the main maritime areas, such as Marsala, Palermo, Catania, and Siracusa, are some of the most beautiful to sail to. These ports were responsible for imports and exports to inland Sicily during the onset of regional trade within the Mediterranean and large cities developed around their harbors. Today, when you sail past, you might decide to stop at one of these historic urban ports to enjoy a few days in a bustling metropolis. Even solitude-loving sailors can enjoy the thrill of being at the center of it all in a good port city.

Departing Palermo and voyaging east, you will sail by the seaside town of Cefalù, which is roughly 38 nautical miles away; setting this town as a waypoint during your passage

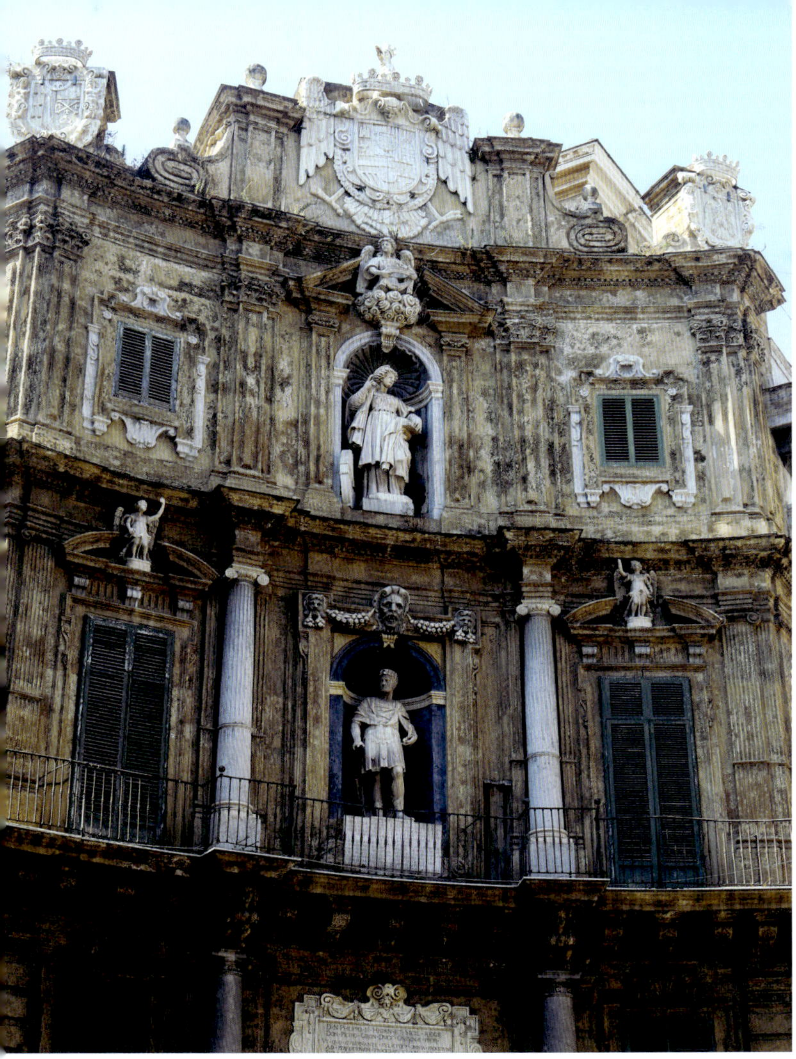

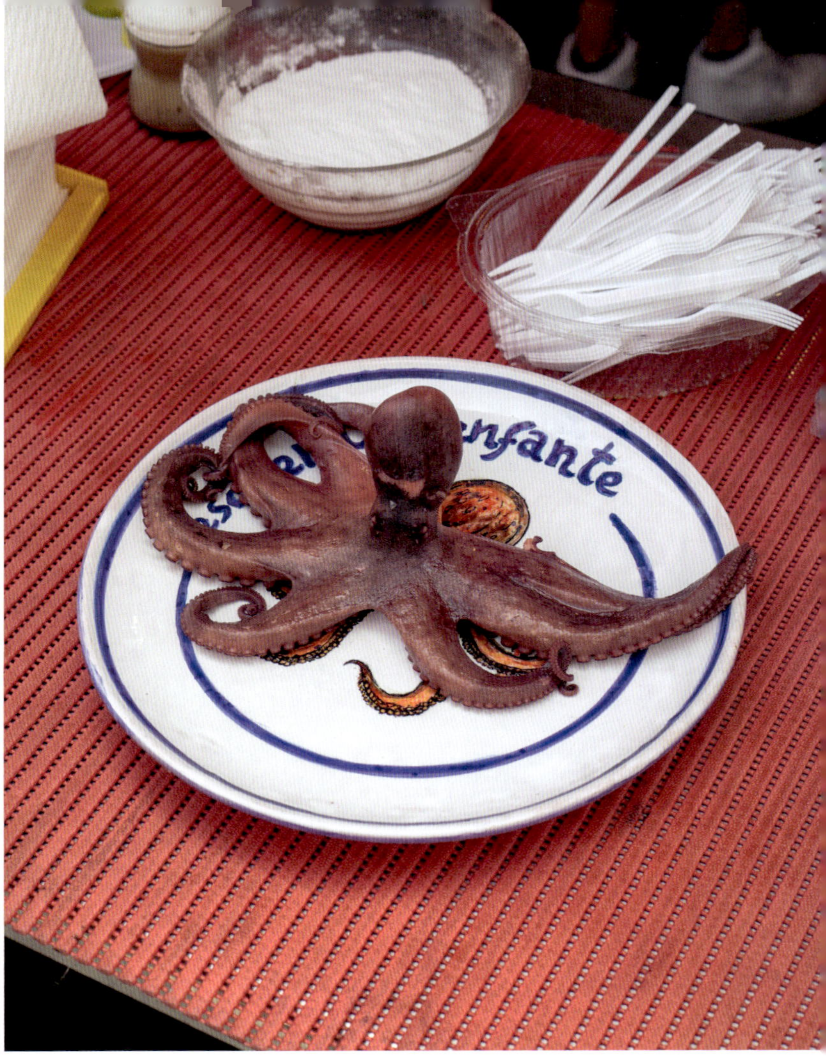

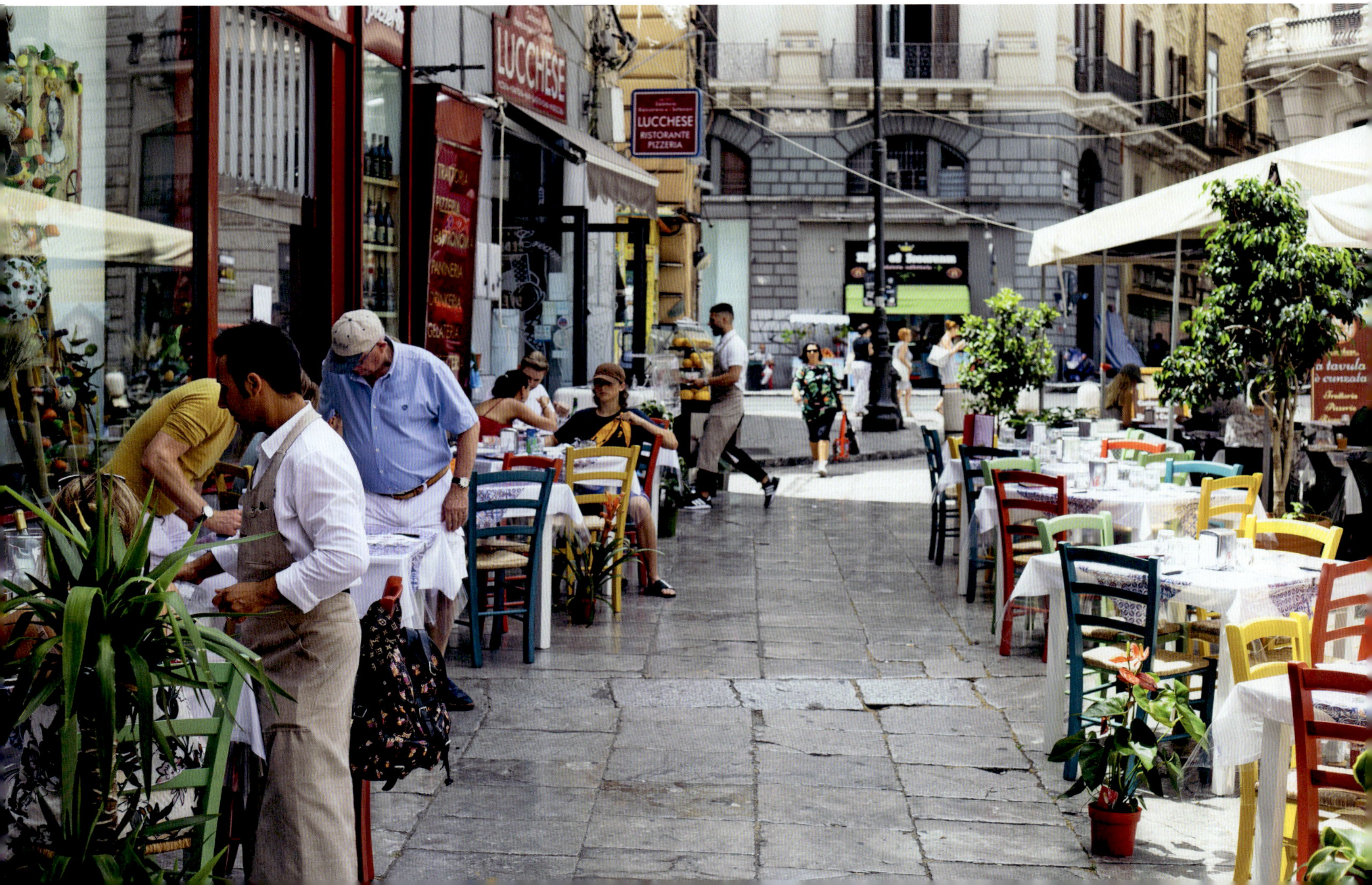
LUCCHESE
LUCCHESE
RISTORANTE
PIZZERIA

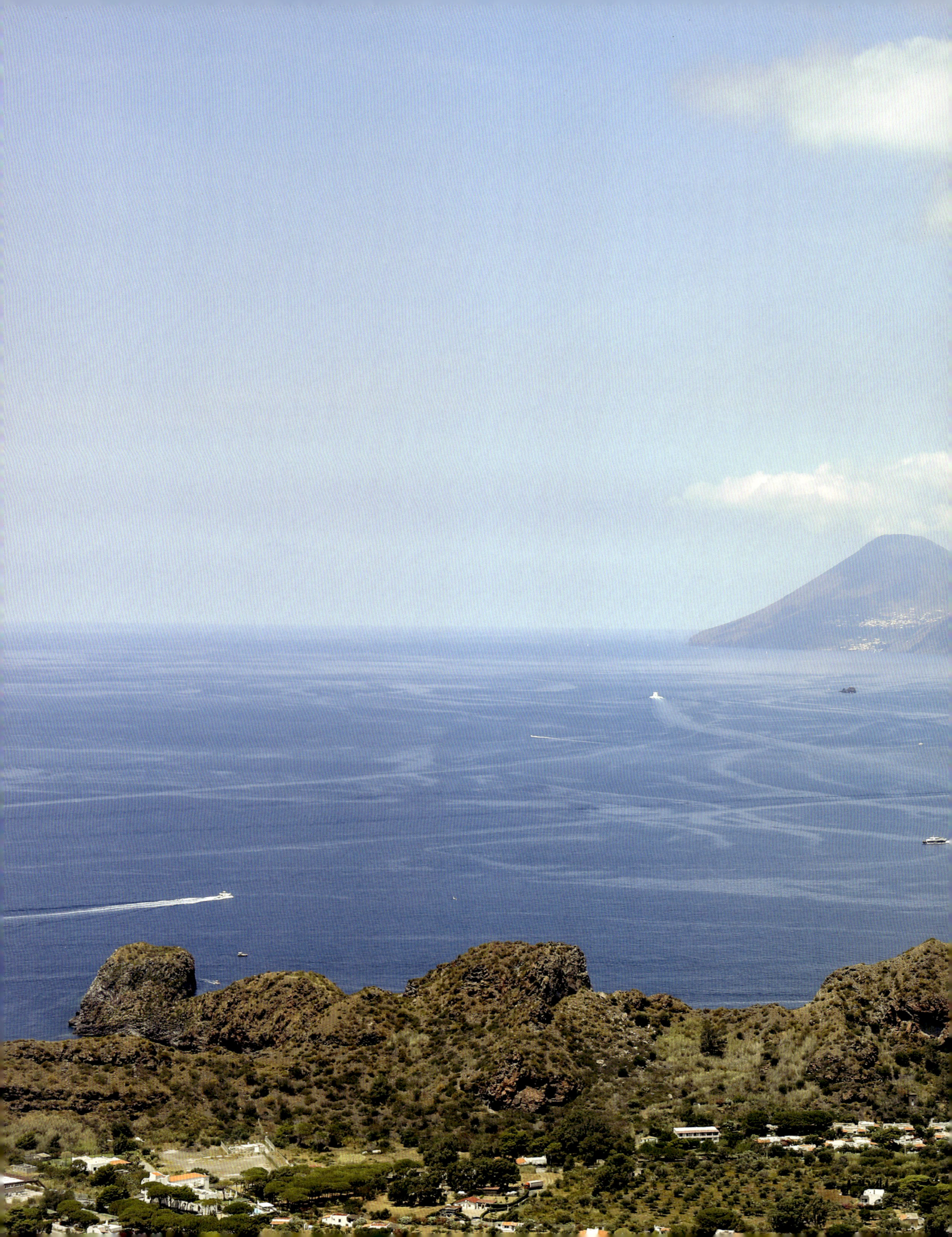

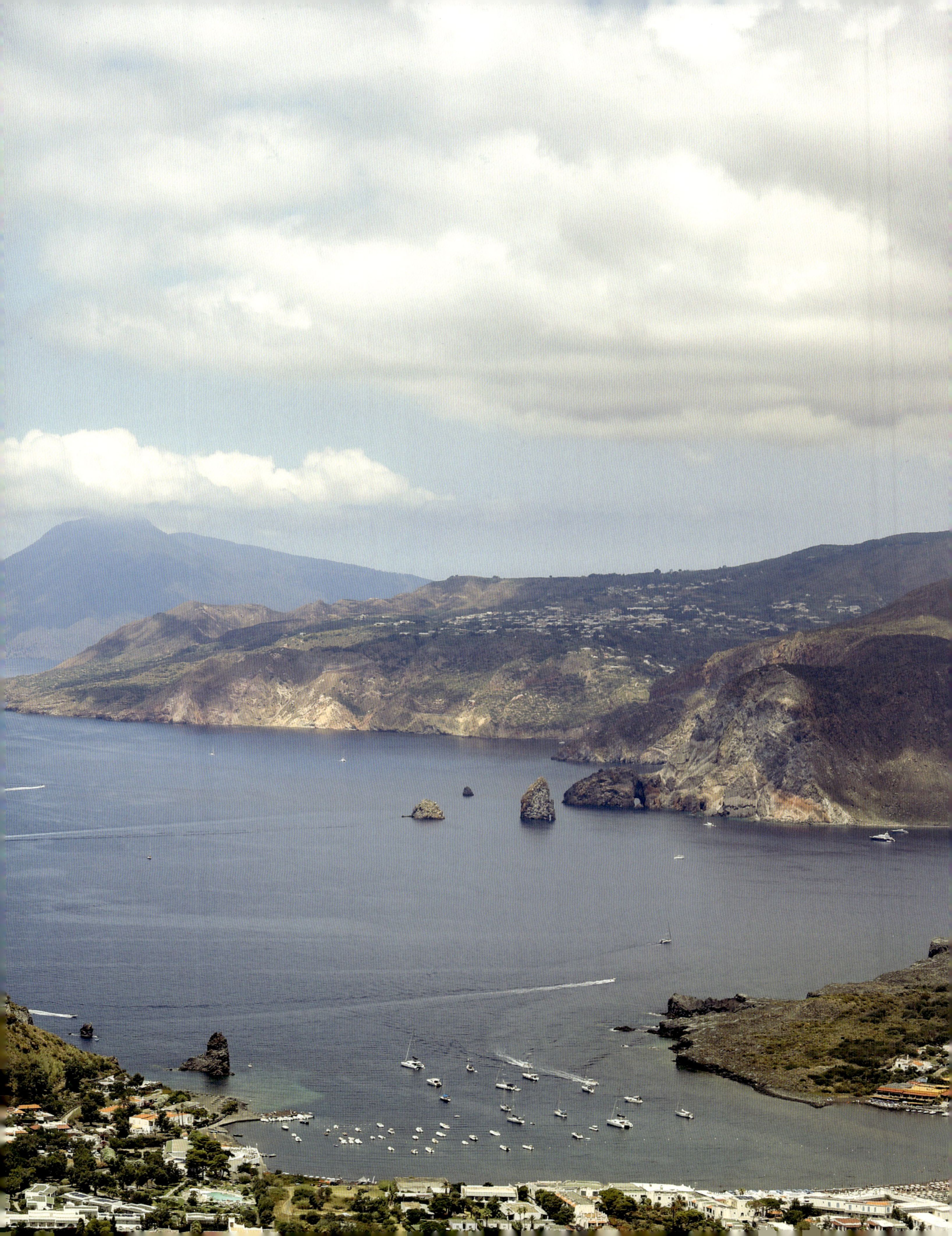

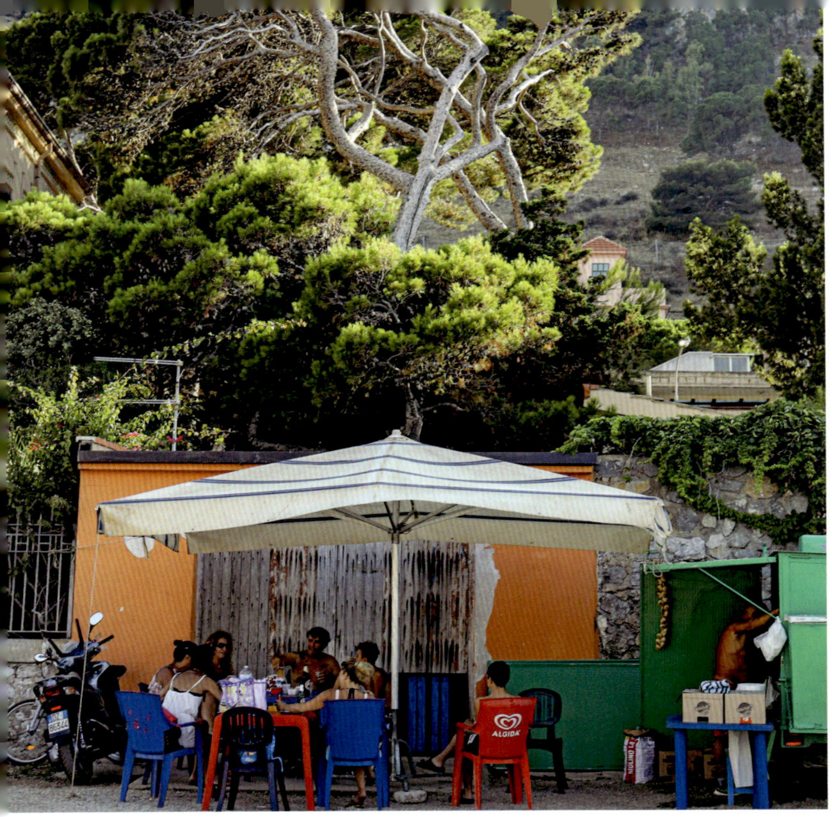
ALGIDA

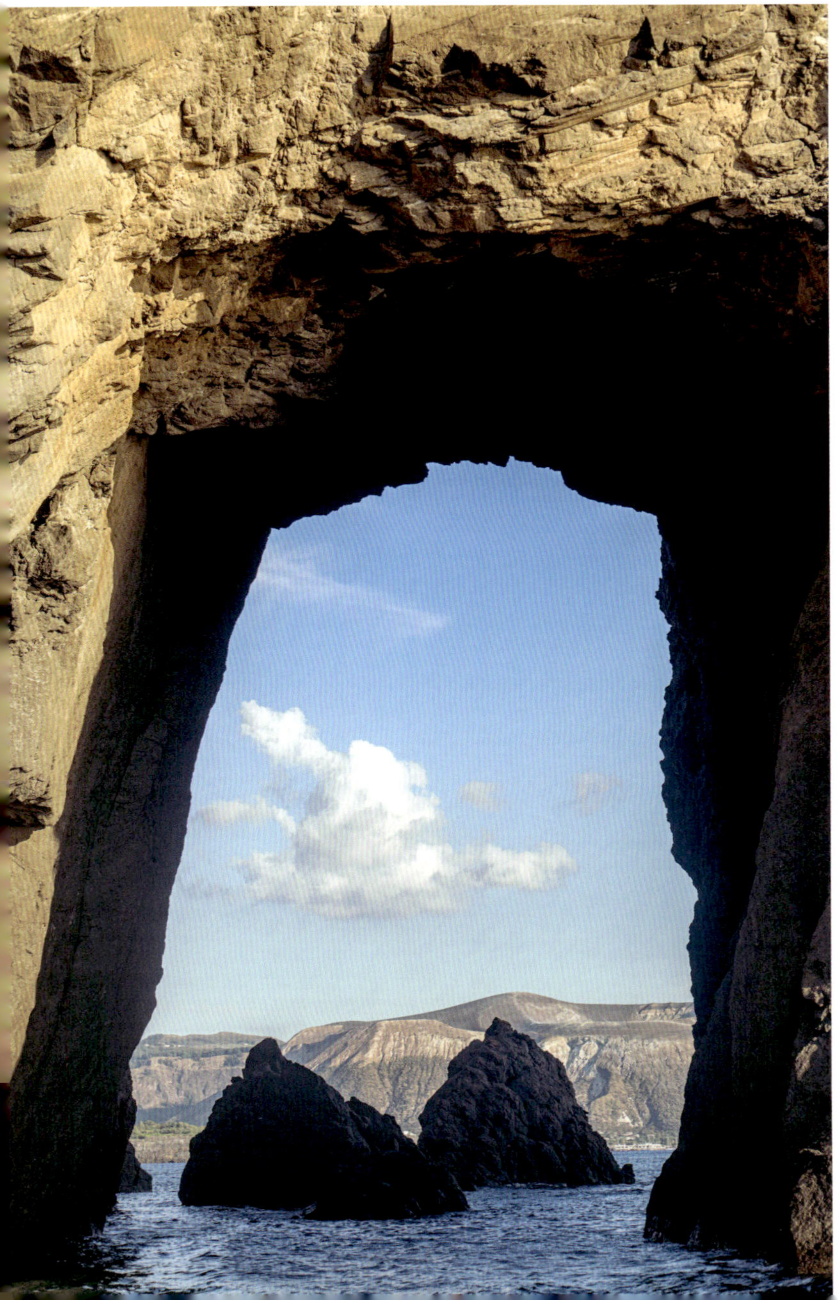

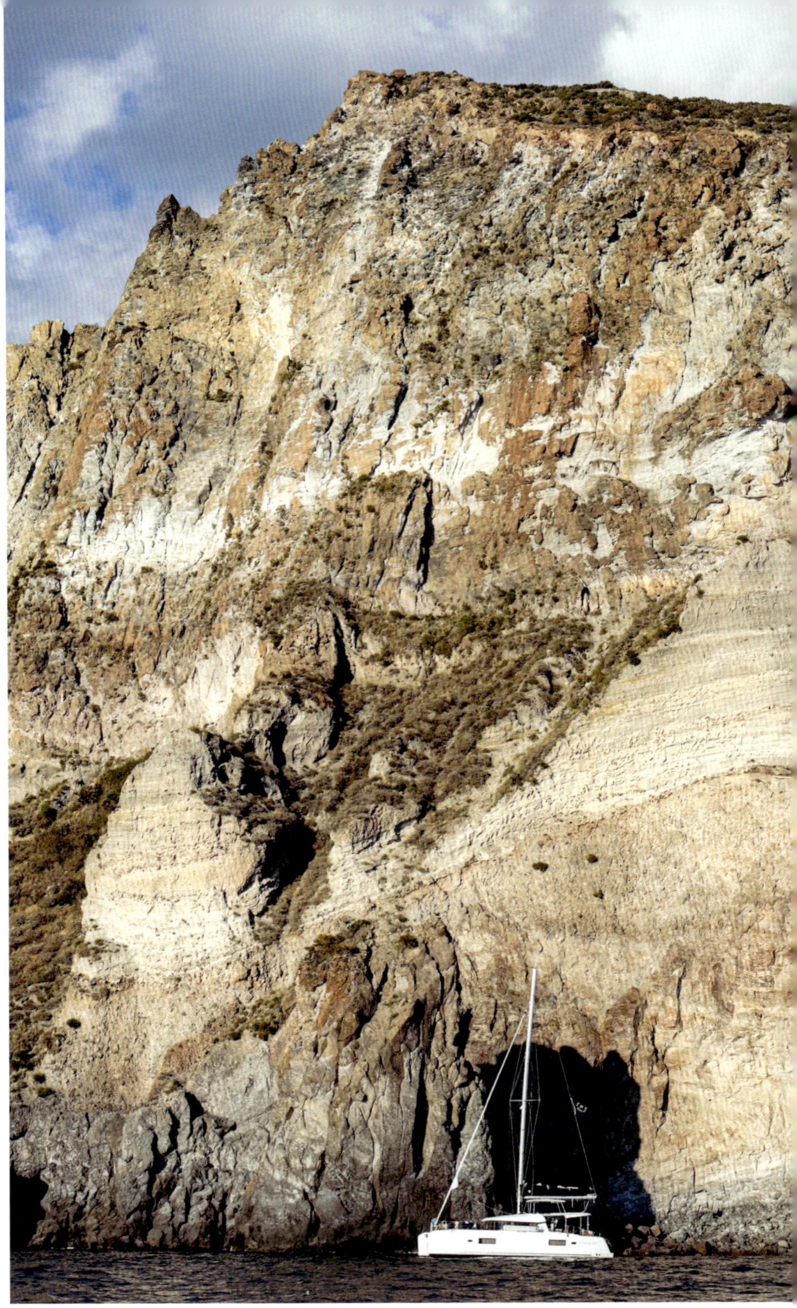

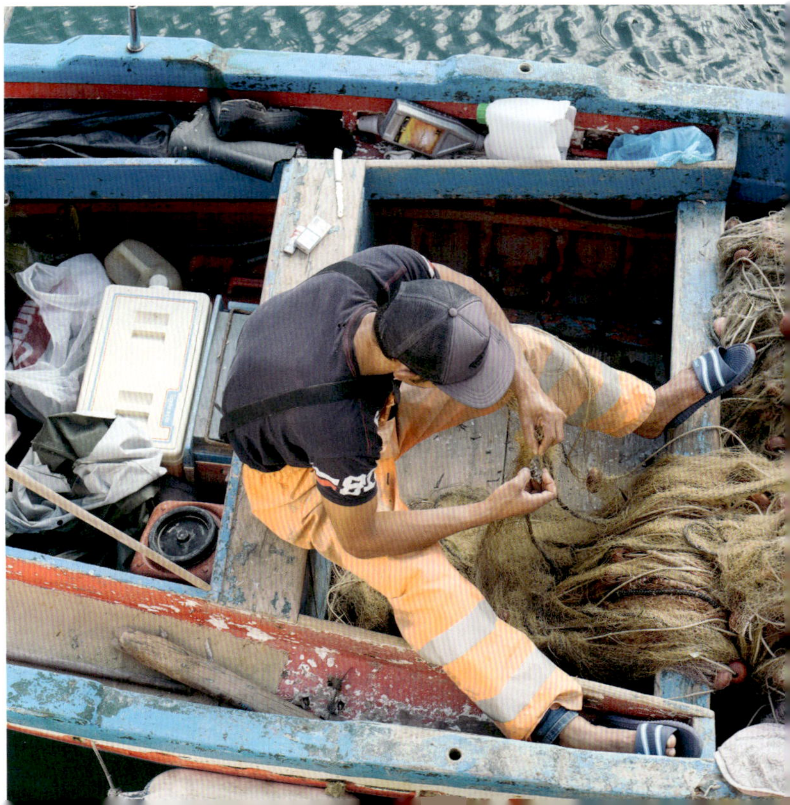

allows you to explore beyond the cityscapes of the larger port towns. This northern coastal beach town is picturesque, with waterfront homes and storefronts chiseled into the hill. Combining centuries-old churches with beach bars gives Cefalù culture, beauty, and leisure facilities aplenty. The waterfront district near Via Carlo Ortolani di Bordonaro has a wealth of unassuming local establishments, perfect for a fish lunch with sea urchins and freshly marinated sardines.

MILAZZO

If you don't care for the energizing hum of an urban port, sail to the port town of Milazzo, located at the northeast corner of Sicily. As the port closest to the Aeolian Islands, it is surrounded by man-made marinas that extend out from the coastline's sandy beaches, protecting fishermen and mariners from the blustery sea during the stormy seasons. Along the western and northern coastlines surrounding this town, inlets can be found with suitable anchorages depending on the weather; because the wind is less predictable during the summer months, however, the decision of where to anchor is often determined by the day's wind report, and the marinas are the only fail-safe option.

LITERARY VISITORS

Many have found themselves compelled and charmed by the beauty of these islands: Aeschylus, William Shakespeare, Oscar Wilde, D. H. Lawrence, Ezra Pound, Cicero, Miguel de Cervantes, Truman Capote, Ernest Hemingway, and so many more. Some of the most prolific travelers—Alexandre Dumas, Jean-Pierre Houël, Guy de Maupassant, Déodat de Dolomieu, and Archduke Ludwig Salvator—who led early expeditions and Sicilian explorations were also completely enchanted. Sicily offers not just fertile ground for agriculture, but also a place of growth for the artistic imagination.

Cruising past Milazzo eastward, you will sail the Strait of Messina. This passageway is narrow and heavy with maritime traffic: ferries crossing the channel, commercial shipping and fishing boats, and mariners sailing the coast of Sicily en route to Catania or, continuing onward, entering the Ionian Sea.

CATANIA

Situated about halfway down the eastern coast of Sicily, Catania is the second-largest city and one of the main ports on the island. It is also one of the most picturesque cities in Sicily, with its landscape dominated by the volcanic giant Mount Etna. The volcano serves as a beacon for the city and has given the landscape of Catania its unique volcanic-rock palette. Close proximity to Mount Etna tells us that the fate of Catania is ultimately linked to the mountain. With slopes molded from that same volcanic rock, certain areas of the city have a somber appearance that contrasts with its lively nightlife and bustling center. A baroque piazza and cathedral sit in the middle of the city. Saint Agatha is the patron saint.

From a berth in the harbor, you can walk into town along Via Etna, which is a long boulevard of elegant shops and restaurants that seems to stretch all the way up to the mountain. Affectionately named "Mama Etna," the volcano is seen by locals as a blessing and a curse. It serves as a symbol of fertility: although it has threatened the city many times throughout history, the rich volcanic soil and fertile landscapes it provides have always given Catania the opportunity to rebuild. Catania enjoys an abundance of agriculture, with beautiful national parks close by and some of the best wines around.

Sicily's landscape is gorgeous; it is an expansive volcanic island that extends to the crumbling, wind-shaped edge of the Mediterranean coast where it cascades into the Emerald Sea. Rolling hills of red soil provide the raw materials for its cuisine and for the complex tones that make Sicilian wines

THE COAST IS LINED WITH SICILIANS EVEN WHEN NO SAND IS IN SIGHT (ABOVE). TUNA AND SWORD-FISH ARE POPULAR IN DEEPER WATERS, BUT FOR A SMALLER CATCH, FISHERMAN GO OUT WITH NETS ON SOLO BOATS (BELOW, RIGHT).

distinctive. For the people of Sicily, the soil, land, and sea are the foundations for their pride, and those same basic elements are among the many reasons sailors plan their voyages to this island.

~

Today, the waters around Sicily—including the Aegadian and the Aeolian Islands—have become a beloved destination for the ambitious sailor. Ferocious wind conditions and unpredictable weather patterns keep many from visiting by way of sea. But those wanderers who know that nothing good comes easy will venture the depths. Once you've conquered the difficulties, the beauty to be discovered is like no other. Sicily reveals its brilliance to sailors who put in the effort and calls them to indulge in its food and drink, to discover its landscapes, so pure and unadorned, and to explore its hidden corners and intriguing past.

AEOLIAN TRIANGLE

Many seafarers believe that the Mediterranean has its own version of the Caribbean's Bermuda Triangle. In this place, a triangle is formed between Ustica off the Sicilian coast, the Aeolian Islands, and the Strait of Messina. Often, in this place, a strange mix of bad weather can be experienced. Many sailors and yachtsmen who've spent years sailing around the Mediterranean seas are convinced that legends of the Aeolian Triangle are to be believed and feared.

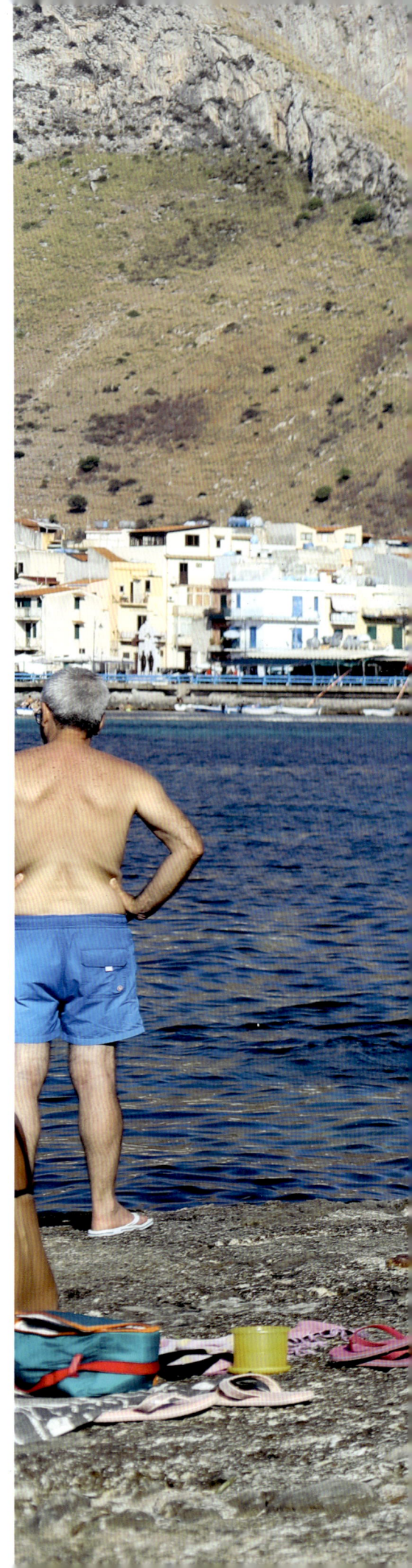

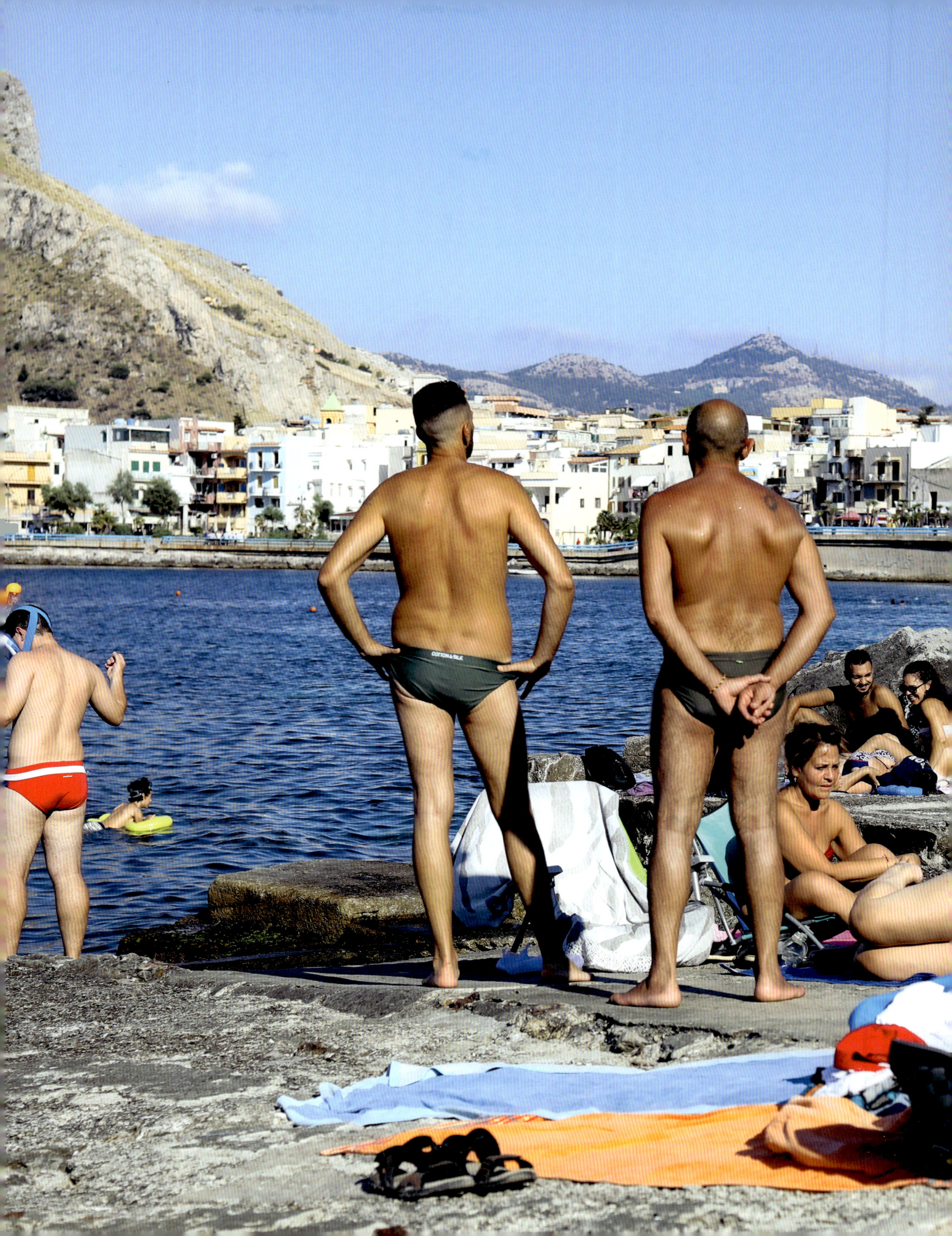
COTTON&SILK

CAPTAIN'S NOTES *COASTAL SICILY*

RECOMMENDED ITINERARY

Taormina
37° 50'36"N, 15° 17'19"E
One of the most famous towns in all of Sicily, Taormina is a popular destination for those sailing along the Strait of Messina. Anchoring is prohibited anywhere along Sant'Andrea Cove north and south of Isola Bella because of the nature reserve. Instead, continue south towards Taormina Bay and anchor in 5.4 fathoms, or use the mooring facilities maintained by George Rizzo. The closest marina is Marina dell'Etna, which is located one nautical mile south from Taormina Bay and is a sheltered refuge from wind conditions.

Aeolian Islands
38° 32'11"N, 14° 55'42"E
The Aeolian Archipelago (see pp.44–55) consists of seven islands sitting north of Milazzo, off the northeast region of Sicily. The islands of Vulcano, Lipari, Salina, Panarea, Stromboli, Filicudi, and Alicudi deserve their own seven-day itinerary.

Palermo
38° 7'37"N, 13° 22'28"E
Palermo is located in the northwest region of Sicily. The harbor itself is not pristine like that of the smaller ports throughout Sicily and is dominated by the sprawling marina. Berth stern-or bow-to where possible, within the Cala Bersagliere inlet, which is characterized by the large Molo, or breakwater. Palermo is a popular resort town with nearby beaches and a ferry service to the Aeolian Islands.

Milazzo
38° 13'52"N, 15° 15'19"E
Berth at Marina del Nettuno, which offers 140 slips with visitors berth options. Yachts can also proceed to the town quay. The marina has good shelter, though a strong sirocco wind can rock boats moored along the pontoons and quay. Anchor outside the pier in depth of 5–8 fathoms only in calm seas. A wrap-around swell can cause monohulls to be uncomfortable.

Syracuse (Grand Harbor)
37° 3'24"N, 15° 16'55"E
The town quay and the Marina Yachting can berth up to 180 yachts, with a maximum boat length of 40 meters. During the summer months, the prevailing wind blowing into the quay can get uncomfortable for smaller yachts, so be sure to keep distance between your stern and the quay when the breeze picks up. The old town is located on a peninsula, which is conspicuous when approaching from the east. If approaching from the south or north following the coastline, it is not easily noticed. South of Syracuse is the Plemmirio nature reserve. Anchoring is prohibited in the area.

Marsala
37° 46'49"N, 12° 25'56"E
There are numerous shoals off the coast of Marsala and care should be given during navigation. Many wrecks lie outside the harbor entrance. Club Nautico Lilybeo is located on the south side of the breakwater and has good shelter, though it becomes uncomfortable during strong southerly winds. There are laid moorings and care should be given while navigating within the pontoons as the depth varies from 1 to 2 fathoms.

Aegadian Islands
37° 56'13"N, 12° 19'23"E
Located just off the west coast of Sicily, between Trapani and Marsala, are the three principal islands that make up this group: Favignana, Marettimo, and Levanzo. Cala Grande lies on the western side of Favignana, and is situated behind the lighthouse. The seafloor is sand and good holding. The island is home to a once-thriving tuna-canning facility that brought work and prosperity. After years of abandonment, the island's facilities are undergoing a revival, and mariners sailing by can view the activity.

RECOMMENDED ANCHORAGES

Cefalù
Favignana
Marettimo
Sayonara Naxos
San Vito Lo Capo

ITINERARY DURATION

7 days, Marsala to Milazzo
4 days, Milazzo to Syracuse
7 days, Aeolian Islands

PREVAILING WIND

On the north coast, prevailing wind during the summer months comes from the northwest. It will blow force 3–4 on the Beaufort scale during the mornings and die down again at night. Wind on the east coast typically comes from the south-southeast and can often blow force 4–5 for days at a time. On the south coast, prevailing wind comes from the southwest. Southerly gales cause heavy swell along the coast and mainly take place during the winter season. Wind during the summer season blows from the northwest on the west coast, and the currents around the western point cause the sea to become confused and can cause difficulties with navigation.

SEASON

Summer sailing season begins in late April and ends in late October, with peak season in July and August.

FOOD

Pasta is a staple in Sicily—an important part of daily life—and comes in all shapes and sizes. *Pasta alla Norma* is found throughout Sicily and is particularly good in Catania. It has a rich, tomato-based sauce with fried aubergine and basil, served with a salted or baked ricotta cheese.

GOOD TO KNOW

Magnetic variance
Magnetic Declination: +3° (EAST)

N
W
E
S
TYRRHENIAN SEA
USTICA
AEOLIAN ISLANDS
STRAIT OF MESSINA
MESSINA
MILAZZO
SAN VITO
LO CAPO
PALERMO
CEFALÙ
MARETTIMO
FAVIGNANA
MARSALA
TAORMINA
SICILY
MOUNT
ETNA
CATANIA
SYRACUSE
STRAIT OF SICILY
MEDITERRANEAN SEA
0
10
NAUTICAL MILES
NOT FOR NAVIGATION

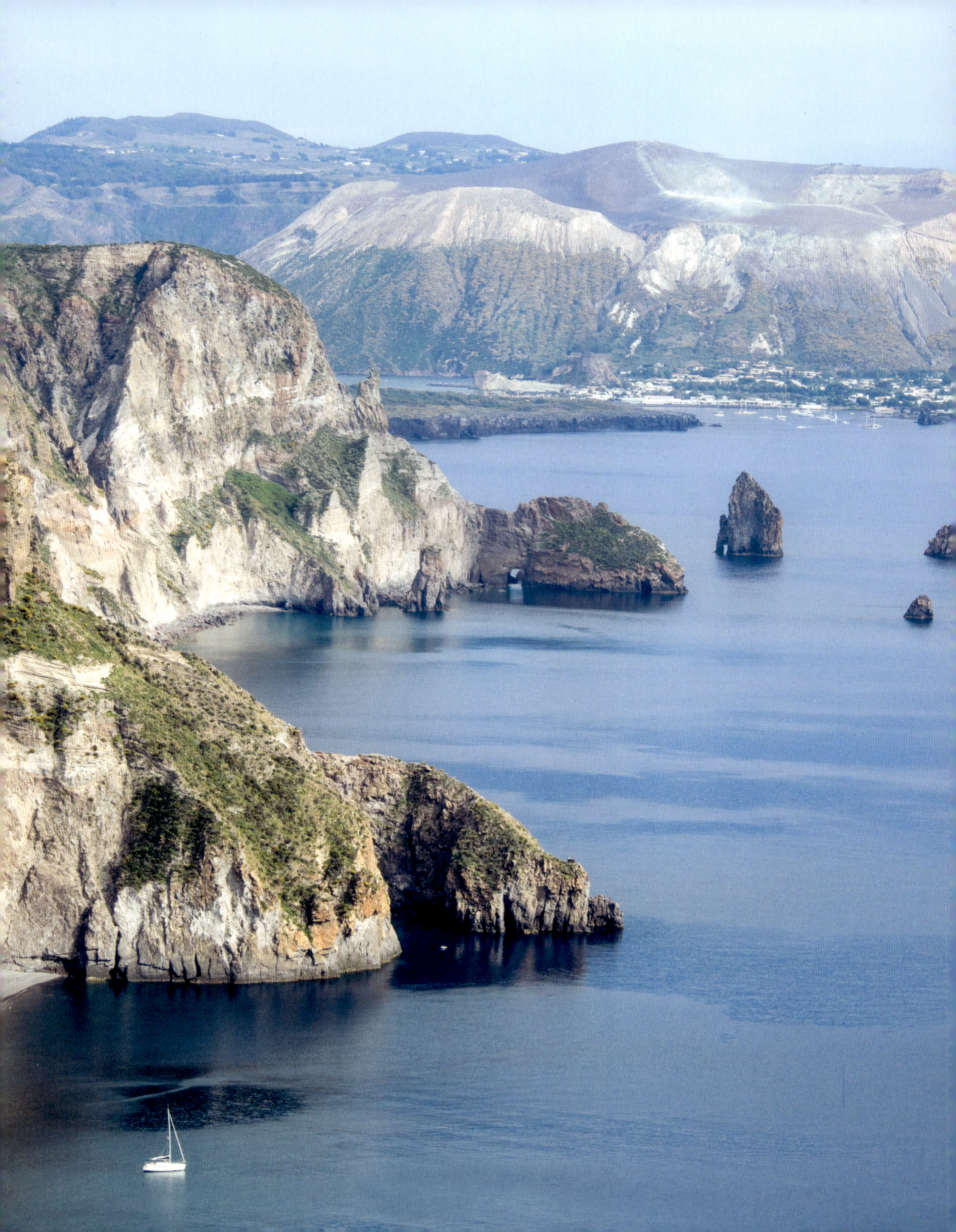

THE VULCANIC AEOLIAN ARCHIPELAGO

SEVEN ISLANDS SIT TOGETHER AT THE BASE OF THE TYRRHENIAN SEA, ONE MORE STUNNING THAN THE NEXT. THESE ISLANDS INVITE SAILORS TOWARD THEIR DRAMATIC SHORES, WHERE THEY ARE WELCOMED BY A RUSTIC WAY OF LIFE.

The Aeolians—seven distinctive islands located in the southern Tyrrhenian Sea that are as vibrant as they are mysterious. Vulcano, Lipari, Salina, Alicudi, Panarea, Stromboli, and Filicudi together make up one of Italy's great sailing destinations. Emerging from the sea during the Pleistocene period, these islands have been reshaped throughout their history. Civilizations first developed here during the early Bronze Age and these waters have been navigated since those early settlements. Today, sailors from all around the world sight their compasses towards the Aeolian Islands to discover its splendor.

During a sailing itinerary to the Aeolian Islands, you'll experience the island edges, home to white pumice mountains and jagged cliff sides that seemingly dive straight into the Mediterranean's indigo seas lined by black sand beaches. These islands are fueled by wine, food, the sea, and the volcanoes—two that are currently active. Fragrances of olives, capers, sea salt, and vegetables ripening in the sun fill the air. Less touristic than their neighboring archipelagos, you'll always be reminded that these islands are far removed from everyday life.

The islands are hard to reach and a sailing itinerary is the most unique way of exploring the archipelago. There are many possible routes when planning a sailing adventure in the Aeolian Islands. Weather can cause the itinerary planning to be difficult and skippers should plan for alternative routes at all times in the event that inclement weather arises and specific anchorages become untenable. Each stop is an easy day-sail away from the rest and routes can be decided at a moment's notice based on the interest of the skipper and their crew.

ISOLA VULCANO

The southernmost island in the archipelago is Isola Vulcano—a popular port to begin the itinerary. Sailing to Vulcano from the mainland coast is a pleasant introduction to the Aeolian Islands—during the passage, you'll observe the islands' natural biodiversity and the layered igneous rock and soil, caused by the volcanic activity. It's also home to a densely wooded forest that lines the hilltops. Towards the southern end of the island, the slopes steeply erode into the edge of the sea.

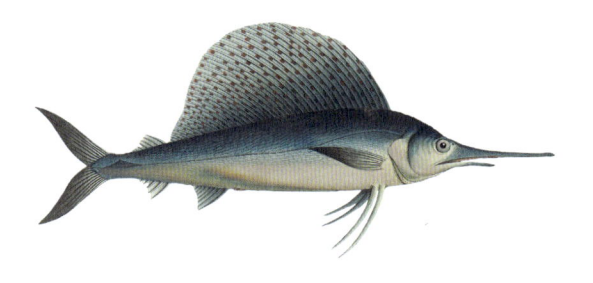

The conspicuous Gran Cratere, the most recent active volcano, dominates the landscape and can be seen from the two main anchorages on the island. Because of its active state, the crater spews bubbling mud pools and hot mineral springs, and the thermal mud bath is a popular activity among sailors visiting the island, a great afternoon activity ashore.

The two anchorages are Porto di Ponente and Porto di Levante, both with access to the village on the island. There is another fantastic anchorage on the southern coast in the bay of Gelso: a short dinghy ride ashore and you'll find yourself on a beautiful black sand beach beneath a vineyard with olive trees lining the southern coast. From the town of Porto di Levante, you can hike to the volcano peak with scenic views of all the Aeolian Islands. Whether you decide to stay overnight or just for an afternoon adventure, Vulcano is a worthy port of call. Cruising north, you can sail towards Lipari and Salina, east towards Panarea and Stromboli, or west towards Filicudi and Alicudi.

LIPARI

Lipari is the largest island and the most inhabited, home to 10,000 residents. Le Bocche di Vulcano is the channel between Vulcano and Lipari, home to pleasant anchorages with dramatic views of nearby islands with a backdrop of the eroding cliffs that plummet into the sea. There are more provisioning options on Lipari than any of the other islands and it is home to the largest fishing fleet in the archipelago. Fishmongers sell large swordfish and tuna with smaller fish like spigola and orata caught daily and sold directly to sailors.

The main harbor is Porto di Lipari, located on the eastern coast of the island. Yacht clubs with piers offering transient slips extend along the quay, where you can berth for a night or two. These marinas are located in the middle of town, with restaurants and bars lining the road adjacent to the docks. A short walk from the marinas will take you into the center of town where you'll be able to enjoy a bustling yet idyllic Italian city.

The western coast of Lipari takes a very different appearance than the more inhabited and developed eastern coast where the town of Lipari is located. If the main port town does not interest you, venture onward to the southwest coves along the island. Sailing to the other side offers an adventurous as well as isolated environment. Spiaggia di Vinci and Valle Muria are exquisitely beautiful secluded coves away from any kind development. The southern cliffs of Lipari are a scenic backdrop especially at sunset where the 1,000 foot eroding edge is illuminated deep orange as the sun sets over the two westward islands of Alicudi and Filicudi.

ALICUDI

The westernmost island of the Aeolians is Alicudi—the least visited island, sitting alone and disconnected from the rest of the archipelago. It is roughly ten nautical miles from Filicudi and a lesser explored island in the archipelago because of the lack of safe harbors and steep underwater slope. Alicudi from a distance appears quintessentially volcanic, with its cone-like shape that drops dramatically into the sea. On the western shoreline is an anchorage that is exposed to the prevailing

---

PORTO BELLO ON SALINA

A restaurant located near the marina named Porto Bello offers delightful local food. The specialty pasta of the restaurant is called Spaghetti "Fuoco," *named after the volcano on Stromboli. The pasta dish is simple with few ingredients: tomatoes, olive oil, garlic, peperoncini, ricotta infornata and basil. Don't let these simple ingredients fool you, this is the spiciest pasta dish you will ever have. The sheer quantity of garlic and peperoncini will be a match for even the biggest spice enthusiasts.*

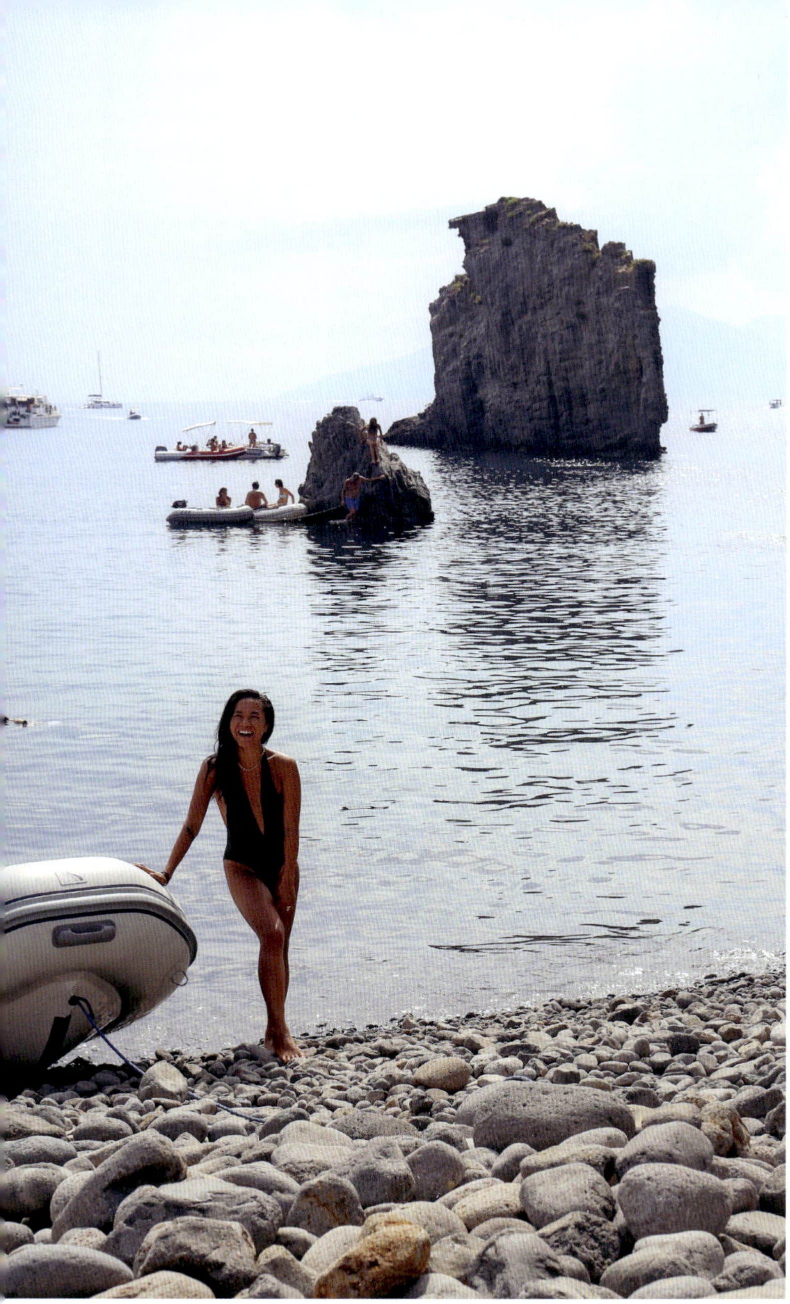

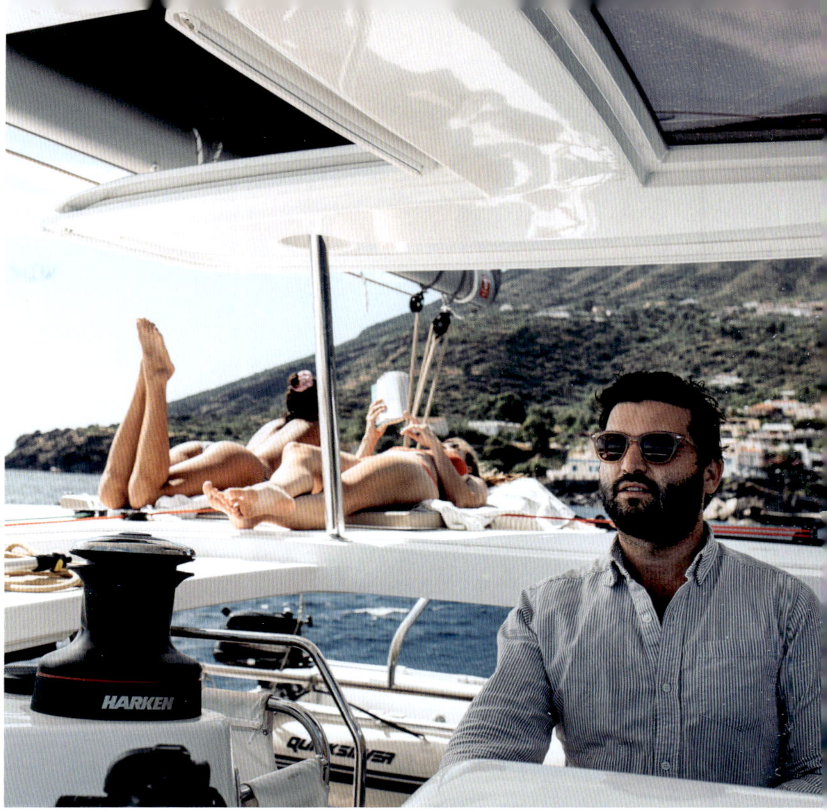
HARKEN

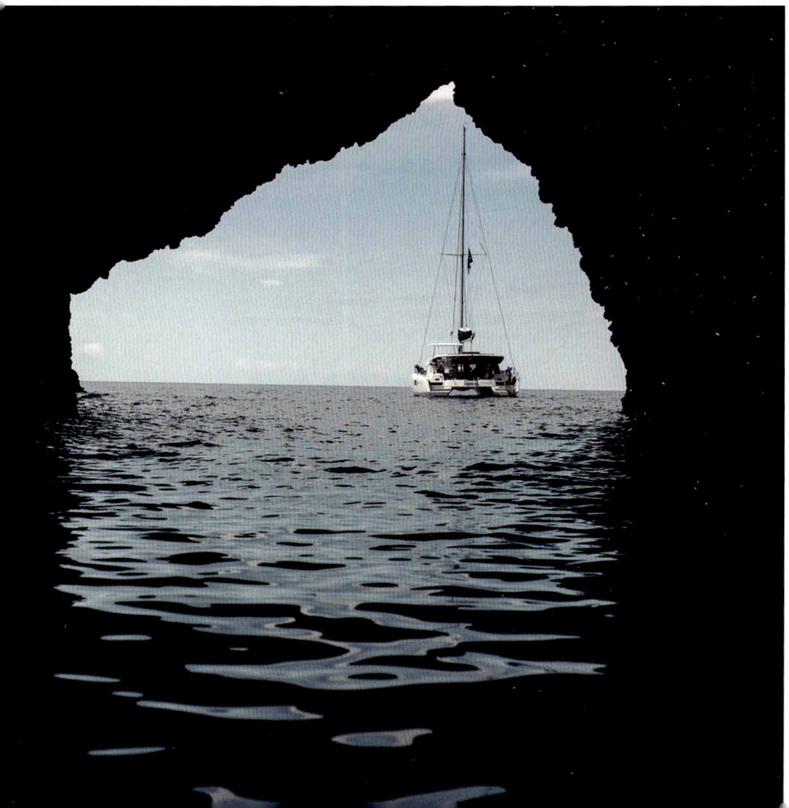

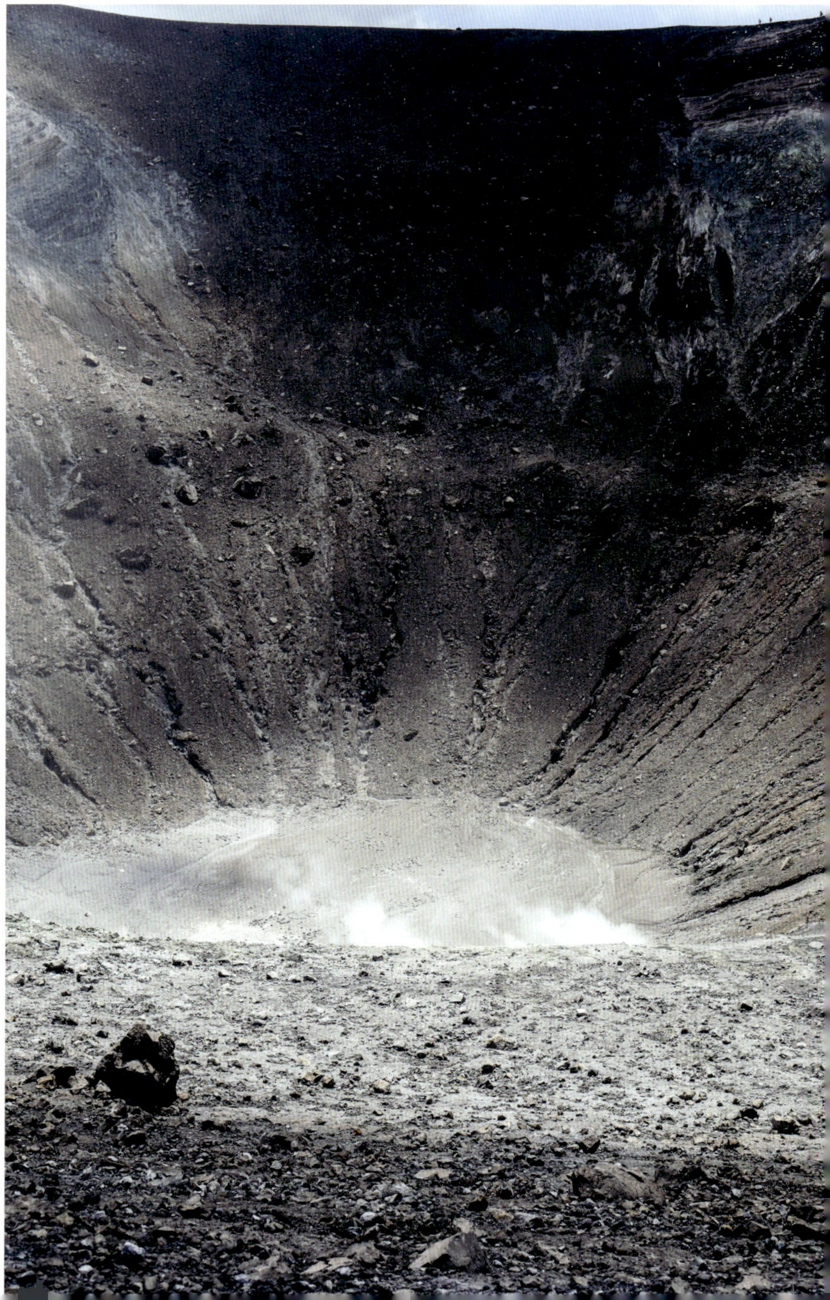

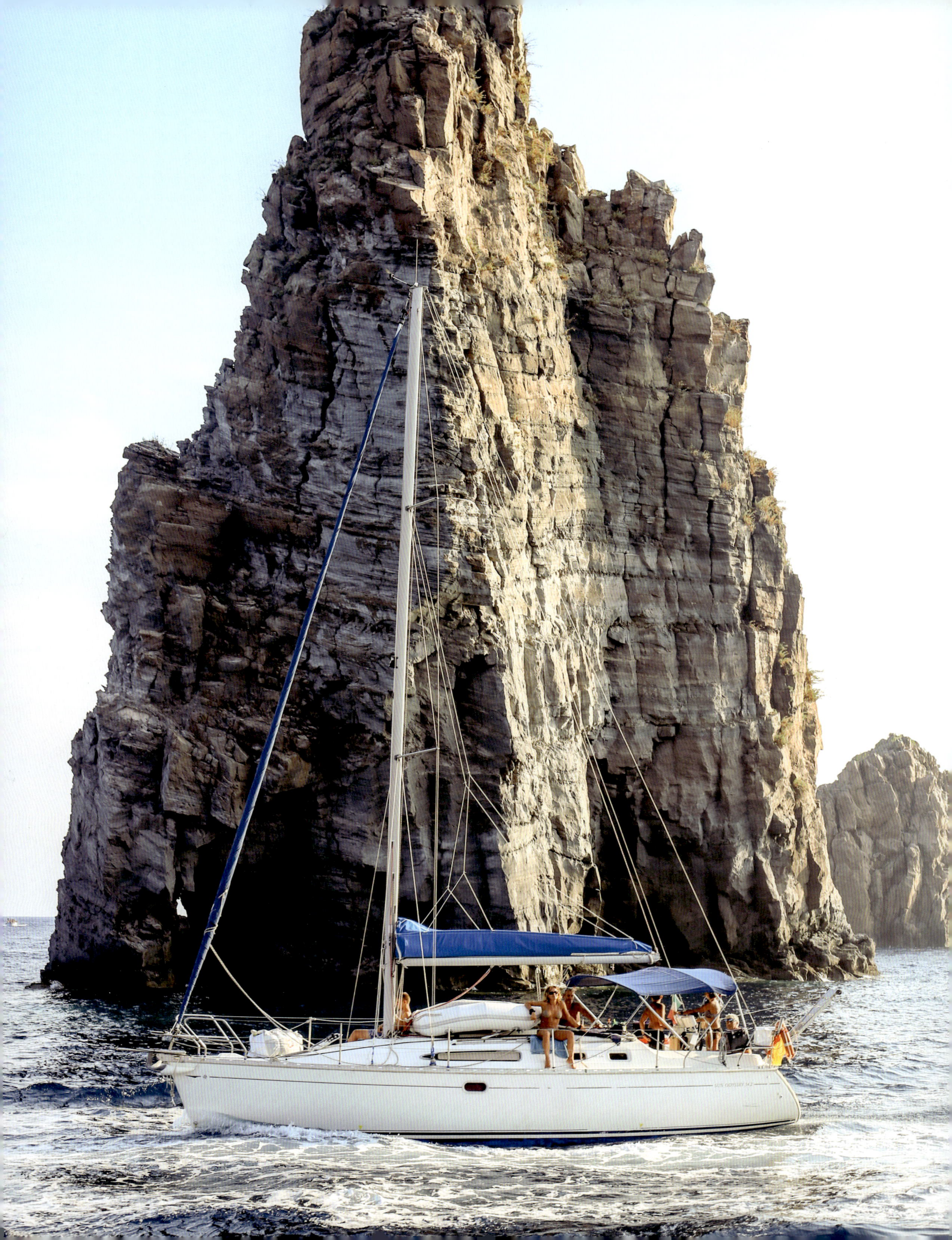

winds and not suitable in any type of rough seas. There is limited space for a boat to drop anchor and the island's harbor-master laid moorings safe for sailors to use when exploring the island. There is a town pier for ferry and supply boats but because it is not situated in a harbor safe from the wind, the island can be shut off from the outside world in rough seas, with ferries unable to dock along the pier. Once arrived and safely anchored off the western coast, a dinghy ride ashore will take you to a sleepy village—home to just a couple of restaurants. With little activity and few coves to explore, Alicudi is for sailors seeking rusticity and isolated charm.

SALINA

Sailing north from Lipari you will arrive at Isola Salina. Easily identified by its twin mountain peaks, Salina is considered the most lush of the islands. The island has become a hub for sailors cruising through the Aeolian, with the main port of Santa Marina Salina located on the eastern coast. Though it contains one of the greater populations of the Aeolian—around 2,000—it has maintained a sense of quaint serenity. In ancient history, it was called Didyma meaning "the twins" because of the two extinct volcano cones. Salina was named after salt-pans in a lagoon that can still be seen on the island.

The islanders welcome sailors by sharing their wines, their cuisine, and always offering stories and anecdotes of this extraordinary place they call home. It's a perfect port of call to re-provision for local wine and other island products to keep for the remainder of your itinerary. Sailing from the port and rounding the north coast, a steep cliff falls into the sea. Above are the hamlets of Malta and Valdichiesa and sailing past you can view the vineyards and groves. Located on the northwestern side of Salina is a popular day anchorage located along the town of Pollara, perfect for spending an afternoon swimming off the boat. Take note when you decide to sail to this cove as, during the summer months, on weekends the cove is full of locals sailing over from the mainland to enjoy their islands.

PANAREA

The island of Panarea is located between Salina and Stromboli. It's the smallest of the seven islands and one that should be on every itinerary. It was the first island to adopt a modern, chic ambiance in the region and is famed as one of the more fashionable isles of the Aeolians. It's undeniably romantic and alluring, the colors and smells are intoxicating, and there is ample reason the island has become home to several elegant hotels. These establishments line the town's edge and are equipped with beautiful lookouts towards Stromboli where you can view the volcano's active eruptions at night. The island is filled with well-established residents, a wealth of restaurants, hotels, and a vibrant social scene.

Panarea has many anchorages perfect for discovering the local culture and off-boat activities. Capo Milazzese and Cala Zimmari, located west of Punta Torrione along the southern coast, offers a safe anchorage with unique geological formations along the cliffs that surround the cove. This is a popular location for snorkeling and, ashore, at the top of the cliff that falls into the cove sits the ruins of an ancient Bronze Age civilization. A short hike to the top offers a stunning view of the cove. After an afternoon anchorage along the southern coast, most skippers will bring their sailboat to the mooring field sitting off Punta Peppemaria, where the nightlife is.

SALINA'S FLORA

On Salina, the volcanic soil is fertile and the island is covered with olive trees, caper bushes, and terraced vineyards. Salina still maintains its terraced farming operations with 11 working vineyards growing Malvasia grapes for wine production.

STROMBOLI

Next in the itinerary is Stromboli—perhaps the most famous of them all. The island is known for its active volcano that has been continuously erupting for 2,000 years. Stromboli is one of the more difficult islands in the itinerary and requires more planning than the others because of the lack of safe harbors. The perfect steep cone-like volcanic shape does not offer any protected coves along the coastline and the bottom only comes up to anchorable depth on the eastern point of the island. Everywhere else the shore drops dramatically hundreds of feet deep as soon as the island meets the sea. You can sail safely along the coast just 30 meters out to enjoy the sights, sounds, and the distinctive sulfur smell of the active volcanic peak.

Rugged and wild is how many locals like to describe Stromboli. The island grows lemons, oranges, capers, grapes, and olives come from its northern and southern slopes. Ashore is a charming town, home to a small welcoming community. Walking the streets you can find a gelateria selling local flavors grown and harvested on the island. There are numerous trattorias serving rustic and traditional menu options and modern restaurants offering fancier gastronomic dishes paired with local island wine.

Stromboli serves as the beacon and spirit of the Aeolian islands, with its volcanic prowess that brings both fear and symbolic fertility to its residents. It has also become a geological muse for explorers and writers for many years. Erupting often, lava flows out of its top, blackening the land and re-molding the earth below. Chunks of pulsating orange rock can be seen from a distance, while shades of glowing lava frequently erupt and light up the night sky. Its deep rumbling emanates from underground and hurls fire into the sky.

FILICUDI

One of the lesser explored islands is Filicudi. Home to two small fishing villages and the archipelago's second-smallest community. There are well preserved ancient ruins scattered throughout its villages dating back to the Bronze Age. It's the second-farthest western island in the group, and sailors come to Filicudi for the true sense of peace and calm that's found there.

The lifestyle is simple and holds a sense of calmness in high regard. Most of the lands are protected parklands, and the entire island has been listed as an UNESCO World Heritage Site. Sailors are greeted with genuine hospitality by the island's residents.

AEOLUS IN GREEK MYTHOLOGY

Greek Mythology tells us that Aeolus was the keeper of the winds and king of the Eolies. He lived on the floating island of Aeolia and was visited by Odysseus in Homer's Odyssey. After experiencing a misadventure, explorers showed up to his home where Aeolus gave them hospitality for a month and offered them winds from the west to take them home to Ithaca. He also gave them an ox-hide bag that contained all the winds, except the western ones. They traveled well for days, but when their native lands were just in sight, Odysseus sank. His men let their curiosity overcome them, and they opened the mysterious bag. The winds roared with such a force that drove the ship all the way back to Aeolus. He refused to help them again and believed their unsuccessful voyage meant that the gods didn't favor them.

HOTEL SIRENA ON ALONG THE SOUTH SIDE OF FILICUDI (ABOVE, LEFT). A TYPICAL SEASIDE SNACK: MUSSELS, SEA URCHINS, AND ANCHOVIES CAUGHT AND SERVED FRESH (BELOW).

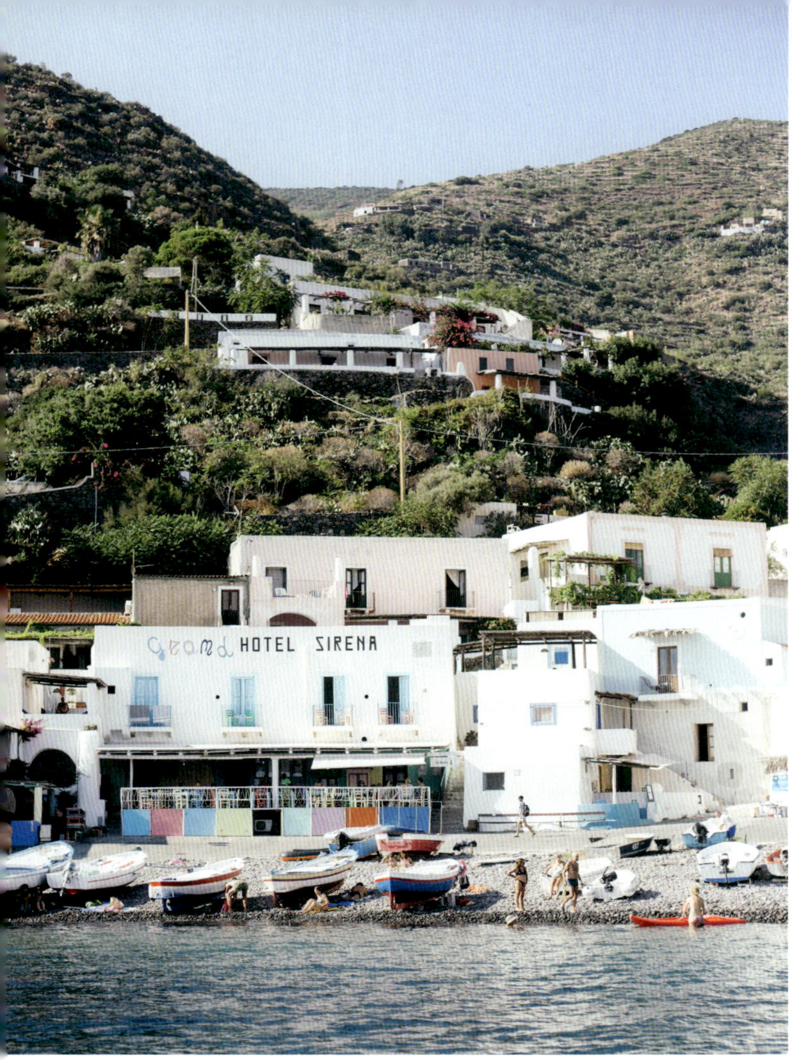
Grand HOTEL SIRENA

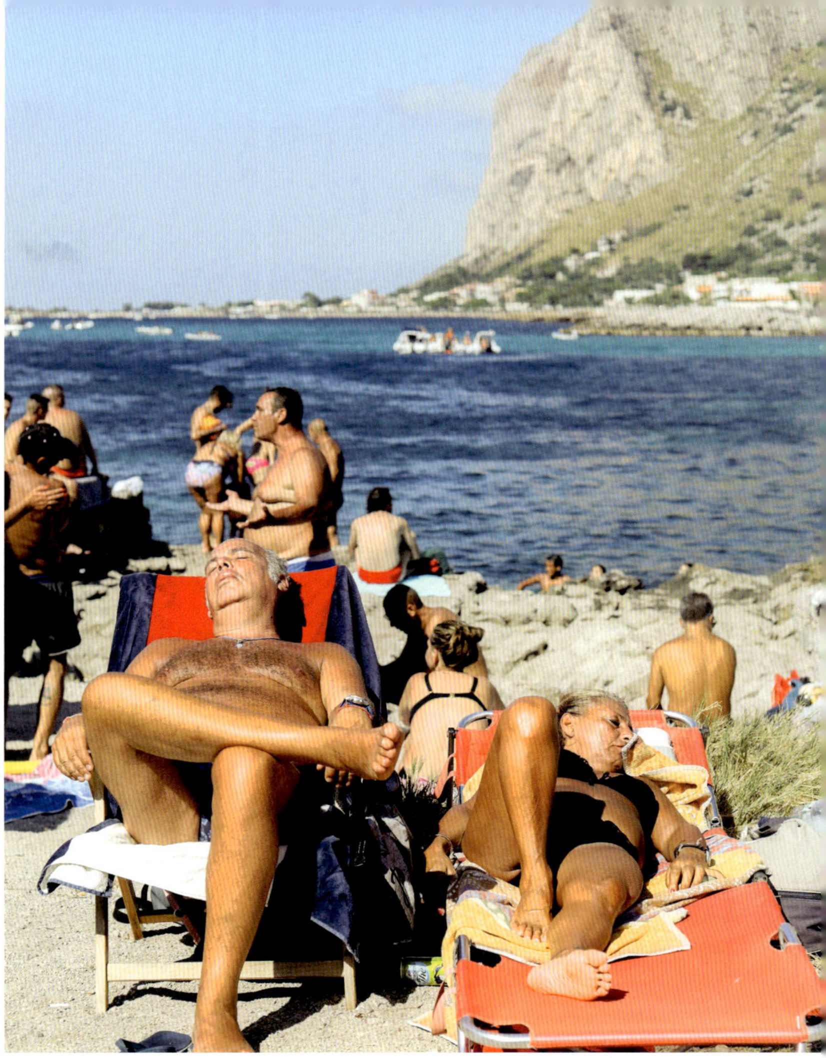

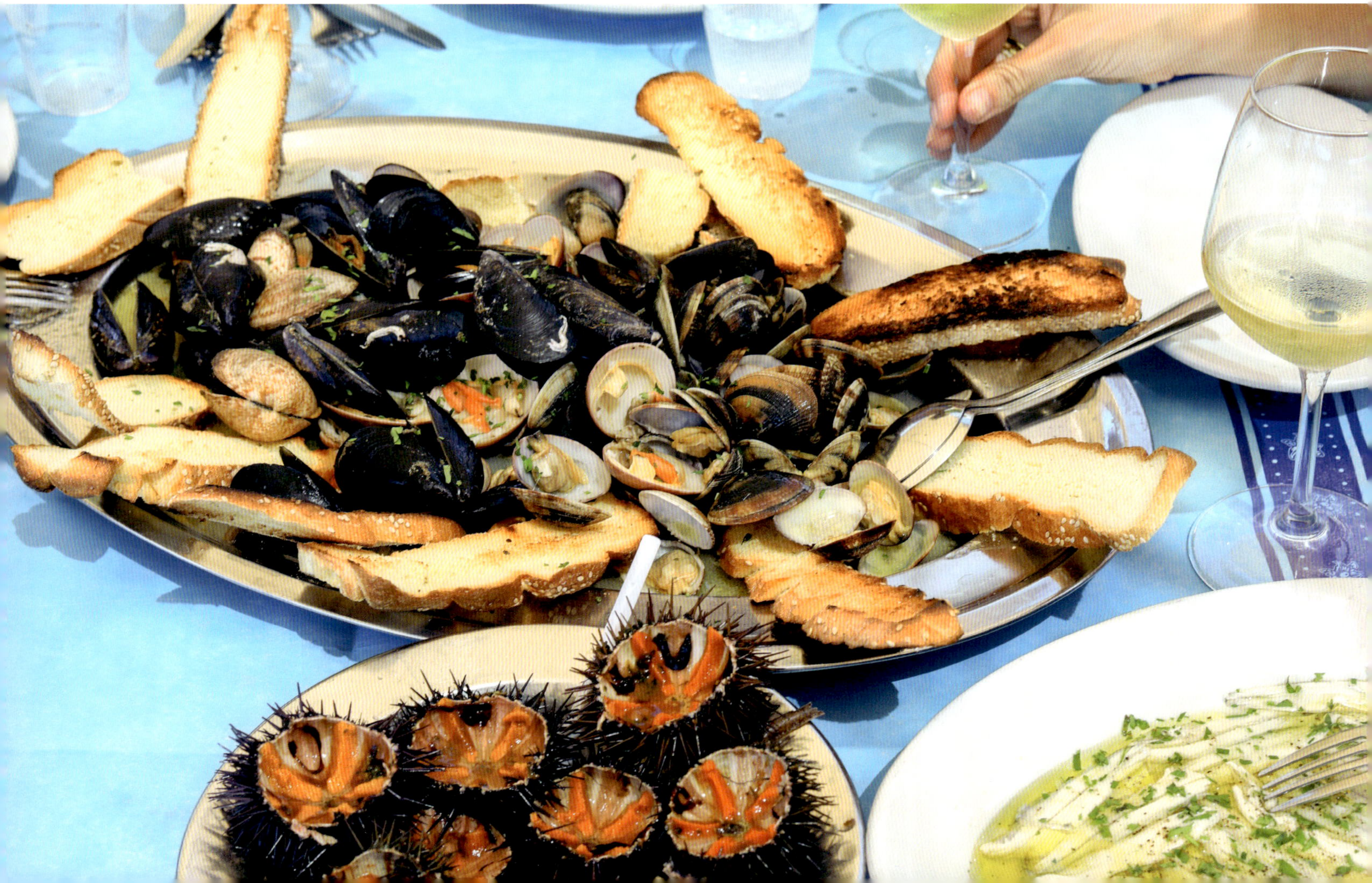

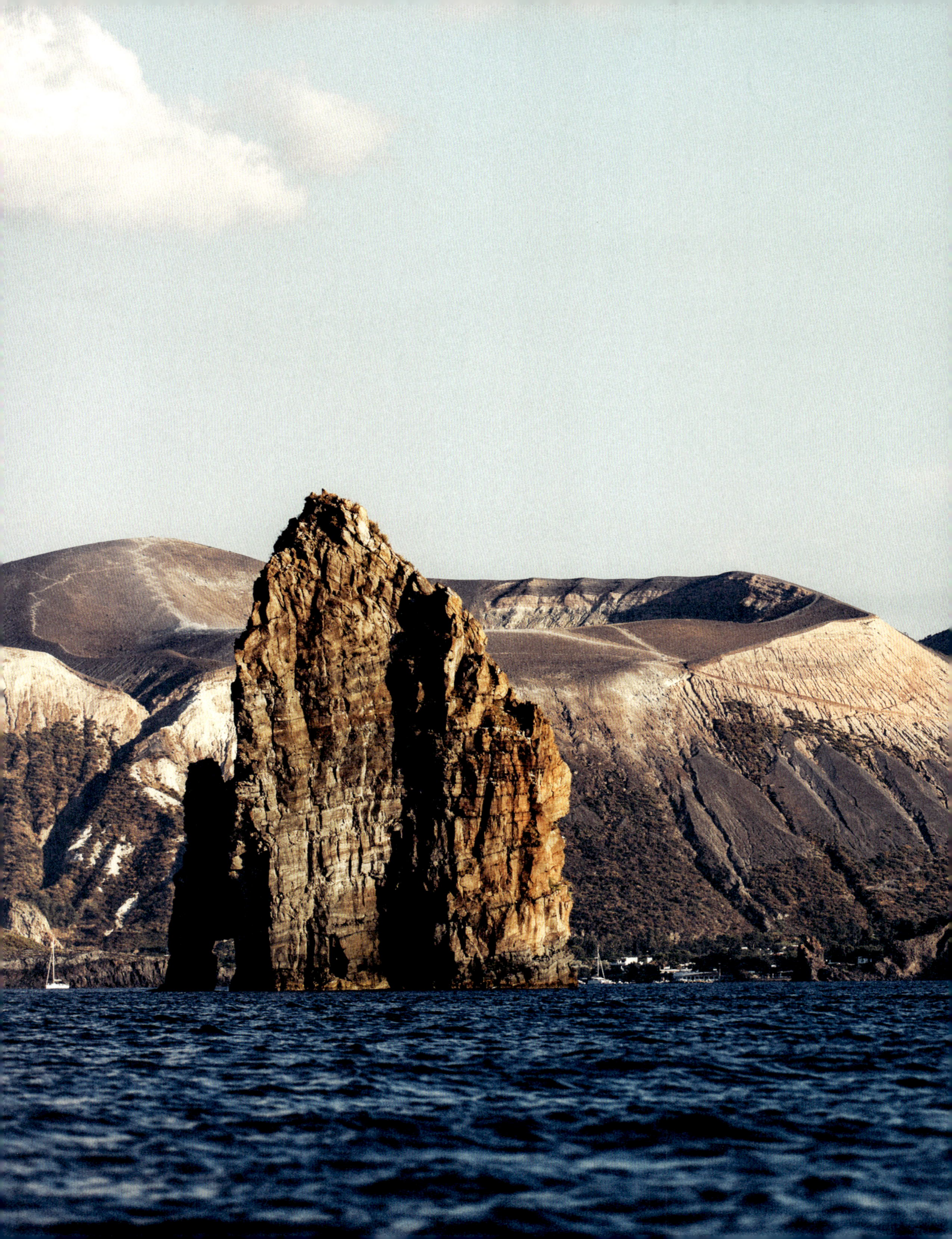

Wandering around the cozy village streets, you'll be welcomed by Italian nonnas who are eager to give you samples of their homemade *arancini*—a delicious Sicilian snack made from leftover rice that is rolled into a ball, breaded, and fried—small batch wines and freshly picked vegetables.

Sailors are perhaps the most common visitors to Filicudi, with roughly 40 sailboats visiting daily during the summer. When the seas are calm, use the harbor's mooring buoys. The official port is located on the eastern side, where there's a ferry with daily service to mainland Sicily. On the south side, you'll find Pecorini A Mare, which is a charming hamlet with the town's cantina, restaurant and hotel.

~

The Aeolian Islands are a part of Sicily's identity. Sicilians praise their beauty and talk about their spirits. The islands are as strikingly beautiful as they are rugged and wild—and food grown from the land is as delicious as it is beautiful. Planning a sailing itinerary is challenging and comes highly recommended to all sailors excited for a true adventure off the beaten path from the other popular locations. Sailing yourself to an island and then hiking into the smoldering volcanic peak is an experience not soon forgotten.

The islanders welcome sailors by sharing their wines, their cuisine, and always offering stories as well as anecdotes of this extra-ordinary place they call home.

AEOLIAN ARCHIPELAGO
ITALY

CAPTAIN'S NOTES *AEOLIAN ARCHIPELAGO*

RECOMMENDED ITINERARY

Vulcano
38° 25′05″N, 14° 57′57″E
Anchoring at Vulcano's harbor can be off-putting because the seafloor consists of a deep ridge that drops off drastically near the shore. Checking the depth-finder on approach, you'll see the reading drops from 300 meters to 100 meters in seconds. Even when slowly entering the harbor, those familiar anchorages of 60–40 meters are still un-anchorable until you line yourself up right along the beach, where the boat can sit comfortably in ten meters of mud. Holding is good, with mud and sand on the seafloor.

Lipari
38° 28′24″N, 14° 57′27″E
Check the weather forecast before deciding to overnight in the main port because the bay of Rada di Lipari is open to the east and southeast wind directions. If a gale-force wind blows from mainland Italy, the berths along the quay can become untenable. Even in a gale pushing from the west, a wrap-around swell can make its way round the point, making for an uncomfortable night's sleep at the dock.

Salina
38° 33′18″N, 14° 52′25″E
Porto-delle-Eolie is the principal yachting center on Salina. Advanced slip reservations are recommended during high season. The marina is protected from the prevailing north and western winds during the summer, but during the strong southeast wind, the harbor can become rough. The only alternative safe marina during strong southerly winds is in Lipari and the marina there is often at capacity with local boats. There is suitable anchoring south of the port, along the island ridge that is protected from the prevailing northwesterly wind. Even here, however, a strong sea will cause a wrap-around swell and can create an uncomfortably rocky evening at anchor.

Filicudi
38° 33′27″N, 14° 33′58″E
Faint-hearted sailors should steer clear of this island. You must be ready to lift anchor and cruise onward at a moment's notice during the night's anchor watch if inclement weather arises; the seas can become violent and the two anchorages are exposed to the sea. The pier in the southern port of Pecorini a Mare also has berth options, going stern-to the quay in calm weather, but keep in mind that the two main commercial boats that pass through have priority and locals will set your lines free if they need to get in.

Stromboli
38° 47′41″N, 15° 14′47″E
Stromboli has the most volatile anchorage of anywhere within the Aeolian Islands. The island is an active volcano and also a perfect circle, providing no coves of any kind. Anchor off the eastern side in the only shallow ridge along the island. If winds are strong from any direction, the anchorage can become unsafe. Many boats end up washed ashore ever year. Drop anchor in ten meters in sand.

Panarea
38° 38′21″N, 15° 04′55″E
The main harbor, located on the eastern side of Panarea, has about 40 moorings that sailors can use when visiting the island, which is well-maintained, with a local team that assists with docking. Laid in deep water, long mooring lines attached to the buoy are handed to sailors while staff recommend where to tie off based on the weather. This anchorage is often rolly because it does not have any protected coves or harbors, and, though it is sheltered from direct western prevailing winds, the wrap-around swell is rough. If heavy winds blow from the west, you can expect gusts up to 40 knots on your bow, blowing from either north or south.

RECOMMENDED ANCHORAGES

Cala Zimmari, Panarea
Punta Pollara, Salina
Punta del Perciato, Lipari
Punta Bandiera, Vulcano

ITINERARY DURATION

8 days recommended

PREVAILING WIND

Prevailing winds during the summer season come from the northwest and west. Squalls can come up throughout the islands but do not last long. Wind can come from the south and southeast, and make many of the anchorages uncomfortable and dangerous when at anchor.

SEASON

Sailing is best between late May through the middle of October. Harbors are closed during the winter season and the winds are unpredictable.

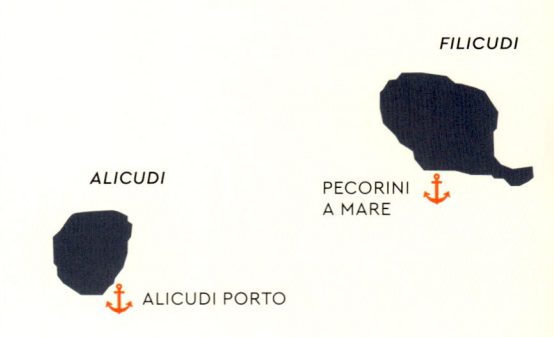

GOOD TO KNOW

Magnetic variance
Magnetic Declination: +3° (EAST)

FILICUDI

ALICUDI

PECORINI A MARE

ALICUDI PORTO

N
W E
S

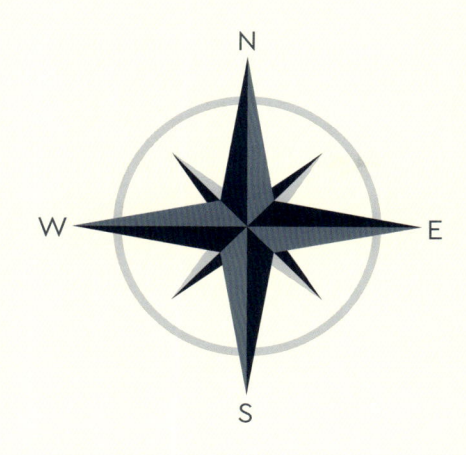

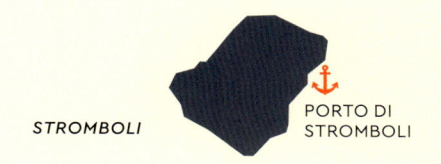

STROMBOLI ⚓ PORTO DI STROMBOLI

THYRRHENIAN SEA

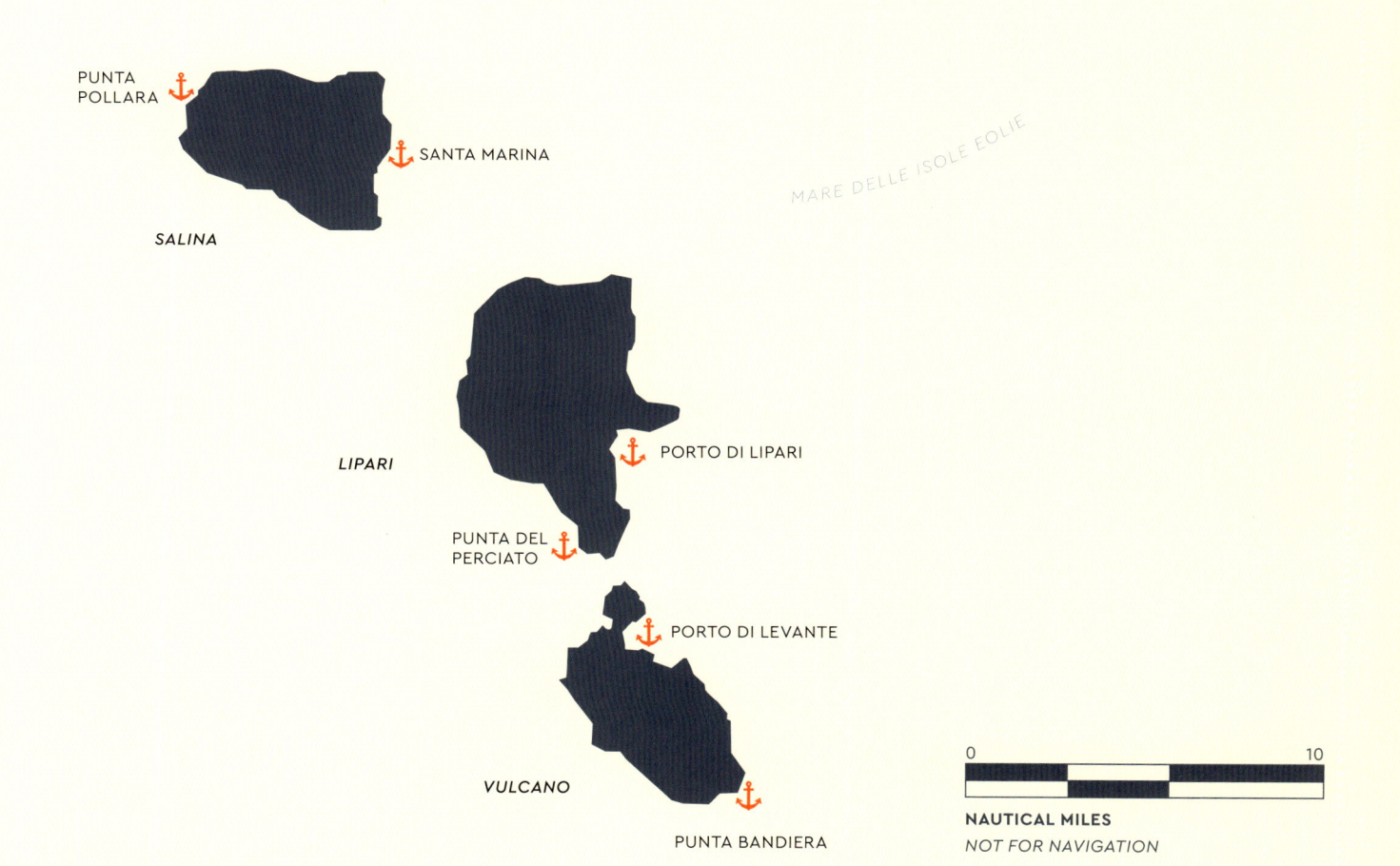

⚓ SANTA MARINA
PANAREA ⚓ CALA ZIMMARI

PUNTA POLLARA ⚓

⚓ SANTA MARINA

MARE DELLE ISOLE EOLIE

SALINA

⚓ PORTO DI LIPARI

LIPARI

PUNTA DEL PERCIATO ⚓

⚓ PORTO DI LEVANTE

VULCANO

⚓ PUNTA BANDIERA

0 — 10
NAUTICAL MILES
NOT FOR NAVIGATION

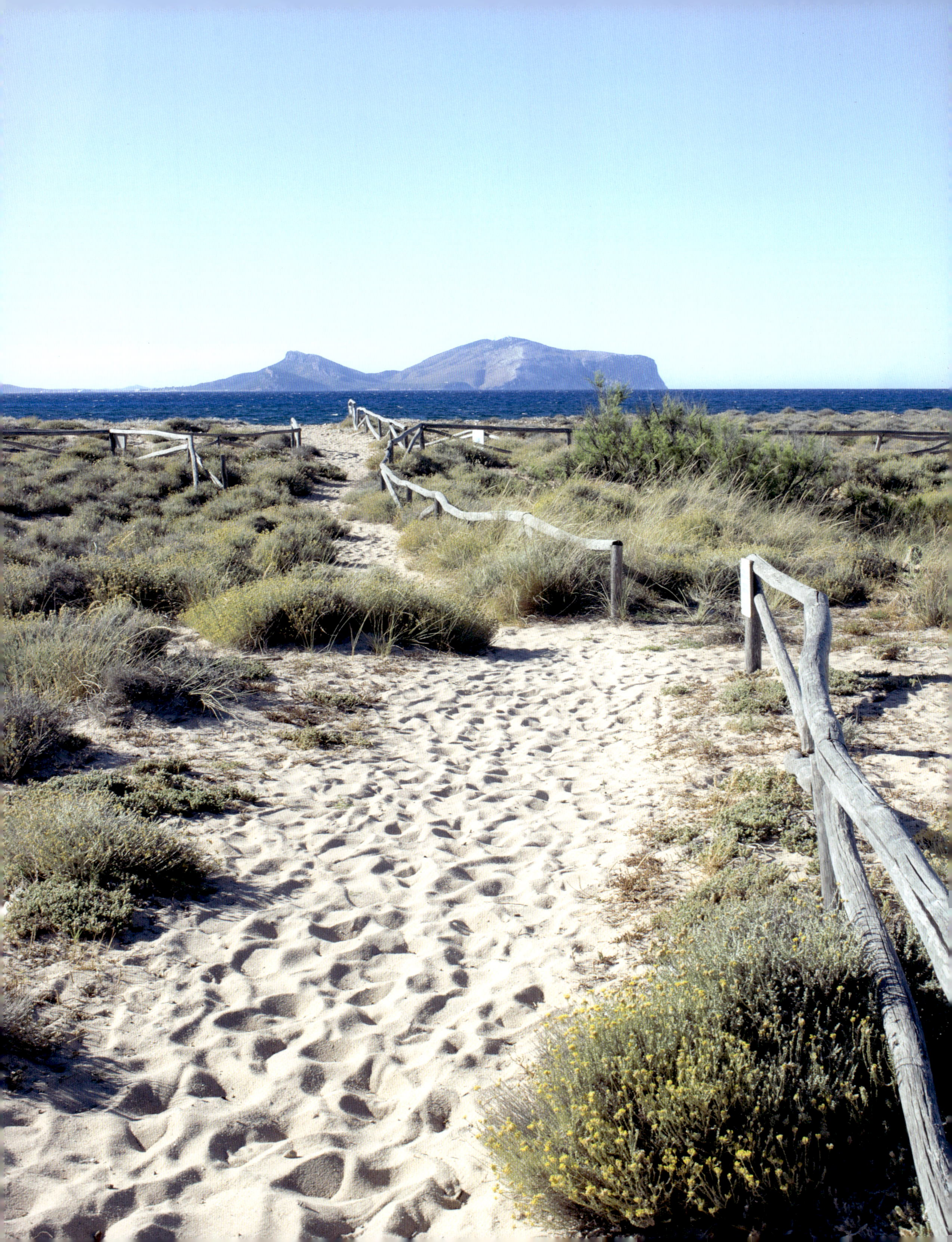

WHITE SANDS OF THE EMERALD COAST

THE NATURAL COAST OF SARDINIA IS UNLIKE ANY OTHER, WITH FINE SAND AND TOWERING BOULDERS MAKING ART OUT OF NATURE. SAIL HERE FOR THE WILD ANCHORAGES AND PLEASANT WINDS.

From the mainland to the numerous islands, the geology of the region feels like an abstract painting and it extends down to the shore where it can be observed continuing underwater through the clear sea. The cluster of islands and the indented coast lined with inlets and coves provide a challenging but rewarding sailing itinerary and are among the finest scenery in the Mediterranean.

The best Sardinian voyaging is along Costa Smeralda, the famous Emerald Coast in the north. Development here is strictly regulated to preserve the natural splendor, especially as viewed from the water because of the influence of a few very rich and very powerful people, most notably Aga Khan IV, Prince Shah Karim Al Hussaini. Roads are built so that they cannot be seen by passing sailors—and houses, no matter how absurdly big, blend into the landscape with natural tone paint and tasteful landscaping. The most expensive sailing yachts in the world gather here annually for the Maxi Yacht Rolex Cup and cruising infrastructure is readily available. Modern marinas are built into the natural landscape as well, and many are unrecognizable from the sea on approach. In many anchorages only the mega yachts give away that hidden in the hills are some of europe's most exclusive addresses—as the shoreline remains unspoilt and retains it's wild beauty.

Sardinia is the second largest island in the Mediterranean has an expansive seacoast of white sand beaches and granite rock formations that create deep inlets and bays. Sardinia's southern point lies just 100 nautical miles from Africa, and to the north Corsica is located only ten nautical miles away across the narrow but formidable Strait of Bonifacio. For much of history the ports of Sardinia were important trading outposts for the great empires of the region, and because of this many of the people of Sardinia settled inland away from the seaside regions as a way to escape seafaring invaders. Disconnected from the sea, the communities developed a pastoral way of life around sheep herding and cheese-making. No written history exists from the Nuragic period here but many traditions on the island, including much of the food, can be traced back to it and significant stone ruins dot the countryside.

Italian is the official language but Sardinian is still spoken on the island and folklore and craftwork traditions remain strong. Stroll through the market stands set up along the promenade in Olbia and you will see gorgeous baskets, intricate embroidery, and pastry breads of delicately woven dough. Towns and villages have their own festivals which are celebrated today alongside the predominant Catholic faith.

The northeast coastline is comprised of Isola Tavolara, La Maddalena archipelago, the famed Porto Cervo, and countless smaller coastal towns and islands each with their own stories. North Sardinia is home to over a dozen uninhabited islands and more than a few cultural treasures. Most Sailors will begin a voyage here from the city of Olbia or Portisco. It's a notably difficult itinerary often with treacherous weather conditions that can force mega yachts and modest sized sailboats alike to remain safe in port for days. But once the weather clears, the emerald waters are unlike any in the Mediterannean with its crystal-like blues and greens that surround small coves lined by impressive cliffs. Nestled towards the head of deep coves are white sand beaches that you'd expect to see in the Maldives, yet here they are for your enjoyment.

ISOLA TAVOLARA

Isola Tavolara is located just south of the Bay of Olbia and is conspicuously recognizable by its steep limestone cliffs that tower 565 meters above the sea and stretch about five nautical miles long. In the west, the cliff dips to a cove and a sun-soaked white sand beach. The eastern side of the island is used as a NATO radio communication station and is off-limits, but sailing past the towering antenna infrastructure that spans mountain peaks is impressive from a distance.

The only viable overnight anchorage is located just south of the western beach which hooks around to form a large bay protected from west and north wind but exposed to the south. There is plenty of room to anchor with the seafloor a mix of sand and weeds. Ashore is a small dock with roughly eight berths that can be reserved by calling the restaurant. Small ferries take day-trippers to the beach from Olbia and the two restaurants, Ristorante da Tonino Re di Tavolara and La Corona, both busy during lunch hours and sparsely populated for dinner when only sailors remain on the island. Adventurous souls can head out for some guided climbing to the peak of the island but it involves technical rock climbing with ropes and most will be satisfied to be awed by the sheer faces of the mountains from the deck of the boat. The beach that lines the anchorage welcomes sailors interested in venturing off their boat and enjoying some time ashore with their feet in the sand.

CAPRERA

Sailing north from Olbia or Tavolara you will enter the La Maddalena archipelago arriving first at Isla Caprera—a largely uninhabited island that has some significant old military infrastructure scattered throughout. The tale of Giuseppe Garibaldi and the unification of the Kingdom of Italy looms large over the island and his retirement home is a museum worth venturing to. Caprera is connected to La Maddalena by a causeway with roads that twist through the mountainous landscape ashore. Along the beaches are restaurants and beach clubs accessed mostly by boat.

LOCAL DISH

Malloreddus is a kind of pasta typical of Sardinia. Also known as gnocchetti sardi or 'little Sardinian gnocchi', after their dumpling-like shape. Malloreddus is made from durum wheat flower, water, and salt and a pinch of ground saffron. Malloreddus alla campidanese is the most common preparation. It is made with fresh tomatoes and Sardinian sausage.

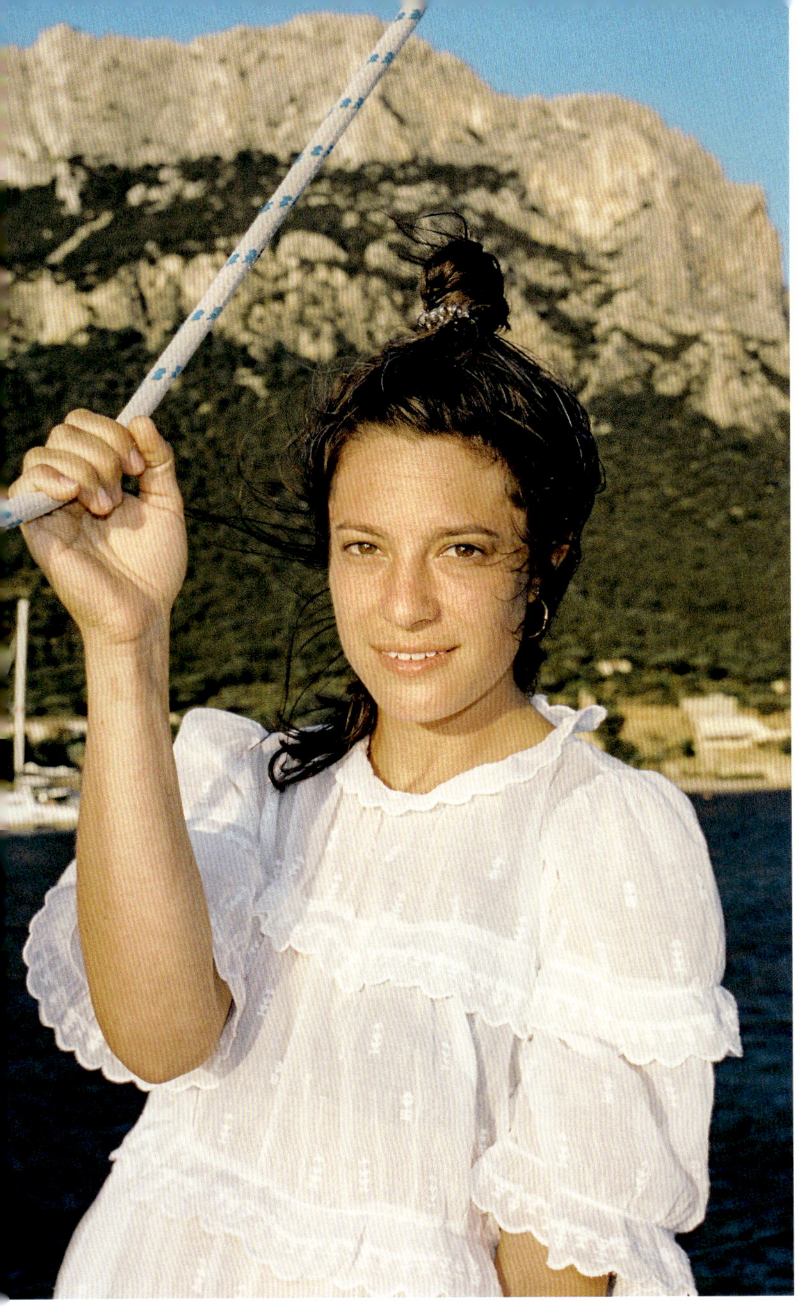

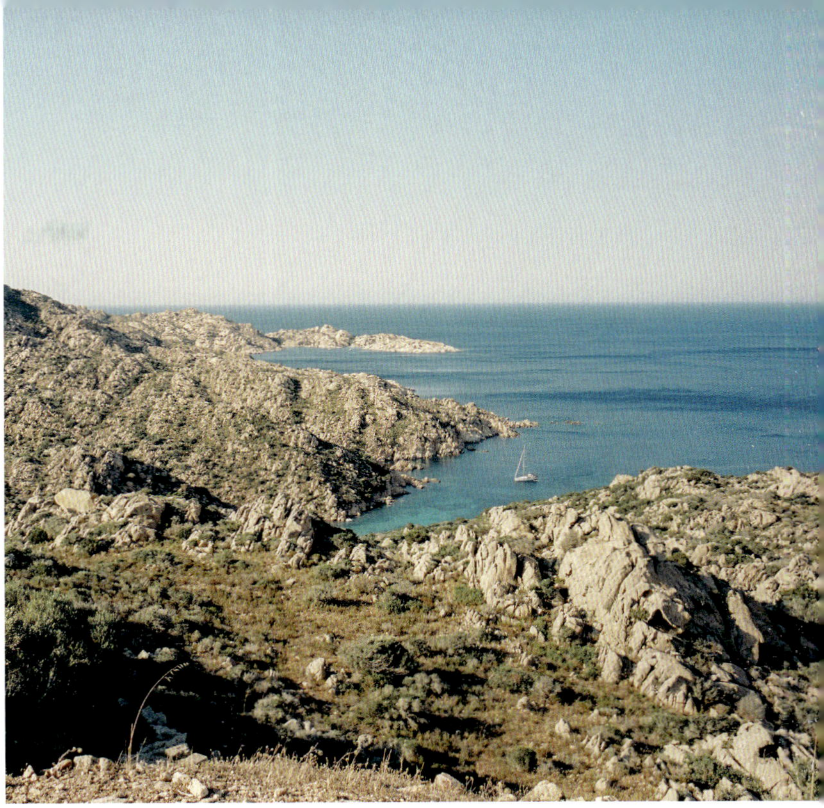

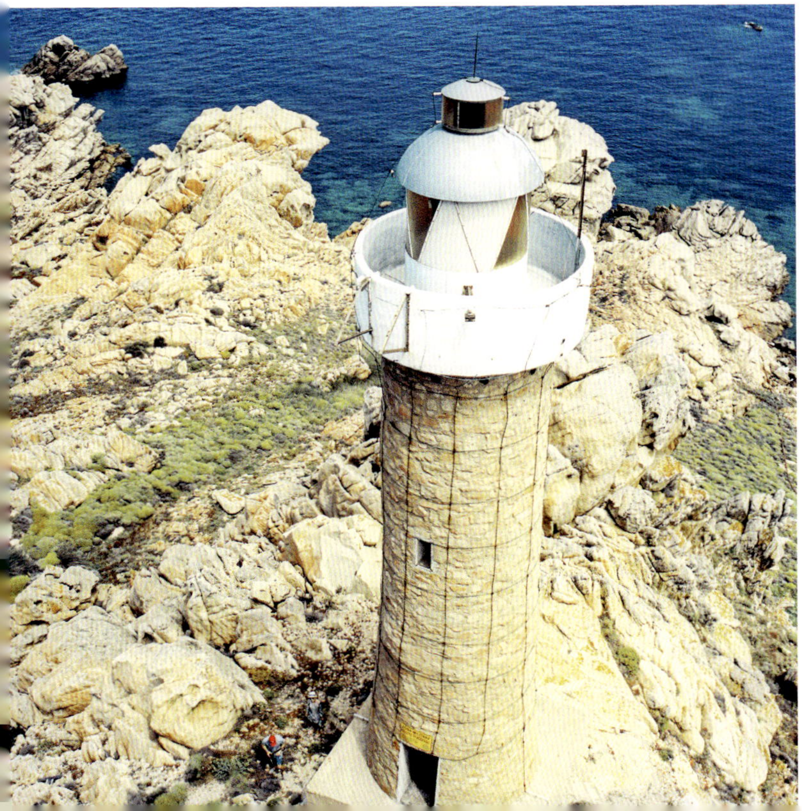

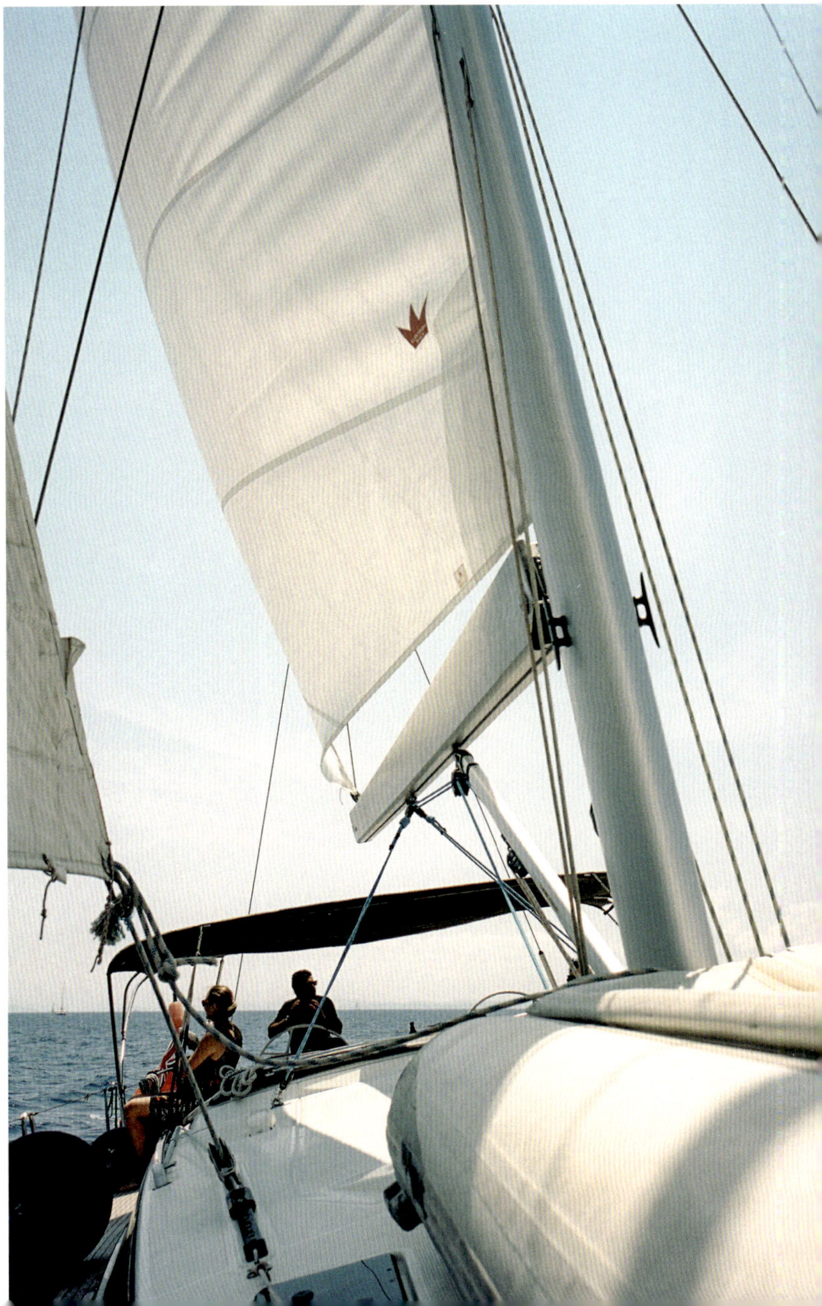

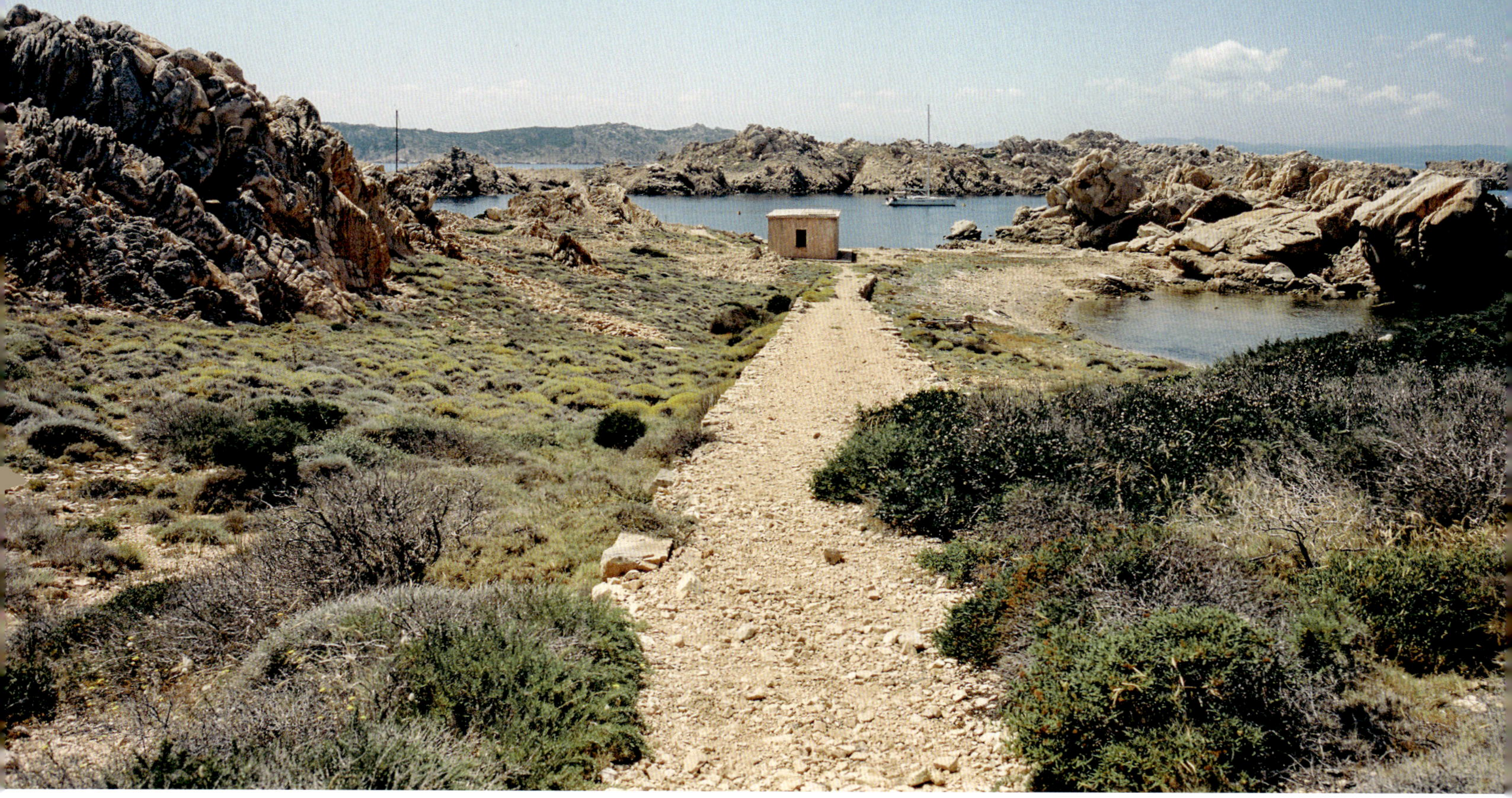

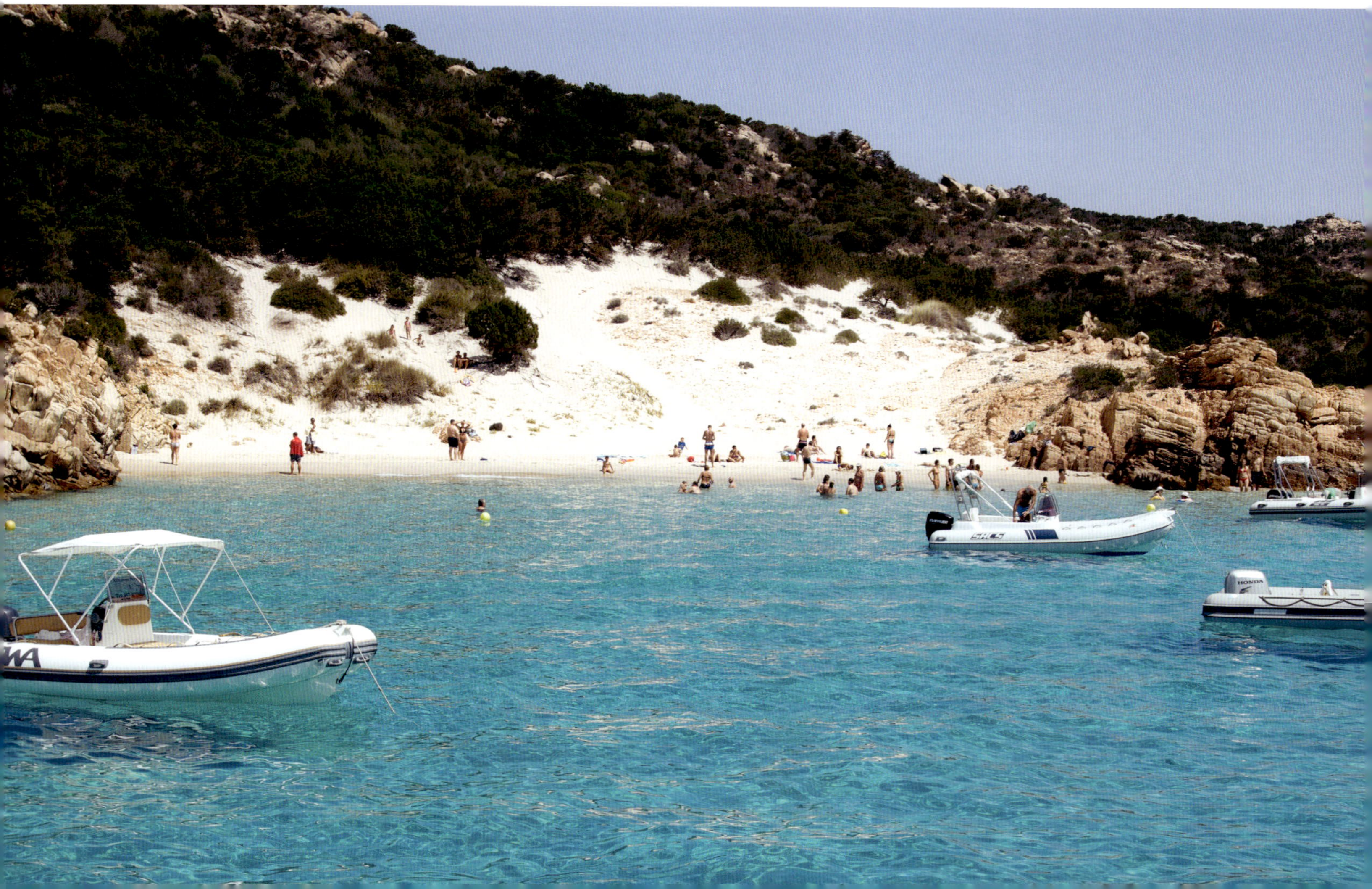

There is no shortage of lunch anchorages in gorgeous deep coves along the rocky shoreline all around the island but overnight stops are mostly in the big bays in the south. A sailing school is headquartered here that teaches a youth program and hosts regattas throughout the summer, anchored in the large Porto Palma you might find yourself completely surrounded by kids in small racing boats one moment, and see the whole pack rounding the corner the next. Cala Portese is the alternative anchorage on Caprera north of Isola Rossa and the anchorage is not safe to anchor in northeast and easterly winds. At the head of the Cala is a white sandy beach with a small restaurant serving snacks and Italian cocktails and a perfect afternoon location to enjoy an Aperol spritz or two.

leaving your boat at the quay to explore La Maddalena and Caprera by road for the day.

LA MADDALENA NORTHERN GROUP

Referred to as the northern group, or "little La Maddalena" are four uninhabited islands named Razzoli, Isola Santa Maria, Budelli, and La Presa, which are home to various isolated coves perfect for an overnight anchorage. Northwesternmost, the island of Razzoli has but one single structure ashore that stands silent sentry over the treachery of the Strait of Bonifacio. A giant aging lighthouse built in brutalist style is still active as a light but no longer houses a lighthouse keeper as it

Sardinia, the second largest island in the Mediterranean, has an expansive seacoast of white sand beaches and granite rock formations that create deep inlets and bays.

LA MADDALENA

La Maddalena is the name of the island group that sits north of mainland Sardinia and is also the name of the largest and most populous island in the archipelago and the name of the only town on the island. Cala Gavetta is the main harbor in town and accommodates transient sailors docked stern-to on the quay but for a quieter night, there is an option for a berth on the floating piers just east of the ferry dock. Going ashore affords you a wander through narrow walking streets lined with fragrant and colorful flowers that overflow from the window boxes of homes that have their shutters flung open to the warm summer air. In the morning at the innermost point of the main harbor fishermen sell the day's catch right off their boat. As the town comes awake tour boats and ferries begin to arrive from mainland Sardinia and the town buzzes with pedestrians eating gelato as they stroll. A scooter rental gives you the option of

once did. Cala Lunga on the western coast of Razzoli is a large bay that opens up into a natural rocky environment that could pass as Mars with redish-orange tinted granite rocks that rise from the water's edge. After anchoring, a quick dinghy ride ashore will take you to a path that leads to the abandoned lighthouse structure.

South of Razzoli is the island of Budelli. Home to the famous Spiaggia Rosa a pink sand beach that today has only a faint hue of pink and is restricted from going ashore onto. Anchor close to it at either Cala Marino or north of Cala Rosa. Viewed from the water this beach is pretty but for a real glimpse of the pinkish hue take the dinghy ashore and land north of the beach to follow a path to an overlook. As the light dims at sunset the magic of Spiaggia Rosa is most poignant. Also ashore on Budelli is a swimming beach in the calm shallow waters where the islands form a triangle (Budelli, Razzoli, and Santa Maria).

AT ANCHOR IN A PEACEFUL COVE ON THE ISLAND OF RAZZOLI (ABOVE). ONE OF SPARGI'S BEACHES (BELOW).

This beach is festive with daytrippers on a summer day and offers pleasant swimming and a long narrow strip of sand to lounge on. Numerous unmarked trails lead around the island and adventurous hikers might make it all the way to the peak of the island and be rewarded with sweeping views of the many gradients of blue water in the surrounding shallows.

~

Home to a variety of charming islands and a rugged and beautiful coastline—Costa Smeralda and the La Maddalena Archipelago is one of the best sailing grounds in all of the Mediterranean. It's vastly different than other sailing itineraries in Italy, let alone the entirety of Europe's waterways. The combination of its isolated coast and offshore islands makes Costa Smeralda best explored by sailboat. Tourism to these places is limited by the exclusivity of the regional resorts, and the itinerary is rewarding for its abundant beauty. There is a nearly endless variety of protected coves for sailors to explore, which means that you could easily spend a week or a lifetime getting to know the region.

CLIFFS OF TAVOLARA

Sometimes the most direct route to an anchorage is not the best one. When approaching Tavolara from the north, round the northeast point of Tavolara and motor alongside the southern cliff face en route to the main harbor. The island cliff falls into the water and steeply continues until the sea floor flattens out roughly a hundred fathoms below. You can crash into the cliffs in a deep keel sailboat here without ever running aground and the experience of staring up past the mast to a towering monolith overhead is a dramatic one.

SARDINIA
ITALY

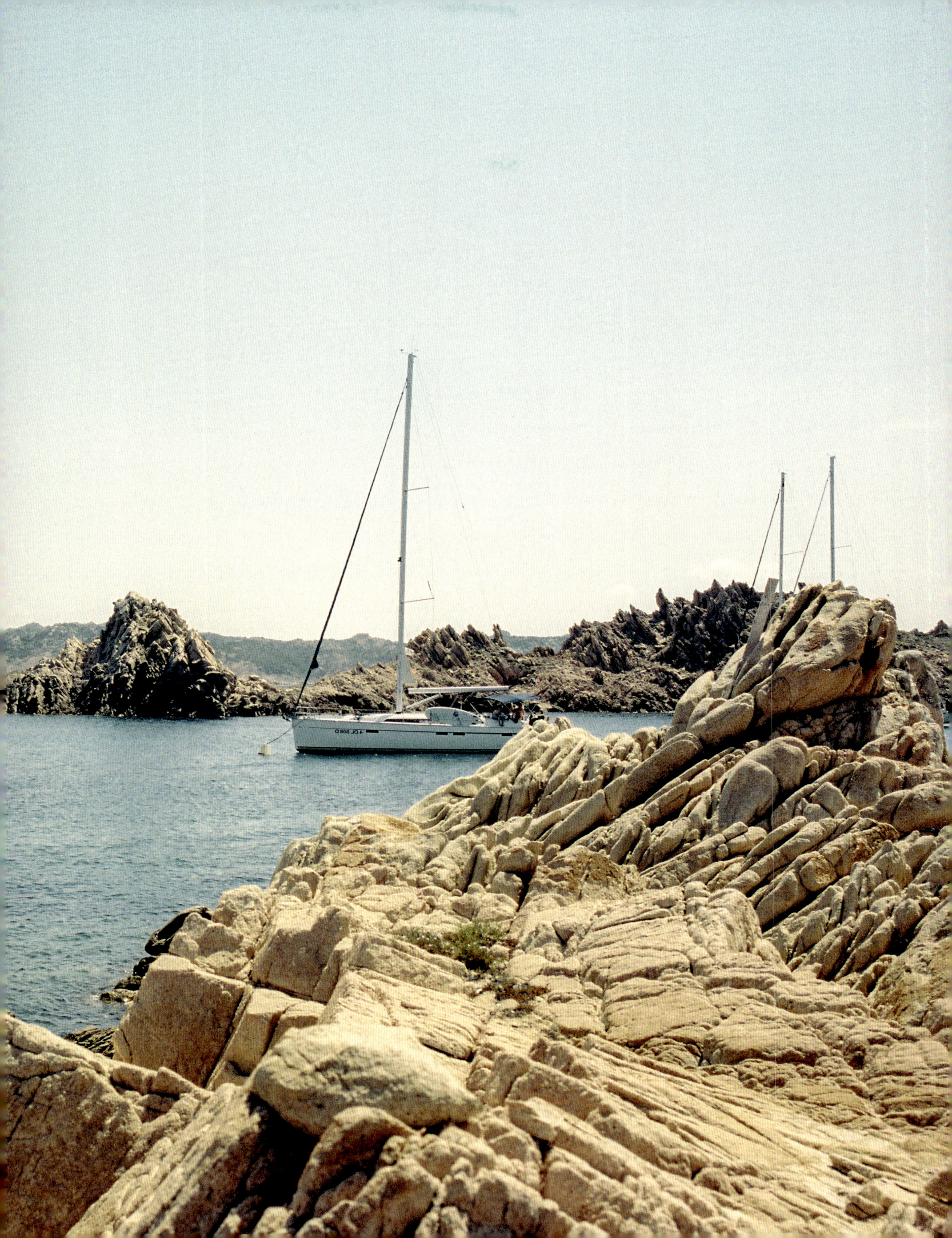

CAPTAIN'S NOTES *SARDINIA*

RECOMMENDED ITINERARY

Olbia
40° 54′58″N, 9° 31′36″E
The large harbor of Olbia is frequented by large ferries and cargo vessels coming and going from all of Italy, France, and Corsica. In the south of the large bay, the marina that caters to yachts has fuel, electricity, and water, and is situated within walking distance of a large supermarket that has good fresh produce and fresh fish.

Tavolara
40° 53′27″N, 9° 40′52″E
Anchor on the south side of the sandy beach for decent protection from every wind except southerlies. Moorings are available close to the beach and restaurants for a fee, or it is possible to anchor further off the beach in sand. Alternatively, arrange with the restaurant on shore to tie up to their floating pier overnight; you just have to be gone by the time the ferries start arriving in the morning.

La Maddalena
41° 12′36″N, 9° 24′30″E
To spend a night enjoying town you can moor stern-to in the historic harbor of Cala Gavetta or head down to the Marina di Cala Mangiavolpe just east of the ferry pier for stern-to docking on their convenient floating piers. Either option allows an easy walk to provisioning and really great gelato.

Budelli
41° 16′53″N, 9° 21′31″E
Anchoring near the famous Spiaggia Rosa gives you good protection from the prevailing northwesterlies. If the wind is south or east, you can anchor in the large, west-facing bay between the islands.

Caprera
41° 11′19″N, 9° 27′03″E
This island, in La Maddalena archipelago, has many small anchorages, which each accommodate just a few boats and fill up quickly in the high season. Anchor in the large Porto Palma for excellent protection from all winds except very strong southerlies. There are only a few mooring buoys, which are preferable if they are available since a grassy bottom makes for poor holding.

Porto Pozzo
41° 11′49″N, 9° 16′29″E
This long, narrow bay on the northern coast of Sardinia offers welcome respite when conditions in the Strait of Bonifacio get rough. Holding at anchor is bad because of thick seagrass, but moorings are available and there is a marina facility with floating docks.

RECOMMENDED ANCHORAGES

Isola del Porco
Cala Portese, Caprera
Cala Corsara, Isola Spargi
Cala Lunga, Razolli

ITINERARY DURATION

4+ days recommended

PREVAILING WIND

As strong westerlies and northwesterlies come through the Strait of Bonifacio they can be bent by the shape of the land into north winds that continue down the coast beyond Tavolara.

SEASON

Sardinia has a wonderful climate with long, hot summers and short, mild winters. spring and fall, temperatures are pleasantly warm. There is a lot of sunshine and little rain. The shoulder seasons offer excellent sailing in April and May or September and October.

FOOD

Much of Sardinian food culture originates in the pastoral highlands, where farmers are known for their sheep cheeses. Pecorino is the most important cheese for export and is sold, both aged and fresh, in every market, but Fiore Sardo is Sardinia's signature. Also a sheep cheese, but with a stronger, more earthy profile than pecorino, Fiore Sardo is aged in three very particular stages before being eaten.

GOOD TO KNOW

Language
Italian is spoken on the streets and taught in schools, but there are still communities that speak the Sardinian language (Sard) at home. Festivals that carry on the traditions of folk music and dance are held in communities all over the island and the importance of these traditions helps keep the language from being lost. The Sardinian language is thought to be the living language closest to Latin as it was once spoken, though it also includes elements that predate Roman influence.

Poseidon's Garden
The local seagrass *Posidonia oceanica* is protected, and it is illegal to drop anchor directly onto it. The grass fouls anchors and makes for poor holding anyways, so avoiding it is in your own best interest. The underwater plant is flowering and produces a non-edible fruit that floats and can be seen in big rafts on the surface along lee shorelines; the floating parts of the plant are known in Italian as *l'oliva di mar*, which translates as "sea olives."

Magnetic variance
Magnetic Declination: +2° (EAST)

La Maddalena Archipelago

Razolli
Santa Maria
⚓ Cala Lunga
Budelli
⚓ Spiaggia Rosa
Isola Maddalena
Isola Spargi
⚓ Cala Corsara
Caprera
⚓ Porto Pozzo
⚓ Cala Portese
⚓ Porto Palma
⚓ *Isola del Porco*

Tyrrhenian Sea

Sardinia

Bay of Olbia

⚓ Olbia

Tavolara
⚓ Porto di Tavolara
Molara

N / W / E / S

0 — 10
Nautical Miles
Not for Navigation

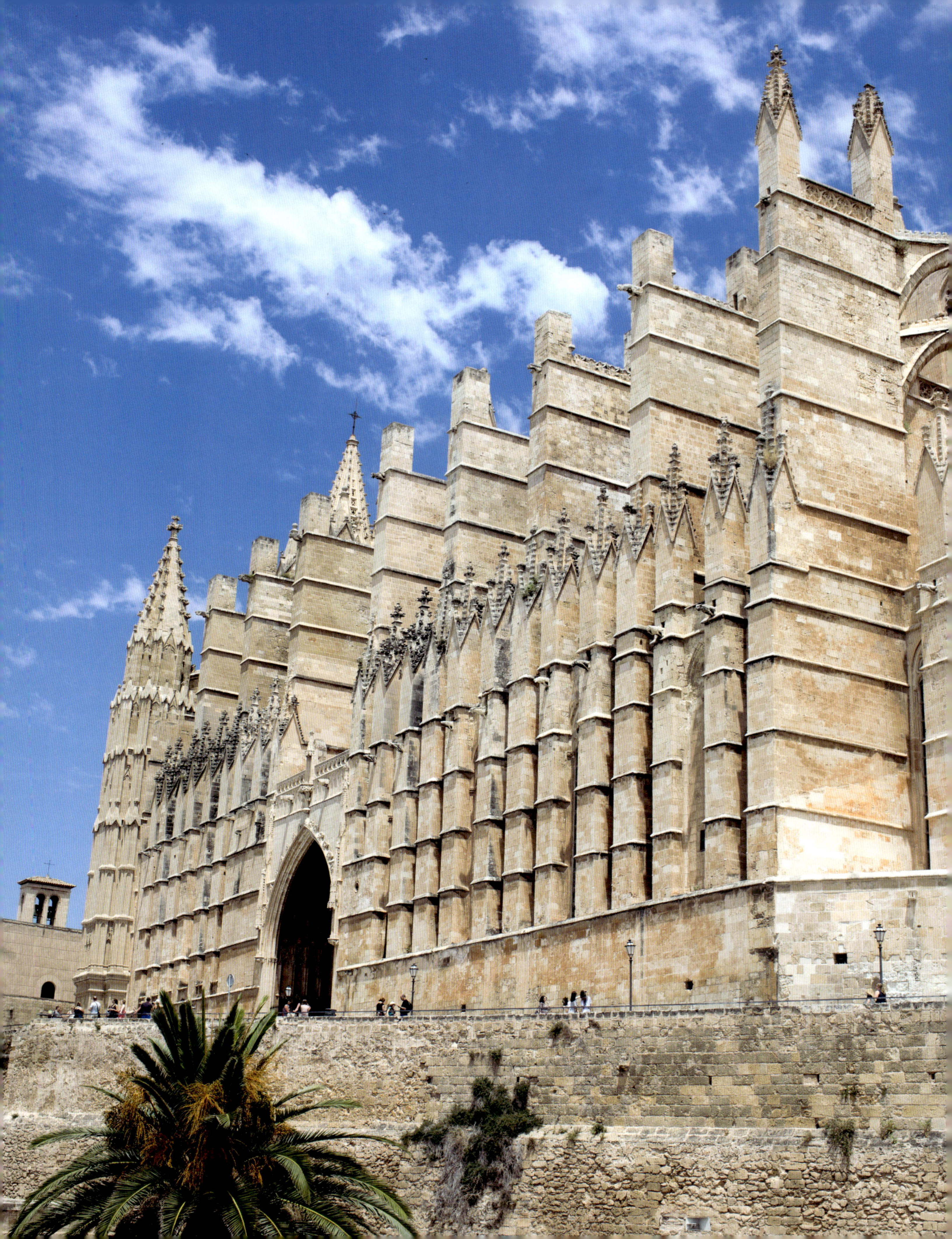

THE GOLDEN HEART OF THE BALEARICS

THE LARGEST ISLAND OF THE BALEARICS, MAJORCA IS HOME TO FISHERMEN, TRADITIONAL TOWNS, AND GLORIOUS BEACHES. YET, DESPITE ITS POPULARITY, IT IS THE AUTHENTICITY OF THE LOCATION THAT KEEPS SAILORS COMING BACK.

The Spanish are no strangers to the sea. Towards the west is the great Atlantic Ocean, and the imposing Mediterranean lines the country's eastern shore. Some 100 nautical miles off the Catalonian coast are the Balearic Islands: popular with Spaniards, foreigners, and mariners alike, and home to one of the largest marinas in all of the Mediterranean. There are four main islands—Majorca, Menorca, Ibiza, and Formentera—with Majorca being the most popular for sailing itineraries within the region.

Majorca differs from many of the great sailing destinations in that it is not a small archipelago with many islands to sail to. Instead, you sail along the coast of the island, anchoring in the *cala*: along the way. A *cala* is an inlet or cove, and here they are in abundance, with stunning white sand beaches and crystal blue waters. Majorca is the largest island in Spain, in terms of both size and population, but, with over half the inhabitants living in the main city of Palma, much of the island is actually sparsely populated, leaving you to explore much of the coast unencumbered by crowds. When the beaches are packed with landlubers, the sea is the obvious place to be.

As in Italy, Spanish culture sings of relaxation and leisure: many of the beaches and *calas* are home to small restaurants serving refreshing beverages and offering local seafood dishes. The scents of olive groves, vineyards, and citrus trees permeate the air as you approach land. Enjoying food is just as important to the way of life as any other aspect of civilization here, and even simple establishments serve incredible dishes. Produce sold at the markets comes fresh from the island.

The culture here expands beyond what is merely productive: *boquerones* fresh from the sea are placed in olive oil to marinate before being served on a plate. You eat this with a crispy bread and a small local beer, in a marriage of simple flavors and bountiful pleasures. This is Majorca; this is why mariners sail these waters. As Majorca is a large island, short sailing voyages can be made from Palma, but, if you're planning on circumnavigating, be sure to allow ten days or more in order to enjoy the pace of local life without feeling rushed.

PALMA

Standing in town and looking out along the waterfront, you will see a sprawling metropolis of sailboat masts, pointing up as far as the eye can see. Marina Port de Mallorca is one of the largest and friendliest port in the Mediterranean and home to thousands of yachts. One after the other, magnificent yachts fill the docks in the port. Many of these are owned by foreign sailors, who keep their boats here in safe harbor to sail the Balearics or to depart for elsewhere in the Mediterranean during the summer months. For sailors cruising on a multi-week itinerary, Palma is the obvious departure location.

Palma has been occupied since Roman times, when it was known as Palmeria. Since then, the city has remained prosperous as a trade center, as can be observed during casual strolling. Palma is mostly car-free and a short walk from the port finds the traveler immersed in medieval streets. Overlooking the harbor, and its focal point, is the gigantic, Gothic Catedral-Basílica de Santa María de Mallorca. Departing Palma for a voyage through the Balearics is a unique experience and leaves any sailor pondering the antiquity of the journey; looking behind while you sail onward, you see the city as it was centuries before, as it has always been.

SANT JORDI AND SES COVETES

The island is diverse but the coastline is consistent, with rough cliffs interrupted by white sand beaches, seamlessly flow into the surrounding environments. Depending on the weather, you can sail clockwise or counter-clockwise to circumnavigate Majorca. Sailing eastward from Palma roughly 25 nautical miles, Sant Jordi is at the end of the point. This is a seaside village, home to a small port with a small local fishing fleet, and on either side of the village are beaches that continue on for miles. Ses Covetes, located west of Sant Jordi, is an open anchorage, where you can find pleasurable refuge along stretches of yellow sand beach. The water beneath your boat is a bright azure and the sand lining the sea floor is soft and inviting. If you sail with a small flotilla, this anchorage is a great place for a raft-up, with sailboats tied one to another to build a small floating village. If not, find a place to drop the hook with no other boats around and feel the joy of seclusion in this beautiful paradise.

A long swim or a dinghy ride ashore and you will find beachgoers in full swing during the summer months. Walk along the sandy shore until you get to one of the many cabanas serving tapas, and fresh and fried seafood; enjoy a refreshing cerveza and enjoy watching your boat float peacefully at anchor.

Back aboard, you can prepare yourself and your fellow sailors a fantastic meal using fresh produce and fish purchased from the markets on the island. *Pintxos* are a local Spanish snack often enjoyed with a refreshing cerveza or with Spanish cava. Thin slices of baguette are cut and topped with a variety of pickles, cured meats, fish, olives, and cheese; it is a perfect boat-snack, to be enjoyed while watching a beautiful sunset.

SPECIALTY

As in other parts of Spain, curing meats is an important culinary tradition and there is a unique local sausage called sobrassada. *Unlike the Italian version,* soppressata, *which is made using a dry-aging process, the Majorcan* sobrassada *is soft and buttery.* Sobrassada *is a combination of minced pork, bacon, salt, and spices including smoked paprika, taking on a color similar to that of chorizo. It is often drizzled with honey and enjoyed with local cheese.*

ANCHORING OFF CABRERA (ABOVE). TRADITIONAL PINTXOS WITH SALT-BAKED WHOLE FISH PREPARED ABOARD THE BOAT (BELOW, LEFT).

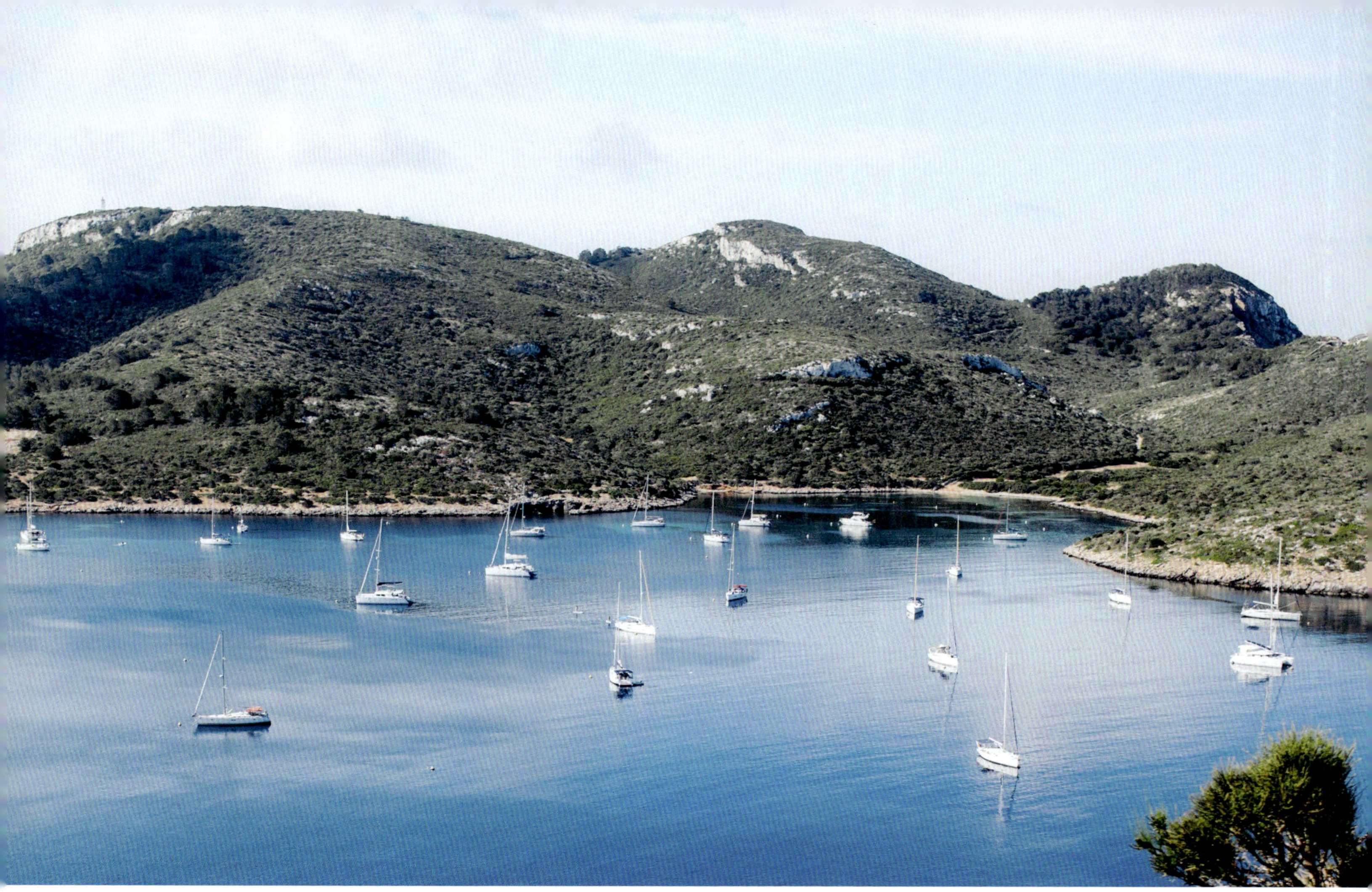

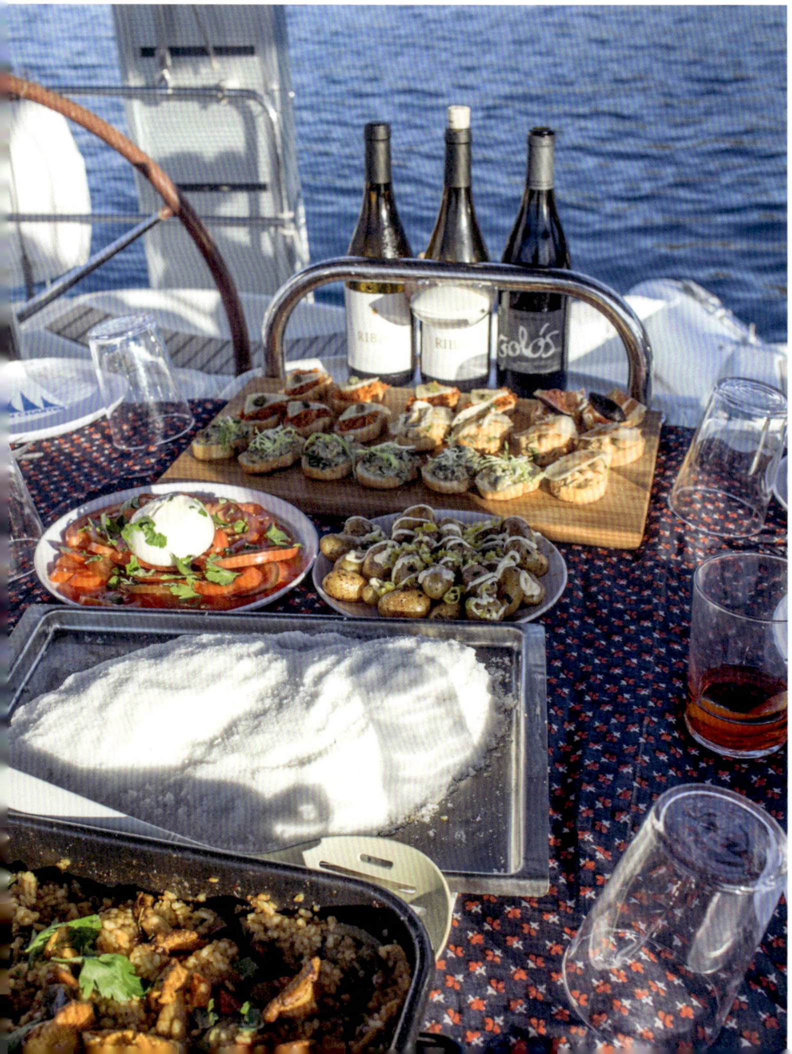

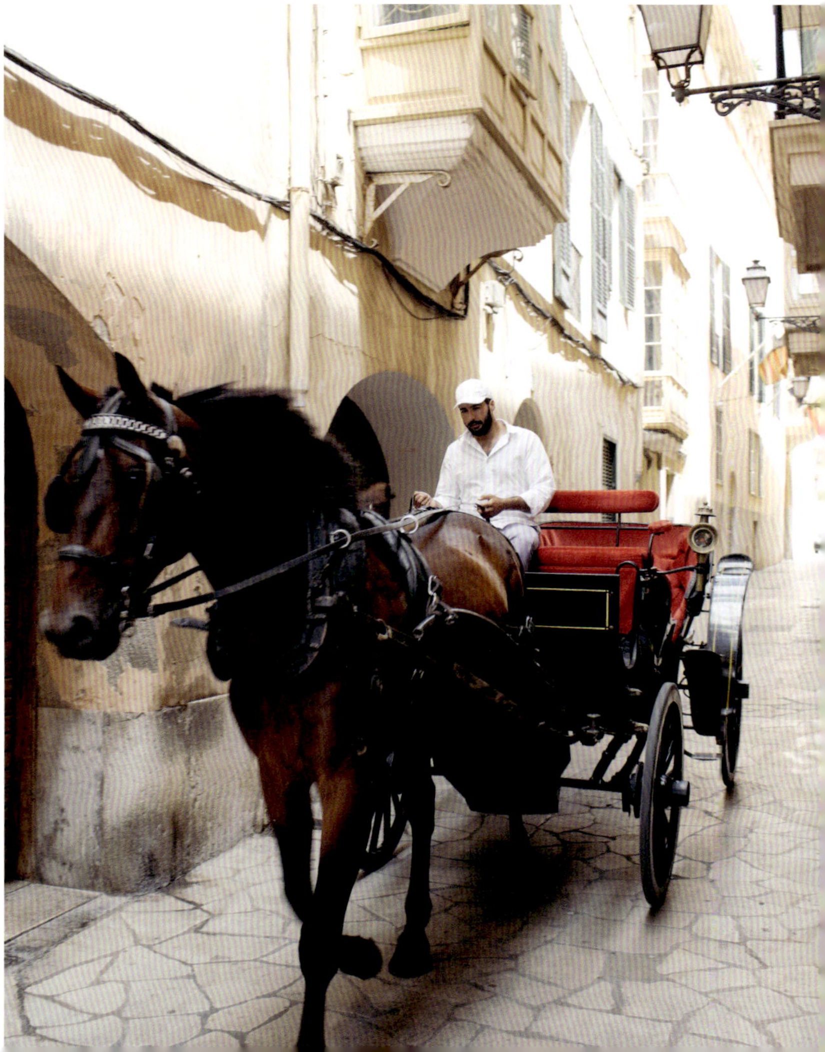

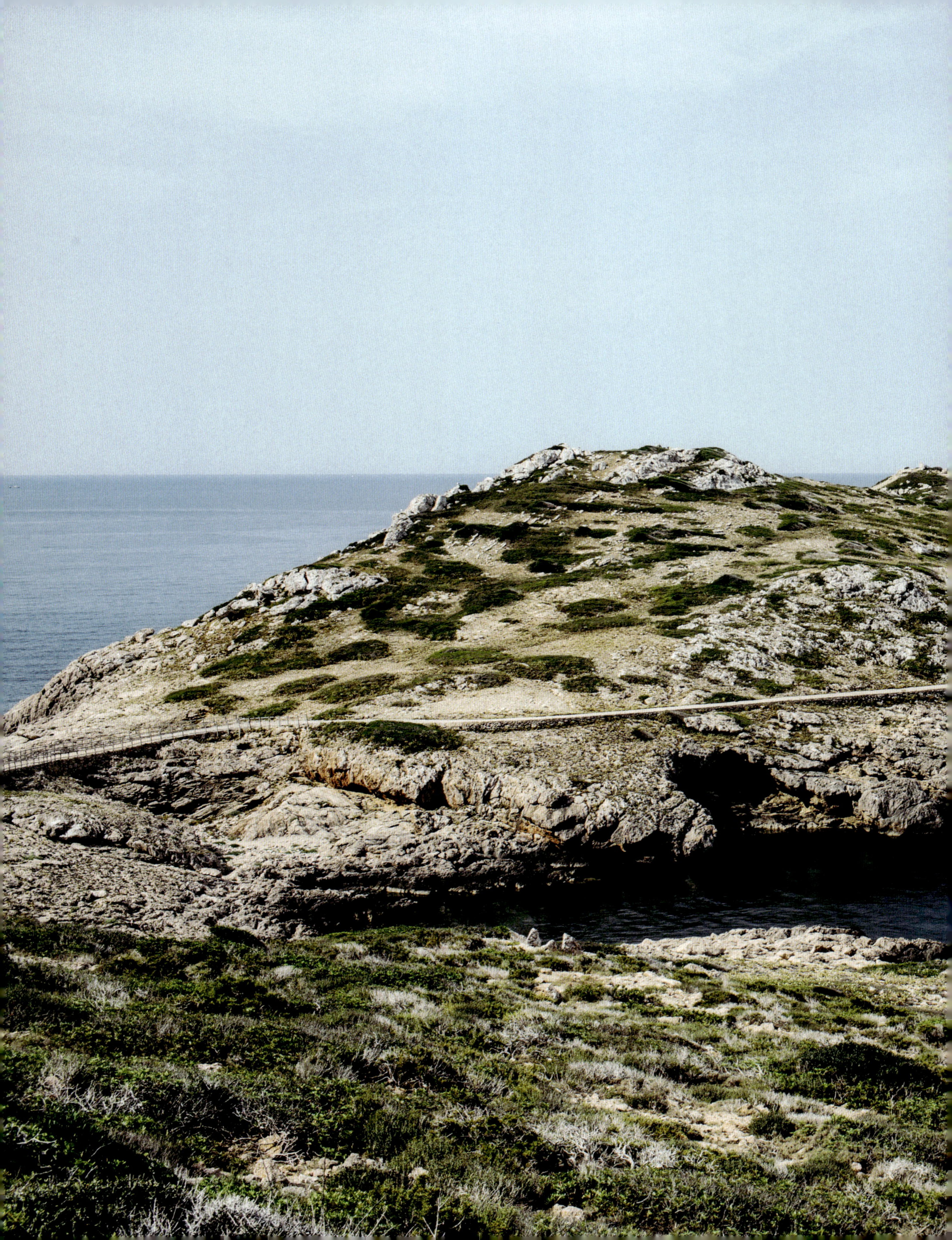

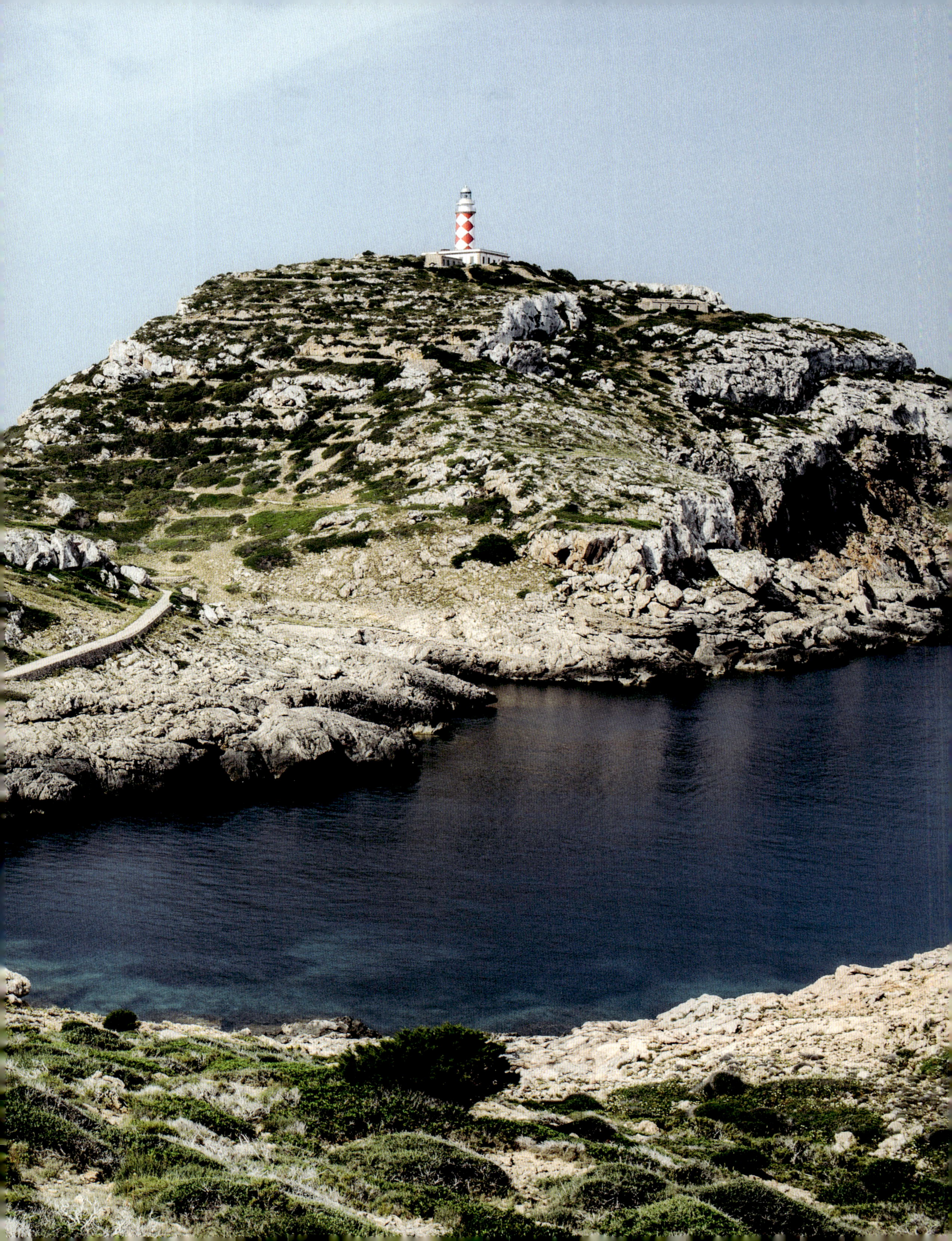

PORTOCOLOM

There are both idyllic and commercial towns lining the coast of Majorca; Portocolom's the latter. Sailing along the eastern coast is easy, with next to no obstacles in your way as you make your passage to your next port of call. Wind is often light and the seas calm. Upon your approach to Portocolom, you'll first be greeted by a large, conspicuous lighthouse, located on the north cliff face at the entrance to the harbor. It stands tall, with the tower painted in white and blue stripes. The entrance of the harbor opens into a large bay with enough water to enter under full sail on calm days. Upon arrival, you will find a marina and a large mooring field with many options for where to moor your boat while you spend the night at the tranquil safe harbor.

One of the highlights of any sailing stopover is walking slowly along the shore, taking note of all the wonderful beauty that surrounds the cove. Going ashore at Portocolom, you'll be met with timeless Majorcan architecture: white buildings with green and blue shutters line the waterfront. Small buildings on the shore have boathouses with carriage doors that open to the water and slanted landings, designed to allow fishing boats to be easily hauled out during the winter season or for repairs. You will see pine trees with wonderfully pleasant fresh scents and droves of lilac flowers that decorate the houses.

PORTOPETRO

Five nautical miles south lies Portopetro, one of the smaller and more peaceful towns located on the eastern coast of Majorca and a perfect port of call while sailing on the eastern side of the island. It retains much of its traditional charm, with most of the homes and small buildings that line the bay built 100 years ago, as you can tell from their colors and the authentic and identifiable Majorcan shutters. The port is a day sail from Cabrera, sailing northeast along the southeast coast of Majorca, and an easy passageway assuming fair seas. The harbor is protected, and, as you sail in through the passageway, you can see the calm waters ahead while you tack back and forth. Drop anchor or dock along the seawall in town.

CABRERA

Sailing towards Cabrera is a nice break from coastal cruising. The natural and perfectly kept island sits ahead peacefully as you sail down from Majorca to this unique and small archipelago; it's possible to experience larger swells the further you sail from Majorca and the closer you get to Cabrera.

The island of Cabrera is wild. It is largely uninhabited and undeveloped other than a few conspicuous buildings: some fortified medieval watchtowers, a cantina serving beer to the fishermen passing by, and a number of lighthouses. As you make your approach, you see the large watchtower boldly sitting on the north point of the harbor entrance. This fortified lookout was built for the purpose of spotting pirates. Fire and smoke signals were used to give warning to the mainland when a potential invasion was on the horizon. Dinghy ashore and hike to the fort to enjoy a stress-free view without the dangers of a pirate invasion.

Another possibility for exploration on land is a hike across the island. You'll be able to explore one of Spain's most important lighthouses, which aids mariners in navigating towards open and safe seas. The windy walkway from the main harbor is lined with unique green and yellow flora that resembles something more like a mystical environment than a pathway in Spain.

PORT DE SÓLLER

Most sailors take to the southern and eastern coasts of Majorca because of the bountiful coves and port towns, home to many marinas and safe anchorages. Along the northwest side of Majorca, however, is a large and devastatingly

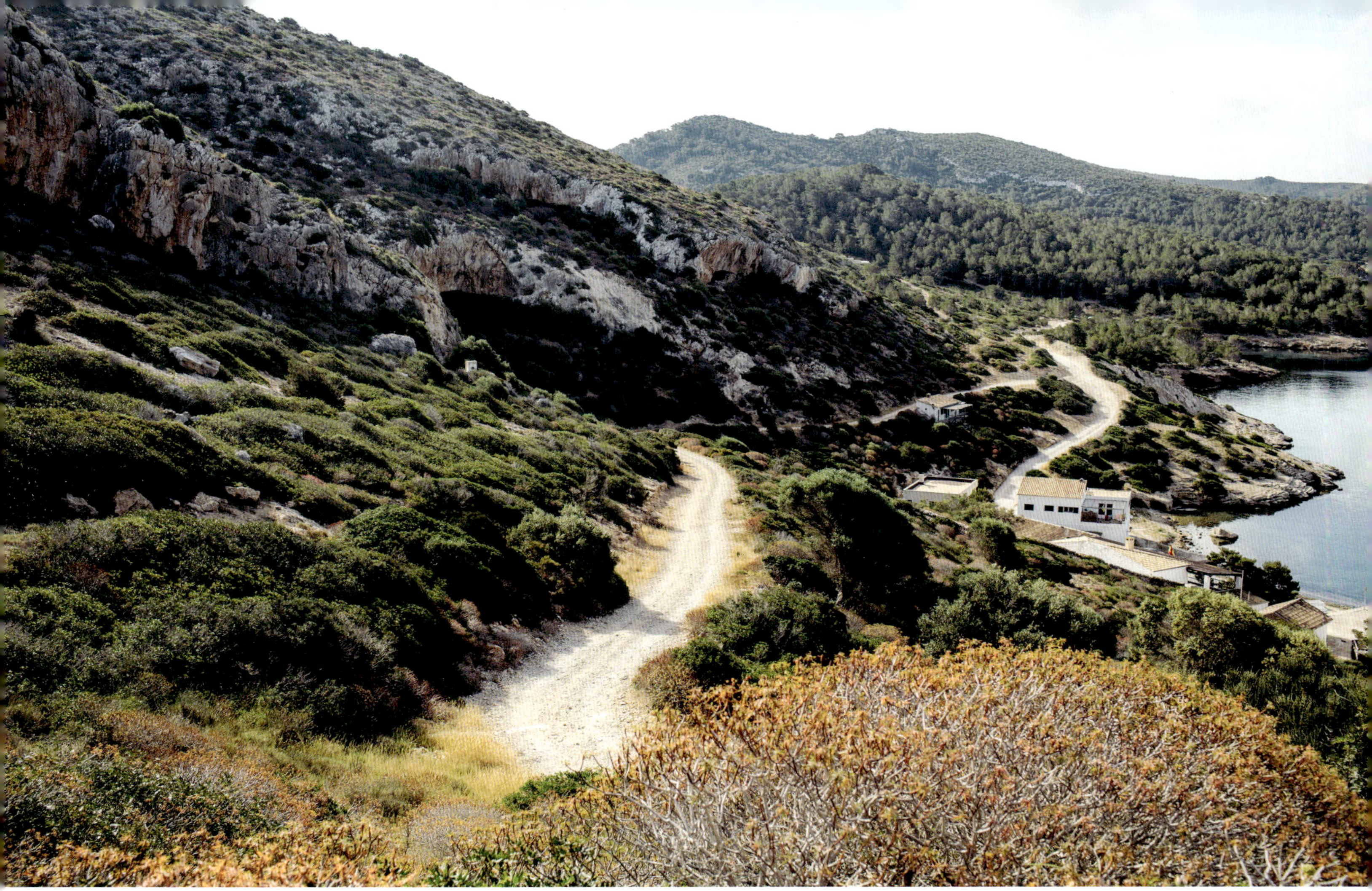

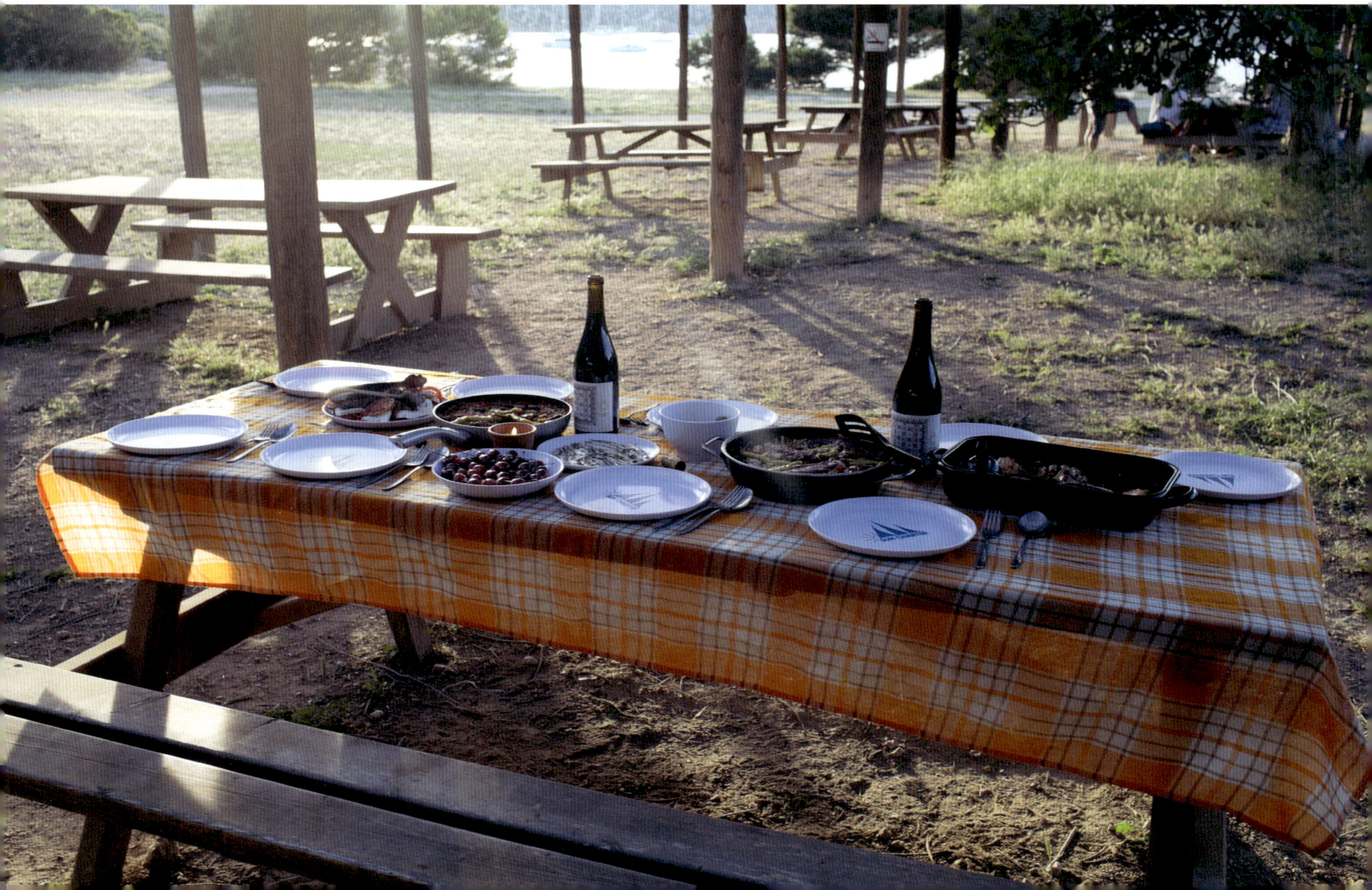

SANT MATIES
7ª MH-2-4-94

beautiful mountain ridge. This leg of the voyage should be timed carefully, as there is only one safe harbor. Located in the center of the coast is Port de Sóller, notable for two things: the home of celebrated Spanish painter Joan Miró, and the endless fields of orange and lemon trees that line the town, offering a sweet-smelling gift to everyone who sails to this quaint seaside village. The town of Sóller is charming, with beautiful architecture, restaurants, and cafés. The harbor is safe from inclement weather, providing shelter in the anchorage and the marinas. Departing Port de Sóller and sailing north, the next safe port is nearly 50 nautical miles away: Port de Pollença. South lies Port d'Andratx and this passage is best made during calm seas.

~

You could spend weeks sailing the Balearic Islands and enjoy every minute of exploring each cala and seaside town alike. The region's rich maritime history is evident throughout the itinerary and the quiet seaside villages are as idyllic as any others in the Mediterranean. The cultures of Majorca, Ibiza, and Menorca are strong and wedded to their traditional ways, just like the sailors who cruise their coastline, enjoying their vistas.

N'ENSIOLA LIGHTHOUSE

This lighthouse on Cabrera has been flashing constantly since 1870 and is vitally important to sailors cruising from Ibiza to Majorca, as well as commercial ships continuing onward towards Italy and France. The light initially flashed every 30 seconds. but in 1929, a new lens in a mercury flotation bath was installed, producing three bright white flashes every ten seconds.

CAPTAIN'S NOTES *MAJORCA*

RECOMMENDED ITINERARY

Palma de Mallorca
39° 34′ 10″ N, 2° 39′ 0″ E
Berth in any of the several yachting facilities set in the large bay. It is one of the largest collective yachting centers in the entire Mediterranean, home to several thousand yachts. Check the local pilot guide for information. The marina is crowded in the high season.

Colònia de Sant Jordi
39° 18′ 45″ N, 3° 0′ 4″ E
Anchor outside the breakwater. The medium-size fishing harbor is mostly for small vessels with depths of less than 1.5 meters.

Port de Sóller
39° 31′ 13″ N, 2° 41′ 10″ E
A suitable anchorage sits in the Bay of Sóller and there is a functioning marina with transient slips for yachts. This is the only protected harbor refuge along the 50-mile stretch of rugged coastline on the northwest side of Majorca. The town of Sóller is surrounded by a spectacular, mountainous ridge, which isolates this town from the rest of the island. The approach is straightforward unless there is a gail from the north and the northwest; the swells and rocky conditions caused by this can present challenges.

Cabrera
39° 8′ 57″ N, 2° 55′ 47″ E
Moor using the national park moorings located in Cabrera port, as anchoring is strictly forbidden. Moorings must be reserved and authorized in advance of arrival, and the harbor patrol will send you away if the moorings are fully reserved. The bay opens to the north and is suitable in virtually all wind conditions.

Portocolom
39° 25′ 11″ N, 3° 15′ 52″ E
Home to a large natural harbor with moorings and slips for over 200 vessels along the Club Náutico di Portocolom, located in the northwest corner of the harbor. The entrance of the harbor is deep with no obstructions. Berth stern-to the south side of the yacht harbor or along one of the two Port Authority jetties.

RECOMMENDED ANCHORAGES

Ses Covetes
Cala Màrmols
Cala Figuereta
Cala Mondragó
Port d'Andratx
Cala de s'Águila
Platja de Coll Baix

ITINERARY DURATION

6 days, recommended for sailing the east and south route

10 days, recommended for circumnavigating Majorca

PREVAILING WIND

The most common wind blows from the south and southwest. During the winter months, the *Mistral* blows from the northwest and the *Tramontana* wind blows from the north. From the end of August through October, the wind is often unpredictable, blowing in all directions.

SEASON

The Balearic Islands enjoy moderate-to-warm temperatures all year round, with highs from June through September and more moderate heat from October through May. There is very little rain in Majorca: October and November are the wettest months, with, on average, six days rain in total. Although the high season is June through August, sailing is enjoyed year-round in Mallorca.

FOOD

Local delicacies and specialties include *sobrassada*, *trempó*, *ensaïmada* and *arroz brut*. *Trempó* is a simple salad comprising tomato, onion, Majorcan green bell pepper, olive oil and salt, and is enjoyed with every meal including breakfast. It is traditionally eaten with the hands only. A savory rice casserole, *arroz brut* is a staple of Majorcan cooking made year-round with different seasonal ingredients. The dish is soupy, with the liquid made from strong meat stock and various seasonal vegetables.

Ensaïmada is a Majorcan pastry made with four, eggs, water, sugar, saim (pork lard), and a mother dough. Some variations are made with filled cream, chocolate, or sweet pumpkin. The use of pork lard instead of butter keeps the pastry savory.

GOOD TO KNOW

Cabrera
Cabrera, while sparsely developed, is an exciting and prominent destination on a sailing itinerary. There is a large bay, where you can reserve moorings managed by the conservation group that governs the marine wildlife park. Registering your vessel before arrival is strictly required, so be sure to have the necessary permits before you set sail.

Magnetic variance
Magnetic Declination: +1° (EAST)

MAJORCA

BALEARIC SEA

- PORT DE POLLENCA
- PLATJA DES COLL BAIX
- CALA TUENT
- PORT DE SÓLLER
- ALCUDIA BAY
- CALA DE S'AGUILA
- DRAGONERA
- PORT D'ANDRATX
- MARINA PORT DE MALLORCA
- BAY OF PALMA
- CALA VARQUES
- PORTOCOLOM
- SES COVETES
- PORTOPETRO
- CALA MONDRAGÓ
- COLÒNIA DE SANT JORDI
- CALA FIGUERETA
- CALA MÀRMOLS
- CASTILLO DE CABRERA & PARQUE NACIONAL
- CABRERA

0 — 10

NAUTICAL MILES
NOT FOR NAVIGATION

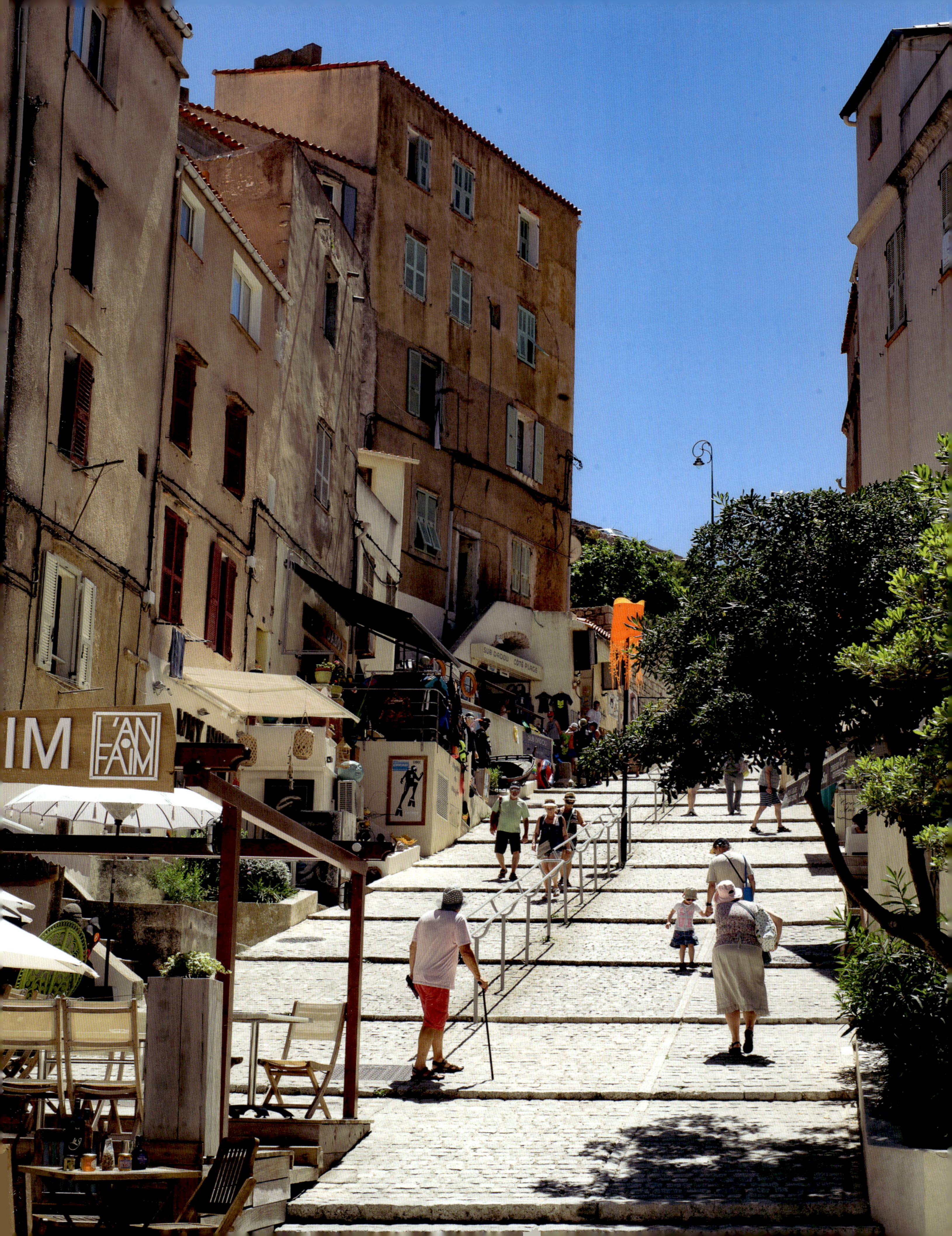
IM
L'AN FAIM

THE CLIFFS OF SOUTHERN CORSICA

THE BEAUTIFUL TOWN OF BONIFACIO OVERHANGS THE MAJESTIC LIMESTONE CLIFFS OF SOUTHERN CORSICA, GAZING DOWN UPON SAILBOATS CROSSING THIS TREACHEROUS STRAIT.

Southern Corsica presents a bold coastline of white limestone cliffs that are as foreboding and dangerous as they appear. Sailors take this coastline and the water around it seriously and explore this itinerary with the caution it deserves. The Strait of Bonifacio presents many of the dangers that keep sailors up at night: magnetic anomalies, hyper-local wind patterns, current rips, steep seas, and a maze of unmarked navigational dangers. Voyaging here is all the more satisfying for these obstacles, however: beyond the danger, you will find beautiful islands, the Mediterranean's most stunning port town, and passage-making that challenges and excites.

The roads along the southern coast of Corsica, as opposed to those in the north, are located well inland, making exploration by sea the best option for seeing the shoreline, and what a shoreline it is! What appears from a distance to be an unbroken and impenetrable barricade of solid stone rising out of the ocean, is, on closer inspection, exactly that. Only in select locations can hikers along the bluff find ways to billy-goat to the water's edge and swim; for the most part, the southern coast is impassibly steep and yours alone to explore by sailboat. Cruise in the shadow of the cliffs and one of the more notable sights is a lighthouse—Madonetta—situated high enough to have a commanding view of the entire strait.

The town of Bonifacio sits over the ocean, perched precariously on limestone cliffs that look like they may topple into the sea the moment you take your eyes off them. This port, and the fortified village above it, have a history that is as storied as the place is stunning. As a skipper, you must know the capabilities and limits of your vessel in order to arrive safely on these shores. The entrance to Bonifacio is foreboding, but it will certainly be a welcome sight to sailors looking for safe harbor as they tuck in under the fortifications.

On days when the Strait of Bonifacio is settled, and not throwing its famously steep swell onto the cliff face in a violent display of indifference to the wellbeing of sailors, there are many beautiful moments to be had outside of the protected bays along the southern shore of Corsica. Should you be graced with such weather, don't lament the lack of wind in your sails—use it to explore the unmarked

STRAIT OF BONIFACIO | FRANCE

wonders. On the other hand, if you do experience the wild conditions for which the Strait is famous, then you can rejoice in that too. Lively passage-making, with reefed sails and a safe harbor waiting for you at the end of the day, is what exploration under sail is all about.

BONIFACIO

The harbor entrance at Bonifacio is so narrow that, until you are right under the overhanging cliffs of the old city, it remains difficult to believe it is there. Buildings within the fortified wall sit right up along the edge of the cliff and loom more pronouncedly as you make your approach. When you do finally spot the small red lighthouse and make the turn into the curved harbor entrance, you come right up against the embattled history of the town. Battlements—some dating back to the Bronze Age and others as recent as the Second World War—tower over you. You get the sense that enterprising locals with large rocks could defeat a well-armed ship in a contest for the high ground here; add gun emplacements and invading forces don't stand a chance. Entering the channel between the narrow cliffs gives you a feeling similar to that of looking up at the night sky.

Inside the port of Bonifacio, you have the option to dock at the marina—a harrowing affair with slime-lines and push boats and people attempting to communicate with you through loud whistles. Alternatively, the cove just outside the marina, to the north of the ferry dock, presents its own set of challenges: when the wind is strong, it blows broadside into this cove and makes the process of dropping anchor and securing stern lines a messy one.

On shore is as quaint a town as you'll find anywhere in the world. Walk up the steps from the harbor and cross a drawbridge to enter the old fortified city; once inside, the modern world is all squeezed into a medieval stronghold. There are shops and restaurants and a post office on the stone walking streets, once you have crossed the drawbridge to enter the fortified walls of the old city. Considering the small geographic area that it occupies on top of the bluff, it is surprisingly easy to get lost in the old city. No grid system dictates these streets; one way you get your bearings is by finding (or stumbling upon) an ocean view—even more breathtaking when you consider you stand above that same ocean on the overhanging edge of the town. Hanging on a stone wall in a narrow alley is a hand-painted wooden sign with an arrow that says "bar with the most beautiful view"—it is not a joke.

At the head of the bay, near the line of tour boats, is a compact supermarket that has everything you need. You can even push your cart all the way to your boat if you are on the floating piers of the marina. If you are in the cove, you can pull your dinghy right up across the street from the market, making this a viable option for substantial provisioning runs. The parts of town below the fortified city, while decidedly less spectacular, still manage to be charmingly French, Corsican, and pleasant.

A number of low-lying islands located in the Strait of Bonifacio are notable for the orange granite boulders that litter the island edges. A marine reserve surrounding the islands forbids fishing of all kinds and, on shore, the

THE STEPS OF BONIFACIO

Legend has it that steps were carved up the sheer cliff face at Bonifacio at night, in secret, by Alfonso V, King of Aragon, during an unsuccessful siege in 1420. It is said that this incredible feat of siege engineering was betrayed by a local woman, who used a treacherous route on the cliff daily to fetch water; once noticed, the invading army was easily defeated. At Bonifacio today, you can hike down the steps all the way to the ocean and swim in a rocky cove under the shadow of the town.

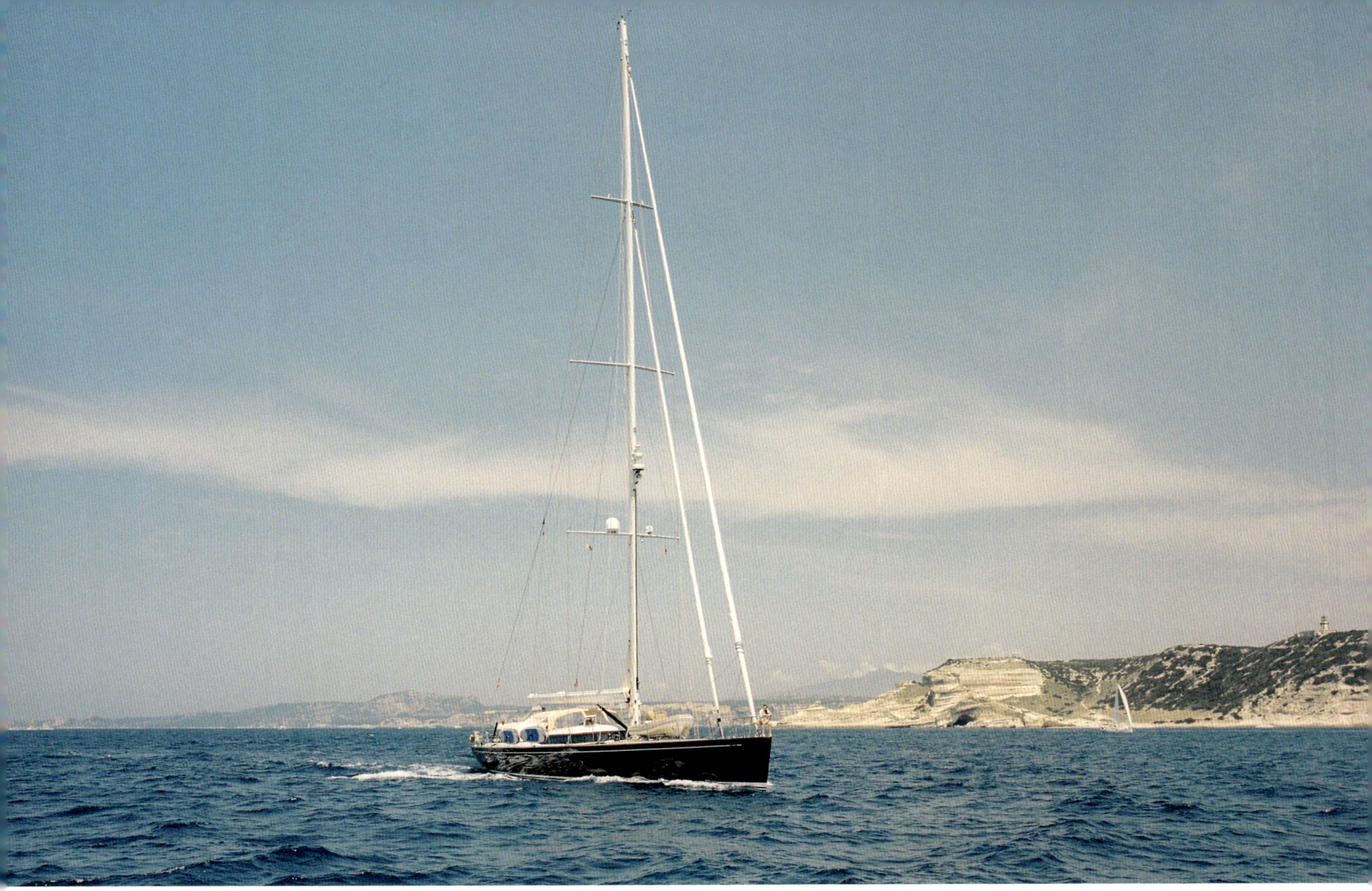
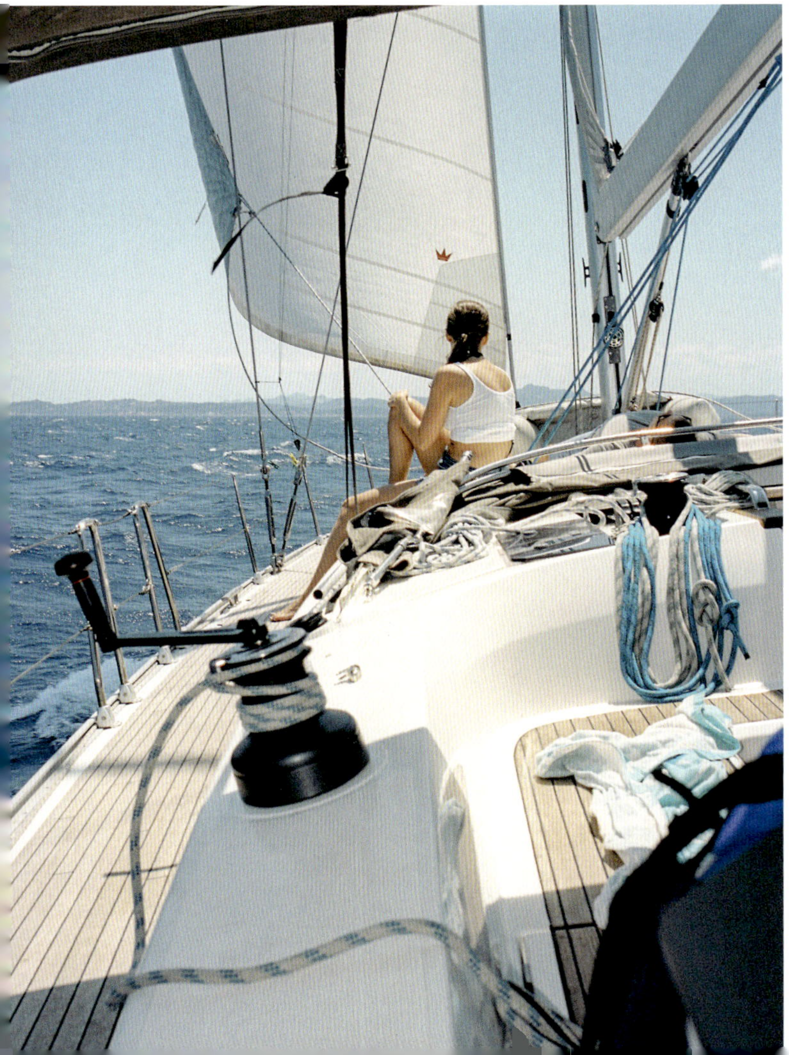
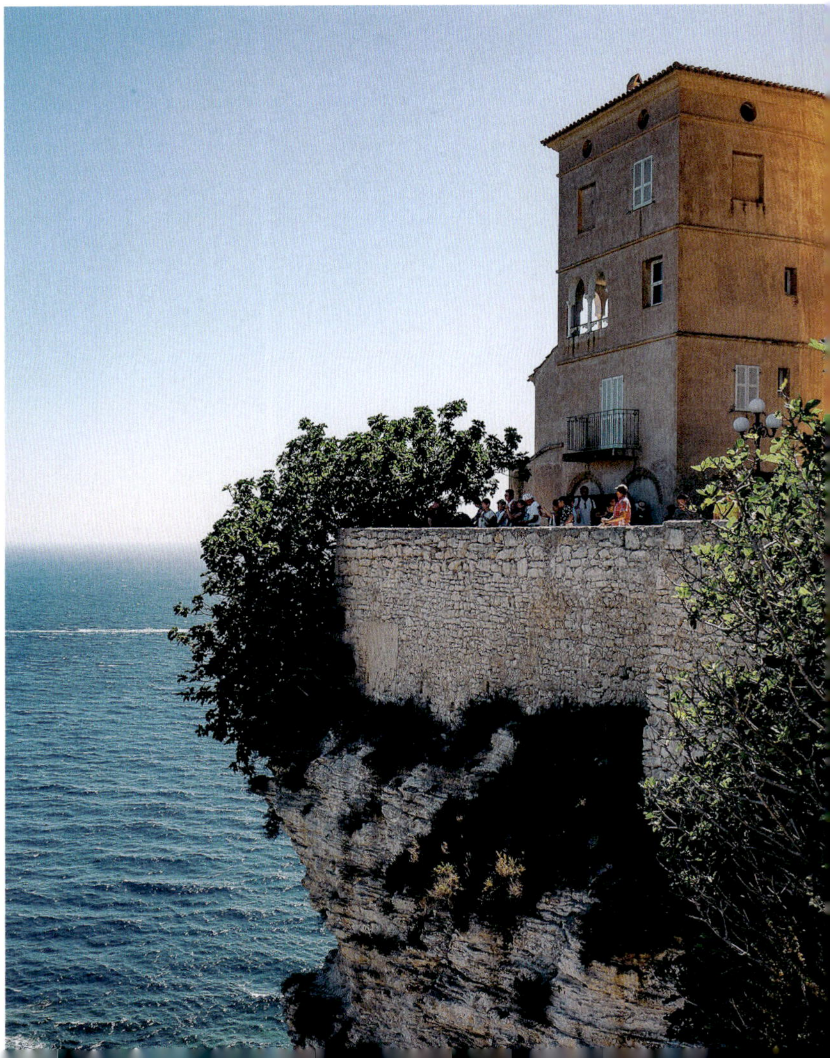

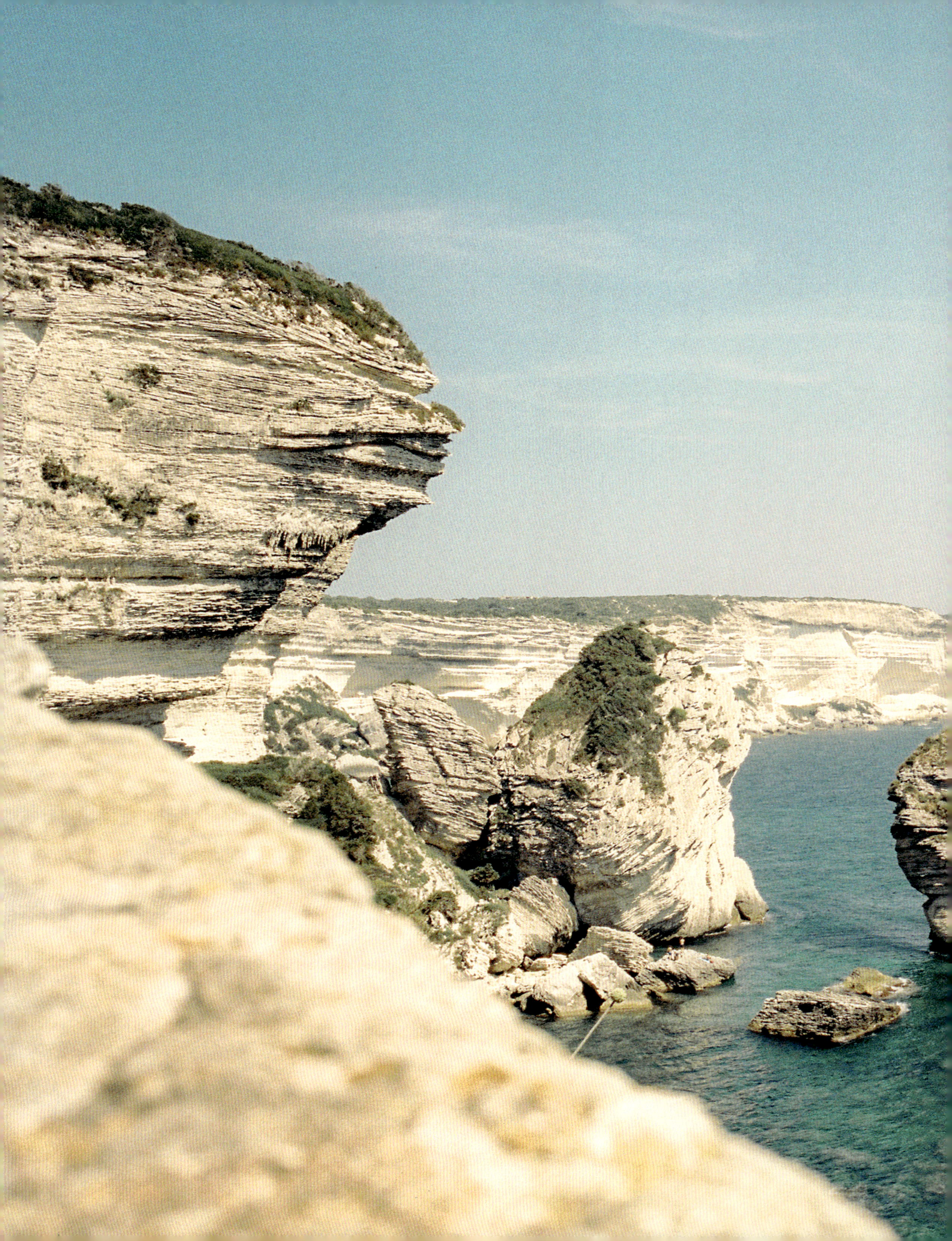

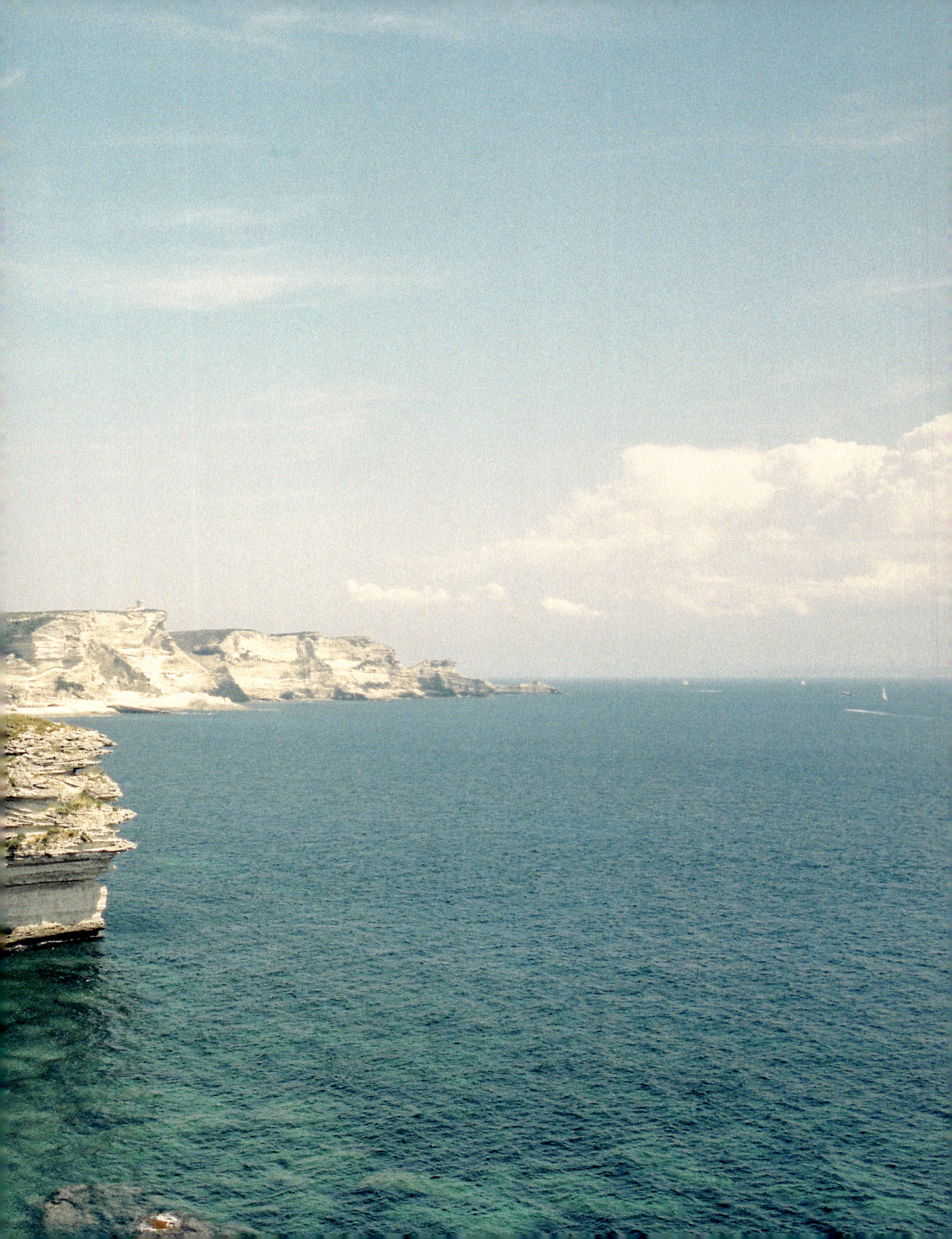

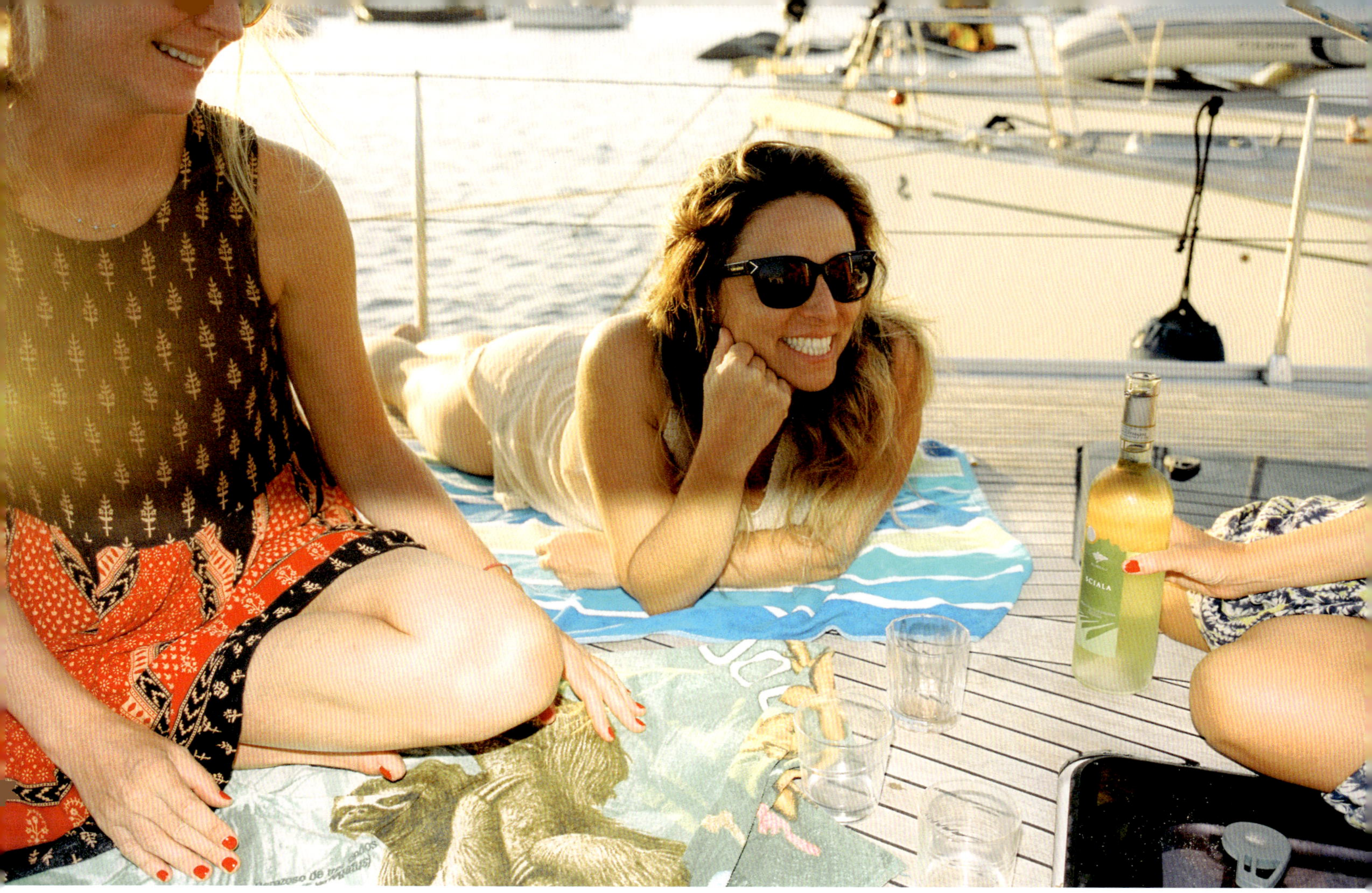

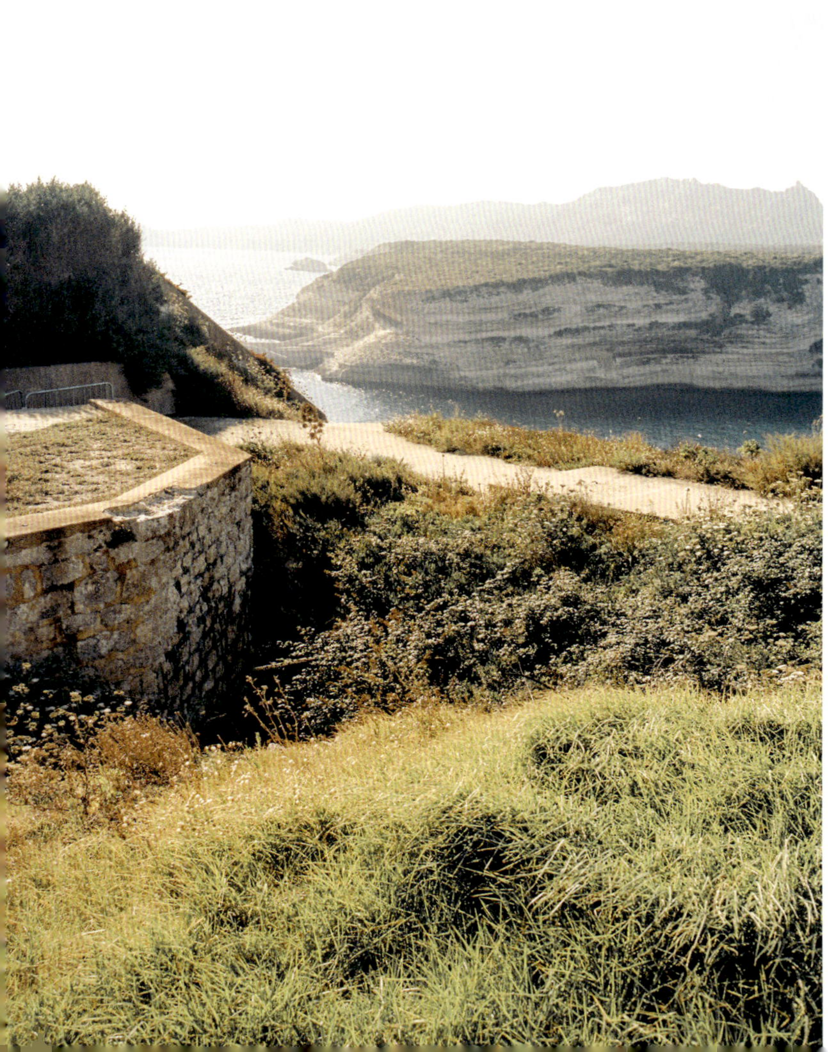

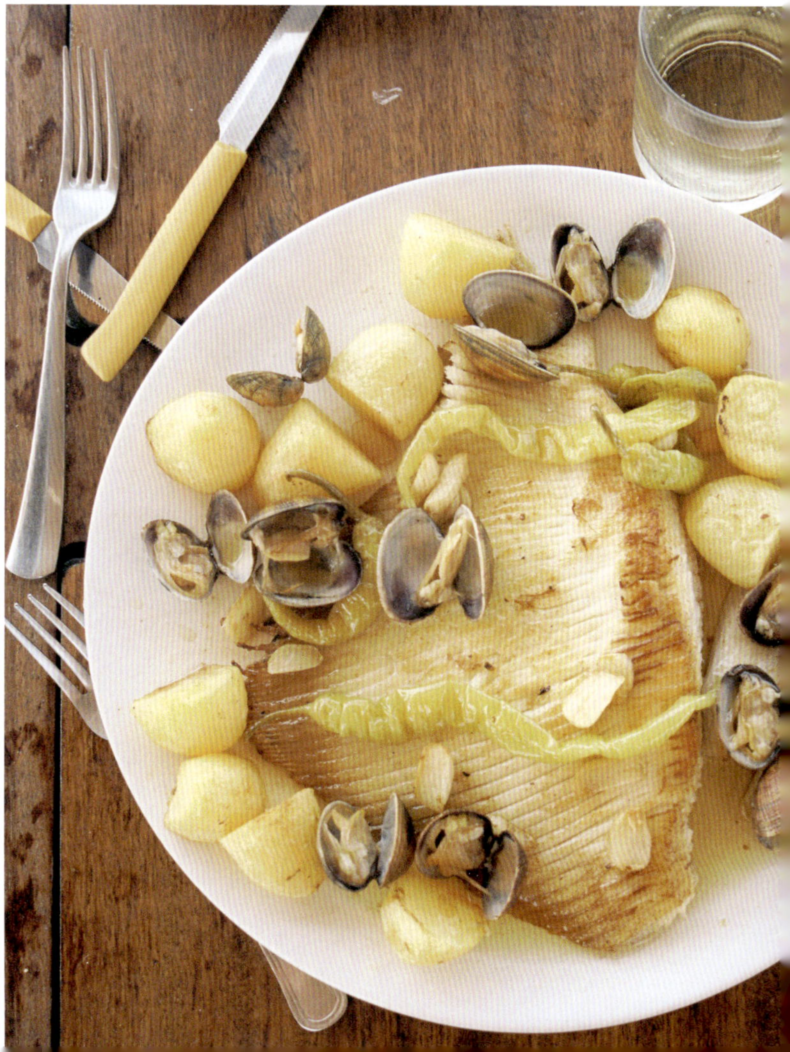

reserve protects nesting birds, which find refuge in the stacked rock formations. These formations cascade from piles on land into the sea. A boulder-strewn seafloor makes for fantastic snorkeling in the anchorages, but can also add to very tricky navigation as you make the approach.

LAVEZZI ARCHIPELAGO

Lavezzi, one of two main islands, is eerily beautiful. The lighthouse that stands on the southern promontory looks appropriately cautionary in its red-and-white horizontal stripes as you approach. This lighthouse was built in 1874 after one of the worst disasters in modern nautical history occurred just offshore here, adding to the beautiful island's dark history. Lavezzi is home to the unmarked graves of over 600 drowned troops, lost here when a French frigate heading to the Crimean War was wrecked along the coast. Anchorages on Lavezzi can offer protection from any wind if you choose the correct one for the conditions. Changing wind directions can be troublesome, since no single anchorage is protected from all sides.

CAVALLO

At a distance, while sailing along the Corsican coast, you can spot poles sticking out of what seems to be an uninhabited reef a few nautical miles from shore. On closer inspection, as you sail towards the outcropping, you notice that these are, in fact, sailboat masts, tucked deep into a cove; what you might have assumed was simply a few rocks is actually an island.

Cavallo is a small, privately-owned island that is home to a few exclusive dwellings and a minimal, but modern, luxury marina. Anyone willing to pay the steep marina fees is allowed to go ashore here, but anchoring nearby does not grant you access. It is an exclusive paradise for those who can afford the cost of the nightly berth at Port of Cavallo. Once ashore, rent bicycles and explore those parts of the island that are not on the grounds of private residences.

There are a number of gorgeous anchorages around Cavallo, and the scenery and swimming are serene, so a visit can be nice even if you stay in the water. Although the island is relatively flat, boulders aplenty give it an interesting and visually impressive structure. Be especially careful when navigating around Cavallo, as the bouldery geography that you see on shore makes for unpredictable shallows underwater. The marking of undersea obstructions on charts is both incomplete and inaccurate, and navigating by sight can be deceptive, as the water color changes not just with the depth of the water, but also with the nature of the sea floor. A shoal that is covered in seagrass may have the deep greens that you would expect from deeper water and sandy depths may appear shallow where they are not.

GULF OF SANTA MANZA

If the northwesterly winds are in full roar during your sailing voyage, you may need to take refuge behind a headland on mainland Corsica. The feeling of escaping a ferocious sea and arriving in a cozy anchorage to rest is a timeless joy. The scrublands around this particular anchorage do little to block the wind, but you will find calm seas and turquoise waters in this large bay. Great wind and calm water make this a popular spot for

FOOD

The French take their food seriously, and so do the Corsicans. Though the sea is full of fish, many of the local dishes are meat-based, with herders working along the coastal hills playing a crucial role in the local cuisine. Dishes like agneau Corse *(roasted lamb prepared with rosemary, potatoes, and garlic) and* civet de sanglier *(wild boar cooked with carrots, chestnuts, garlic, fennel, and spirits) are found on the menus at traditional restaurants.*

A TYPICAL DAY AT ANCHOR (ABOVE). LOOKING DOWN AT THE NARROW ENTRANCE TO BONIFACIO BAY (BELOW LEFT). BOAT FOOD: SKATE WING WITH SPANISH POTATOES, CLAMS, AND BANANA PEPPERS (BELOW, RIGHT).

windsurfers and kiteboarders, who will zip around your boat as you sit at anchor. The main ring road around Corsica leads past the head of the bay, so there are beach bars and restaurants with good food scattered along the shore; you can beach your dinghy right at the tables on the sand.

In the north is a small *calanque* similar to those found on the Côte d'Azur. Enter only in shoal-draft boats and only in calm weather, with a lookout posted on the bow. If you find space inside, this is a viable anchorage for a night among the rock walls and sparse, evergreen vegetation.

The town of Bonifacio sits over the ocean, perched precariously on limestone cliffs that look like they may topple into the sea the moment you take your eyes off them.

CAPO PERTUSATO

Venture here, to the southernmost point of Corsica, only in settled weather. The anchorage is deep and the holding suspect. Minimal protection from swell is provided by tucking to one side or the other of the cape. The cove is not protected and any swell that rolls through the Strait of Bonifacio is ever present.

Take your dinghy into what appears to be an unassuming sea cave west of the large rock formation that resembles a sphynx; it opens up into a most unusual lagoon. The overhanging cliffs on all sides of this circular limestone chamber open up to the sky, allowing beams of sunlight to illuminate the shallow water inside a lagoon that is something like a cave with a giant skylight. There is a rocky beach under the looming walls, where you can rest and look out through the arched passage to the sea beyond, and up through the round gap to the sky above.

~

Corsica's south can be wonderfully challenging at sea, and sailors hoping to exercise their coastal cruising knowledge and skill should look to this itinerary. The variety of unique coves that line both the southern coast and the archipelago between Corsica and Sardinia will have you always wanting to push a little further and see what lies around the next corner. Entering Bonifacio is a feeling that will linger in the hearts and minds of sailors lucky enough to experience it.

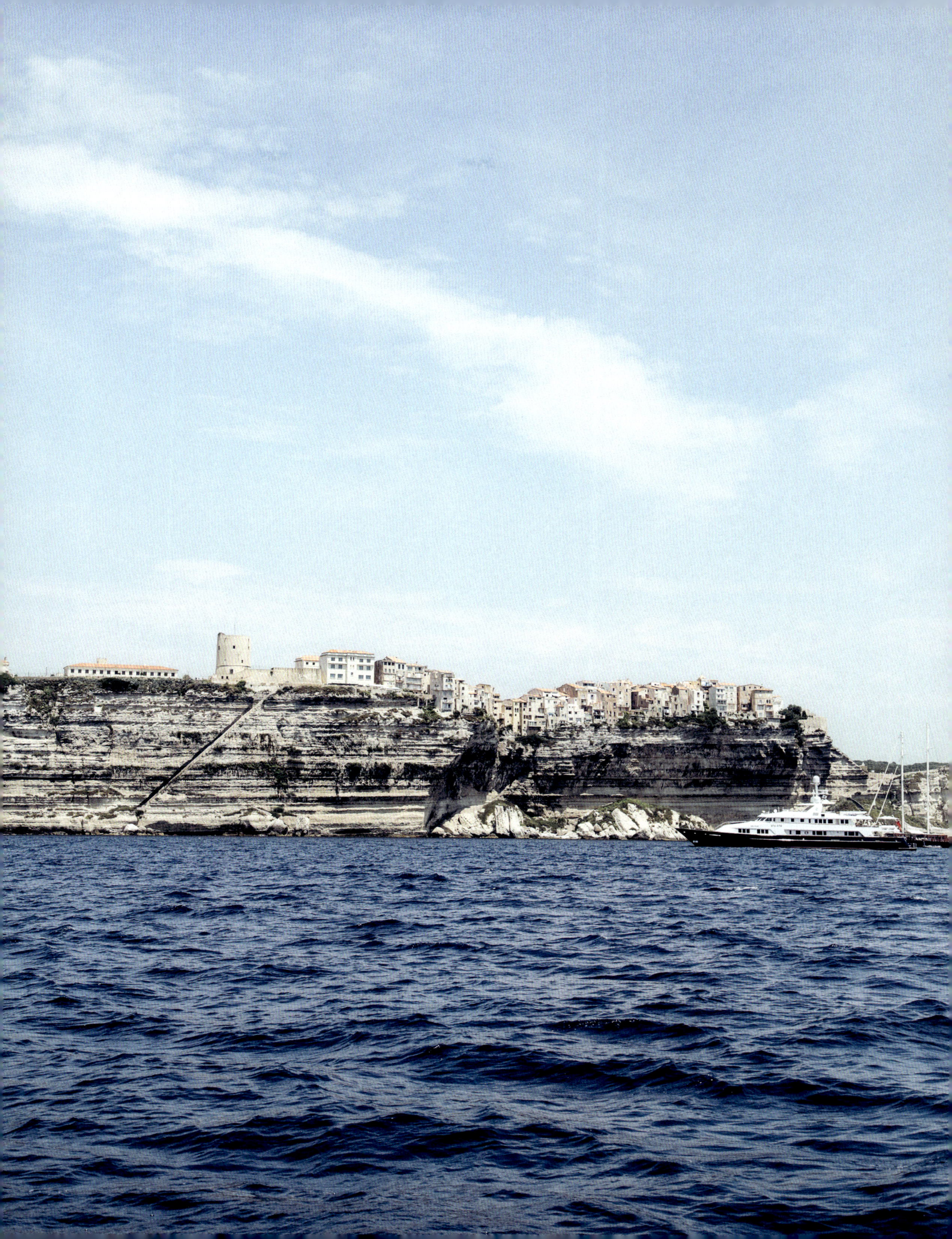

CAPTAIN'S NOTES *STRAIT OF BONIFACIO*

RECOMMENDED ITINERARY

Bonifacio
41° 21′ 34″ N, 9° 15′ 56″ E
Entering Bonifacio is a rite of passage for sailors. Once inside the dramatic harbor you can moor at the marina or in the nearby cove, both outfitted for stern ties with lazy lines. At the marina there are dock workers to help you with lines and even someone in a push boat that helps maneuver boats into tight spots when needed. In the cove, it helps to have someone ready to swim or take the dinghy to pick up the lazy lines from where they are attached to the rocks on big iron rings.

Lavezzi
41° 20′ 14″ N, 9° 15′ 04″ E
Tight anchorages strewn with boulders make rigging a stern tie a good idea, especially in shifting wind conditions. You will need to get creative when tying off to the large boulders, with some combination of swimming and rock climbing.
There are a few moorings specifically for the day tour boats that you can use if you arrive after their last trip of the day (and can be sure to be out of their way in the morning). These moorings are in very deep water in a very narrow inlet, so in heavy conditions they can not be trusted to keep you off the rocks.

Cavallo
41° 21′ 34″ N, 9° 15′ 56″ E
Entering the marina at Cavallo is expensive, but it buys you access to parts of the beautiful and exclusive island that are otherwise off-limits. Bicycles can be rented from the marina; the island has lovely roads and no cars.

Gulf of Santa-Manza
41° 24′ 44″ N, 9° 13′ 32″ E
This large bay has great holding and plenty of swing room to anchor. For something cozier try the *calanque* on the north side, where a stern line will be necessary to keep you from swinging if the wind shifts.

RECOMMENDED ANCHORAGES

Cala di Zeri
Cala di Paragnano
Capo Pertusato

ITINERARY DURATION

4+ days recommended

PREVAILING WIND

The wind on the southern coast of Corsica is sculpted by the island's geography. Coming down from Provençal France, it is funneled into the strait between Corsica and Sardinia and channeled into locally higher strengths that give these waters their fearsome reputation. Normal summer winds are force 3–5.

SEASON

Corsica has a sunny, hot summer from June to September. During the busy season—which is the French and Italian holidays from mid-July to late August—the anchorages and marinas can be crowded.

FOOD

French bakeries take pride in their work. They make a limited amount of delectable bread and pastries, which will sell out by late morning, so be sure to visit the local boulangerie when you wake up to provision the boat for the day.
The mountainous wilderness of inland Corsica has populations of wild boars that are hunted to make wonderful cured sausages, often flavored with the local chestnuts that find their way into so much of Corsican cuisine.

GOOD TO KNOW

Language
French is the lingua franca, but Corsican is an ancient language that is closer in relation to Italian and much more closely tied to the strong Corsican culture that makes this coast so uniquely charming. While there are no true monolingual Corsican speakers left, you will hear Corsican spoken on the boules court among old-timers.

Magnetic Variance
Magnetic Declination: +2° (EAST)

Strong local magnetic variances have been reported in the region.

CORSICA

GULF OF SANTA-MANZA

⚓ PORTO-VECCHIO

CALA DI PARAGNANO

⚓ BONIFACIO

⚓ CAPO PERTUSATO

CAVALLO
⚓ CALA DI ZERI
⚓ PORT OF CAVALLO

ARCHIPELAGO OF LAVEZZI

LAVEZZI
⚓ CALA LAZARINA

STRAIT OF BONIFACIO
MEDITERRANEAN SEA

0 — 10
NAUTICAL MILES
NOT FOR NAVIGATION

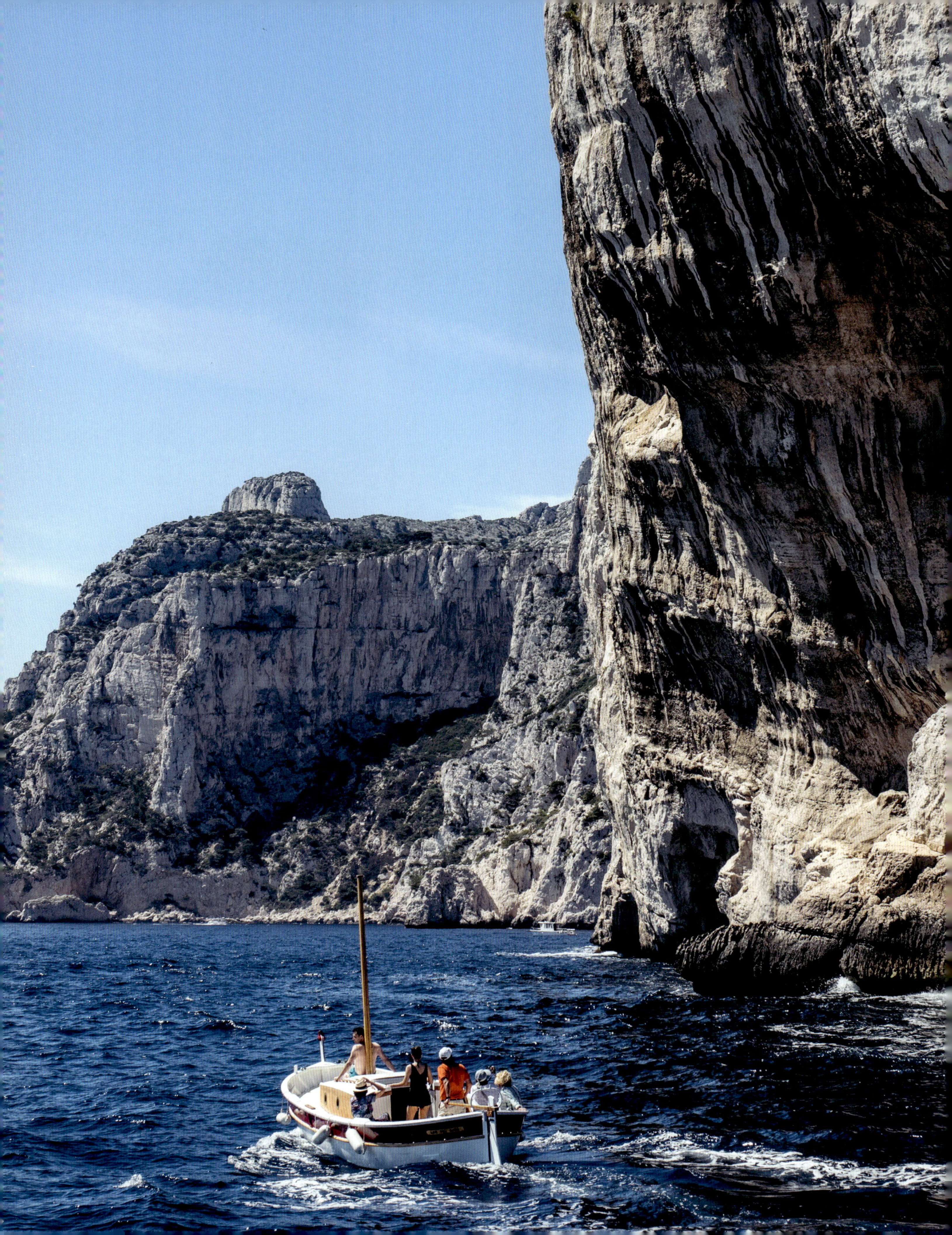

THE MANY SHADES OF CÔTE D'AZUR

THE FRENCH RIVIERA IS WORLD-RENOWNED FOR ITS GLAMOUR AND BEAUTIFUL BEACHES. BUT DESPITE ITS PRESTIGIOUS NAME, THIS COASTLINE OFFERS RUSTIC CHARM AND EXCEPTIONAL SAILING.

Hemingway's *The Garden of Eden*, Picasso's foray into ceramics, Brigitte Bardot's *La Madrague*, F. Scott Fitzgerald's *This Side of Paradise*, Vincent van Gogh's seascapes. To even list the works of great art produced in and about the French Riviera could be a lifelong project for a dedicated curator. This is a place that inspires. Hillsides fragranced with fresh lavender tumble into the clear blue Mediterranean waters. In countless seaside villages, life slows with the heat of the summer into a leisurely stroll, a drift in the sea. The language here, like the English of the American South, is spoken in a slow drawl that belays the unhurriedness of it all. Provençal French is a dialect of honest farmers and hardworking fishermen. The French Riviera is their not-so-hidden gem, shining bright from any angle you view it.

Stretching between the cliffs of Cassis and the independent microstate of Monaco, the French Riviera—or "Côte d'Azur" as it's known to the French—exudes a cultural passion for sailing. The traditional fishing boats here carried sailing rigs and the more modern history of recreational sailing has a strong presence on this coast as well. It's not unusual to see a regatta on the horizon with 100 boats under their full press of sail. They are out there for the love of sailing as much as for the coastline that they are tacking to. Whether you come primarily for the sailing or for the Côte d'Azur itself, you'll be delighted by the interplay of how they come together—a classic pairing like Chardonnay and Gruyère, or butter on a freshly baked baguette.

Along this coast there are ancient towns where the fortified walls, originally built to protect against pirates and invaders, still stand doing their best to keep out the big power yachts and helicopters that buzz around them with the annual influx of the rich and famous. Events such as the Cannes Film Festival and the Monaco Grand Prix are like a siren song for mega yachts and their patrons who recognize the beauty here too, even if they are only enjoying it through the tinted windows of their upper deck lounges. On a sailboat the beauty is inescapable and becomes a part of you even as you become a part of it. Sailboats and the sailors who ply them are an important part of this landscape, and by sailing here you are laying your brush on the canvas and contributing to the Côte d'Azur seascape that has inspired so many.

Like the start of any sailing itinerary, there are critical decisions you will make in your planning that shape the experience. Make sure to allot Côte d'Azur the time it deserves. End to end, you could transit the entire region in just a day or two with good wind; but remember that you didn't come here to breeze over the details, so don't rush past this amazing Provençal coastline. Be sure to taste the Pastis on Embiez, swim to the beach at the very end of a *calanque*, smell the wildflowers along the path in Port-Cros and, most importantly, leave time to discover the unexpected moments of bliss that you are sure to find in some lazy lunch anchorage in the shadow of the lavender-lined shores.

MASSIF DES CALANQUES

Spanning 20 kilometers along the coast from Marseille to the east towards Cassis is Parc national des Calanques. Under the shadow of Mont Puget this coastline is rugged and imposing. The area has only been protected by a national park since 2012, but the impenetrability of this terrain left it largely undeveloped even before park status. A *calanque* is a fjord-like formation of limestone walls making up a very narrow and deep water inlet. Entering a *calanque* in a sailboat is a dramatic experience that is not to be missed while sailing here. Make sure to spend some time just exploring before you find a spot within one of the *calanques* to drop anchor. Do not deprive yourself of the thrill of seeing your mast dwarfed by sheer vertical limestone walls on both sides as you cautiously enter a narrow winding inlet with no visible end. There are many hikes ashore and you will see people high on the cliff walls following trails that lead them to the rocky beaches commonly found all the way at the head of the coves.

ÎLE DES EMBIEZ

Further east along the coast is a peninsula that extends south before Toulon, and on the southwest of this peninsula an island. This little island, just a short hop from the mainland, is the home of the Paul Ricard Oceanographic Institute and the gravesite of Paul Ricard on a dramatic bluff that faces the Mediterranean Sea. Before he dedicated his legacy to ocean conservation, the late Mr. Ricard used his capacity in his family's wine business to popularize a local Pastis that was traditionally made from aniseed and aromatic local herbs in provincial France. *Ricard Pastis Marseille* is now loved worldwide and emblematic of this region of France. His beloved island Embiez has a few restaurants and a very nice protected harbor with berths available for visiting yachts.

Well sheltered from westerlies and southerlies, there are anchorages to either side of the harbor entrance with delightful views and pleasant swimming to be had. A small market ashore is remarkably well stocked for its size and offers basic provisioning and, of course, pastis. A hike to the scenic memorial or a lazy wander through the uncrowded streets is a perfect way to spend an afternoon if you care to leave the boat along this enchanting coastline. Whether you go ashore or not, the charm of Embiez is tangible and the scenery sublime.

FRENCH SAILORS

There are more than 20,000 new boats registered in France each year. Many of the largest and most popular sailboat manufacturers in the world are French. Jeanneau, Beneteau, Lagoon, Fountain Pajot, Prestige, Dufour, Amel, Nautitech, Outremer, Catana, Bali, and many more are all French shipyards and their engineers are defining what high-performance cruisers look like with the release of their new models each year.

LOCALS BUYING AND SELLING FISH IN MARSEILLE IN FRONT OF THE MARINA (ABOVE, LEFT). TRADITIONAL SAILBOATS CRUISING ALONG IN FRONT OF A SEASIDE TOWN (ABOVE, RIGHT).

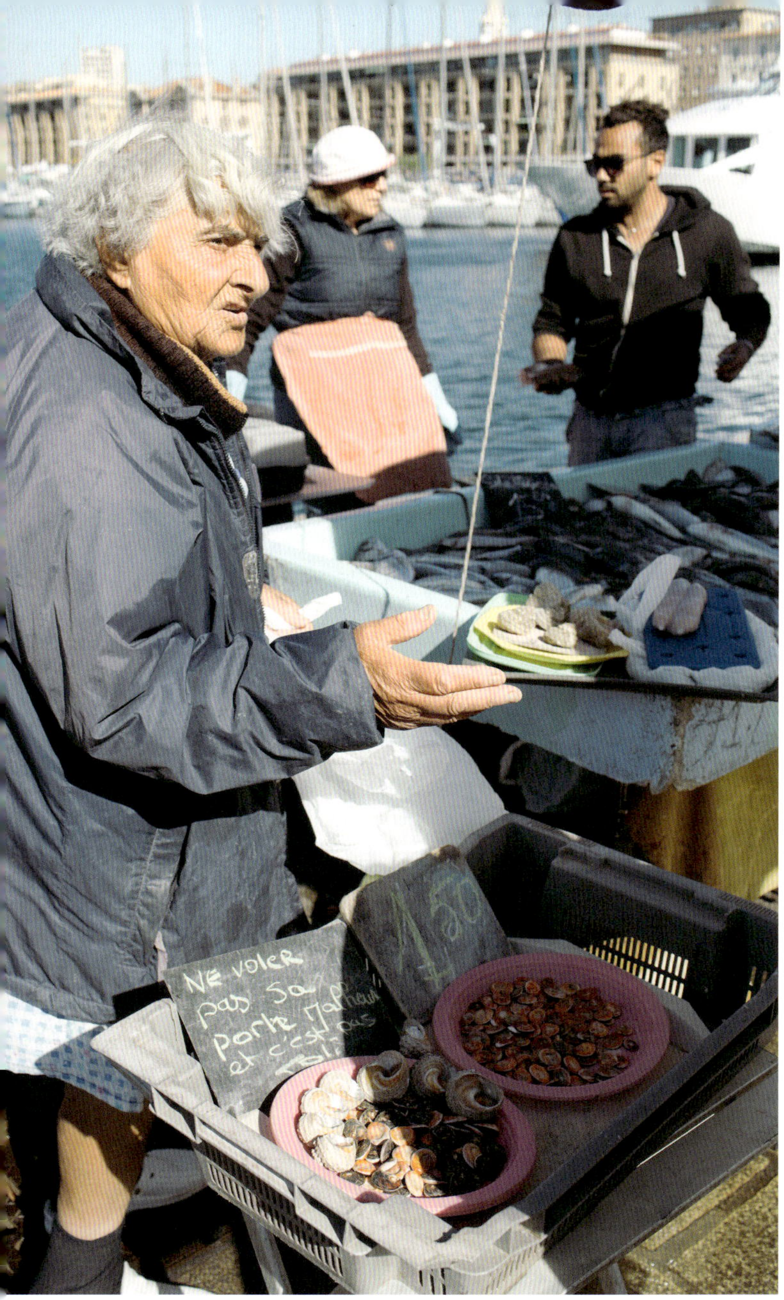
NE voler
pas sa
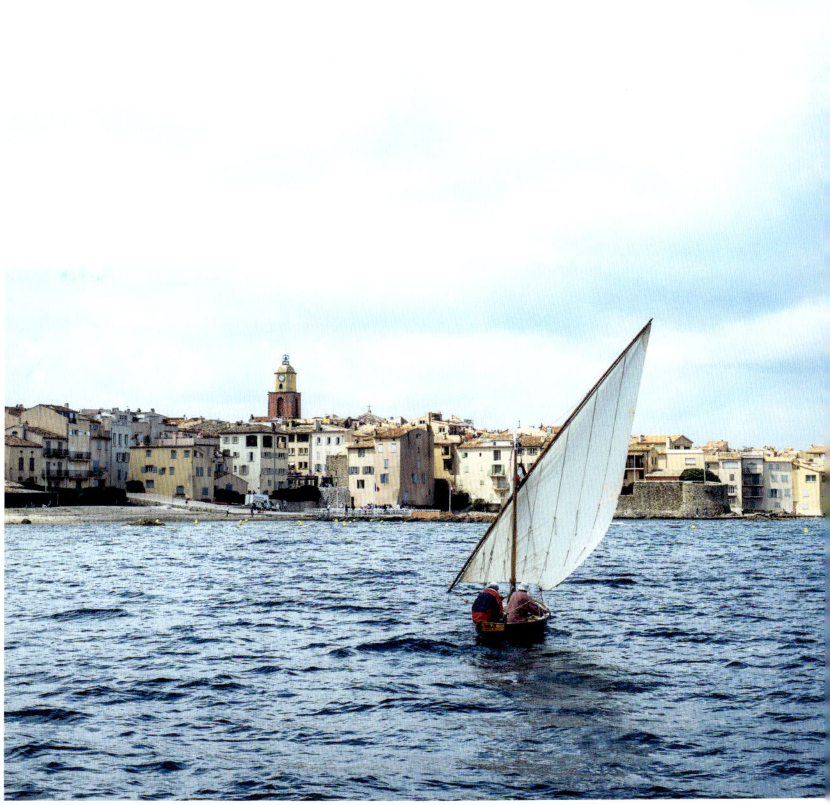
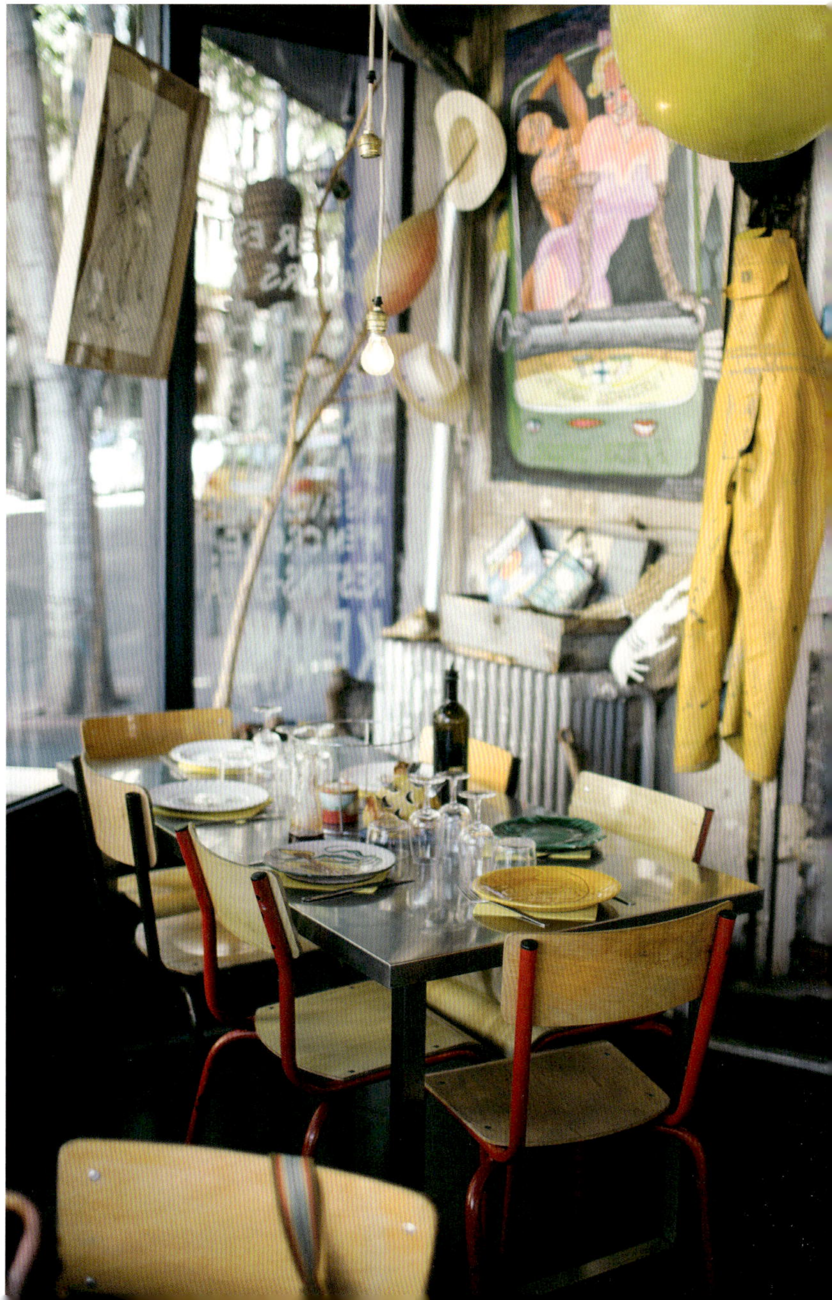
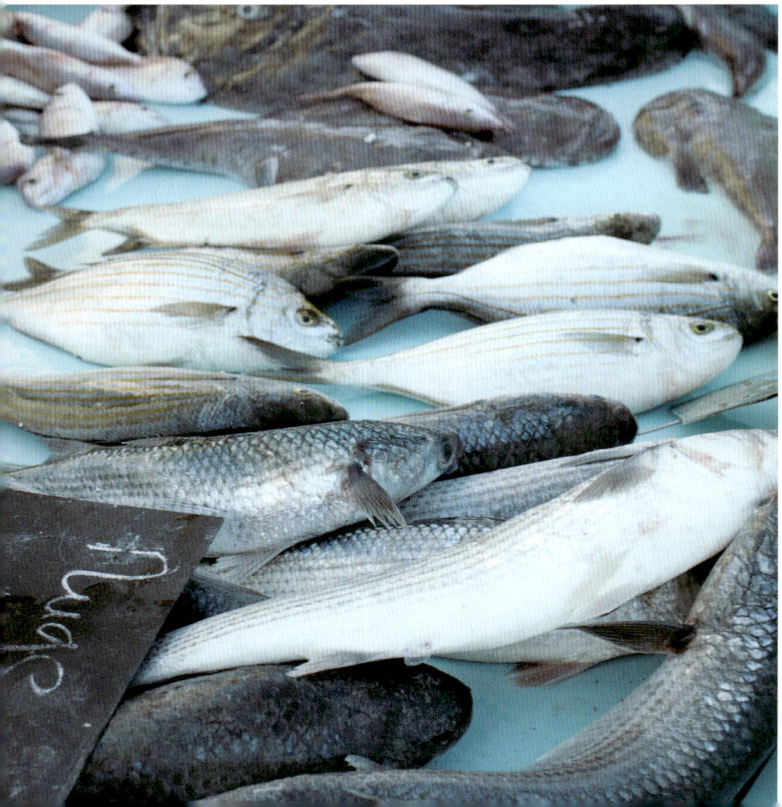

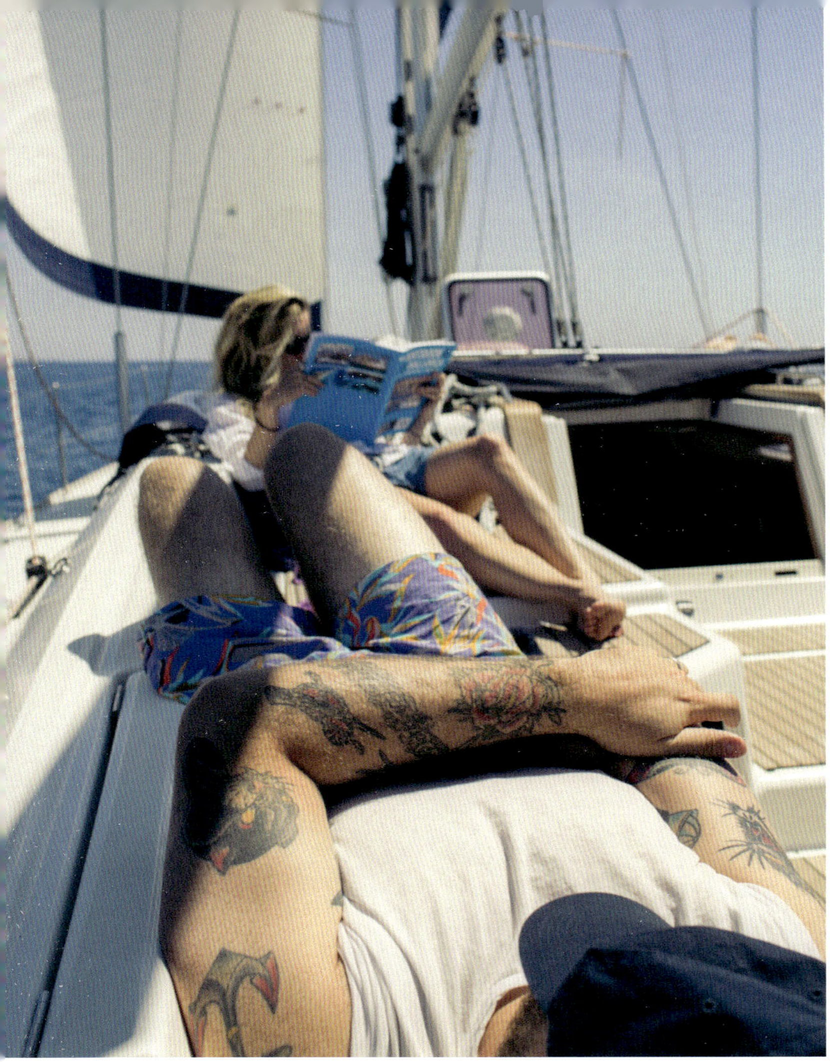

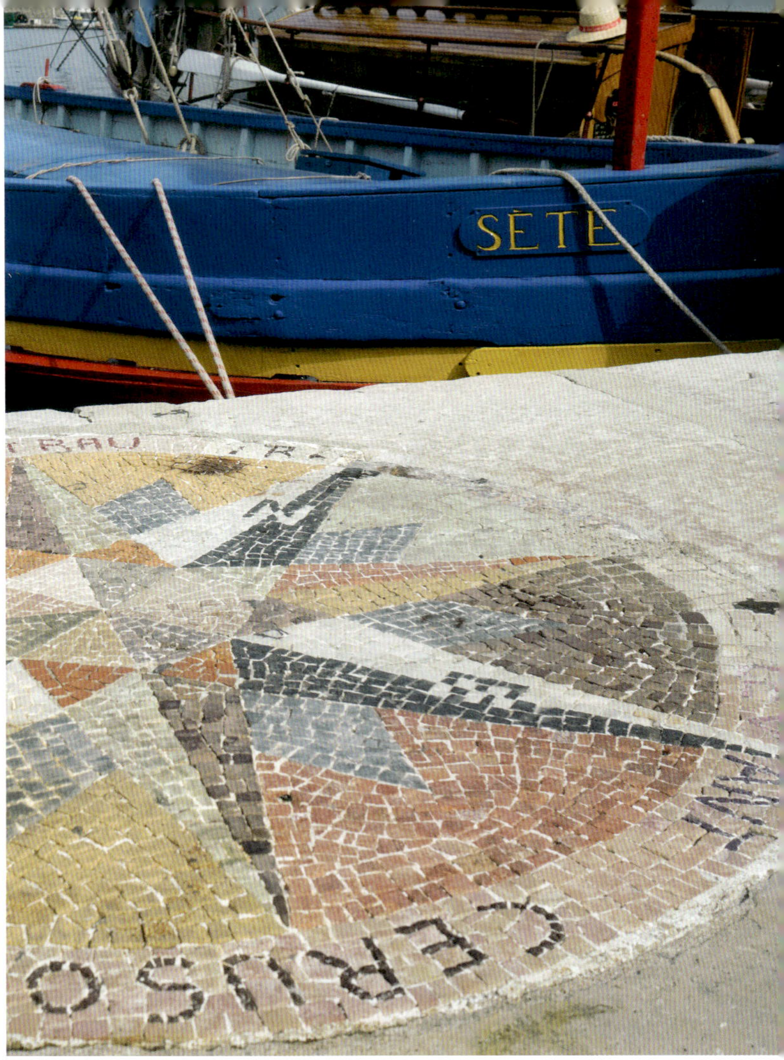
SÈTE

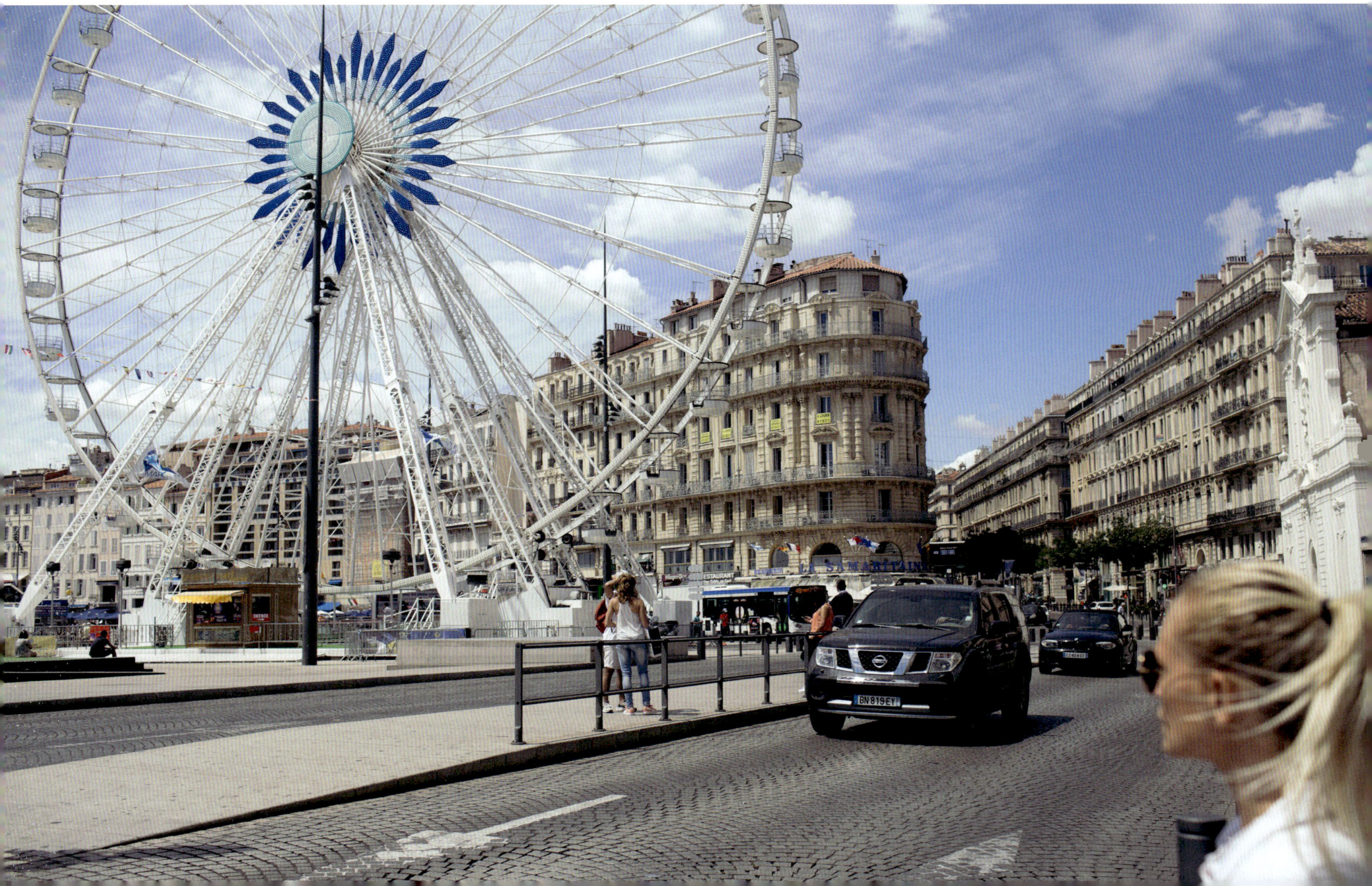

PORQUEROLLES

Located centrally in the Côte d'Azur region is a group of well protected islands with hiking trails and spectacular beaches. Sailing east or west, this is an obvious stop and should not be missed. All of the islands sit within site of the mainland but don't let that fool you into assuming these are calm protected waters. When conditions build to force 4 or above, expect this crossing to be a formidable one and take appropriate caution.

Le Parc national de Port-Cros spans across multiple islands and includes the waters up to 600 meters offshore in its strict environmental protections. Porquerolles, the name used for the island group as a whole, also refers to the most populous of the islands. A large marina facility in Porquerolles has ample dock space to leave your boat while you explore the town. Bicycles for rent allow you to cruise the island and visit spectacular beaches. The beaches on this island that are accessible by bicycle may also be accessible by boat in settled weather, but the town is at least worth visiting as a charming summer community. You'll see almost no motorized transport, quaint restaurants with tables spilling into the pedestrian ways, and church plazas. A botanical garden in the center of town is free to enter and has local flora and fauna labeled with both Latin scientific and French common names.

The island of Port-Cros is only sparsely developed with its two biggest populations belonging to a military base and a nudist colony that presumably don't intermingle much. There is a single hotel on the island that looks much the way it did when it was built about 100 years ago and still has many of the same amenities including a sea breeze in lieu of air conditioning. The restaurants ashore are busy for lunch when tour boats bring hikers to the island for the day to explore on foot. As part of the park, smoking is not allowed anywhere on Port-Cros, which is a distinctly un-French suppression of personal freedoms that people happily oblige to protect the island from the risk of forest fires. There are mooring balls in a fairly well-protected harbor for boats under 14 meters and there is room to anchor around the corner in less well-protected waters.

SAINT-TROPEZ

Continuing east and rounding Cap Lardier leads you to a vast bay opening eastward and therefore providing decent protection from the strong north-easterlies that can ravage the riviera. Home of some of Europe's most expensive properties, the drive into Saint-Tropez can take hours sitting in traffic jams

> Saint-Tropez sits on a long peninsula that makes for a very large anchorage—accommodating vessels of all shapes and sizes.

of Ferraris and Rolls Royces, all the more reason to breeze in on the water, and drop anchor outside the harbor, where you can row into town and tie up. A sailboat is the perfect vehicle to take you to this enchanting old harbor, with its lighthouse at the entrance and charming old town above. Saint-Tropez sits on a long peninsula that makes for a very large anchorage, accommodating vessels of all shapes and sizes.

"Les Voiles Latines"—a boat festival for latin-rigs that celebrates the Beauty of Mediterranean maritime heritage held annually in May—packs the harbor with traditional fishing boats that have been lovingly restored by rowing and sailing clubs from the area. A visit during this time makes it hard to secure a transient spot in the inner harbor, but a walk along the

READING AND RELAXING AT ANCHOR (ABOVE, LEFT). THE FERRIS WHEEL IN MARSEILLE'S OLD PORT (BELOW).

seawall during the festival is like a trip back in time. Just a few blocks inland from the harbor is a charming market that springs up every Tuesday and Saturday morning in a city park. The market has a healthy mix of fancy and local, with the produce section featuring local farmers selling their crops.

~

Côte d'Azur is undoubtedly one of the world's great sailing destinations. French sailors know and love this coastline and their love of sailing here is felt all over the world. There are French adventurers cruising on their sailboats in every corner of the world and they all got their start right here.

LOCAL DISH

Of note on this southern coast is the fisherman's stew. This is not the Bouillabaisse that is a staple of French cuisine but a more provincial creation simply called soupe de poisson, *which is a lot more like being served a big bowl of gravy. Salty and thick, you can see how this would be a favorite of the hardworking early-rising fishermen from the region. On the side you'll get a plate of shredded Gruyère and toast baked hard like croutons but not broken up. To enjoy it like a local, put the cheese on the toast and float it in the stew until it soaks in soft and the cheese starts to melt.*

CÔTE D'AZUR
FRANCE

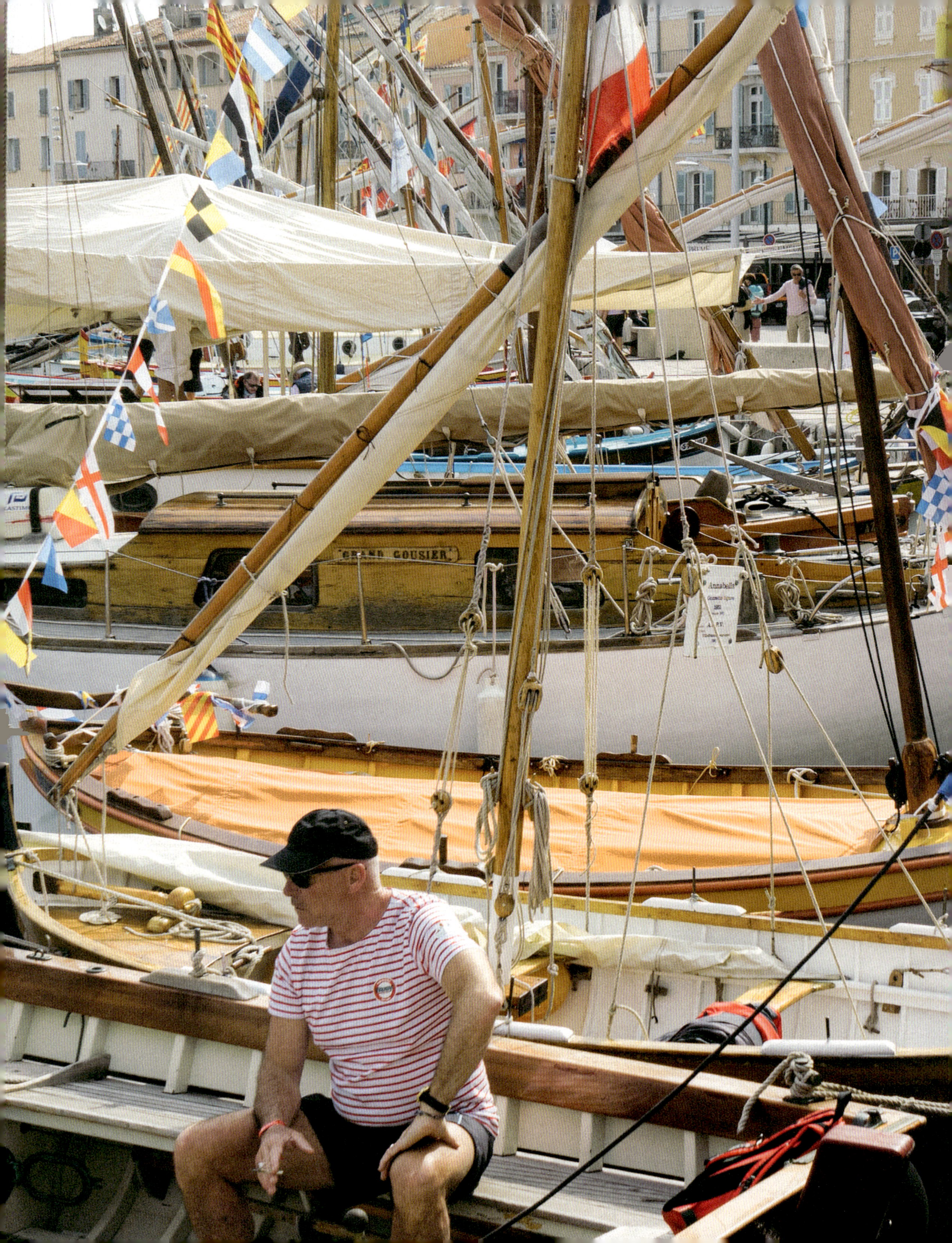
GRAND GOUSIER

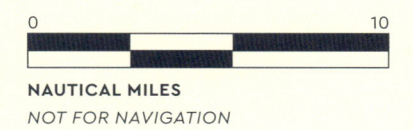

Map labels:
- MARSEILLE
- LE TORPILLEUR
- CALANQUE DE PORT-MIOU
- CALANQUE DE PORT PIN
- ÎLE DES EMBIEZ
- SAINT-MANDRIER-SUR-MER
- MEDITERRANEAN SEA
- FRA[NCE]

0 — 10
NAUTICAL MILES
NOT FOR NAVIGATION

CAPTAIN'S NOTES *CÔTE D'AZURE*

RECOMMENDED ITINERARY

Saint-Tropez 43° 16′09″N, 6° 38′23″E
Berth in the inner harbor if you would like to be at the heart of the action. Otherwise, anchor west of the lighthouse at the harbor entrance in ten meter's depth.

Île des Embiez 43° 04′84″N, 05° 47′21″E
Berths available at the marina on the north side of the island can be reserved in advance. Depths of 3 meters accommodate most sailboats in stern-to docking with laid moorings as bowlines that are tailed to the quay. Entering the marina in strong northerly wind can be dangerous, but once inside it is well-protected.

Port-Miou 43° 12′01″N, 05° 31′00″E
A safe harbor for overnighting in the *calanques*, Port-Miou has moorings and stern lines for visiting yachts—far simpler than dropping anchor in such narrow spaces. The inner part of the harbor is administered by a yacht club and there are walkways along the cliff, allowing you to step off your boat and go ashore. Electric and water is available. The outer part of the harbor has only moorings and stern lines. Anchoring is prohibited.

Port de Porquerolles 43° 10′19″N, 6° 12′1″E
The Hyères have a variety of options for safe harbor depending on the wind and swell direction. The harbor at Porquerolles has the best all-around protection in the group. This large harbor has ample berths and moorings for visitors and is easily spotted by looking for the old signal station on the top of the hill behind it to the south. Water, electricity, and fuel are available here and there is a repair facility as well.

Port-Cros 43° 0′0″N, 6° 24′0″E
Berths fill up quickly here, so make sure to arrive early if you want to be on the dock. Moorings are available in the harbor for boats under 14 meters and it is also possible to anchor outside the harbor in less well-protected waters.

Saint-Mandrier-sur-Mer
43° 04′45.9″N, 5° 55′27.1″E
This charming little seaside enclave of the Toulon area has ample berths for visiting yachts and nice marina facilities. The shore is lined with classic French seafood restaurants serving fish straight from the sea, brought in by the fleet of small fishing boats in the inner harbor. French naval ships come and go through the channel just past the breakwater.

RECOMMENDED ANCHORAGES

Anse du Bon Renaud
Calanque de Port Pin
Le Torpilleur
Rade de la Badine
Île de Bagaud

ITINERARY DURATION

5–10 days recommended

PREVAILING WIND

The usual summer winds for the coastline east of Marseille are southeasterly and moderate: around force 4. Strong winds—the *Mistral*—can come out of the northwest, especially on the western end of this itinerary along the *calanques*, where winds blow out of the Rhône river valley and carry cold dry air out to sea towards Corsica. The *Mistral* is a wind that is legendary for its destructive capacities—especially during winter, when it is most common. It will kick up a vicious sea state with very little warning. Upon making your first weather check for the week, take some time to make marina reservations in advance for any nights that seem like they might bring force 5 or above. Strong winds here will surely bring big seas. This effect is strongest when closer to Marseille and tapers off a little as you get back towards Nice. If northwesterlies are in the forecast, staying to the east of Toulon will generally keep you in calmer conditions.

SEASON

The Côte d'Azur has around 300 sunny days a year, so summer is long. Winds for sailing are best around August and September.

FOOD

French food needs no introduction. Visit any seaside restaurant for the classics of French coastal cuisine, or book a table at a fine-dining establishment to experience formal food at its height.

GOOD TO KNOW

Navigating calanques
The charts here are limited in their accuracy, and the towering limestone walls of *calanques* will block GPS antennae, making your position reading inaccurate. Keep a spotter on the bow as you enter, to communicate clearly about possible obstructions ahead. Many of the bigger *calanques* are divided in half by a line of buoys, to signify one side where anchoring is allowed and another that is to be left open for navigation. Drop anchor and tie a stern line to shore in all but the biggest of the *calanques*, as the depth of the water and the narrowness means you won't have swing room to sit on anchor alone.

French language
Sailing here is so popular that marinas are plentiful and large. But the prevalence of boat ownership and a national passion for sailing also means that finding space in these large, plentiful marinas is not always easy. A passable knowledge of French will bring a more hospitable reception and possibly even dock space in a marina that would have been "full" if you had tried to ask in English.

Magnetic variance
Magnetic declination: +2° (EAST)

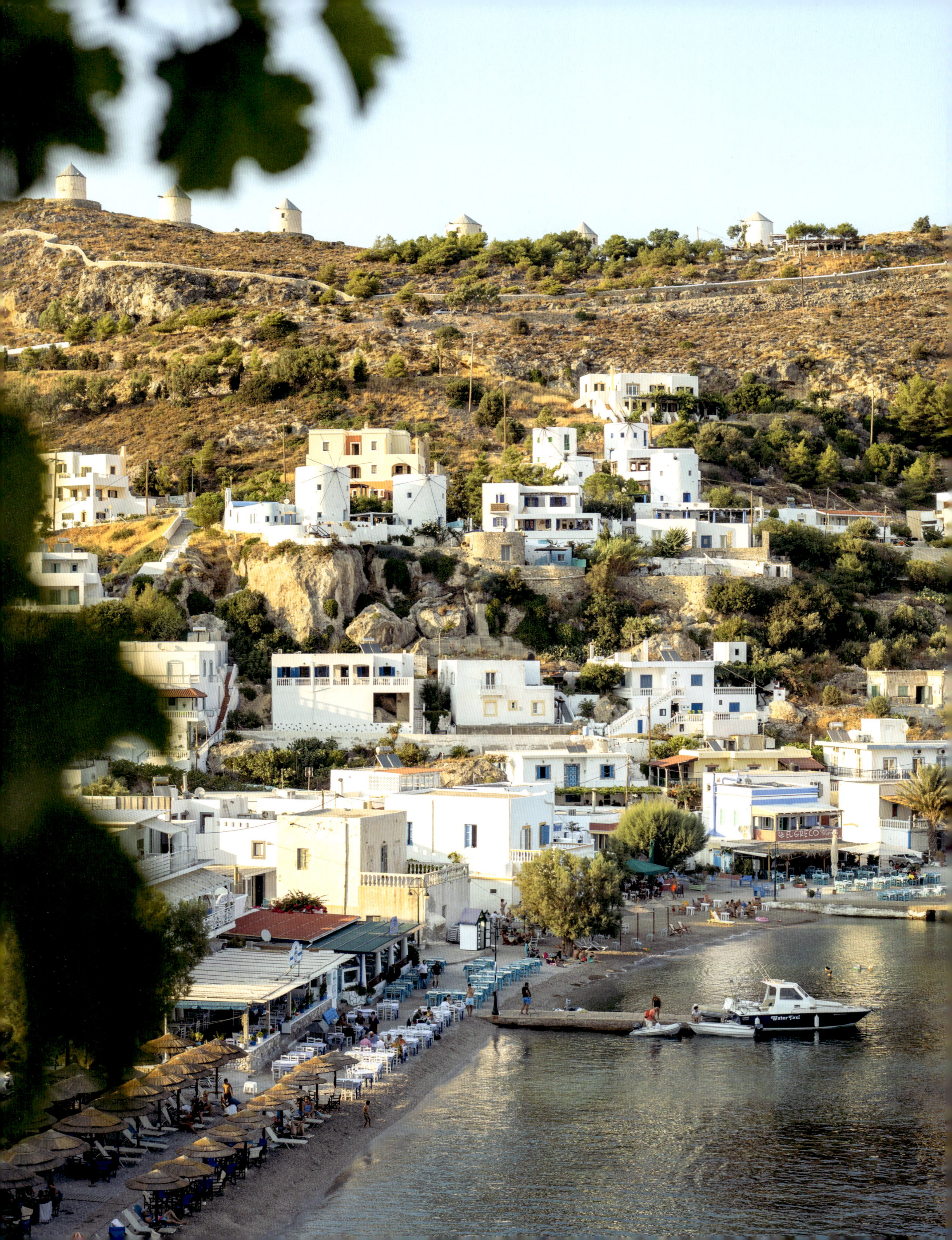
EL GRECO
Water Taxi

CLEAR WATERS AND PEBBLE BEACHES

THE DODECANESE IS A PLACE WHERE EAST MEETS WEST: 15 GREEK ISLANDS JUST A STONE'S THROW FROM THE TURKISH COAST. THESE ALLURING ISLANDS ARE RICH WITH HISTORY—A TRUE SAILOR'S PARADISE.

Located in the southeast Aegean Sea, the Dodecanese Islands are dramatic and exciting; drastic cliffs slope down into the sea with protected anchorages scattered throughout the rural and rustic itinerary. Fifteen picturesque islands with a mix of glamour and rustic vibes make up the archipelago, and there's good reason they became popular with ambitious sailors setting out for solitude and excitement. Planning a voyage here is thrilling—the changing scenery from north to south provides tremendous juxtaposition from the busy ports of Kos and Rhodes to the smaller island communities that lie in comparative obscurity. No two communities are alike with the history, migration, and merging of cultures that influenced this region. These islands have been ruled by Ancient Greek civilizations, Byzantines, the Ottoman, the Italian Empire, and were finally assimilated by the modern Greek state in 1947. Since then, the Dodecanese Islands have become a popular travel destination with the islands of Kos and Rhodes serving as the two bustling tourist hubs, though other villages have maintained their quaintness with only local residents of fishermen, sailors, and the occasional summer visitor.

This archipelago is one of the less frequently sailed itineraries in Greece. Its main islands encapsulate changes brought on by tourism, while some smaller islands here still hold onto their traditional ways of off-the-grid living.

Though people have resided in the main towns for thousands of years, the way of life in town is a modern one; but just a few nautical miles away, there are nearly uninhabited coves, with people in the lone structures still living as their ancestors did. These scattered islands hug the Turkish coast running from northwest to southeast, in line with the prevailing *Meltemi* wind which blows north-northwest during the summer months. Kos is located in the middle of the archipelago and mariners departing on their voyage likely will decide to cruise the northern or southern islands based on the local weather and wind reports for the week. The wind largely dictates their decisions to sail along the leeward coast of the islands or duck behind the vast sheer cliffs that cascade above the coastline and take refuge to avoid any inclement winds predicted.

The islands are indeed Greek, but have a different history than much of the rest of Greece. Unlike many of the other regions with towering ancient artifacts, the Byzantine Empire's comparatively modern—some structures just 600 years old—influence is most evident throughout the area. Massive forts sit atop many of the islands, seemingly glaring down at you. As you sail alongside these picturesque historical artifacts pursuing leisure, you can easily imagine the intimidation of worrying about cannon fire flying above as you approach on a medieval ship as an enemy combatant. Patmos and Leros have two of the largest Byzantine fortified castles that were built around the 11th century. With the castles in sight nearly everywhere you sail in the area, it's a reminder of the antiquity of these islands and their longstanding maritime history. And, at the same time, it remains rustic and untouched, which makes diving off the bow of the boat after dropping anchor in a secluded cove all the more exciting and really unique.

KOS

The island of Kos has a protected marina where many of the boats in the archipelago reside year round. It also happens to be one of the busiest spots in the Dodecanese. A once sleepy, bohemian town that had a touristy overhaul throughout the past 30 years, Kos bears the brunt for the majority of tourism in the northern parts of the Dodecanese. Years ago, this village had few residents living within its old city walls and was known for its traditions of fishing and farming. As time went on and the surge of tourism swept across the western parts of Europe, Kos took to the economic opportunity, while exchanging many of the islands' traditional ways of life for trinket shops and guided activities. Despite this sometimes regrettable evolution, the marina is protected from wind and weather and there is plenty of provisioning to prepare for the voyage, making Kos an ideal starting point for a journey into the surrounding lesser developed territories.

PSERIMOS

Sailing north from Kos is the island of Pserimos, a lovely and sparsely inhabited place that's home to a few little villages and scattered homesteads where people can be found living a relatively self-subsistent existence, similar to their ancestors's way of life before tourism swept through the islands. The most recent census reported a population of 80 residents, with most of them living in the single town that holds the island's namesake. Vathy is a cove that's popular with yachters passing by. Here you'll find a large bay that opens to the west and looks out towards the Turkish coast. This cove is uninhabited, other than a small fishery on the southern end that has nets laid in the bay for aquaculture. Pserimos is barren and isolated, with cascading beige textures that permeate the land and meet the aqua blue water creating a distinctive color contrast. Joining fellow boaters to rest peacefully at anchor is one of the joys of exploring as a sailor. Diving off the boat into clear water in a newly found cove is a simple pleasure unmatched by many in this world.

KALYMNOS

Kalymnos lies north from Pserimos and is home to many extraordinary coves that are protected from the prevailing wind. One of the best coves to drop anchor in is Palionisos, located along the northeast side of the island; a non-touristic cove serving locals and sailors. This emerald blue inlet is captivating and inviting, with its surrounding dramatic cliffs that provide protection from the wind. Onshore there are just three small but welcoming restaurants that offer simple and delicious fare—it's all about traditional low-key food, and genuine conversations taking place among sailors who dinghy ashore for a cold beer and a break from boat life. Dinner is grilled lamb, fresh seafood to order, and local wine. There are 20 mooring buoys in the harbor and the option to anchor stern-to along the cliff face or in 15 meters of water behind the mooring field. Winds

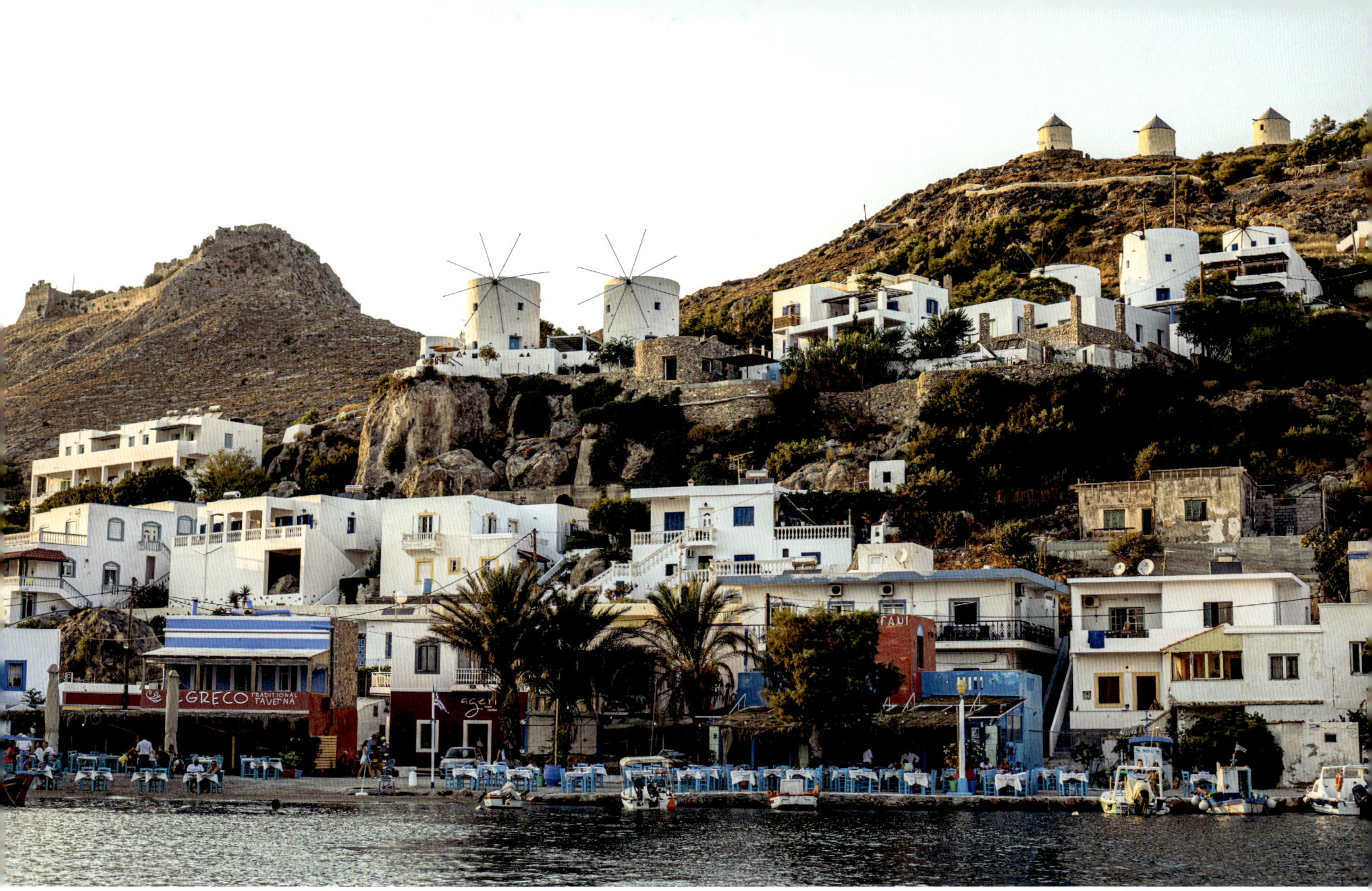
GRECO TRADITIONAL ΤΑVΕΡΝΑ
ageri
FANI

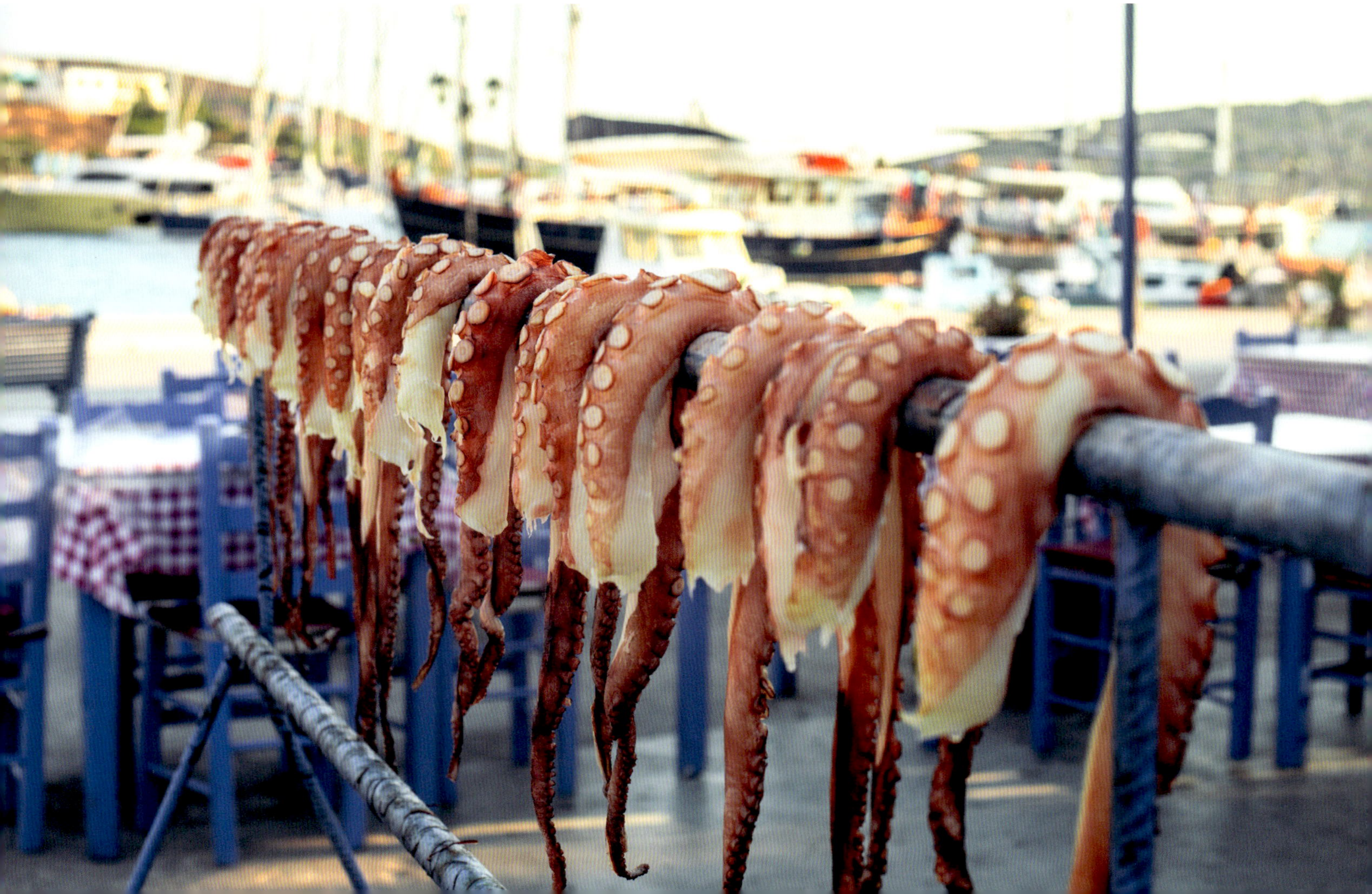

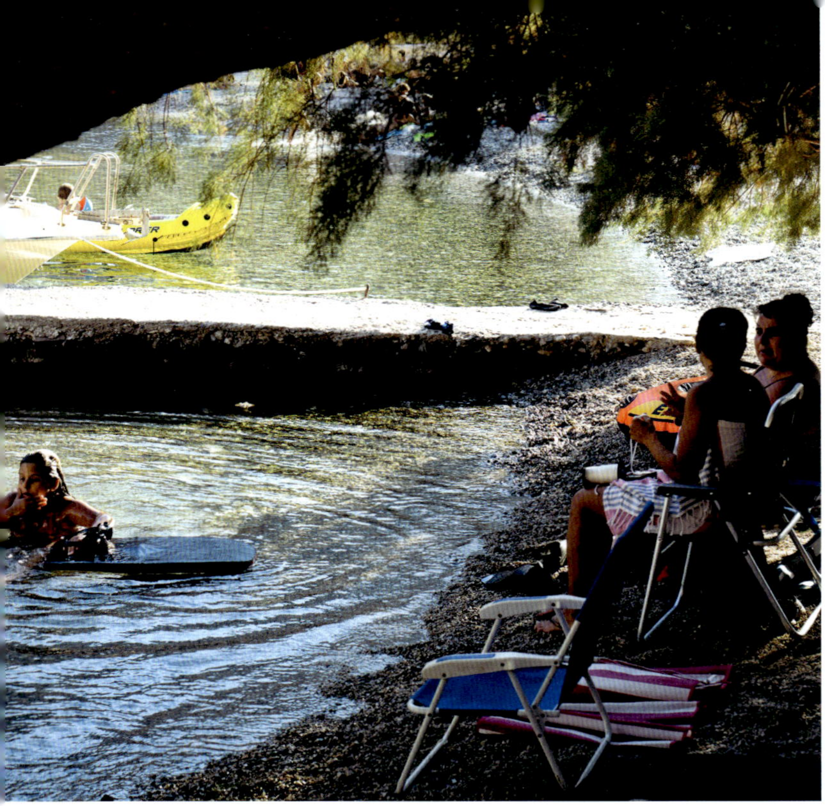

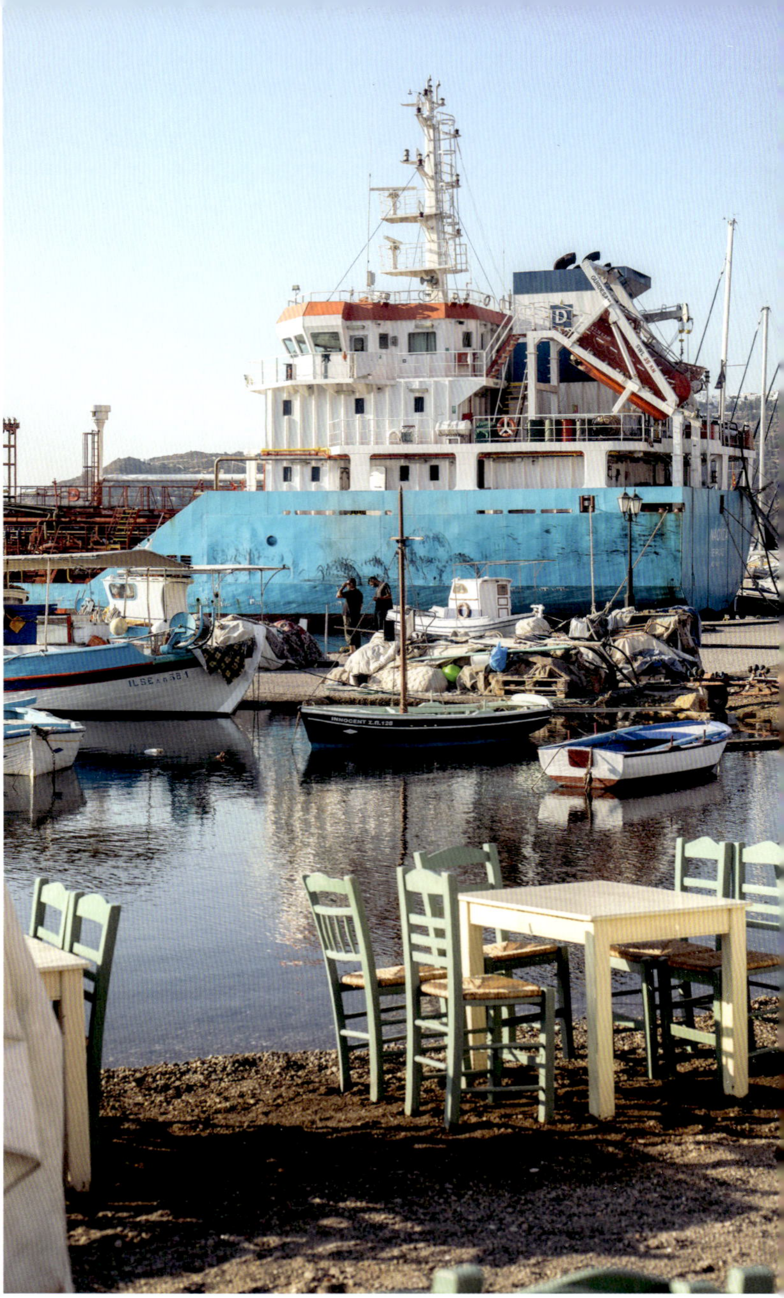

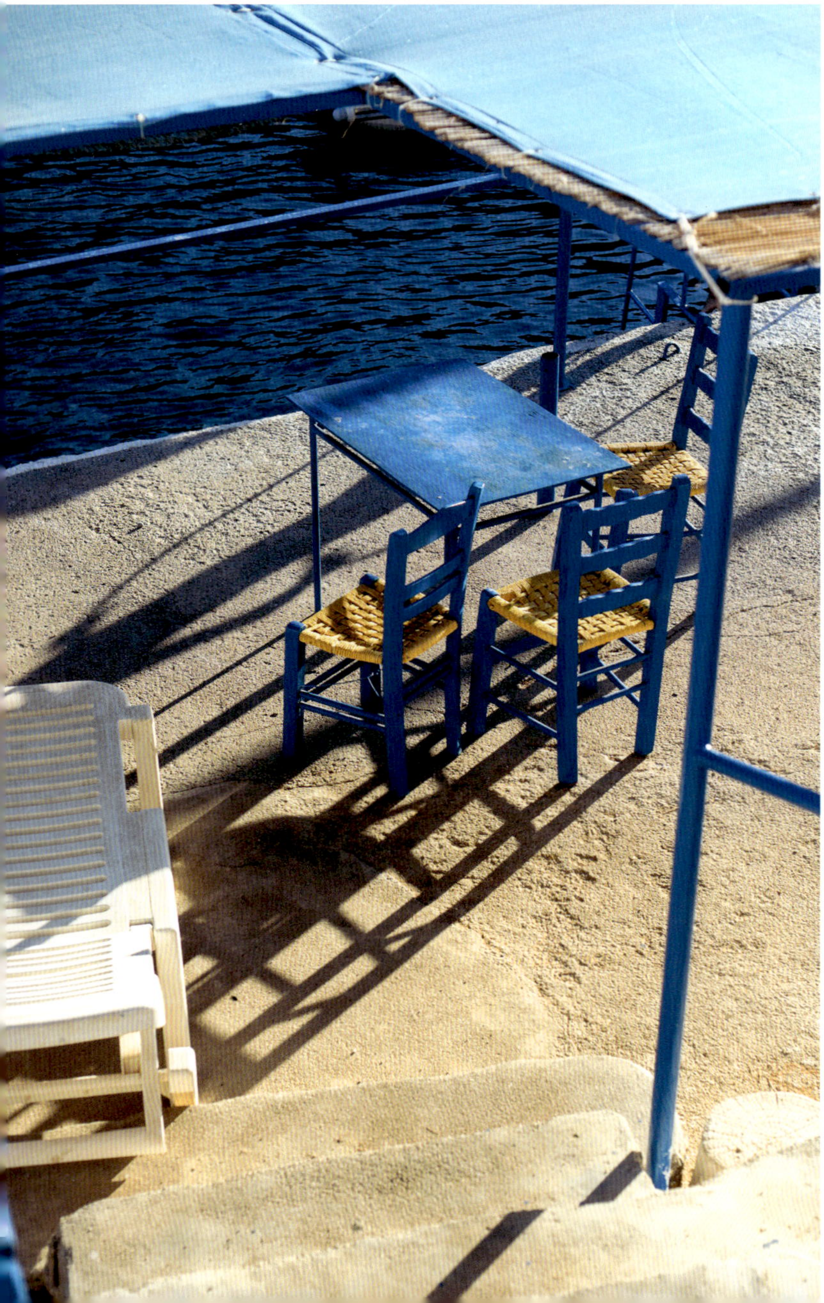

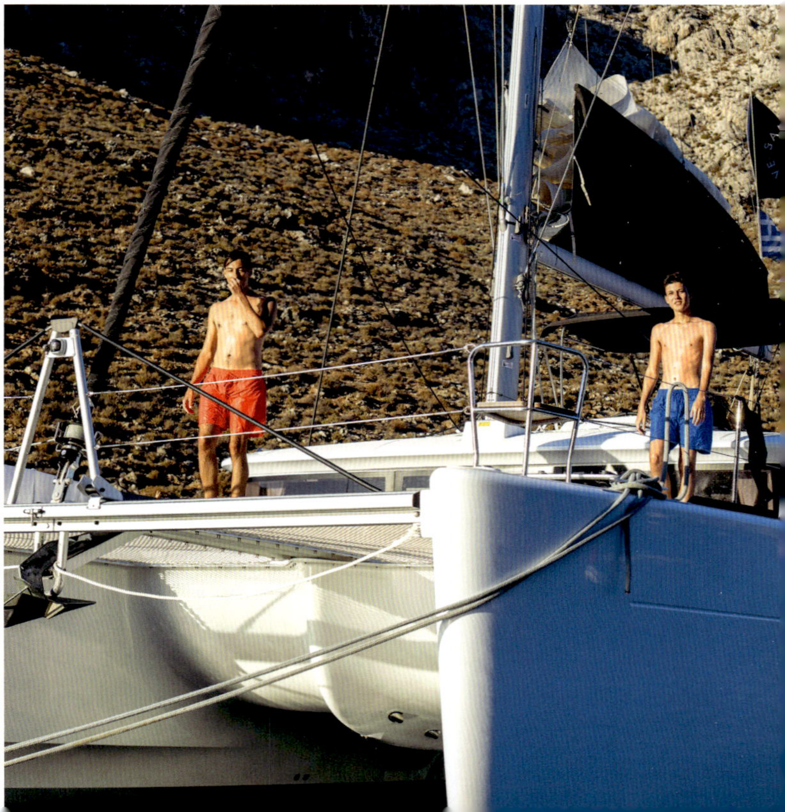

naturally pick up in the evening hours and the nights can be blustery with gusts commonly reaching 25 to 35 knots.

Further north on Kalymnos is Chondri Miti, a rarely visited inlet and home to one remote homestead. There are no roads to be seen— only an old donkey path leading into town. It's difficult to believe places like this exist so close to the bustling island of Kos, as the isolated homestead seems lightyears away from the chaos that can seem hard to escape just miles away; a wild and untouched place accessible only by boat. Anchor here and swim ashore, you will be greeted by a large herd of wild goats with 2,000-year-old ancient ruins as their home.

PATMOS

Sailing northwest you'll find the island of Patmos. Perhaps the most prestigious in the group, it's still easy to see that Patmos had a day when times were simple and traditional. Pulling into the island feels wildly impressive and eerie. The island is back-lit from the western sunlight and its cliffs appear even more bold, rugged and dramatic in the sunset hours. It's stark and mysterious, lined with blue and white show-stopping villas. Still somewhat sheltered from modern development, Patmos has maintained its traditional architecture and atmosphere. It's filled with village settlements, scenic beaches and traditional tavernas.

The history of the island stands out for mariners cruising here. A towering Byzantine fortress is built on the highest peak of the island, protecting an idyllic hamlet sitting just below. At the center of this historical narrative is the monastery of Saint John, the backdrop for his prophetic visions of the end of the world that were dreamed up in a nearby cave. It's interesting to think about how such harsh revelations were brought to life in this remarkably serene place.

As the northernmost island in the Dodecanese, there's a sense of wildness and barren beauty to be found here. It's comprised of three volcanic peaks that are joined by narrow isthmuses. With its gorgeous beaches, this small sea-horse shaped island has been turned into an idyllic stopover for jet-setters and elite travelers. Often sailors are skeptics of hype, because at some point these once-hidden gems become overrun with an influx of tourists. Sailors sometimes feel the responsibility to be protective of these places. When more people start to come, the inevitable fear is that a place can lose its traditional charm.

LIPSI

Lipsi is an island that is known for its simple charm and humble appearance. Its lack of roads and old-world Greek appearance make Lipsi a blissfully serene spot. When arriving at the island by sea, numerous blue-domed churches cover the horizon. Naturally, this fishing village has a number of low-key but exceptional seafood restaurants serving the catch of the day, and paired with dark-colored local wines. Some of the most delightful and friendly people inhabit this island. Many locals still live off of traditional methods of farming and fishing, and life is laid-back, quiet and relaxed. It's filled with Greek-style

---

LOCAL DISH

On the island of Lipsi there's a cozy restaurant called Dilaila that's known for its traditional Greek-style tuna. When visiting, you are instantly met with a sense of authenticity and Greek pride—it's evident that locals here still enjoy and embrace their humble of their way of life. Owned by a fisherman, the tuna is caught daily in local waters and immediately flash-frozen on the boat. It's then grilled and served with a simple lemon rosemary sauce.

EVERYTHING IS IMPORTED TO THE ISLANDS AND LARGE OIL AND GAS SHIPS COME IN DURING THE NIGHT, DOCKING ALONGSIDE THE CRUISING BOATS (ABOVE, RIGHT). A TYPICAL DINNING TABLE (BELOW, LEFT).

white and blue houses and a coastline of cozy beaches. This tiny, lush island stands out for its unspoiled natural landscapes. You can spend a day on the boat travelling from secluded beach to secluded beach, enjoying the mezmerising water, without bumping into another soul. And, once the sun has set, you can visit one of the low-key but exceptional seafood restaurants serving the local specialty (as featured in highlights). There are three main anchorages on the south side of this island, and it's nice to stay further out to enjoy the scenic landscapes and natural beauty. Every restaurant on Lipsi acquires its food from local farms and fishermen, and there's an abundance to go around, with only a few restaurants and bars that usually serve only islanders and sailors. Lipsi today is like Lipsi of old, and as long as there are fish in the sea and crops to grow hopefully Lipsi of tomorrow will be like the Lipsi of today.

LEROS

Sailing south from Lipsi towards Kos brings you to the island of Leros. The island has a charm all its own that comes from its dramatic landscapes, brown-hued highlands and fertile valleys. Much of this island's income is from the practice of sending ships to North Africa every year to fish for sponges. Leros has rounded hills on high and lush countryside along the shore that's full of green forests with hibiscus, jasmine, bougainvillea, and oleander growing wild. The beautiful town of Pantelis located on the eastern side offers protection from the *Meltemi*. Cruising on the eastern side of the island, sailors can anchor close to the harbor or drop cliffside just south of the harbor entrance. It's exceptionally picturesque with views of the idyllic Greek village ahead and windmills spinning on the hill and, true to the region, a Byzantine fortress sitting atop of the peak. Leros has a repertoire of secret beaches, laid back tavernas, and 20th-century Italian influences that make it unlike its neighbors in the best way. This distinct vibe on Leros comes from its extraordinary historical connection to Benito Mussolini. The Italians took over in 1912, and he poured money into the islands to make Leros his base for imperial ambitions. Often slipping under the radar, Leros offers more benevolent landscapes and a serene attitude that makes this little-visited place very inviting.

~

Every voyage to these islands will differ from sailor to sailor. One of the interesting elements of cruising an itinerary is the ad hoc sailing network that forms in shared waterways. Often, sailors will see each other from island to island. Faces of other crew members become familiar, and experiences and information are shared. Returning to Kos after a week of discovery creates such a feeling of nostalgia for what was just experienced, as well as excitement for coming back one day to explore these same waters again. Cruisers with unlimited time could spend months discovering the Dodecanese, as each new cove lends itself to distinctly varied natural beauty and Greek charm.

> Sailors have a greater freedom to explore the lesser known coves and bays, beyond the tourist trail.

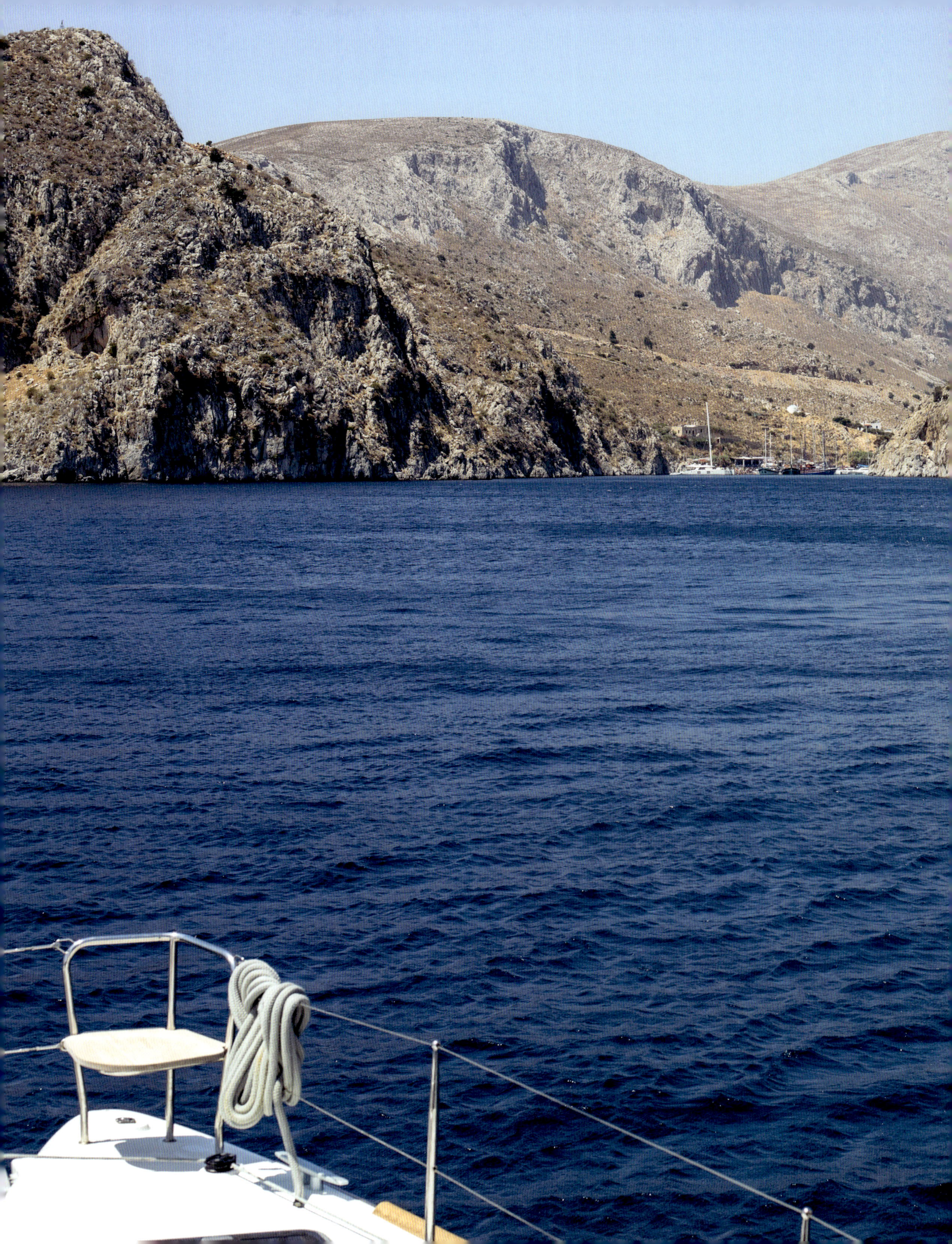

CAPTAIN'S NOTES *DODECANESE ISLANDS*

RECOMMENDED ITINERARY

Kos
36° 53′56″N, 27° 17′23″E
Berth alongside Neratzia castle in Kos town old harbor. The town is home to both medieval and later Turkish architecture, with some Italian additions. Souvenir shops and cafés line the waterfront and the beaches are filled with enthusiastic tourists. Best to use Kos as a provisioning stopover only and depart for the less crowded islands.

Palionisos, Kalymnos
37° 2′20″N, 26° 58′30″E
Moor in the uncrowded bay of Palionisos, located in a large cove that is open to the southeast, using the moorings laid and maintained by the restaurants in the cove. Anchor behind the moorings in deep water go go stern-to the cliff.

Pantelis, Leros
37° 8′42″N, 26° 52′2″E
Lakki is the largest port on Leros, and there are also suitable marinas in Partheni and Alinda. The recommended anchorage on Leros is at Panteli, an idyllic town on the eastern side of the island. Protected from the *Meltemi*, there are three berthing options. The town has a small cement pier: mostly home to the town fishing boats and some local pleasure crafts. Sailors can go along dockside if there is space during the summer season, though the pier is reportedly closed in the off season, when fisherman take up the available space for their commercial use. With local economies shrinking and fisheries struggling, it is good practice to support fishermen hoping to create a flourishing economy through traditional practices.

Patmos
37° 18′32″N, 26° 32′51″E
Berth stern, or bow, to the quay along the northwest part of the bay. The *Meltemi* gusts can bear down, beam-on, across the seawall. Drop anchor in sand and mud in good holding. The bay is open to the southeast and, in moderate wind from this direction, can become uncomfortable. Anchoring in harbor is restricted because of commercial boats and gas tankers coming in and out during the night; this is an odd sight but also a pleasant reminder that we're all sharing the same waterways.

Lipsi (also Leipsoi)
37° 17′42″N, 26° 45′53″E
Berth bow-to either side of the town pier. The inner harbor has been dredged to 3–5 meters and the bottom is sand, mud, and weeds; be sure to have a good anchor set, as the holding is not great. During strong *Meltemi* wind, yachts should consider anchoring in the bay to the east in Ormos Kouloura.

RECOMMENDED ANCHORAGES

Vathy, Pserimos
Sykate, Kalymnos
Panteli, Leros
Agia, Leros
Katsadiá, Lipsi
Makronisi Kasou, Lipsi

ITINERARY DURATION

7 days recommended, sailing the northern route beginning from Kos

12 days recommended, sailing the entire archipelago

PREVAILING WIND

During the summer season, the prevailing wind is the *Meltemi*, pushing southward from the north-northwest. This wind blows strong in July through September, when it will regularly blow force 4–6 on the Beaufort scale.
The wind is less continuous in June and October, blowing force 2–4. As the *Meltemi* blows south, the wind first hits the north and west side of the islands and, at full strength, gusts off the lee side of the islands are considerably stronger than the wind strength on the open sea.

SEASON

The shoulder season is the optimal time to sail the Dodecanese, in June and in September. July and August are the two warmest months and also the windiest. During the winter season, violent wind can blow from the east and west, causing rough seas.

FOOD

The Dodecanese are sea-bound people, who are used to dishes with big flavor. In the northern islands, fishermen historically cultivated sea sponges, which live in the waters around Kalymnos, lining the seafloor. This led them to be expert at lobster fishing as well. In these islands, sun drying was the preferred way of preserving catch and sun-drying octopus, fish, and lobster influences the island's gourmet cuisine.

GOOD TO KNOW

Off-Season Sailing
Though temperatures stay moderate all year, most boats are tied up and docked for the winter months. Those willing to sail during the off-season will find the *Meltemi* unpredictable and the sea state recognizably different. Sometimes in the spring, rare but strong easterly sea breezes funnel over the Turkish coastline and create large waves and swells. Perhaps locals know what to do, but visitors cruising by can easily be caught off guard; what appears to be a safe harbor situation may not be tenable in easterlies.

Magnetic variance
Magnetic declination: +4° (EAST)

AGATHONISI

ARKI

MARATHOS

LIPISI

PORT OF PATMOS

KATSADIÁ

MAKRONISI KASOU

PATMOS

N
W E
S

LEROS

AGIA

PORT OF LEROS

PANTELI

LAKKI

SYKATE

PALIONNISOS

MEDITERRANEAN SEA

VATHI

KALYMNOS

VATHY

PSERIMOS

TURKEY

KOS TOWN

KOS

0 10
NAUTICAL MILES
NOT FOR NAVIGATION

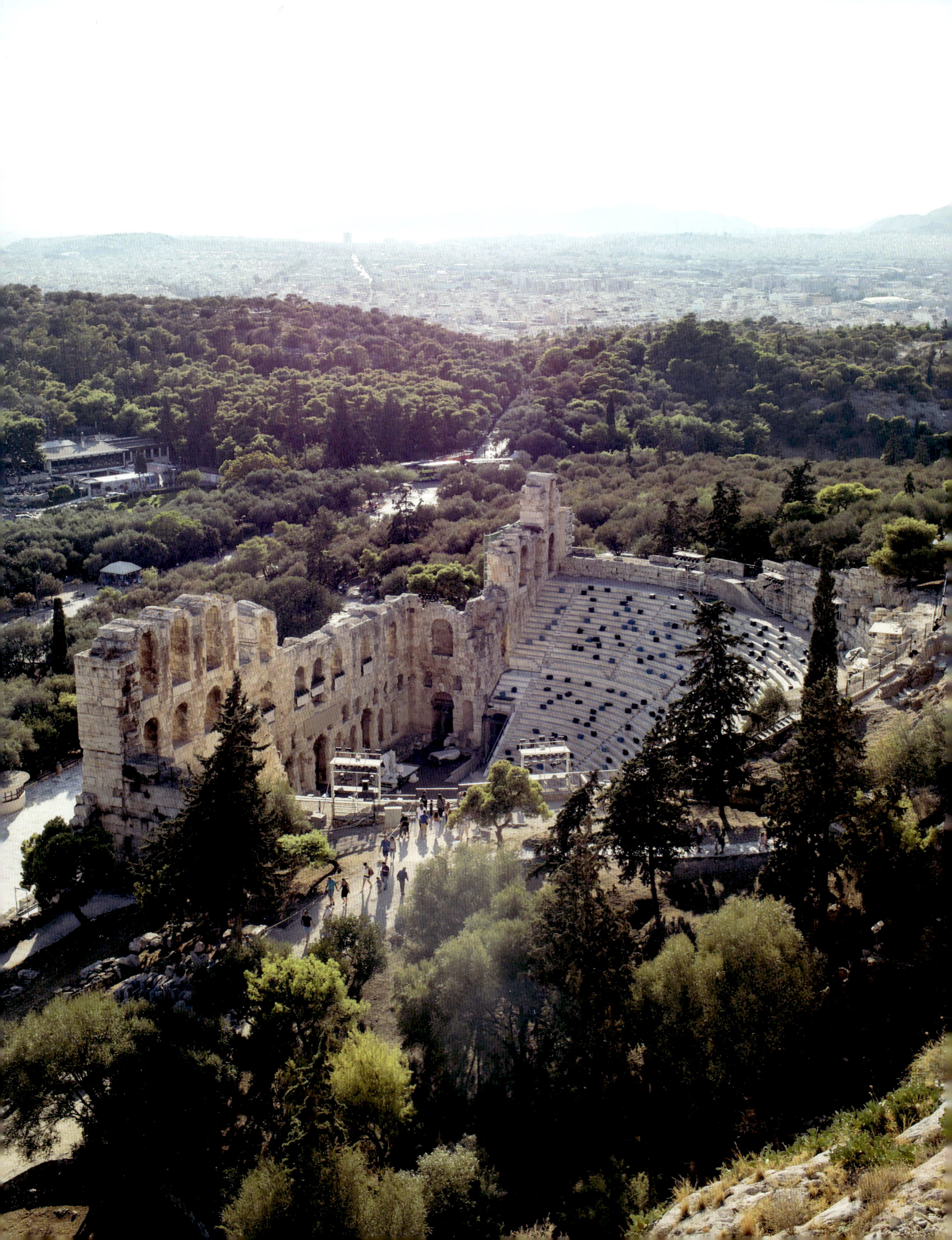

FROM ATHENS TO THE SARONIC ISLANDS

JUST A SHORT SAIL FROM ATHENS, PAST THE GRAND TEMPLE OF POSEIDON, ARE THE SARONIC ISLANDS AND THE PELOPONNESE COAST. THIS SPIRITED LOCATION FEELS ESPECIALLY FREE, PUNCTUATED BY CHARMING TOWNS AND SECLUDED COVES.

The Aegean Sea is generously endowed with islands—Greece has more than any other country in the Mediterranean. Deciding which islands to visit during your sailing itinerary is not easy, with each region home to a unique maze of land and water and providing endless sailing opportunities. The word "archipelago" was the original Greek name for this sea; it translates simply as main sea, and this was indeed the center of the world for one of the history's great seafaring civilizations. In modern usage we refer to island groupings as "archipelagos," but this is the original and proper, capital-"A" Archipelago, and the standard by which others should be judged.

Setting sail from Athens, an exploration of the Saronic Islands takes you south along the east coast of the Peloponnese peninsula and can easily include Hydra, Dokos, and Spetses, which sit just past the Saronic Gulf. Sailors can visit Salamis, Aegina, Poros, and some mainland destinations such as Epidauros at their leisure. Hydra, a sleepy island that is home to a single town with no automobiles, is a highlight of this itinerary and often the turnaround point for sailors doing a round trip from Athens. The Saronic Islands, with their tucked-away anchorages and seaside villages, are a tranquil getaway and a perfect adventure for sailors departing the busy urban life in Athens and seeking adventure.

The history of these islands is immense, and to sail among them is to partake in a living reenactment of how people have ventured out into the world since ancient times. When the waves stand up tall and a rain squall blacks out the sky you feel the respect for the sea that sailors throughout time have felt. Then, when the sun shines bright and a fresh breeze fills your sails, you feel the love for the archipelago that inspired poets and soldiers alike.

A truly remarkable thing about sailing south from Athens into the Saronic Islands and beyond is the layers of literature that you transverse under sail: Homer was here; Plato made this passage and Henry Miller sailed here as well.

AEGINA

The island of Aegina sits centered in the Saronic Gulf. Home to enjoyable, easygoing towns with protected harbors, it is often the first port of call during a Saronic Islands itinerary. The main port has a proper seawall in an unusual arrangement, with the harbor for large boats closer to town than the small-boat harbor. Sailors deciding to spend an evening moored along the quay will enjoy the laid-back attitude of the locals, wandering past vendors who sell fresh and local produce off wooden boats that have been modified into farm stands. Shops onshore feature a plethora of products made with pistachios that grow on the island. Take a walk off your sailboat and wander the streets, where you'll be welcomed by beautiful neoclassical buildings in bright colors, picturesque cafés, and restaurants offering fresh fish caught by the island's many fishermen.

Across the island to the east, summiting the prominent peak, you will find the Temple of Aphaia—an impressive ruin in an impressive location. Taxi there to enjoy the sunset and have an amazing view without the crowds of the acropolis. Aegina, being an island, has escaped most of the package-tour hordes that are so prevalent around Athens, and this spectacular temple is a significant one.

Prior to the rise of Athenian naval supremacy in the 6th century BC, Aegina was the thalassocracy (naval empire) to beat. The wealthy merchants and political rulers of this island had the biggest fleet and the best trade network of the whole pre-Hellenic Greek world until the Athenians ultimately triumphed through direct military action against Aegina.

South of the port lies the seaside town of Perdika, which is a very popular overnight anchorage. The town is small with a number of charming tavernas offering classic Greek island foods like grilled whole fish and halloumi cheese served with local honey and crushed pistachios. One nautical mile from Perdika is the uninhabited island of Moni. A quick sail to the island offers a quiet respite from populated Aegina. The south-facing cliff has a small deep cove that is wonderful for swimming into sea caves; snorkel into the one with the narrow tall entrance and you can follow it all the way to a dimly lit stone beach inside the cavern. Sunlight coming in through the mouth of the sea cave bounces off the water and provides a spectacular light show on the rocks overhead. On the north side of Moni is a beachy cove with one sleepy restaurant. Dinghy ashore and hike to the summit for sweeping views in all directions.

POROS

Separated from the Peloponnesus peninsula by a narrow channel, residents of Poros have easy access to mainland amenities, but Poros doesn't sacrifice its island charm.

The main town on Poros is located on the southwest coast. The harbor runs along the town and has two separate points of entry depending on the side from which you approach. Buildings border the waterfront and boats anchor stern-to the seawall throughout the entirety of the town. In the late afternoon, once all the sailors come into port after the day's voyage, boats squeeze in next to one another with fenders out and the

---

LOCAL DISH

The island of Spetses is home to a famous village fish dish: Psari Spetsiotiko. *It is a baked dish that might make use of bream, bass, cod, or even thicker steaks of halibut, hake, or haddock. The fish is baked in tomato sauce and topped with a golden crust of breadcrumbs. Sampling the local specialty on arrival to a new island is a fantastic way to immerse yourself in the culture and this dish is both delicious and distinctly local.*

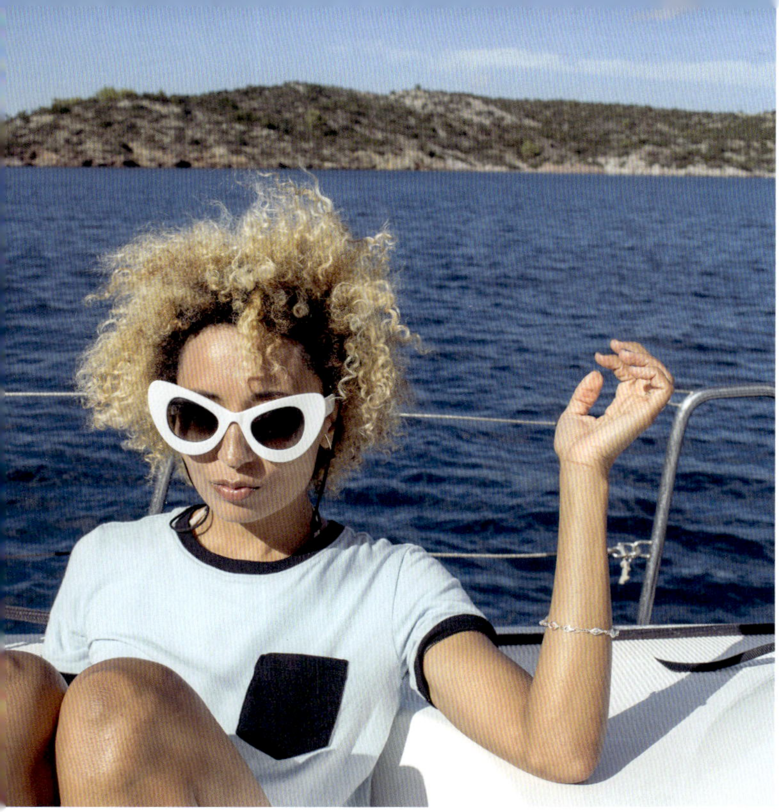
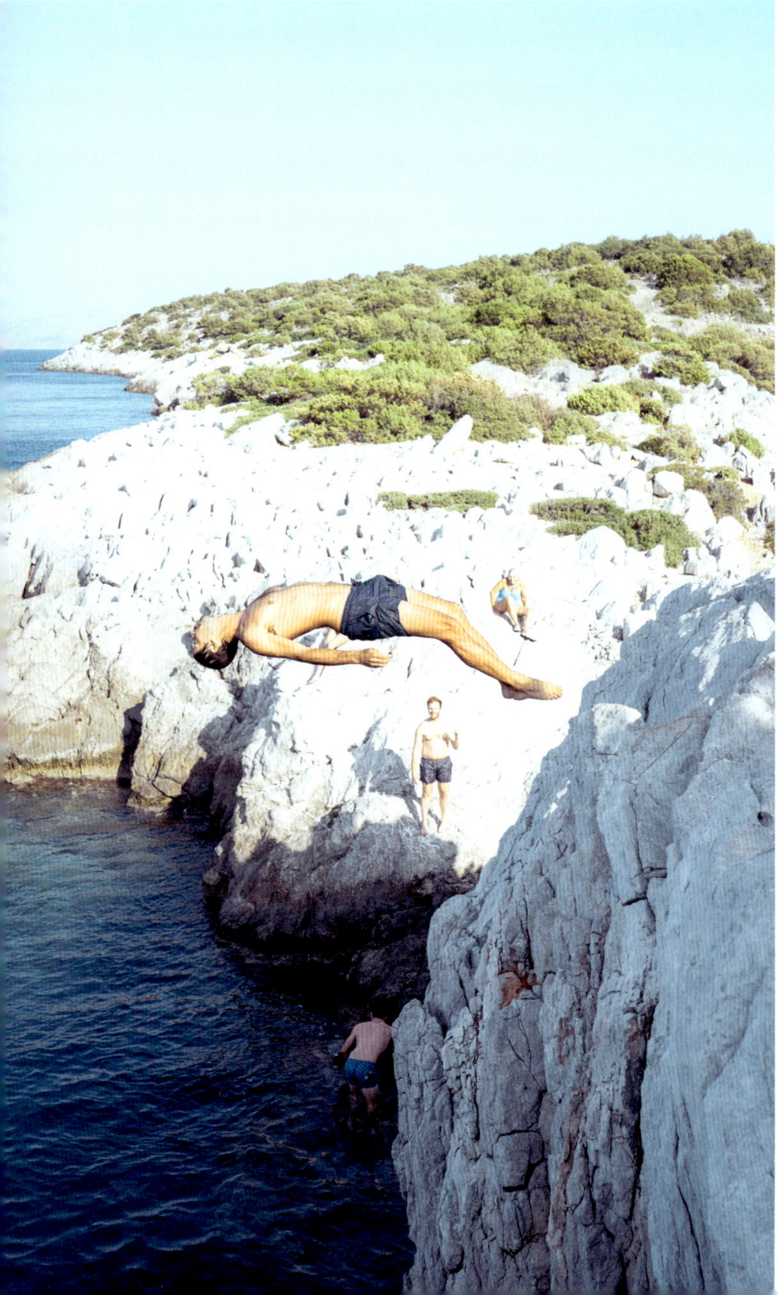
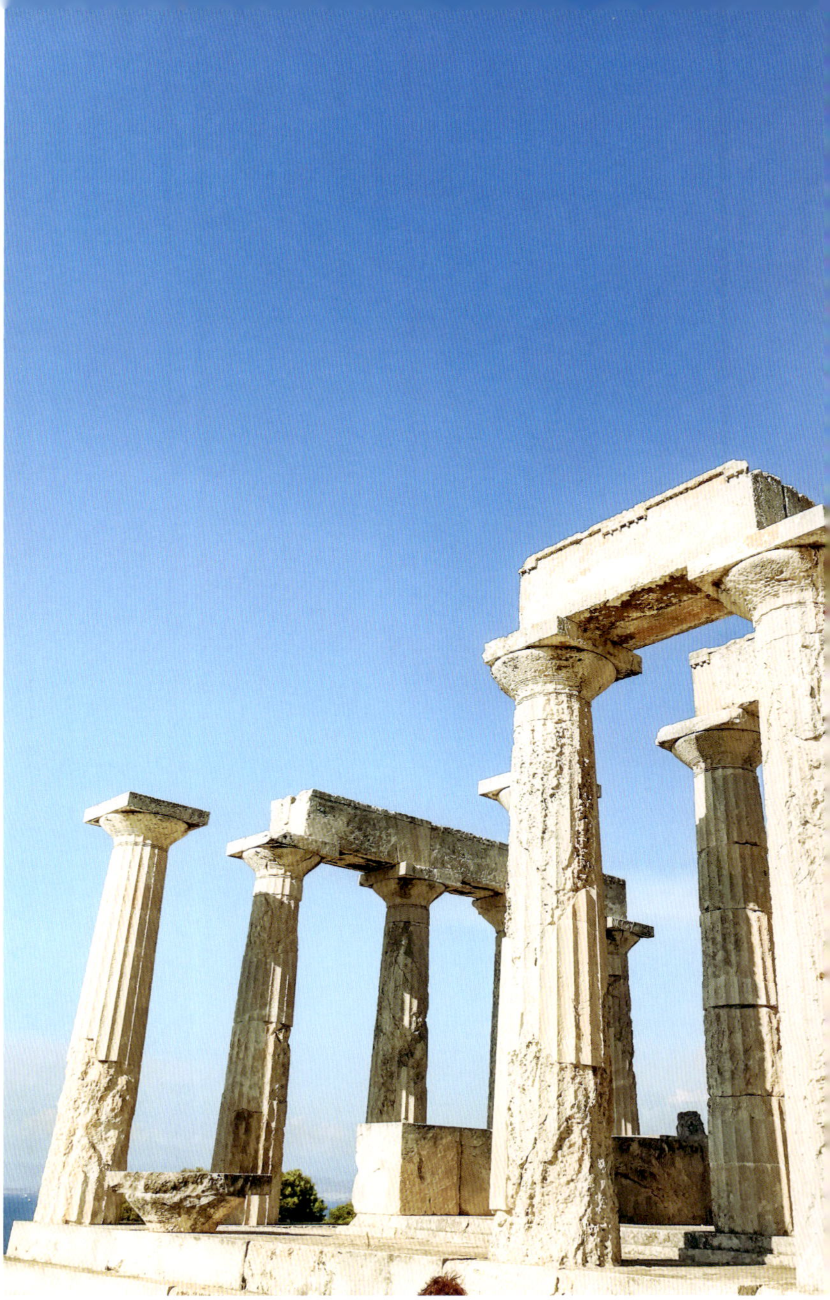
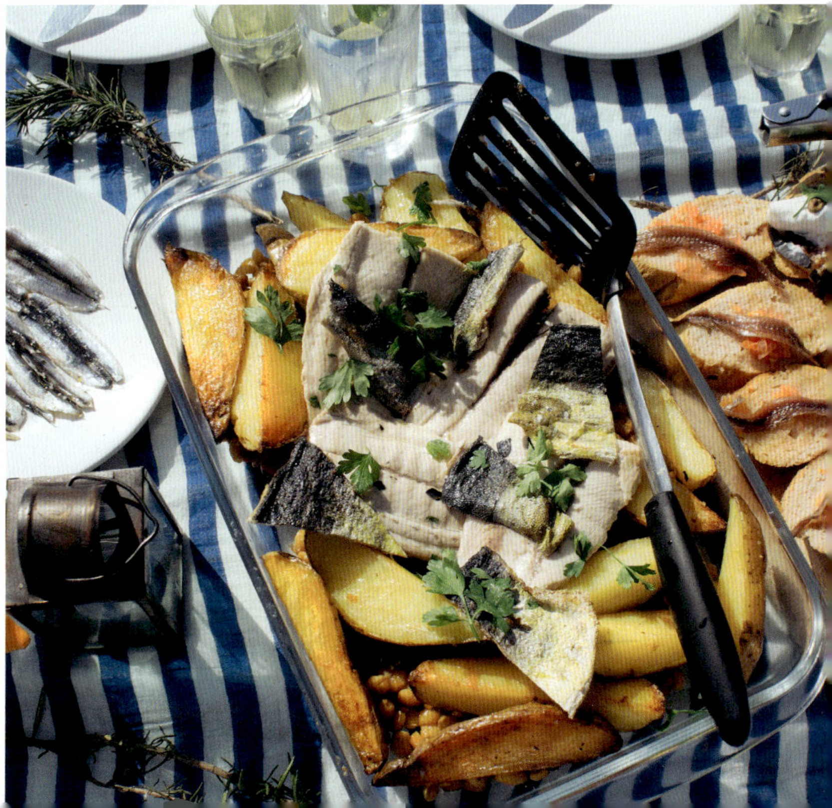

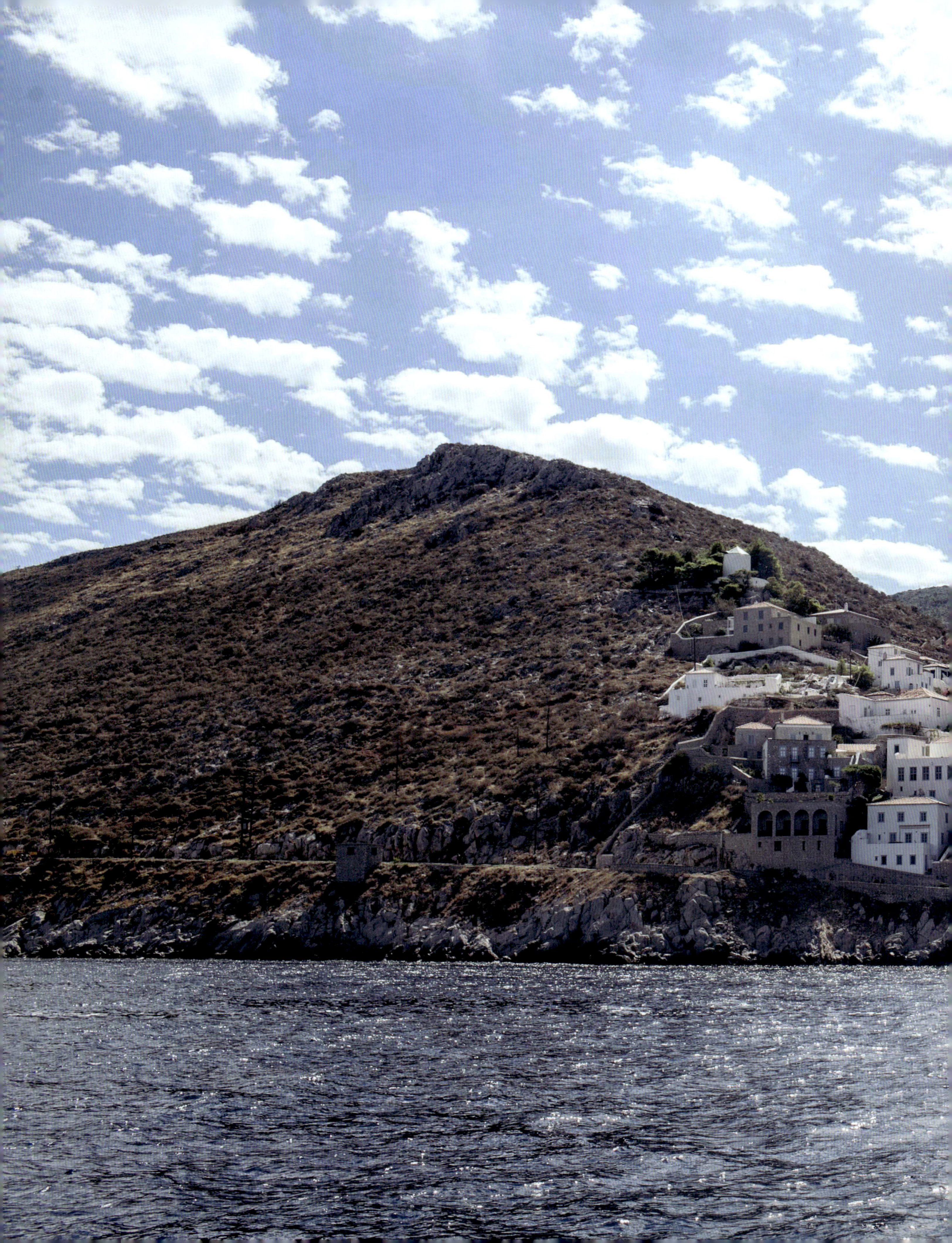

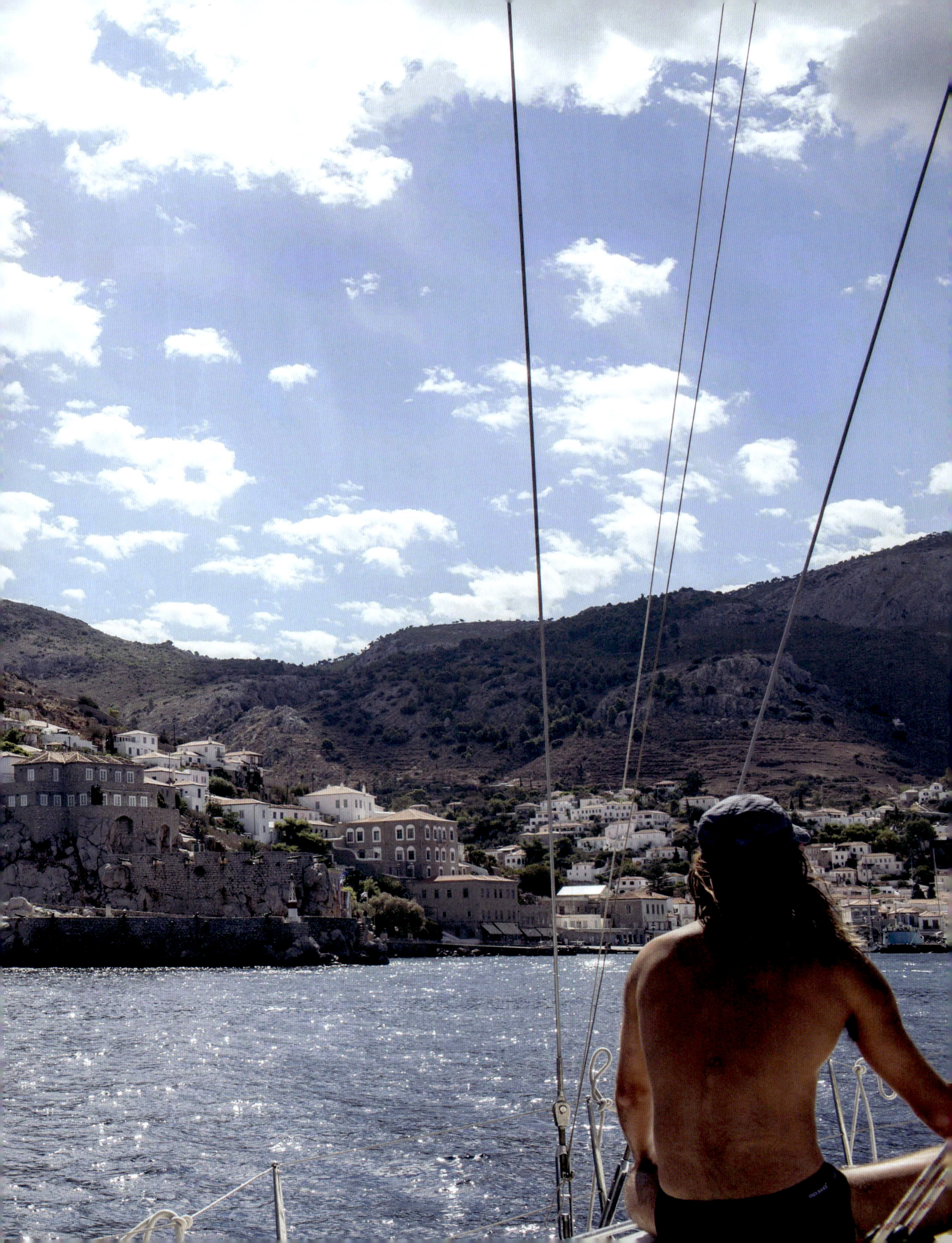

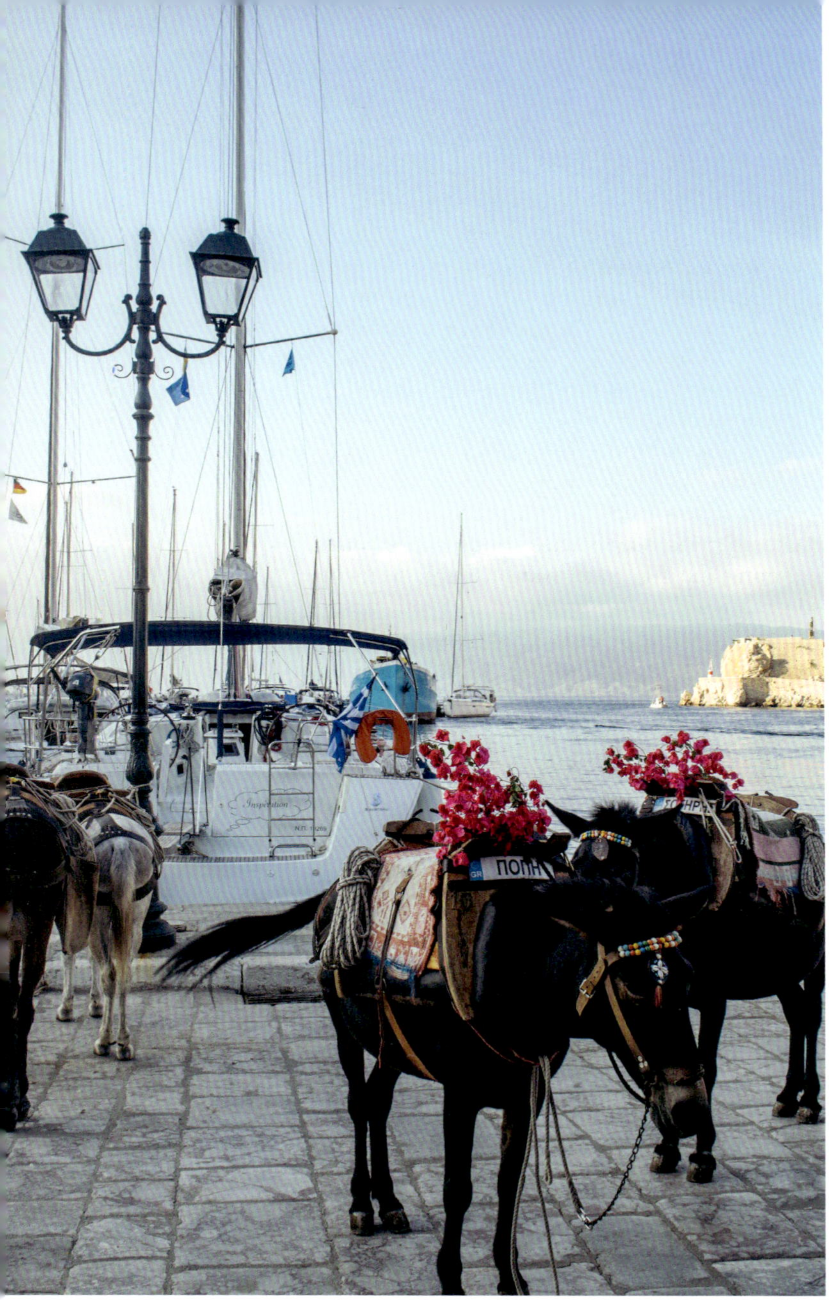

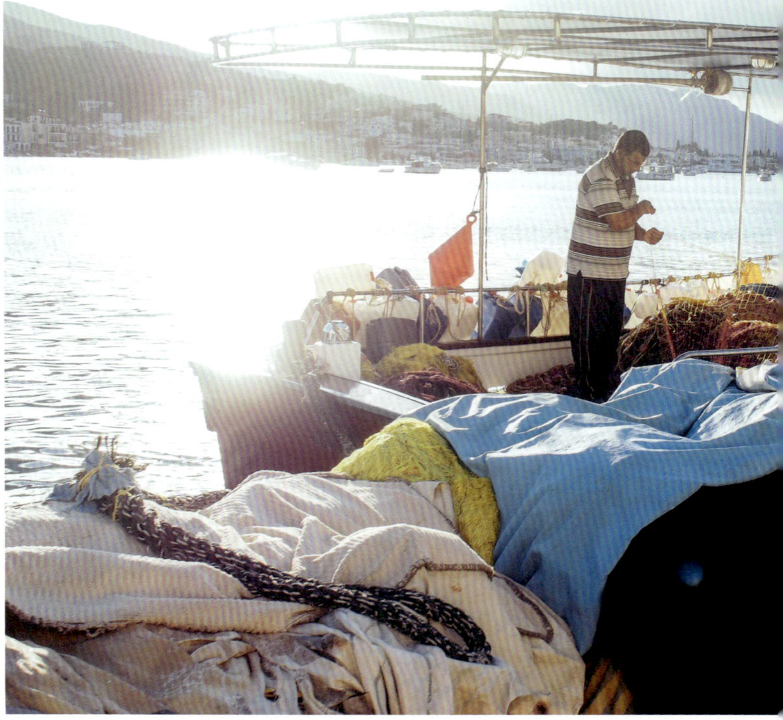

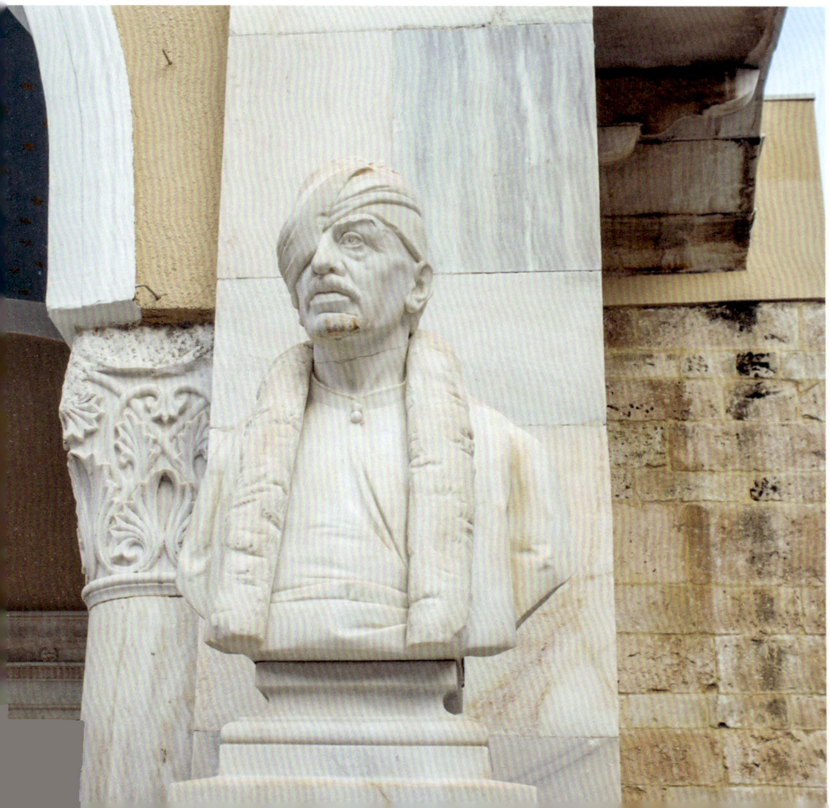

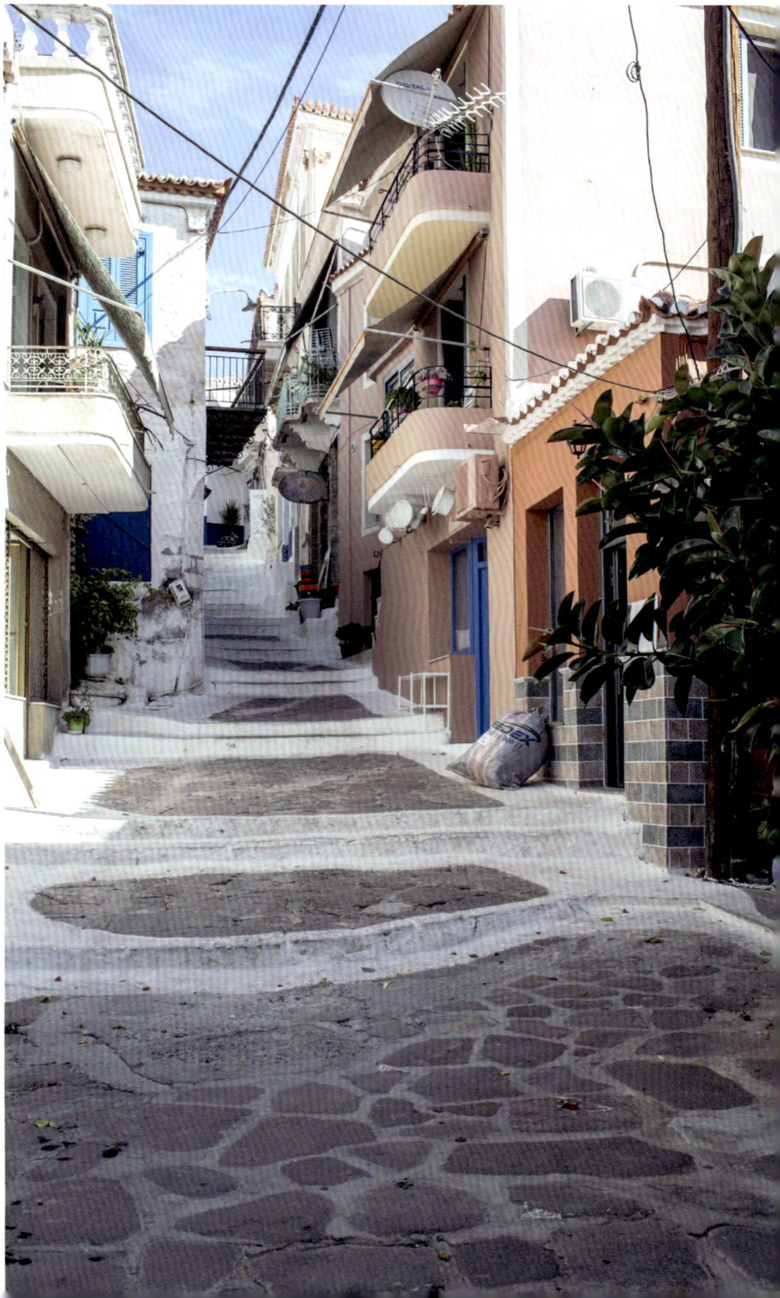

town is painted by the masts that tower over the buildings. With plenty of restaurants as well as cafés to explore, sailors stroll the seawall and find a table at which to settle.

Poros is also home to numerous sheltered coves, providing anchorages well-suited to an afternoon or an overnight stay. Neorio, Elies, Russian Bay, and Bistiou Cove are inlets home to stunningly clear waters with lush cypress trees—for sailors interested in a quiet night away from the port. Be sure to check the weather forecast when deciding where to anchor for the night, as even the more protected southern coves can get rolly in a strong westerly breeze.

EPIDAURUS

Nestled along the northeast shore of the Peloponnesus peninsula is the seaside village and harbor of Epidaurus—not technically a part of the archipelago but inside the Saronic Gulf. The town itself is small and charming but without the old-world idyllic Greek architecture found on the islands. Still, there are nice cafés along the waterfront, full of locals enjoying their everyday life. Anchoring outside of town along the undeveloped northern shoreline feels like a secluded slice of Aegean calm. There are magnificent sunsets and being anchored away from town is blissful, as there are no sounds of cars or people, just you and your friends swaying peacefully at anchor.

Just south of Epidaurus harbor is a snorkeling location on a shallow sandy shelf, with ancient ruins that sunk below sea level in an earthquake many years ago. The underwater ruins nowadays are just rows of stones but you can still feel like a treasure hunter braving the unknown as you swim from the boat to seek them out.

HYDRA

Entering Hydra is not for the timid. Like the mythical sea creature of the same name, this harbor is a contentious foe and not all who face it leave unscathed. Because the inner harbor is small but the town is so wonderful, boats drop anchor and raft up in lines two-or-three-deep, spider-webbing lines to each other in a collaborative effort. The harbor here is not as well protected as it looks and a northerly swell with some west in it can bend in and wreak havoc. Add to the mix the local water taxis, ferries, supply ships, and fishing boats coming and going and you have a recipe for at least a few dings and scrapes, and sometimes much worse fates, for boats who enter. Hydra is worth the effort. The steep climbing village surrounding the harbor has been a treasured getaway since the 19th century, when wealthy merchants built "captains' mansions" there. In the 1950s and 1960s Hydra was home to a community of artists, many of whom were expats living in Greece, including the musician Leonard Cohen and author Axel Jensen.

As fishing boats navigate the melee of yachts to their dedicated spots in the inner harbor you should scurry across to the seawall if you want to get first pick of the day's catch. The locals (Hydroits), some of them looking

---

AMPHITHEATER

Epidaurus is notable for its ancient theater, which is located on the grounds of a significant archeological site in the mountains above the harbor.

A short taxi from the dinghy dock and you will arrive at one of the largest amphitheaters in Greece. Built in the 4th century BC, it is still active today and enjoyed by the public. If you are lucky, in the summer months, you'll be able to see a classic Greek play performed here. To test the acoustic perfection of amphitheater design, have someone stand in the very center of the circular stage and recite poetry while you try out seats in the audience—even at the very top you can hear people remarkably well.

DONKEY'S, LINED UP IN FRONT OF THE SEAWALL, ARE THE ONLY MODE OF TRANSPORTATION ON HYDRA (ABOVE, LEFT). A FISHING BOAT IN THE HARBOR OF POROS (ABOVE, RIGHT). THE STREETS OF POROS (BELOW, RIGHT).

like they must be 100 years old, will already be there waiting as the fishermen tie up. Happy-looking alley cats wait opportunistically for fish scraps or the occasional charity of a whole sardine that gets tossed to them on the seawall by bartering fishermen.

Take time to wander the steep paths of Hydra and you will see the local delivery donkeys working hard to bring everything that is needed up staircased alleys that no truck could service. At the end of the day, wander out of town to the east along the main path and grab a cocktail at the aptly named Sunset Restaurant. Bring a bathing suit, as there is wonderful swimming from the rocks below the bar if you need to cool off.

DOKOS

The barren and dramatic island between Hydra and Spetses makes for a wonderful respite. Dokos supposedly has 18 residents but you will be hard-pressed to find them. This large island has steep and formidable cliffs on the southern side and a large protected bay that is devoid of infrastructure on the north. Anchor to swim on the west side of the anvil-shaped peninsula on the northeast of the island. This narrow inlet, just outside a larger bay, is deep and requires a stern tie to keep a boat from swinging. Once secure, you can snorkel along the outside wall to see dramatic underwater rocks and cliff jump from the shoreline into deep water. Enjoy the beautiful sunset colors here from the deck of your boat or go hiking onshore, among olive trees that are many hundreds of years old. In the depths below is one of the oldest shipwrecks ever discovered; artifacts from the wreck can be viewed in a museum on Spetses.

SPETSES

Perhaps more metropolitan than other islands on this itinerary, Spetses has no shortage of gourmet restaurants or fancy boutiques. Sailing into Spetses, most yachts will anchor outside the small inner harbor of Baltiza Creek. While there is depth in there for a sailboat it is often too crowded with local boats to find a space. The protection outside, in the big Spetses main harbor, is sufficient, but to deal with the swing room of dropping in deep water you will see many boats run long lines to the shoreline.

About a 20-minute walk northwest along the coast brings you to the Bouboulinas museum, where you can immerse yourself in the history of Laskarina Bouboulina, who led the rebel Greek navy against the Ottomans in the early 19th century and is credited with turning the tides of seapower in the region, allowing the Greek independence movement to triumph. Her house is open to the public with museum tours daily.

~

There is too much to see and do here for a quick visit. If you decide to spend only a week sailing here you will realize quickly that you need to return at least once, and probably again after that. Experiences in these islands will be significantly enhanced by reading along as you sail; it is easy to get lost in the rich cultural history of the region even from afar but as you glimpse the evening light dancing on the water below you, the stories will take on new and deeper meaning. To sail here is to be a part of history.

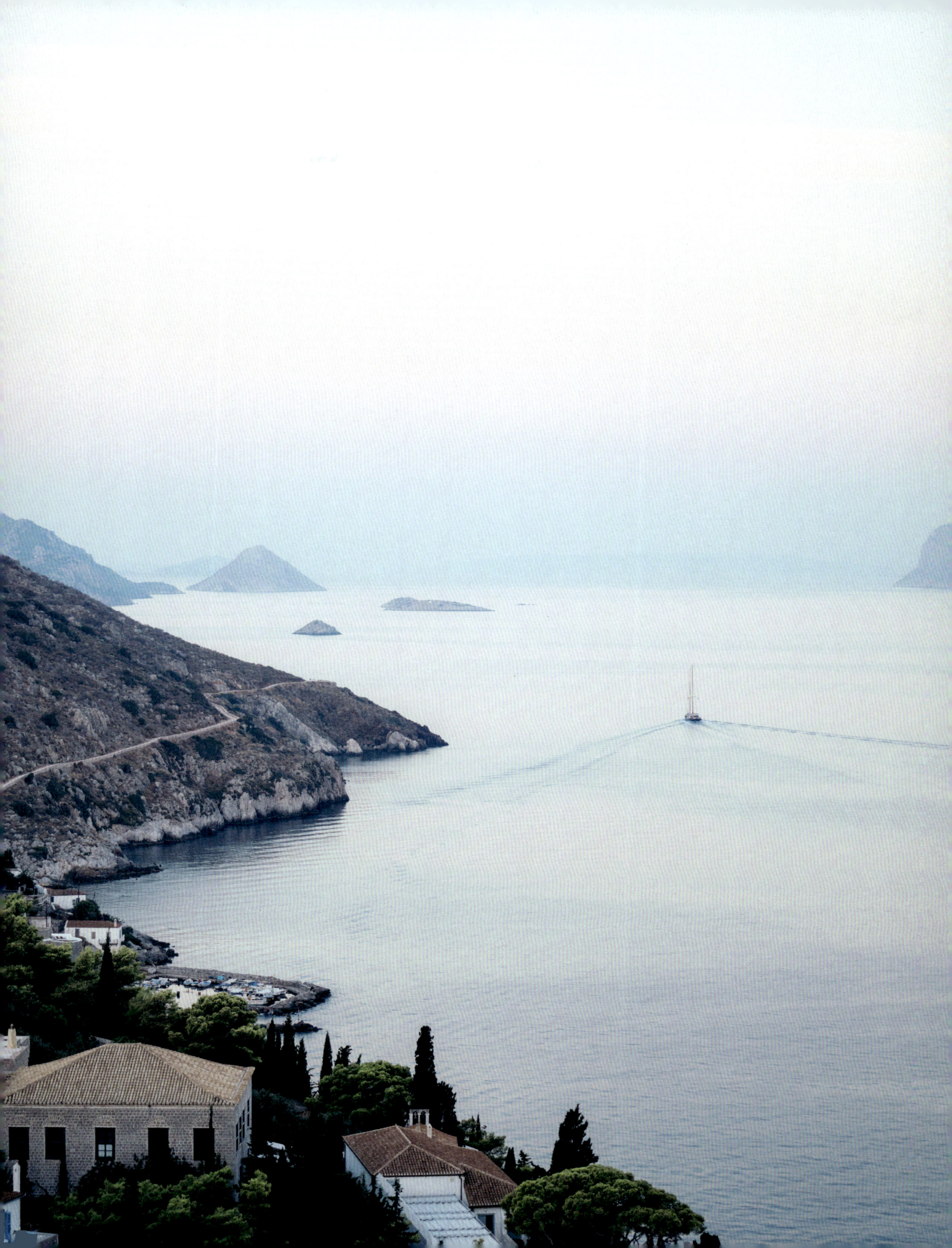

CAPTAIN'S NOTES *SARONIC ISLANDS*

RECOMMENDED ITINERARY

Poros
37° 29′47″N, 23° 27′09″E
The quay in the main town stretches nearly two nautical miles from one end to the other. Berth anywhere that there is space by dropping anchor in the channel and backing down, tying stern lines ashore. A lack of laid mooring lines along the quay is made particularly difficult by the fact that the chain where former lines were attached is still on the bottom; you must be sure to drop anchor far enough away from the quay so that your anchor does not get caught along the chain located in the center of the channel.

Hydra
37° 21′05.2″N, 23° 27′57″E
Sailors who enter this adventure of a harbor are quickly schooled in the local mooring style, which involves rafting boats into a spiderweb of dropped anchors and stern lines close enough together to enable you to walk from one boat to the next. So many anchors get tangled here that a diver for hire waits around every morning. To add to the organized chaos, hotel shuttle boats come and go constantly through the wild maze of yachts.

Dokos
37° 20′58″N, 23° 20′39″E
Anchor in a variety of locations around the large bay on the north side of Dokos, or tuck in and anchor with a long stern line to the rocks in "anker bay," the small inlet on the northeast corner of the large anchorage. The island is nearly uninhabited with only a few residents living the traditional rural island lifestyle.

Aegina
37° 44′43″N, 23° 25′40″E
As you enter the harbor in Aegina, keep an eye out behind you for the hydrofoiling ferries that approach with alarming speed and don't slow down until they are right at the harbor entrance. On busy days, a port official will be standing on the rocks of the breakwater directing you towards open berths. If you don't get direction, just take any spot you see and dropping anchor with plenty of scope to hold your stern off the seawall.

RECOMMENDED ANCHORAGES

Moni, Aegina
Sunken City of Epidaurus
Saint Nicholas, Hydra
Kelevini Islands
Megalochori, Agistri

ITINERARY DURATION

7+ days, from Hydra to the Athens area

PREVAILING WIND

The Saronic Gulf is sheltered from the bigger swell of the Mediterranean Sea, but can still get quite rough when conditions build. The Saronic area is two distinct regions as far as wind is concerned, with the coast around Athens in a different microclimate than East Poros and Hydra. The *Meltemi* (north) wind begins around mid-July and builds to full strength in August and early September, dying down towards the end of September. During that time it can be up to force 5–6. The *Meltemi* is strong in the middle of the day and usually dies down at night but can sometimes last for days at a time. The wind that comes from the mountains of the Peloponnese, the Katabatic, can build quickly but only lasts a few hours.

SEASON

Greek summers are hot and dry, making the sea the best place to be. Winter, from November to March, can be quite cold and bring ferocious weather. Occasional spring showers in the months of April and May give way to clear skies for a summer of great sailing that lasts into October, when it starts to get cool again.

FOOD

Horiatiki—what we know in English as a "Greek salad"—is more accurately translated as "village salad." and it contains all of the best and freshest things growing in the garden. Many Americans in particular have been led astray in their own country by disappointing "Greek salads" made using sad tomatoes far from the bountiful village gardens of Greece. Taste it here anew and you will discover just how powerful a few good ingredients can be when prepared skilfully by the hands that grew them.

GOOD TO KNOW

The Med moor
A common technique for securing boats in the harbors of Greek islands is to drop anchor and back stern-in to a seawall with taught stern lines. The process of getting a boat into a *Med moor*, as this arrangement is called, can be a difficult one. Crew communication is of utmost importance, as the skipper typically needs to be both giving commands and getting observations from someone on the box controlling the anchor windlass and also coordinating with at least two line handlers in the stern, who are communicating with people onshore. In light and favorable winds this can seem very easy, but if you put a crosswind into the equation, everything gets harder.

Magnetic variance
Magnetic Declination: +4° (EAST)

ATHENS
SARONIC GULF
AEGINA
PORT OF AEGINA
MEGALOCHORI
PERDIKA
MONI
AGISTRI
N
W
E
S
EPIDAURUS HARBOR
POROS
PORT OF POROS
GREECE
KELVINI ISLANDS
HYDRA
DOKOS
IDRA
DOKOS
SAINT NICHOLAS
0
10
BALTIZA CREEK
SPETSES
NAUTICAL MILES
NOT FOR NAVIGATION

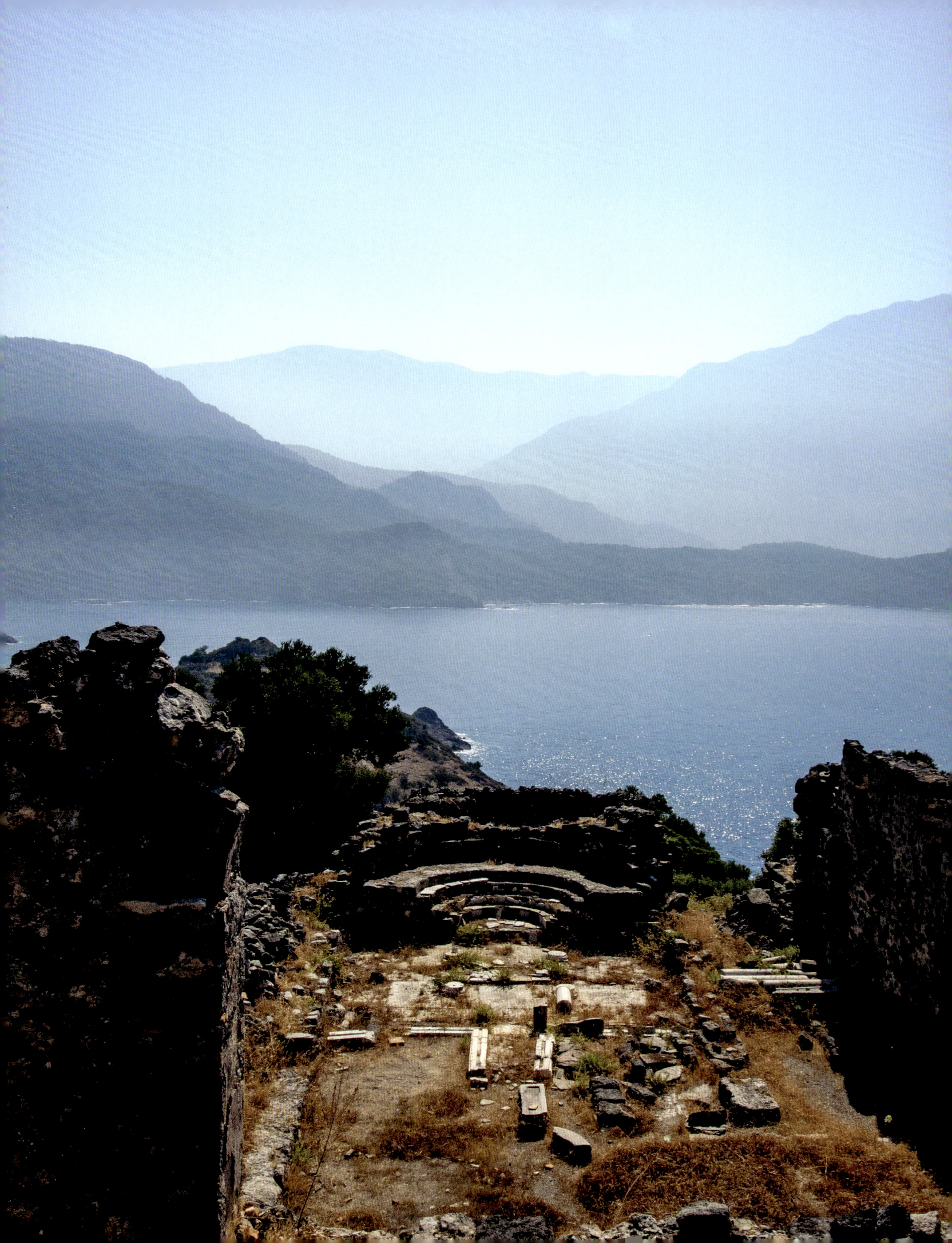

LIVING HISTORY IN THE GULF OF FETHIYE

SAIL TOWARDS THE EASTERN MEDITERRANEAN TO BE GREETED BY LOCALS WITH A WARM WELCOME. THE LANDSCAPES STRETCH ALONG FOR THOUSANDS OF MILES FROM GREECE TOWARDS SYRIA, WITH NATURAL BEAUTY AS FAR AS THE EYE CAN SEE.

The sea is a rich, deep turquoise and its shoreline a bold, evergreen teal; Turkey offers over 8,000 kilometers of coastline and is one of the most attractive sailing destinations in all of the Mediterranean. Travelers have dubbed this region the "Turkish Riviera," in reference to its sunny shores and beautiful coastal retreats. Turkish people, however, have long known that this is a place for relaxation and rejuvenation on the sea. This particular part of the Aegean Sea offers serene, calm beauty, with a storied history of sailing for exploration and discovery.

Voyagers know that it's important to have an understanding of the culture amidst which they find themselves, and this is especially true for sailors cruising along the Aegean coast. This land was prosperous under the ancient Greeks, the Romans and the Byzantine and Ottoman Empires, with each era leaving a mark on modern-day Turkish society. The country was part of the Ottoman Empire until 1923, when Mustafa Kemal Atatürk, a prominent military general who moved up the ranks during the First World War, paved the way for a modern Turkish state. Atatürk formed a secular democracy by separating mosque and state.

The safe passage of sailors in and out of Turkish ports is good for business today, just as it has been since the days of the ancient Greeks and Romans, and the Persian Empire before that. As a sailor in these waters, you are offered the same hospitality that has been offered throughout the millennia: safe passage and a complimentary beverage—it is the social rule of law. Turkey has a culture of hospitality that runs in a clear line through its long and diverse past. The honest tradition is to provide comforts for others, especially travelers. The people here share their own identity through kind acts: offering a coffee or tea, maybe even partaking in trade, and sending people happily on their way. Historically, this was the end of the Silk Road, which governed trade between Europe and Asia, with nearly all goods entering Turkish ports in one form or another. Through every passing exchange—whether it was with Persia, China, the Arab world, India, Egypt, or European empires—the Turkish remained hospitable, while also being steadfast in their own identity and ideals. Turkey bridges gaps and welcomes travelers.

The coast is alluring for many reasons besides the hospitality. Sailing the Turkish itinerary is exotic for anybody not from this region of the world: the food, language, culture, and even the liquor are all distinct. You can hear the call to prayer five times a day echoing along the coast. When docking alongside a restaurant, you'll be greeted like family and treated as the personal guest of the restaurant owner. Food is aromatically packed with intense and pleasurable flavor. In many ways, life here can be simple: a perfect day is spent drinking a glass of rakia, sitting on a comfortable pillow playing a game of backgammon.

GÖCEK

On the western side of the bay are the attractive harbor and charming town of Göcek, a premier yachting center and home to six marinas with wonderful restaurants, markets for provisioning, hotels, and, of course, a Turkish bath. Göcek is the perfect location from which to start your sailing itinerary and is centrally located among the most interesting of the surrounding islands and bays. Sailors from all over the world walk the docks as they gear up for their adventurous journeys along the majestic coast; they cart provisions and supplies to their sailboats along the docks, full of excitement as they look out to the almost shockingly pristine bay. An intoxicating smell floats in the air, coming from the Turkish pine trees that line the shore.

The town of Fethiye, roughly ten nautical miles away, is not only the largest town in the area, it is also one of the only towns nearby. It is busy: full of local residents shopping in the open-air markets. Home to the largest marina in the region, ECE Marina, the town is popular among sailors stopping to reprovision or simply to enjoy the town.

GEMILER ISLAND

Sailing eastward crossing the bay you'll pass Gemiler Island. Part of the allure of sailing in Turkey is the opportunity to explore the diversity of the significant historical ruins here, which span over a 3,000-year period. Bringing your sailboat to nearby anchorages, you can see these ruins up close and outside of museums or tedious tours. Anchoring at Gemiler island for the night affords you the opportunity to wander an early Byzantine settlement. Though tour guides are available, you can easily dinghy ashore for your own adventure, allowing your imagination to wander with you and building a mental image of how the magnificent buildings that once stood strong here might have looked.

Many scholars believe that this island was once a healing retreat run by a wealthy Byzantine-era man named Nicholas of Bari, or Saint Nicholas of Myra. He was born just 30 kilometers from here and is the patron saint of sailors, so he would have had no problem making the journey from the mainland to his island! It is thought that wealthy Christians living in Constantinople would make the journey to this island during the summer months, for vacations and to be healed by the wonderworker himself.

As you sail by, you can see why he might have stopped and stayed for a while. Walking among the expansive and surprisingly intact stone ruins you will see the tile-mosaic flooring of the original churches; you can picture Nicholas himself having stood on those floors.

WALK IN FETHIYE

Fethiye is home to a fish market, with the fresh catch sold to mariners, travelers, and residents. Restaurants surrounding the market will prepare purchased fish in any way you prefer and served along side dishes called mezzes. Another impressive dish found in Fethiye—testi kebabi—is chicken or lamb cooked in a claypot. Waiters will present the flaming pot to the table and the server will crack it open expertly, using a special hammer.

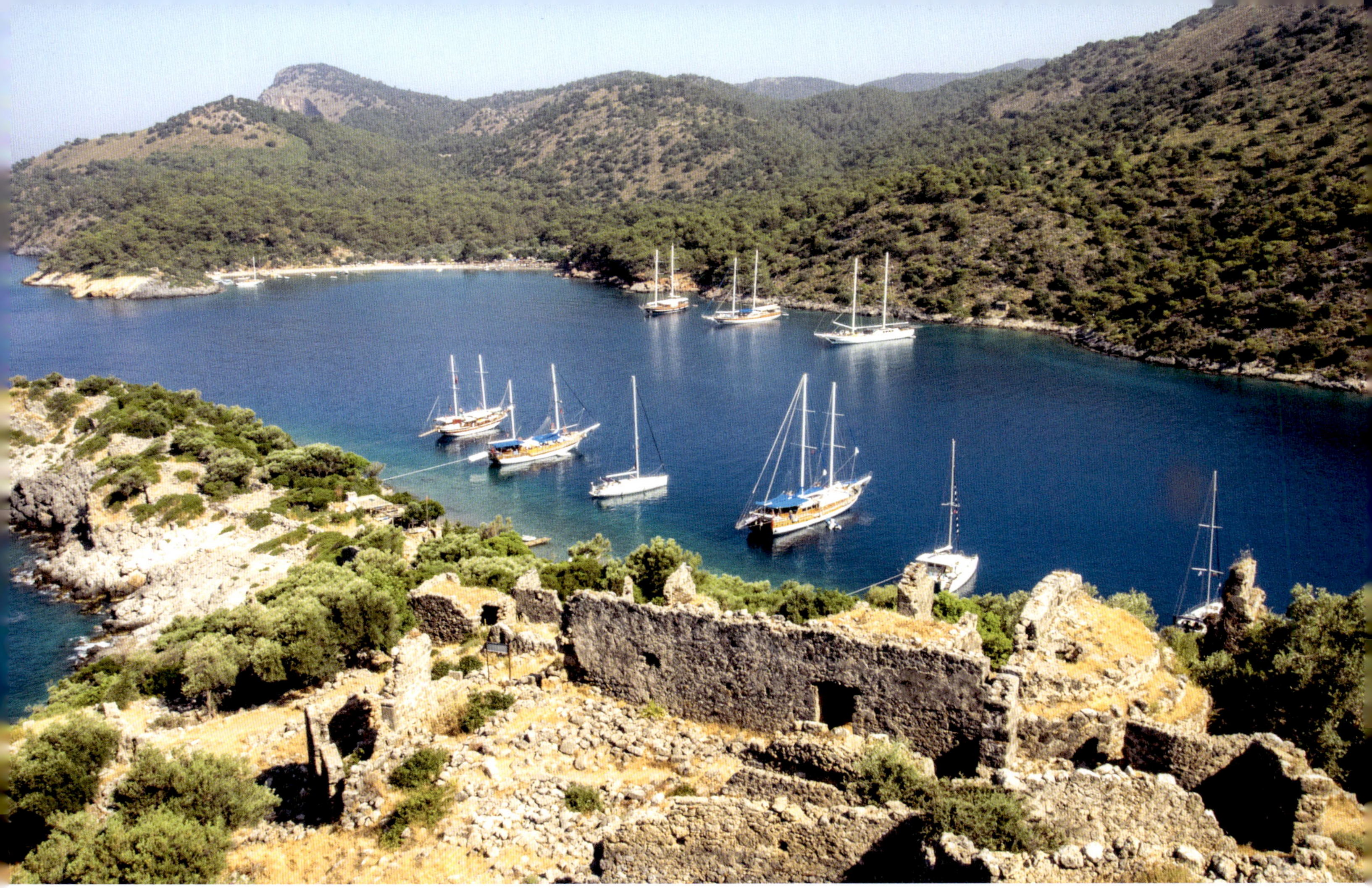

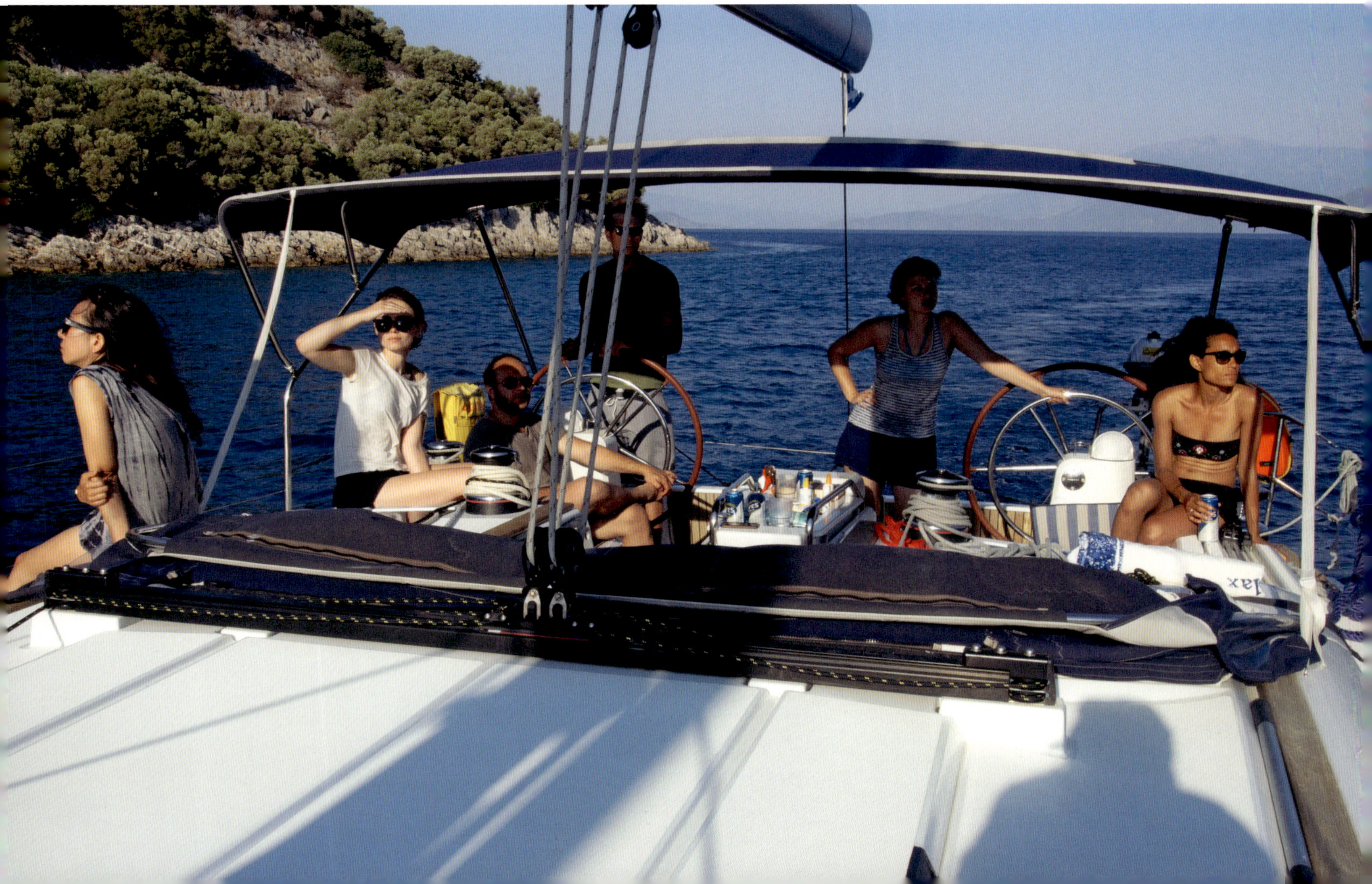

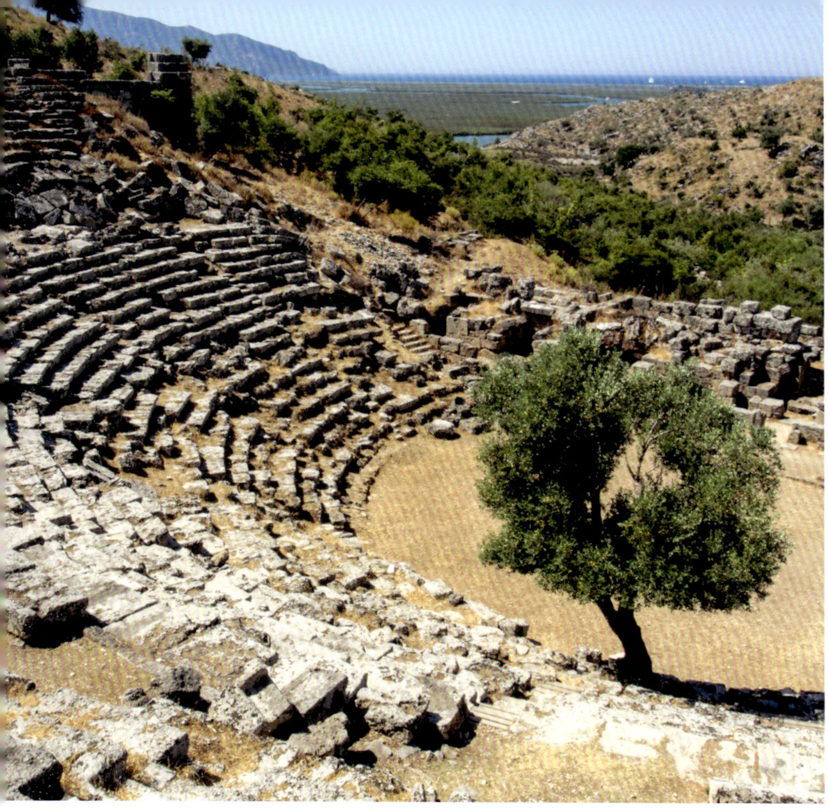

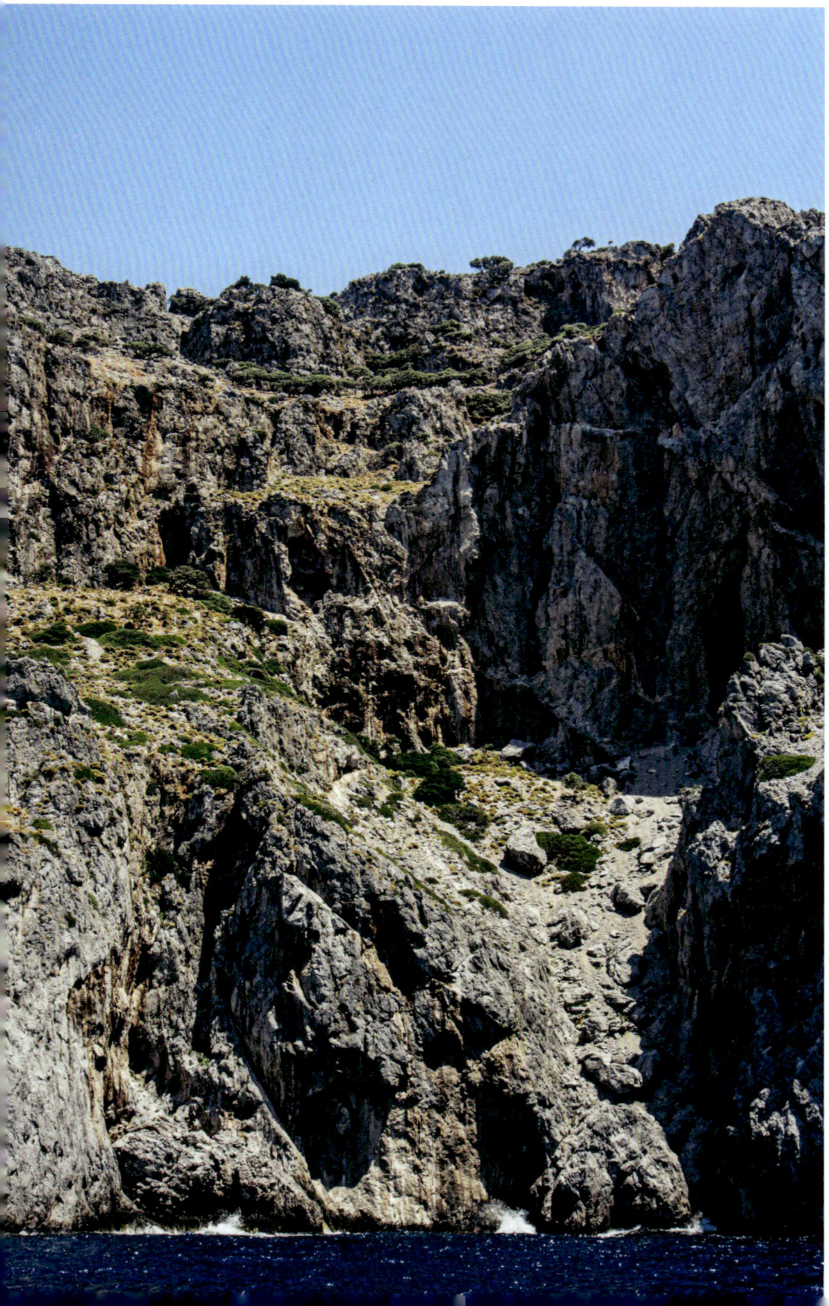

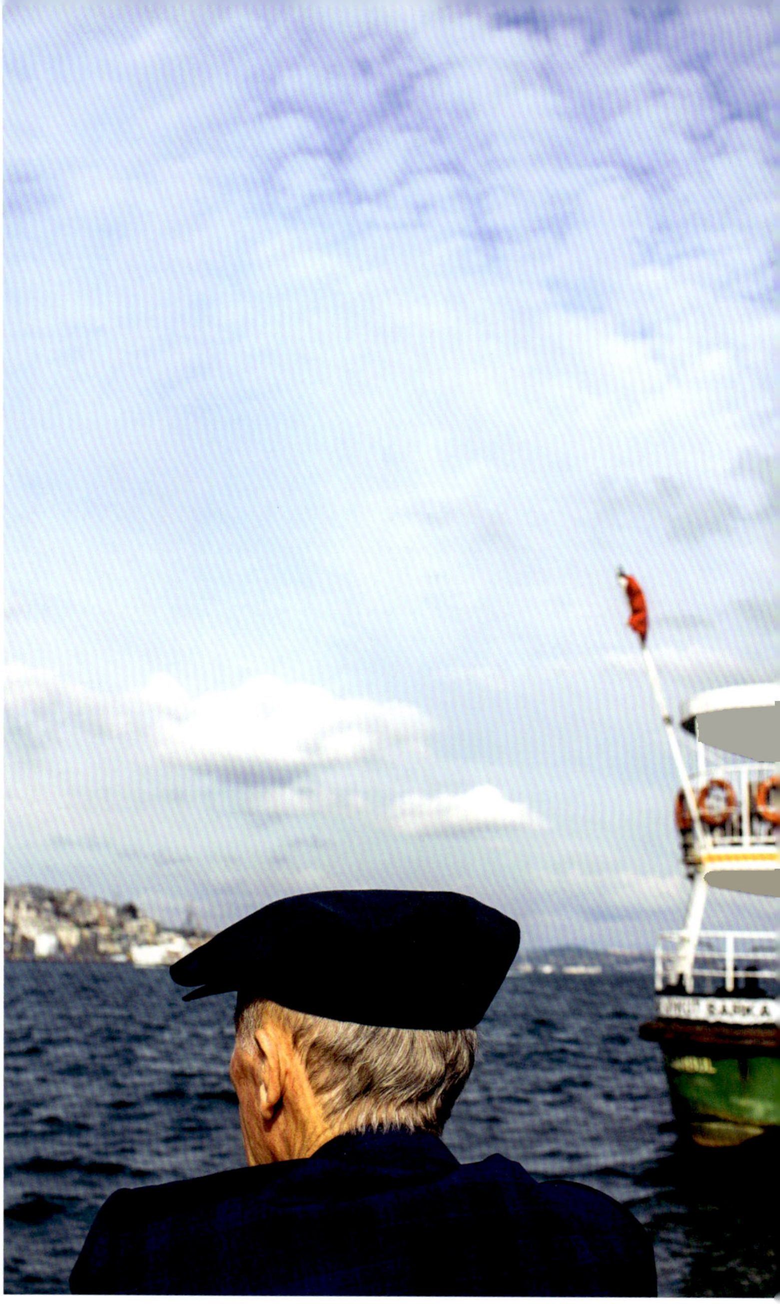

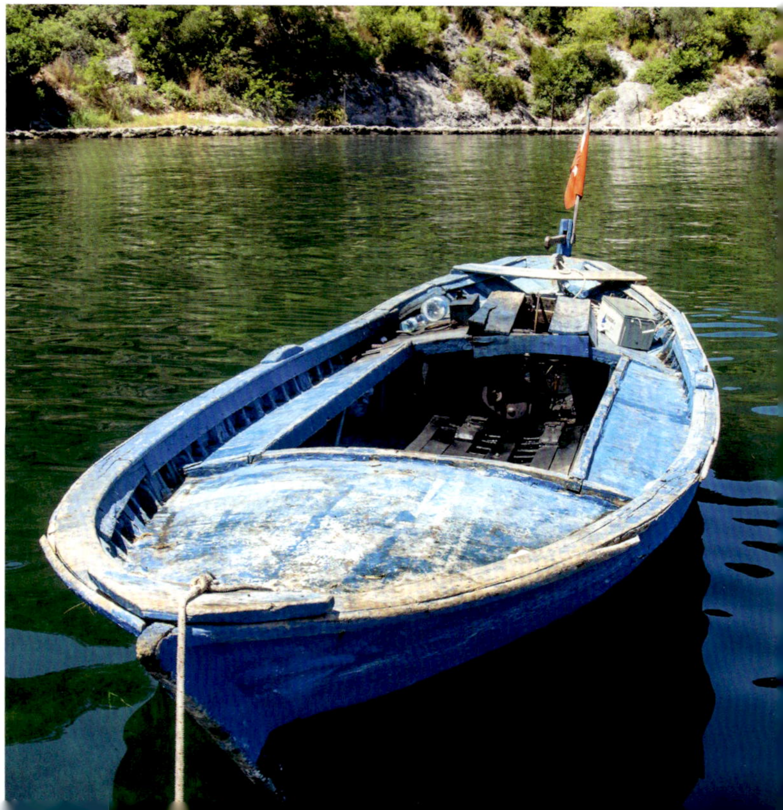

COLD WATER BAY (SOĞUK SU KOYU)

Cold Water Bay, south of Fethiye, is a charming cove, welcoming sailors with open arms. There is a restaurant located at the top of the ridge, just a short walk from where sailboats sit at anchor, moored stern-to at the edges of the cove. Take a swim off the transom of your boat and you'll quickly realize how the bay received its nickname. An underwater stream flowing down from the mountains above feeds into the bay. The surface of the water is the warm Mediteranean, but plunge a meter below and you'll be shocked by a refreshing blast of cold water.

The restaurant mainly caters to the sailors enjoying a night's stay during the summer months. Ali is the owner of the restaurant and an experienced yachtsman himself. You can often find him in his runabout boat assisting sailors while they moor in the cove. Be sure to order the restaurant specialties: a Turkish wild boar curry and freshly caught sea bass grilled over hot coals.

DALYAN RIVER

The Dalyan River is located west of the Gulf of Fethiye in the district of Marmaris and a day's sail along an open sea passage. The coastline along the way has limited safe anchorages and the nearest safe port with easy access to the river is the town of Ekincik, a small beachy village popular among locals during the summer months. Ekincik has a large bay with suitable anchorages and is home to two marinas. Here, you can hire a local guide aboard a traditional wooden fishing boat to take you on a tour of the Dalyan River.

The river itself is a winding maze that begins at the Köyceğiz lake, home to the rare blue crab and loggerhead turtle, along with other marine life that spawns in the brackish marshland waters. Entering the mouth of the river is a terrific experience. Fishermen walk along the mudbanks in shallow waters on the (controversial) hunt for the blue crab: the practice has been debated for over 30 years, with a lack of effective regulation of sustainable fishing practices meaning that some argue the creature shouldn't be fished at all.

A slow motor up the river, past thick reeds and rushes along the banks, takes you to Kaunos, an expansive, ancient Carian acropolis, now in a state of magnificent ruin, that dates back to the 10th century BC. Legend has it that King Kaunos, grandson of Apollo, built this city. It became an important trading port between the East Mediterranean and the Aegean Sea. Control over Kaunos was key to empires far and wide. They exported salt, slaves, pine resin, salted fish, and black mastic, and was a major ship-building port. It is speculated that the city fell into ruin after the time of the Byzantine Empire, due to rising water that made it difficult for merchant ships to sail along the river's banks. Walk up through the walled city and you will see the Aegean Sea with views back to your boat anchored in Ekincik.

KAUNOS AND TOMB BAY

Back in the gulf, a sail in this area will take you by extravagant tombs, including that of King Kaunos, carved out of the dusty stone cliff face along the shore. The Lycians believed the dead would enter the afterlife on a magic winged creature, and the larger and taller the tomb, the better off they would be

---

HOME OF THE GULETS

The gulet is a Turkish-built, twin-masted boat with a gaff sail and several foresails, often built with a mahogany hull. These boats are characterised by large deck space and comfortable accommodations, and the construction of these wooden vessels gained international notability beginning in the 1970s as a result of increased tourism along the Turkish coast, especially between Bodrum and Göcek.

EXPLORING THE THEATER IN THE VAST RUINS OF KAUNOS (ABOVE, LEFT). A TURKISH MAN GAZES OUT ALONG THE RIVER (BELOW, RIGHT).

in their afterlife. These tombs were carved into the side of the hills, with the entrances designed as extravagant temple facades, with ornate columns and archways. Those who were buried here would line the interiors with their wealth, but chambers inside are now empty after hundreds of years of looting.

Sailing in Tomb Bay is a pleasant leg of the journey. The bay is busy with fellow sailboats enjoying the afternoon breeze and majestic wooden *gulet* sailboats motoring along with their sails filling the sky. Mainland Turkey wraps around like an arm, with various islands blocking any larger waves from entering the bay. With your sails full, you will glide along towards the next stopover, enjoying the views of the beautifully carved tombs from your boat.

There are no modern towns in the area to speak of, but small, family-run restaurants offer a rustic home-cooked meal to anyone sailing by. There are a number of coves, home to small wooden docks, that cater to cruising yachts sailing by.

TERSANE ISLAND

Tersane Koyu Restaurant on Tersane Island is a prime example of a slow food restaurant. The only way to access this restaurant is by boat and the restaurant has built a small dock along which sailors can moor. This off-the-grid, family-run restaurant, powered by generator, is reliant on the personal gardens on the island and the fish the family catch themselves daily. The owner has a drove of his own lamb to which he personally tends, and if you have a group of eight sailors, they will prepare the house specialty: whole roast lamb with rosemary, cooked slowly on a spit over open flames. There are lobsters that are caught and kept in cages along the dock and honey, cheese, olive oil, and bread made on Tersane Island for purchase. The bay is peaceful, with a small wooden dock accommodating ten sailboats and room to drop anchor running a stern-line ashore.

Waking up the following morning in the Bay of Tersane, and seeing the family residents prepare Turkish tea and coffee for the sailors along the dock, you are reminded that the only way to get to this location is by boat. The natural quiet and calm, enjoyed as you swab the decks and swim in the still waters, are unmatched by many other experiences in life. This place embodies Turkish hospitality and the appreciation for mariners visiting these lovely shores.

~

Sights, sounds, and the indescribable feelings of a place are all nuanced and varied throughout the different sailing itineraries in the Mediterranean, but Turkey stands out as a phase change from the rest of the area. The coastline is one of the Mediterannean's longest stretch of undeveloped natural lands and is also home to some of the oldest ruins, perfectly intact after thousands of years. And, although the Turkish waters of the Aegean Sea are a day's sail from Greece, and the passage to Sicily across the Ionian Sea can be made in less than a week, Turkey feels exotic for most sailors new to the area. It is an itinerary that should not be overlooked by those with a desire to explore and experience beautiful nature and wonderful culture.

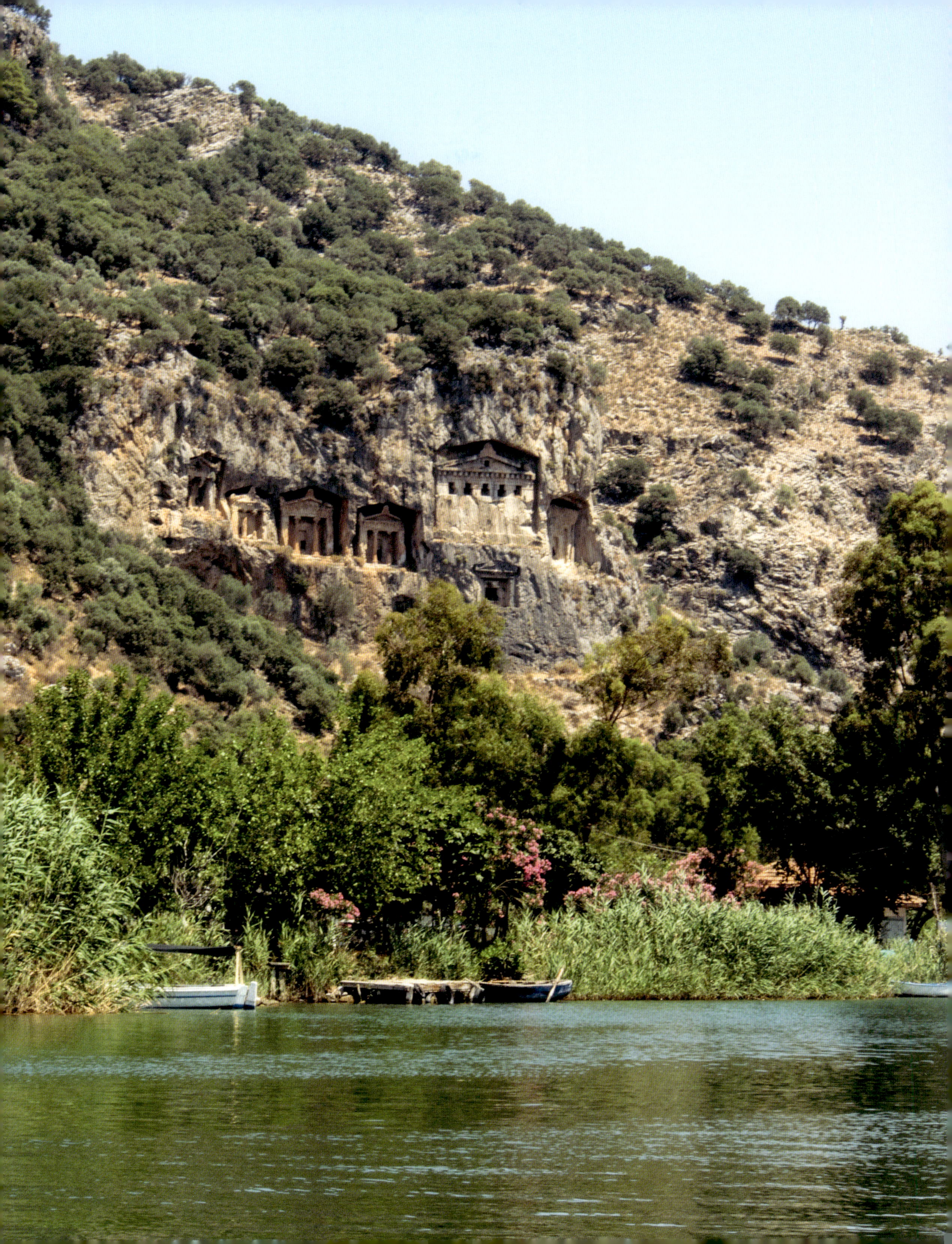

CAPTAIN'S NOTES *GULF OF FETHIYE*

RECOMMENDED ITINERARY

Göcek Yacht Club
36° 45′ 2″ N, 28° 56′ 8″ E
Göcek is the largest yachting facility along his part of the Turkish coast and the base for most charter operators. It is home to six marinas, all providing transient slips for mariners. A local pilot guide will indicate the appropriate channel to hail for each marina; docks are set up with Med moorings, go stern-to the dock. The harbor offers safe anchoring with easy dinghy access to shore for provisioning and supplies.

Fethiye
36° 37′ 34″ N, 29° 6′ 9″ E
Berth at the ECE Marina yachting center for marine services, water, and electricity. The marina berths up to 460 boats and yachts up to 60 meters in length can safely dock. Anchoring is possible outside the marina along the bay, with reasonable shelter from south winds.

Cold Water Bay (Soguk Su Koyu)
36° 33′ 48″ N, 29° 4′ 58″ E
Anchor stern-to, dropping anchor in the center of the bay. At depths of 3–5 fathoms, up to 15 boats can anchor with a stern line attached to the shore. Ali and his team, who own the restaurant on shore, assist with setting stern lines and will direct you where to anchor. There are no marina facilities. A path from the beach will take you to the restaurant, perched on a ledge that looks over the bay.

Tersane
36° 40′ 33″ N, 28° 54′ 51″ E
Berth along the floating dock managed by the one restaurant ashore. The dock is well-maintained with mooring lines. Alternatively, drop anchor in the middle of the bay and tie a sternline to the secured metal blocks drilled into the rocks onshore. Restaurant staff can assist with dock lines and provide facilities to mariners.

Ekincik
36° 49′ 26″ N, 28° 33′ 49″ E
Berth along the concrete quay managed by My Marina Yacht Club, with water depths of 3–5 fathoms. Power and water are provided, and the yacht club has a terrace restaurant and bar providing services for mariners staying at the marina. Anchor in the middle of the large bay in 4 fathoms. Southern winds can cause large swells to enter the bay.

RECOMMENDED ANCHORAGES

Gemiler Island
Göcek Adasi
Bedri Rahmi Koyu
Tomb Bay
Ince Koy

ITINERARY DURATION

6 days recommended

PREVAILING WIND

June through September are the summer months, with dry and hot sunny weather. From November through May there is increased rainfall and the temperatures can drop. The sea is often calm within Tomb Bay with the coastal passage towards Marmaris windier with more rough seas.

SEASON

May through October

FOOD

Here along the Gulf of Fethiye, the slow food movement has been thriving since its humble origins. Homey restaurants —surrounding the bays will use vegetables the owners grow themselves; the fish comes from the sea in the bay and animals are raised in the hills above. There's no better place to enjoy a meal here than in these great establishments.

GOOD TO KNOW

Common Aegean fish
Fangri (sea bream), *kalkan* (turbot), *lipsoz* (large-scaled scorpion fish), *palamut* (bonito), and *tekir* (red mullet) can all be found in the waters of this region.

Anchoring technique
Most bays are small and deep, with limited space to anchor with swing room. With steep seafloors along the edge of many of the bays, it is usual for a yacht to drop anchor in the middle of the bay and back down, tying a stern line to shore. Let your anchor free-drop until it hits the seafloor, then slowly reverse towards shore before tightening the windless and securing the anchor line.

Magnetic variance
Magnetic Declination: +5° (EAST)

TURKEY

KÖYCEĞİZ GÖLÜ

KAUNOS

DALYAN RIVER

EKINCIK

GÖCEK

TOMB BAY — GÖCEK ADASI

BEDRI RAHMI KOYU

TERSANE ISLAND

DOMUZ ISLAND

INCE KOY

FETHIYE

SOĞUK SU KOYU

GEMILER ISLAND

GULF OF FETHIYE

0 — 10

NAUTICAL MILES
NOT FOR NAVIGATION

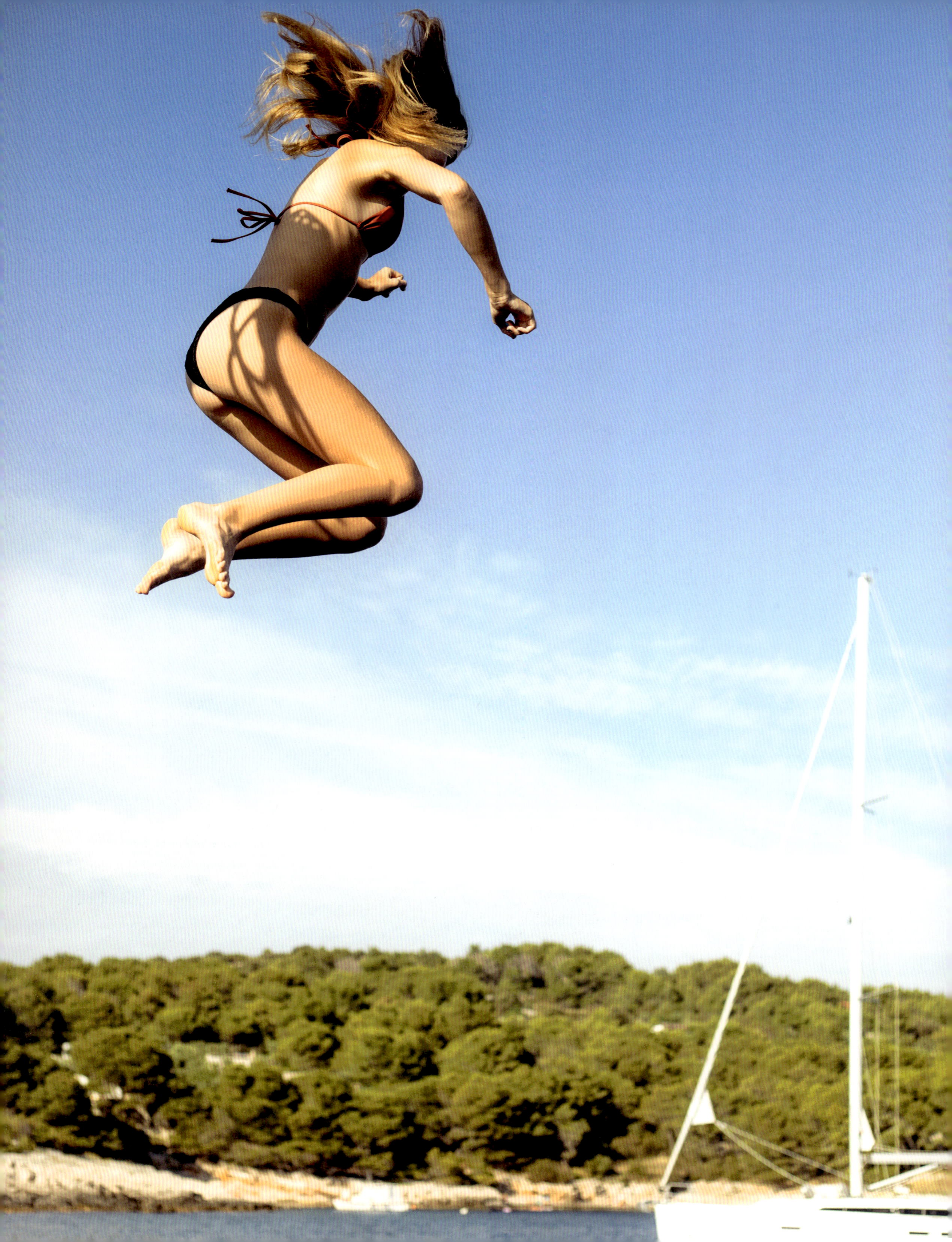

THE ARCHIPELAGO OF A THOUSAND ISLANDS

CROATIA MAY BE ONE OF EUROPE'S YOUNGEST COUNTRIES, BUT ITS ANCIENT COASTS HAVE WELCOMED MARINERS FOR MILLENNIA. IN THE NORTH LIES THE ŠIBENIK ARCHIPELAGO—A PLACE FOR SAILORS SEEKING SOLITUDE AMONG THE RUGGED LANDSCAPES.

Sailors in the know flock to Croatia. The country has become one of Europe's most popular sailing destinations over the past few decades and for good reason. It's shockingly beautiful and with around 1,200 islands home to the second largest number of islands in all of the Mediterranean. From the northern province of Istria and extending down the coast to the border of Montenegro, Croatia is lined with various archipelagos boasting island life that is vibrant and distinctly varied from mainland culture. Along the Northern Dalmatian coast lies the Šibenik Archipelago, and while parts of Southern Croatia can feel crowded with sailors, these islands have remained unspoiled and exude a spirit of ruggedness. It's possible to find quiet, tucked-away anchorages even in the height of sailing season. This makes for some one of the most relaxing and mellow cruising grounds for sailors looking to get off the beaten path and venture into a lesser explored territory.

The Dinaric Alps tower dramatically over the coastline along mainland Croatia with the mountain slopes cascading to the deep blue Adriatic. Characterized by its mostly barren terrain, the Šibenik Archipelago runs northwest along the coast towards the southeast and ends just south of the mainland city of Šibenik. Looking from the islands towards the Dinaric Alps in the winter months, you would see snow-capped mountains pushing cold, wintery weather downward to the coastline.

For sailors cruising here during the summer months, the Northern Dalmatian coast is a true paradise, and those same mountains provide a dramatic backdrop. This area is a refuge comprised of wild and undeveloped islands that offer a seemingly endless number of coves to anchor and explore along the shoreline. Thousands of inlets hug and line the Croatian mainland coast, with a few that have rustic restaurants serving the regional foods; here, you'll find exuberant amounts of figs which are often served with *pršut*, a dry ham that's specially cured in the mountains above the sea. There are hand-crafted cheeses from the nearby island of Pag, local lamb, and fish that's caught daily by island fishermen.

The archipelago is a string of many islands with a seemingly endless number of crags and coves to overnight in lovely isolated nature. When sailing along this route, you'll hear the sounds of seagulls swarming around these deserted landscapes, and you might even see a lone fishing boat making its way to one of the restaurants sitting along the coastline. These dining spots only host locals and occasional sailors who are cruising by, taking safe refuge from the sea for a night before continuing their journey onward. Much of the joy that comes from sailing the Šibenik Archipelago is found within the calmness of the sea in these safe anchorages. Both Zadar and Šibenik are beautiful historic cities built during the Venetian empire, with buildings and streets made of ancient blocks of white limestone. There are local markets with farmers selling the products they harvested themselves in their fields and gardens. The vendors are typically older Croatians living a traditional life, many of them with soil under their fingernails, conveying the authenticity of the local farming.

OTOK ŽUT

A popular yet remote island near Zadar is the island of Žut—a place with no ferry service, limited fresh water, and no electricity sources other than generators and solar power. Roughly a 30 nautical mile sail from Zadar, Žut is rich with charming inlets and a large peaceful bay called Luka Zut. When entering the bay, there are two marinas upon the approach: first is the Adriatic Croatia International Club, commonly referred to as the ACI Marina, which is a nautical tourism company that operates 16 marinas throughout Croatia. The other marina is privately owned and managed by a restaurant named Restoran Fešta—a timeless and idyllic establishment. In the middle of such a wild island lies this upscale, true gastronomic restaurant that's equally elegant and rustic, historic but modern. Walking ashore after docking, there are only two structures to be found—the restaurant and the shed where the diesel generator lives which provides their electricity. Restoran Fešta has a cellar that showcases some of Croatia's finest wine options with the servers doubling as their sommeliers. The food isn't exactly simple, but it's not overly highfalutin either. Each day, fishermen pass by to deliver a variety of freshly caught fish. One of their specialty dishes is the mixed seafood crudo, with other menu specialties varying based on the catch of the day. Though Restoran Fešta isn't necessarily a place for the budget sailor, the full experience of dining here while sailing in the region is highly unique and worthwhile.

DUGI OTOK

Only a few nautical miles from Žut is the island of Dugi Otok, home to the Telašćica Nature Park. In 1988, the Croatian government turned Telašćica Bay into a nature park which restricted any new developments and declared strict environmental protection regulations. When approaching by sea, this bay appears more vibrant than other areas on this route, as it's a landscape that's dominated by trees and lakes which creates a contrast with the many barren surrounding islands. As one of Croatia's largest bays, the narrow entrance opens up into the lake-like body of water. Here, the local winds blow from the north with a light but consistent breeze. The calm, serene waters make sailing north into the bay and tacking back and forth while making way towards the anchorages a delightful experience. There are a few rustic

---

VELIKA PROVERSA CHANNEL

Kornati and Dugi Otok were once one landmass. However, Croatia's mainland has been sinking into the Adriatic Sea at a rate of over a metre every thousand years. The passageway between the two islands is now navigable, but a bit of human assistance is required. In the 1980s, the canal was dredged by 4 meters and widened to 15 meters with buoys guiding mariners through the channel. Sailing Mala Froversa, you pass the unearthed foundation of an old Roman villa, which had been built on solid ground and now sits underwater.

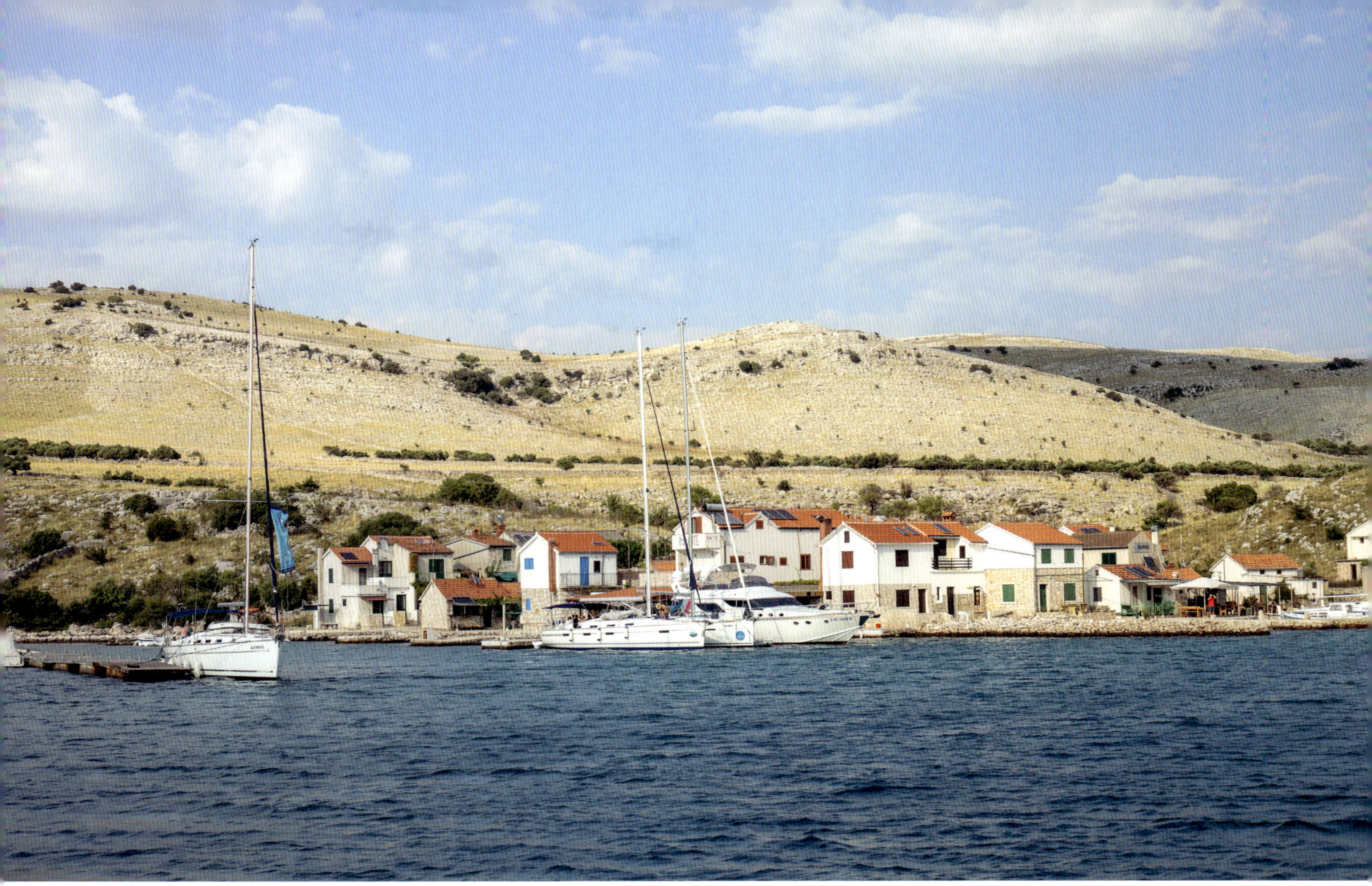

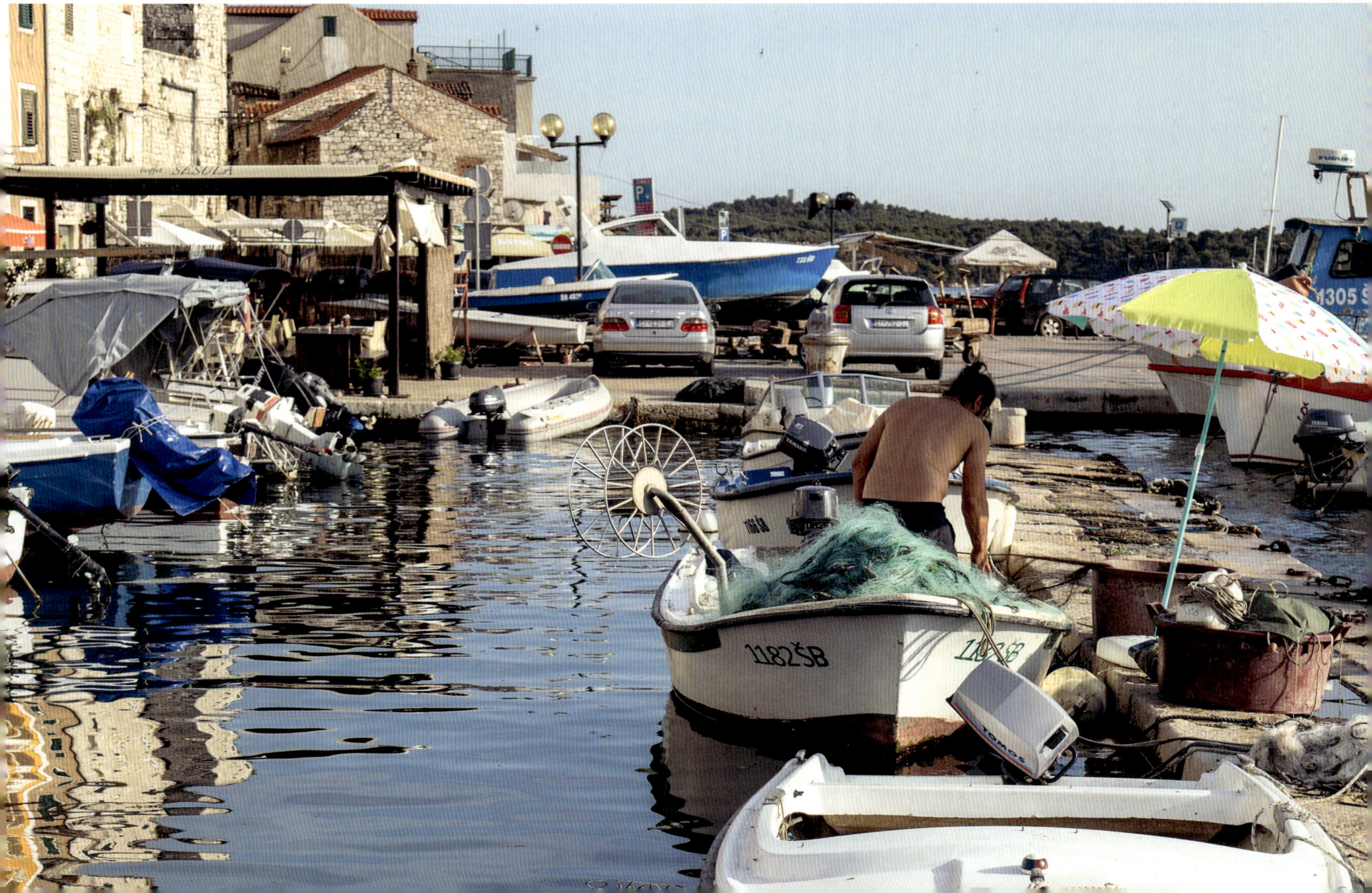
1182ŠB

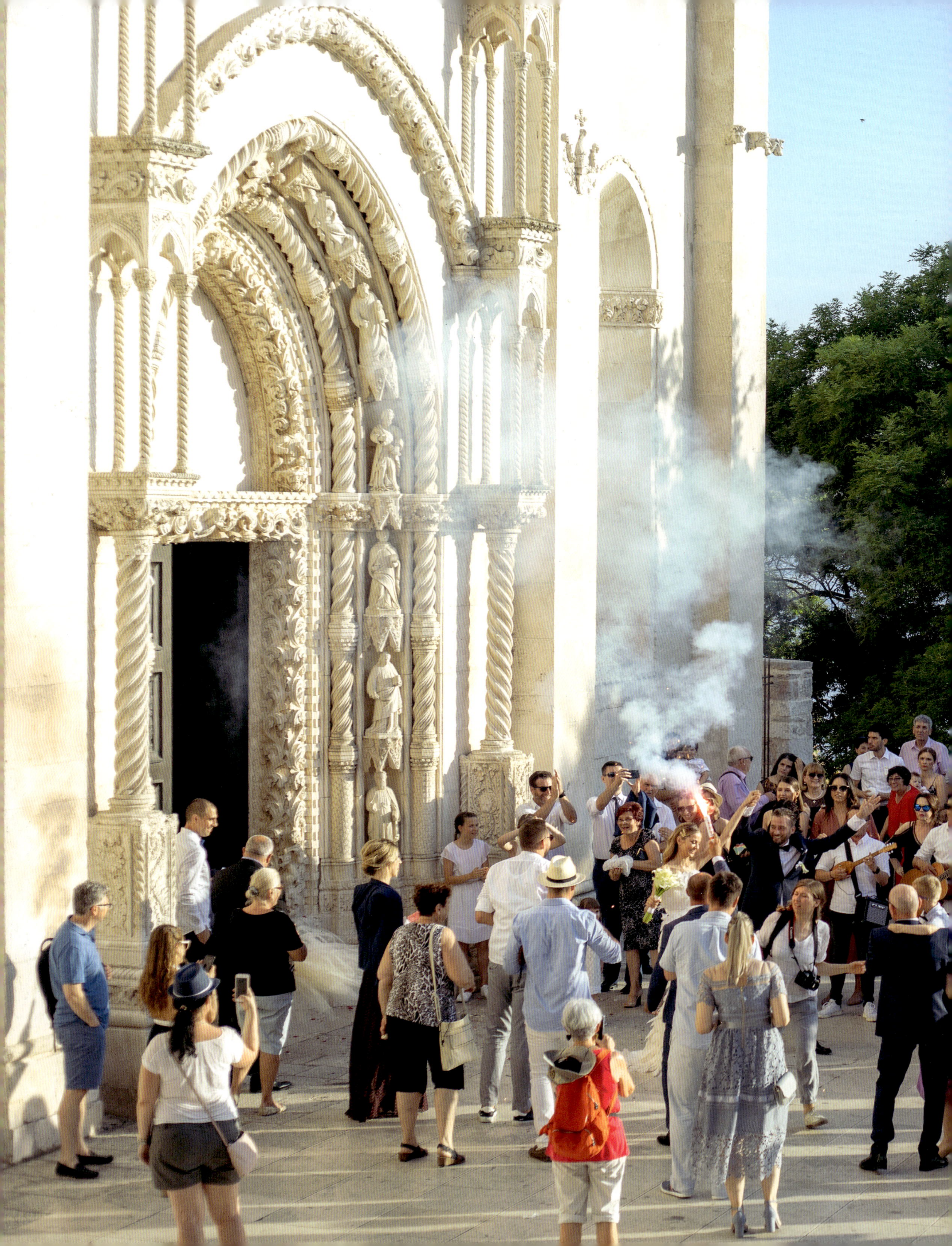

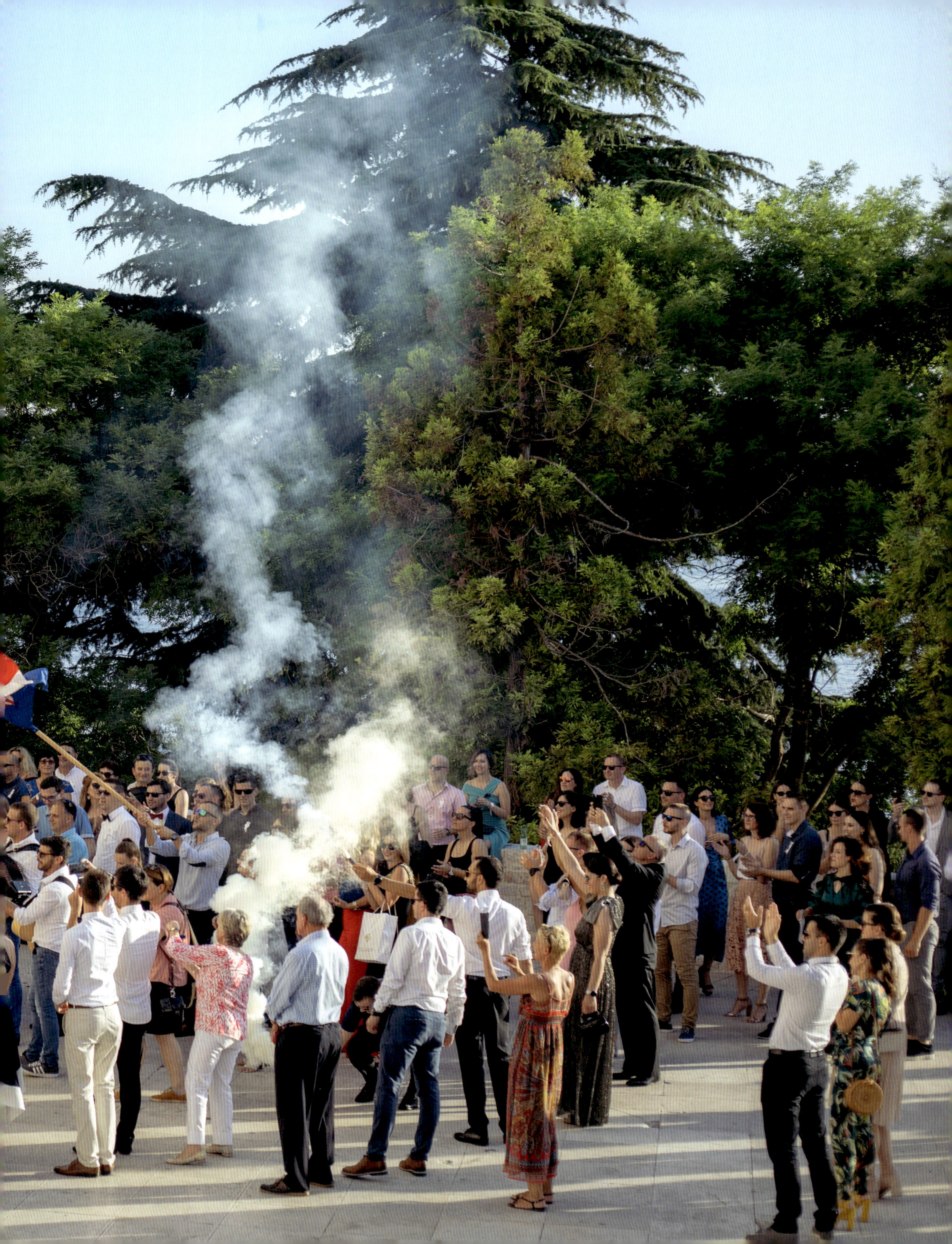

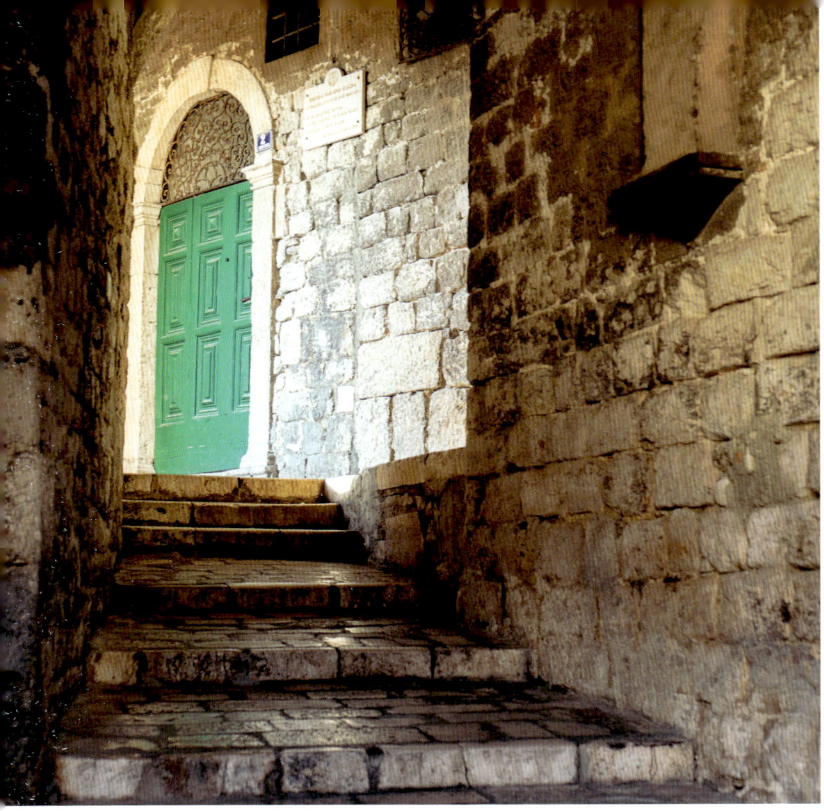

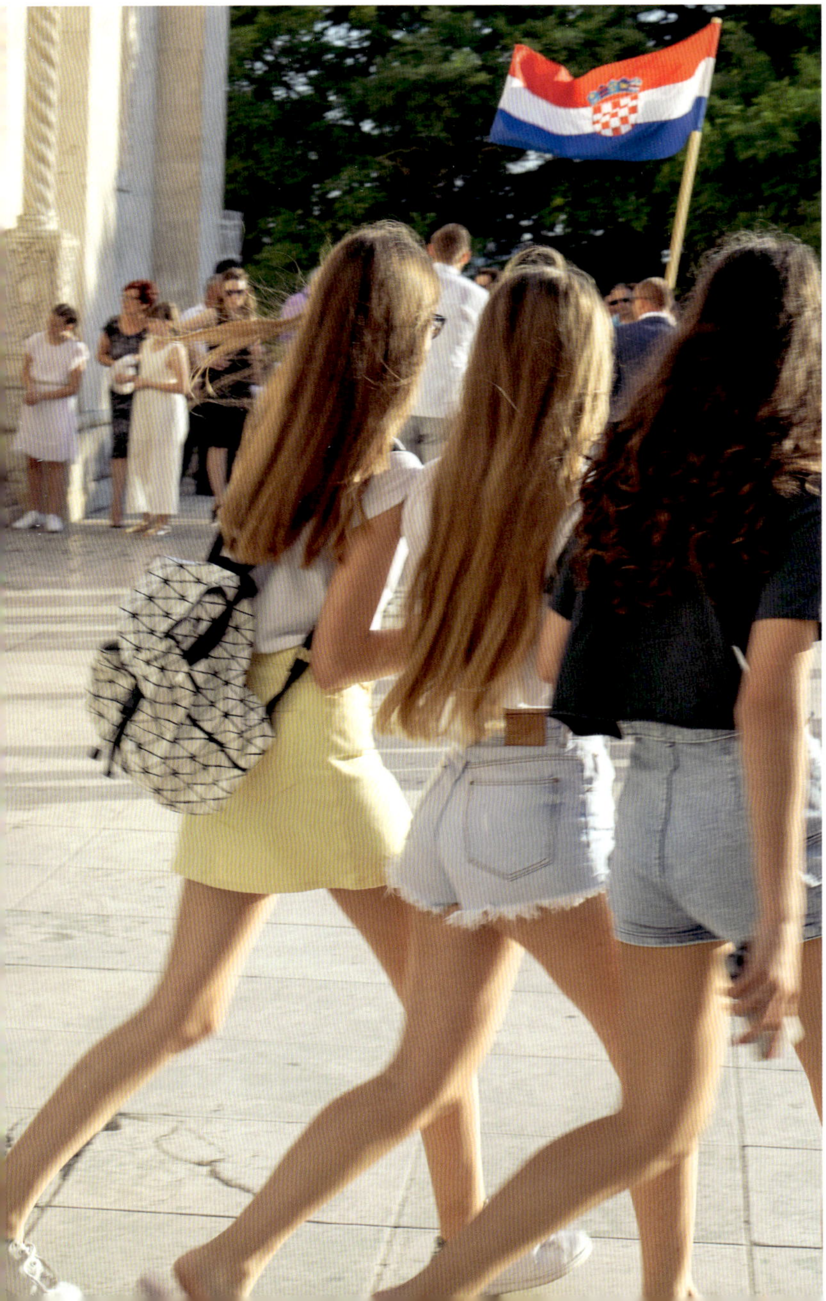

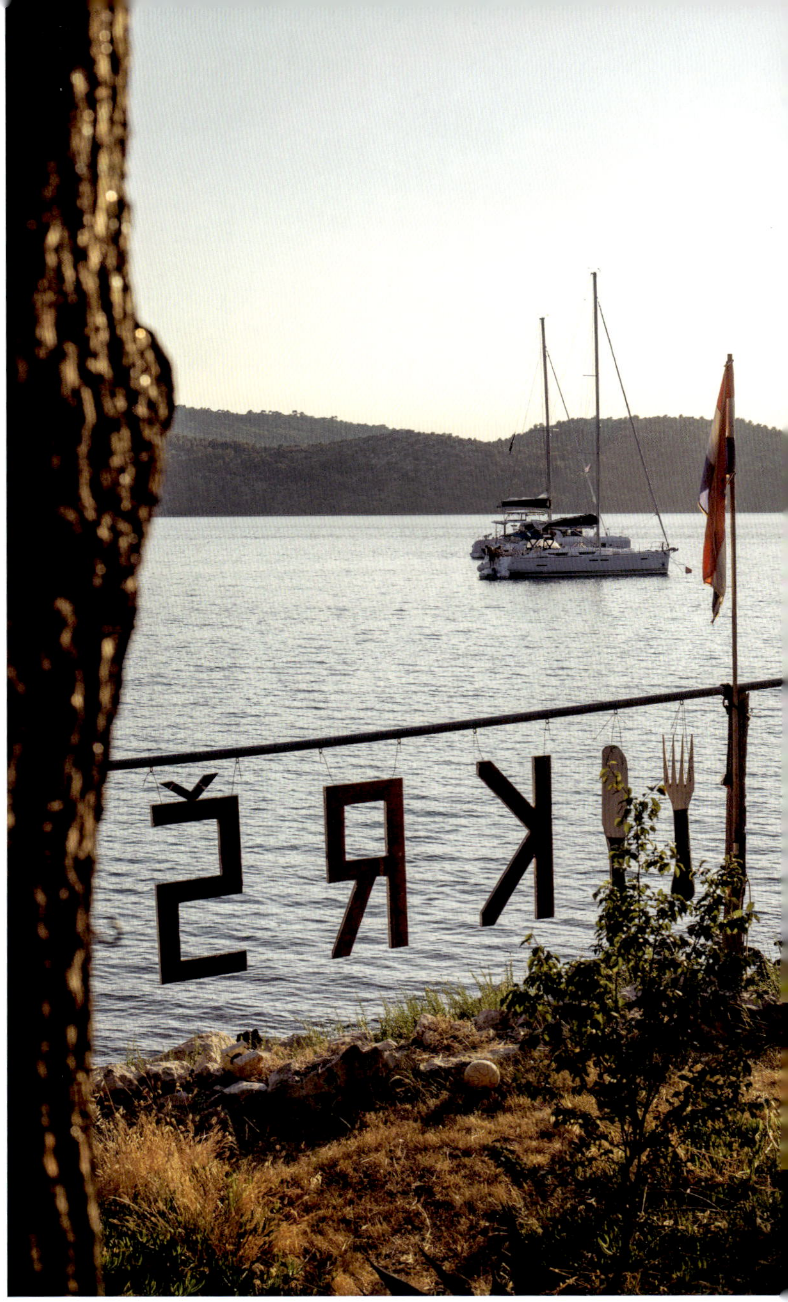

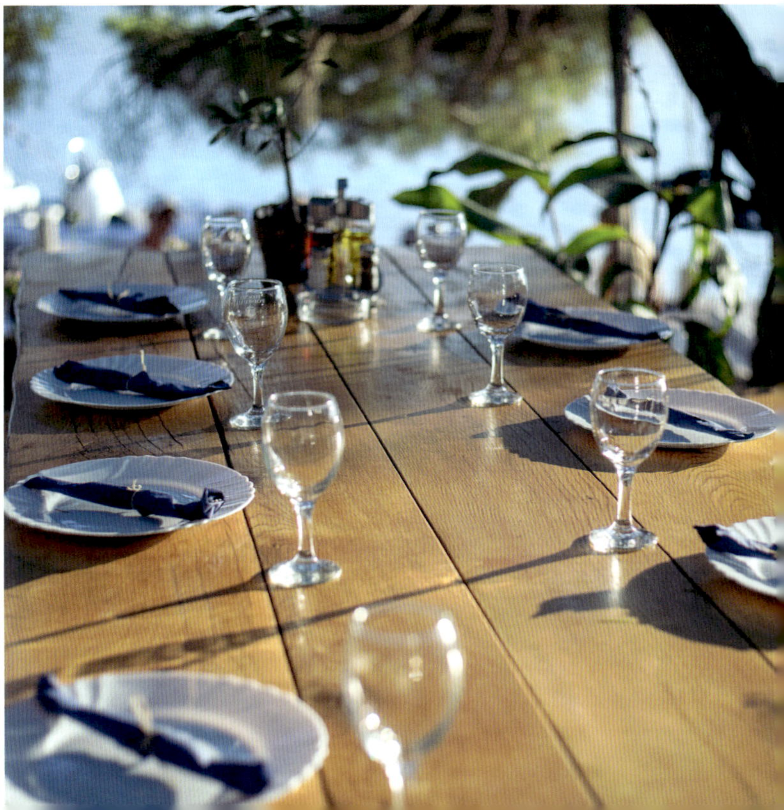

restaurants tucked away in coves that serve simple foods such as grilled meats, fresh and locally-caught fish, and homegrown vegetables that are either prepared as a stew or grilled. If you're not interested in dining out, there are numerous uninhabited inlets throughout the national park where you can drop anchor and enjoy an evening on the boat, fully immersed in the wilderness and surrounded only by the sounds of birds or natural wildlife limestone that feels like sailing to the moon. Tracks sloping down into the sea are very bare, other than a few scattered patches of olive trees in terraced-lined plots of land. There are a few villages along the western side of Kornati welcoming sailors with their island hospitality, and most of the hamlets are home to at least one restaurant that's open during the summer season. The stark, lunar magic of these islands has been bewitching

> Both Zadar and Šibenik are beautiful historic cities built during the Venetian empire, with buildings and streets made of ancient blocks of white limestone.

and whatever music or conversations are happening onboard your boat. During the day, tour boats from Šibenik cart tourists back and forth to the unique saltwater pond on the island. A 30 minute hike around the pond takes you to ocean-facing cliffs with dramatic views of the Adriatic. Looking out from above, all that can be seen across the horizon is a seemingly endless deep blue sea and only on a very clear day you might glimpse eastern Italy far off in the distance.

The islands surrounding Telašćica appear to be endless, with passageways between them like a labyrinth in the sea that makes for exciting sailing, tacking, and jibing through narrow channels. Most of the islands are uninhabited and, other than a few sparsely scattered homesteads, many of the residences here are only used as summer vacation homes. Though some have turned their properties into hospitable restaurants for sailors passing by, others have kept their seaside cottages as simple places to be enjoyed in solitude and serenity. Regardless, anchoring nearby is always welcomed by all.

KORNATI

Located south of the Telašćica Bay on Dugi Otok is the island of Kornat and the Kornati National Park—an island covered in white

sailors cruising by for decades. Moorings are usually placed in front of the restaurant for sailors interested in dining onshore and select towns have handmade marinas with seawalls laid by the limestone island rocks. The crystal clear waters make the approach eerie for sailors new to the area because looking down from the boat creates an optical illusion, with the seafloor appearing closer than it really is.

There are no hotels on Kornati so if you're not sailing here, the only places to stay on the island are a few select, private rental options that can be arranged by a broker. Vrulje is a little settlement on Kornati that's comprised of 40 houses with moorings that are available at the taverns and the bay has buoys for sailors to use for a fee. There are no scheduled ferries from the mainland, so getting to the rental property must be carefully coordinated. When sailing here, you'll find over 20 pleasantly secluded coves and harbors that are perfect for dropping anchor to explore. With about 16 restaurants on Kornati, these places each offer fresh fish and traditional aromatic lamb dishes that are unique to the region. Serving mostly mariners who are sailing by, many of these restaurants now run on solar energy.

KOBONAS ARE AN IMPORTANT PART OF CROATIAN CULTURE (ABOVE AND BELOW, RIGHT).

~

Choosing the Šibenik Archipelago itinerary offers endless routes appealing for any sailor with interest in cruising in a quiet and relaxed location. Hundreds of islands comprise the archipelago, most offering safe anchorages. The towns are scarcely spread throughout and mainly located on mainland Croatia, but, even still, sailing to a nearly uninhabited island home to just one family-run restaurant, looking far off in the hills, you may spot a Roman, Byzantine, or Venetian structure along the treeline. Going ashore, you'll find Croatians living a rather traditional life largely off the grid in protected bays, to the delight of any sailor.

SHEPHERDING

Sheep herds have indirectly shaped the sight of Kornati, with man-made stone walls roughly 2 meters tall running from the east to west shoreline and dividing the island. The island lacks a natural water source and each animal requires a particular amount of green pasture to survive, which is managed carefully by shepherds. The number of sheep in a herd is determined by the resources available, so sometimes shepherds allow only two or three sheep to live in a pasture at a time. The many walls allow them to control these pastures and prevent sheep escaping their bounds.

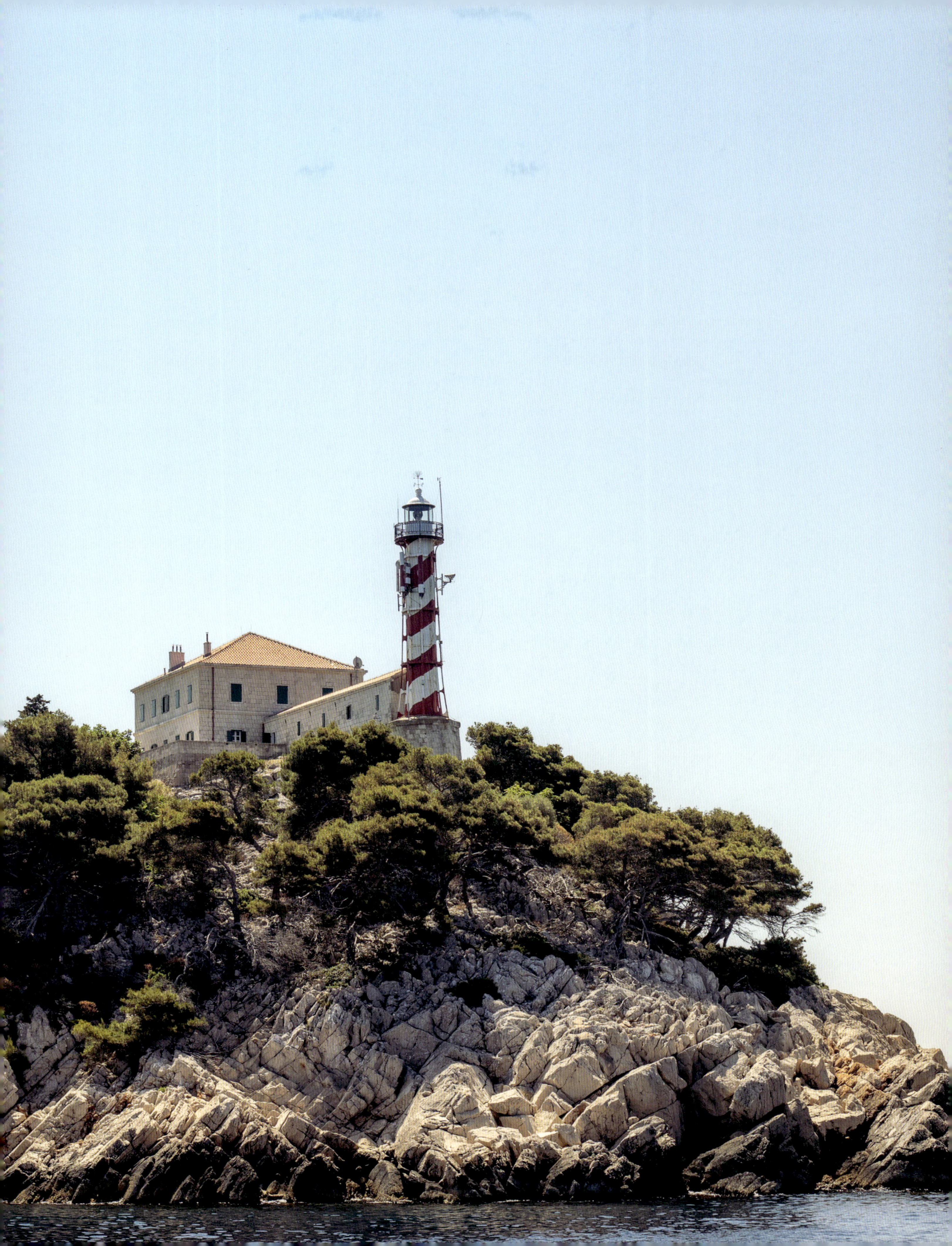

CAPTAIN'S NOTES *ŠIBENIK ARCHIPELAGO*

RECOMMENDED ITINERARY

Kršovica, Telašćica, Dugi Otok
43° 54′36″N, 15° 9′42″E
The Telašćica nature reserve is located on the sound end of Dugi Otok, within a large, lake-like bay. Park officials maintain a series of designated moorings throughout the bay. Anchoring here is also permitted. Krsovica is a small cove located along the upper east side of the bay, with about ten moorings and a small rustic restaurant that serves mariners anchored in the cove.

Luka Žut, Otok Žut
43° 52′57″N, 15° 17′13″E
Berth at Marina Zut or Marina Festa in Luka Zut, a bay safe from all wind. During a strong *Bura* wind (see below), the bay can become uncomfortable, with large swells entering the marina. There are laid moorings and safe anchoring along the north coast of the bay.

Uvala Virlje, Kornati
43° 48′36″N, 15° 18′2″E
The island of Kornat is nearly uninhabited. Uvala Vrulje is a small, protected cove located along the western side of the island, offering protection from the *Bura* and the *Jugo* wind. There are roughly ten homes clustered together here, home to three family-run restaurants. This town is built in Dalmatian style, from limestone rocks. An ancient seawall stands, where boats dock stern-to the quay. Moorings are available opposite the hamlet andmaintained by the restaurant establishments. Anchor at the north end of the bay.

ACI Marina Piskera, Kornati
43° 45′34″N, 15° 20′42″E
Well protected from the *Bura*, this Marina is part of the Kornati National Park. The amenities include a bar, restaurants, water, and basic provisioning. There are 120 slips and, during high season, mariners should make reservations to berth, especially if the *Bura* and *Jugo* whip up. The marina is located on the small island of Panitula Vela, across from Vela Piškera. The location is beautiful, with bright blue waters and a white, moon-like island landscape.

Uvala Stupica Vela, Žirje
43° 38′3″N, 15° 41′22″E
This claw-like cove is protected from the *Bura* and exposed to the *Jugo*. The bay has approximately 20 moorings that cost up to 300 Kuna a night. The center of the bay is very deep and anchoring is only possible along the coast of the bay. There is also room to anchor along the north side. A rustic family run restaurant is located ashore serving fresh-caught fish and lamb raised on the island. Unlike Kornati, Žirje is wooded with thick green pine trees that cover the island.

RECOMMENDED ANCHORAGES

Telašćica, Dugi Otok
Otok Katina
Levrnaka, Kornati
Uvala Opat, Kornati
Uvala Potkucina, Kakan

ITINERARY DURATION

7 days recommended

PREVAILING WIND

See "Southern Dalmatian Coast, Croatia" (pp. 144–155)

SEASON

Sailing season is best between late mid-June through mid-October

GOOD TO KNOW

Local winds
Sailors cruising here should be prepared to encounter the two powerful local winds. The *Bura* blows in from the east and rushes down the Dinaric Alps, where it gains great strength as it is funneled westward, towards the Adriatic Sea. The *Bura's* sleepier and less rampant cousin is named the *Jugo*, beginning at the mouth of the Adriatic, where it pushes its way up the coastline and causes large swells that often flood the towns. It is often accompanied by strong lightning storms that can last for days at a time. The island vegetation is shaped by these winds, and entire towns have been structured around them, as homesteads exposed directly to the *Bura* will not stay intact or be habitable for very long. Though most sailors take refuge during this wind, others sail straight through it while cruising the Zadar Archipelago.

Magnetic variance
Magnetic Declination: +4° (EAST)

CROATIA

PAG ISLAND

⚓ ZADAR

DUGI OTOK

⚓ KRŠOVICA
⚓ TELAŠĆICA

OTOK KATINA ⚓
⚓ ŽUT MARINA
⚓ LUKA ŽUT

OTOK ŽUT

⚓ LEVRNAKA
⚓ UVALA VRULJE

KORNATI

⚓ ACI MARINA PISKERA

⚓ UVALA OPAT

KORNATI ISLANDS

OTOK KAKAN
⚓ UVALA POTKUCINA

⚓ ŠIBENIK

OTOK ŽIRJE ⚓
UVALA STUPICA VELA

ADRIATIC SEA

0 — 10
NAUTICAL MILES
NOT FOR NAVIGATION

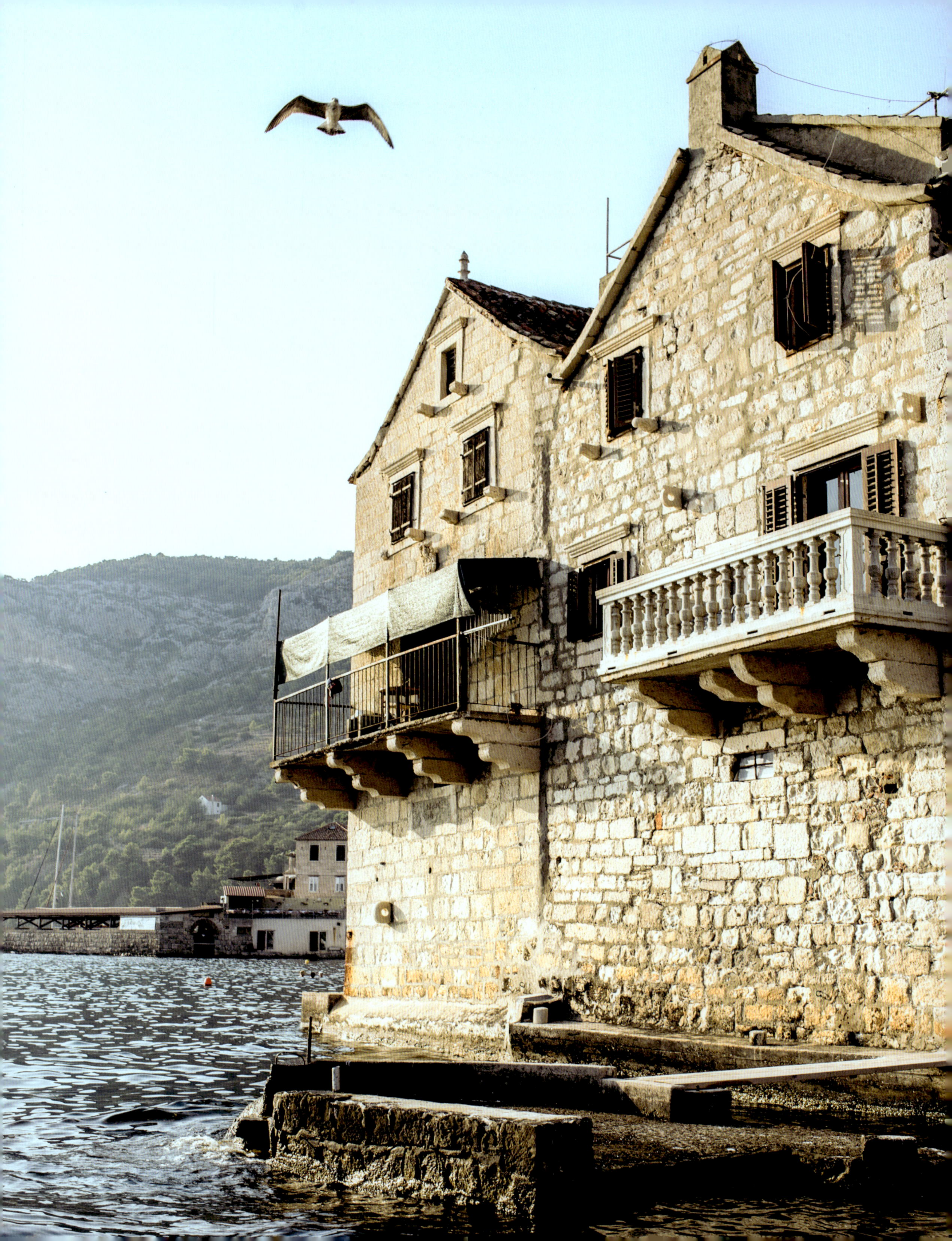

THE TRANSPARENT WATERS OF DALMATIA

CLEAR SEAS, LOCAL WINE, AND LIMESTONE QUAYS IN VENETIAN-BUILT FISHING VILLAGES—THE COAST OF SOUTHERN CROATIA IS ONE OF THE MEDITERRANEAN'S GREAT SAILING DESTINATIONS.

There's something about Croatia's stark, sweeping islands and imposing mountainous coastline that draws sailors from far and wide. The waterline wears a marble skirt of exposed rock that guides you to ancient palaces, medieval walled towns, and simple fishing villages full of charm. The colors of Croatia are simple and well defined on the landscape: deep blue, vibrant green, decadent ivory. The Adriatic Sea is so clear that it is possible to get lost in the optics of it. In such transparent waters, it is hard to tell the water depth: diving off the boat can feel like a leap of faith when you have an unrestricted view of the bottom as much as 15 meters below your keel. Sailing into a narrow cove gives you the dreamlike experience of gliding, suspended over the rocky bottom that is perfectly clear below.

Dalmatia has played host to seafaring empires for many hundred years and you will sail passed abandoned fortifications from the span of European history. Across the Adriatic Sea from Italy, this land was an obvious next step in territorial expansion for everyone from the Venetians to the Austro-Hungarian Empire. Conquerors looking to expand their influence discovered that these islands are a key strategic piece in the world-domination puzzle. During the Second World War, there were secret allied airfields on the islands, and, in the Cold War, this land was teetering between ideologies, ready to tip the scales of military might at any moment.

Formerly a part of Yugoslavia, Croatia has been an independent state since 1991. The breakup of Yugoslavia was both brutal and visible on the world stage—a trauma not forgotten even on the more remote islands. Years later, Croatia is thriving. Its cultural identity is stronger than ever and the country produces world-class wines, delectable truffles, cheese to die for, and sailing journeys that are distinct and memorable.

The central Dalmatian Coast is home to one of the largest charter fleets in the world, with thousands of sailboats lining the marinas from Rogoznica to Split. Šolta, Brač, Hvar, and Vis are the key island destinations. Seaside family homes line the quiet and tranquil coves. *Konobas*, traditional restaurants that embody the cultural heritage of Croatia, offer homemade wine, freshly caught fish, and pasture-raised meat, often served by the head of the household. The smoke from a wood-fired outdoor oven can lead you to a sleepy *konoba* in an otherwise quiet cove; the night's special will be what they have fresh from the day's fishing and farming.

Little has changed since the Venetian Empire developed much of the Dalmatian Coast during the 11th century. Coastal towns are maritime hubs, with the village center revolving around a waterfront promenade referred to as a *riva*. Docking inside the old ports and sleeping aboard your boat puts you in the best real estate there is. Step off your boat and stroll the *riva*, the very heart of the town, where locals and sailors alike gather for morning espresso and congregate for evening drinks.

SPLIT AND THE MAINLAND

Split is the capital city of the central Dalmatian region and a lovely location from which to begin a sailing excursion. The old city is centered around the summer palace of the Roman emperor Diocletian. The walls of this immense palace, which he built for his retirement, still surround the neighborhood that sprung up inside long after the palace itself was abandoned. The stone houses in Split are timeless and the narrow alleyways are delightfully confusing. The old part of town is busy with tourists and pedestrians who roam along worn marble alleyways that wind between the stone buildings.

Diocletian was a lover of historical artifacts, so Split is littered with treasures from before even his time, such as Egyptian sphinxes and ancient Greek pillars. Finding these is like a treasure hunt through the town, though many are hidden in plain sight. Split is the busiest port in the region, with a massive ferry terminal that services all of the islands and connects to Italy, but don't let that discourage you from enjoying an overnight stay in town; the yacht marina is tucked away from it all and very well protected from wake and swell.

Thirty nautical miles north of Split is the town of Trogir, a quintessential medieval fortified city situated in the narrow channel between the island of Trogir and the mainland. Approaching by land or sea, you experience the sense of good fortune that travelers throughout time have felt upon arriving here. A walk through Trogir today is a stroll through a 14th-century village, perfectly intact and lived in just as it was 800 years ago. Only the cobblestones, worn smooth by centuries of foot traffic, betray the town's age. Every day, in small wooden boats, the fishermen set out to sea from the inner harbor, just as they have for generations.

HVAR

The island of Hvar is large and long, and, conveniently, two of the main harbors are located a day's sail from both Split and Trogir. It is a booming Croatian island with Hvar Town at the center of the chic cosmopolitan ambience for which the island is famous. Walking along the yacht-lined *riva* of the gorgeous, thousand-year-old city, you will see what draws people here. In season, there are dance parties offering bottle service any night of the week and late-night pizza and shawarma street-food stalls open late, but you can also find authentic Croatian food in establishments serving local wines that are paired perfectly with the cuisine. The shops,

---

THE CASTLE ABOVE HVAR

Take a short hike up well-graded switchback trails to the castle above the walled town of Hvar for incredible views overlooking the harbor and the surrounding islands. From here you can see Sveti Klement, a long island across the channel and popular destination for sailors seeking solitude in a more natural and unspoiled environment. Make sure to wander the castle and explore the dungeons, where cells carved into the cliff have an eerie, haunted feeling.

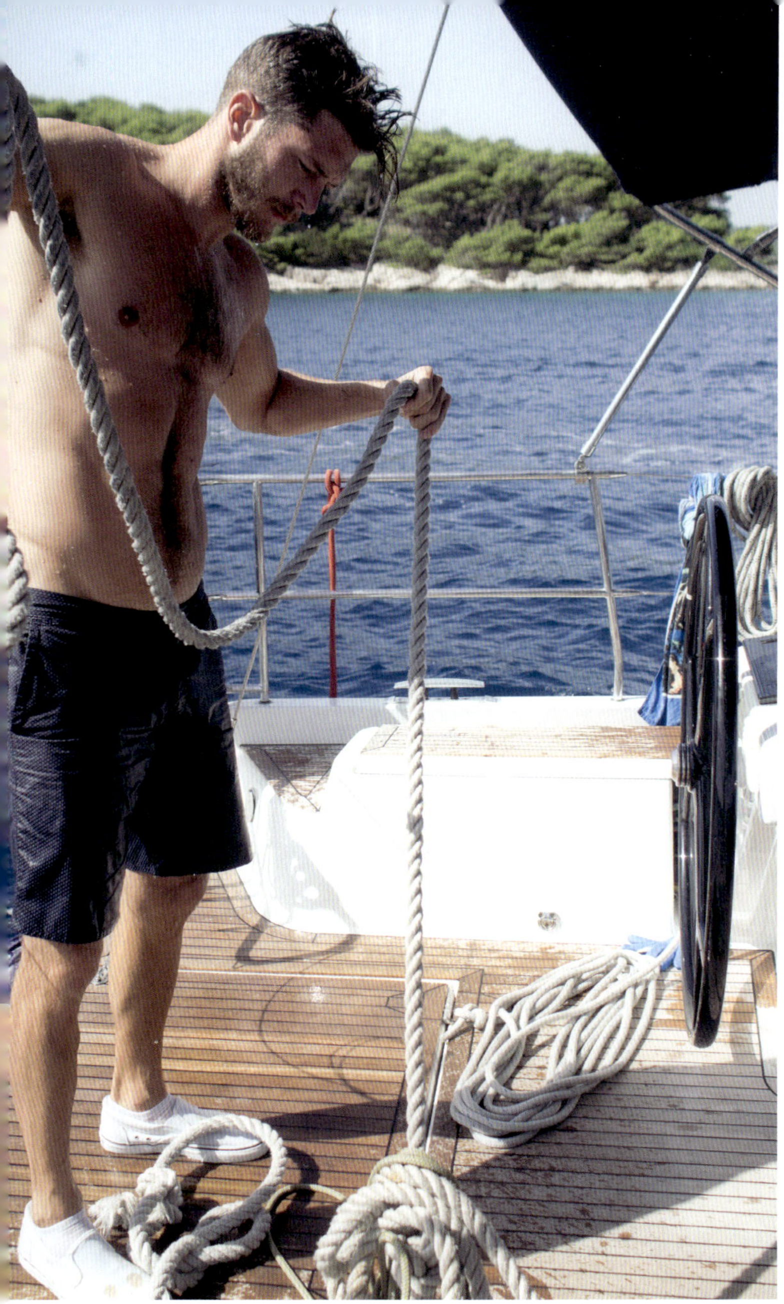
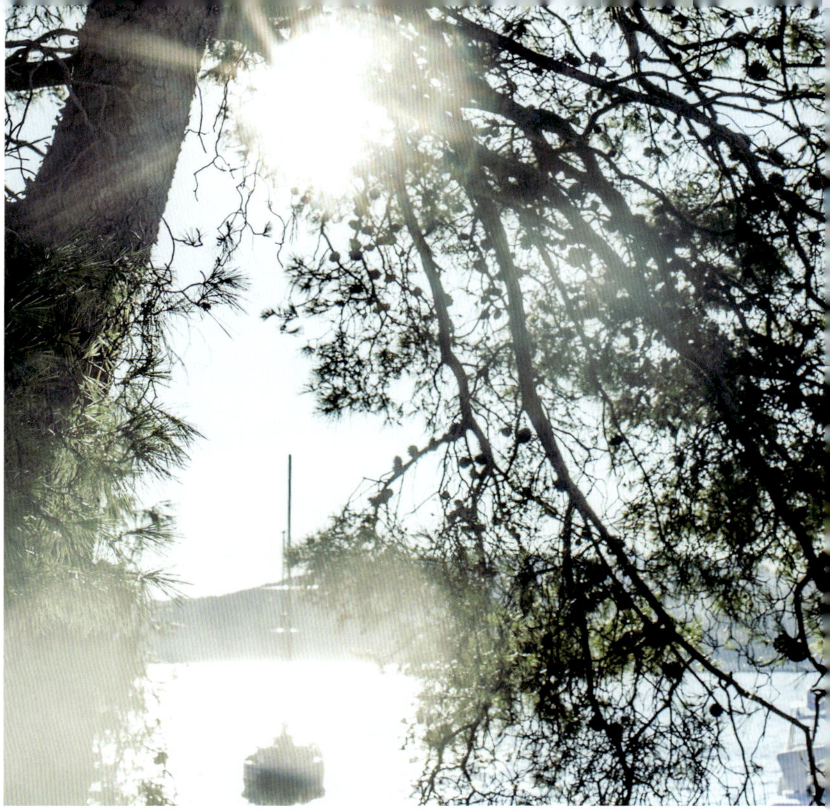
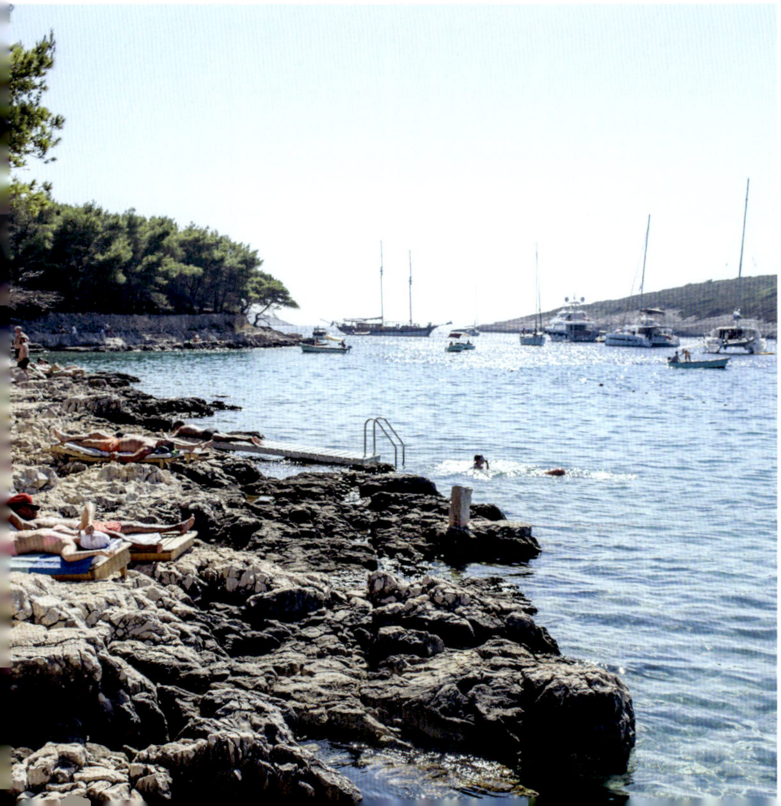
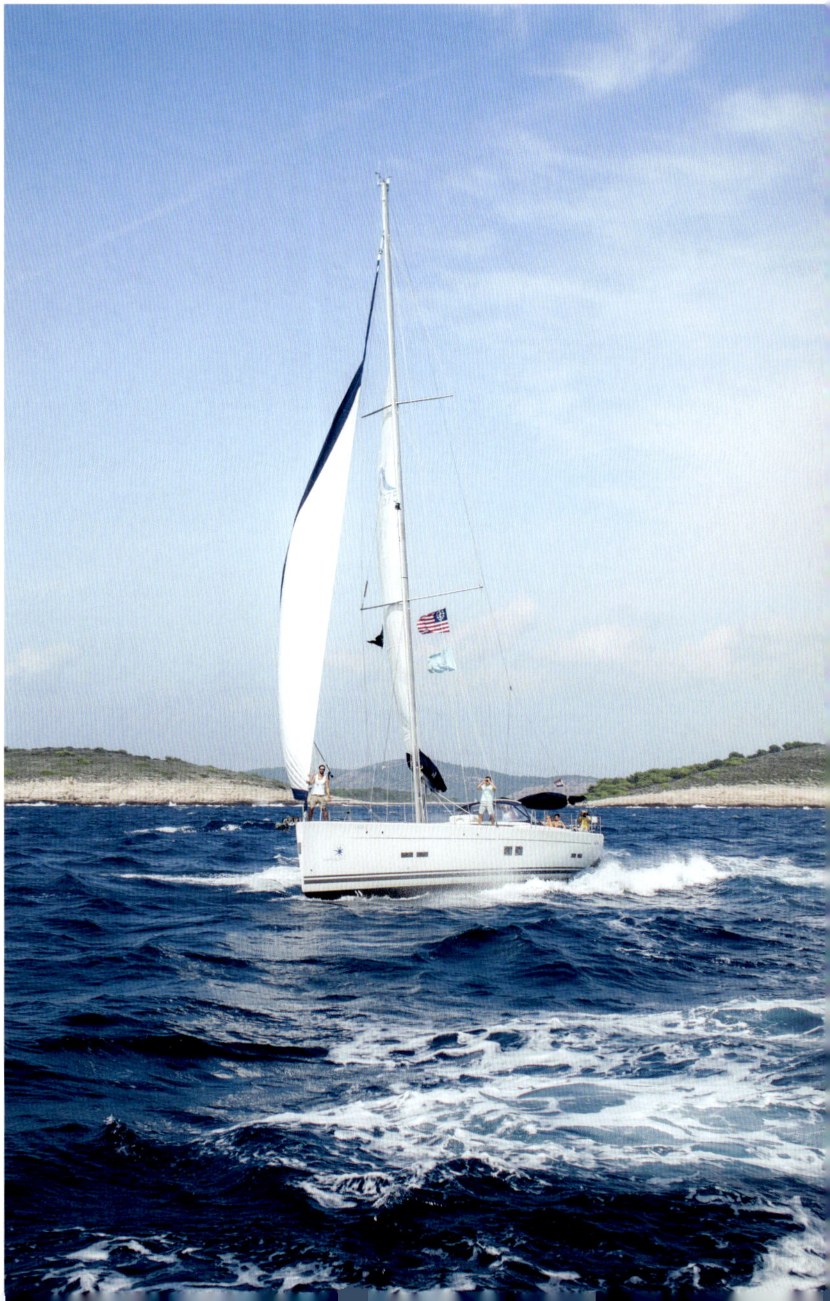

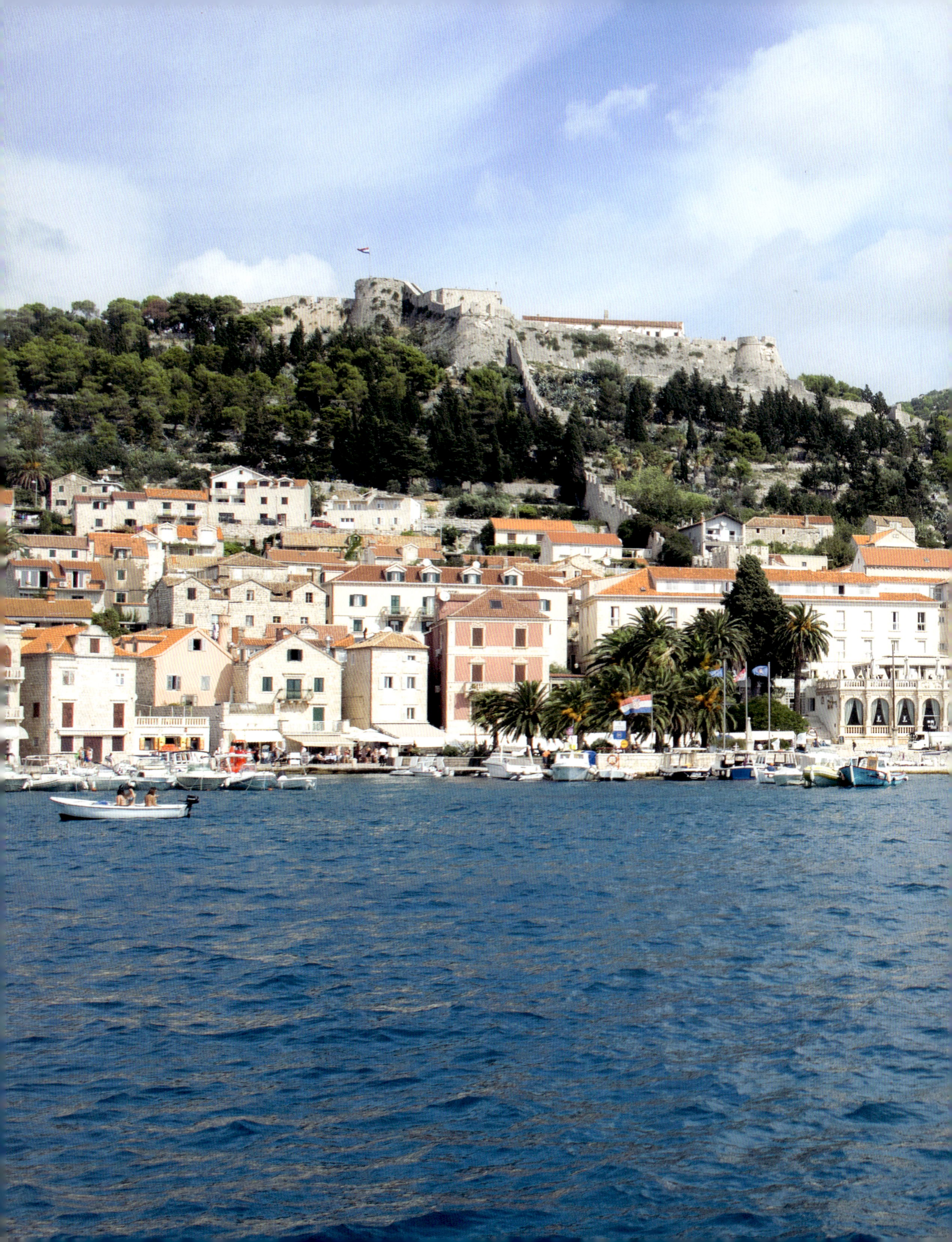

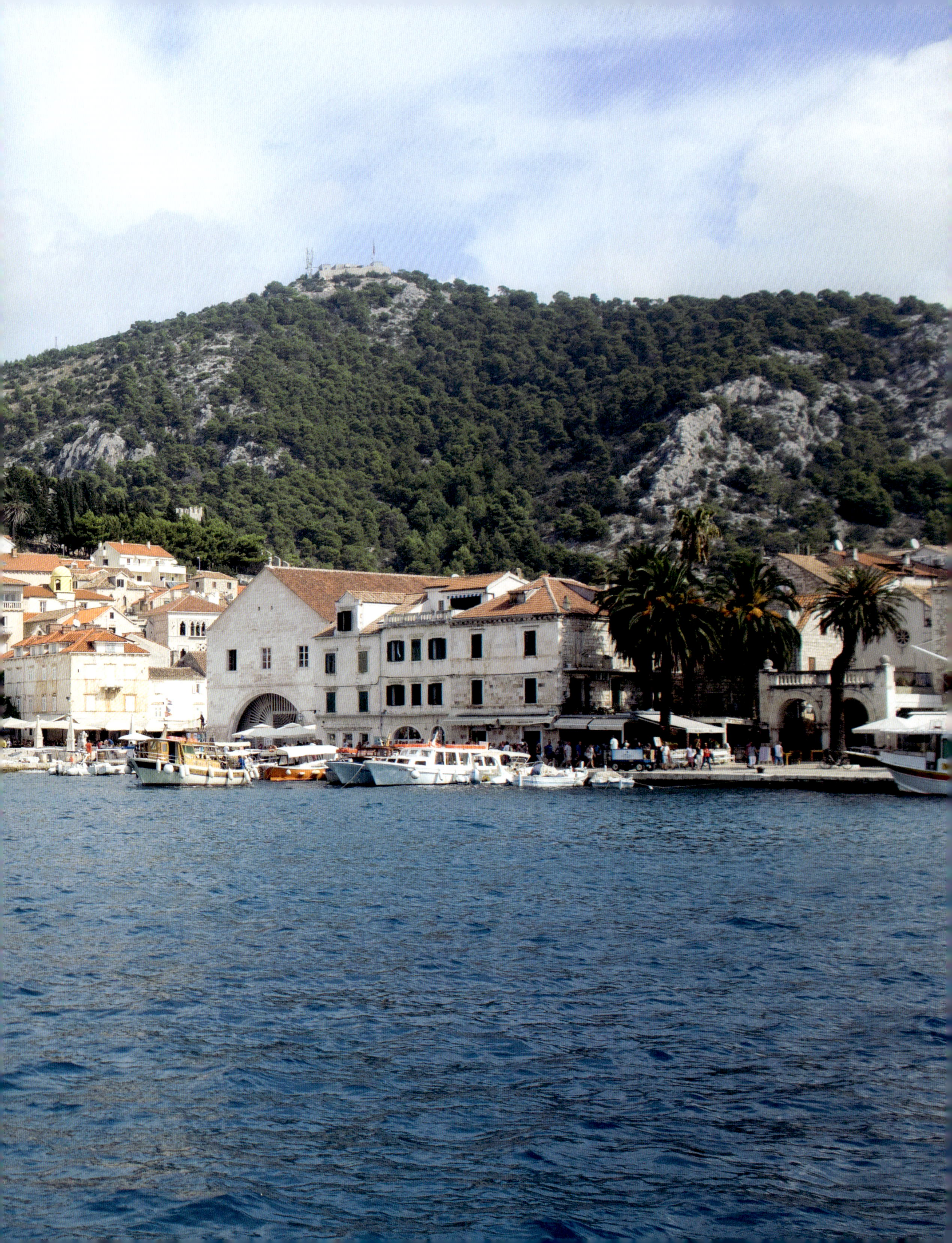

restaurants, hotels, and nightclubs inhabit the grand architecture in and around the old city walls. Whether you are cruising a humble boat or spending a night aboard a mega yacht, there's something for everyone in Hvar Town; it's a perfect stop for unloading a crew of salt-stained sailors into town for a night off.

Along the edge of the farmers' market, in the upper plaza by the cathedral, are small storefronts selling locally produced goods. While these lacks the designer styling of the streets inside the walls of the old city, the real goods of Hvar are sold right here. Head to the wine and prosciutto shop run by Igor, a local man passionate about food, wine, and the Croatian way of life. It's a hidden gem in this shiny town. They have all the best cheeses, cured meats, and wines produced on the island and are generous with their tastings and their stories as you learn about what makes each flavor unique.

The sleepier of the two big towns on the island of Hvar, Stari Grad is no less charming. While many of the towns in the region have a Venetian feel to them, Stari Grad actually floods like Venice, leaving you wading through the streets near the harbor when the wind blows hard from the west. Stari Grad has a very well stocked market for reprovisioning and a fantastic local farmers' market, open every morning at the head of the harbor.

VIS

The island of Vis is one of the furthest from mainland Croatia and one of the closest inhabited islands to Italy. Historically, it was strategically important as a naval defense base, and was prominent during the Second World War and the Cold War. History buffs will do well to take the military-history tour of the island, which takes you (with headlamps) into submarine tunnels and abandoned missile silos. The island has two main harbors: Vis Town on the east, and the smaller Komiža in the west. The interior is charming, and hiring a scooter for the day is a great way to explore the island and see, smell, and taste all its wonders. Vis has an ambience unlike any other and it is worth venturing into its fertile upper valleys to experience it.

Vis Town has a large, well-protected harbor with a 9th-century church sitting prominently on a small peninsula in the middle. As you enter the harbor, you will see rows of sailboats docking stern-to along the stone seawall that runs along the town *riva*. Vis Town was built in typical Adriatic fashion, with large rectangular blocks of limestone forming the foundation of everything from the walkways to the three-story homes and shops. Each day during the summer months, hundreds of sailboats gather here and sailors sit outside the coffee shops enjoying after-sail cocktails, food, and laughter.

In the hills above Vis Town are vineyards, each producing their own wines, which they will sell to you right out of the cask. If you neglect to bring your own bottle, the vineyards that don't have bottled vintages on hand will happily fill a plastic water bottle with whatever they are currently pouring and send you on your way. Some of the better vineyards, such as Rokis or Magic have a

---

LOCAL DISH

Lamb, octopus, fish, or vegetarian by special request, however, you like it, peka *is a Croatian national treasure. Literally translating to "cooking under the lid,"* peka *must be cooked in specially shaped cast-iron dishes that have high pointed tops allowing for steam to rise off the ingredients but not escape, and rims around the top for stacking coals to create the proper heat. To order* peka *at a restaurant, you normally tell them a half-day in advance of mealtime since cooking times vary from three to five hours depending on the size and contents of the* peka.

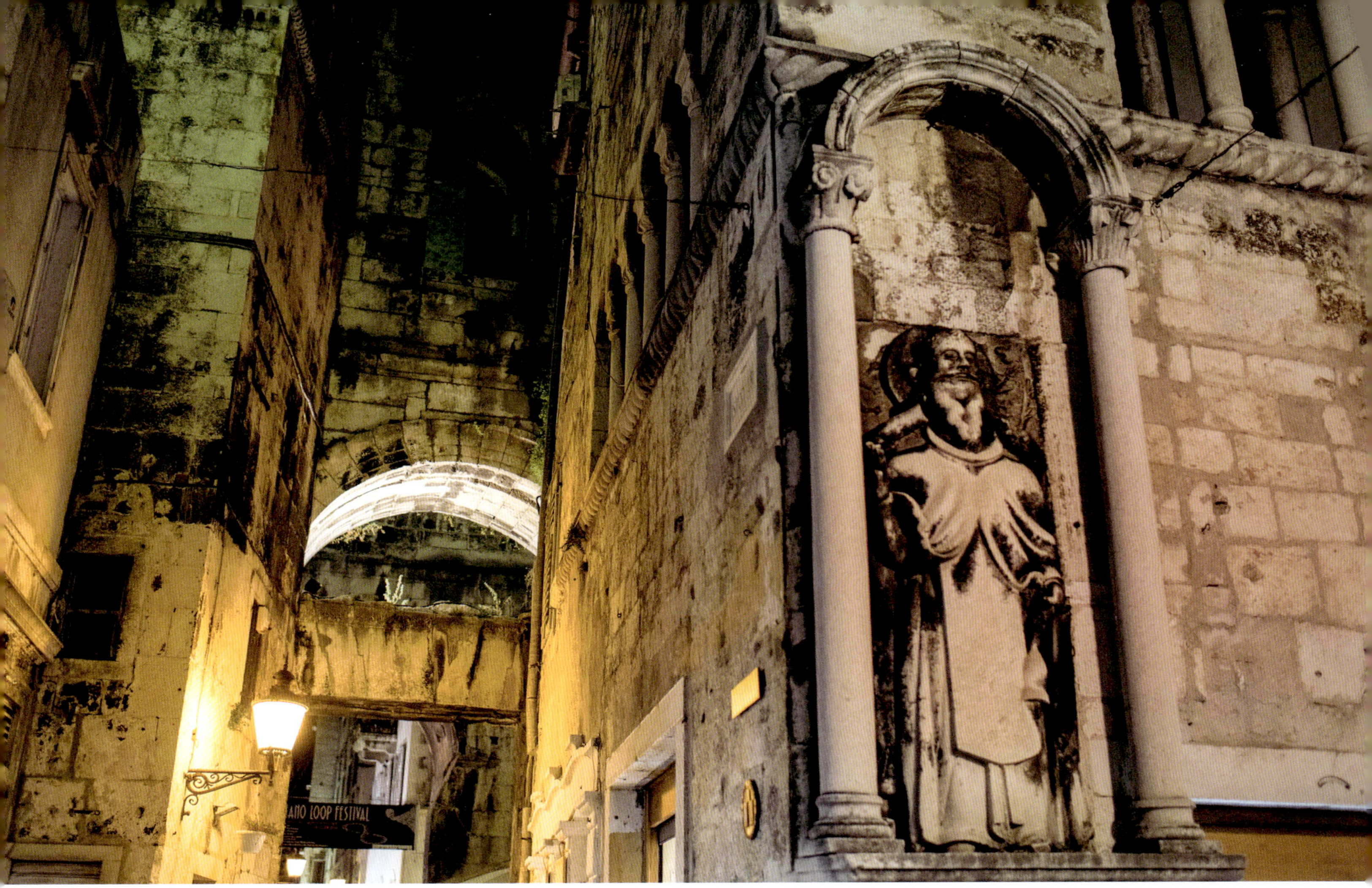
LOOP FESTIVAL

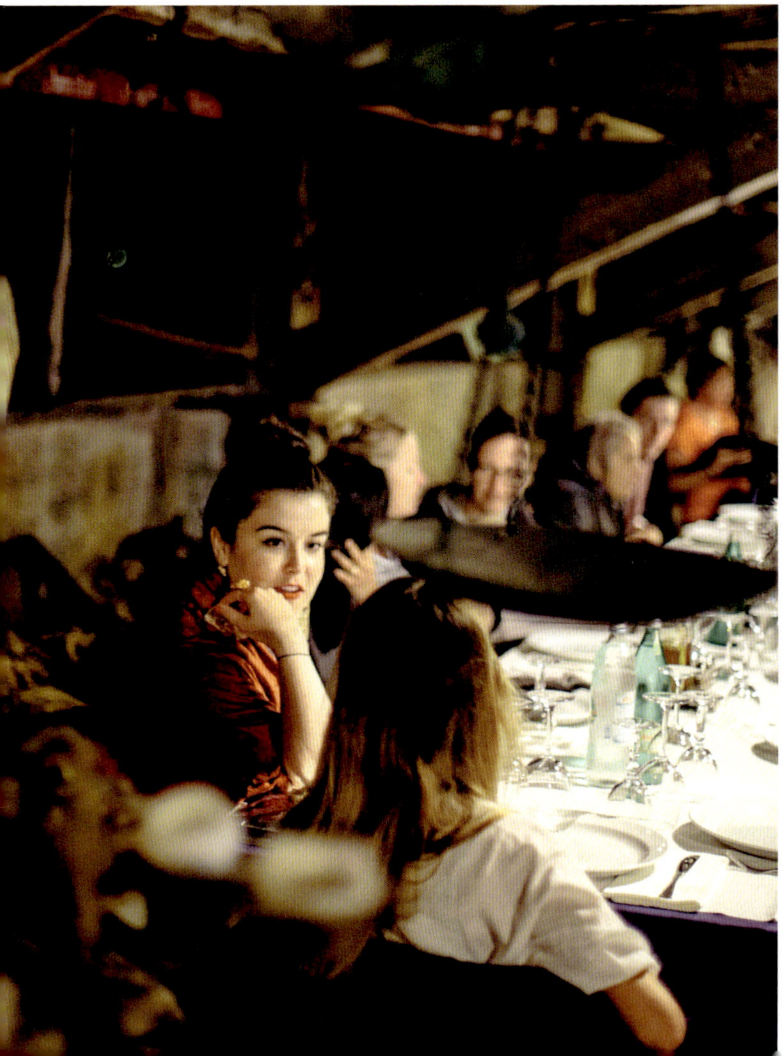

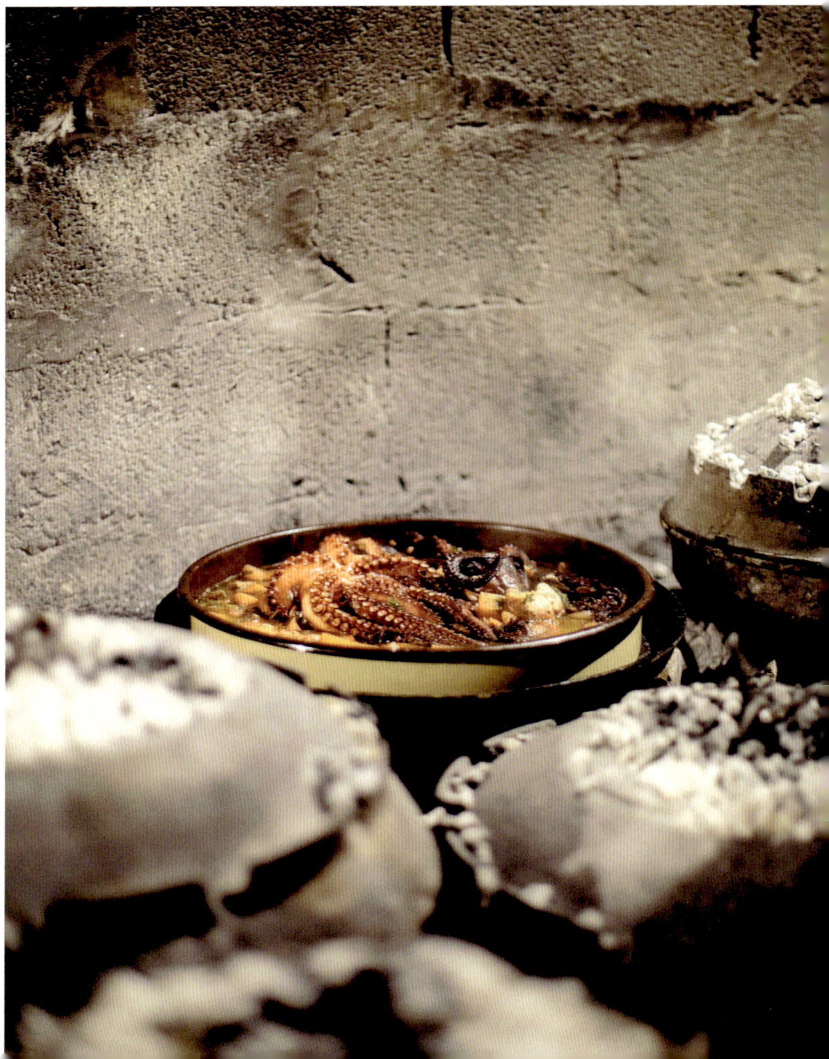

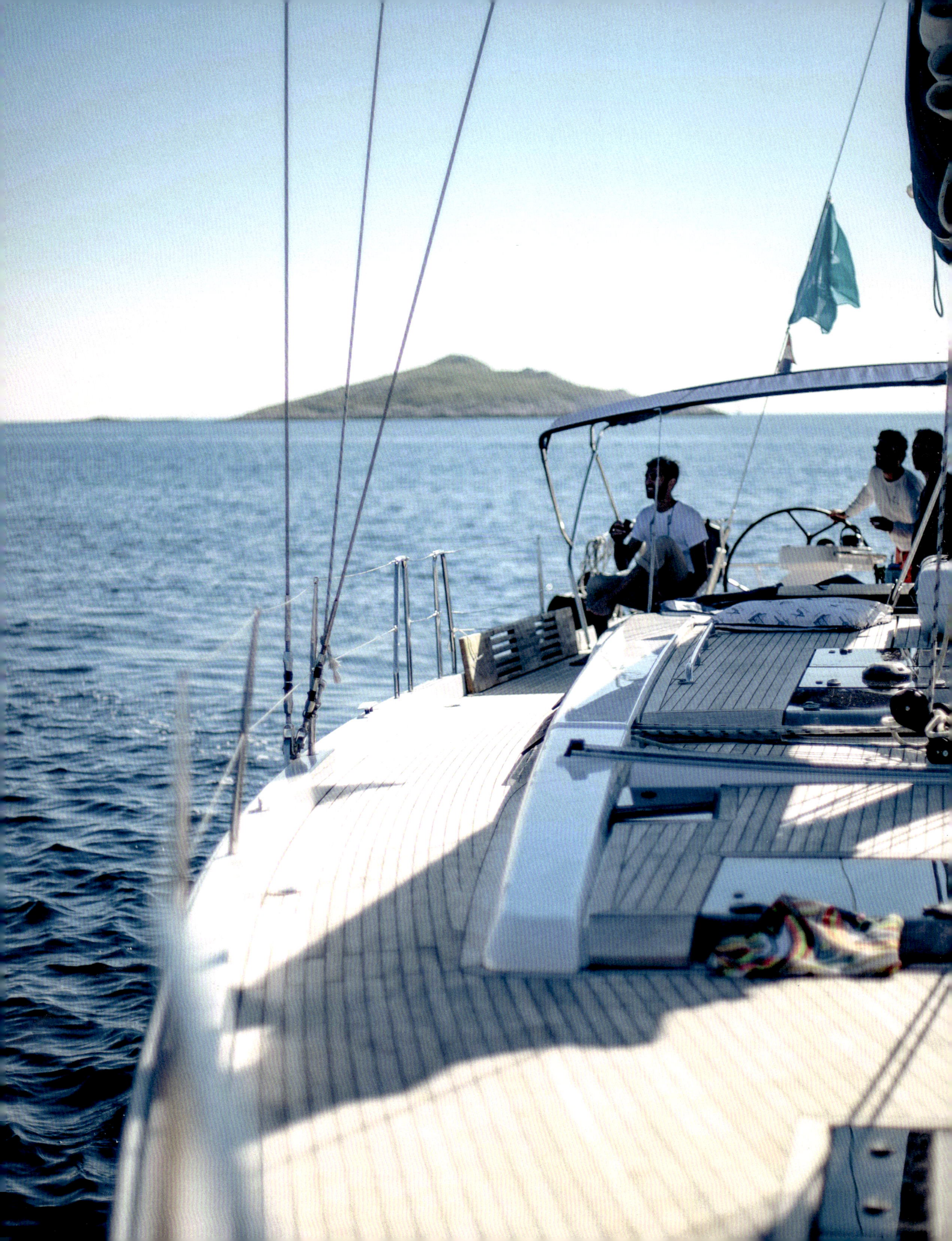

konoba on site, where you can sit out among the vines if you have a reservation. Mention you are sailing when you make your dinner arrangements and they will send a ride right to your boat on the *riva* and drop you off again after the meal.

KOMIŽA

On the far side of the island, in a less well protected harbor, is the town of Komiža. It is everything you could ask for in a small Croatian island town. Prominent churches sit in the foreground, with steep cliffs as a backdrop. Along the water's edge is the church of Our Lady of the Pirates, which was named after the town was ransacked by pirates (a common problem for Komižeans in antiquity); days later, the statue of the Virgin Mary that was stolen from the church floated, miraculously, right back into town. Apparently, after committing such sacrilege, the pirates' boat had foundered on the getaway.

The church of Saint Nicholas, on the hill above the town, is also distinctly nautical. "Saint Nick" is the patron saint of sailors: in Komiža, every year on December 6th, the local fishermen drag the hull of a retired wooden boat up the hill and burn it on the church grounds. A walk up to the church brings you along the main road out of town, which cuts through olive groves. The sweeping vista of the town and the harbor from the church is worth the walk, even if the church itself is rarely unlocked and open to visitors.

BIŠEVO

Under a grand limestone precipice on the eastern shores of Biševo is a Blue Grotto, where the only light inside a cavernous sea cave comes from underwater passages. This is a natural wonder that was made more accessible by enterprising locals using a little well-placed dynamite: the bigger entrance allows to offer boat tours of the grotto. Many sailors go to Biševo for the Blue Grotto alone, then do the tour and leave, but there is more to the island. On the western shores are beautiful coves, carved into the limestone landscape. After your tour of the cave, sail around to this far side, where you can anchor and swim from your boat: the singular restaurant on shore, Konoba Tomić, offers small seafood snacks and drinks.

~

Up and down the Adriatic coast there are lovely experiences to be found. In the Dalmatian Islands, the loveliness is everywhere you look. The pull of these islands is unavoidable. Even with their enormous popularity among sailors, they are still underrated—there is just no rating high enough to do them justice. Each new town on each new island brings with it a whole world of sensation and beauty. Freshly grilled fish and perfectly cooked *peka* pair with a burgeoning local wine scene to forge remarkable culinary experiences. Sweeping limestone shorelines along cliff-edged mountainous islands come together with remarkable medieval villages for a spectacular sailing adventure.

> The central Dalmatian Coast is home to one of the largest charter fleets in the world, with thousands of sailboats lining the marinas from Rogoznica to Split.

CAPTAIN'S NOTES *DALMATIAN ISLANDS*

RECOMMENDED ITINERARY

Trogir
43° 30' 58" N, 16° 14' 57" E
There are five premier marinas located in and around Trogir, providing safe berths and yacht services. These marinas are full from Friday through Sunday with charter boats that depart Sunday morning and return Friday night. They are otherwise empty. Trogir old town is a beautiful ancient city with a moat, creating an island connected to the mainland by two bridges. Along the waterfront is the public *riva*, and yachts can berth here. It is a splendid opportunity to see the small town up close.

Vinogradišce Bay, Paklinski Islands
43° 09' 25" N, 16° 23' 21" E
This bay is protected from all except southerly winds, which kick up a large swell and make the cove uncomfortable. Use the moorings in the bay or anchor along the outer edge. The bay is surrounded by a small number of beach clubs and restaurants, with docks to tie the dinghy. For a quieter stay, anchor at any of the three uninhabited coves to the west. For marina services, dock at Marina Palmizana, which has 180 berths sheltered from all winds.

Lučica, Brač
43° 18' 37" N, 16° 26' 40" E
This cove is located on the south-west side of Brač island and is characterized by its tree-like shape. The bay has laid moorings managed by the restaurants onshore, which can be reserved in advance. It is very deep and anchoring is only suitable in few select locations.

Šešula, Šolta
43° 23' 37" N, 16° 12' 37" E
Located south of the town of Maslinica on the island of Šolta is Šešula, a protected inlet that curves inland. There are a series of moorings that run parallel to the inlet; boats are to tie bow lines to the mooring and run stern lines ashore, to be tied off to the fixed bollards attached to the shoreline. This cove is protected in all winds. The Konoba Šešula and Šišmiš restaurants provide quality food and offer facilities to mariners. A short walk across the hill is the small town of Maslinica, providing provisioning and restaurants.

Komiža, Vis
43° 02' 42" N, 16° 05' 12" E
The large bay provides shelter from the north, east, and southeast winds and is exposed to southwest and west winds. During strong southerly winds, mariners should seek refuge in Vis Town, as the bay can become violent and hazardous.

RECOMMENDED ANCHORAGES

Plaža Porat, Biševo
Uvala Krknjaš, Drvenik Veli

ITINERARY DURATION

8 days recommended

PREVAILING WIND

Perhaps the most famous of the Adriatic winds, the *Bura* blows from the north to northeast and is common during the winter season, though it comes at any time of the year. Like many of the winds in Croatia, the *Bura* will be present often for a few days at a time. This wind is cold and dry: it begins in Siberia and travels towards the Dinaric Alps, where it gains great speed as it funnels down toward the Adriatic Sea. It strikes with a powerful gust of often up to 15 knots, followed by a short period of no wind at all. The levanat is a moderate wind that brings good sailing conditions before it turns into the *Bura*.

When the *Tramontana* blows it is often an indicator that extreme weather conditions will follow. This wind often lasts a day before becoming unpredictable and shifty. By contrast, the *Mistral* is the preferred wind for sailors during the summer season. It is a refreshing breeze that often begins around noon and dies off around sunset. At times, this westerly wind can reach up to 30 knots, but it is usually more like 15. The *Jugo* wind blows onto the Adriatic from the Sahara and causes winds and choppy waves as the wind builds, moving up the Adriatic Coast. The *Jugo* can bring sporadic rain and fierce thunderstorms as the isolated system makes its way northwest.

SEASON

Sailing season is between mid-June and mid-October.

FOOD

Povrće Lucice is a vegetable dish made with local varieties including eggplant, zucchini, and cabbage. These are cooked in an earthenware dish with water, a splash of wine, local herbs, and are garnished with thinly sliced potatoes.

GOOD TO KNOW

Magnetic variance
Magnetic Declination: +4° (EAST)

CROATIA

ADRIATIC SEA

- TROGIR
- SPLIT
- UVALA KRKNJAŠ
- *DRVENIK VELI*
- ŠEŠULA
- *ŠOLTA*
- BOBOVIŠĆA
- MILNA
- LUĈICA
- *BRAČ*
- STARI GARD
- *SVETI KLEMENT*
- MARINA PALMIŽANA
- VINOGRADIŠCE BAY
- HVAR TOWN
- *PAKLINSKI ISLANDS*
- *HVAR*
- *VIS*
- VIS TOWN
- KOMIŽA
- TITO'S CAVE
- BUDIKOVAC ISLAND
- PLAŽA PORAT
- *BIŠEVO*

0 — 10

NAUTICAL MILES
NOT FOR NAVIGATION

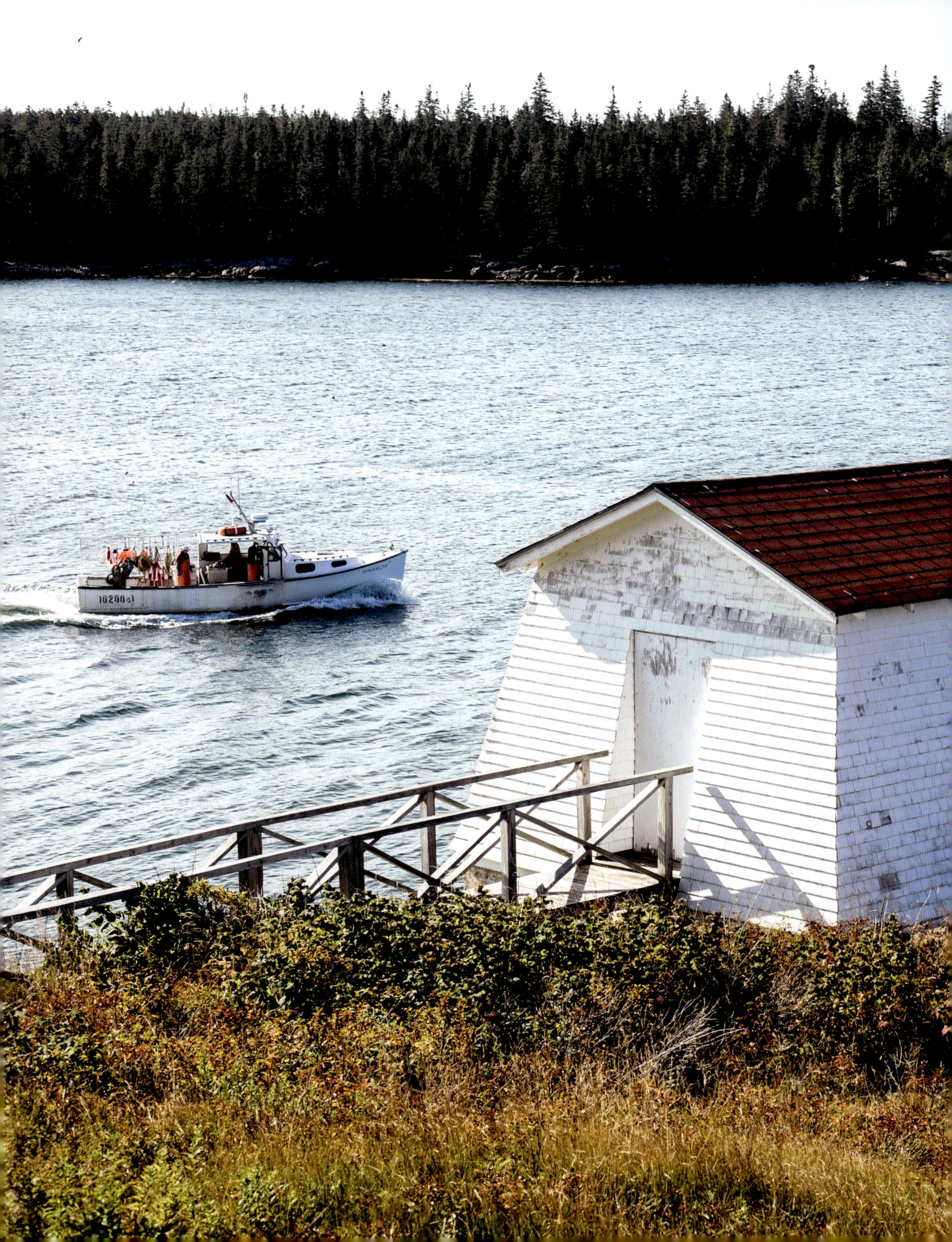

THE JAGGED COASTLINES OF MAINE

COLORFUL BUOYS ATTACHED TO LOBSTER TRAPS BOB UP AND DOWN IN THE WATER IN THIS NEW ENGLAND BAY. GLACIERS FORMED THE RUGGED COASTLINE, AND ITS COMPOSITION HAS IN TURN SHAPED THIS REGION'S WAY OF LIFE.

In Maine waters, the tradition of sailing is not a mere novelty. Fleets of historic sailing ships work commercially to take passengers on voyages around the islands and bays, and classic wooden boats are lovingly kept by passionate owners in almost every harbor. Voyaging here, you will experience this coastline the way sailors have for hundreds of years. Watch a gaff-rigged schooner drop anchor and furl sails while fog rolls in along the hemlock-lined coast and you will understand the simple truth of Maine's official state slogan: "The way life should be."

Communities have practiced the maritime trades along the coast of Maine since its early settlement. With the skills passed down from generation to generation, the working waterfront is alive and well. Oyster farmers can be seen working the tides, traditional tall ships dot the horizon, and lobstermen haul their daily catches. Witnessing these traditions takes you on a journey back in time, but it is also the reality of the present. When sailing here, you can clearly see the importance of the ocean to Maine's famed way of life.

Maine is a cerebral sailing destination and a puzzle of interplaying elements: tide, wind, fog, current, and a complex labyrinth of shoreline and shoals. There is a high variety in the geology of Maine's coast—it presents a complicated mix of brackish inlets, isolated coves, rocky shoals, marshy bays, and un-inhabited islands. Rare is the passage in Maine where you can let the autopilot steer. But, for all the hazards, the rewards of sailing here are rich. Overall, Maine has more coastline than California; a coast that runs just 225 miles from Canada to New Hampshire actually consists of about 3,500 miles of shoreline, not including all of the state's island coasts.

This jagged coast makes for exciting navigation through tricky passages; cruise here with extreme caution. Spend the evenings studying the charts and plan as best as you can for the unknowns that tomorrow will surely bring. Four-meter tides in the mid-coast region make the difference between high and low tide drastic. The change in the shape of the shoreline is astonishing for those uninitiated in the intricacies of such a large tidal range. Bays that are a vast expanse of open water at high tide will shrink to rivulets running through the mud at low tide. As the tide begins to ebb, it is as if the earth billows to the surface and

> Communities have practiced the maritime trades along the coast of Maine since its early settlement.

PENOBSCOT BAY | USA

reveals the mud, ledges, and rocks that lay below. Then, on a flooding tide, the ocean envelops it all back into its icy depths.

This coast is recognized as one of the greatest places to voyage in the world. Hundreds of miles of sawtooth seaboard, offering an abundance of islands and coves, make Maine a true playground for cruisers. Amazing experiences await all along Maine's vast coastline, but, if you don't have all summer to explore, then look to the Penobscot Bay region for a near-perfect slice of what Maine has to offer. Those seeking natural landscapes, solitude, and cultural authenticity are drawn here during the short sailing season, running from June to October. But, even with cruisers seeking summer enjoyment amid this rugged and wild landscape, the coast of Maine remains true to its heritage, and pleasure boaters are careful to give way to commercial activities. This region is home to one of the most substantial fisheries in the United States, and is the largest lobster exporter worldwide.

Gliding through cold green waters past a lone pine ledge, you will hear only the occasional luff of the sails, water lapping the bow, and the gulls in the air. Around you are anchorages in every direction and navigable passages around each island. In the Penobscot region alone there is too much to see and do for a guide to do justice, but a few places here really shouldn't be missed.

PULPIT HARBOR

Home to both the recreational sailor and the working mariner is Pulpit Harbor, on the northern side of North Haven Island, which lies in the center of Penobscot Bay. This multi-forked inlet provides ample protection from every wind. Going left or right at the harbor entrance, just past Pulpit Rock, gives sailors two very different Maine experiences. Turn right at the floating lobster pound and you'll enter Cabot Cove, which is the summer compound of one of the great American families—the Cabot family. Clay tennis courts and a fleet of immaculately maintained classic wooden sailboats speak to the heritage of this holding. Going left takes you to a small-town commercial lobster pier. Past a tidal dam at the head of the harbor, in an old salt pond, there's an oyster farm. After dropping anchor, dinghy ashore and walk up the hill or take a ride in the bed of a passing truck to the North Haven Oyster Co. farm stand, where bags of 50 or 100 oysters wait in a 1950s refrigerator by the side of the road. If nobody is working, just leave cash in the box.

The evolution of the working waterfront of Maine, specifically within the commerical shellfish industry, has brought a transition from wild foraging to aquaculture. In Pulpit Harbor salt pond, local oysters are cultivated by an entrepreneur, who lives in a floating cabin anchored in Cabot Cove. Clamming has always contributed to the economy on Maine's coast, but wild shellfish are not as easily harvested as they used to be. Oyster farms like the North Haven Oyster Co. provide a sustainable source of Maine shellfish. Sitting on the bow of your sailboat, shucking local oysters while anchored in the cove where they were harvested, is the absolute best way to enjoy them.

WINDJAMMERS

Maine has a thriving business of sailing on traditional tall ships called windjammers—the same sailing vessels that could have plied this coastline 100 years ago. They are staffed by youthful crews, who carry tethered rigging knives on their belts and sing sea shanties out loud as they hoist heavy sails. There are no winches onboard, no jiffy-reefing or roller-furling. These boats offer traditional sailing experiences in a style that's rarely found elsewhere.

ABOARD A CLASSIC WOODEN SAILBOAT (ABOVE). A TRADITIONAL LOBSTER BAKE WITH CLAMS, CORN, POTATOES, AND LOBSTERS STEAMED IN FISHING NETS (BELOW).

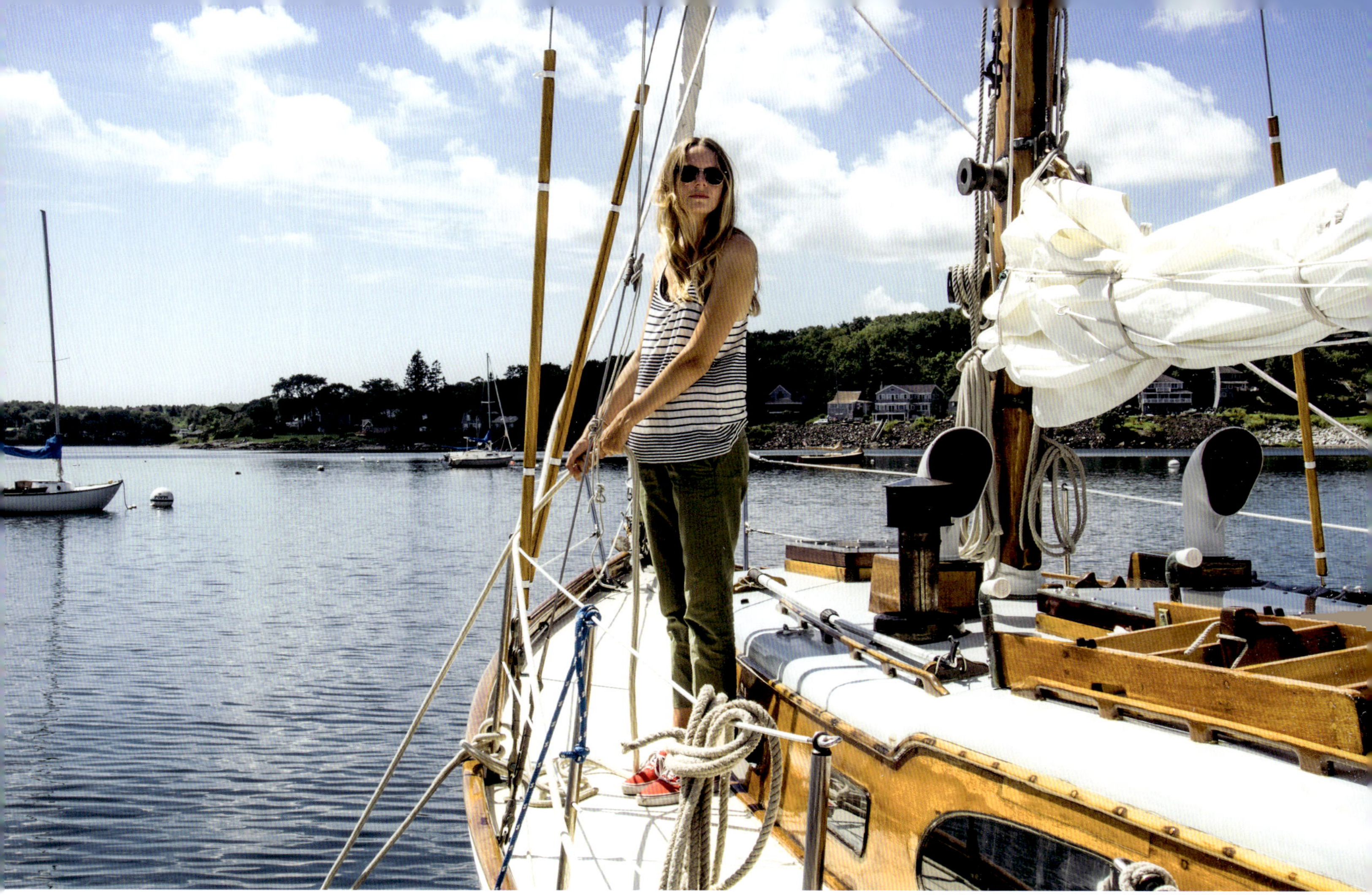

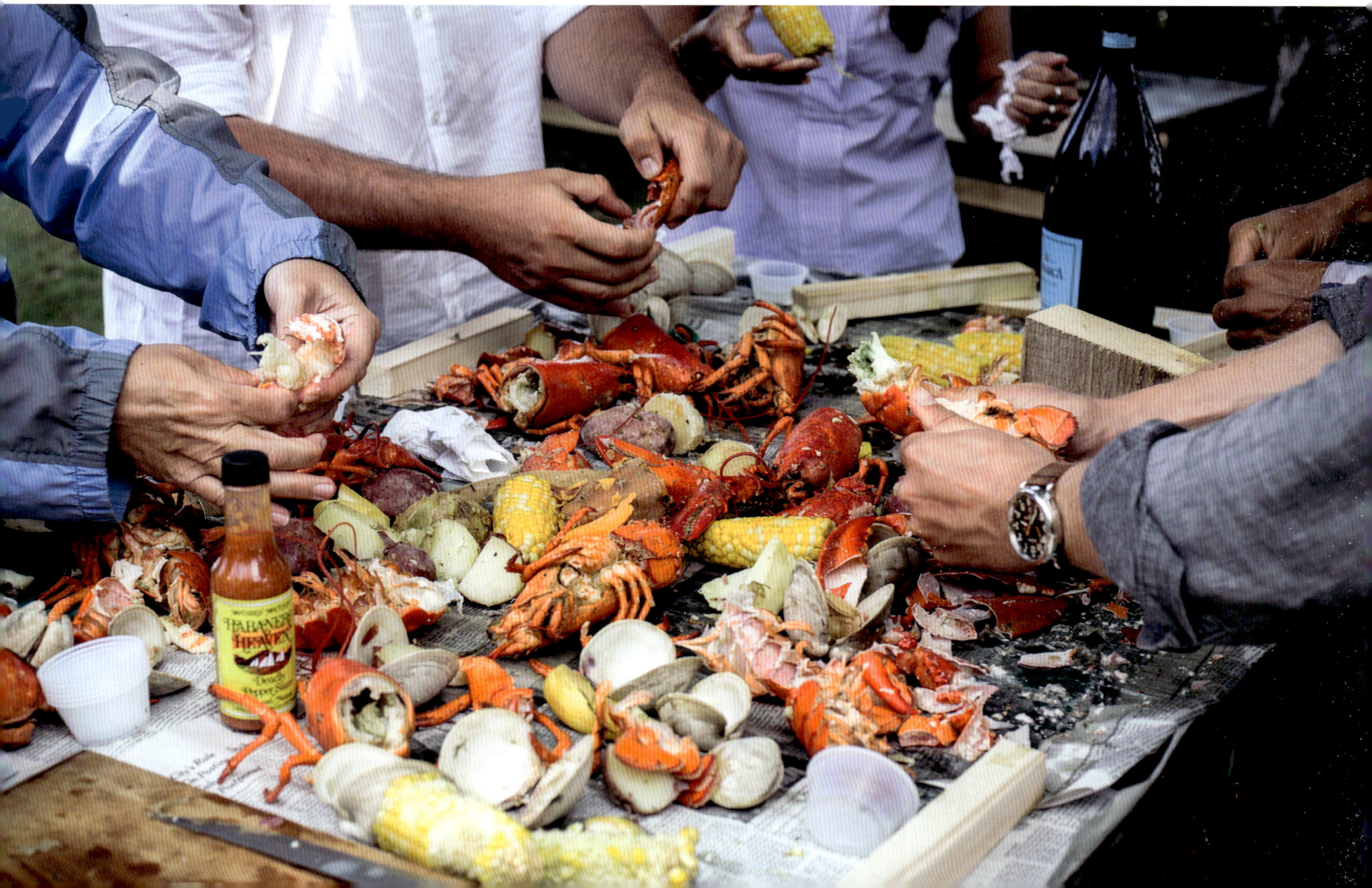

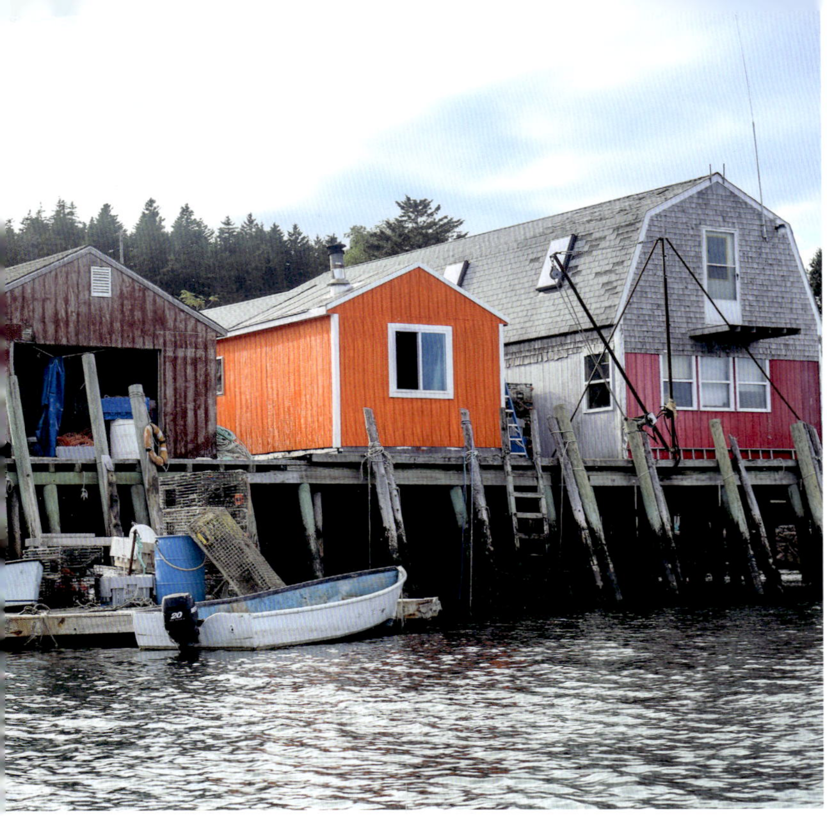

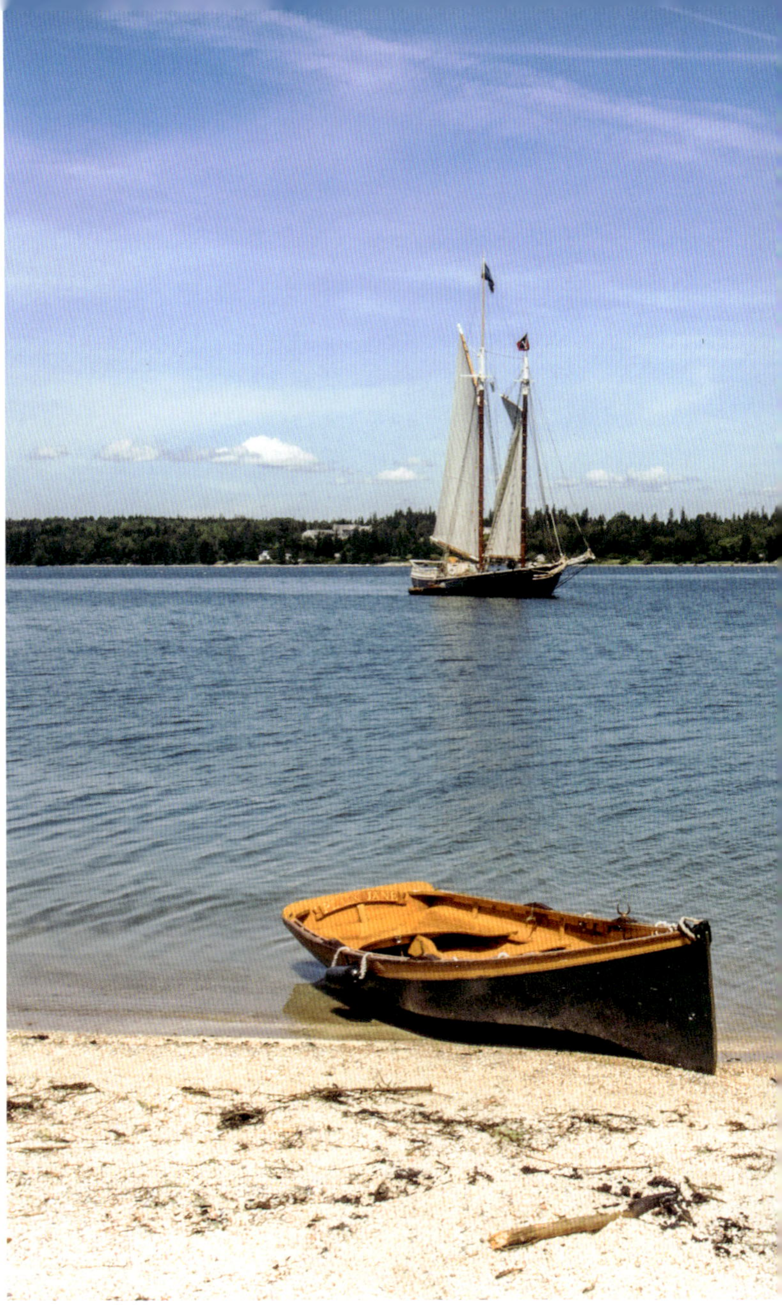

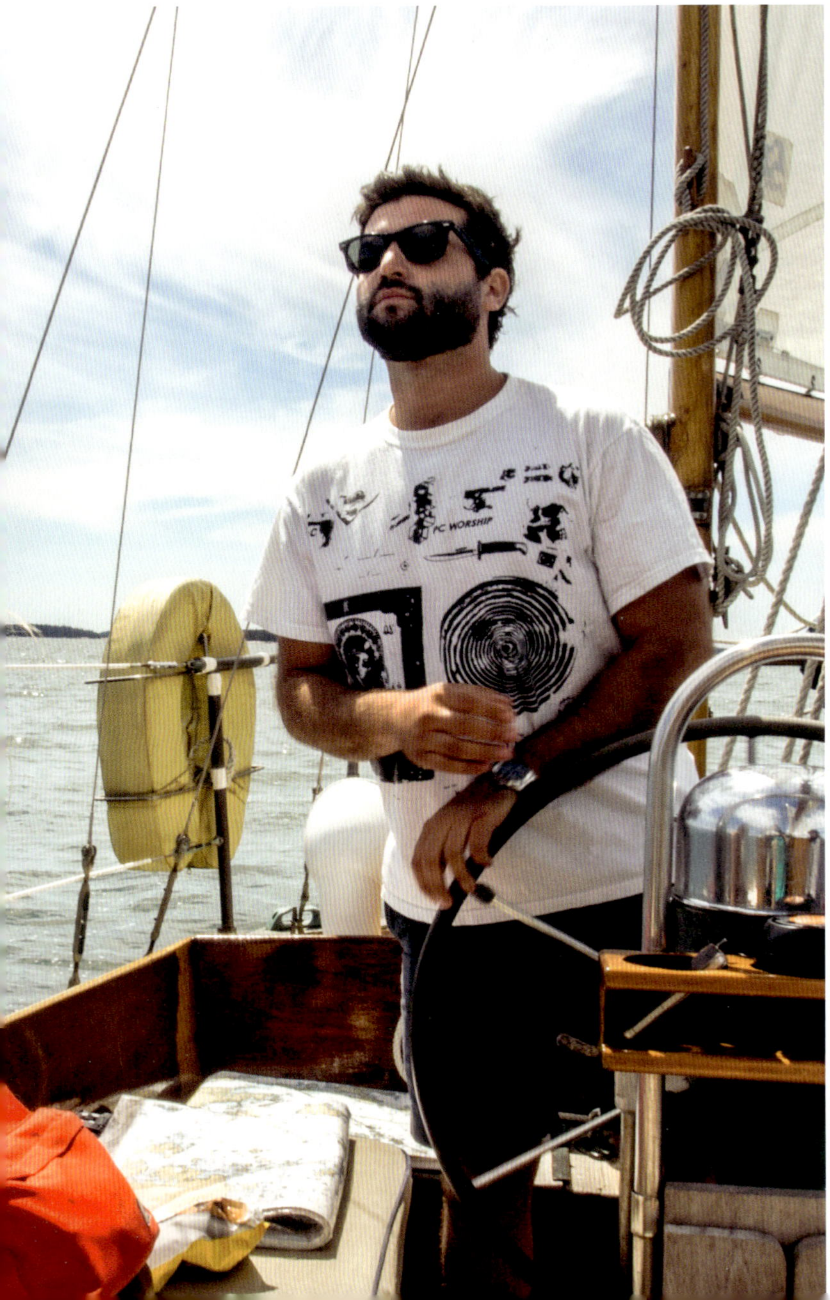
FC WORSHIP

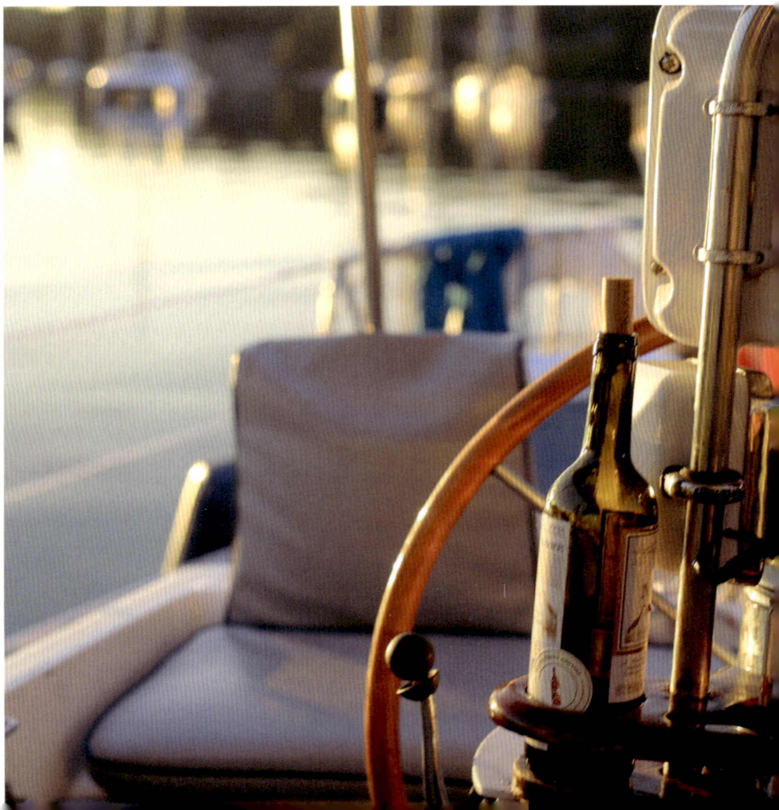

WOODENBOAT HARBOR

Big Babson and Little Babson Islands, at the eastern entrance of the Eggemoggin Reach, create the shelter for what is known locally as Woodenboat Harbor. There is ample room to drop anchor, with good holding in sand and mud, or, if you prefer, there are moorings that are well-maintained available for a nightly fee. In the mooring field, you will find yourself surrounded by the most beautiful collection of classic boats.

The Wooden Boat School in Brooklin is a perfect lens through which to view sailing in this area. The old and the new come together to create an intentional way of living on this coast. The art of boatbuilding is a tradition that defines the working waterfront. At one time, boats for work and trade were the foundation of the economy, and without traditional boats in Maine, there was no other work to be found.

Today at the Wooden Boat School, people gather from around the world to pass on the knowledge and traditions of boatbuilding and its associated crafts. Apart from construction techniques, they also teach sailing exclusively on wooden boats. Seeing students glide past in a beautiful *Herreshoff 12 ½ Footer* really is a stirring sight. Visiting sailors are welcomed to walk around the campus, tour the shop spaces, and enjoy the view of Eggemoggin Reach.

STONINGTON

Continue sailing clockwise around Deer Isle and you will journey through a famous thoroughfare, busy with lobster boats. Midway through the thoroughfare, the conspicuously labeled Opera House on the hillside of a town alerts you that you have arrived in Stonington. This small coastal town has the largest commercial lobster fleet in the entire state. Go ashore for great food from the surprisingly gourmet local scene and incredible coffee, roasted on the island by a shop named 44 North Coffee on Main Street. Don't miss the Marlinespike Chandlery: part antique store and part art gallery of the nautical sort, where mind-boggingly complex decorative knots are on display.

MERCHANT ROW

While sailing this coast, take the time to enjoy the passage through Merchant Row slowly. This is a well-traveled cut through a maze of islands. Popular here is Hells Half Acre, where a pleasant, protected anchorage leads you to a small uninhabited island that has all of the magic of the Maine coast wrapped up in a half acre of rocks, trees, and clear green water over granite and tidal flats. Rockweed drifting past the boat at anchor is the only disturbance in the mirror surface of the cold water on a calm day.

It is not uncommon to see the schooner *Mary Day* ghosting along with its topsails up on a light wind day, barely making a knot of speed, sailing slowly down Merchant Row. The commitment to a traditional sail in this community means that some of the windjammers don't even have engines—a rarity in a place with such strong currents; they instead rely on push boats to get in and out of port and commit to moving only with the wind each day. Even experienced captains will benefit from booking passage on these traditional crafts, as there is much to learn in modern sailing by witnessing old traditions.

GLACIAL GEOLOGY

Sailing past the steep beach on Hog Island at the eastern end of Eggemoggin Reach, you'll see boulders that look like they were placed there by some unimaginably powerful force. They were! This coastline was shaped by glaciers, and these rocks are glacial erratics, carried here in the ice pack. Glaciers were last here during the Pleistocene epoch, around the same time that early humans were first arriving in North America.

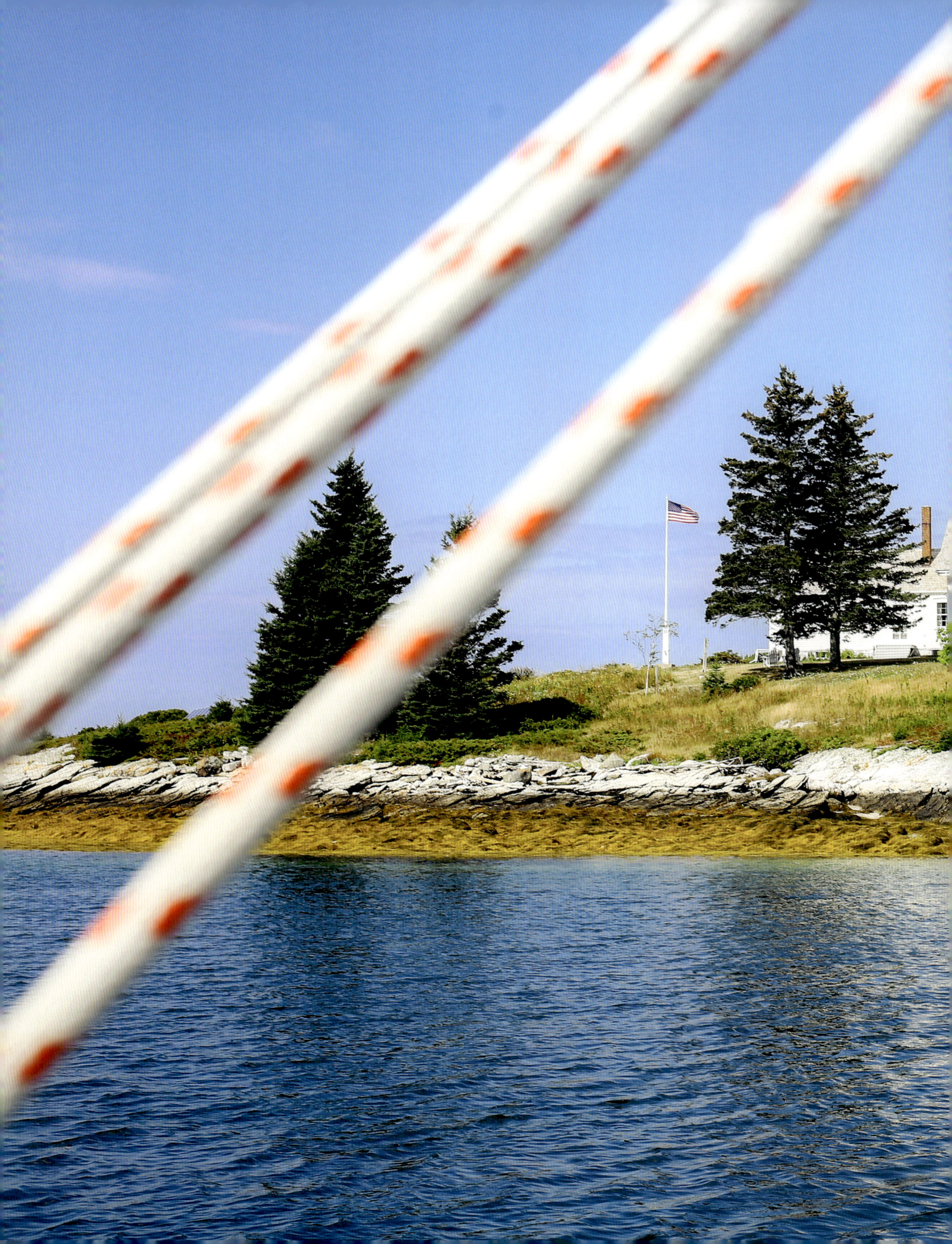

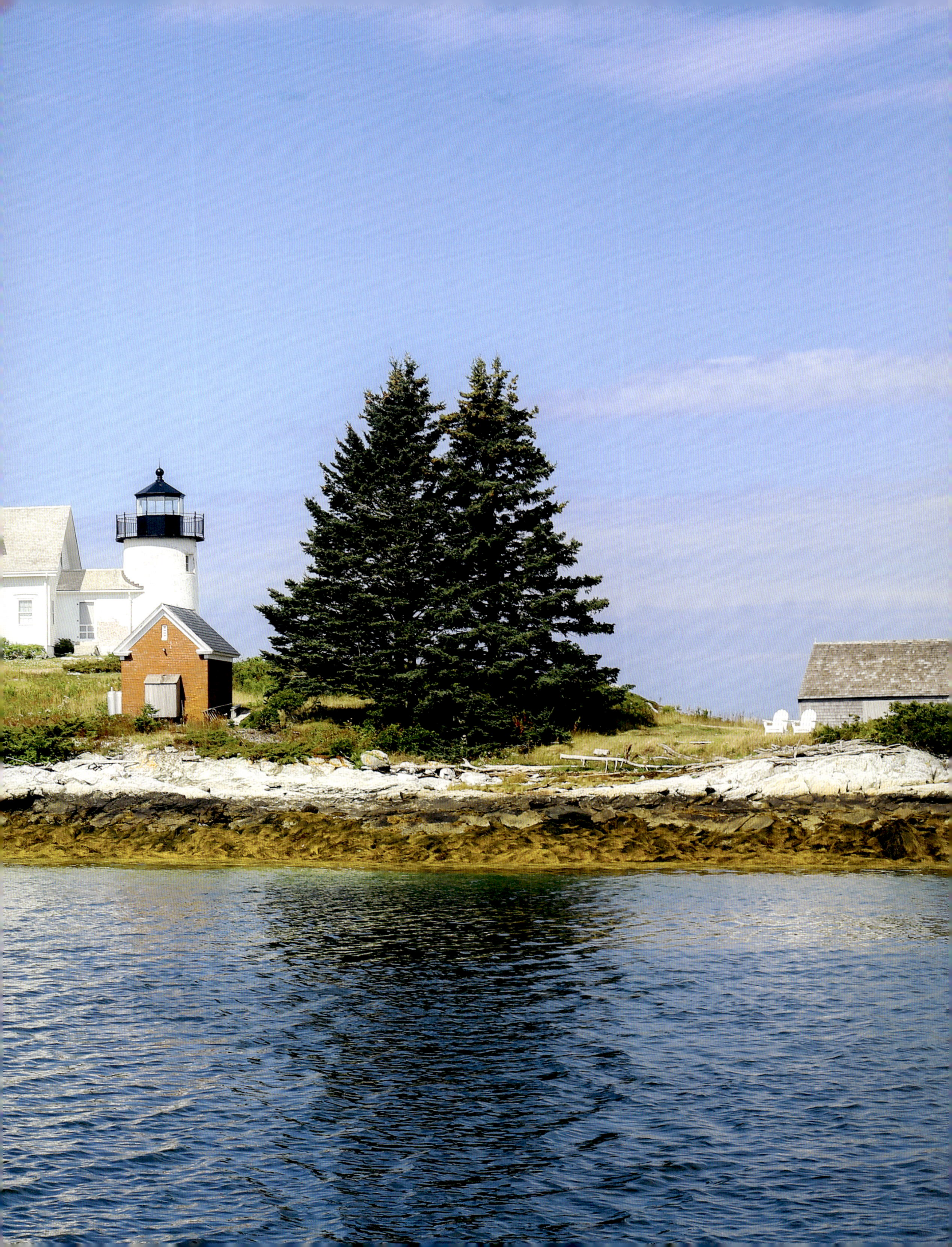

The windjammers add majesty to the local scenery as they weave between the islands and drop anchor in rocky coves.

VINALHAVEN

Vinalhaven, one of the larger islands and centrally located in Penobscot Bay, is the quintessential Maine commercial port. Sailors passing through know that you can't pick up a mooring buoy here without first obtaining permission from the owner. Local boats are protective of their scarce resources, and they have been known to set yachtsmen adrift in the middle of the night for trespassing on moorings. This shouldn't steer you away though, as this is a place with old-world Maine charm. The Victorian-era house of the well-known pop artist Robert Indiana, which he called the "Star of Hope," sits in the center of town, and the town's storied relationship with both—house and artist—is a tale of the tenacity of the traditions that pervade here.

~

Many sailors return year after year to cruise this coastline in the summer months, and still discover previously unknown idyllic coves. The anchorages are vast in number, enough for each captain to have their own favorite hidden place, tucked away along the shore. Pilot guides such as *A Cruising Guide to the Maine Coast* can give assistance to even the most seasoned of local sailors. Walking the docks in seaside towns is a great way to meet "old salts," who might share stories of cruising the coast. If you are lucky, they'll even share their favorite wilderness anchorages. The difficulty of navigating these waters brings people from across disciplines together—yachtsmen and fishermen, amateurs and professionals—to share stories and knowledge. Maine is worth a wander, but to explore safely here takes prudence and vigilance.

LOBSTERING TRADITIONS

Maine's lobster fishery is one of the best examples of a well-managed wild-stock fishery in the world. Seven days a week, there are real mariners rising with the sun to stake their claim on a natural resource that has the ability to bring great wealth or financial ruin. Lobstermen give little regard to sailors exploring this itinerary for leisure; it's common to be woken in the early morning hours by the roar of a lobster boat engine, even in the most secluded of coves. You may hear sailors complain about the wake, fumes, and noise, but to eliminate this would be to lose a stitch in the fabric of Maine's culture.

PENOBSCOT BAY
USA

ROWS OF LOBSTER TRAPS ALONG THE DOCKS IN VINALHAVEN. TRAPS ARE COLOR CODED, AS ARE THE BUOYS IN THE SEA.

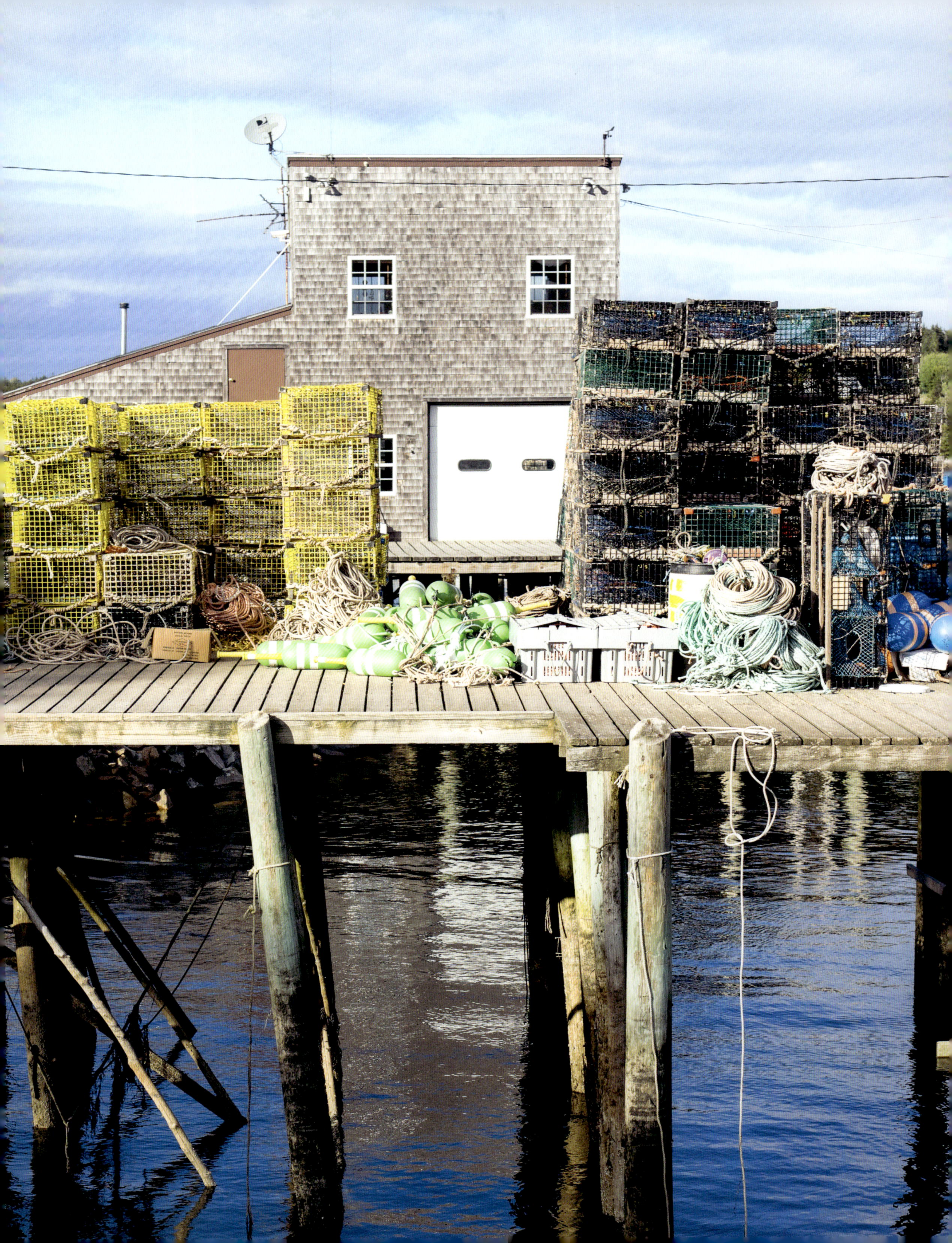

CAPTAIN'S NOTES *PENOBSCOT BAY*

RECOMMENDED ITINERARY

Carvers Harbor, Vinalhaven
44° 02' 32" N, 68° 50' 14" W

Most of the moorings in Carvers Harbor belong to local lobstermen and there are alotted moorings available for transient sailors. The nightly cost is clearly signposted and payment is placed in a watertight canister on top of each mooring. It is possible to anchor at the nearby Green's Island with access to town by dinghy. The entrance of the bay has an active lighthouse and the bay is secure from most winds.

Stonington, Deer Isle
44° 09' 22" N, 68° 40' 00" W

Moor or anchor outside the channel along the Deer Isle Thoroughfare. Transient slips are available at Billings Diesel & Marine, just a short walk from town. Billings is one of the busiest diesel repair shops along the Maine coast and has mechanics on hand and many parts in stock. There are scattered islands throughout the Deer Island Thoroughfare with many suitable overnight or day anchorages.

Bucks Harbor, Brooksville
44° 20' 15" N, 68° 44' 10" W

Moorings are available for visiting yachts, or call ahead to Buck's Harbor Marina for dock space, ice, and fuel. There is a small market onshore with staple goods for provisioning; it is attached to an upscale restaurant welcoming to mariners, with reservations recommended. Harbor Island is located in the center of the bay, blocking any swell that could enter at the mouth of Buck's Harbor.

Pulpit Harbor, North Haven
44° 09' 15" N, 68° 53' 02" W

This is a protected bay which is located in the northern part of North Haven; Billys Cove and Crockett Cove are located within it. Pass between Pulpit Rock and Mackerel Point to enter into the harbor. Anchor or pick up a mooring. There are no facilities onshore but you can use the town pier for dinghy tie-up.

RECOMMENDED ANCHORAGES

Hells Half Acre
Hurricane Island
Isle Au Haut Thorofare
Crockett Cove and Goose Cove, Deer Isle
Back Cove, Swans Island
Winter Harbor, Vinalhaven
Frenchboro, Long Island

ITINERARY DURATION

5+ days recommended

PREVAILING WIND

Northern Maine is often referred to as "Down East," in a turn of phrase that is confusing to most outsiders. Most people visualize north as "up" on a map. A southwesterly prevailing wind through the summer months explains this terminology, which was used by travelers under sail to refer to the easy, downwind travel to the northern coast. Bad storms in Maine tend to bring winds that are opposite to the prevailing. These, coming down from the Canadian Maritimes, are referred to as "Nor'easters" and respected for their cold fury. Sailors are wise to respect the conventional wisdom not to set out in a Nor'easter. Luckily, Maine has a coastline full of some of the coziest and best-protected harbors any sailor could wish to hunker down in.

SEASON

Sailing season begins in June and ends in early-October, though weather can become inclement at the beginning and end of the summer months, with June often being cold and rainy. In the winter months, recreational water activity shuts down and only lobster fishermen are boating commercially.

GOOD TO KNOW

Tides
A strong and ever-present force on Maine's coast is the tide, which ranges upwards of 4 meters in the mid-coast region and higher still when moving north. A rock dangerous at low tide may be passed easily at high tide, and a passage made safely at high tide may become impassable as the water drops. A clock is equally as important as a compass in these waters, but time alone doesn't explain the intricacies of tide in the Gulf of Maine. As this enormous mass of water moves up and down the coast, it stirs up significant currents coming in and out of the deep bays.

Navigation
Maine is home to 3,168 islands, which are all registered as either private or state-owned on the official Coastal Island Registry. On such a rocky coastline, with vast tidal range, there are thousands of ledges exposed at low tide that disappear at high water. In order to be, officially, an island and not a ledge according to the Maine tradition, a landmass must have at least one tree growing. Take a look at any chart, and you'll see island names are reused regionally and often in befuddling ways. In Bar Harbor, nearby islands are named: Sheep Porcupine, Burnt Porcupine, Long Porcupine, and Bald Porcupine. In Casco Bay alone, there are no fewer than four "Crow" islands, five if you count Crow Island Ledge. Additionally, there are around 26 islands sharing the name "Bar Island" on the coast of Maine.

Fog
An old salt might jokingly explain that the traditional way to navigate through thick Maine fog is through "potato navigation." It's simple: stand on the bow of a boat with a 50-pound bag of potatoes and, depending on your headway, throw a potato dead ahead every ten seconds or so. If there's a splash, rest assured that there is water ahead. A soft thud could mean land, a hollow thud could be another boat, and getting hit by another potato surely means there's a boat headed right for you.

Magnetic Variance
Magnetic Declination: -15° (WEST)

Map of Penobscot Bay and Surrounding Waters

PENOBSCOT BAY

BROOKSVILLE

- BUCKS HARBOR
- EGGEMOGGIN REACH
- LITTLE DEER ISLE
- BABSON ISLANDS
- WOODENBOAT HARBOR
- HOG ISLAND

WEST PENOBSCOT BAY

- NORTH HAVEN ISLAND
- PULPIT HARBOR / CABOT COVE
- GOOSE COVE
- DEER ISLE / STONINGTON
- HELLS HALF ACRE
- JERICHO BAY
- SWANS ISLAND BACK COVE
- LONG ISLAND FRENCHBORO

EAST PENOBSCOT BAY

- WINTER HARBOR
- MERCHANT ROW
- ISLE AU HAUT THOROFARE
- ISLE AU HAUT BAY
- HURRICANE ISLAND
- VINALHAVEN / CARVERS HARBOR

GULF OF MAINE

0 — 10 NAUTICAL MILES

NOT FOR NAVIGATION

N / E / S / W

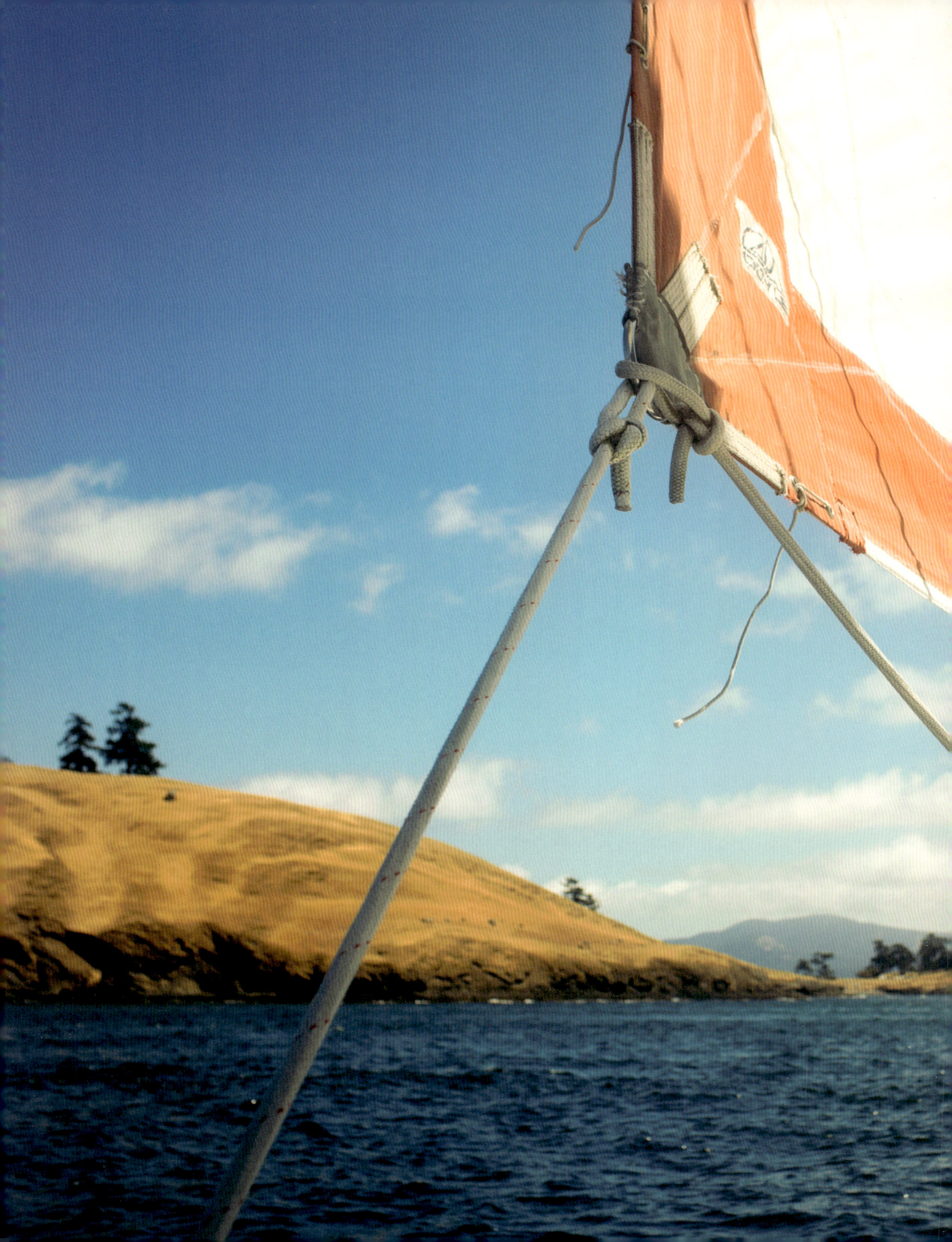

THE UNTAMED PACIFIC NORTHWEST

A GRAND ARCHIPELAGO ALONG AN EVEN GRANDER COASTLINE, THE PACIFIC NORTHWEST IS A BREATHTAKINGLY WILD AND BEAUTIFUL PLACE. ABOUNDING WITH WILDLIFE, IT'S ONE OF THE BEST PLACES IN THE WORLD TO SEE ORCA WHALES.

Cold green waters rush in and out of narrow passageways between densely forested islands. Behind tree-lined hills, there are distant snow-capped peaks that sit like sentinels of the Salish Sea. In the deep waters below your keel exists a world of kelp forests, giant crabs, jellyfish swarms, families of seals, and pods of orcas: ocean so wild that it overflows with flora and fauna. Wildlife in this landscape of abundant resources contends with harsh elements to survive. A large tidal range makes for massive amounts of water moving on fast currents that change throughout the day. Predators and prey alike—the orcas, sea otters, and salmons—all have to be quick and smart to survive. To sail here, you must be the same: indecision in such strong currents and fast-changing conditions can make or break your voyage.

The San Juan Islands are at the northwest corner of the continental United States and the southern end of the truly wild Salish Sea. The first people to settle this region, more than 5,000 years ago, are still represented today by a large population of indigenous people living along the border between Washington State and Canada. The tribes identify as part of the "Coastal Salish," ethnically and linguistically related peoples of the Pacific Northwest Coast. Their presence in these waters is not solely historical, this region has a strong culture carried forward from its pre-Americanidentity, and it is apparent in everything from the local cuisine to the politics of the islands and towns. Inhabitants of this region, of native ancestry or not, tend towards a nature-centric perspective; it is more common to see a "Blue Marble" Earth flag flying from people's homes than the "Stars & Stripes" of the United States.

Here, the sailing community is one of the largest in the United States, and cruising the San Juan Islands is undoubtedly the best way to explore the archipelago. The larger islands are serviced by the Washington State Ferries, which offers year-round service to the major ports and an expanded network in the summer months. There are also seaplane docks in the main ports that have regularly scheduled routes. Many of the smaller islands are excluded from these networks, however, and are reachable only by personal boats.

Residents on these more remote islands rely on their own boats and hired floatplane pilots to access amenities: an idyllic, but often rather complicated existence.

Sailing the San Juan Islands presents a maze of channels and passages leading into deep bays around stunning promontories. You can begin your voyage near Seattle, south of the San Juans, or alternatively, in the northern towns of Bellingham or Port Townsend, which provide easy access to the archipelago. Route planning is as much about the tidal currents as anything else; with speeds upwards of eight knots in some passes, it is possible to be completely barred from making any headway at all and to be carried backward, even if you run the motor at full throttle. For this reason, your passage is limited to those times when the tide is in your favor and the welcome lull of slack tides. You may well have just a few daylight hours to make headway in certain passages. Navigating these waters at night is not advised because of floating trees, known as "deadheads," from local logging, which can puncture your hull if you do not keep a careful watch. The necessity of using favorable tides to get anywhere gives the sailing here a pace all its own that is in sync with the natural world around you.

During the short cruising season, from May to August, boat owners are out in force. With such a small window to enjoy this wonderland, there is no time to waste. Orcas in the water, seals on the shoreline, humpback whales on the horizon, eagles in the sky, sea anemones under your fingertips, deer in the forest, and you at the helm of a sailboat.

FRIDAY HARBOR

Located on San Juan Island, this harbor town is a popular destination for sailors and is probably the busiest port of the archipelago. It is also the main hub for most visitors. Several times a day, the Washington State Ferries arrive from Anacortes, full of fresh-faced explorers using the boats to broaden their horizons.

Taxis, shuttles, bicycles, and mopeds are available for rent should you want to get out of town and explore the island, but there is plenty to keep you entertained as you walk around near the docks. While your boat is at anchor or docked at the San Juan Island Yacht Club, make sure to take a walk to the floating seafood market and check out the fresh local prawns and shellfish kept in saltwater tanks, as well as the salmon and other fresh fish in their coolers. The market is in a houseboat located on the docks and the people running it are knowledgeable about the local seafood, so this is a great provisioning stop. Visit the grocer nearby for regional produce as well as lavender products from an organic lavender farm on the island and be sure to browse the bottles from some of the many local vineyards and breweries.

A vibrant local art scene, featuring work that could be described as earthy and spiritual, is represented in the many galleries and shops around town. Enjoying a delicious blackened salmon sandwich on the waterfront, you can take your time to sit and watch an eagle circle the harbor, and, by the end of the afternoon, you will possibly be also feeling quite earthy and spiritual.

> Orcas in the water, seals on the shoreline, humpback whales on the horizon, eagles in the sky, sea anemones under your fingertips, deer in the forest, and you at the helm of a sailboat.

ROCHE HARBOR MARINA ON THE NORTH OF SAN JUAN ISLAND (ABOVE).

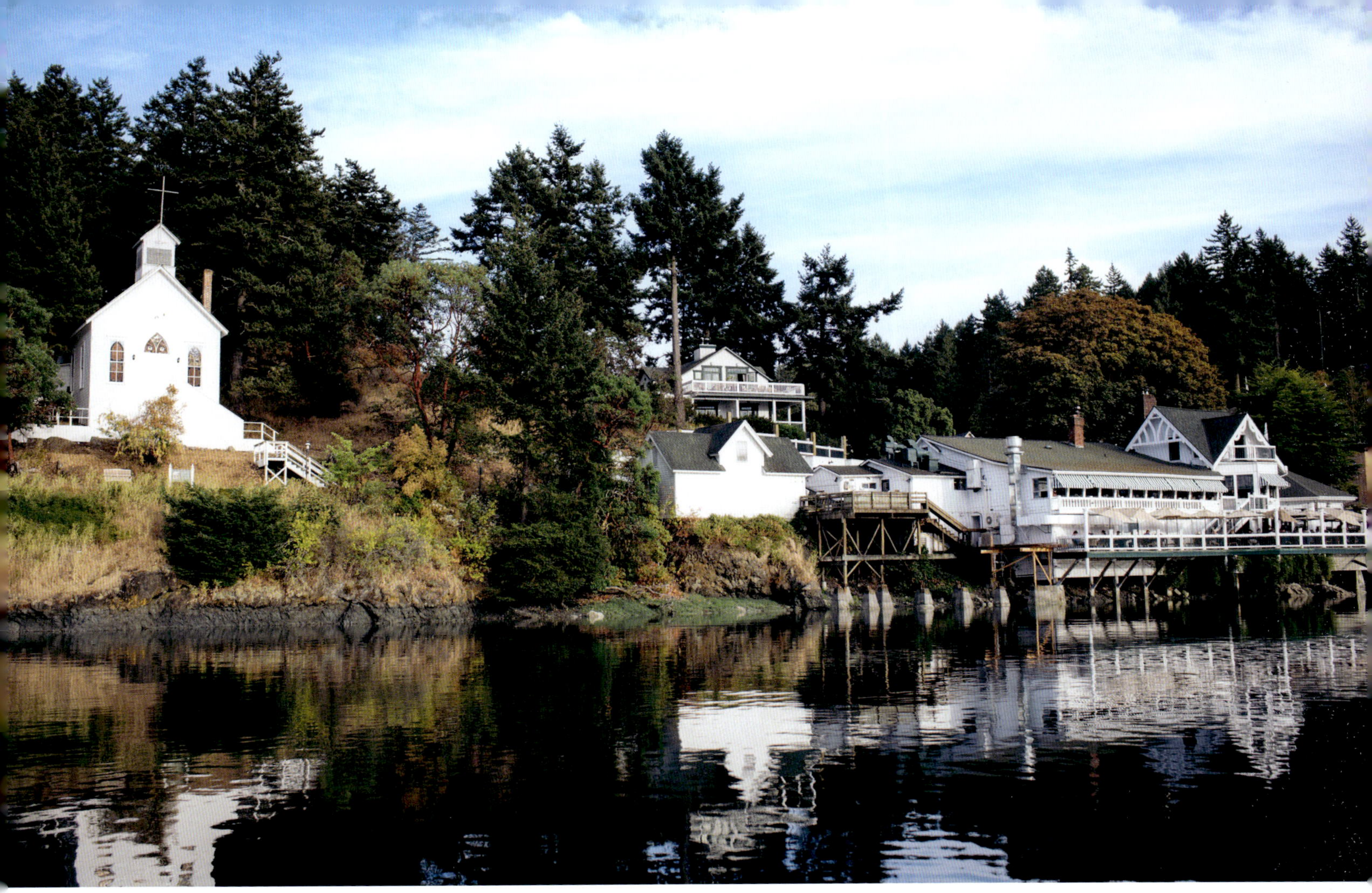

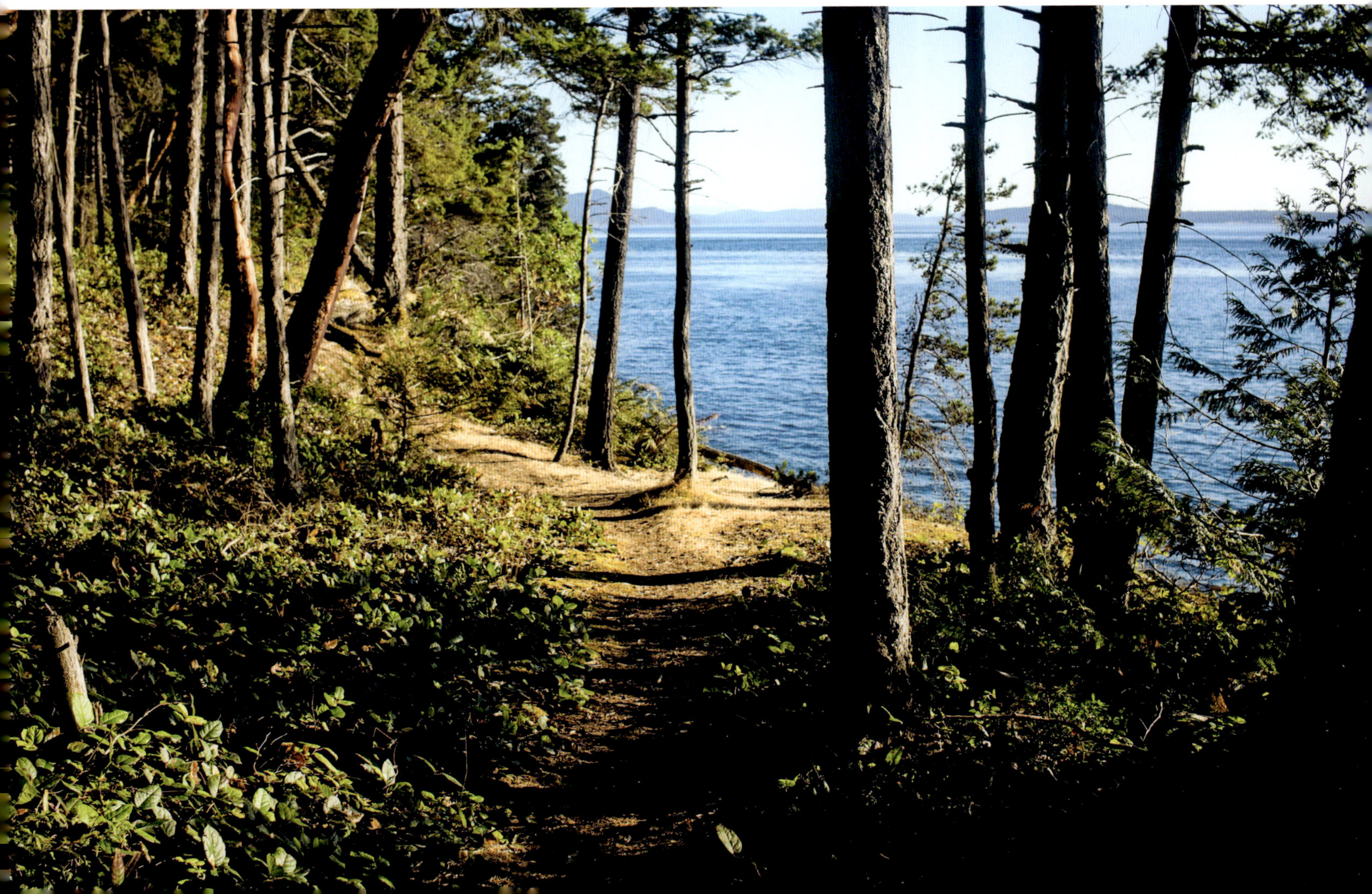

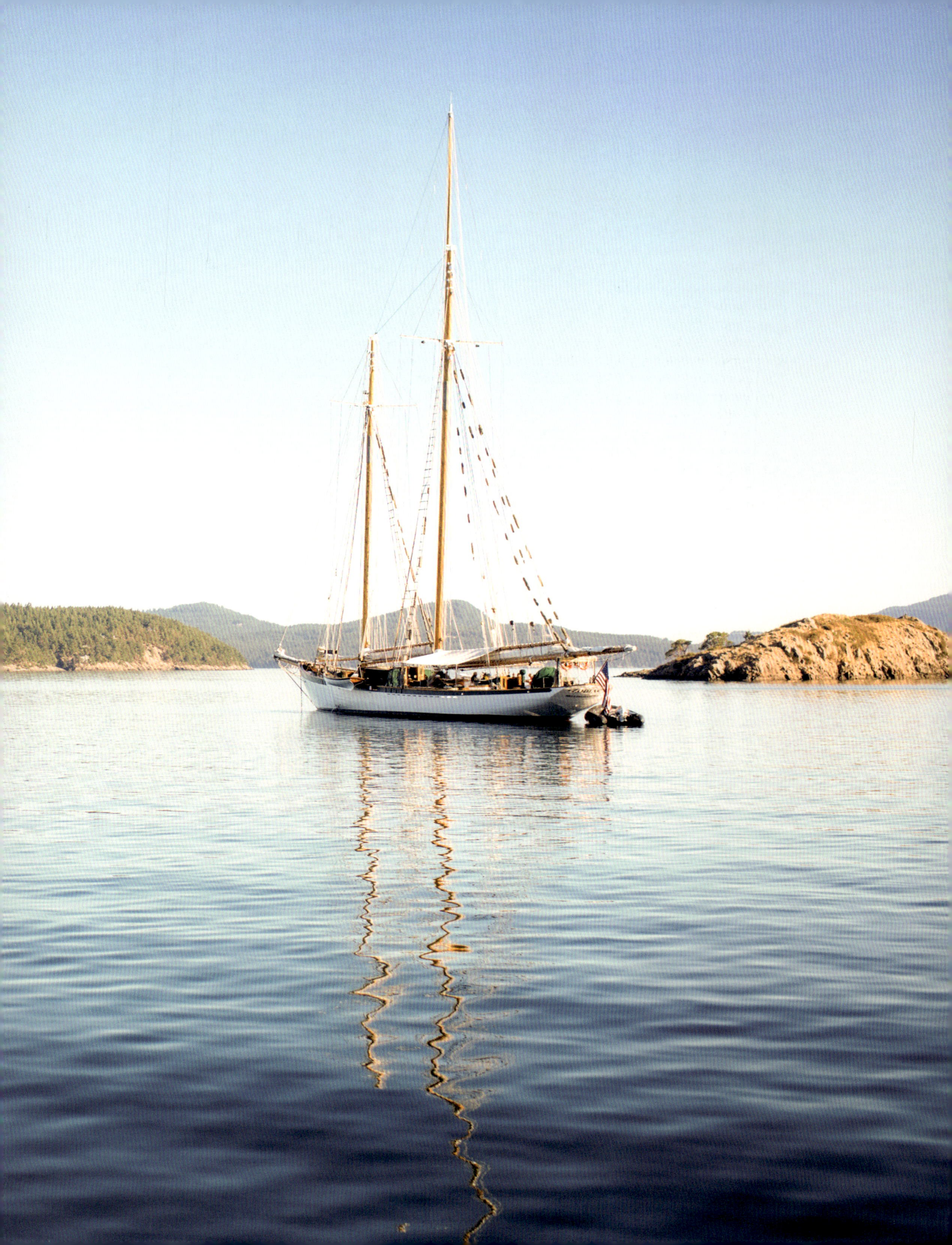

ROCHE HARBOR

An old mining port turned private resort, Roche Harbor was, historically, an industrial town for employees producing mortar and concrete on San Juan Island. Nowadays the employee housing is all high-end guest accommodation and gorgeous gourmet restaurants. Sailors stop here for the nice resort and a five-star meal overlooking the water. Ample dockage is available and you will find yourself among fancy boats at the marina. The resort offers three distinct restaurants on the waterfront surrounding the inner harbor, and a coffee shop open during the summer. Lime Kiln Cafe is the least formal of the three and a wonderful option for a no-fuss, quality meal in a gorgeous historic setting. At sunset every day, the staff of the Hotel de Haro perform an act of multi-national patriotism, in a ceremony where they lower the flags of Roche Harbor, Washington State, Canada, Great Britain, and the US, while playing the respective anthems for each and firing off a canon to the applause of yachts in the harbor.

An outdoor sculpture gallery across the road from the resort has a rotating display, presented on eight hectares of land. Allow yourself some time here: you really have to hike to see it all. There is a gorgeous natural lake on the property and a lawn where you can enjoy a picnic in the presence of incredible art. A small Catholic church—Our Lady of Good Voyage—sits perched on the steep shoreline, overlooking the boats.

SUCIA ISLANDS

The sandstone of the San Juans is laid bare on the Sucia island group, resembling a hand with five long, slender fingers. This designated state park has wonderful anchorages throughout and camping facilities. It offers picnic sites with shelters, and places to access potable water on shore. Keep an eye out on the crumbling limestone shoreline—in 2012 there was a significant discovery of dinosaur fossils made here—but leave whatever you find, as fossil collecting is strictly prohibited without research permits. Whale-watching boats will steam past this anchorage, headed north in search of humpbacks in the open water, but they do not put people ashore. The forested trails on the island are the prize of those who guided themselves here.

STUART ISLAND

This island is the end of the line for the San Juan group and has the remote feeling of being "on the edge;" people who have homes and cabins here are looking to tuck away into a quiet corner of nature. To peer out past the San Juans, make the hike to Turn Point Lighthouse, which overlooks the Canadian border. The hike itself is pretty flat and passes local homes built in remote locations, as well as a private airstrip in a field. Handwritten wooden signs at every juncture will help to guide you. The hike comes out on a point that has dramatic cliffs on either side and a lighthouse ahead.

The island has two bays: Reid Harbor is your best bet if you plan on anchoring here—it's characterized by a long, mud-bottom bay with a little dock, protected from all sides and a good place for sitting out foul weather.

ORCA SPOTTING

Off the west coast of San Juan Island is Lime Kiln Lighthouse. The water just offshore is where the whaleboats go looking for orcas in the summer. Pods are carefully monitored in the region and individual members are known to the knowledgeable naturalists aboard the ships, who help keep track of the population. Orcas, known colloquially as "killer whales," are in fact the largest species of dolphin. They live in complex family groups and communicate in "dialects" that are passed across generations—behavior cited as evidence that they are capable of cultural learning.

A SCHOONER SITS AT ANCHOR IN A PROTECTED BAY IN CALM WATERS BEFORE THE WIND PICKS UP.

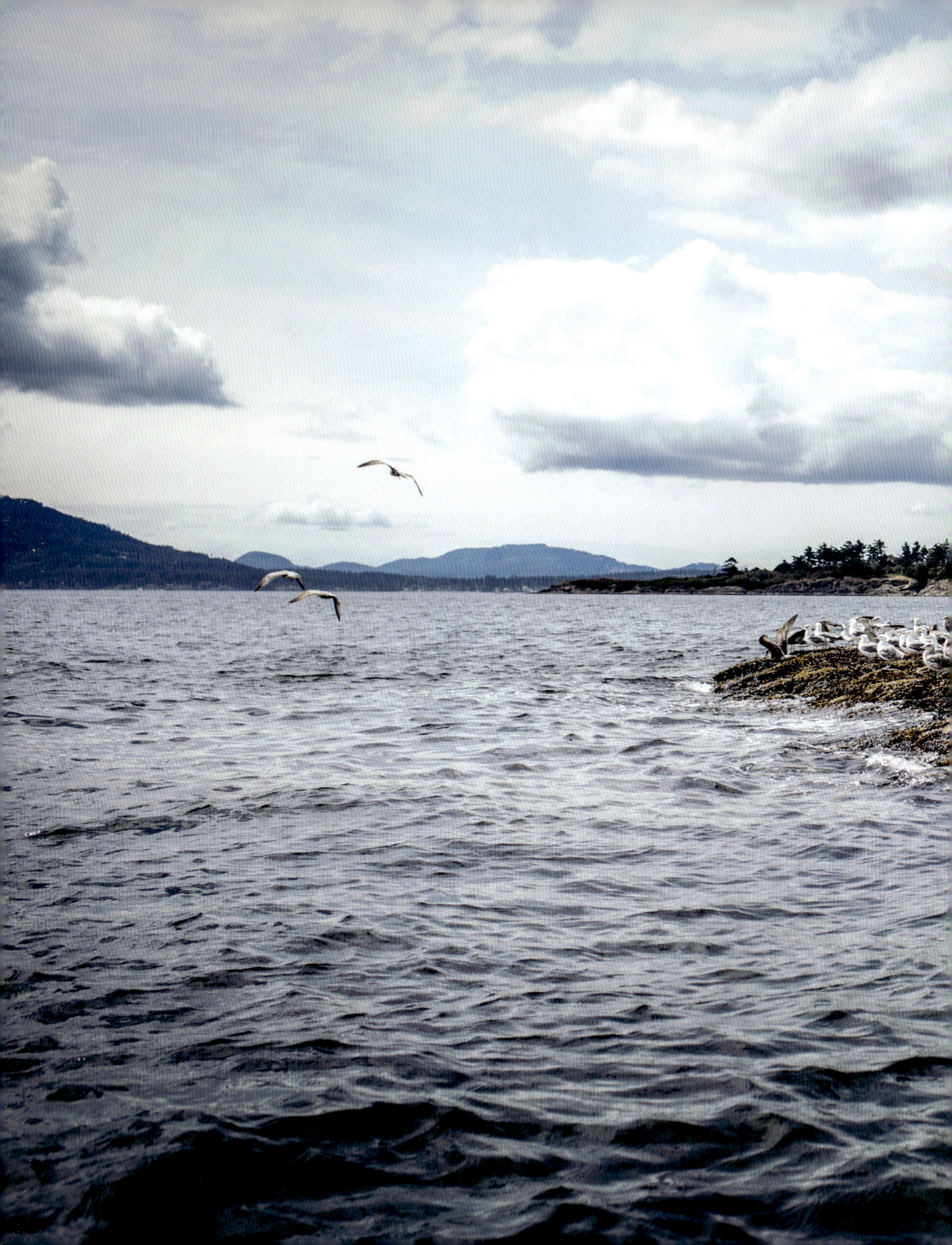

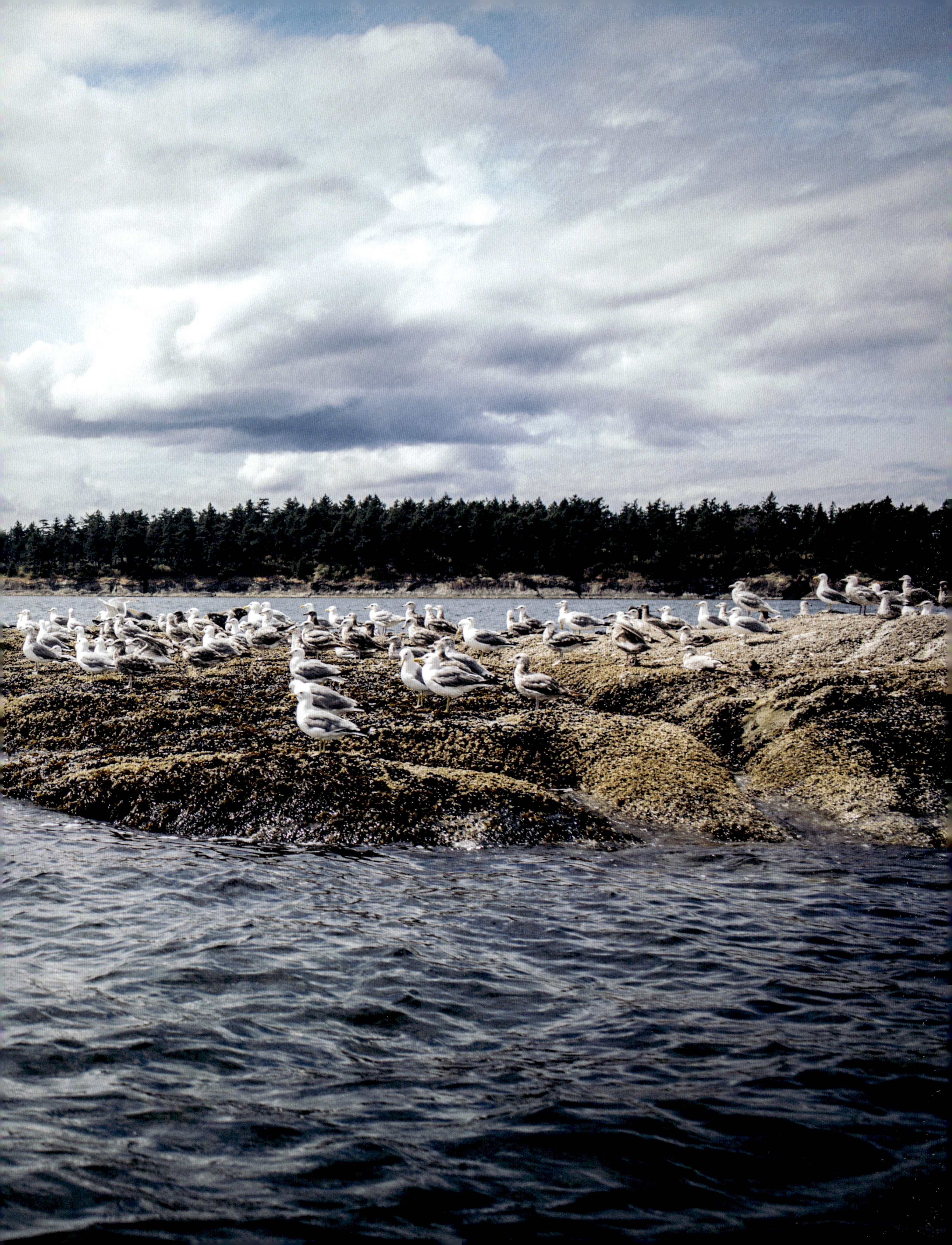

On the other side of the narrow arm of the island is Prevost Harbor, which is not as well protected. There are no stores or restaurants aside from an honor-system souvenir stand that has some hand-printed T-shirts: you can take one and mail payment when you get home. The local schoolhouse has just a few students per year and shuts down in years when not enough families stay the winter.

JONES ISLAND

Famous for its tame wildlife, Jones Island (also a state park) has hiking trails that will bring you passed deer with no fear of humans. More wildlife abounds here, but don't expect the eagles and blue heron to let you get close. The forest of *Madrona* trees has a rich red color and well-marked paths. *Madrona* trees have a peeling bark and stretch out over the water on steep shorelines throughout the area. Their outside layer is ashy white and, as this bark peels away, it reveals a reddish-brown; below that is a dense, harder trunk that is light grey-brown. There are several mooring balls for visitors to stay on while they explore the island. If the moorings are all taken, anchoring is possible but tricky, in a tight spot with large tidal range, so don't stray far from the boat.

ORCAS ISLAND

Orcas Island's Eastsound is known for an afternoon thermal breeze that gives lovely smooth sailing among the forested hills and mountains. Sail right into Cascade Bay to find Rosario Resort—off the beaten path, tucked into a cozy wilderness anchorage. Stepping into the Moran Mansion at Rosario takes you back in time to the early 1900s. Built by a wealthy shipbuilder, the mansion features collections of photographs and model ships that make it as much a museum as part of a leisure resort. The mansion is open to the public for self-guided tours a few days per week; concerts are performed in the impressive music room on a 1913 Aeolian organ featuring 1,972 two-story tall pipes.

The spa at the resort is a welcome respite for sailors, especially if you hit some cooler rainy weather (and this can happen any day of the year in the San Juans). Staying at the marina gets you a discounted spa access, and you can sit in soothing hot water overlooking the temperate evergreen shores. A cozy restaurant in Eastsound offers water views and serves classic north-west fare: hearty and honest food that features local ingredients and plenty of fresh seafood. Locally caught oysters, venison, and regional Washington wines will definitely invigorate your spirits.

~

This is a sailing destination that stands out for its wilderness and the people who have carved a living out of the landscape. The layered trunk of the *Madrona* tree, which grows only on this coast, provides a perfect metaphor for a sailing location that has hidden wonders around every serpentine corner. Rarities abound here; under every veneer of this landscape is another discovery and, for those willing to take the time to go deeper, there is always more to find.

THE INTERTIDAL ZONE

As the ocean ebbs and flows each day, it gives curious wanderers the opportunity to explore the intertidal region. This land is neither the ocean floor, nor does it belong to the islands, but supports a unique ecosystem of species that have adapted to the constant "dunking and drying out." Plants, animals, and even lichen, live in this dynamic area and they can be observed closely on a stroll along the water's edge at low tide.

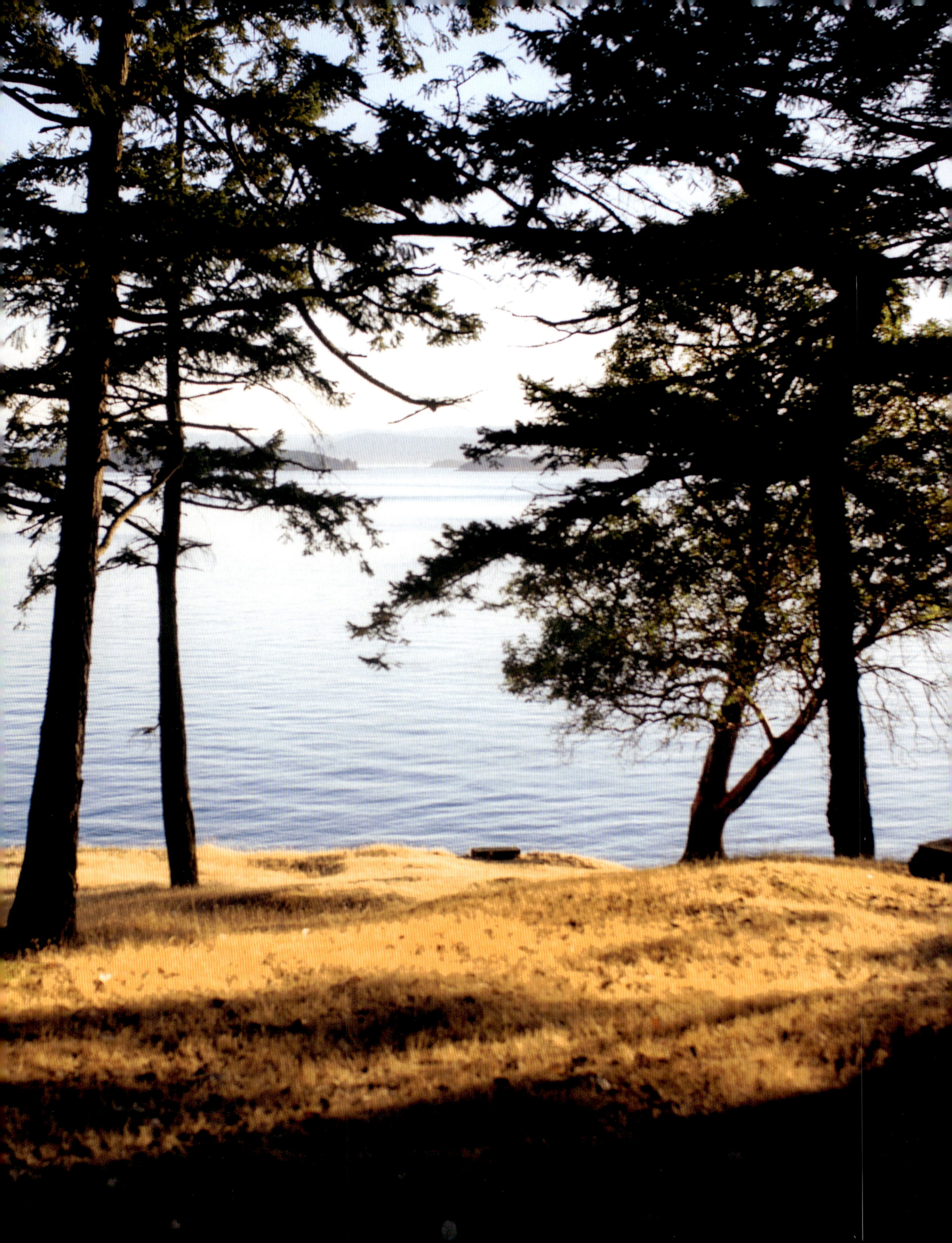

CAPTAIN'S NOTES *SAN JUAN ISLANDS*

RECOMMENDED ITINERARY

Friday Harbor, San Juan Island
48° 32'13"N, 123° 00'48"W
The protected marina at Friday Harbor has ample dock space and offers easy walking access to downtown Friday Harbor. The San Juan Island Yacht Club is located onshore with facilities for transient mariners. Provisioning is available, and water and electricity are provided for yachts. Anchor or use the laid moorings to the north and to the east of the port.

Sucia Islands
48° 45'40"N, 122° 53'37"W
The state park campground on Sucia is only accessible to those who have their own boats to get them there. Restroom and potable water facilities are available onshore in the summer months. There are numerous bays in which to anchor, with Echo Bay, located on the eastern side of the island, the largest. If the wind is blowing strong from the east, opt for Shallow Bay on the western side of the island.

Stuart Island
48° 40'14"N, 123° 11'30"W
Stuart Island has two bays. Reid Harbor is a long, mud-bottom bay with a little dock, protected from all sides and a good place in foul weather. Pevost Harbor, on the east side of the island, is protected by the neighboring Satellite Island. Both harbors are laid with moorings in their most protected areas.

Jones Island
48° 37'06"N, 123° 02'47"W
The state park maintains several mooring balls that you can take on a first come, first served basis. Anchoring here is more difficult, with little swing room and large tides; you need to know the local conditions intimately. The island is uninhabited but there is a small dock that can accommodate up to six small yachts docked port-or-starboard-to.

Roche Harbor, San Juan Island
48° 36'37"N, 123° 09'38"W
The well-appointed marina here has full amenities, including power, water, and pump out. A few restaurants, ranging from casual to more formal, give you options for dining out. Roche Harbor is also a US port of entry, where yachts can declare customs when entering US waters.

Rosario, Orcas Island
48° 38'47.4"N, 122° 52'14"W
Berth at the marina facility here for access to the resort restaurant and spa, located along the east side of Eastsound. Anchoring in Cascade Bay is difficult because of deep water. There are nine moorings laid outside the marina, but do not moor during southern wind, as the bay can become very choppy.

RECOMMENDED ANCHORAGES

Westcott Bay Shellfish Co., San Juan Island
Fossil Bay, Sucia islands
Marine State Park, James Island
Spencer Spit State Park, Lopez Island

ITINERARY DURATION

4+ days recommended

SEASON

Although the Pacific Northwest receives significant amounts of rainfall, there is a rainshadow effect from the windward mountain ranges on Vancouver Island that keeps this particular region relatively dry.

The best months to sail here are July and August. Hearty sailors continue into early October and brave the cold days. June tends to be rainy and foggy in a weather pattern referred to as the "June Gloom."

FOOD

The culinary scene in the Pacific Northwest is an earthy one. Chefs focus on seasonal and wild ingredients harvested from both sea and land. Visiting the markets you'll see a similar emphasis on what is local and what is ripe seasonally.

GOOD TO KNOW

Tides
Tides here have unusual complexities that make them hard to predict. The west coast of North America has mixed semidiurnal tides, meaning that there are two tides, of differing magnitude, each day. The Pacific Northwest, with its labyrinth of narrow deepwater channels and large freshwater rivers flowing down from the mountains, has a much more complicated tidal pattern, affected by local factors. Know that even the best tidal models are wrong occasionally, even under the best conditions, and the opportunity for error here is greater than normal.

Magnetic variance
Magnetic Declination: +15° (EAST)

Map of the San Juan Islands

STRAIT OF GEORGIA

SUCIA ISLANDS
FOSSIL BAY

PEVOST HARBOR

STUART ISLAND

REID HARBOR

ROCHE HARBOR

JONES ISLAND

ORCAS ISLAND

ROSARIO

WESTCOTT BAY SHELLFISH CO.

SHAW ISLAND

ROSARIO STRAIT

SPENCER SPIT STATE PARK

FRIDAY HARBOR

JAMES ISLAND MARINE STATE PARK

HARO STRAIT

DECATUR ISLAND

SAN JUAN ISLAND

LOPEZ ISLAND

VANCOUVER ISLAND

SALISH SEA

0 — 10
NAUTICAL MILES
NOT FOR NAVIGATION

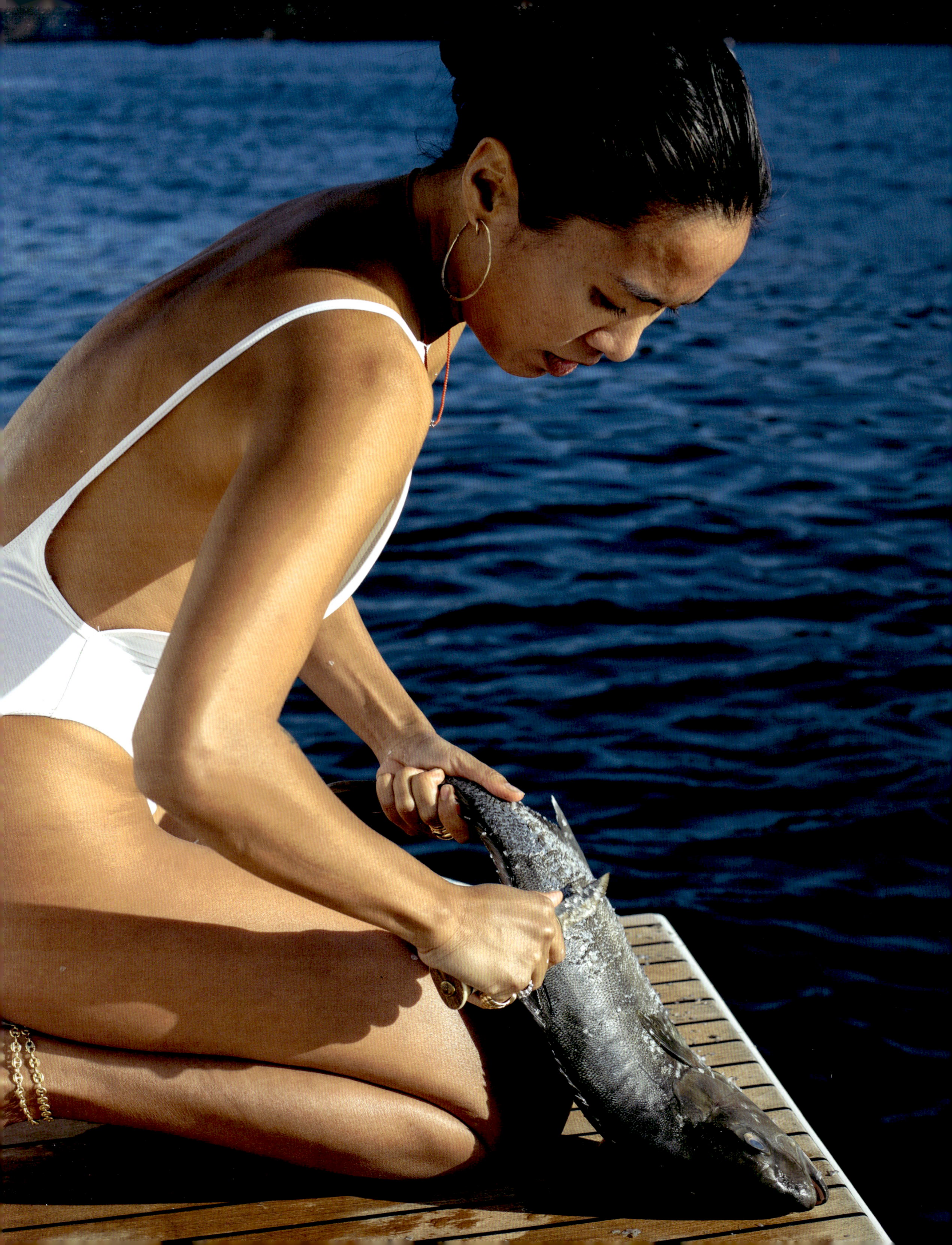

CALIFORNIA'S WILD ISLAND

CALIFORNIA IS A PLACE WHERE VAST OPEN SPACE FLOWS INTO GRIDLOCK TRAFFIC. YET JUST 20 MILES FROM THE MAINLAND, CATALINA IS A SPARSELY POPULATED ISLAND THAT LOOKS MORE LIKE GREECE THAN THE CITY OF ANGELS.

Row by row, the boats on the island of Catalina are aligned in an orderly grid throughout the island's many coves. Setting out beyond the harbor is to discover what the wilderness has to offer. The Channel Islands are a first taste of voyaging into the Pacific. California needs no introduction. Culture flows from here to the far reaches of the globe through music, art, film, politics, and style. Sailing culture along this golden coast is shaped by the vastness of the Pacific Ocean and the gold rush spirit with which Californians set out to enjoy it. Like surfers and skateboarders that characterize the Cali style, sailors here manage to be simultaneously laid back and extreme. It is multicultural and embodies a diverse population that has made its home in an arid mountainous landscape crested with valleys and sandy beaches along an expansive coastline.

Off this sprawling coast you can sail to Santa Catalina Island, a wild and beautiful paradise situated just 31 nautical miles from one of the largest sprawling metropolises in the world. The island is considered as a sanctuary by mariners and nature lovers alike. The string of islands that contains Catalina is called the Channel Islands, and the archipelago hovers close to the western horizon of the continental United States. You will be welcomed by fresh coastal air, endless sunshine, explorations ashore, and beautiful hiking options that all exist in a unique microclimate. Hues of orange light permeate the landscape during the summer months, and the island becomes a lush green color with blooming wildflowers throughout the winter season.

Catalina is 22 miles long and 8 miles across at its widest and its highest point reaches 2,097 feet at the summit of Mount Orizaba. Exploring this barren landscape during the dry season it feels like an arid Mediterranean island but, during the rainy season when the flowers are in bloom, the island is naturally vibrant. Today, there are wild bison grazing in the fields, palm trees lining the sandy beaches, and eucalyptus growing wild on the hilltops. The coastline is rugged but the inlets, coves, and harbors are inviting. Today Catalina Island has a population of roughly 4,100 people with nearly everyone living within the town of Avalon.

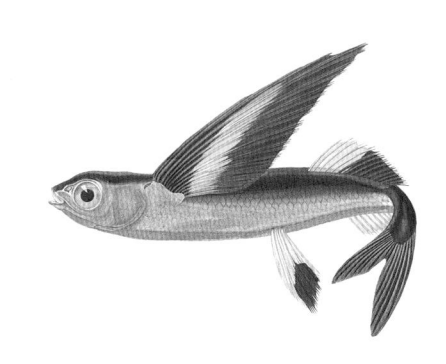

Sailing to Catalina takes four to six hours from any of the ports found in the Los Angeles greater area: Marina del Rey, Redondo Beach, Huntington Beach, Dana Point, and Newport Beach. You can also choose to cruise north from San Diego for a slightly longer journey offshore. The bay between mainland California and Catalina is often calm, and land is never out of sight when sailing to Catalina from the east. But, as with any voyage, weather conditions can change at a moment's notice. Upon arrival, use the mooring buoys owned and managed by the Catalina Island Conservancy who regulate the island's environmental state with strict regulations. Anchoring is permitted here, but you may have issues finding a place to set in between the massive mooring fields that fill the main harbors.

AVALON

Most people who know about Catalina know the town of Avalon and its long-standing history as a getaway from Los Angeles. Find it by sailing to the eastern edge of the island, it is the main entry point to Catalina Island and a popular port of call during a Catalina sailing itinerary. Entering the large harbor you will find hundreds of moorings located in the bay to be used on a first-come, first-served basis. While the town of Avalon is busy, the rest of the island is nearly uninhabited and remains untrammeled by development.

On your approach, standby at the harbor entrance and hail the harbor patrol boat over VHF radio. They will guide you in and assign the mooring based on your boat's size. Larger boats are assigned a mooring in deeper water, and smaller boats are placed nearer to the shoreline. The anchoring area for Avalon is located outside the breakwater just west of the Catalina Casino building, which is conspicuously located on the north side of the bay. The giant Casino is one of the most noticeable structures as it's built in a Mediterranean style Art Deco design: this isn't a gambling hall, it was named for the Italian use of casino as simply a gathering place. This building was a state-of-the-art construction in 1929 to show "talkies"—movies with sound were cutting edge technology—and host big bands in the enormous ballroom. The movie theater is still active, and if you're staying for multiple days, check the listings for a unique experience.

The brightly colored Green Pleasure Pier that extends into the bay can't be missed. The pier has a dinghy dock that offers easy access to town and the Chamber of Commerce and information visitor center sits right over the water with information and maps to guide you. There are about 20 restaurant options, a bait and tackle shop for fishing, and various local boat rental operations all within a few blocks right along the esplanade. From ashore,

> **Sailing onward after a stay in Avalon, you'll find yourself in a different landscape with rolling hills cascading into the Pacific Ocean.**

you can explore the charming town and have an insightful glimpse into the history and civilization of Santa Catalina Island. You can restock with provisions for the rest of your Catalina itinerary where you'll likely be sailing to uninhabited coves with nothing but swimming holes and wild beaches.

ISTHMUS COVE (TWO HARBORS)

Sailing onward after a stay in Avalon, you'll find yourself in a different landscape with rolling hills cascading into the Pacific Ocean. Located on the western side of the island, Two Harbors is a sailors' destination and home to roughly 400 moorings in the surrounding coves, a campground, a general store, and one restaurant. Two Harbors doesn't attract the number of visitors that flock to Avalon—it's a location that's truly geared towards sailors.

RIDING THE BOW DURING THE APPROACH TO CATALINA (ABOVE, LEFT). A VIEW OF CAT COVE (ABOVE, RIGHT). ONE OF THE HIKING TRAILS ON CATALINA (BELOW, RIGHT).

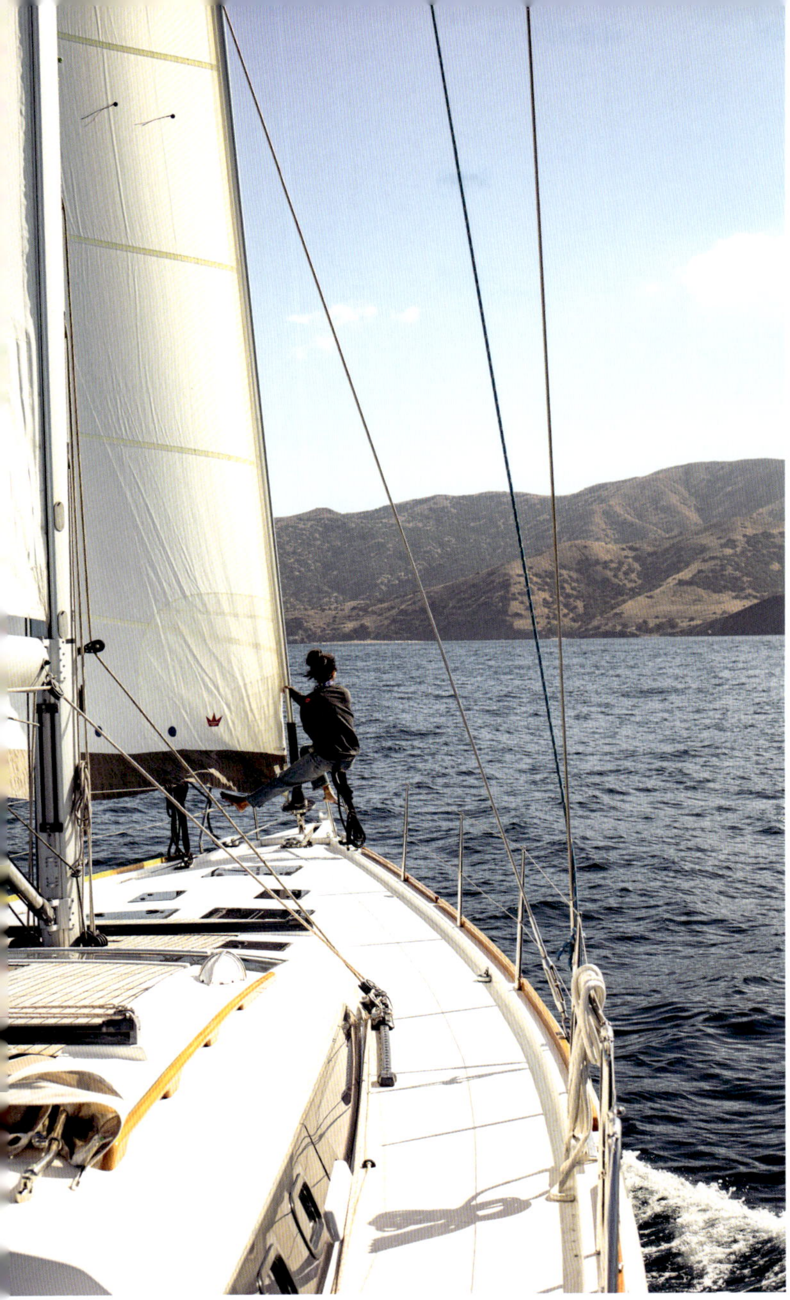
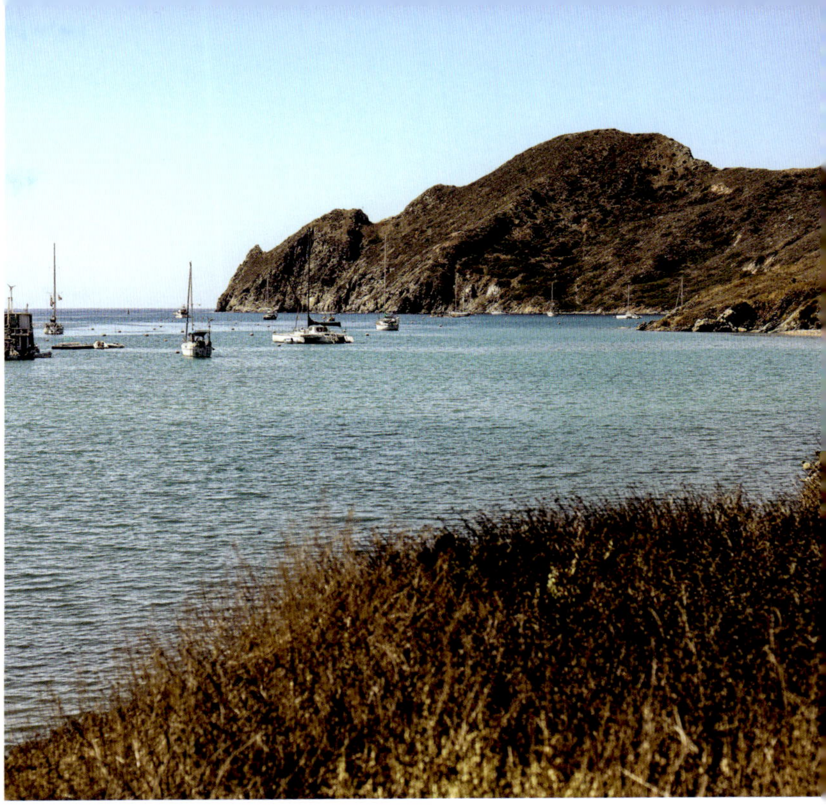
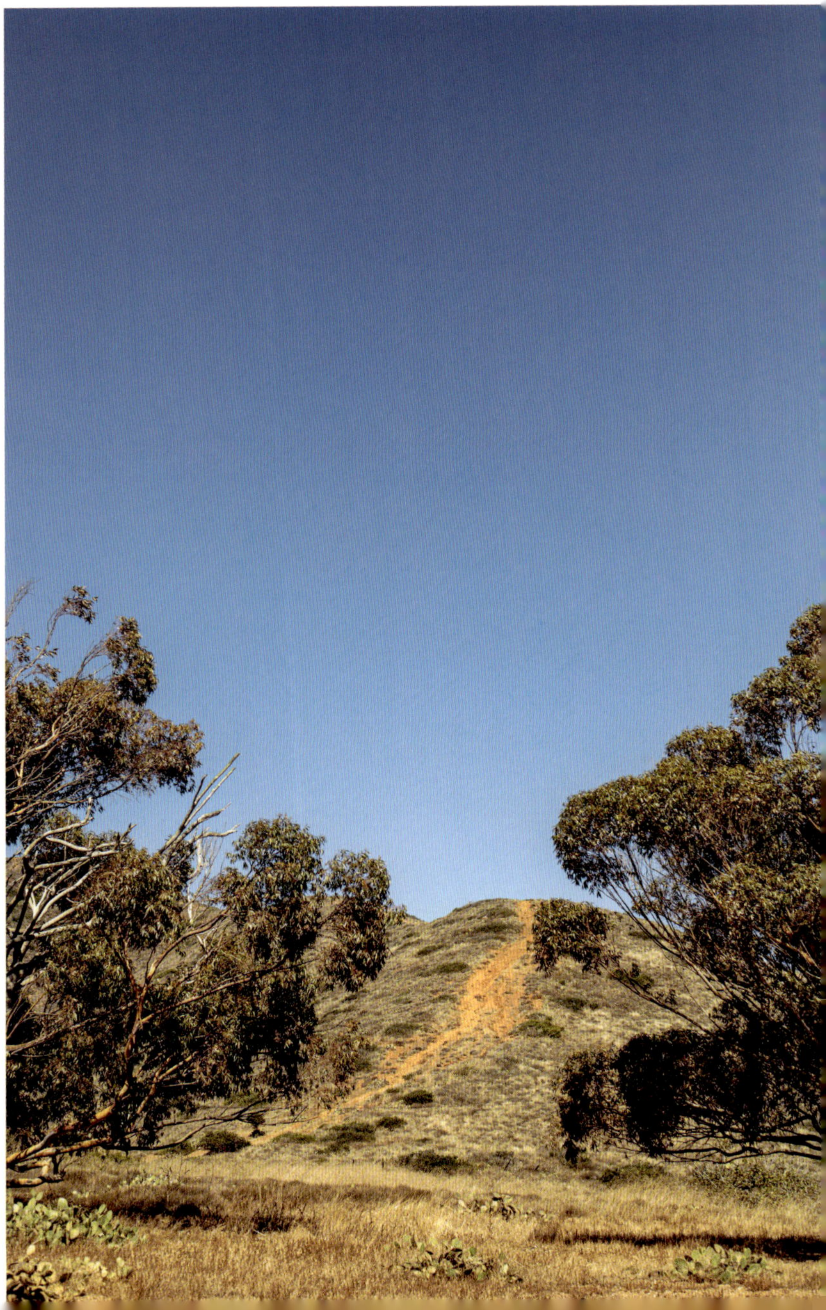
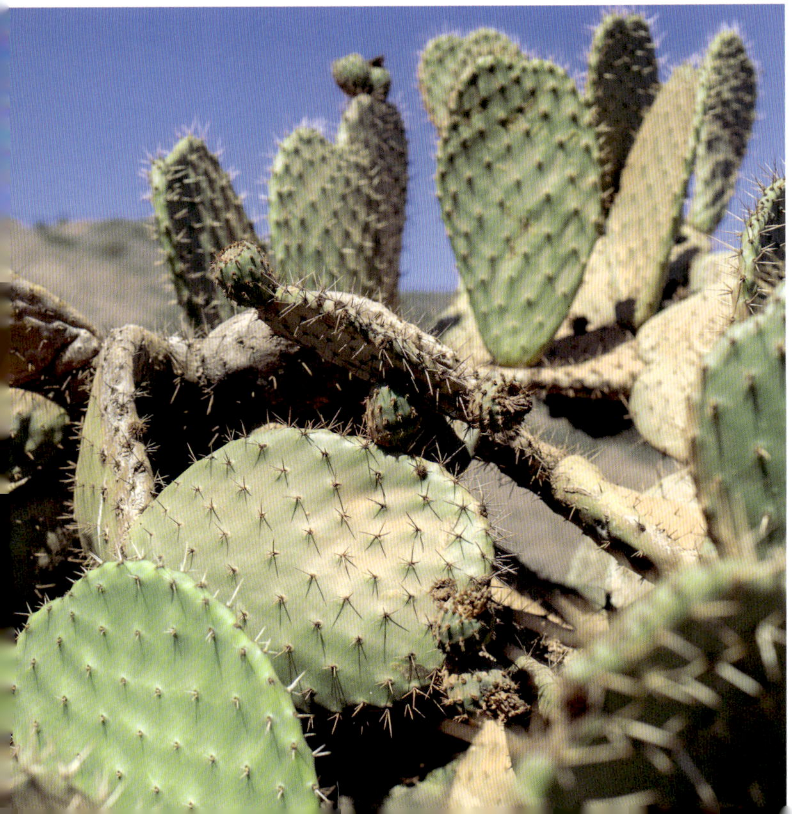

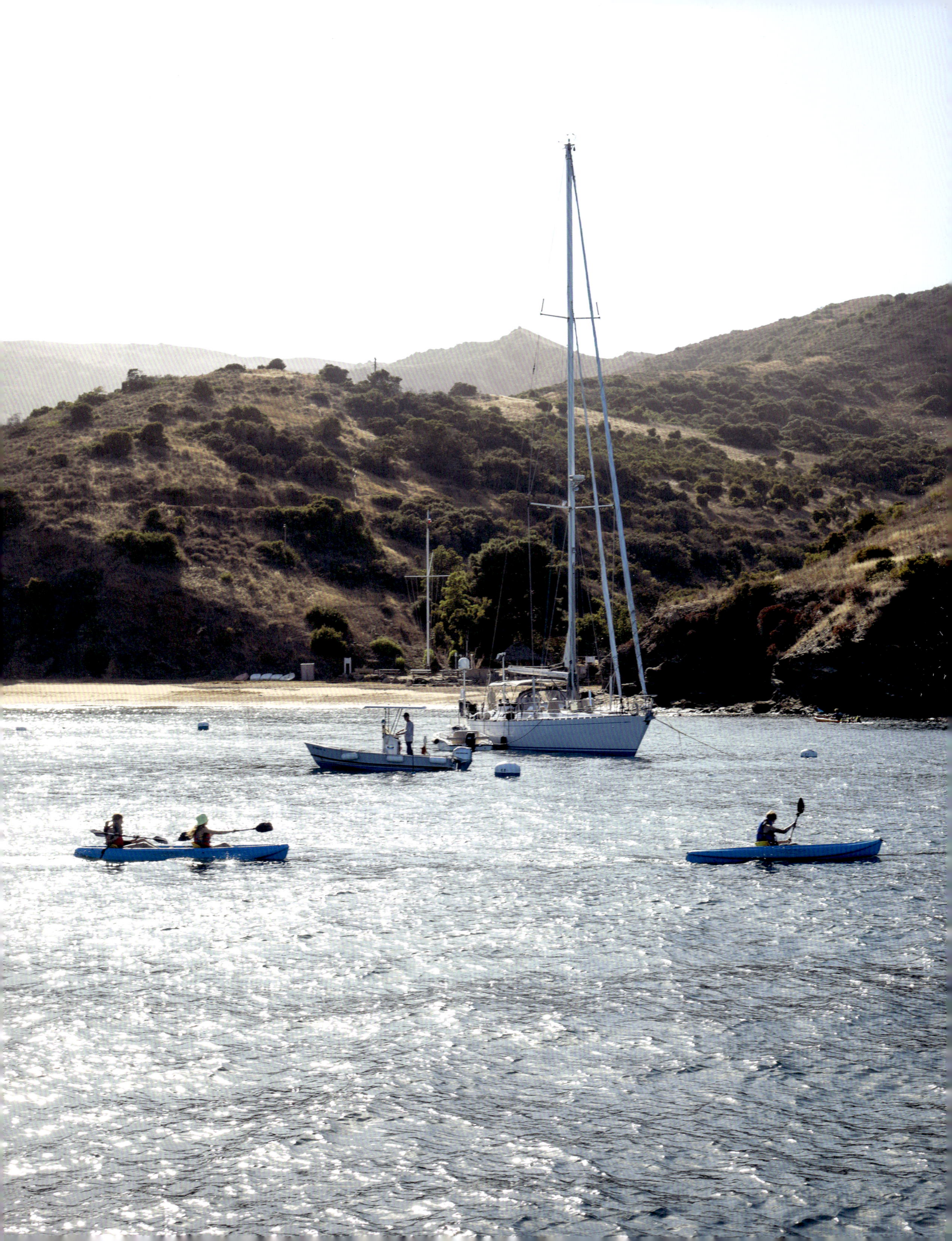

Isthmus Cove is one of the two primary destinations on Catalina Island, which is located on the northeast side of Catalina and protected from the westerly prevailing wind. Anchor directly in Isthmus Cove for easy dinghy access to the small town. Alternatively, there is a launch boat that will shuttle sailors to and from their boats to shore for a small fee. The anchorages sit between two arid and dusty hills. The moorings are situated with the bow and stern ties that keep moored boats facing the shoreline, and the stern facing towards the sea. The shore is lined with palm trees along the sandy beachfront, and the restaurant and its small shop are open to visitors year-round. You can reprovision food and find local wine that's produced on the island.

FOURTH OF JULY COVE

Another welcoming mooring field pleasant for an overnight anchorage is Fourth of July Cove. Located between Cherry Cove and Two Harbors, it supplies 42 moorings in a deep water anchorage that allows boats to enjoy the cove in depths of around 100 feet. It's a short dinghy ride to Isthmus Cove—a small, oblong bay that sits roughly 300 feet into the land with a slanting, inclined pebbly beach. The hillside that slopes steeply from the valley is covered in a local shrub called *adenostoma*, an evergreen that has small leaves with clusters of flowers sprouting from the branches.

Home to the Fourth of July Yacht Club, a private association with club facilities built along the shoreline. Although much of the island has been made into public managed land by Catalina Island Conservancy, there are still many private regions. The members-only Fourth of July Yacht Club is not open to the public. Sailors can use the moorings in this cove overnight, but to go ashore you need an invitation from a club member.

Regardless of the exclusive nature of the onshore facilities, Fourth of July Cove is a splendid anchorage and the yacht club ashore paints an old-world Americana setting that can be enjoyed from your boat. The shoreline surrounding the harbor is rocky, offset by the cliff that jets up to the ridgeline. This is a beautiful location for snorkeling and, depending on the season of your voyage, you can swim from the back of your boat all along the shoreline.

EMERALD COVE

This secluded cove is one of the unparalleled natural gems of Catalina Island. Located a few nautical miles from Two Harbors, Emerald Cove is accompanied by a beautiful sandy beach and boasts world-renowned snorkeling and diving. Emerald Bay has 102 moorings with an anchorage that's located southeast of Indian Rock and large enough for five to ten boats, depending on the weather conditions. Like the other mooring fields on the island, when making the approach, hail the harbormaster on your VHF radio to tell him your location and the patrol boat will come to your boat to assign a mooring ranked for your sailboat. Dinghy ashore to the sandy beach and enjoy the numerous hiking trails located in the cove.

CABRILLO BEACH

Sail to Cabrillo Beach when you want to spend a night in a quiet cove. It's is a beautiful anchorage located in a dramatic setting. Designated as a boat-in campground, sailboats can anchor off the beach and kayaks can reach Cabrillo from Avalon or Two Harbors. Located between Rippers Cove and Goat Harbor, Cabrillo Beach is immediately east of Little Gibraltar Point, which is recognizable by the steep hillside that sits behind a rocky inlet. There are no moorings here and the cove is moderately protected from the west/northwest, making it best suited for anchoring in prevailing westerly conditions. With room for only five or so sailboats at a time, Cabrillo Beach offers an alternative overnight setting that's away from the busy mooring-laid harbors.

The beach is mostly cobblestone, with some sand near the water's edge. With an abundance of fish, snorkeling in the cove is highly recommended. If Cabrillo Beach is too crowded to drop anchor, the next cove towards the east with a suitable anchorage is Goat Harbor. It's less protected than Cabrillo Beach, so be sure to check the weather forecast before deciding to anchor for the night.

CATALINA HARBOR

Opposite Isthmus Cove sits Catalina Harbor, or "Cat Harbor," as the locals call it. This is arguably one of the most strikingly beautiful anchorages in Southern California. Two Harbors is located at the base of a valley with two mountains towering above on either side. Being the narrowest part of the island, you can walk from Catalina Harbor to Isthmus Cove in about ten minutes by following a dusty dirt road that's lined with fragrant eucalyptus trees.

Cat Harbor is on the western side of the island, and Lobster Point jets towards the sea with the mouth of the harbor facing south, opening towards Outer Santa Barbara Passage. The harbor is protected from the prevailing winds and sheltered by the point. A dramatic rocky cliff not only protects the harbor from heavy seas but also shelters it from any high wind. The water is a light aqua color that matches beautifully with the reddish-orange arid soil that's found on the island. You can see wild American bison roaming the fields near the cove. In 1924, some 14 buffalo were left on the island after being used in a movie scene that was shot on the island. Today there are approximately 150 living on the island, monitored by the Catalina Island Conservancy.

~

The island's accessible location from mainland California makes a Santa Catalina Island sailing itinerary as easy as it is enjoyable. With an abundance of moorings properly maintained by the Catalina Island Conservancy, overnights are easy and accessible. For sailors interested in finding their own adventure, hidden coves with suitable anchorages are scattered throughout the island. Going ashore to explore the towns and hike along the mountain ridges is an essential part of the sailing itinerary. Beaches are located along most anchorages and home to world-class snorkeling and dive opportunities. A Catalina itinerary could be as short as one night or as long as a week. Regardless of how long you stay, it's a perfect sail to step outside the hum of Los Angeles.

CATALINA ENVIRONMENTAL LEADERSHIP PROGRAM

Created by Jean-Michel Cousteau's Ocean Future Society and the Catalina Island Camps, CELP is a part of a global environmental education program with a location on Santa Catalina Island. The camp focuses on environmental and outdoor educational programs for students of grades four through 12. CELP is dedicated to environmental stewardship and sustainability education. Its location is in Howlands Landing, a camp location since the 1920s and a CELP since the 1990s.

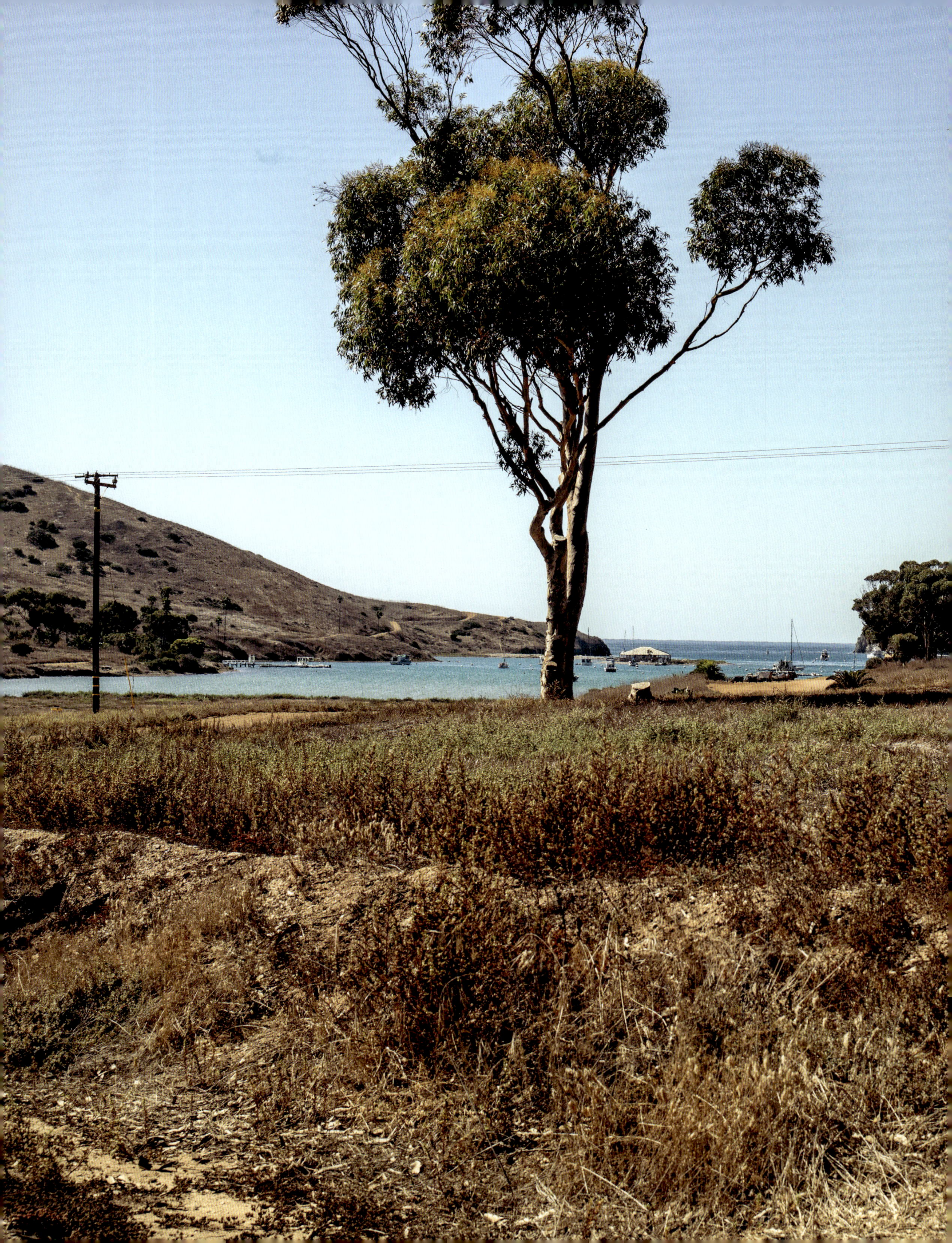

CAPTAIN'S NOTES *SANTA CATALINA ISLAND*

RECOMMENDED ITINERARY

Avalon
33° 20′45″N, 118° 19′26″W
Avalon has the largest mooring field on the island, with 315 moorings laid in the harbor. During the summer months, the harbor is packed with boaters and advance reservation is recommended. Hamilton Cove, Descanso Beach, and Lover's Cove all have laid moorings and are in close proximity to Avalon. The bay is protected from all except northeast wind.

Isthmus Cove (Two Harbors)
33° 26′34″N, 118° 29′44″W
Moor using the 249 laid moorings located here. The cove is protected from westerly and southernly winds and exposed to the north and east winds. Anchoring within the mooring field is prohibited and yachts can anchor at the entrance of the bay. The harbormaster will assign a mooring to you upon your approach. Mariners should have the boat registration numbers available before radioing in.

Catalina Harbor
33° 25′40″N, 118° 30′33″W
This is the most protected harbor on the island and often referred to as a "hurricane hole," where mariners can take safe refuge during gale-force wind. There are 99 moorings laid in the harbor and room for up to 200 boats to anchor. A dinghy dock can be found on shore and a launch service will shuttle sailors from the shore to the mooring field.

RECOMMENDED ANCHORAGES

Emerald Cove
Cherry Cove
Fourth of July Cove
Shark Harbor
Wells Beach

ITINERARY DURATION

3 days recommended

PREVAILING WIND

Prevailing winds are north and west, with a westerly breeze being the most common. Wind can clock around and blow from the northeast often during the summer months, in a weather pattern known to meteorologists as a Catalina eddy, or coastal eddy. This spiral weather pattern is caused by strong winds blowing from offshore and low-pressure winds blowing from the coastal south. The Catalina eddy can bring cooler weather and fog.

SEASON

May through September is the high season, with water temperature the warmest in mid-summer. Southern California's mild year-round weather allows for mariners to cruise Catalina Island at any time, though temperatures can drop during the cold winter months.

FOOD

Catalina Island fishing is legendary, with schools of mackerel, sardines, and smelt. Larger fish such as yellowtail and white seabass also live in the waters. The sight of any of these fish on a Catalina menu is a sign of fresh and locally caught seafood. Look out, also, for Catalina spiny lobster.

GOOD TO KNOW

Moorings
All of the coves and harbors on Catalina use the same mooring system. Boats are to be secured on the bow and stern of the boat and each mooring has both a bow and stern weight, with the bow hawser connected to the stern hawser by the spreader line. Each mooring has a pick-up pole and a boat hook is not required. The pick-up pole is attached to the bow hawser by the eye-loop. When approaching the mooring, be sure to have the crew on the bow to firmly tie the bow hauser to the bow cleat. The spreader line is attached to the eye-loop. Once the bowline is secure, walk the spreader line to the stern of the boat and secure the stern hawser to the stern cleat.

Local fauna
Urocyon littoralis catalinae (the Santa Catalina island fox) has been resident on the island for at least 5,400 years and is a subspecies found only here, as is the Santa Catalina Island harvest mouse (Reithrodontomys megalotis catalinae)—another species monitored by the non-profit Catalina Island Conservancy. Other species to look out for are mule deer, American bison, and California ground squirrel.

Magnetic variance
Magnetic Declination: +12° (EAST)

N W E S

EMERALD COVE
CHERRY COVE
FOURTH OF JULY COVE
ISTHMUS COVE
CABRILLO BEACH
WELLS BEACH
CATALINA HARBOR

SHARK HARBOR

SANTA CATALINA ISLAND

AVALON

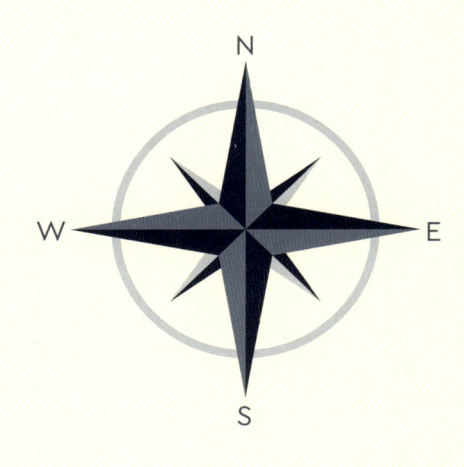

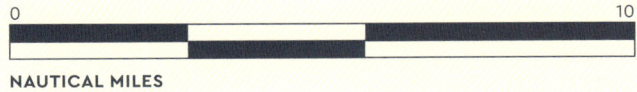

SAN PEDRO CHANNEL

NORTH PACIFIC OCEAN

SANTA BARBARA PASSING

0 — 10
NAUTICAL MILES
NOT FOR NAVIGATION

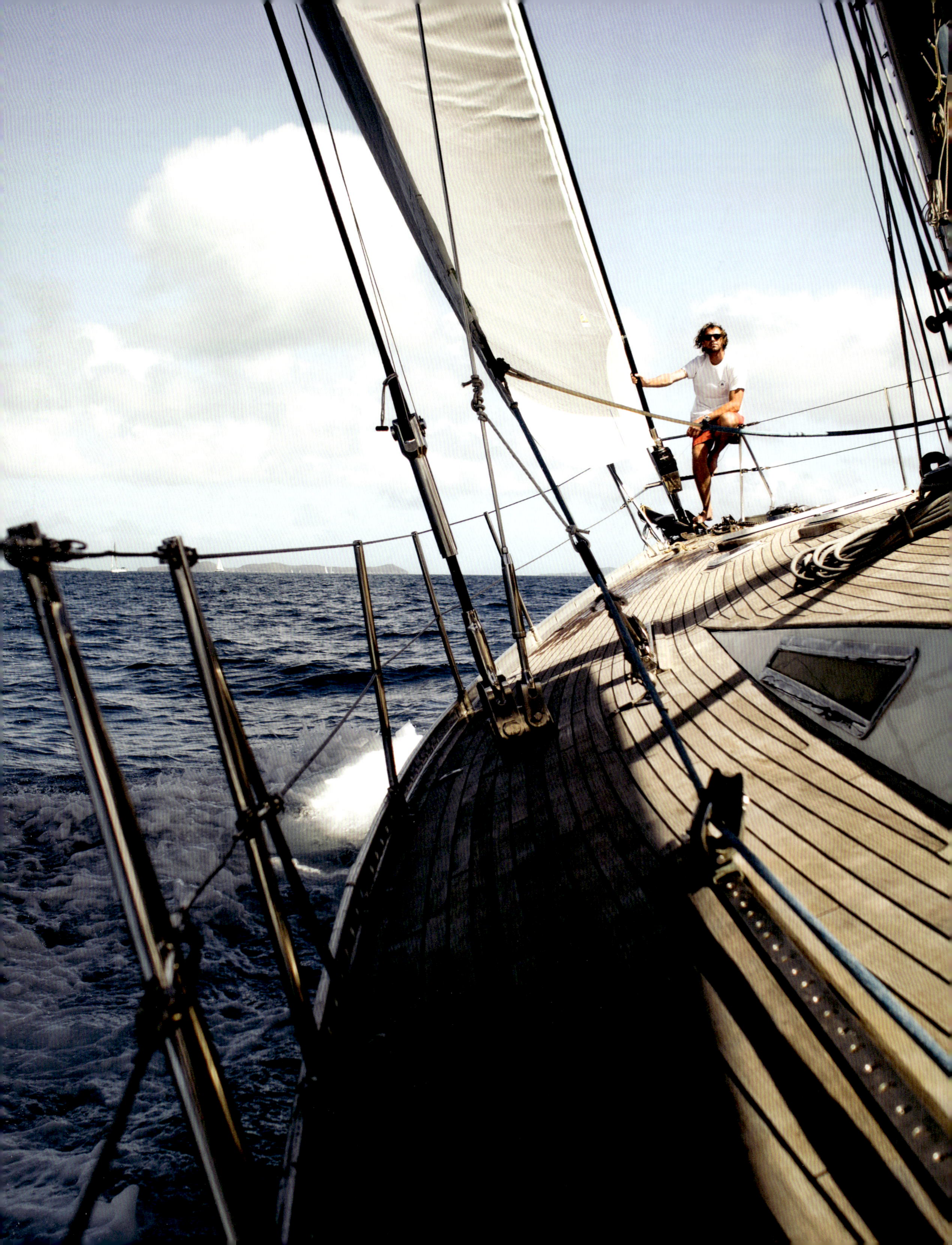

A SAILOR'S PARADISE IN THE TRADEWINDS

A VOYAGE TO THE POPULAR CHARTER DESTINATION OF THE BRITISH VIRGIN ISLANDS IS ALL ABOUT COMPANIONSHIP, CAMARADERIE, AND SHARING STORIES WHILE SAILING FROM ONE RUM SHACK TO THE NEXT.

If the Caribbean strung together is considered a sailor's paradise, the British Virgin Islands deserve a special category of praise for their role in earning that reputation. In a small area relative to much of the Caribbean lie a group of islands with nearly flawless sailing conditions for any mariner cruising in the archipelago. Sailing here is a lifestyle; the winds blow from the east all winter and rarely change direction, so the navigation is dynamic yet simple with easy passageways that do not cause a fuss when sailing. You can't tack without missing a rum bar perched along a beach. With inviting anchorages scattered throughout the islands, it is accessible to new sailors and a favorite of experienced old-timers.

The island of Tortola is at the center of the cluster, with roughly 30 surrounding islands extending to Anegada in the north and stretching southwest to Norman Island. The greater archipelago includes not just the BVI but also the United States and Spanish Virgin Islands, which extend westward towards Vieques and south to Saint Croix. Differing from many Caribbean nations which are comprised of a single main island like Martinique or Dominica, the BVI is a cluster of smaller islands. This gives cruisers the ability to find coves in any direction with ease. Over the years, sailing charters have developed into a prominent business, providing easy access to rental boats for competent skippers.

These Virgin Islands are no strangers to the seafaring life. Dating back to the early civilizations that inhabited this land some 3,000 years before Christopher Columbus dropped anchor off Saint Croix, the Ciboney, Igneri, Taíno, and the Kalinago settled these islands and sailed the waters. Columbus named the Virgin Islands after the patron saints of maritime navigators Saint Ursula and her martyred maidens: *Santa y las once mil virgenes*. Though the artifacts remaining from the pre-Columbus era are limited, it's safe to assume that many of the anchorages, hikes, and snorkeling areas that sailors still voyage to were frequented by pre-Columbian people, and much of this land has remained naturally unchanged, appearing just as it has for thousands of years.

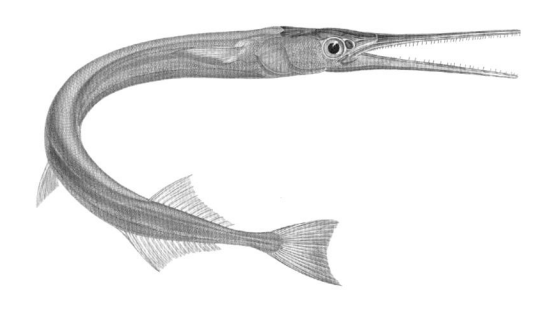

DEPARTING

As one of the most regularly sailed itineraries worldwide, there's no right or wrong way to plan your voyage. The abundance of islands clustered with such close proximity allows for sailors to sail with the wind conditions in the spirit of the moment. Some skippers will take their crew through a circumnavigation of Tortola while others will zig-zag, jumping from island to island—Norman Island and then to Marina Cay, North Sound, on Virgin Gorda, and then sail south to Cooper Island. The ability to choose your own adventure is one of the pleasures of the BVI. Most of the prominent marinas are located on the south coast of Tortola, which is a common location to start your charter. Road Town is the main harbor and the capital of Tortola, home to most of the provisioning and supplies for sailors cruising the region.

After departing, there are two common options for beginning a sailing itinerary—downwind towards Norman Island or upwind towards Virgin Gorda. Both routes offer great sailing, so it comes down to what a skipper and crew decide is best for the overall flow of the voyage.

NORMAN ISLAND

One of the famed islands here is Norman Island—home to the infamous floating bar Willy T's, which was situated in its largest cove called The Bight until the permanently anchored ship sank in 2017 during the unprecedented devastation of Hurricane Irma. Now reborn on a new vessel, the bar is known for its abundance of sailors who can be seen arriving by dinghy and tying up alongside. Willy T's attracts all sorts, and on any given day you might see people casually in absurd costumes, dressed formally for a dinner reservation at nearby Pirate's Bight, or perhaps jumping off the roof naked—all together enjoying an afternoon or evening drink as sailors do. Sailors will be sailors, a global community that stands for comradery—in BVI and the rest of the world. At Norman Island, most sailors will pick up a mooring in The Bight, but there are in fact six different coves you can anchor in depending on various weather conditions, with each one bringing something unique to the sailing experience.

SALT ISLAND

With all of these islands situated in such close proximity and with an abundance of coves for anchoring, the itinerary options are endless. If you don't care for the boisterousness of Willy T's, you can sail to Salt Island. Drop anchor on either the northern or western side of the island and dinghy to shore for land exploration. Most boats pick up a mooring on the western cove and swim on the Wreck of the Rhone, which is a sunken UK Royal Mail Ship from 1867, popular for both freediving and snorkeling.

One of the lesser ventured activities is hiking around Salt Island, which remains completely uninhabited other than a few families of goats that roam freely around the lush green fields. There's a goat path across the island that takes you from the salt pond to the southern point of the island, where there are unimaginably beautiful views of Cooper Island and the Caribbean Sea. Pelicans dive freely into the natural mangrove harbor, with the sound of goats rummaging nearby. As one of the quieter places in the group, Salt Island has many hidden corners to discover—look closely and you may even find a piece of ancient volcanic glass that exists from the island's early creation.

TORTOLA

Only during rare southerly wind conditions should you sail to Rogue Bay, a beautiful small cove on Tortola's north shore often unreachable from the large swell that wraps around the point during the prevailing easterly winds. When conditions are good, however, you can sail there, and visit the Lava Flow Beach, from any number of locations on

ISLANDERS NET-FISHING IN CANE GARDEN BAY, AMBERJACK ARE COMMON FISH CAUGHT USING THIS METHOD (ABOVE). LOBSTER BEING SORTED IN ANEGADA REEF (BELOW, RIGHT).

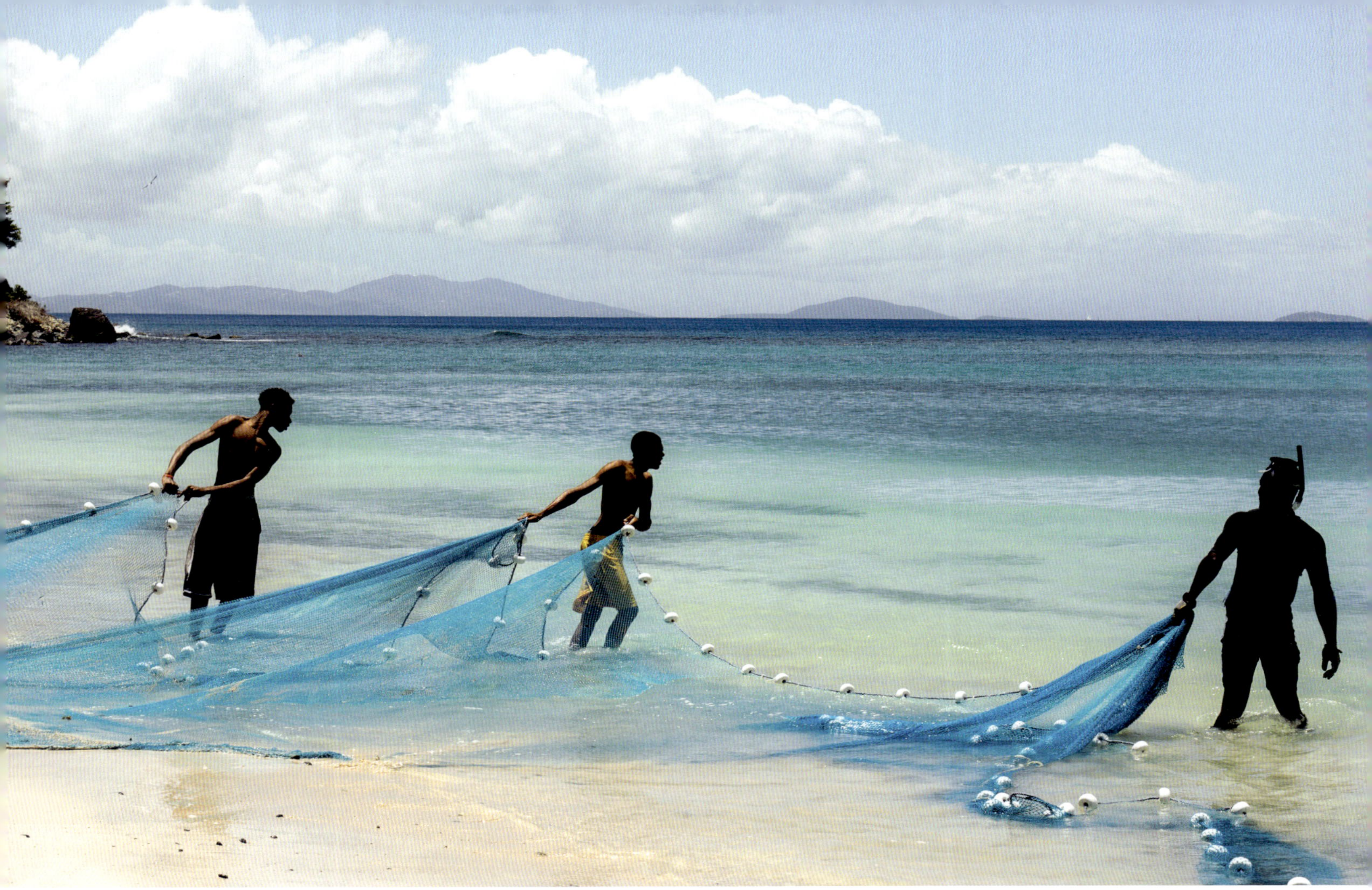
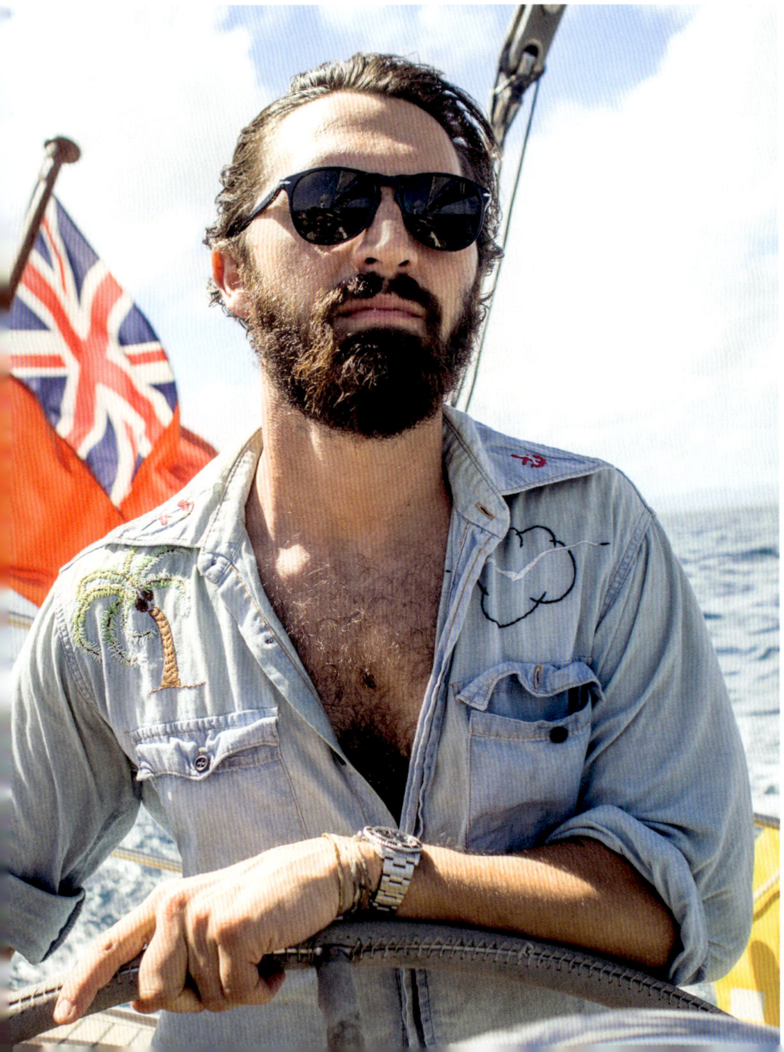
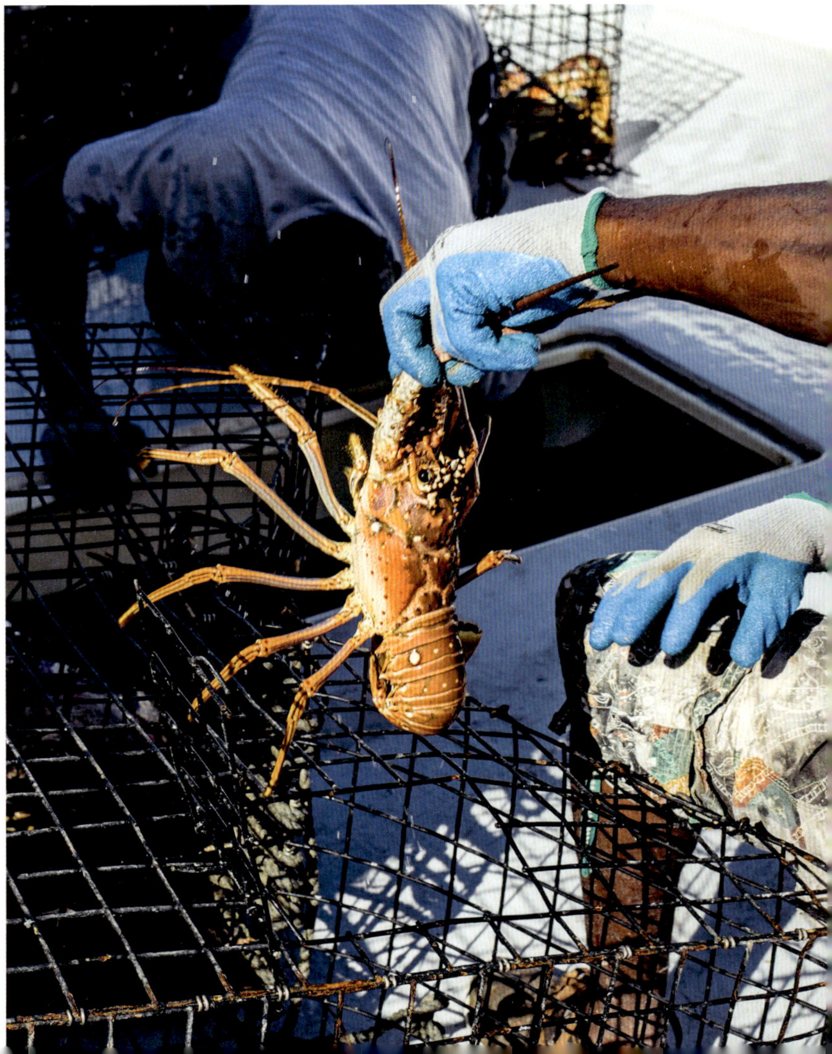

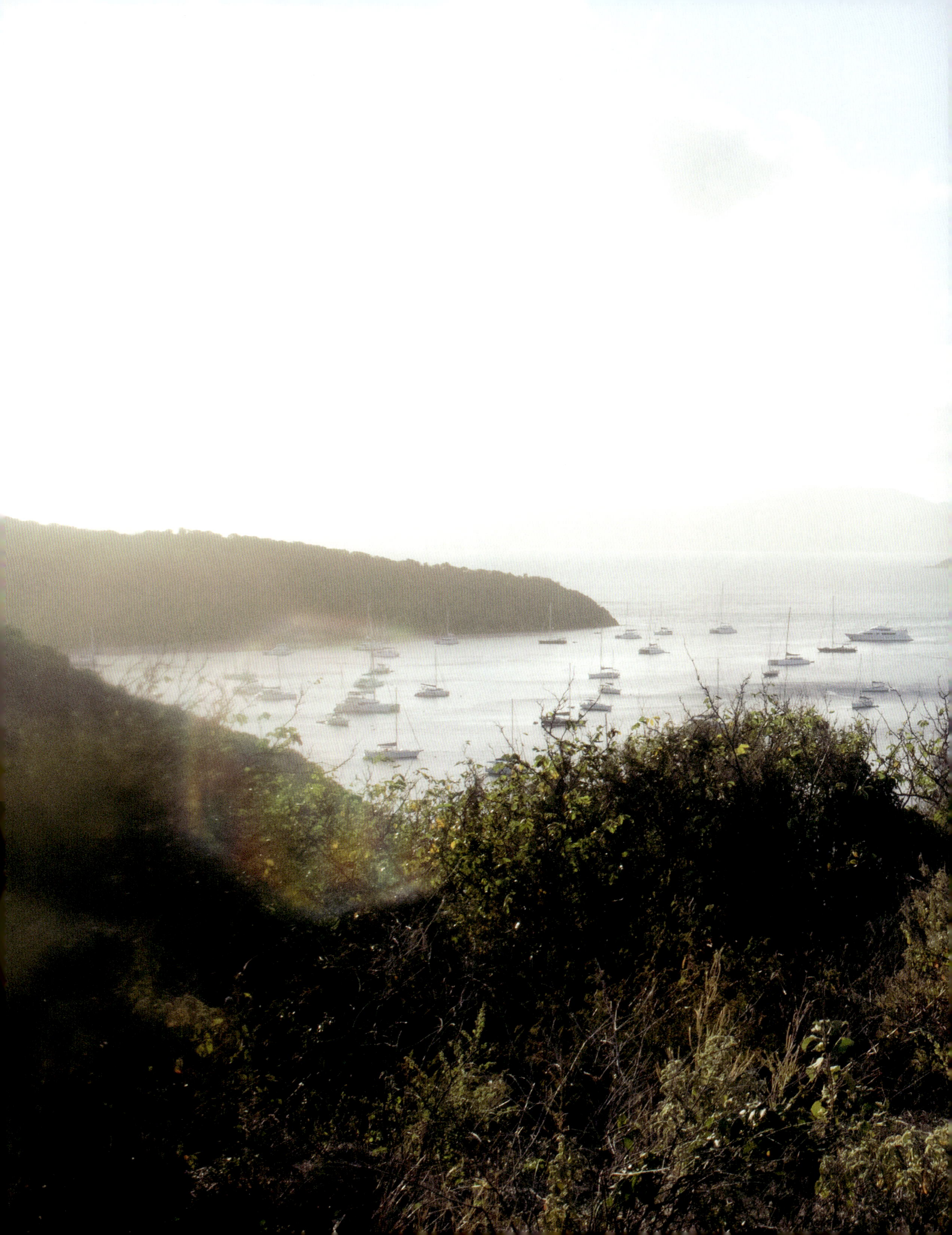

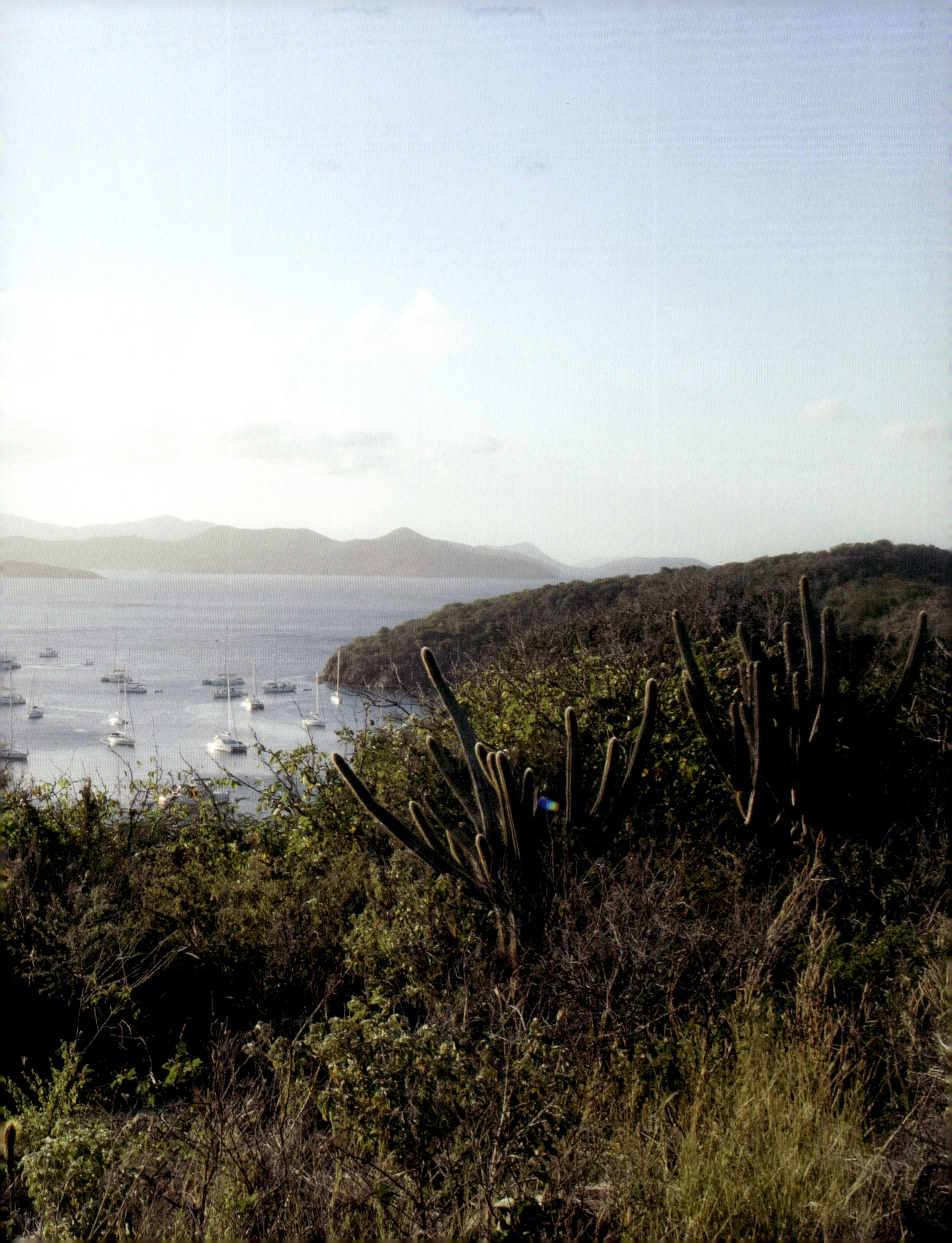

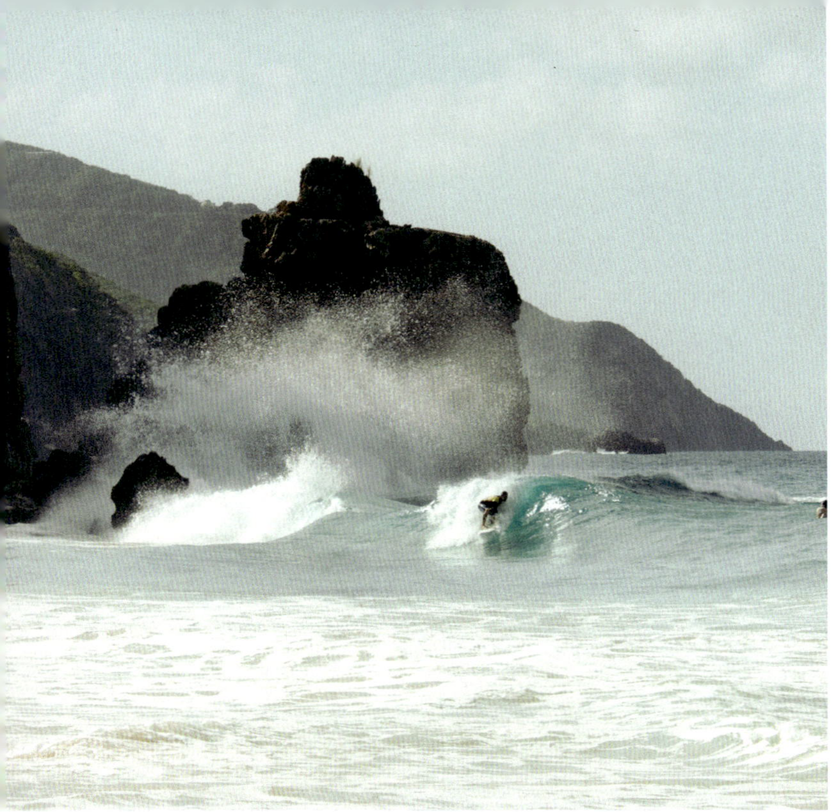

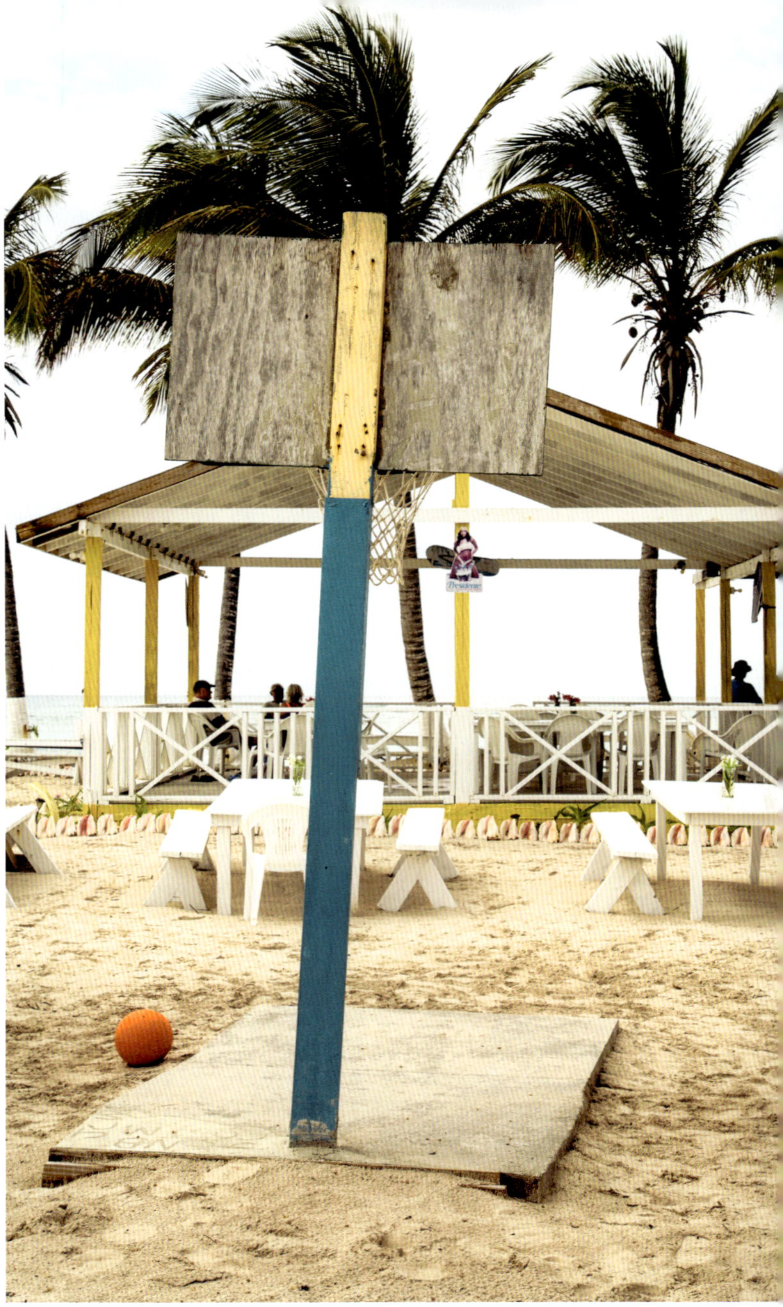

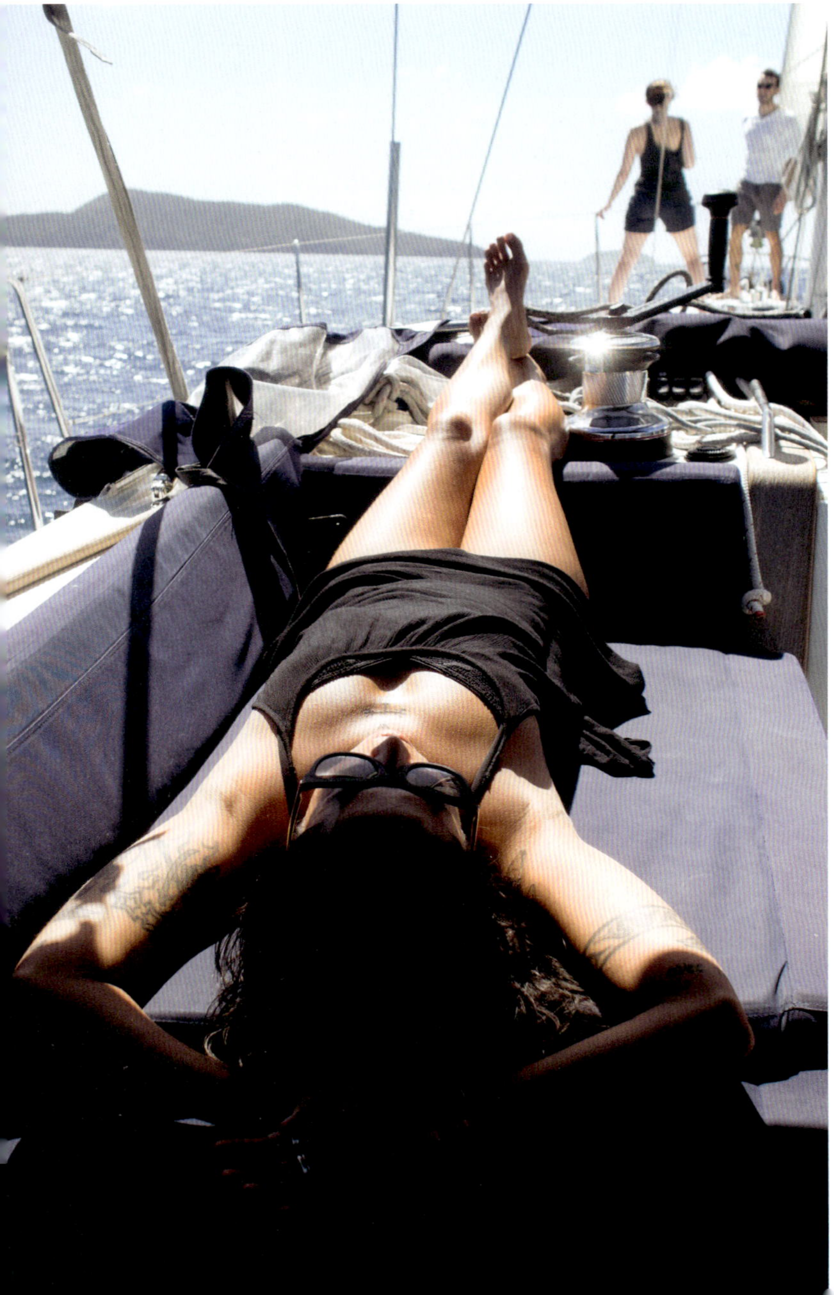

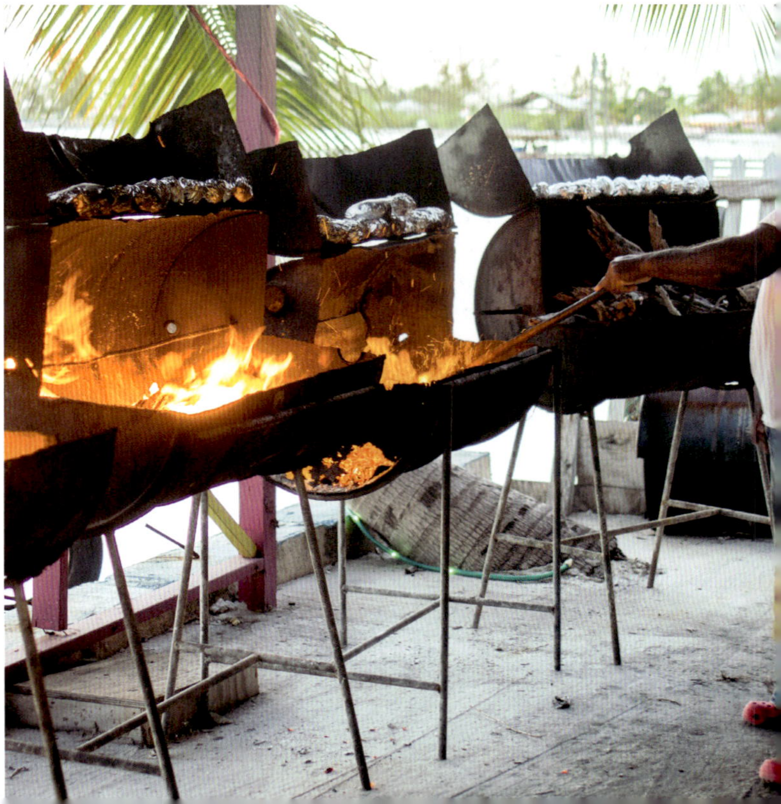

your itinerary. From Norman Island, you can sail north along the western point of Tortola, sailing past West End and continuing onward to Jost Van Dyke, the most north-westward inhabited island. From Jost Van Dyke, Lava Flow is only 12 nautical miles. Alternatively, sailing from Norman Island towards Lava Flow, you could decide to sail northwest up the Sir Francis Drake Channel, rounding Beef Island and making the passageway by Great Camanoe and Guana Island.

The beach in the bay called "Lava Flow" earned its name with locals because of ancient black volcanic rocks that "flow" from the hillside to the white sandy beach and into the water. This spot is one of the best hidden surf beaches on Tortola. From land, you can only access the beach by hiking down a steep wooded path and boats can only anchor on extremely calm seas. It's a beautiful sight by boat, but be careful if you decide to dinghy or swim ashore, as the slope of the sand along the shoreline is steep and the waves will barrel even in a light groundswell. After landing ashore successfully, you'll be greeted by soft white sand that your feet will sink into with every step, creating the nicest foot massages. Palm trees line the beach, with a tropical wooded area just behind them. There's a high probability that you could be the only person there, or maybe just accompanied by a few people who also know of this hard to access secret beach. Looking back at the boat peacefully resting at anchor, you might have an overwhelming feeling of satisfaction in knowing that you've done the right things in life in order to end up exactly where you are.

ANEGADA

The northernmost island in the archipelago requires more sailing time, usually on a pleasant beam reach, depending on which island you set out from. With the trade winds blowing normally, leaving from Gorda Sound offers the nicest tack. Anegada is unlike the others. In a chain of mountainous volcanic islands, Anegada was formed by a coral reef and is just a few meters above sea level at its highest point. Hurricanes have been known to completely wash over the whole island.

Large in land mass but low in elevation, Anegada has a completely different feel to it with flamingos wading in the mudflats and a white-sand shoreline that goes uninterrupted for miles. There is only one good harbor on Anegada and it's only good when it's good; being exposed to the south, the anchorage can become rolly aboard your vessel during the evenings. Even the island ferry dock—the locals' only access on and off the island—goes out of service in strong southerlies.

Most sailors will spend their evenings anchored off of Setting Point, which offers an easy dinghy ride to numerous lobster shacks and local restaurants. A lesser explored anchorage west of the main harbor is Pomato Point, a shallow sandy location away from the restaurants and home to an endlessly pristine beach with typically only a few sailboats surrounding it. Pomato Point can be affected by wrap-around swell so stick to settling for overnights unless you have a moderately calm sea in the forecast.

ANEGADA'S NORTH

Anegada's northern coast is not accessible by sailboat, but is well worth a visit. From the anchorage, dinghy ashore and hop in the back of a local pickup truck rigged up with bench seats to bring people around to the myriad of lovely beaches on the reefy north side. Cow Wreck Beach on the north coast got its name from a barge transporting cows wrecking on the outer reef here and the apparent cow skeletons you could see while snorkeling on a calm day. Needless to say, they serve a great hamburger, and on a good day their billiards table is level enough to get a game playing barefoot with what must be one of the best views for a billiard's table anywhere in the world.

SURFERS IN ROGUE BAY DURING THE CHRISTMAS WINDS (ABOVE, LEFT). THE IDYLLIC RUM SHACK AT COW WRECK BAY, ANEGADA (ABOVE, RIGHT). LOBSTERS ON THE GRILL AT POTTER'S BY THE SEA (BELOW, RIGHT).

MICHIGAN
YARE
GREAT LAKES 86
BOMBA'S
SURF SIDE SHACK
YOU WANT to KEEP
DRINKS
Piña Colada
Virgin Colada
Xmas

THE SHACK WAS B 1976 OLD SCHOOL

J-2076

bomba's shack

GAS, GRASS OR ASS
NOBODY RIDES FOR

For THE MONTH
OF SEPTEMBER
Extended Happy Hour
Friday + Sunday
4pm-8pm
3 Beers for $7
3 Mix
T-Shi
2 fo
1 fo

Bomba doesn't drink alcohol so he don't wanna mingle inside

KEYSTONE STATE
PMF ONE
PENNSYLVANIA

MCH 449
MINNESOTA

MICHIGAN
STROHS
GREAT LAKES

you Have
to carry new
to be a m
Bomba Do
Have to do
that. I talking
Gre yo Dog

WISCONSIN
2BOMBA
America's Dairyland

O MOON
America's Dairyland

KWY-5
ISCONSIN

UTAH
477 ZP

PENNSYLVANIA
LANCEX
WWW.ST TE.PA.US

Bomba
ain't get
Panties
For X-Mas
or New
Years, So
Ladies Make

JOST VAN DYKE

Sailing southwest from Anegada roughly 25 nautical miles, just a short hop from Tortola's west end is Jost Van Dyke, one of the most emblematic of all the islands in the region. Culture seems to flow from here to the other islands and you'll see this island's signature style emulated elsewhere in the form of signed t-shirts and flags hanging from driftwood rafters of the local establishments or signature cocktails, but the authenticity of it all here is unmistakable. Foxy's music bar sits on one end of the sandy main street that runs along the water in Great Harbour. Most nights, the party spills out into the street and onto the beach as the dance floor at Foxy's attracts sailors like flies to honey.

White Bay, just to the east of Great Harbour, has all of its action during the day. Ashore is the famous Soggy Dollar Bar, named because dinghies are not allowed on the beach so sailors traditionally swim ashore for a drink. It's been around long enough that Soggy credit card wasn't an option, although they happily accept them today. Soggy Dollar is home to the 'Painkiller' cocktail, invented here by the owners who produce them with great efficiency for the hordes of day-trippers coming over from nearby Saint John and clearing customs for the day. For a more mellow vibe, wander down the beach and over the small rocky bluff in the middle to Ivan's Stress Free Bar—if there is no one behind the bar you are welcome to make your own drinks and leave some cash in the till.

Around the far side of Jost to the west sits a protected anchorage where you can set out on a hike to the Bubbly Pool, a neat geological feature when there is a northerly swell for the way that waves crash into a narrow inlet, making for an aerated shallow-water lounging pool just beyond the thundering rollers. If the sea is too big this feature becomes unsafe, so heed local warnings before going in and don't try to swim out to the ocean.

While the route options are endless, it's the innate camaraderie of sailing here that brings the Virgin Islands to life. Whether it's sharing a fresh catch with fellow boats nearby, a Frenchman teaching a fellow sailor his boat-bread recipe, or a casual conversation between captains about favorite surf breaks over rum at a beachside shack, the Virgin Islands remain a meeting point for the world's sailing community. It's a place where there is more interest in this mode of travel and the experience of seeing the world by way of water than almost anywhere else. Chances are, if you have sailed in the Virgin Islands, you'll be returning. Most do. With its paradise white sandy beaches, abundant National Parks, and vibrant turquoise waters, this Caribbean archipelago is a place that calls visitors to come back. A sailor could cruise the BVI a hundred times and still find new coves to tuck in and enjoy.

THE PAINKILLER COCKTAIL

The Painkiller is a native island drink with disputed origins. Many established in the Islands have claimed to be its creators, including the Soggy Dollar Bar on Jost Van Dyke.

Recipe: 2 oz. rum
4 oz. pineapple juice
1 oz. orange juice
1 oz. cream of coconut
Grated fresh nutmeg
Pineapple wedge garnish

ANCHORED OFF SETTING POINT, ANEGADA. THE WATER COLOR IS UNLIKE ANYWHERE ELSE IN THE BVI. WHERE MOST OF THE ISLANDS ARE VOLCANIC, ANEGADA IS A LARGE SANDY REEF THAT STRETCHES OVER 20 MILES.

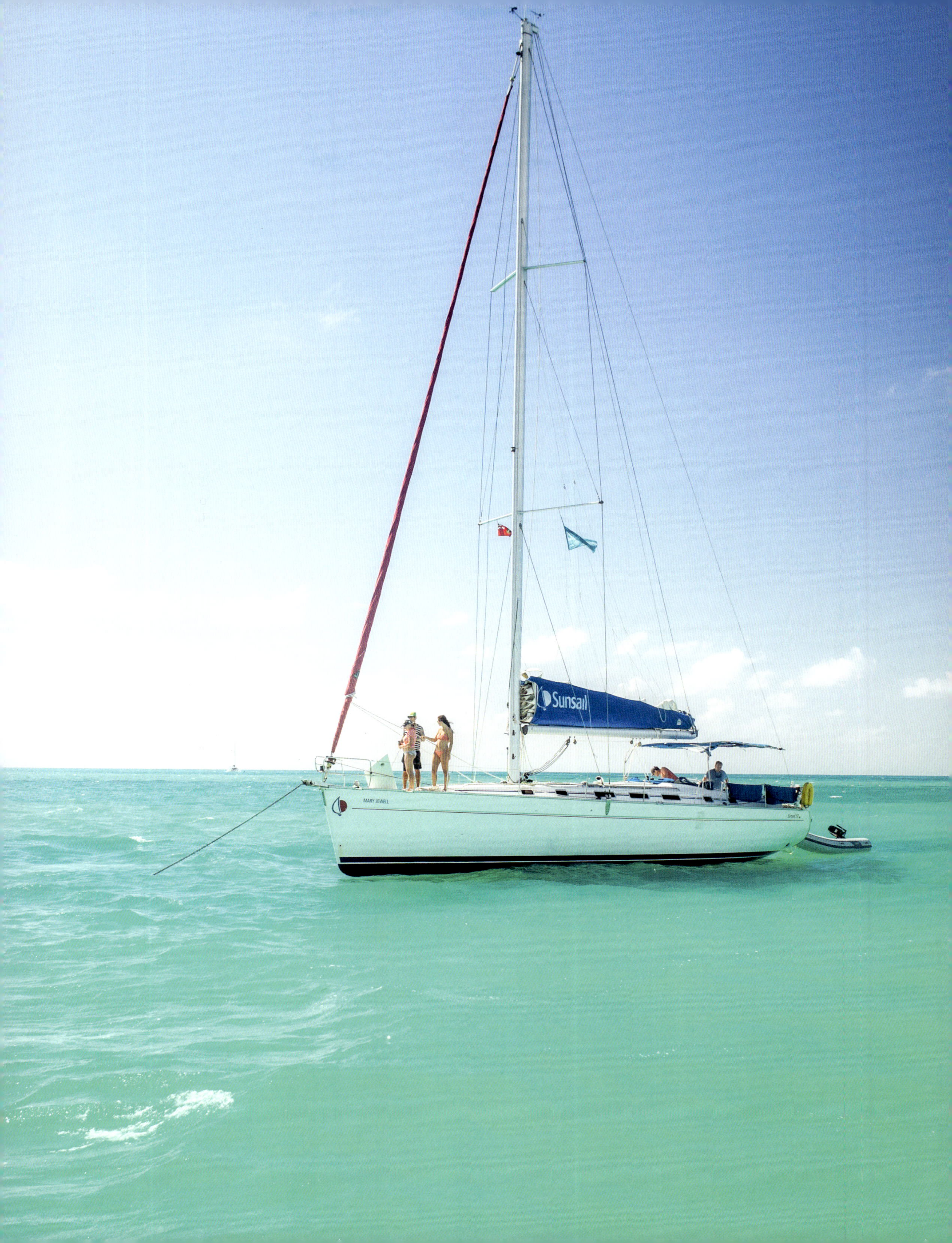
Sunsail
MARY JEWELL

CAPTAIN'S NOTES *BRITISH VIRGIN ISLANDS*

RECOMMENDED ITINERARY

Setting Point, Anegada
18° 43'22"N, 64° 23'02"W
Follow the channel markers closely towards the anchorage in Setting Point, as there are shallow reefs on either side of the channel. After rounding the final buoy, use the laid moorings or anchor, keeping a close eye on the depth. The seafloor is light sand and depth can shift from year to year. Be sure to swim on your keep to be sure you have enough clearance with the seafloor. Expect your keep to be 30–60 centimeters from the seabed.

Manchioneel Bay, Cooper Island
18° 23'10"N, 64° 30'54"W
Moor using the laid buoys. There are 30 guest moorings that accommodate vessels up to 18 meters. The moorings tend to be full by 12 noon and 15 orange buoys at the south end of the bay can be reserved in advance. The seas in the bay are consistently calm though strong gusts of wind can reach up to 50 knots, often in the evening. The Cooper Island Beach Club offers a coffee shop, microbrewery, rum bar, dive center, and a beachfront restaurant.

The Bight, Norman Island
18° 19'5"N, 64° 37'14"W
Moor in a large bay protected from the easterly prevailing wind. There are approximately 76 buoys available in The Bight, with approximately 17 more located in Privateer Bay and Soldier Bay together. The Bight's center is very deep and with poor holding, but there is good anchoring on the south and western edges of the bay.

Great Harbor, Jost Van Dyke
18° 26'24"N, 64° 45'03"W
Moor using the designated buoys located in the harbor. There are 30 moorings available and 15 moorings are reservable and managed by Foxy's bar. Larger boats can anchor outside the mooring field and other yachts should not anchor within it due to poor holding and limited space. Anchor in three meters of sand located along the southwest entrance of the bay, keeping clear of the reef along the shore.

White Bay, Guana Island
18° 28'22"N, 64° 34'38"W
Moor in White Bay using the 11 designated mooring buoys managed by Guana Island resort. The bay is protected from southerly and easterly winds and mariners should avoid this bay during a northern swell, as the bay can become very uncomfortable. Anchoring is not recommended as there are many dead coral heads. Larger yachts can anchor past the mooring field.

Savannah Bay, Virgin Gorda
18° 27'43"N, 64° 26'01"W
Anchor inside the reef along the yellow sand beach in the lagoon. This is one of the lesser-explored anchorages in the archipelago and offers a quiet and calm overnight stay. The entrance of the lagoon is not marked and mariners should make the approach slowly and during daylight.

RECOMMENDED ANCHORAGES

Devils Bay, Virgin Gorda
North Lee Bay, Fallen Jerusalem Island
Little Harbor, Peter Island
Manchioneel Bay, Cooper Island
Rogues Bay, Tortola
Prickly Pear Island
South Bay, Great Dog

ITINERARY DURATION

7 days recommended

PREVAILING WIND

The trade winds are fairly consistent, blowing from the northeast direction with a moderate breeze of force 3 to 4. Winds during the winter months (referred to as the "Christmas" winds) tend to be stronger, reaching near-gale and, occasionally gale-force wind.

SEASON

Sailing is best from December through May. Hurricane season begins in June and goes through November, though many sailors still cruise through the islands at this time. For the Hurricane season, most boats are taken out of the water and put on dry dock.

FOOD

This island once had a productive salt pond facility that shipped salt as an export until the mid 1970s. Even today, during certain periods when the salt pond is dry, you can scrape up the island's salt which is still harvested in small batches.

GOOD TO KNOW

Volcanic origins
Most of the British Virgin Islands were formed volcanically and it is easy to sail between them on a line of sight with good visibility of the mountains rising out of the sea. Anegada in the north is the exception and is a low lying reef-formed island. When you set sail for Anegada it will be below the horizon and your first glimpse of it will be the tops of palm trees that line its southern shore.

Magnetic variance
Magnetic Declination: +12° (EAST)

British Virgin Islands Map

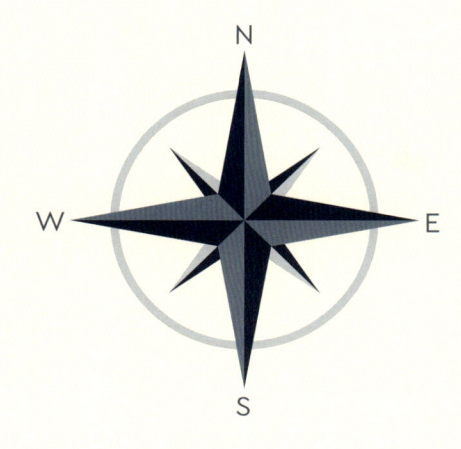

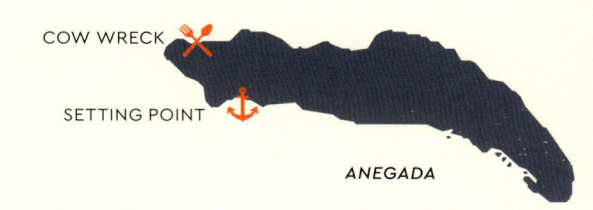

N / W / E / S (compass rose)

Anegada
- Cow Wreck 🍴
- Setting Point ⚓

NORTH ATLANTIC OCEAN

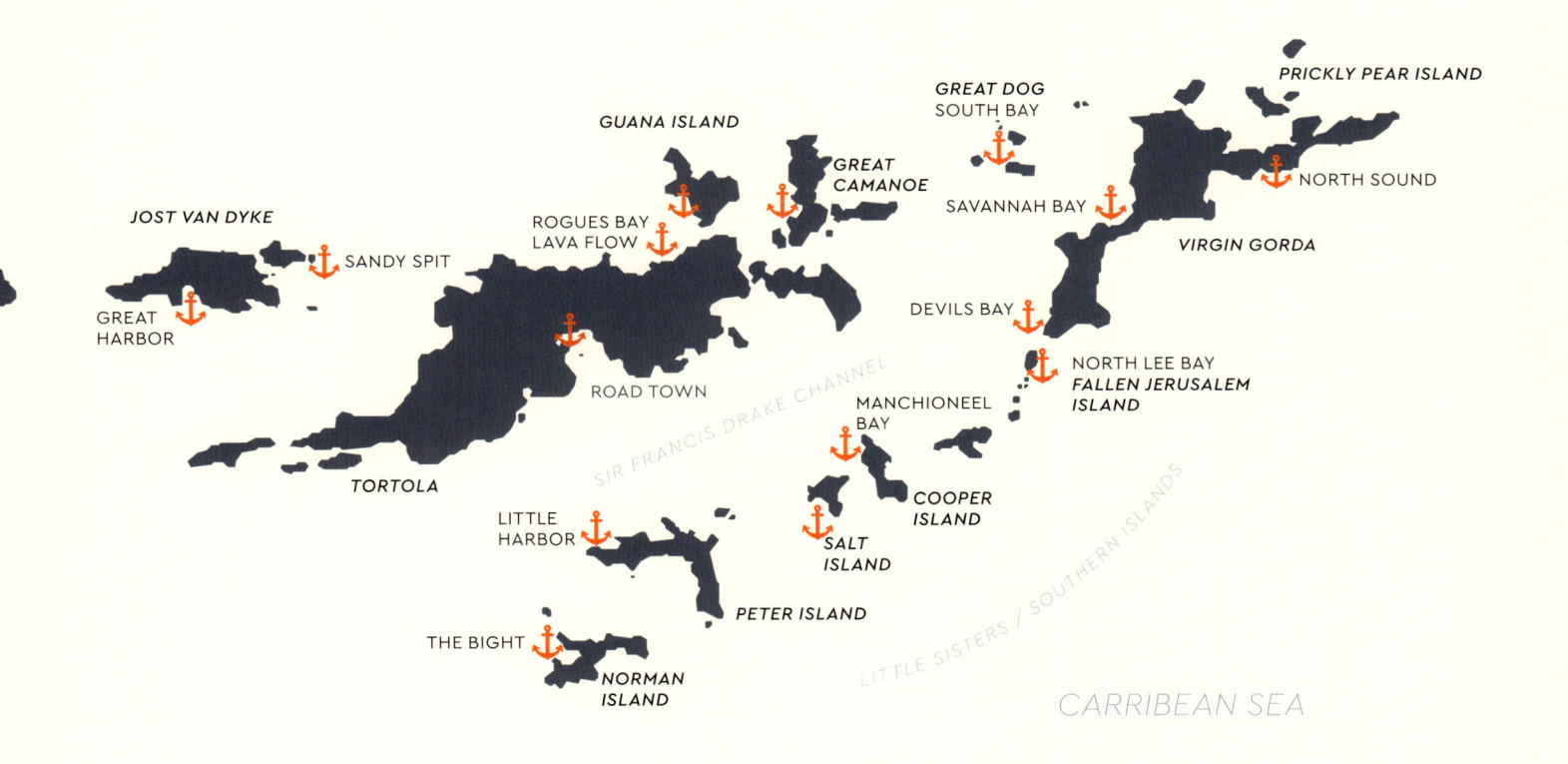

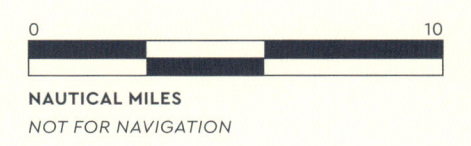

Main Islands

- **JOST VAN DYKE**
  - Sandy Spit
  - Great Harbor ⚓
- **TORTOLA**
  - Rogues Bay / Lava Flow ⚓
  - Road Town ⚓
- **GUANA ISLAND**
- **GREAT CAMANOE**
- **GREAT DOG SOUTH BAY** ⚓
- **PRICKLY PEAR ISLAND**
- **VIRGIN GORDA**
  - North Sound ⚓
  - Savannah Bay ⚓
  - Devils Bay ⚓
  - North Lee Bay ⚓
- **FALLEN JERUSALEM ISLAND**
- **PETER ISLAND**
  - Little Harbor ⚓
- **SALT ISLAND** ⚓
- **COOPER ISLAND**
- Manchioneel Bay
- **NORMAN ISLAND**
  - The Bight ⚓

SIR FRANCIS DRAKE CHANNEL

LITTLE SISTERS / SOUTHERN ISLANDS

CARRIBEAN SEA

0 — 10
NAUTICAL MILES
NOT FOR NAVIGATION

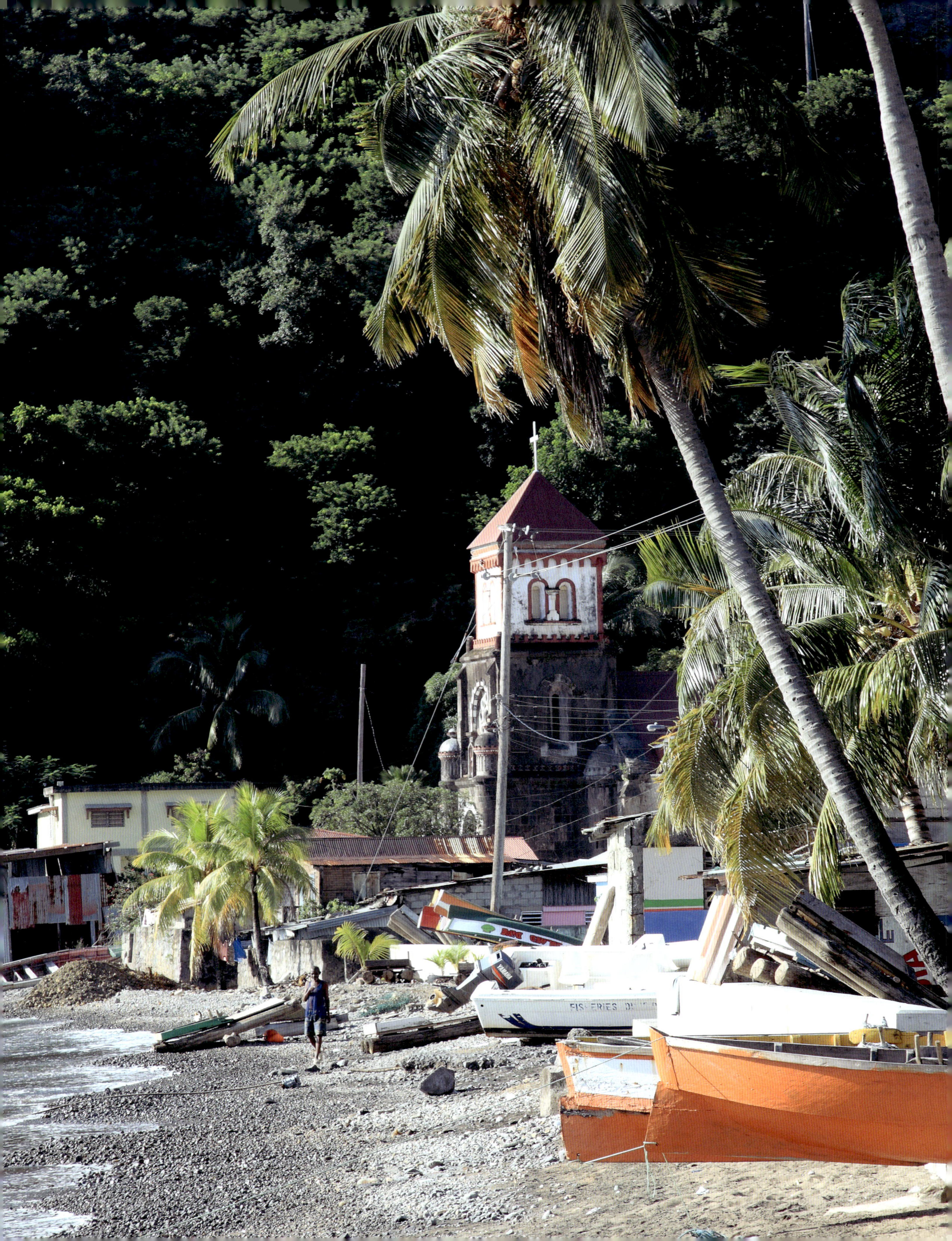

A PASSAGE BETWEEN ISLAND CULTURES

THESE ARE TWO CONTRASTING ISLANDS SIDE BY SIDE WITH THE FIERCE MARTINIQUE PASSAGE FLOWING BETWEEN. TO THE NORTH, DOMINICA IS A WILD JUNGLE, "NATURE'S ISLAND." SOUTH IS MARTINIQUE, A MODERN FRENCH ISLAND, LUSH, AND BEAUTIFUL.

There is an art to cruising the Caribbean: navigating between the islands also takes you between cultures, and a good sailing itinerary highlights the joy of traversing both the physical and abstract boundaries. The Caribbean is a mix of independent sovereign nations, commonwealths, and territories, each of which is home to a unique cultural heritage, and natural and geological environment. Dominica and Martinique are located in the Lesser Antilles, which lay like a string of pearls between Grenada and, arching north and west, Puerto Rico. Sailors love these islands and cruising them in their entirety is a rite of passage for the modern sailor.

Dominica to the north is wild, lush, and tropical, dubbed "Nature's Island"—it is said to be the only island in the Caribbean that Christopher Columbus and his men would still be able to recognize today. Martinique, south of the channel, is governed by France as an overseas department and the local culture is a marriage of French traditions and Caribbean flavor.

Sailing between Martinique and Dominica spans a gap that is as wide as any in the Antilles; the sail itself takes less than five hours, but politically, culturally, and geographically, the islands are different worlds, bound together only by what separates them: the oceanic waters. For sailors who cruise the entire island chain, from Venezuela to Florida, this crossing stands out as one of the most beautiful for the contrast in the islands that it connects. The tumultuous waterway itself, known for its rolling seas and fierce winds is called the Martinique Passage, or the Dominica Channel, depending on which island you sail from.

MARTINIQUE

The volcanic peak of Mount Pierre is important for Martinique and is omnipresent as you sail around the island. Its saturated greenery reaches from one side of the island to the other. From afar, the island looks calm and quiet, and a steady tradewind pushes your boat along its coast. On clear days, when a deep blue sky connects with the lush land, it is especially dramatic and beautiful. Sighting Martinique from the bow of a sailboat making its approach to the islands is soothing to the eyes and calming to the spirit.

The sandy beaches are lined with restaurants that welcome sailors with open arms; they fill tables with spectacularly fresh seafood and delectable imported provisionings from France. The attitude, food, language, and style here blend Carribean and French culture. While listening to the radio and enjoying a local *Rhum agricole* at a shack under a palm tree, you'll hear Serge Gainsbourg, Harry Belafonte, and MC Solaar all in one mix. At one point in time, Martinique was one of the most fashionable islands in the Caribbean, and the architecture retains the sense of French maritime chic and a nautical Art Deco style.

LE MARIN

The harbor town of Le Marin is the likely starting point for this itinerary. Tucked in a large bay along the southern coast of Martinique, Le Marin is just 23 nautical miles north of Saint Lucia and the main hub for sailors, home to one of the Caribbeans largest yachting centers. The protected cove, surrounded by a mangrove forest, is home to hundreds of boats peacefully sitting dockside, with a crowded bay full of cruising boats swaying at anchor. Many of these boats are laid up and waiting for their owners to come back to the islands and sail away. The approach through the reef is difficult, with the outlines of shoal banks scattered on the chart like patch-work.

There are numerous great French-Caribbean restaurants at the marina serving up examples of multicultural cuisine: *steak au poivre*, for example, with Martinique peppercorns and a side of cassava fries. It has the taste of France, refined in its technique and method, but what makes it so unique are the fresh and diverse Caribbean ingredients.

Farming is central to the island's economy; walk from the marina towards the farmers' market that sells produce and tropical fruit and you'll see the wonderful abundance. There is an incredible variety of local spice mixtures influenced by French *herbes de Provence*, but made with local island aromatic flavors.

FORT-DE-FRANCE

Setting sail north from Le Marin you will find Fort-de-France, the capital of Martinique and one of the largest and liveliest cities in the Windward Islands. There is a safe anchorage under Fort Saint Louis if you care to drop anchor and explore ashore. The streets are lined with shops and restaurants, perfect for people-watching. There are cruise-ship docks along the jetty on the northside of the bay, which leads to big swells of tourists coming and going on any given day. Sailing into Fort-de-France when the big cruise ships are not docked at port will lead to a more enjoyable and less crowded Caribbean island city experience.

SAINT-PIERRE

Saint-Pierre is the most northern settlement before the Martinique Passage with a suitable anchorage. The town sits at the bottom of Mount Pierre and is one of the most idyllic and picturesque ports in Martinique. This historic coastal town was largely destroyed during the 1902 volcanic eruption that killed the entire town's population, sparing just two lives. The steep slopes surrounding this part of the island make for tricky anchoring and on any given day during the sailing season, you

---

RHUM AGRICOLE

Rhum agricole is made from freshly squeezed sugar cane juice rather than molasses, a technique unique to French Caribbean islands. Go ashore to any beach bar in Martinique for a famous ti-punch. *The drink, which is pronounced "tee paunch" by locals, has a heavy pour of Martinique's Rhum agricole with a little lime juice and a splash of cane syrup.*

A KID SKIPS ALONG THE WATERFRONT OUTSIDE A RUNDOWN RESORT IN MARTINIQUE (ABOVE). BOATS AT ANCHOR LOOKING WEST TOWARDS THE CARIBBEAN SEA (BELOW).

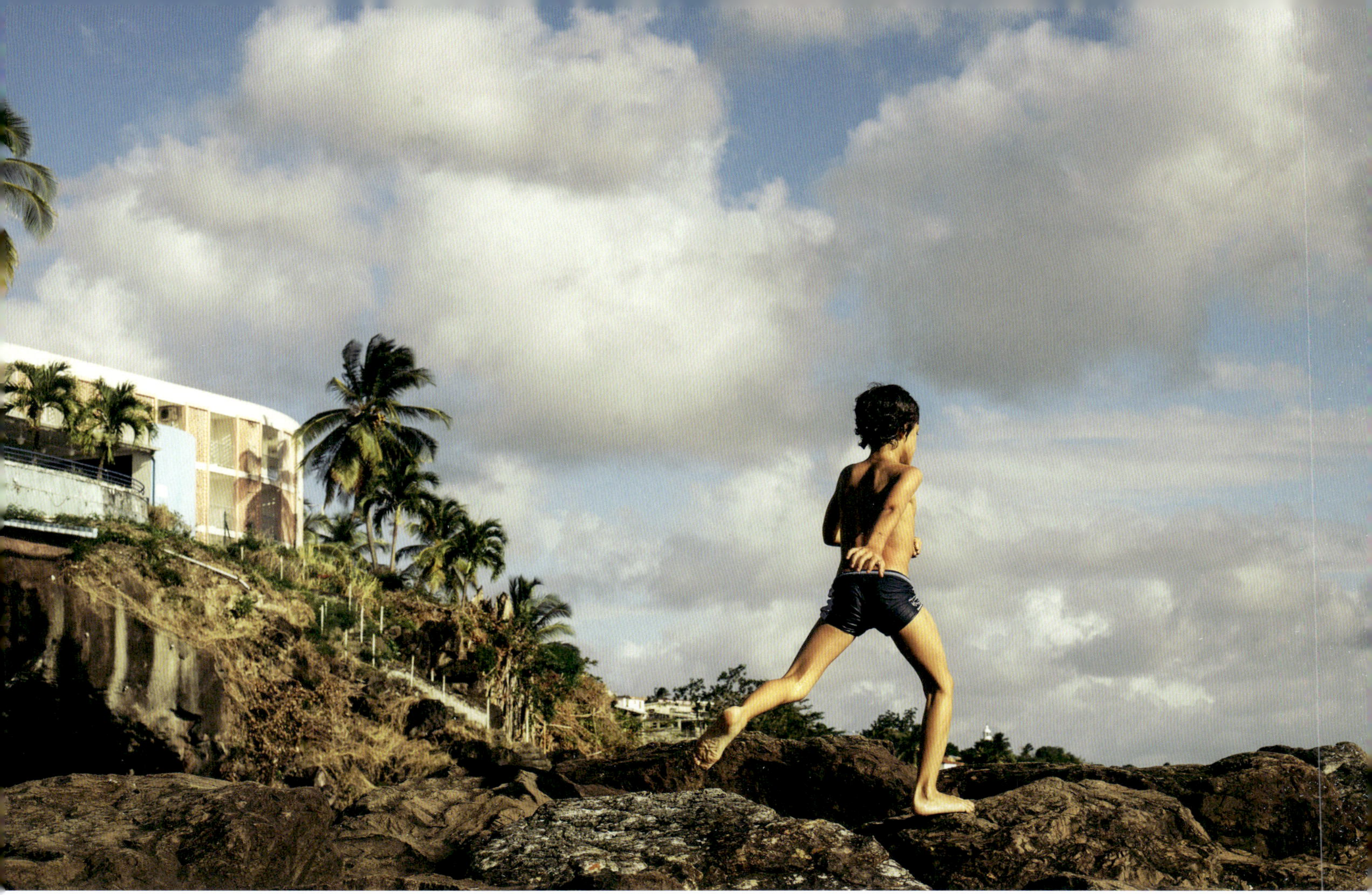

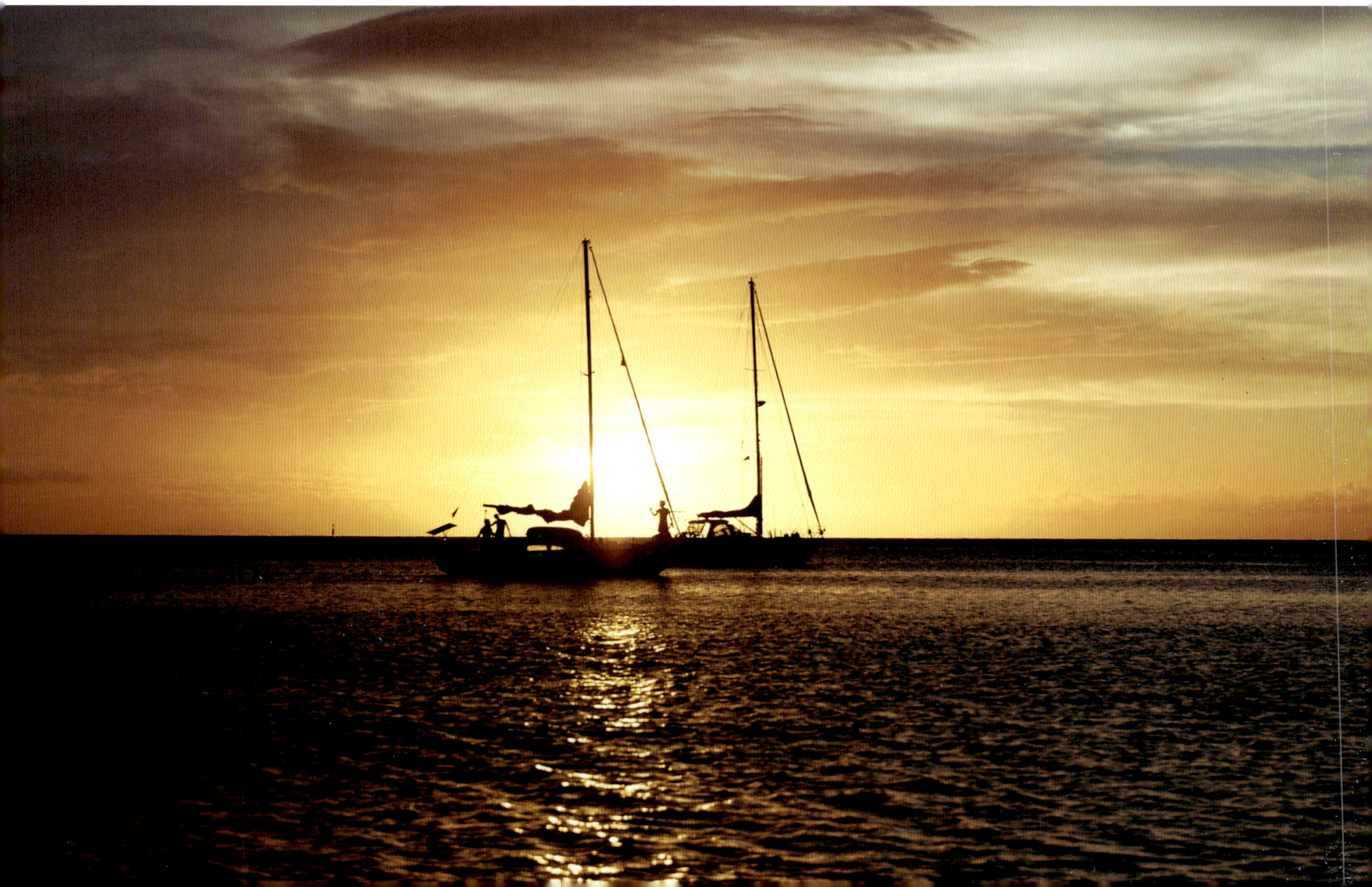

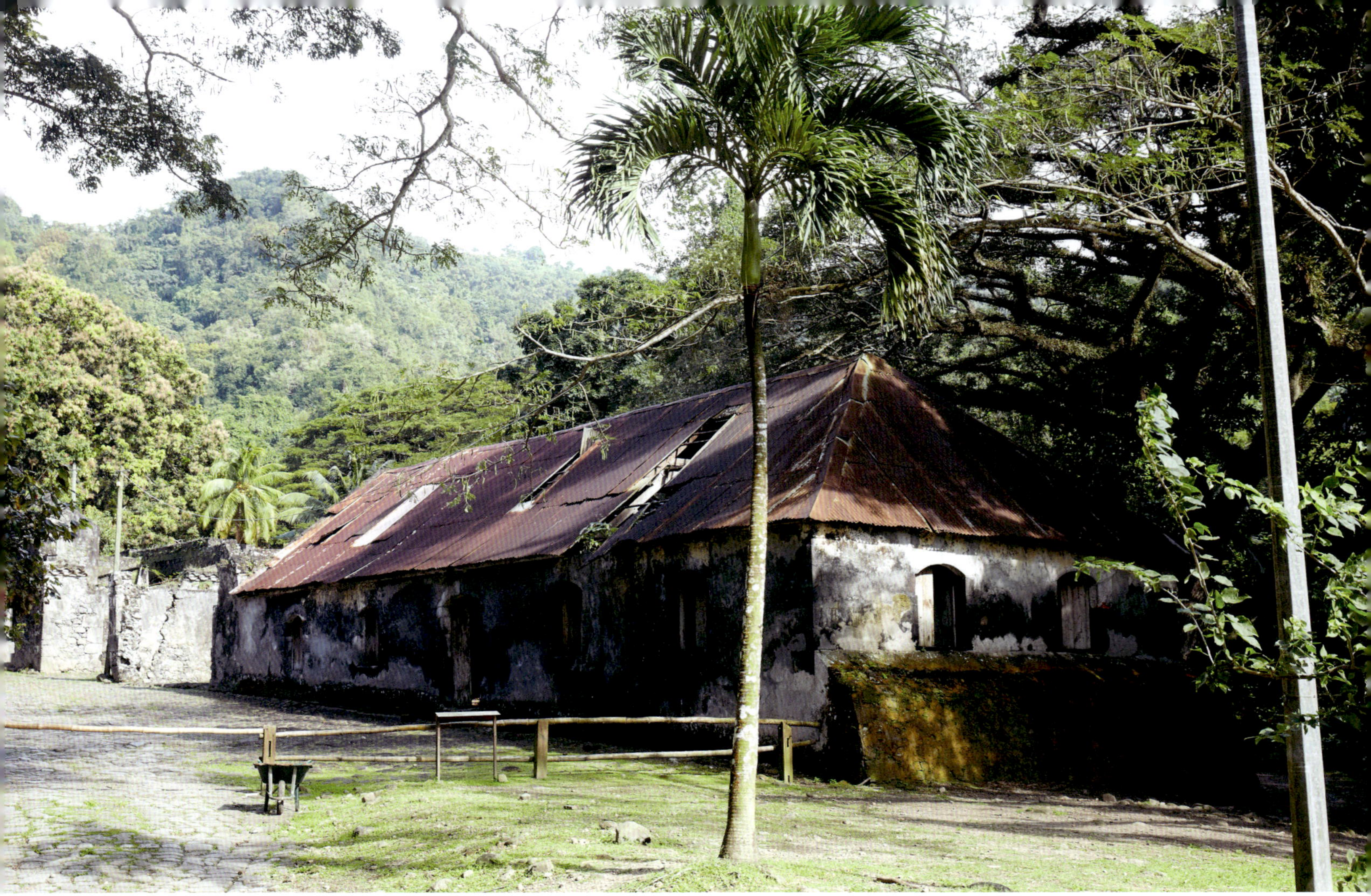
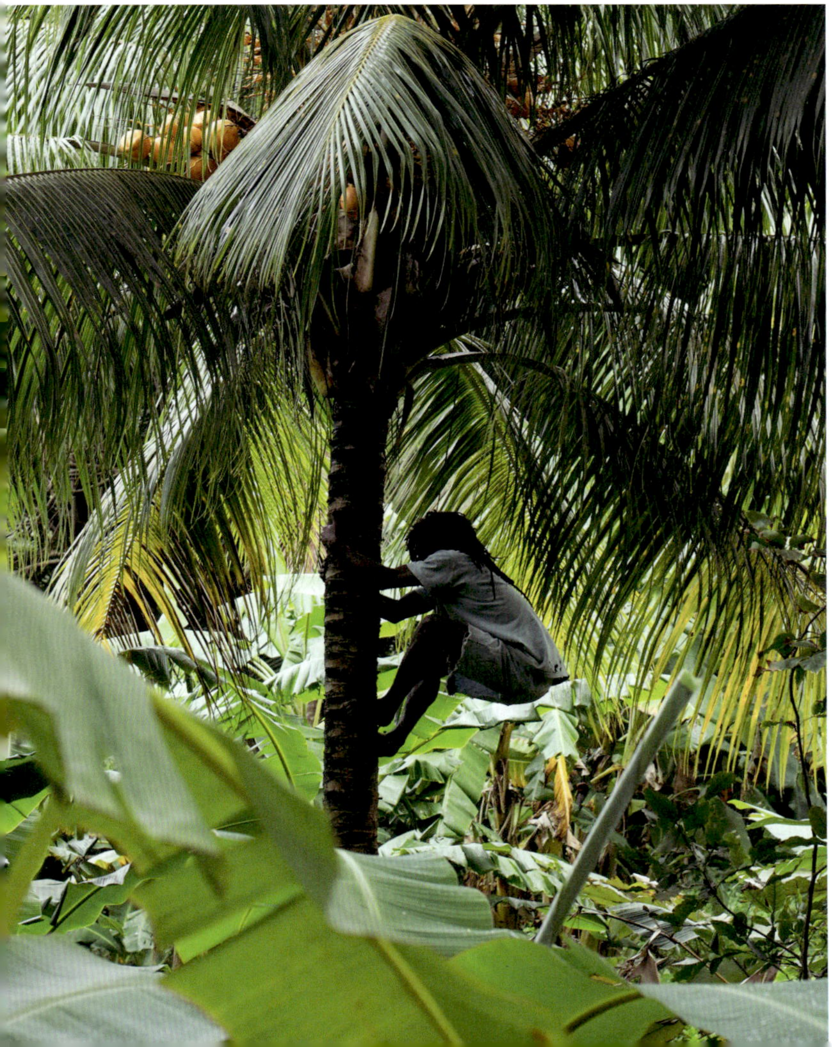
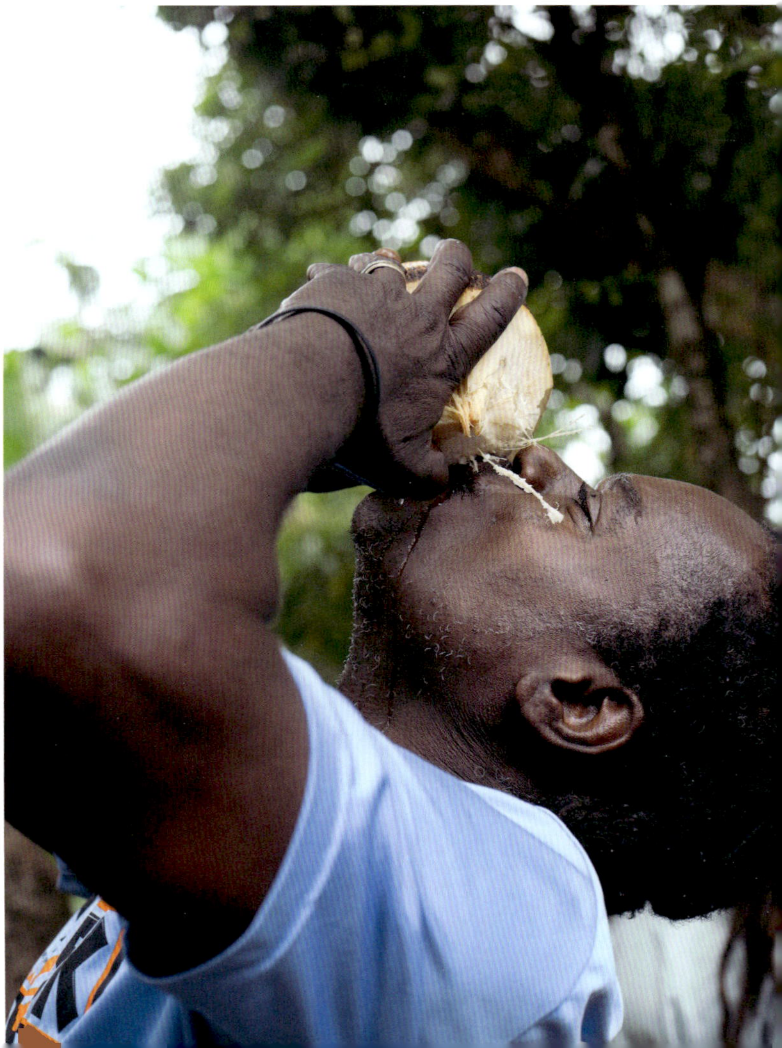

might see an anchoring gone wrong, with a sailboat washed up along the black volcanic sand beach.

MARTINIQUE TO DOMINICA

The sail from Martinique to Dominica is a voyage of discovery. Leaving Saint Pierre, you'll make the passage across roughly 25 nautical miles of open ocean, with Atlantic-size rolling waves and heavy winds. On either side of the passage lie the now-dormant volcanoes that overlook the channel. Mount Pelée on Martinique towers high over the sea (even the rough swells that constantly push through the channel seem like ripples from its lofty mountaintop). Clouds hover at the peak, creating dark shadows over the tops of the waves as you sail from one island to the other. When the sun is beaming and peering out from behind the clouds, the same waves appear more beautiful, but are no less treacherous as you sail onward.

DOMINICA

Dominica contrasts with Martinique both visually and culturally, and as you approach the island by sea, every sailor aboard will know that they have arrived on a distant shore, fundamentally different from the land from which they set out to sea that morning. Dominica is a steep and mountainous island with a sprawling jungle. The dramatic slopes drop into the ocean and there are limited areas in which you can safely anchor. Difficulty getting to the island helps to make it one of the less tourist-heavy islands in the Caribbean. Its relative obscurity in the world of travel is the allure for any sailor seeking true adventure.

Dominica is rich with history and the island's maritime heritage is noticeable along the coast. The first European to sail past Dominica was Christopher Columbus, who traveled alongside a fleet of 17 galleons with some 12,000 men during his second passage to the Caribbean. According to his ship's log, Dominica was first sighted at about five o'clock in the morning on November 3rd, just at the end of the hurricane season. Columbus and his ships had the same dilemma that sailors are still facing today—there are limited harbors—so he declined to make landfall, but noted in his log the alluring feel of this ancient volcanic outcropping.

Once you round the southwestern corner of Dominica and are safely sailing on the leeward side of the island, there are two suitable anchorages: the more southerly, sleepy and rustic anchorage of Roseau south, or the more robust and well defined Portsmouth in Prince Rupert Bay, further up in the northwest.

Scattered hamlets along the coastline have homes that are mostly wooden and painted in colorful green and yellow hues, blending in nicely with the forested island landscape. The western shoreline has mostly dark-colored stone beaches and few suitable anchorages for cruisers; residents of this coast live a simple life that revolves around building wooden fishing boats and harvesting food from the jungle and the sea.

ROSEAU

Roseau isn't a bay but rather a slightly more shallow area of the southwestern coastline that is open to the sea. There is often wrap-around swell, which can make for a rolly evening if you're sailing in a monohull boat, making the anchorage more popular among

---

KALINAGO TERRITORY

Also known as Carib Reservation, this settlement—the last remaining domain of the Kalinago people—is located in a remote region of the eastern mountains of Dominica, overlooking the Atlantic Ocean. The self-governing community was established in 1903 on roughly 1,500 hectares of land. Visitors can explore the village with its traditional Kalinago buildings.

catamaran sailors. When approaching Roseau from the south, typically after a rowdy sail from Martinique, there are "boat boys" who come up in their small craft to greet you and offer assistance. Since the harbor, aside from a small area that quickly fills up, is mostly too deep for anchoring, many sailors rely on the boat boys to secure a mooring for their stay in the southern part of the island.

A short dingy ride away from the moorings is the main town of Roseau. In the early mornings you can find fisherman selling their fresh catch in downtown Roseau at the New Market, a central outdoor bazaar located along the waterfront. The island markets are where local residents shop, purchasing their food direct from the farmers. A robust local agriculture is important here because the island does not have a main industrial harbor, and large shipping vessels are not always able to dock due to the waves and weather along the shoreline. Taking a stroll through the New Market, you will find tall stacks of sweet pineapples that have been freshly picked alongside piles of cassava root and seasonal fruit. Spices such as cinnamon, ginger, and pimento are also available.

> The Caribbean is a mix of sovereign nations, commonwealths, and territories, each home to a unique cultural heritage and natural and geological environment.

Seafood is caught by the local fleet of traditional fishing boats, and vendors are required to have a permit to sell their catch. A popular local workaround for fisherman without the proper permits is to drive around at fast speeds with their fish (often as large as four-foot long mahi-mahi) piled up in the back of pickup trucks. Islanders driving by keep an eye out for these fishermen and then speed alongside, chasing them until there are enough interested buyers in pursuit to warrant the pickup pulling over, at risk of arrest, to quickly sell the entire catch.

INLAND DOMINICA

One of the pleasures of sailing to Dominica is having the opportunity to explore the tropical jungle that thrives in the island interior. This is the steepest island in the Caribbean, and you see just how lush the jungle really is when climbing up the hills in a taxi or passenger van with an island guide. The roads are not well maintained and only one main roadway connects the north to the south along the east coast. Winding pathways serving as roads have been cut through some of the island, but, because of the steep slopes and the density of the forest, many places in the interior are not accessible by car. The roads that do exist are rough due to erosion and prone to mudslides caused by the abundant rainfall.

~

The joy of making headway through a windswept sea while rolling waves throw spray over the deck of your boat. The warm comfort of gourmet food prepared with fresh ingredients and served to you on a black sand beach. The sense of adventure as you pour over the charts while making landfall in a new place. The gratification of making new friends in far away places. The thrill of exploring a rich jungle ecosystem. These diverse experiences are made possible by a diverse itinerary across two islands so close and yet so different.

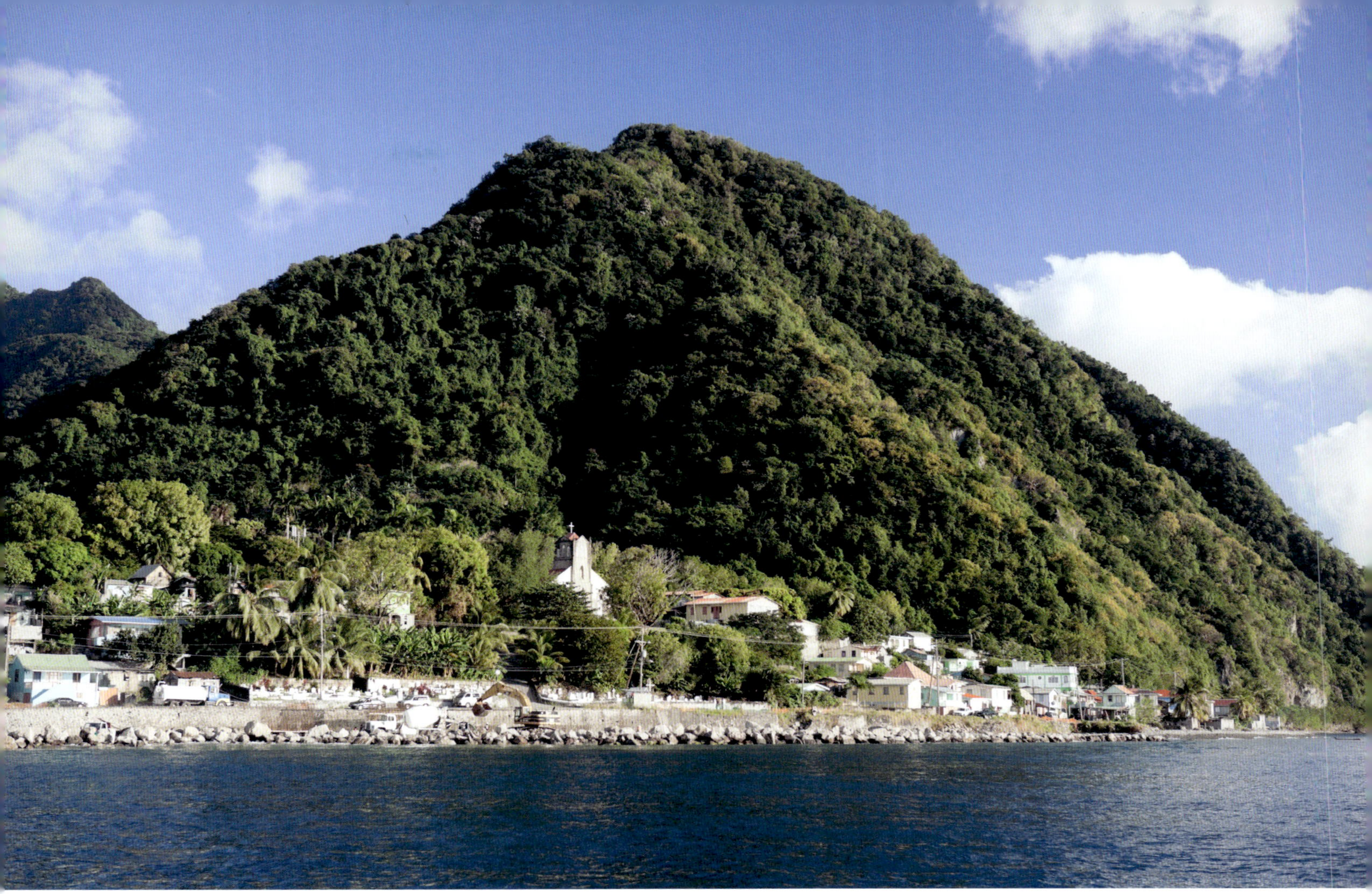

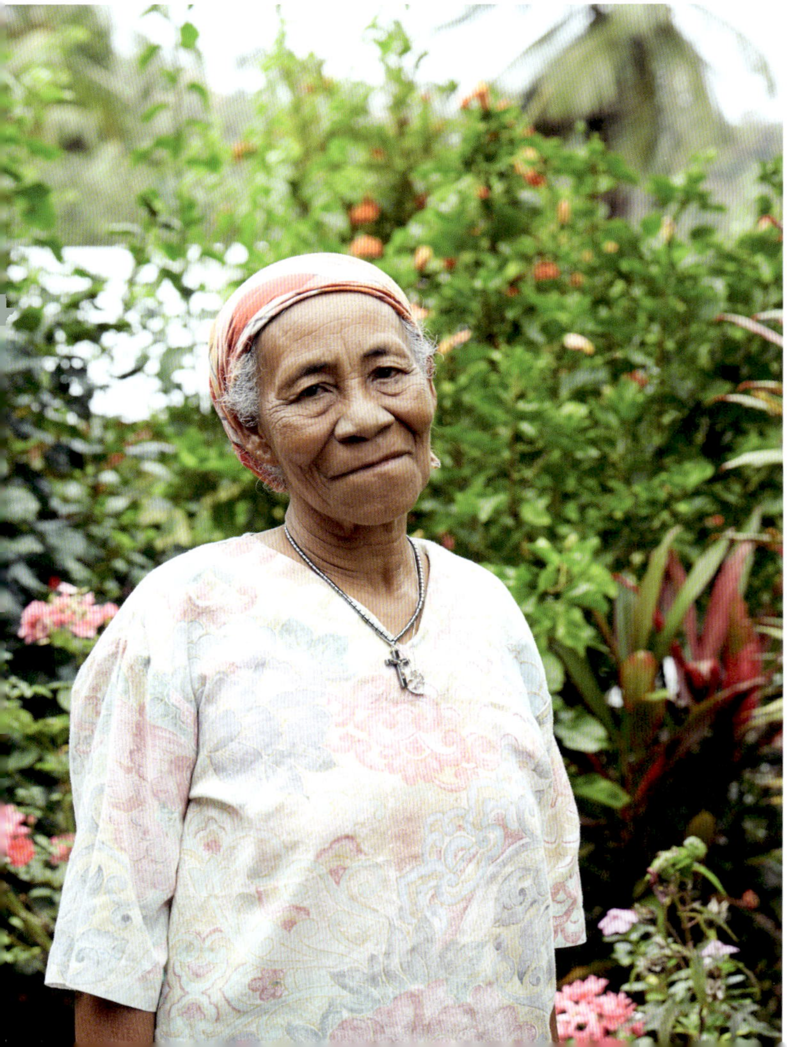

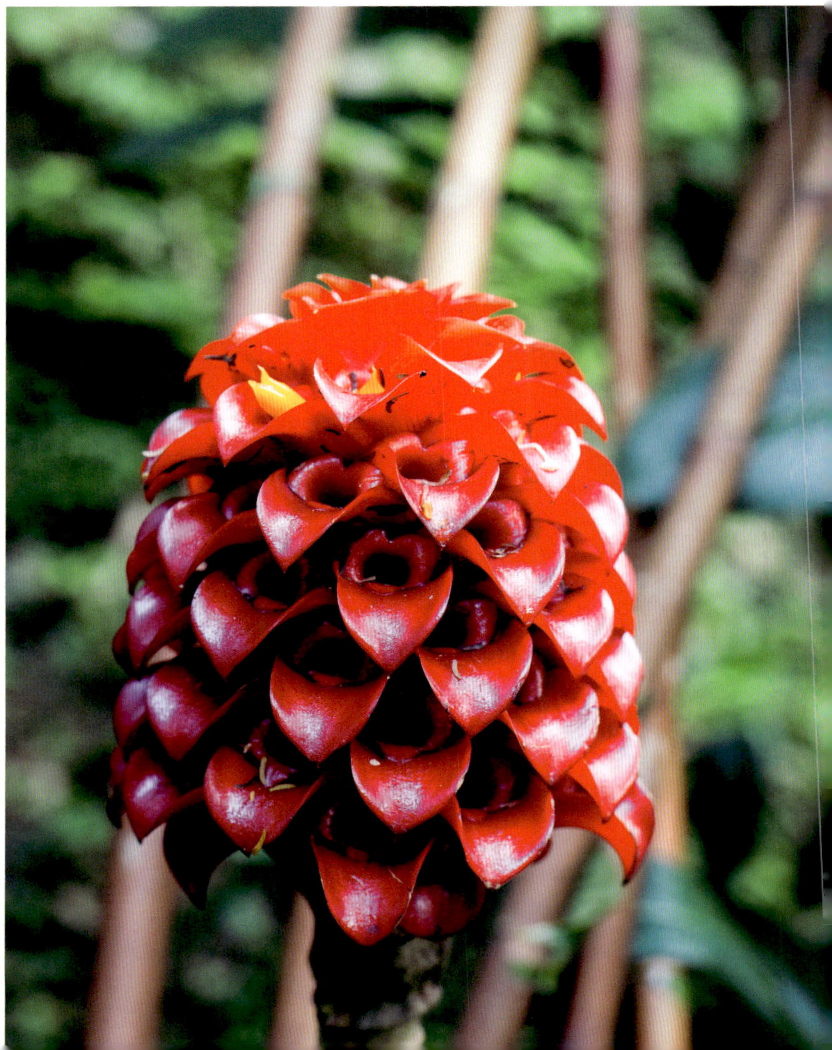

CAPTAIN'S NOTES *DOMINICA & MARTINIQUE*

RECOMMENDED ITINERARY

La Marin, Martinique
14° 28' 4" N, 60° 51' 59" W
This is a French port of entry with do-it-yourself customs computers located in the marina mall. All mariners entering Martinique from Saint Lucia should clear customs upon arrival. Choose from over 160 slips located in Marina du Marin or anchor outside the channel markers. Stay clear of the shoals located in the middle of the bay; navigation at night should be minimized, as the shoals are sometimes difficult to spot.

Grande Anse d'Arlet, Martinique
14° 30' 5" N, 61° 5' 25" W
Anchor or moor using one of the many laid mooring buoys located along the south and north sides of the large bay. Anchor in 5 fathoms in sand with good holding. Do not anchor too close to shore because the reef extends into the bay. Take a dinghy anchor to set away from the dock, as swells can cause dinghy damage.

Saint-Pierre, Martinique
14° 44' 29" N, 61° 10' 42" W
There is adequate depth along the underwater shelf to anchor in 4 fathoms on the north and south sides of the town dock. The shelf drops quickly to over 13 fathoms, however, and mariners should anchor off the town beach. Saint-Pierre makes for a suitable overnight anchorage in all weather except heavy northerly swells.

Citronier, Dominica
15° 16' 45" N, 61° 22' 38" W
Use the mooring buoys located south of Roseau and the town of Citronier, just north of Anchorage Hotel. Moorings are laid in deep water (nearly 14 fathoms). Anchor off the town of Newton, south of the customs dock, in 5 fathoms. The orange moorings are maintained by "boat boys," who assist with dock lines upon your approach.

Portsmouth, Dominica
15° 33' 53" N, 61° 27' 46" W
Anchor in Prince Rupert Bay, located on the northwest corner of the island. The bay is safe from all weather except during a southwest gale. The "boat boys" look after the boats at moorings during the evenings to ensure mariners are safe from piracy, and will notify a skipper during inclement weather. "Boat boys" are reliable and work for tips. Big Papa and Purple Turtle are the beach bars ashore with their own dinghy docks to use.

RECOMMENDED ANCHORAGES

Anse Caritan, Martinique
Anse Noire, Martinique
Anse Mitan, Maritinique
Fort-de-France, Martinique

ITINERARY DURATION

5 days, if making the passageway north or south continuing onward

8 days, if only voyaging Dominica and Martinique

PREVAILING WIND

The trade winds are fairly consistent, blowing from the northeast direction with a moderate breeze on the Beaufort scale. Winds during the winter months (referred to as the "Christmas winds") tend to be stronger, reaching near-gale and, on occasion, gale-force wind.

SEASON

Between December and April is the best period to sail Dominica and Martinique. The shoulder months of November, May, and June also provide steady wind. The twice-yearly hurricane seasons begin in July and November.

FOOD

Rum on Martinique is distilled using pressed sugarcane and called *Rhum agricole*. This differs from other rum in the Caribbean, which is distilled from molasses, the residue from turning sugarcane into sugar. Popular rum brands are Rhum J. M, Neisson, Clement, Saint-James, as well as Habitation Saint-Etienne.

GOOD TO KNOW

Indigenous people
The Arawak and the Island Kalinago were the first seafaring peoples to arrive on Martinique and Dominica, voyaging north from the South American coast in wooden *dugout canoes*. There are an estimated 2,000 indigenous Kalinago residents still living on Dominica.

Hiking on Dominica
One of the joys of sailing to Dominica is going ashore and exploring the lush jungle. Dominica is known as the "Nature Island," and for good reason. Its steep slopes have prohibited industrial development, sparing the dense jungle from ruin. Recommended hiking trails include the Boiling Lake hike, the hike from Rosalie to Freshwater Lake, and the Waitukubuli National Trail, segments 4, 9, and 13.

Magnetic variance
Magnetic Declination: -14° (WEST)

PORTSMOUTH

DOMINICA

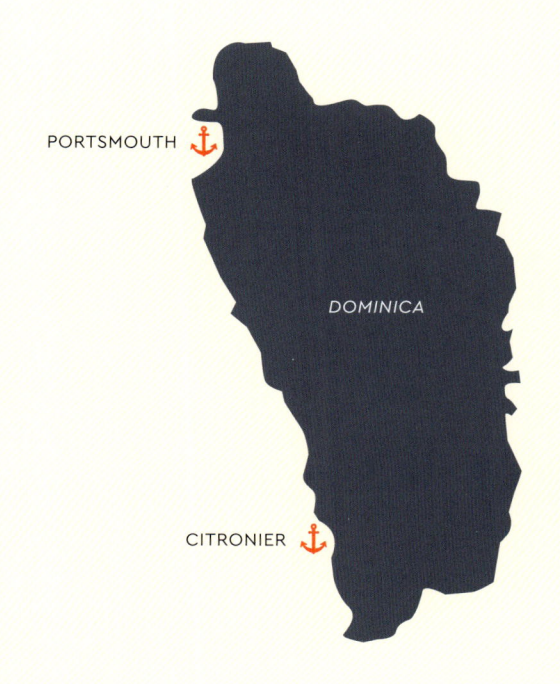

CITRONIER

N
W E
S

CANAL DE LA DOMINIQUE

MARTINIQUE-PASSAGE

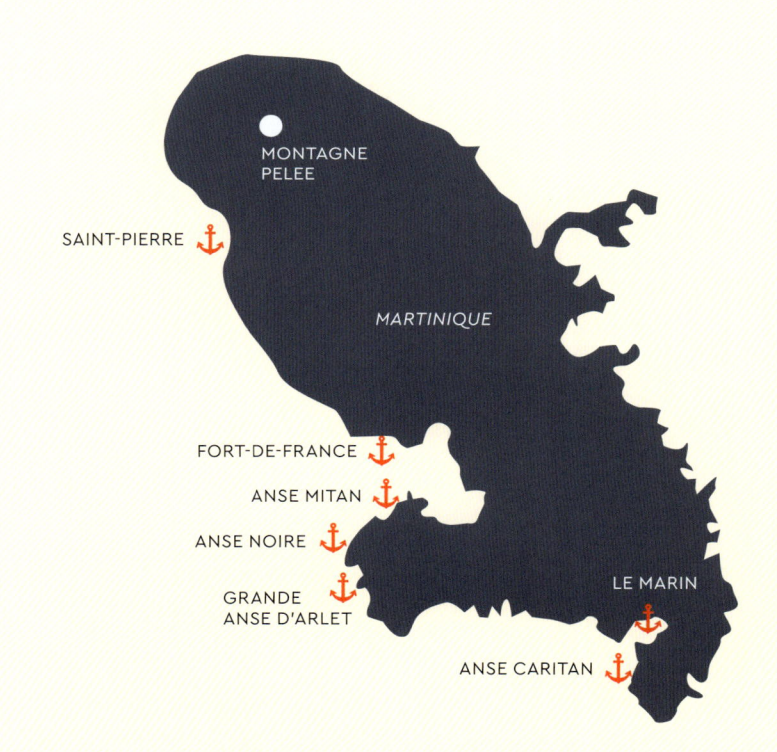

MONTAGNE PELEE

SAINT-PIERRE

MARTINIQUE

FORT-DE-FRANCE
ANSE MITAN
ANSE NOIRE
GRANDE ANSE D'ARLET

LE MARIN
ANSE CARITAN

CARRIBEAN SEA
WINDWARD LESSER ANTILLES

0 — 10
NAUTICAL MILES
NOT FOR NAVIGATION

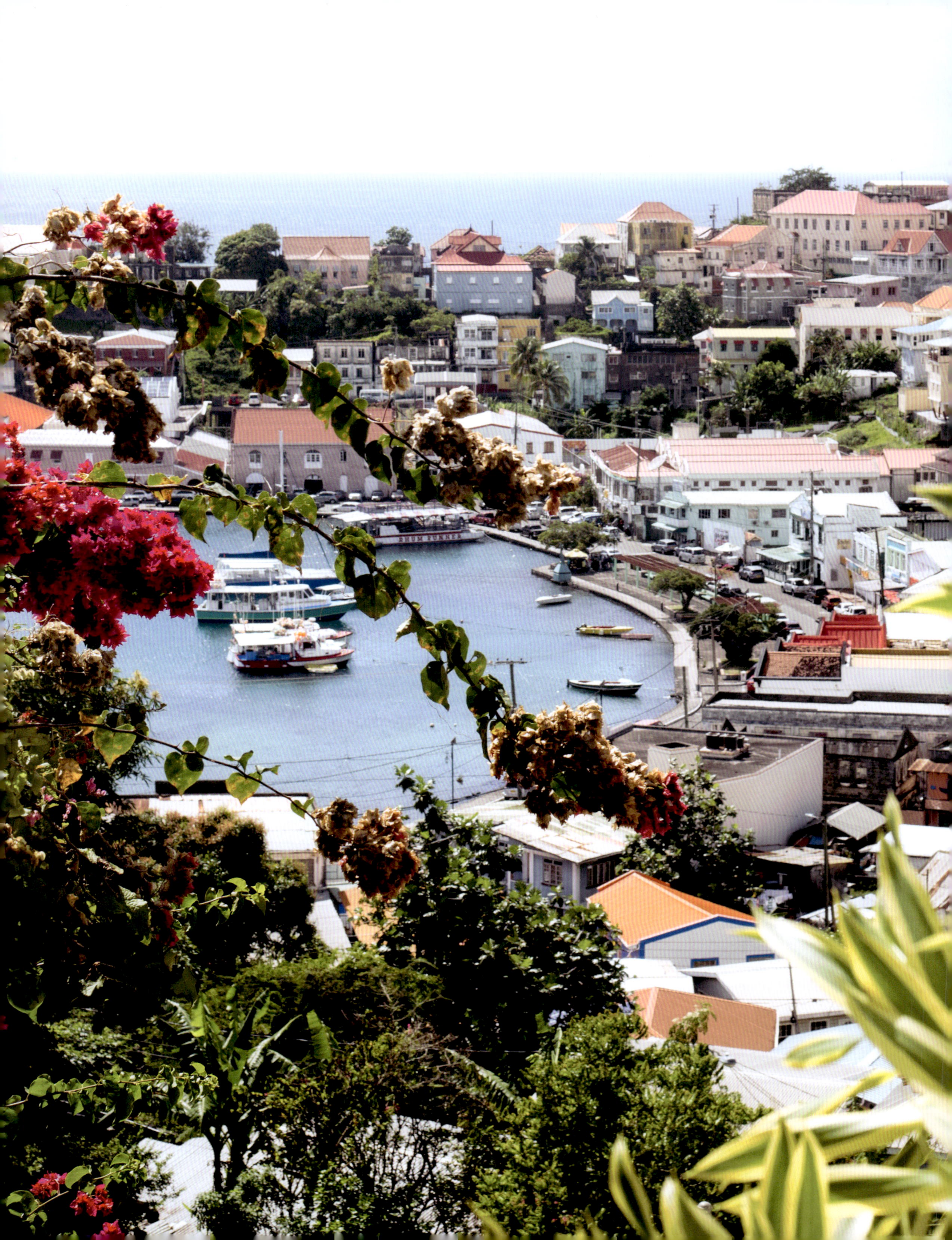

CORAL REEFS AND SECLUDED BEACHES

GRENADA, WITH ITS HILLY TERRAIN, IS FAMED AS A PRODUCER OF SPICES. JUST A SHORT PASSAGE AWAY LIES THE GRENADINES ARCHIPELAGO—DOTTED SANDY ISLANDS WITH ANCHORAGES SCATTERED THROUGHOUT.

As you sail along the west coast of Grenada, small settlements dot the shoreline connected by a road along the water's edge. The land above the coast climbs dramatically to densely forested mountaintops where mona monkeys swing from the trees. On the horizon ahead are green islands fringed by reefs, and your sails are trimmed to take you there across deep and wild waters. Strong ocean currents, confused seas, and active undersea volcanoes all conspire to keep you away, but venturing into the Grenadines is a journey worth embarking on.

The Grenadines is the group of 32 odd islands extending about 50 miles between Saint Vincent and Grenada. These southernmost of the Windward Islands are so extraordinary they are worthy of an entire winter's exploration. The archipelago is a mix of sandy cays and small volcanic islands that together creates biodiversity sparsely seen in the Caribbean. St. George's on Grenada is the preferred departure port for the southern Grenadines with its position giving sailors options to explore along the craggy south coast of Grenada and take advantage of the trade winds for an out-and-back voyage.

Saint Vincent, the Grenadines and Grenada are part of the Lesser Antilles, both use the East Caribbean Dollar, and both are part of the British Commonwealth, however the islands have two separate sovereign governments. Sailing between the two countries requires clearing in and out of customs in a process that is subject to island time.

The history of Grenada, Saint Vincent and the Grenadines is awash with change. Territories were handed back and forth between the British and the French, slavery brought culture from many disparate regions of Africa, and it all blended into the unique culture seen on the islands today. English is the national language here but take a trip ashore and you'll hear Grenadians speaking a distinct Creole English dialect that mixes words from throughout the island's political history. Sail here and you'll be met by a unique and enjoyable way of life, the natural pace of things is slow and the beauty of the islands is objectively magnificent.

ST. GEORGE'S

St. George's is true to its roots, architectural details convey the antiquity of the city and its role as an important port. Even with the growing number of luxury hotels and its cruise ship dock, Grenada's principal harbor is a working waterfront servicing this small island nation and providing for the residents. Commercial fishing boats that go out for tuna are tied up next to the 17th-century brick warehouses that run along the harbor's edge, bigger ships moor right in the center to load and unload their freight. Beginning a sailing voyage in St. George's offers wonderful provisioning options for the boat embarking on a voyage through the Grenadines. The official market is the large outdoor plaza in the center of town but it caters more towards tourists looking for souvenirs than a yacht chef searching for their provisioning. Follow the locals to the street markets that spring up along the main road where farmers sell fresh produce out of the back of pickup trucks every morning. Traditional *Ital* food stands, the unmodified vegetarian cuisine of the Rastafarian movement, offer fresh juices and delicious fruits.

A walk to the fish market first thing in the morning gets you the best selection of freshly caught seafood. One busy stand is run by a no-nonsense woman who swings her machete high above her head to get clean steaks of enormous mahi-mahi and tuna. Fish are laid out on butcher block slabs for you to select from, they are carried here at sunrise by the fishermen who are docked at the long pier just behind the market. Beside her booth is a metal table with heaps of recently caught and still unsorted prawns and shrimps. Purchasing one kilo of the local crustaceans you will get a grab bag in a wide array of sizes and colors, from white jumbo prawns the size of your hand to tiny little pink shrimp.

RONDE ISLAND

The sail between Sauteurs on the north point of Grenada and the island of Carriacou can be a difficult because the sea is often choppy from a combination of the islands funneling wind and open ocean currents upwelling. The private Island of Ronde offers a welcome respite from this melee midway through the crossing.

Navigating the passage is made more difficult by an active underwater volcano, marked as "Kick 'em Jenny" on the charts. Mariners must keep at least a nautical mile away, and further if the current eruption threat level is high. Ronde Island is the geographic sister of Kick 'em Jenny and has the rough edges of a recently formed island. Cliffs drop straight into the ocean and crumble onto sandy beaches that hug the shoreline. Only a small seasonal fishing village exists on one end of this otherwise uninhabited island. Two possible anchorages are only marginally protected and not recommended for an overnight in anything but stable weather and calm seas.

CARRIACOU

Thirty years ago there were only eight cars on the island. The first taxi driver on the island still plies the streets today and if you hop in the front seat with him you can get great stories about just about anything and anybody that you pass. He'll lament the island traffic that can be occasionally experienced when there is livestock on the road and blame it on the fact that there are now several taxis and over 100 cars (by his estimations). There is also a radio-net on channel 9 VHF ship's radio that cruising sailors tune into every night at

SPICES

Grenada is known for its spices—nutmeg will be ground fresh onto every rum punch ordered. The tree that grows both nutmeg and mace, two spices produced from the same plant, has been cultivated here since 1843, when it was brought by a British trader.

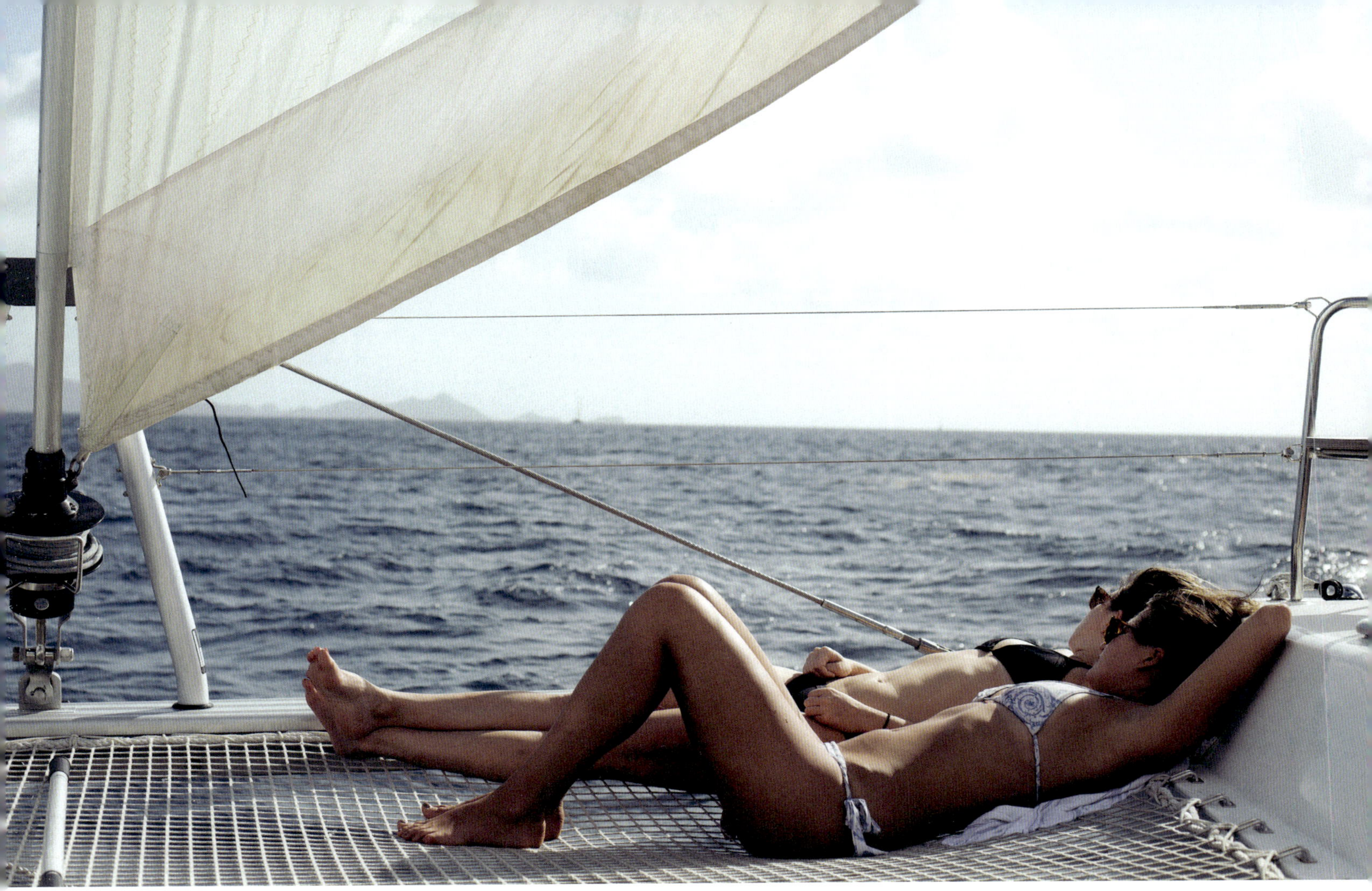

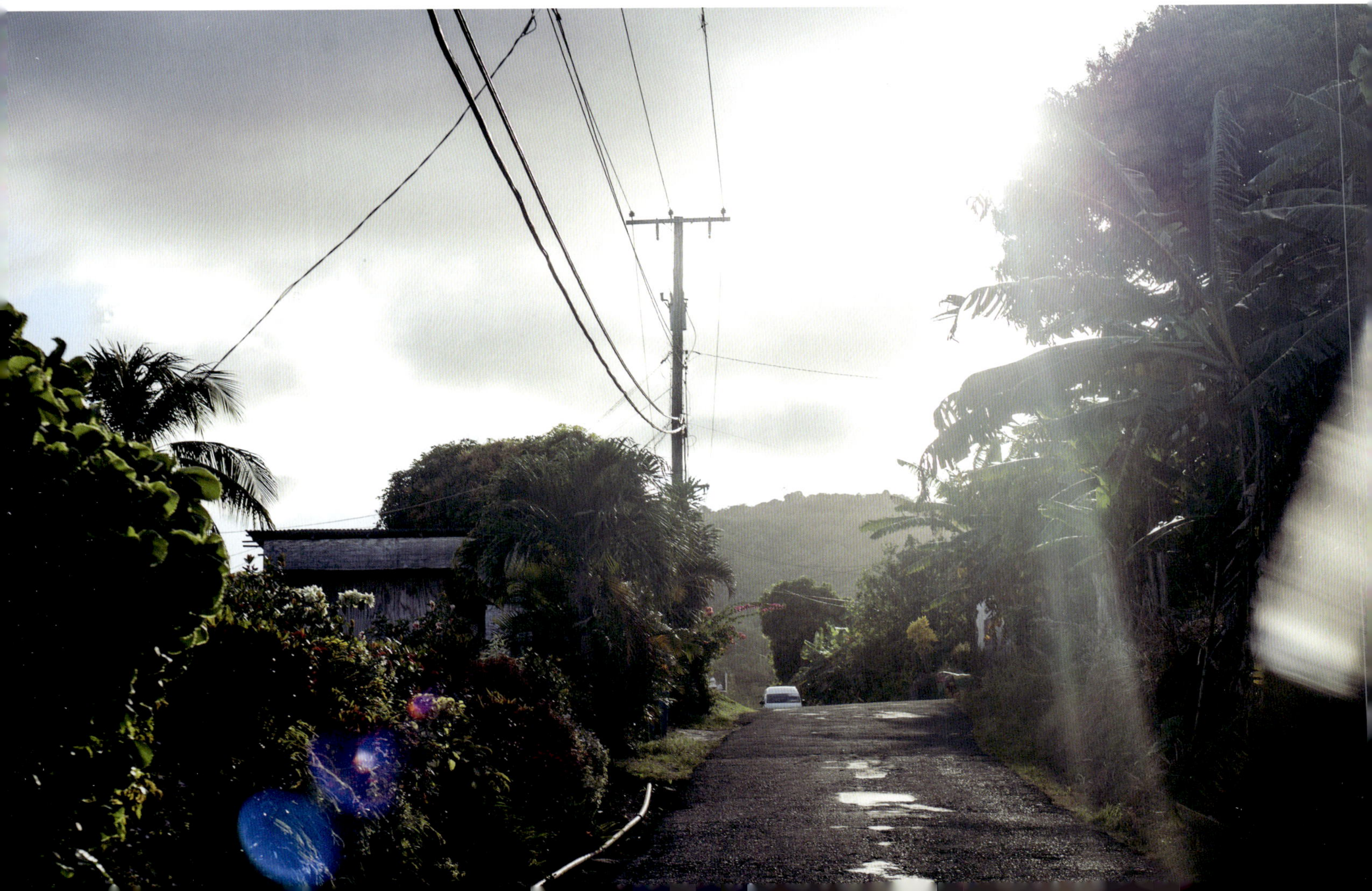

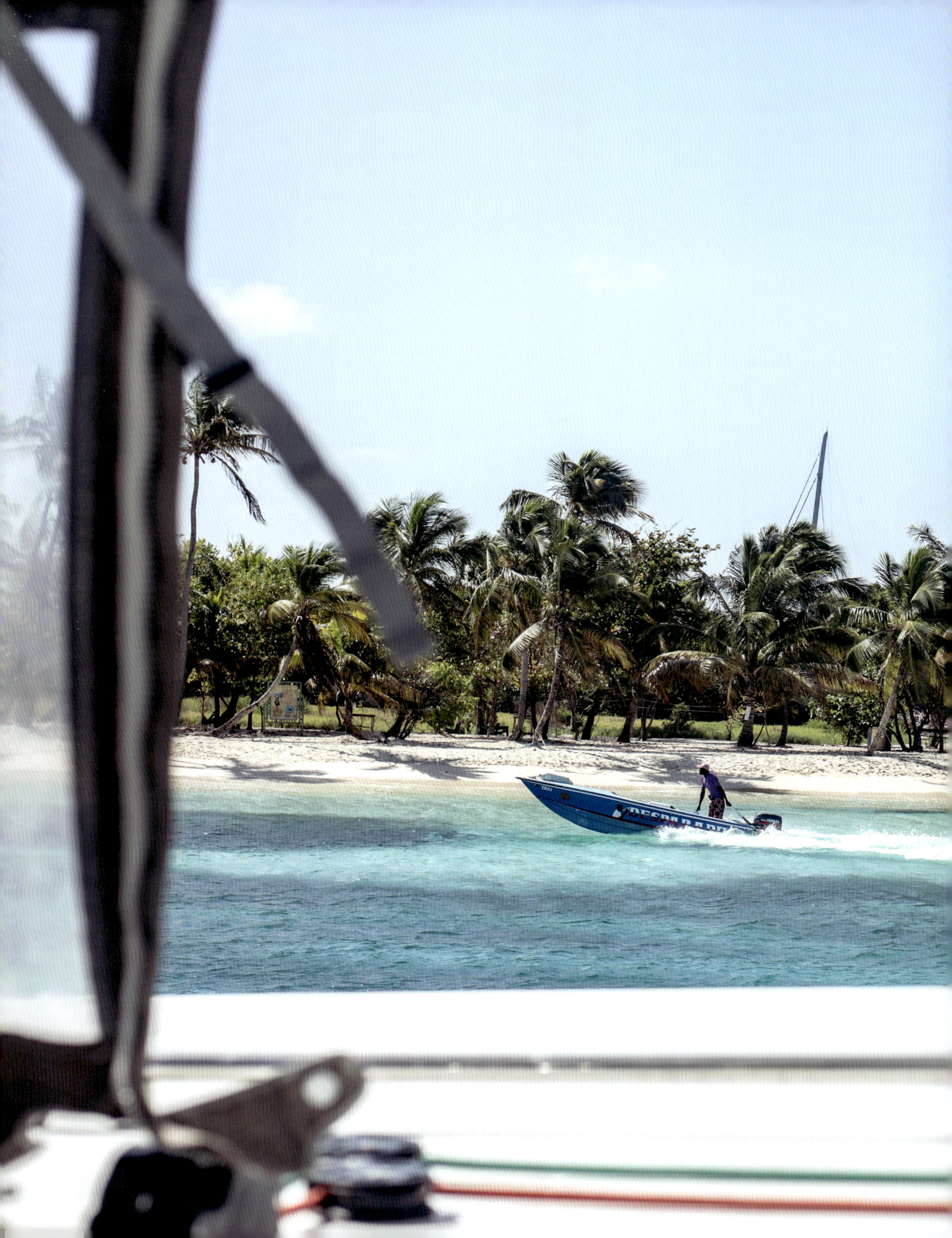

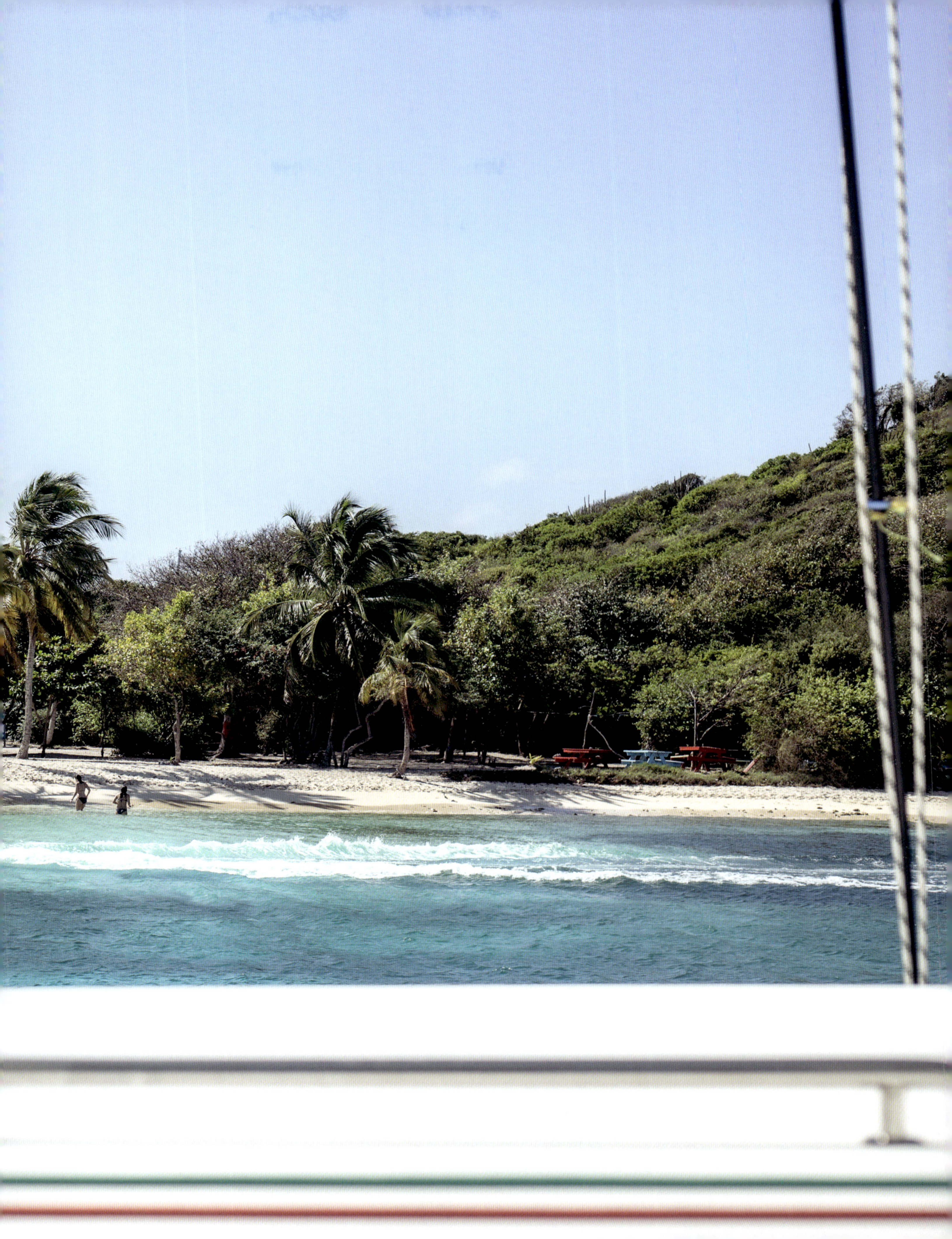

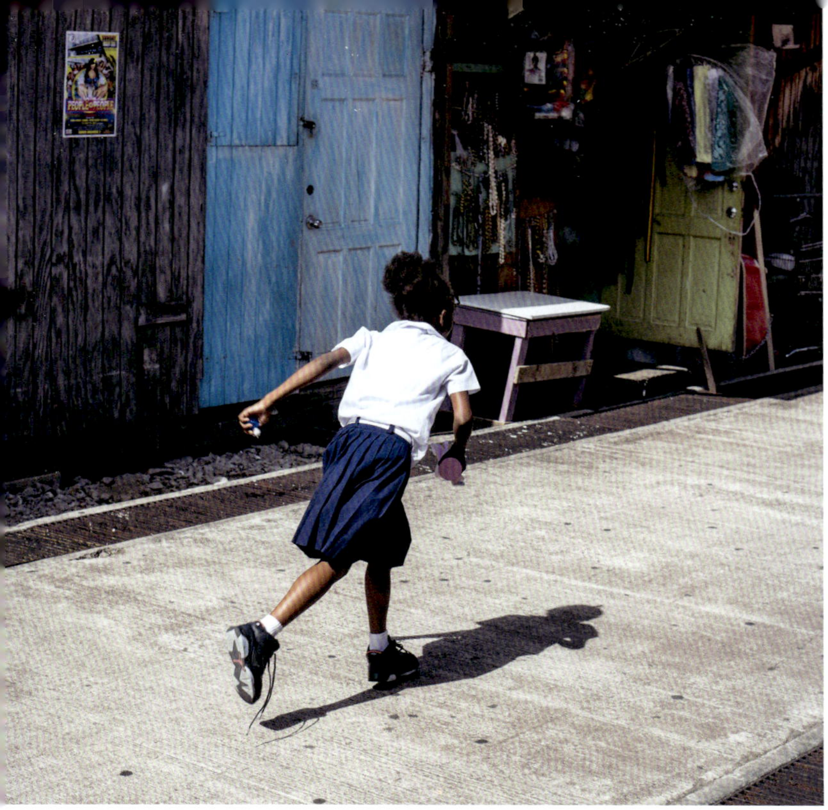

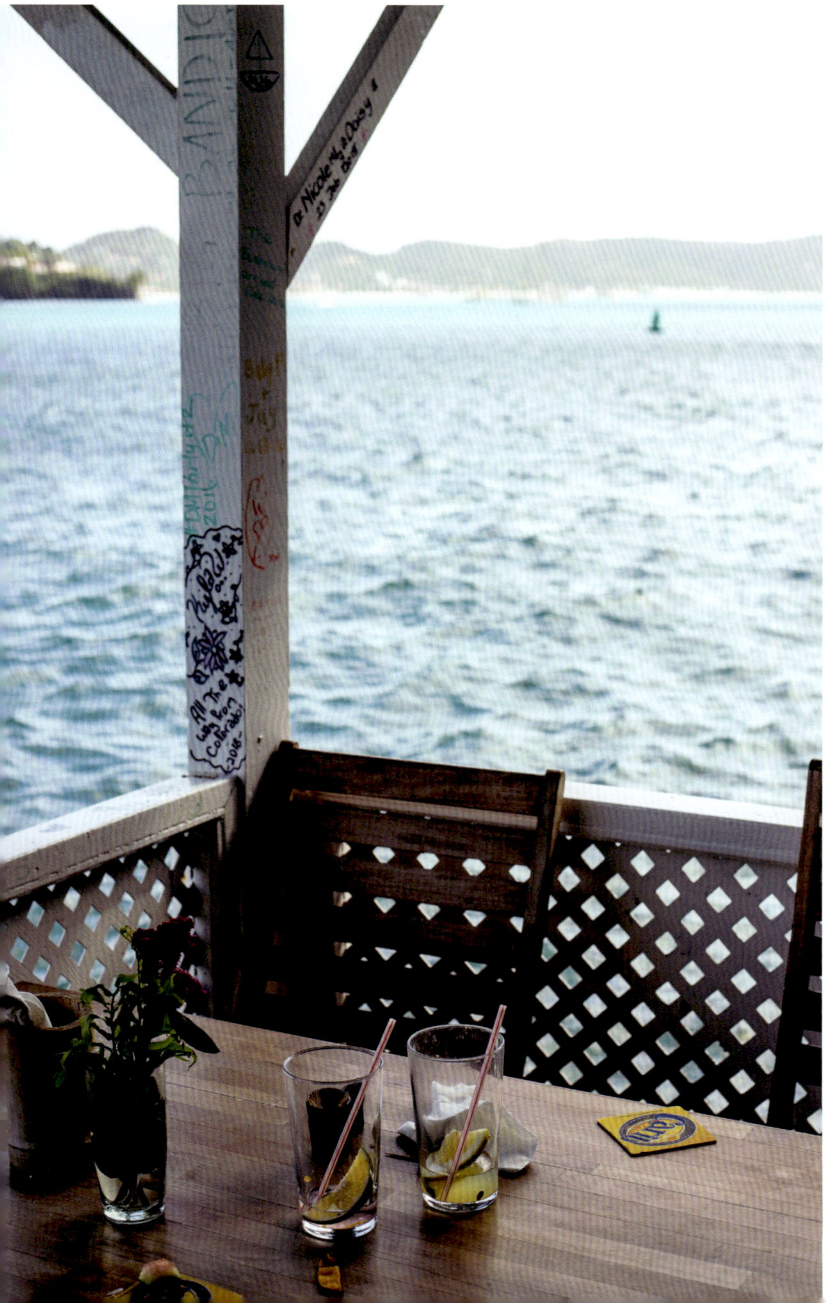

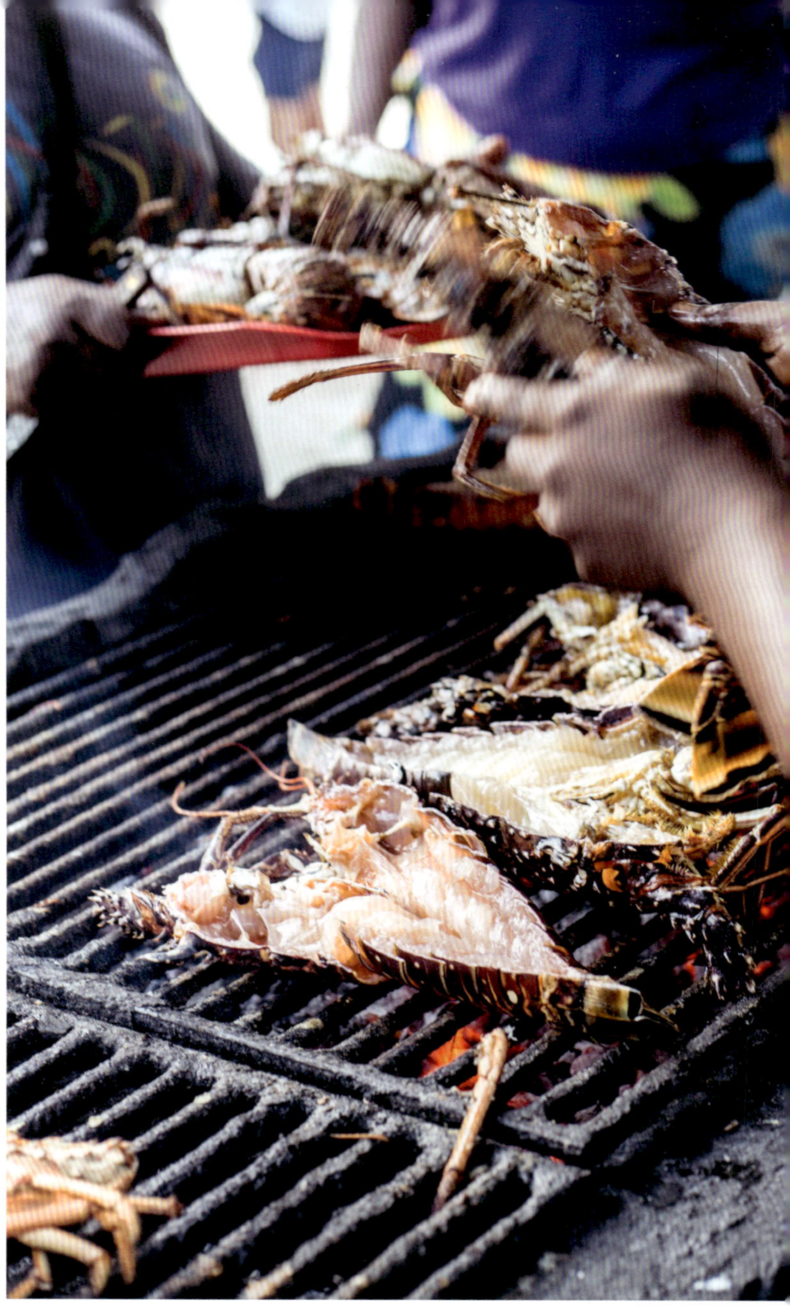

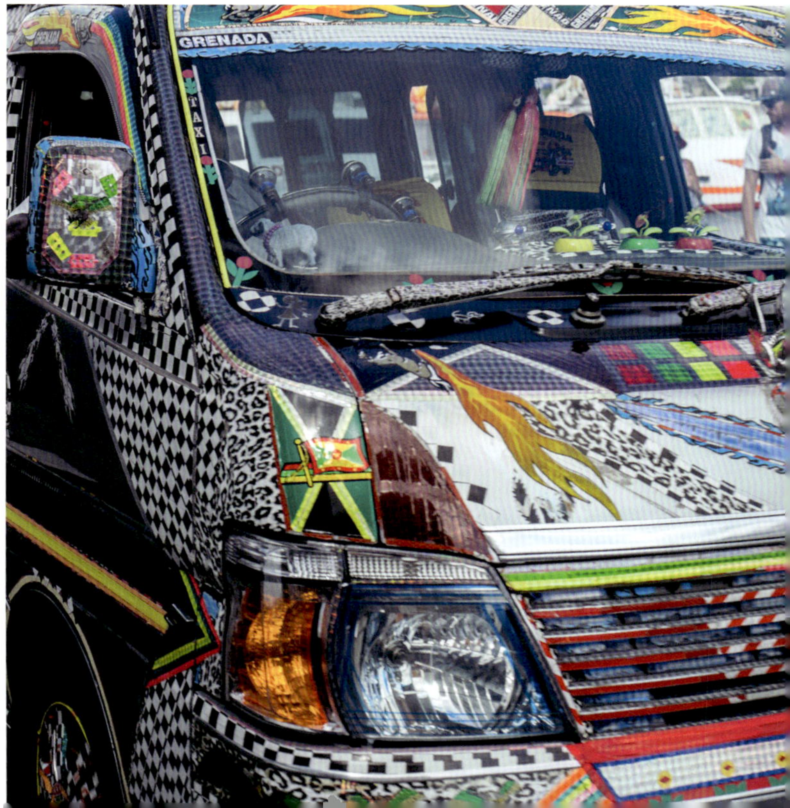
GRENADA

7pm to chat about the goings-on about the island and the evening's social engagements. Even if you are just passing through it's worth listening in to the conversation to get a feel for the pulse of the place.

Carriacou is governed by Grenada and is the northernmost island before you sail towards Saint Vincent and the Grenadines. Tyrell Bay on Carriacou offers very good protection from the tradewinds and is a large anchorage that can accommodate many boats. The presence of a well-equipped local boatyard for repairs makes this a spot where transient sailors tend to congregate and stay put for a while.

The open horizon to the west offers remarkble views of the sun setting over the Caribbean Sea off the back of your boat while you float at anchor. Dinghy ashore and enjoy a local feast at the "Lazy Turtle" or any of the local seaside restaurants offering fish and rum. A fisherman harvests a unique Caribbean oyster that is about the size of a coin. After you finish your anchoring procedures, he'll often dinghy alongside your boat and sell these small but fantastically sweet and delicious shellfish.

HAPPY ISLAND

Adding to Union's layers of Caribbean charm is the aptly named place, Happy Island, located between the harbor of Clifton and Palm Island. Happy Island is just a bar, and that's all. This man-made island is home to Janti Ramage, a local who built the outpost by scavenging conch shells from nearby beaches. After seven years, it grew to the size where he could lay the floor to what would become one of the greatest bars in the world. Like a sovereign state, Janti keeps watch of his patrons. Happy Island serves sailors' thirst for rum punch topped with freshly grated nutmeg. Today, a cement seawall helps it to stay put in a storm and offers a perfect place to sit and dangle your feet in the water as kite surfers cruise by.

SANDY ISLAND

Sitting just west of Carriacou in the protection of its lee is a small skinny island with a few palm trees growing along a fine-grained white beach. Sandy Island is protected parkland and moorings are provided for visiting boats. Ashore is the allure of the desert island: once you have arrived, the humdrum of outside life leaves you alone and you settle into a pace that is solely the wind in the palms and the waves lapping at the sand. A perfect anchorage before sailing north or as a stop on your way back south.

UNION ISLAND

Union Island's steep volcanic peaks are a monument on the horizon as you head north from Carriacou into Grenadines. The two pointed precipices stand out from the other surrounding islands as you approach. There are various nice anchorages on Union. The main town of Clifton is a perfect Caribbean enclave with a big protected harbor and a sleepy colorful village that has everything you need. Docks are available for a fee that offer freshwater to top off your tanks and ample protection inside the reef. Walking along the main street in town you will find a daily farmers market in a park with remarkably good local produce and fruit. There is also a market for all of the imported goods that come in on the ship that is called 'Big Ship Club' and has lots of supplies.

TOBAGO CAYS

The Tobago Cays area is a vast marine park northeast of Union Island surrounded by a barrier reef and encompassing a few uninhabited islands. This stunning playground attracts sailors from islands north and south. The expansive reef system makes entry difficult and care must be taken to stay in the channels, many of them unmarked, and away from the coral heads. Once inside the horseshoe reef, the lagoon is very large. The protected waters are home to many sea turtles and plenty of fish, rays, sea stars, and coral on the outer reef. The current running around the islands can be quite strong so snorkeling parties should take the drift into account when planning their exploration.

Locals in their colorfully painted and cleverly named speedboats are busy in the park offering a wide variety of services. Ice, trash pickup, and souvenirs will all come right to you and each one will offer to arrange a lobster cookout dinner on the beach at Petit Bateau. Employ their services and they will take care of you for this wonderful semi-communal feast that happens nightly around sunset on the beach. Your chosen guide will reserve picnic tables for you and purchase the lobsters to bring to the grills where local chefs from Union Island cook your spiny local lobsters over the coals. Bring your own beverages. No shoes are necessary for dinner or the dance party in the sand that might get going if a steel drum band starts up as the night goes on. The party goes on until the chefs are cleaned up and the generator shuts down for the night, cutting power to the bare light bulbs strung between palm trees. In the moonlight and the silence, as steel drums are handed onto boats for their trip back to Union, you can spend a quiet moment on the beach looking out at the masthead lights of sailboats anchored in the channel.

PETIT SAINT VINCENT

Petit Saint Vincent is a private island with an exclusive resort that features private villas scattered throughout the hills and beaches. The spa on the island is world-class and appointments are open to visiting sailors only after the guests of the island have had a chance to book them. Also open to sailors is a well-appointed beach bar that serves good food and has comfortable lounging with great views. Going ashore here you pay triple the local going rate for a beer but it buys you access to some of the incredible service and gorgeous facilities that the guests of the island enjoy.

MAYREAU

Off the northern end is a high promontory connected to the island by a narrow strip of beach. Salt Whistle Bay on the leeward side offers great protection as you get in close to the beach but is a remarkably rolly anchorage out towards its mouth. The beach is lined with local establishments on the southern end and has beautiful bright sand and coconut palms along its entire stretch. On the windward side of this peninsula, there is a long beach that is perfect for kiteboarders of all skill levels and will often be dotted with colorful kites. The "Last Bar Before the Jungle" sits at the mainland end of the beach and has fabulous breezy views of it all and a ping pong table in the sand under the palm-thatched roof.

~

Many sailors enjoy the many wonders of the Caribbean and never make it as far south as Grenada and the Grenadines. Those who venture this far are rewarded with spectacular islands in a pristine sea. A sense of adventure abounds in these far Windward Islands that will have you wanting to keep seeing what is next over the horizon as you sail.

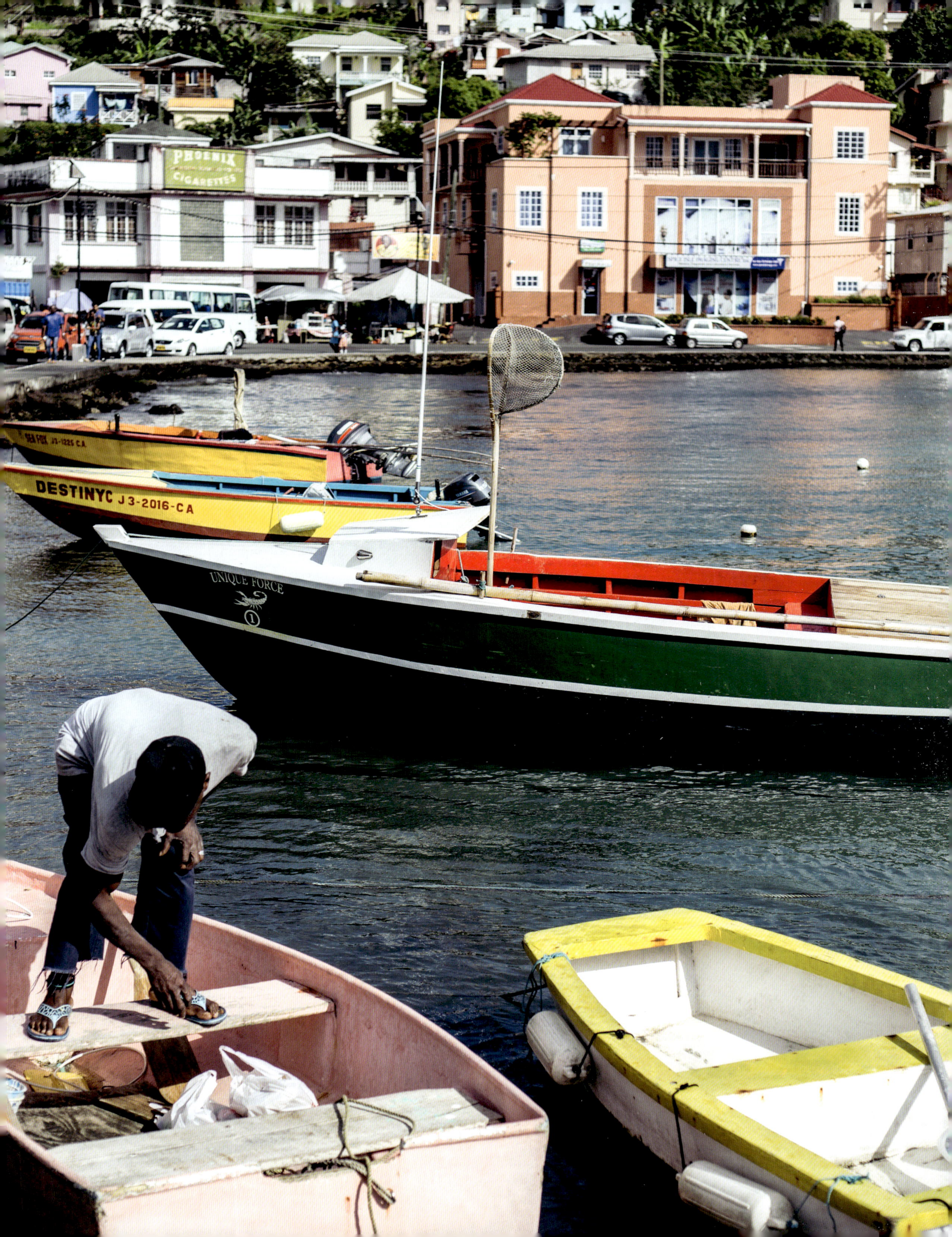
PHOENIX
CIGARETTES
DESTINYC J3-2016-CA
UNIQUE FORCE

CAPTAIN'S NOTES *GRENADA & GRENADINES*

RECOMMENDED ITINERARY

St. George's, Grenada
2° 02′ 43″ N, 61° 44′ 53″ W

The main harbor on Grenada is divided into the yacht harbor to the south, and the commercial harbor to the north. Port Louis Marina has ample slip space and facilities for visiting yachts of all sizes. To buy ice, take your dinghy to the gas station.

Clifton, Union Island
12° 35′ 43″ N, 61° 24′ 51″ W

Moor or anchor inside the reef: "boat boys" driving a locally built wooden dinghy zip past delivering supplies to boats from shops onshore. The outer reef does nothing to block the trade winds on this eastern side of the island and all of the dockings are stern-to, relying on your anchor to hold against the wind, so make sure to get a good set with plenty of scope in case it begins to blow in the night.

Tobago Cays
2° 37′ 57″ N, 61° 21′ 27″ W

Moorings here are included in the park fees that you will pay. Anchoring is allowed but the moorings are plentiful and well maintained in order to discourage boats from dropping anchor on the seagrass, which is an important food source for turtles. A ranger's boat comes around a few times a day and collects the park entry fee for everyone on board.

Salt Whistle Bay, Mayreau
2° 38′ 52″ N, 61° 23′ 29″ W

Moorings towards the outside of the bay tend to get rolly when there is a swell running, but the closer you tuck into the beach the calmer it gets. Steady winds coming over the low sand spit allow for shoal-draft boats to nose right into the beach and anchor safely very close to shore. Roughly 30 yachts can fit in the bay at anchor.

Tyrell Bay, Carriacou Island
12° 27′ 37″ N, 61° 29′ 28″ W

Locals in small boats will offer mooring buoys for a fee. Alternatively, anchor further out towards the mouth of the large bay. A shipwreck in the middle of the anchorage is marked on the chart and should be avoided. Fuel and water are available at the boatyard dock.

RECOMMENDED ANCHORAGES

Chatham Bay, Union Island
Ronde Island
Sandy Island
Petit Saint Vincent

ITINERARY DURATION

7–10 days recommended

PREVAILING WIND

Trade winds during the winter will provide good sailing most days: around force 5 out of the east-northeast. Temperatures are cooler and more comfortable, while the trade winds blow from December to May. The rainy season is hot and humid with not so much wind for sailing.

SEASON

Grenada is closer to the equator than most of the Caribbean islands and therefore has less variation between winter and summer temperatures. It is also further out of the hurricane belt, although notable hurricanes have damaged the island in the past. There is more rain May to November, and June to August are the wettest months.

FOOD

French influence is apparent in the island's many well-seasoned seafood dishes and Indian and Carib Amerindian influence is also seen in the island's cuisine. The *oildown* is the national dish and Grenadians also use the term to refer to a neighborhood party where they serve it cooked over an open fire. An *oildown* is a stew of sorts that is cooked in fresh coconut milk until all the milk is absorbed, leaving coconut oil in the bottom of the pot. Every family has their own *oildown* recipe and the style and flavor can vary wildly. If you try it and don't fancy it at one establishment, be sure to sample others when you come across them. Common staples in an *oildown* are breadfruit, flour dumplings, green banana, potatoes, and yams layered into a big pot, slow-cooked and never stirred, spiced to preference using the islands huge array of local spices.

GOOD TO KNOW

Kick 'em Jenny
An undersea volcano named "Kick 'em Jenny"—near Ronde Island, in the crossing between Grenada and Carriacou—is active and daily alerts are issued about the danger level. The nautical exclusion zone gets bigger or smaller depending on the current threat. What appears to be a tranquil stretch of ocean on the surface may have untold dangers lurking underneath.

Fishing
If you have the gear to troll off the back of the boat, don't miss the opportunity to fish the waters between Grenada and Carricou. This stretch has a strong current where an undersea ridge pushes ocean water up from the deep, causing schools of fish to gather here for feeding. Always be sure to have the proper fishing licence for the waters that you are sailing in and follow local regulations.

Boat commerce
A good relationship with the local "boat boys" (some of them actually old men) can get you just about anything you need on these islands. Michelangelo on Union Island is a speedboat taxi driver, who can also arrange dock reservations, gets you a lobster cookout in Tobago Cays, brings you an emergency canister of cooking fuel on Mayreau.

Magnetic Variance
Magnetic Declination: -14° (WEST)

CANOUAN

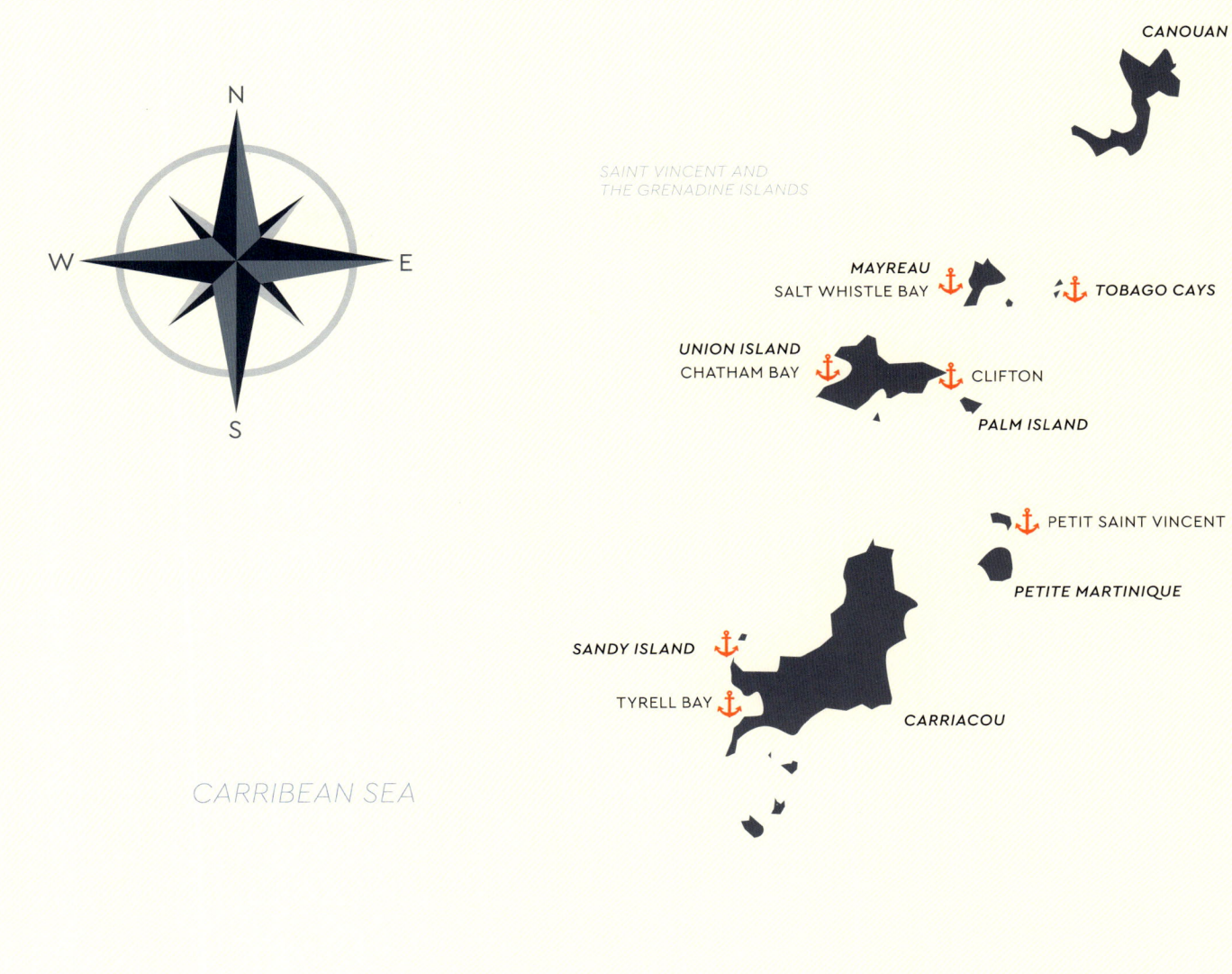

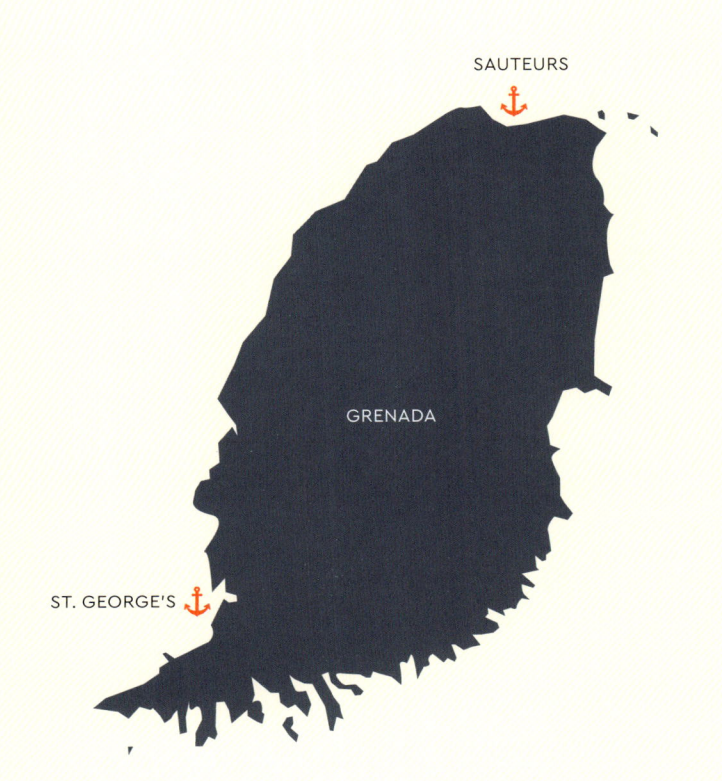

SAINT VINCENT AND
THE GRENADINE ISLANDS

MAYREAU
SALT WHISTLE BAY ⚓ ⚓ TOBAGO CAYS

UNION ISLAND
CHATHAM BAY ⚓ ⚓ CLIFTON
PALM ISLAND

⚓ PETIT SAINT VINCENT
PETITE MARTINIQUE

SANDY ISLAND ⚓
TYRELL BAY ⚓
CARRIACOU

CARIBBEAN SEA

CORN STAY ⚓
BAY   RONDE ISLAND

KICK 'EM JENNY

ATLANTIC OCEAN

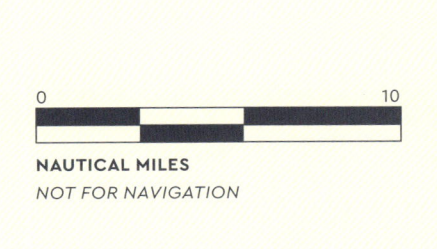

SAUTEURS ⚓

GRENADA

ST. GEORGE'S ⚓

0 — 10
NAUTICAL MILES
NOT FOR NAVIGATION

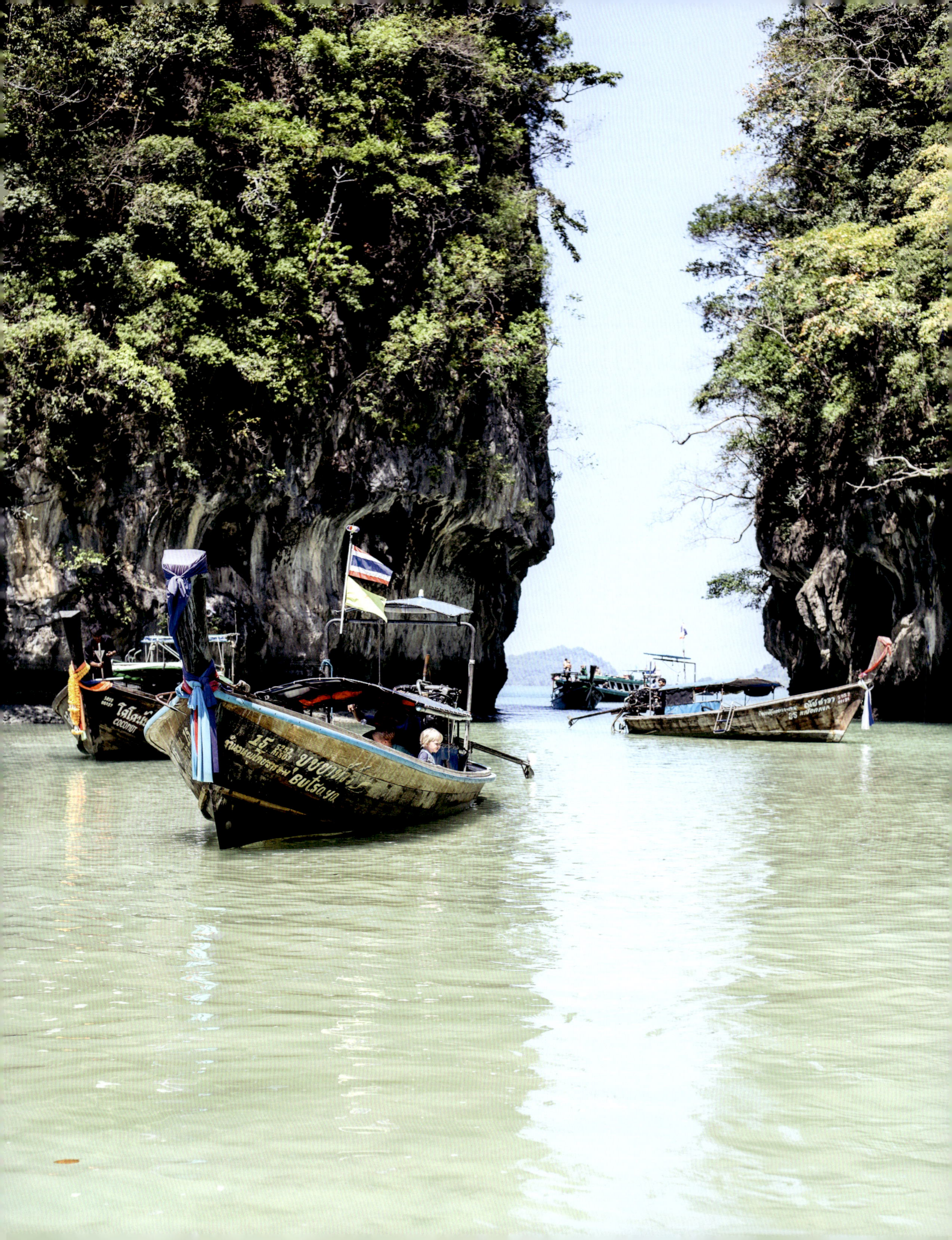

THE LIMESTONE CLIFFS OF THAILAND

THE ANDAMAN SEA IS A SEEMINGLY ENDLESS COASTLINE THAT STRETCHES FROM MYANMAR DOWN TO MALAYSIA. BETWEEN THE ISLAND OF PHUKET AND KRABI, HOWEVER, IS A TUCKED AWAY PARADISE WITH VERDANT CLIFFS AND TURQUOISE WATERS.

Referred to by residents as "the Kingdom," Thailand is enchanting. Sail this fairy-tale coast and you'll discover jungles enveloping otherworldly rock formations, wildlife on both the sea and land, and welcoming people, who love this region with all their heart. Bursting with flavors and powerful scenery, life is friendly and people are gracious. The coastline is endless, with over 1,000 nautical miles of shore in the Gulf of Thailand and along the Malay Peninsula, where you'll find the Andaman Sea, home to some of the most interesting sailing anywhere in the world. The most established yachting center is located on Phuket Island, a location not foreign to hospitality and tourism.

Thai people often describe their country as looking like the head of a smiling elephant: Bangkok sits in the elephant's open mouth and Phuket is down at the curve in the trunk. East of Phuket is Phang Nga Bay—a dimple in the wise old elephant's rough skin.

This vibrant itinerary takes on different forms and color palettes from Phang Nga Bay down into the Andaman Sea, even in the tone of the water. Cruising from north to south, you see the slow change of water clarity over the course of a long day's sail: one starts the morning in cloudy, caramel-colored river water flowing out of the mangrove channels, and anchors in clear blues and greens in the evening. An enormous river delta at the head of Phang Nga Bay is what makes the water rich in sediment and dark in color. In the south, the sediment has settled out, leaving you in the clarity of the Andaman, with all of its colorful reefs and abundant marine life visible as you sail and swim.

PHANG NGA BAY

Phang Nga Bay is the enchanting home to hundreds of islands and rock formations that rise from the shallow bay, reaching high into the sky. The northern islands are a surrealist masterpiece, with towering limestone pillars that balance on slender foundations and are topped with funny bouffants of vegetation. Ocean swell doesn't make it through the maze of islands to the north and you'll have fair conditions as the wind pushes you along. The bay is wide but unexpectedly shallow for such a vast expanse of water; if you don't keep a close eye on the charts and stay in the many natural channels, you'll see your depth sounder display some uncomfortably low numbers.

The danger of running aground is real and tidal currents can be strong, so you'll want to factor this into your itinerary and not assume that you can sail straight lines across what appears for all the world to be a lot of water.

Find a *hong* (sea cave) or two to explore as you make your way around the bay: a cave entrance will open into a large, atrium-like center that is open to the sky and home to its own micro-environment. In the interior lagoon of a *hong*, steep cliffs rise out of the water on all sides with vines and lush growth clinging to the rock walls. Wandering into these open-air caves is nearly indescribable and, at first impression, you might think these remarkable places were created by supernatural forces. Be sure to time your adventure with the rising or falling tides, leaving before the waters are too high to exit or too low to navigate, and always keep your safety as the first priority.

KO PANYI

Entering the river delta area in the north of Phang Nga Bay, you will find the island of Ko Panyi, where a densely populated small village sits on stilts, above the water and is referred to as the "floating village." It was originally formed by nomadic Malay fisherman, who settled on Ko Panyi in the eighteenth century. Over time, these nomads put down roots and built permanent structures, with large wooden pilings set into the mud below. Since its humble early beginnings, the community here has grown to around 360 families, and today has a population of over 1,500 people.

Despite the rise of tourism in recent years, the village still relies largely on fishing as its main revenue source. Along the docks are net pens, where live fish are kept. If you peer into them through the murky water you can sometimes see enormous fish being kept alongside oysters and anything else that can be kept in this way.

Anchor along the river, on the east side of the village, in ten meters of water and dinghy to the floating docks to explore. There are a few restaurants "on shore," which mostly cater to day tours that arrive on speedboats for lunch, but they will remain open for dinner if you place your order ahead of time. Since this is a fishing village, ordering from the wide variety of seafood listed on the restaurant's menu is the way to go. Included are delectable barramundi fish, prepared a variety of ways using ingredients harvested on the mainland. Also sold are large local oysters, cultivated in the brackish waters and served raw or in a delicious lemongrass soup.

The ecological importance of the delta around the village is recognized globally and it was designated as a wetland of international importance by UNESCO in 2002. Its vast network of mangrove forests spawns an abundance of fish and shelters over 80 bird species. Hire a local guide to pick you up at the anchorage in a shoal-drafted longtail boat and take you into the miles of natural channels. You'll see white-bellied sea eagles, collared kingfishers, and the Pacific swallow flying above in great numbers.

Sailors share the waterway with village fishermen using longtail wooden boats to cast nets and traps for crab, shrimp, and fish. Drop a baited line while under sail and you might be so lucky as to catch a mahi-mahi or a barramundi—anything caught will be the perfect fish to cook aboard while at anchor along this dramatic coast.

KO YAO NOI AND KO YAO YAI

Two large islands sit in the middle of Phang Nga Bay: Ko Yao Noi and Ko Yao Yai, separated by a shallow passageway. Although a number of modern resorts have been developed here recently, these islands remain rural and traditional. The population is mostly made up of Thailand's Muslim minority group and life for the islanders has a traditional tone.

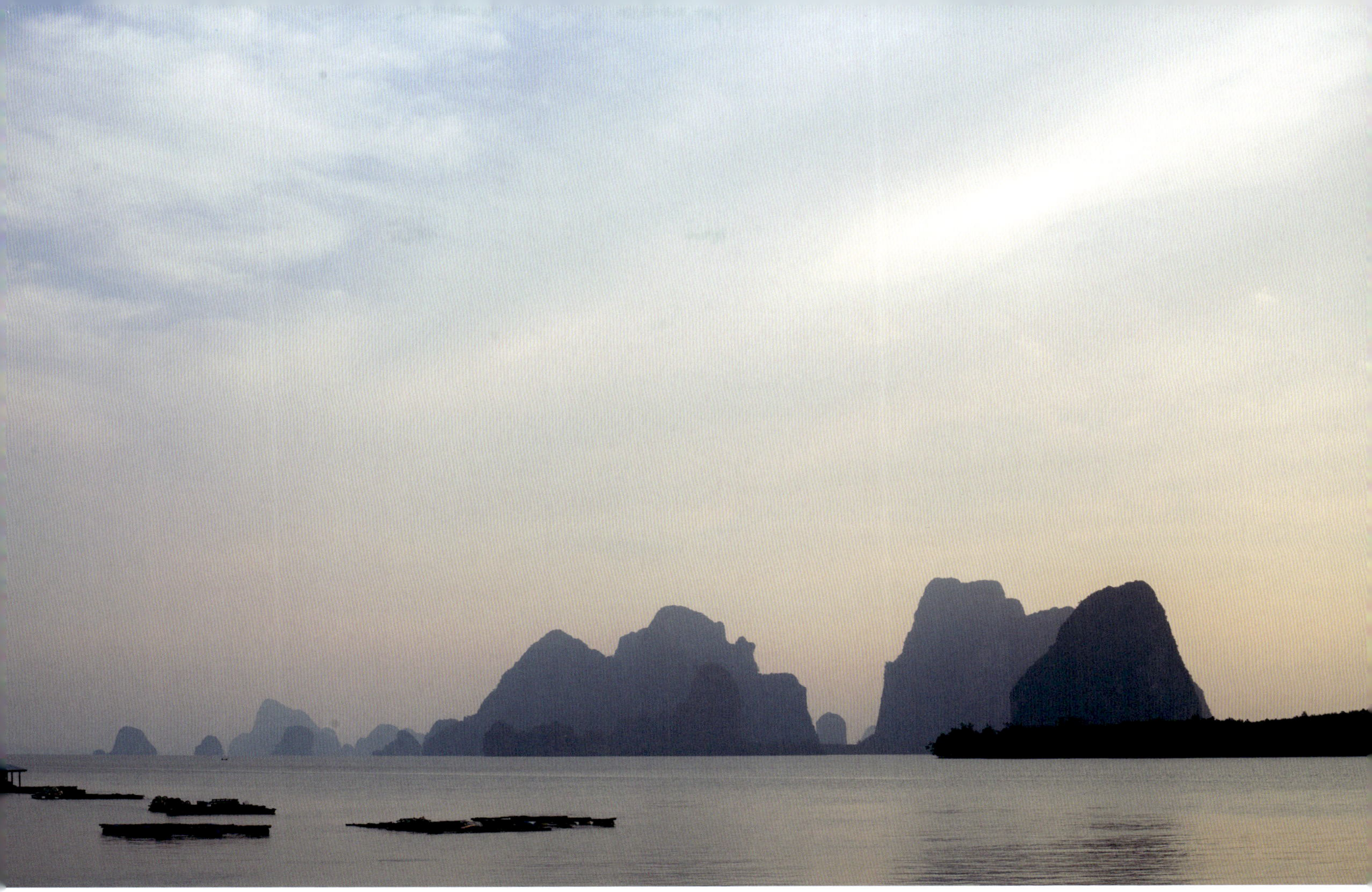

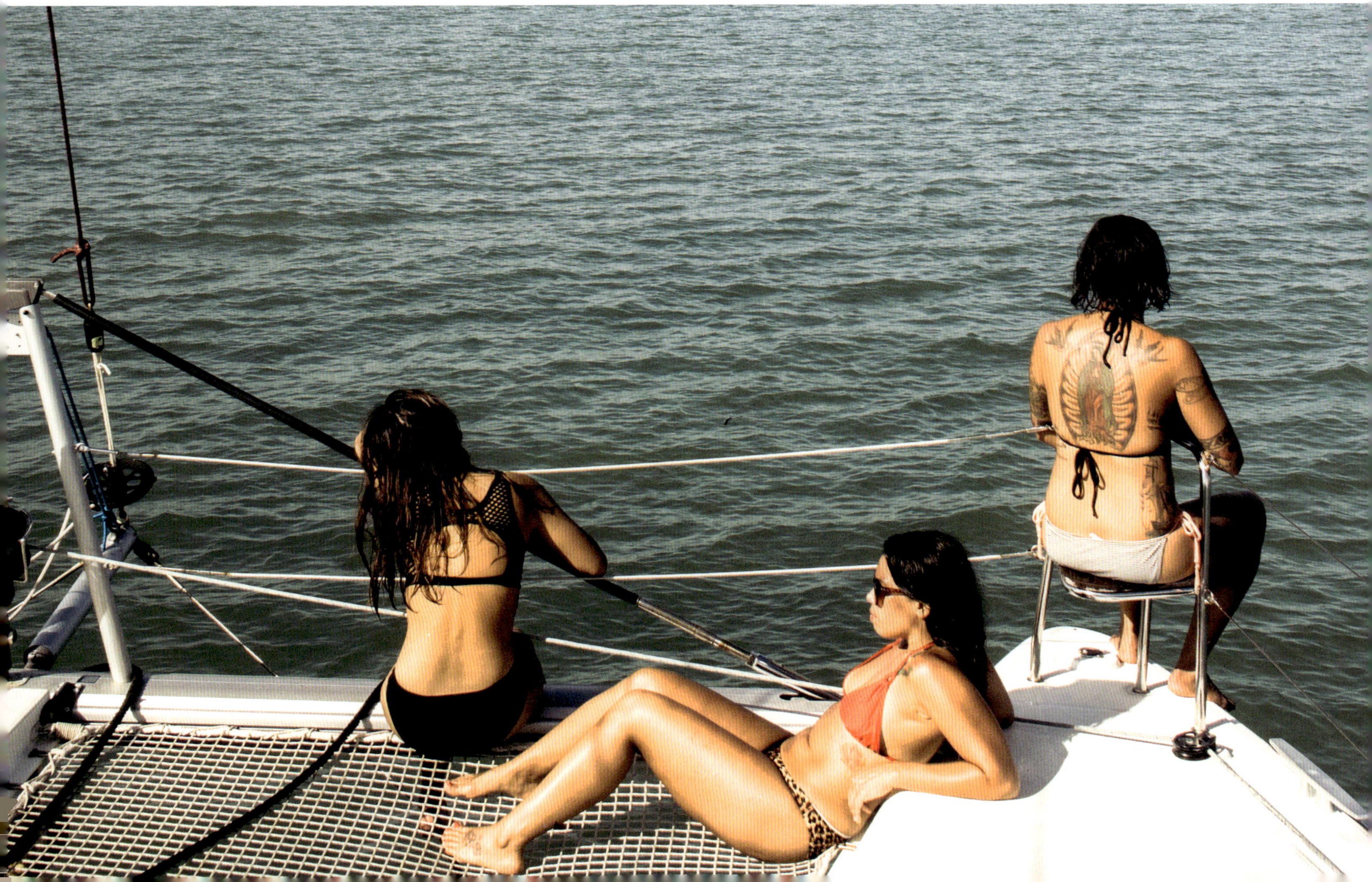

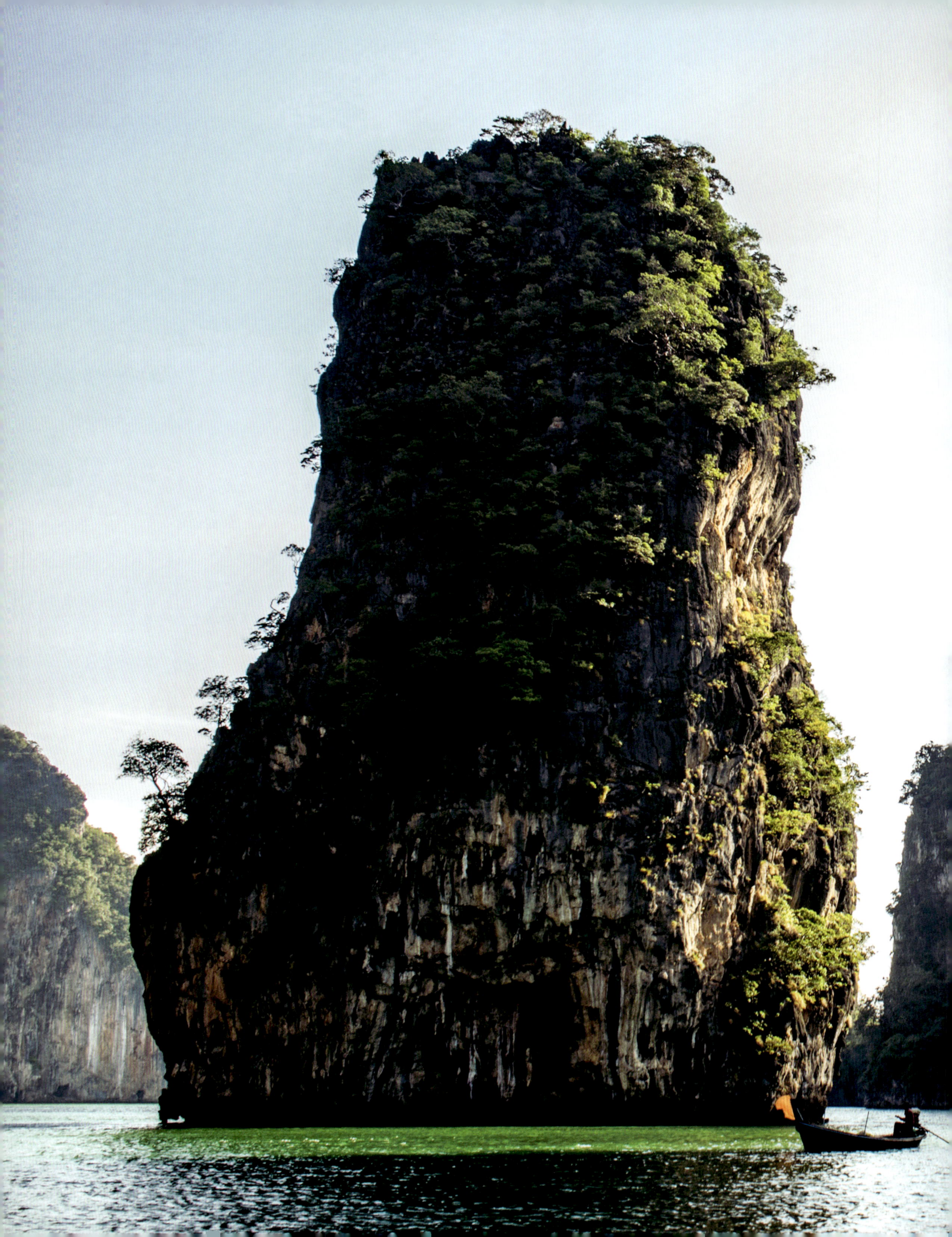

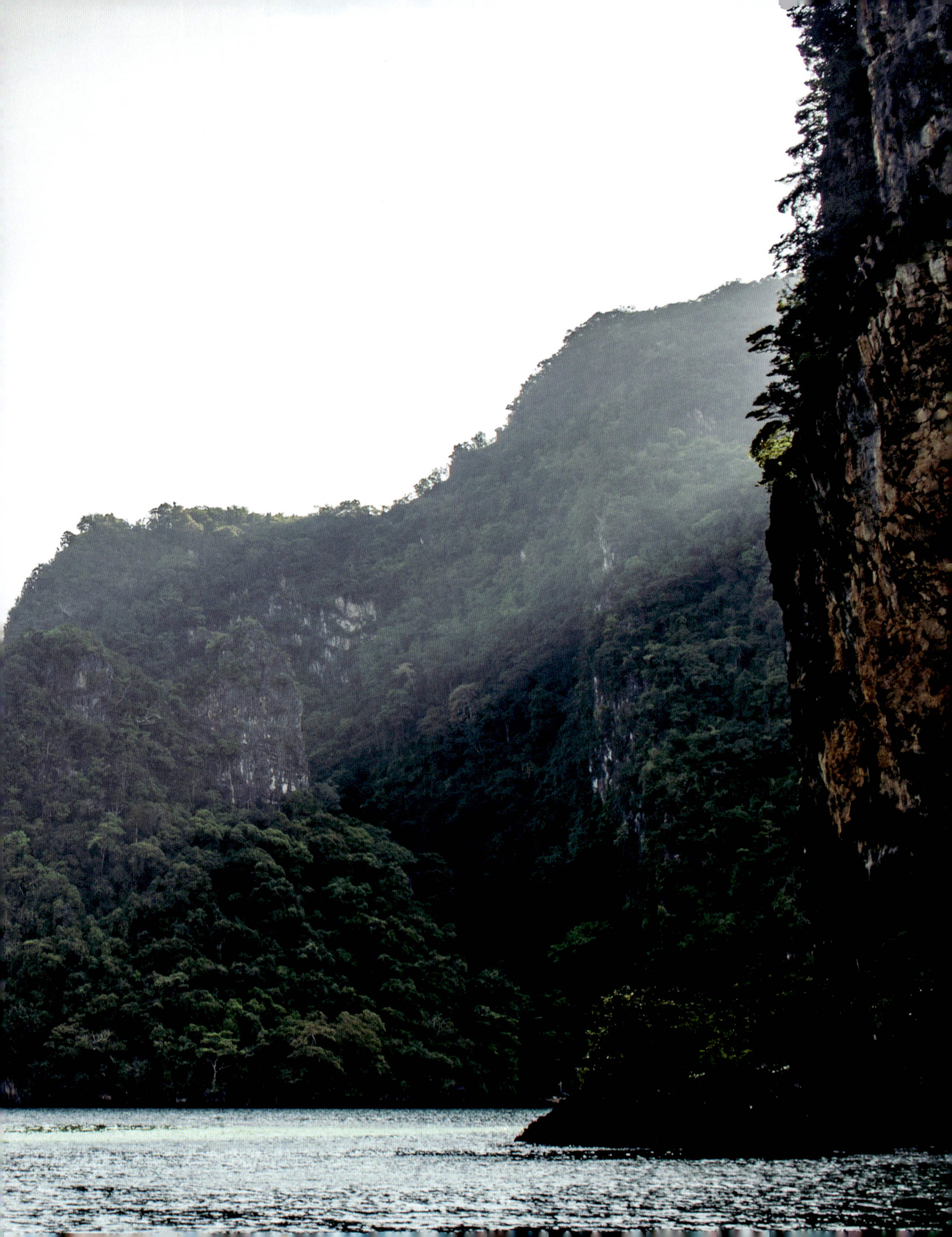

The two islands are lush, and geographically appear more similar to Phuket than the nearby Hong Island, even if they are a world apart culturally. Going ashore will take you back in time, giving you an idea of life on the island of Phuket before it became a major tourist destination. The interior of each island is worth exploring, though you will be dependent on dirt bikes and scooters. You will see the rows of thin, tall rubber trees that are tapped for sap to produce natural latex.

The islands are located in the center of the sailing itinerary and are a convenient port of call while sailing north to south. On a picturesque sandy beach on the western side of Ko Yao Yai are a number of small restaurants serving local seafood to their patrons, who sit on plastic chairs and tables right at the water's edge. Fresh fish are laid out for you to choose, and there are saltwater tanks with live shellfish and the local delicacy, mantis shrimp: these are grilled and served with a chili, lime, and cilantro dipping sauce.

RAILAY AND TONSAI BEACHES

Moving out of the silty waters of the north brings you to crystal-clear tropical waters and white sand beaches. Thickly forested mountains with breathtaking limestone walls and overhung rock amphitheaters hide caves and vistas that are yours to discover.

Across the bay from Phuket, towards the east, is Krabi Province, a mountainous part of mainland Thailand known for the steep and towering cliffs that stand over the sea below. Railay Beach is on a mainland peninsula but not accessible by roads because of the impenetrable mountains that block land travel to Krabi own. The beaches are lined with hotels and tourists are brought in by longtail boats. There is a pleasant anchorage that offers you the ability to explore Railay and spend an afternoon in the bustle of the popular beach. Of particular interest is the cave where phallic statues are set up as altars to fertility; also, the wonderful "food truck boats" that nose into the beach and take orders while you stand knee-deep in the surf. Getting a massage on the sand in the shade of a mango tree is always going to be nice, even if you are in the midst of a crowd of people doing the same thing.

Sharing the anchorage is another valley, also isolated by its inaccessibility, and you can hike here from Railay over the steep rocky bluff (though better to just take your dinghy around). This world-renowned rock climbing location has a very different feel from Railay. Climbing backpackers will often settle into the rustic, affordable bungalows, high in the jungle here, for months at a time. The eclectic bar scene as you wander the jungle paths is distinctly bohemian and you'll meet people from all over the world in this small valley.

KO PODA

Not far from the hustle of Railay beach is a group of islands with great snorkeling, idyllic beaches, and world-class deepwater solo rock climbing. Arriving at these islands from Railay will remind you why sailboats are the best way to see the world. In the sunset light you will see the adventurous tourists, who managed to hire a longtail water taxi to take them out for the day, returning to their hotels. Meanwhile, you enjoy the quiet evening on deck in the lee of a jungle-capped spire, next to a sandy beach that is hidden between cliffs.

KO RACHA YAI

Sitting south of Phuket Island is Ko Racha Yai, an island notable for its white sand beaches and emerald waters. Differing greatly from the northern region of Phang Nga Bay, this island is located in less protected waters. Sailing here from the Phi Phi Islands, Phuket or Krabi, you'll likely cruise through rougher waters with larger swells. This is a good opportunity to explore open-water sailing, however, as Ko Racha Yai is about 25 nautical miles from its closest neighbor.

DRIED CHILIS AND ANCHOVIES, ESSENTIAL INGREDIENTS OF THE THAI CUISINE (ABOVE, RIGHT). GOONG OB WOONSEN, A TYPICAL DISH FROM SOUTHERN THAILAND (BELOW, LEFT). CRABS PURCHASED FROM A LONGTAIL FISHERMAN (BELOW, RIGHT).

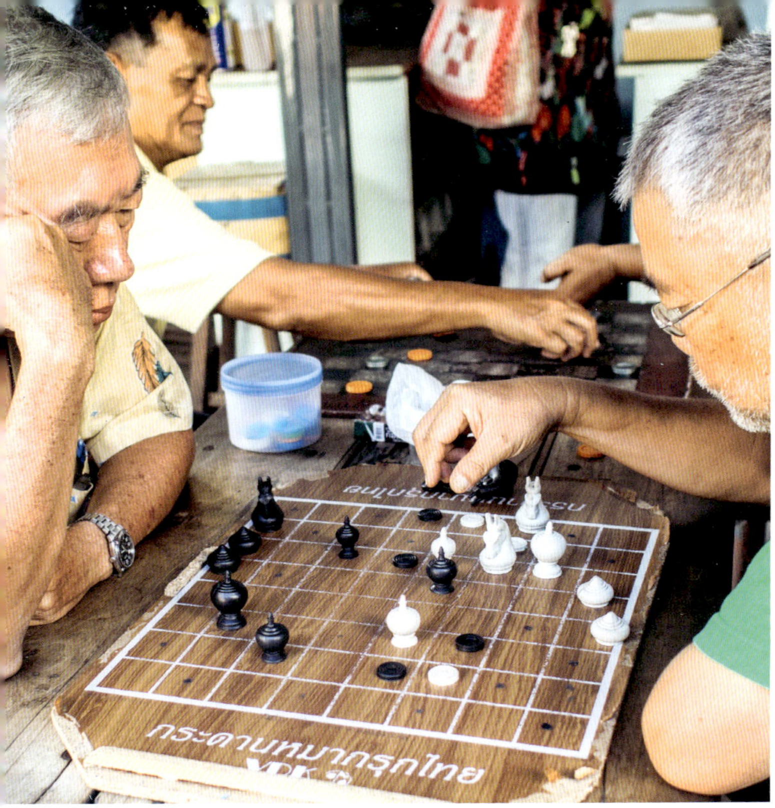
กระดานหมากรุกไทย

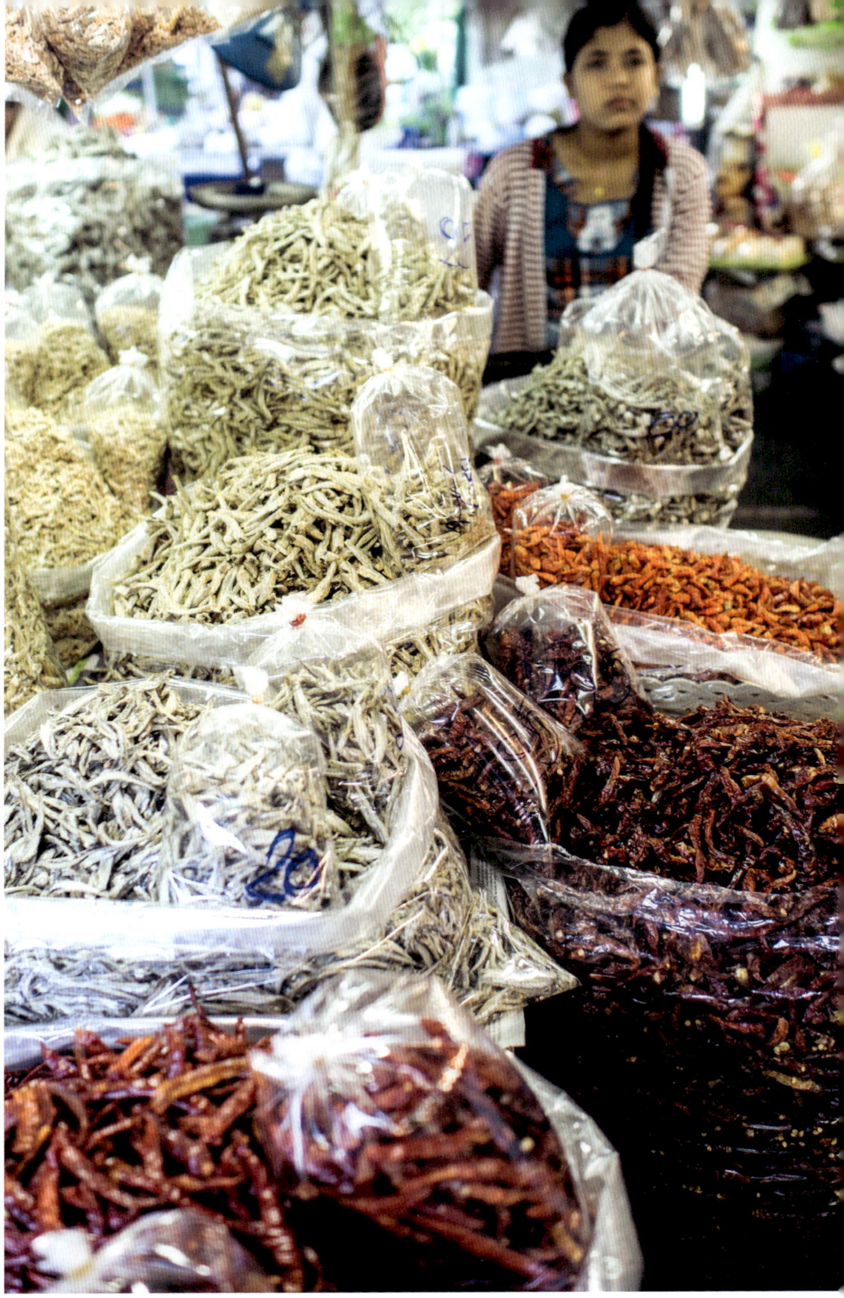

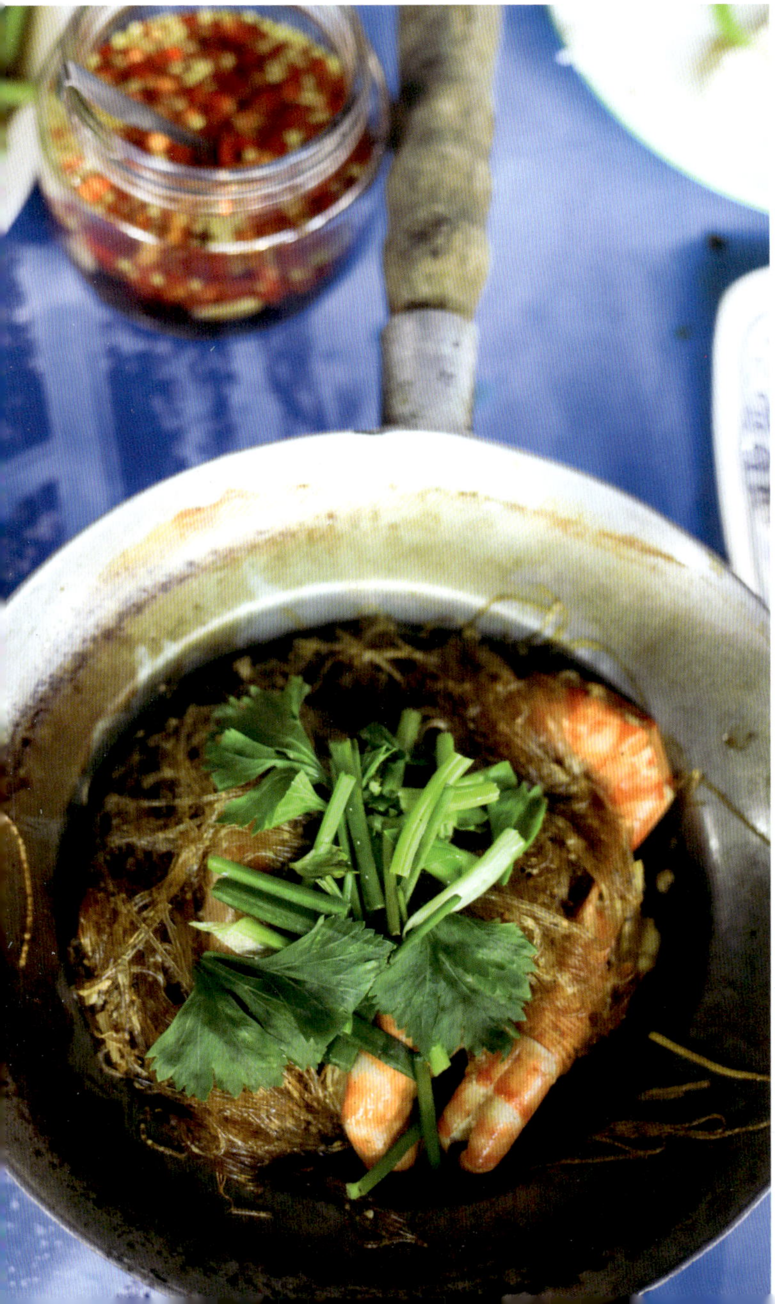

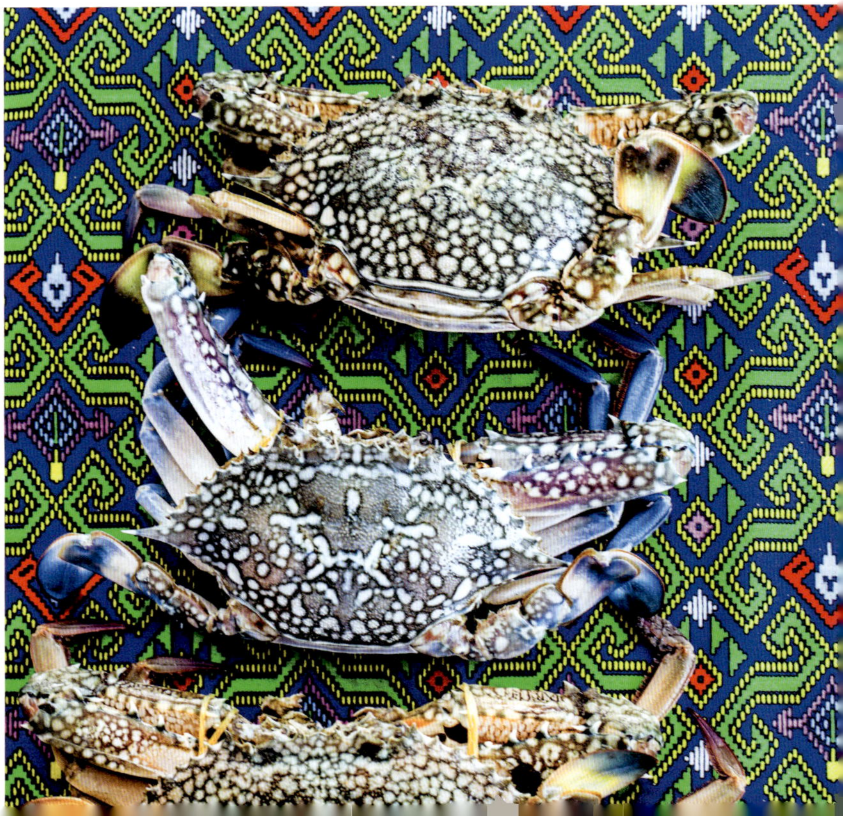

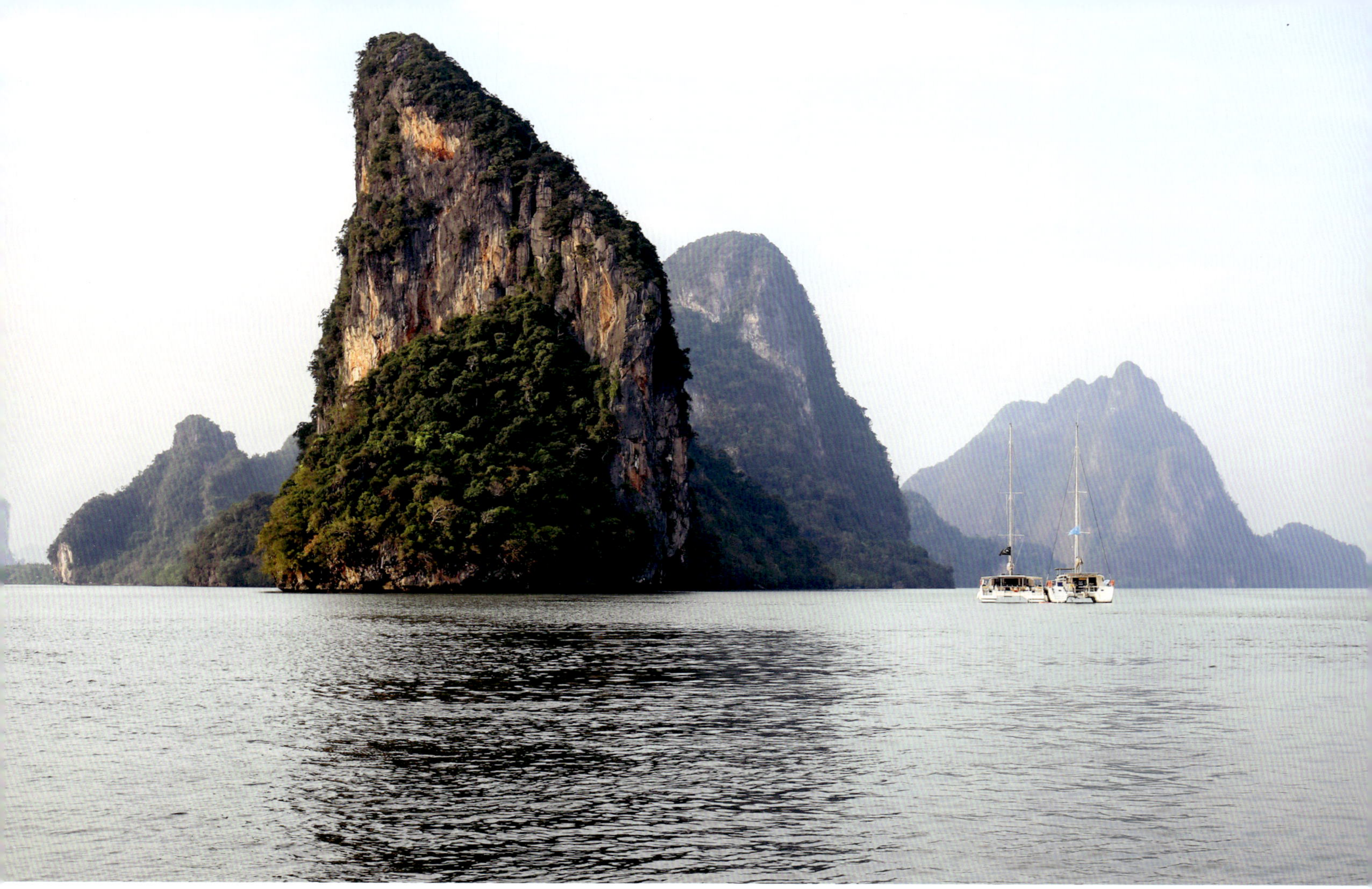

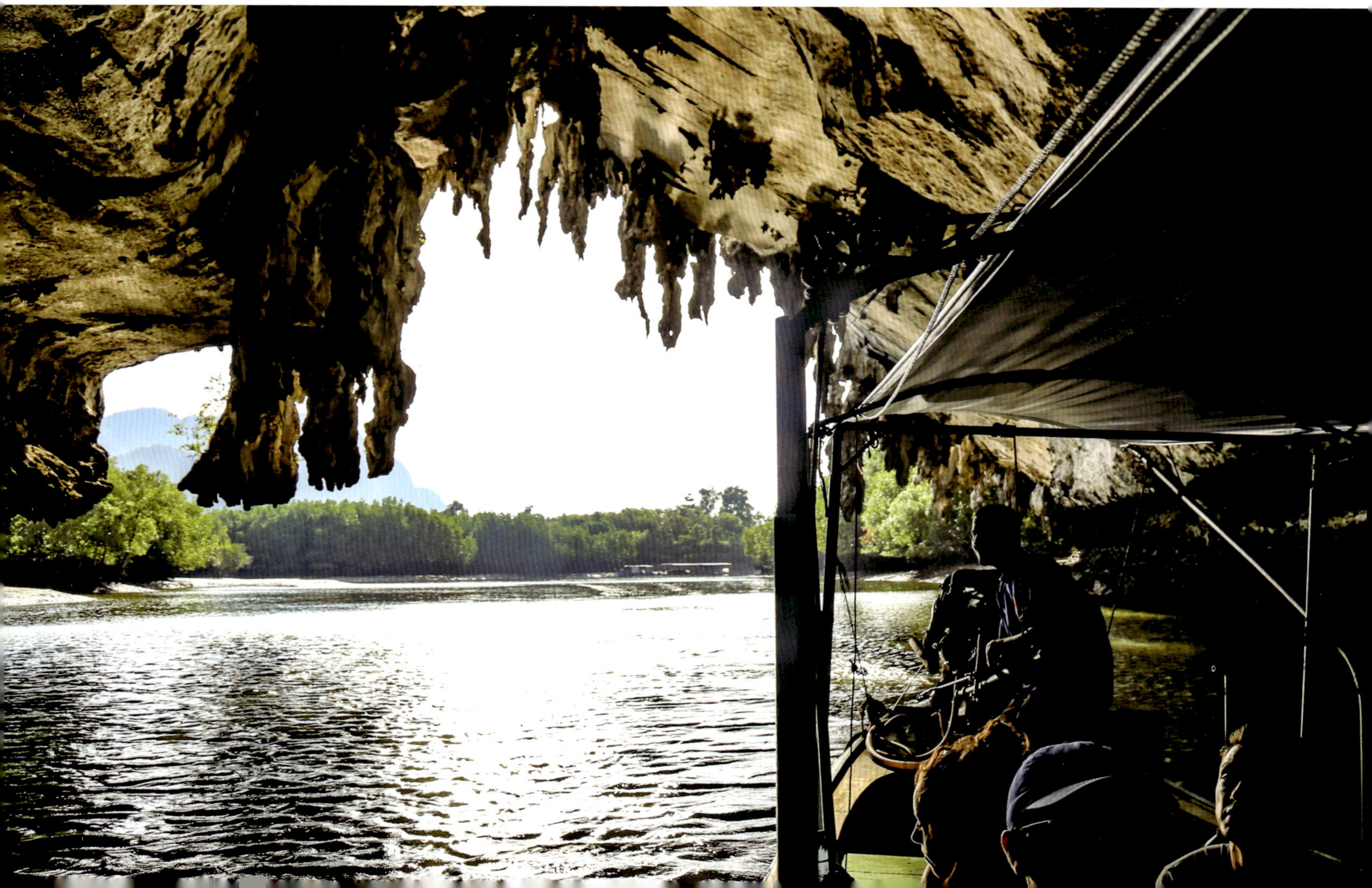

Patok Beach is protected from the prevailing easterly winds during the winter season and is a beautifully suitable anchorage with white sand and crystal-blue waters sitting beneath your keel. The island itself is relatively small—much of it uninhabited and forested. Beside the white sand along Patok Beach is a luxury resort that has a good cocktail bar.

Busy during the day with boats taking tourists back and forth from Phuket, parts of this sparsely inhabited island can become overwhelmed by day-trippers. Tour boats leave Patok Beach in late afternoon, however, as the serious sailors are just arriving from a day's sail, and by early evening the island is quiet and serene. Going ashore on a walk towards the village where islanders live, you will pass water buffalo grazing in fields along the dirt roads and islanders tilling the land.

KO PHI PHI

In the anchorages of Ko Phi Phi, longtail boats zip past at all times of the day, from early morning to late at night: tourists taking rides to remote beaches for romantic sunset moments or, possibly, vacationers off to go snorkeling at Monkey Beach. On shore there is a charismatic chaos, with hundreds of hotels and guesthouses jammed into packed alleyways full of tattoo shops, food stalls, and every imaginable color of Chang Beer-logo tank top. Mixed drinks are literally sold by the bucket to excited groups of party-seeking travelers getting ready all day to go all night at the dance clubs along the beach.

Sail here for the raucous good times and the perspective that they lend you. Phi Phi has become a beacon for backpackers wandering this part of the world over the years, and, during a trip ashore, their slightly rambunctious lifestyle is evident. The activity contrasts greatly with the experience a sailor will have just around the corner, anchored off a jungle cove with monkeys on the cliffs high above your mast top. It sparks inevitable feelings of gratitude for the experience of seeing these islands in another way. Which isn't to say that Ko Phi Phi isn't fun. In fact, this island is developed around fun. Fire dancers on the beach outside the flashy dance clubs are there to push your evening into a surreal and hedonistic indulgence of the senses.

Ko Phi Phi Island itself is large and lush. Dramatic limestone cliffs are on display along the coast as you sail towards the island's anchorages. No single anchorage is particularly well protected, so pick your night's stay carefully with the latest weather forecast in mind. Ko Phi Phi must not be overlooked during your sailing itinerary in the region: although the main town is not for everyone, the island is beautiful, with dramatic *hong* on the southern coast and anchorages aplenty.

~

Sailing in Thailand is an opportunity to go on an adventure. The navigation is exciting, the locations are exotic, the food is tantalizing, and the people are amazing. The coastline of Phang Nga Bay, in particular, lends itself well to exploration by sailboat. Calm waters and spectacular islands lend this bay a majesty that lingers in your imagination long after you leave.

ISLAND NAMES

Knowing a little basic Thai can help you navigate the Andaman, where many islands have identical or very similar names. To help differentiate islands that share the same name look for the name of the island group added to the end: for example, Ko Hong Krabi and Ko Hong Phang Nga.

RAFTED UP ANCHORED OFF OF KO PANYI (ABOVE).
LIMESTONE STALACTITES IN A CAVE LOCATED IN
PHANG NGA BAY (BELOW).

CAPTAIN'S NOTES *PHANG NGA BAY*

RECOMMENDED ITINERARY

Ko Hong Phang Nga
8° 13′12″ N, 98° 30′05″ E
Anchor along the shore of Ko Kaya and enjoy dinner on your boat while the tour boats reign in the big *hong*. As they start to leave for the day, the enormous cavern will be yours to explore. At low tide bring water shoes to walk the sand flats, and at high tide, you can access areas via dinghy.

Ko Panyi
8° 20′23″ N, 98° 30′20″ E
Proceed upriver past this village and anchor in good holding northeast of the last village pier. On the tidal change, current will switch directions, so prepare your swing room accordingly. Dinghy tie-up is available at the main town dock or at any of the restaurants.

Ko Poda and Ko Dam
7° 58′09″ N, 98° 48′18″ E
In calm conditions, anchor in deep water near the hidden beach on the west of Ko Poda and tie a stern line to rock formations onshore. In force 3 winds or above, moor north of Ko Dam, to the west of the sand spit that is visible at low tide.

Monkey Beach, Ko Phi Phi
7° 44′41″ N, 98° 45′42″ E
The bustling town on Ko Phi Phi can be accessed via either of the island's main bays, and your choice should be made depending on the forecast. Prevailing winds will most often put you at Monkey Beach, where you can moor or anchor. If you decide to take the long dinghy trip to town, follow the channel that the longtails use to approach the beach; alternatively, flag a passing longtail for a ride into town.

Maya Bay, Koh Phi Phi Le
7° 40′46″ N, 98° 45′53″ E
Moor here, along the northern cliffs outside the snorkeling zone, which is roped off with buoys. Access to the shore is controlled by the local park rangers, who will advise you as to current restrictions and fees. This dramatic setting is one of the most protected environmental zones in the region for good reason: years of tour boat traffic have seriously damaged the reefs, and restoration efforts are ongoing.

Ko Racha Yai
7° 36′33″ N, 98° 21′48″ E
Moor towards the southern side of the harbor for excellent snorkeling along the shoreline all the way out to the point. Dinghy to the floating pier off the main beach for access to shops and restaurants on shore.

Ko Yao Yai
7° 58′48″ N, 98° 34′03″ E
Anchor off the beach in 2–4 fathoms; a clay bottom makes for difficult holding to the south of the hotel pier. Dinghy to the pier or land directly on the beach.

RECOMMENDED ANCHORAGES

Hong Island
Ko Yao Noi
Railay Beach
Ko Roi

ITINERARY DURATION

7+ days recommended

SEASON

Phuket has two seasons annually: a northeast *Monsoon* season, running from October to May; and a southwest *Monsoon* season, running from June to October. Light but steady winds characterize the former, with temperatures around 85 degrees Fahrenheit. Dry and sunny weather prevails. In the latter, southwest winds reach force 2–6 and the climate becomes humid and rainy.
The wind direction will have you favor anchorages on the east side of islands or in sheltered bays. There is still safe sailing in Phang Nga Bay as far south as Ko Phi Phi, but expect to encounter larger swells as you venture south. It is wettest during September and October when there can be extended periods of rain lasting up to five days.

FOOD

There is wonderful food to be had everywhere you look in Thailand, and the markets are no exception. As you shop for the boat, be sure to find a local fresh market and buy a selection of fruits that you have never seen before in your life. With a basket full of Noi Na (custard apple) and Sala (snake fruit), your own culinary creations await.

Kanom jeen (Phuket yellow crab curry)
The waters surrounding Phuket have an abundance of crab. One dish that highlights this delightful seafood is *kanom jeen*, a dish found throughout Thailand but is particularly unique in and around Phuket. It is made using a thin round rice noodle served with nam ya pu, a spicy coconut milk-base with crab and southern-style herbs, vegetables, fruit and seasoning mixed together. It's sweet from the coconut-milk, spicy from the curry, and supple from the crab meat. Simply delicious.

GOOD TO KNOW

Hongs
Exploring the *hongs* of Thailand is an experience no sailor should miss, but proper precautions and respect should be exercised at all times. *Hongs* that have local guides for hire are your safest bet; there is no substitute for local knowledge, especially in variable tidal conditions that can make the cave entrances dynamic. When exploring on your own, respect wildlife by never running your dinghy motor inside a *hong*, where noise and pollution can be detrimental to the sensitive ecosystems.

Park fees
On this itinerary, you have the privilege of sailing through multiple national parks. As sailors, we have come to experience natural beauty, and we can think of park fees as a way to contribute directly towards marine preservation and enforcement.

Magnetic Variance
none

THAILAND

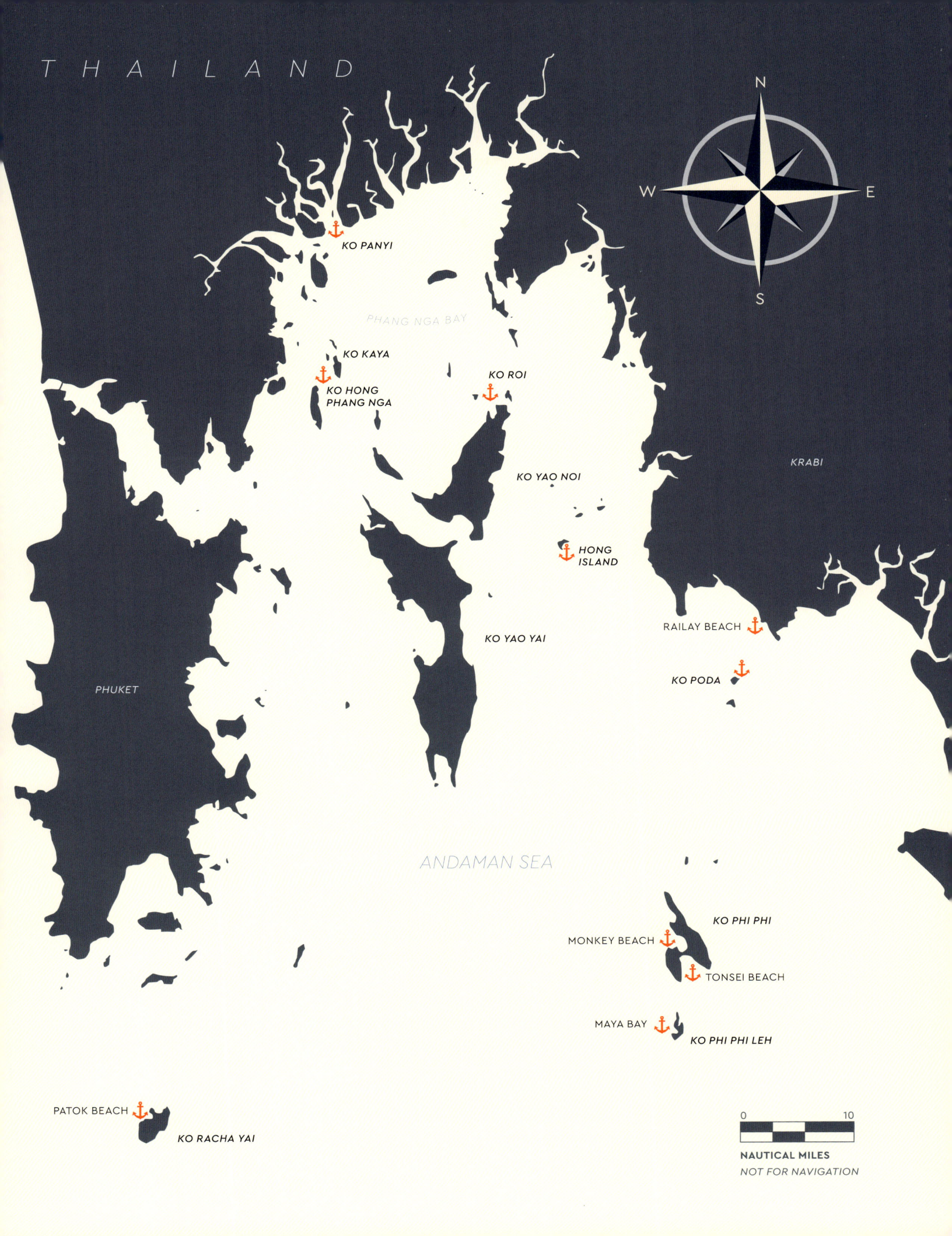

PHANG NGA BAY

⚓ KO PANYI

KO KAYA
⚓ KO HONG PHANG NGA

⚓ KO ROI

KO YAO NOI

⚓ HONG ISLAND

KRABI

KO YAO YAI

RAILAY BEACH ⚓

⚓ KO PODA

PHUKET

ANDAMAN SEA

KO PHI PHI
MONKEY BEACH ⚓
⚓ TONSEI BEACH

MAYA BAY ⚓ KO PHI PHI LEH

PATOK BEACH ⚓
KO RACHA YAI

N / W / E / S

0 — 10
NAUTICAL MILES
NOT FOR NAVIGATION

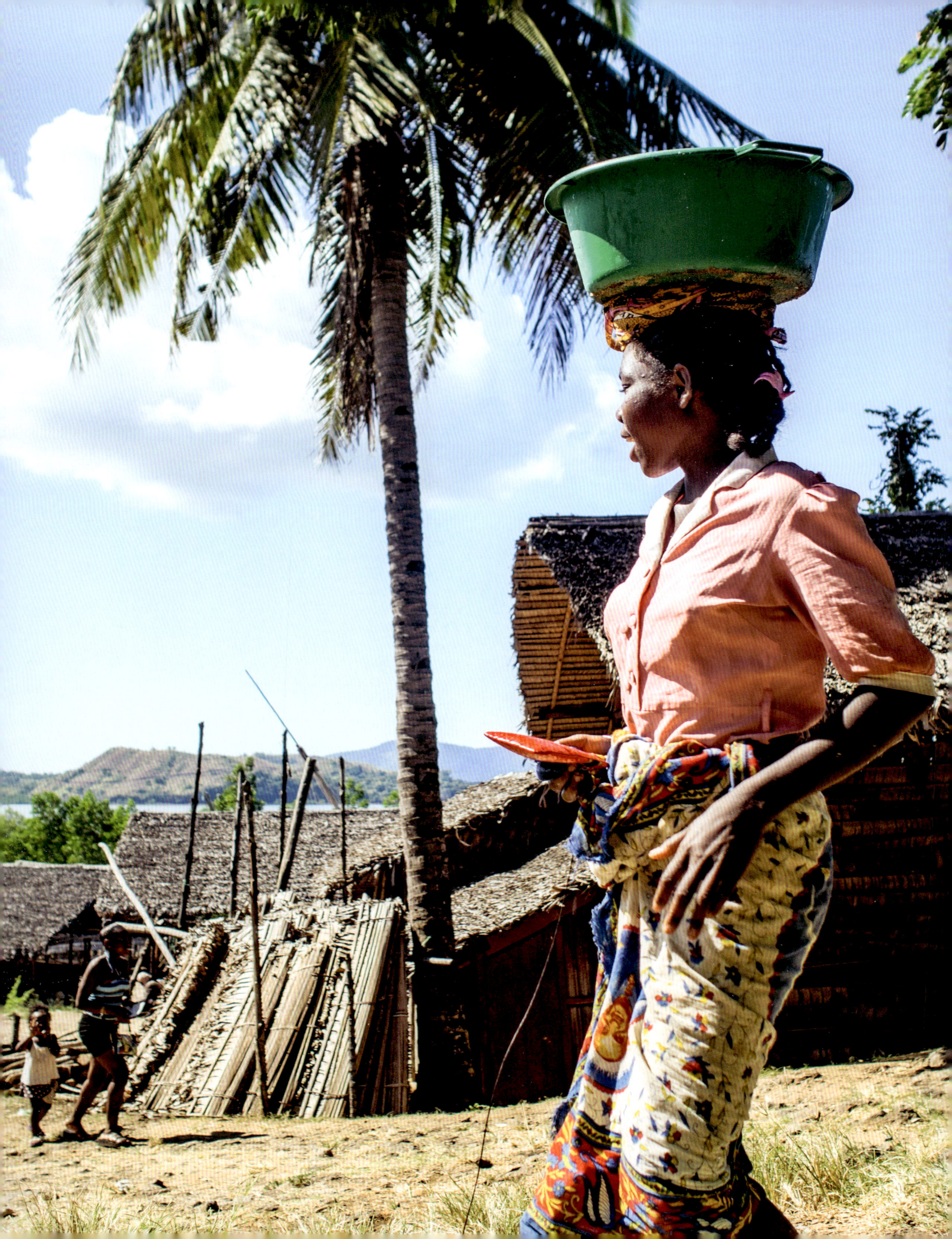

THE TROPICAL NORTH OF MADAGASCAR

REMOTE VILLAGES AND UNTOUCHED SANDY BEACHES STRETCH AS FAR AS THE EYE CAN SEE. SAIL ALONGSIDE TRADITIONAL DHOW SAILBOATS AND DISCOVER THE UNIQUE BIODIVERSITY OF THIS SPECIAL ISLAND.

Sitting off the southeast coast of Africa is Madagascar, the fourth largest island in the world, and one of the great sailing locations. The island evolved in isolation, separated from mainland Africa—it's famed for its largely endemic array of wildlife and biodiversity. Nosy Be is a small archipelago located along the northwest coast of Madagascar and by far the most popular sailing destination in the country. While world cruisers get to set their eyes on a diverse landscape dotted with archipelagos and a rich agricultural land, it is the mix of culture and nature that brings this itinerary to life.

In Madagascar, you will find rural populations scattered throughout its lush coastline and densely forested inland regions living a life based on principles of sustainability. Economically speaking, Madagascar is a poor country with an estimated 75 percent of the country's population living on less than two dollars per day. However, a sailing itinerary along the coast offers very different perspectives. The standard of living is less associated with monetary income, and more reliant on self-sufficiency, exchanging local goods rather than using imported products. The coastal communities appear to hold a greater value on communal gains than individual wealth. For those of us living modern lives, sailing to these small communities is an eye-opening experience, and a principle reason to plan a sailing itinerary along this coast.

Madagascar's geological history is unique and interesting—splitting off from mainland Africa before early humans inhabited this part of the world, so evolution of the ecosystem happened here without human influence. Archeologists believe that the first people arrived by outrigger sailing canoes—an early form of the *Dhow* sailboat that's traditional of the Sunda Islands—and settled in Madagascar between 200 BC and 500 AD. They would have discovered a wilderness unlike any other on Earth, lush and untouched. Since then, Madagascar has experienced waves of migration with sailors exploring from South Asia, East Africans arriving on the island, and more recent Portuguese, French, and British mariners arriving from the north—each having an impact on the island's culture. The diversity of the island reflects these many influences.

The history of French trade and incredible local biodiversity gives Madagascar a layered cuisine that's both fresh and sophisticated. With fertile hills and healthy soil, farming here produces flavorful abundance; and with a healthy ocean teeming with life as it's backdrop, Madagascar is poised to have great food. Downwind from a vanilla plantation, the air is light and sweet. A walk through the countryside here will inspire the chef in all of us, as even the wind carries playful mixtures of the local flavors. Agriculture is the foundation of the economy here through the cultivation of coffee, paddy rice, vanilla, and cloves.

Nosy Be and the surrounding islands are a hub for both sailors and tourists in Madagascar, with more than half of the country's visitors traveling to this region annually. The islands are a true example of unspoiled coastline with raw terrain and beaches untrammeled by modern development.

CRATER BAY, NOSY BE

Most itineraries begin in Crater Bay, a lively settlement that rests on the south-west point of Nosy Be, a few miles down a bumpy dirt road from Hell-Ville (Andoany). As both the capital and the largest city, Hell-Ville is the hub of commerce here and is rather pleasant despite its name. The roads are lined with zebu, a local cattle carting goods from one market to another. Provisioning is sufficient, and the local markets are filled with freshly harvested produce of every kind. Nothing is imported and the vibrant colors of earthy vegetables and fruits on display at the market creates a feast for the eyes. There are supermarkets available for locals and expats with bigger budgets, and the aisles are lined with imported French wines, cheeses, and local foie gras. Sailors stopping over in Crater Bay often wind up in the town of Madirokely, home to a central outgoing mainstreet with bars and restaurants that are filled with locals and expats enjoying live music and festivities most nights of the week. Lively is the appropriate way of describing this little strip, with nearly everyone in seemingly good spirits. Any safe harbor where sailors tend to stick around for more than just a few days is going to have some fun activity. Sailors find places where stories can be shared over affordable food and drink; somewhere with a pleasant spot to see what local life on land entails, before heading out to sea again.

After departing Crater Bay, it's common to sail counter-clockwise around Nosy Be, with the first leg of the itinerary sailing towards Nosy Komba. From there, you can sail along the east side of Nosy Be en route to Nosy Mitsio. After spending a few days in the northern islands, sailing south with an overnight anchorage in Nosy Sakatia located on Nosy Be's western coast is recommended. South from there is Russian Bay and Nosy Iranja, two popular locations during the itinerary.

NOSY MITSIO

Sailing north from Nosy Be, you'll find a small archipelago that's roughly 45 nautical miles away and made up of about a dozen islands. The main island is dotted with a few small farming villages. There are no stores or even a supply shop ashore. A five kilometer long white sand beach lines the main cove. Upon arrival, you will find a very different and traditional way of living. Nosy Mitsio

---

DHOW: THE LOCAL BOATS

Sailing from island to island, you can't help but notice the stark contrast between modern sailboats and the native Dhow, with its latin-rig, triangular sail configuration. On a breezy day, these Dhow rigs can gain speed but many of the seasons in Nosy Be bring little to no wind; local sailors use the wind at all times of the day and drop anchor or drift when it dies down, sometimes waiting hours and even through the night until they are able to sail onward.

A QUIET VILLAGE LOCATED ON THE BARAMAHAMAY RIVER. MOST COMMUNITIES HERE ARE LOCATED ALONG THE WATER (ABOVE). A DHOW CANOE RESTING ON A BEACH ON NOSY MITSIO (BELOW).

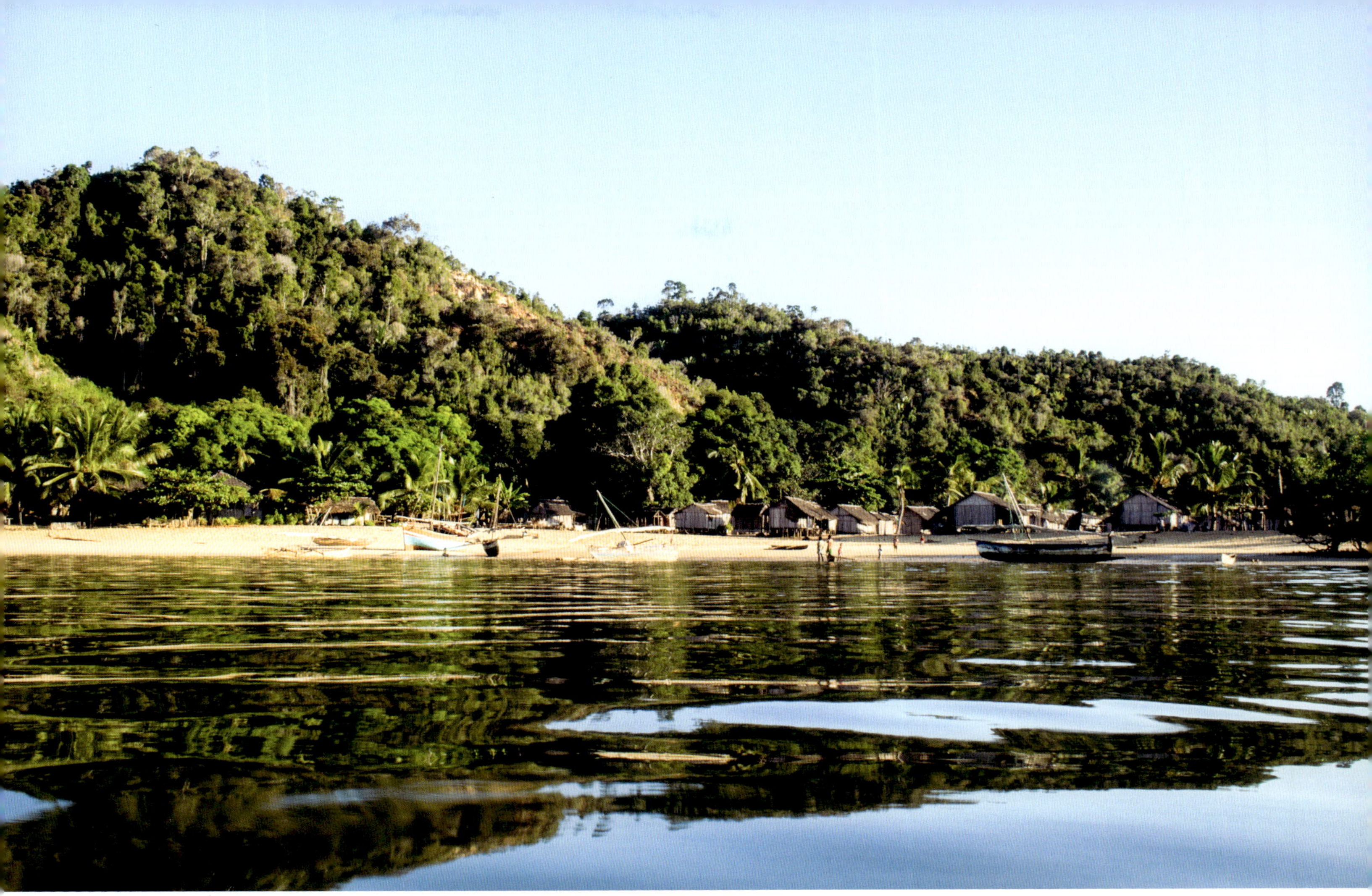

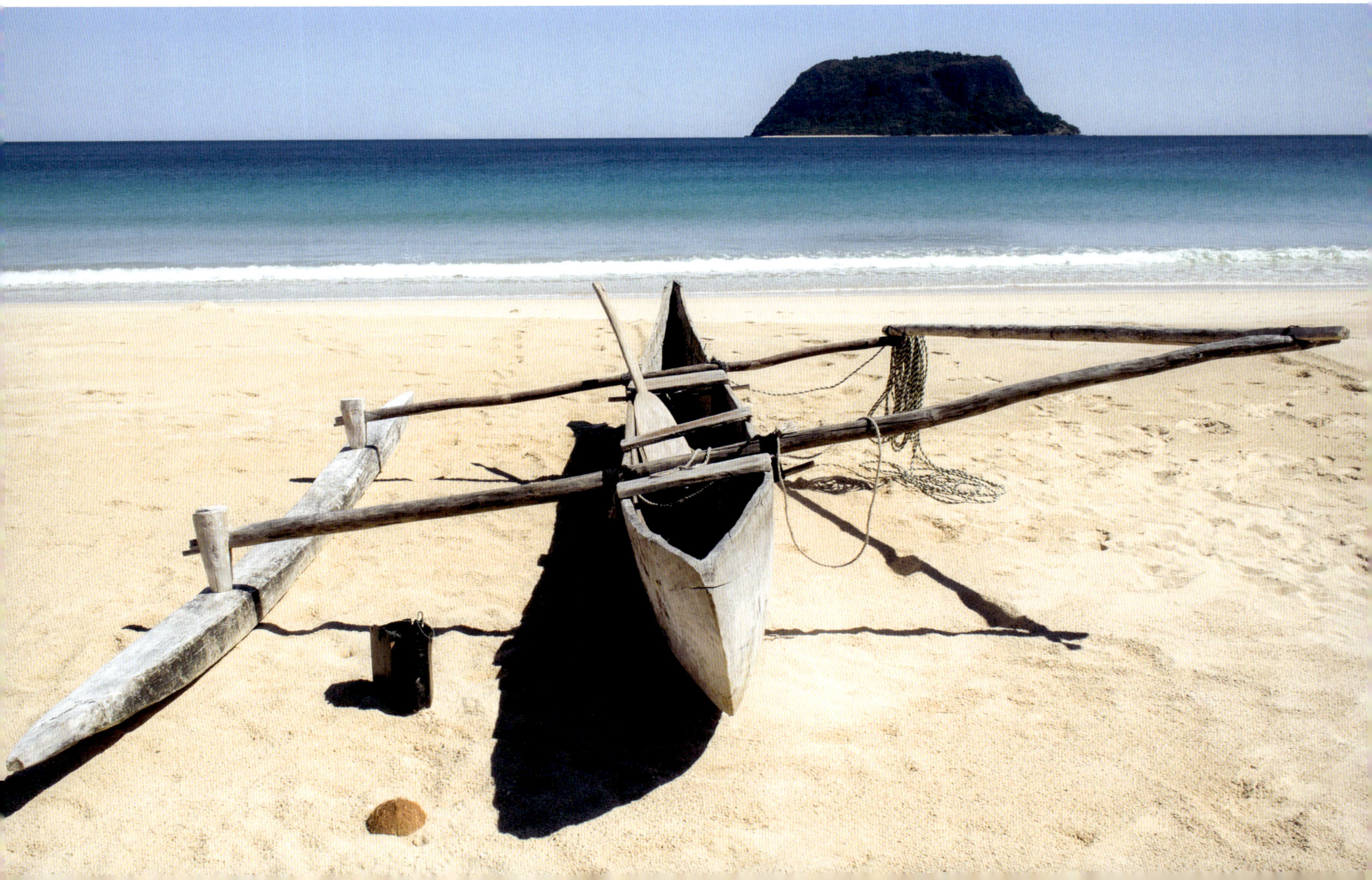

125 MARQUETTERIE

Biby
Havantsika

DROIT·DE·VISITE
à Nosy Komba
Prix: 4000 Ariary

PARC Lemuriens

is completely isolated and the few villages on the island trade only minimally outside of their communities, unlike Nosy Be which is home to resorts accommodating mostly French and Italian tourists. Nosy Mitsio has remained more untouched by modern ways of life. The island is lush with palm trees along the beach where the settlements are built.

The bay is large with plenty of space to anchor in calm and protected waters. It's surrounded by a large expansive white sand beach that extends along the bay with various villages located along the shoreline. Houses in the villages are mostly one-room huts built on wooden stilts with thatched roofs and they are clustered together creating an organized community. A short dinghy ride ashore leaving your sailboat behind safely at anchor, you can explore the beautiful beaches and villages on the island. The locals welcome sailors to walk through their village and often barter supplies for local-caught fish and fruit. There are hiking trails to the island's summit where you can enjoy stunning views of the main harbor and look down on your boat resting in the protected waters of the island's lee. Nosy Mitsio is a calm and relaxed paradise and multiple days should be allocated to explore the archipelago when sailing the area.

When anchoring near a remote village such as those on Nosy Mitsio, it is a kind gesture to dinghy ashore with gifts to introduce yourself. Although many of the residents now do business using currency, it hasn't always been this way. It's difficult to spend money if you don't live in Hell-Ville on Nosy Be and the sail from Nosy Mitsio south to Nosy Be on a wooden *Dhow* is a full day's voyage. When appropriate, gifting items to the communities upon your arrival is a sign of respect for anchoring in their community. You can offer school supplies, clothing, or fish caught while trawling behind your boat.

TSARABANJINA

After spending a few days exploring the various islands in the northern archipelago, most sailors turn their itinerary south towards Nosy Be. Along the way is the small island of Tsarabanjina. Surrounded by coral reefs and covered in layers of thick greenery, this small island is located between Nosy Be and Nosy Mitsio, perfectly suited for an afternoon stopover to swim off your boat. Only one suitable anchorage exists here,

> When anchoring near a remote village such as those on Nosy Mitsio, it is a kind gesture to dinghy ashore with gifts to introduce yourself.

which is located off the southern point of the island. Along the beach is an exclusive resort with private bungalows and a bar made from the island's traditional timber. The bar welcomes sailors for tropical drinks and freshly caught seafood dishes. Take note that an overnight in this anchorage is only suitable in very light winds and not recommended by local mariners. Good snorkeling can be found on either side of the beach. The resort itself is private and offers an exclusive ambiance to only a few lucky patrons at a time and sailors are able to experience a taste of it.

NOSY IRANJA

South of Nosy Be, located a few nautical miles from mainland Madagascar, is Nosy Iranja. The island is home to some of the most tranquil turquoise waters and surrounded by mangrove trees that feed into an electric blue colored sea. A well positioned lighthouse has been constructed at the top of this island, which is also home to the school on the island. Nosy Iranja is a hatching ground for both green turtles and hawksbill

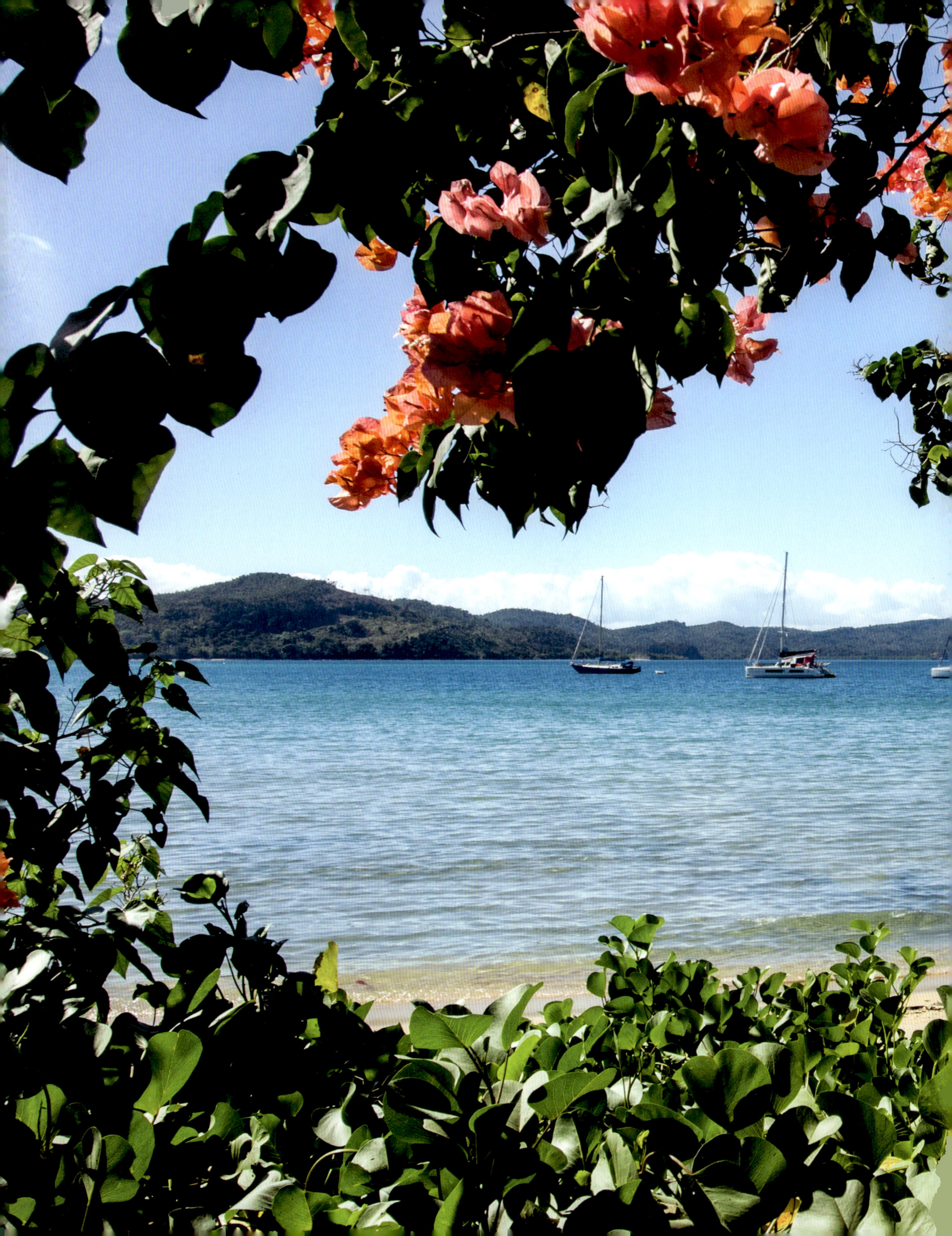

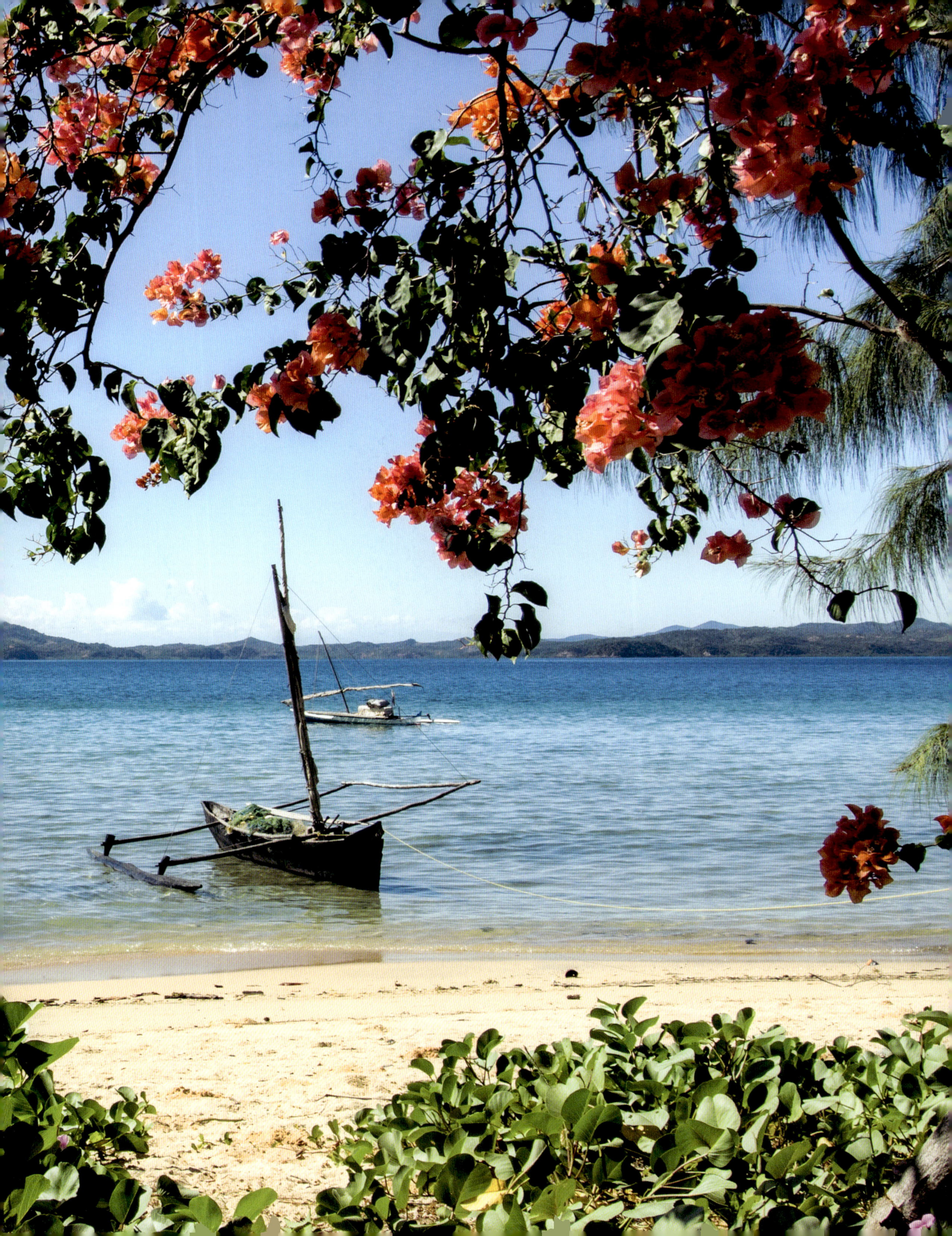

turtles, which can be seen swimming around the anchorage. These turtles can grow up to five feet long and are easy to spot from the boat as they come up for a breath in between dives to snack on the seagrass below. There is a long spit of white sand that connects the main island of Nosy Iranja with its southeast point. Anchoring along the eastern coast off the sandy spit makes for a perfect location for swimming with the turtles and having easy access to dinghy ashore.

RUSSIAN BAY

Ambavatoby, or Russian, Bay is 25 nautical miles from Nosy Be, located on mainland Madagascar at the tip of the Ampasindava Peninsula. Sheltered from the sea and surrounded by vibrant green hills that are completely covered with jungle, Russian Bay is a remarkable environmental ecosystem that's frequented by pods of dolphins, whale sharks, and other unique species. It serves as a mating ground for local humpback whales, while the beaches are a nesting place for sea turtles. The bay is also lined with exceptional coral reefs. Taking a dinghy ride ashore, you will find a gorgeous forest that's inhabited by lemurs, wild boar, birds, bats, and the Madagascar fish eagle, one of the rarest raptors in the world. On land, there are scattered fishing villages along the waterfront, and the community is largely made up of boatbuilders and fishermen that happily welcome you ashore to explore their domain. Most of the villagers speak only Malagasy, so a smile and some pantomiming goes a long way in making new friends.

~

Few locations are as remote and beautiful as Nosy Be and also home to adequate charter facilities. The reasonable size charter base located on Nosy Be offers services for sailors cruising the region. It's not an easy itinerary to plan, however. Even with yacht services in Nosy Be, resources are scarce and advance planning is advised. Sailors require local knowledge to navigate these waters. With over a three meter tidal drop, many bays become empty at low tide and one misjudgement could cause you to wake up with your boat in the mud. Most maritime charts of the region are outdated and inaccurate, but with the onset of new satellite imagery and digital chart plotting software, planning your sailing voyage in remote parts of the world like Nosy Be becomes more accessible each year. The real joy of sailing this itinerary is the cultural experience. The malagasy way is kind and welcoming, and their islands are enchanting. With the proper preparation and skills applied, any sailor can plan a voyage to Nosy Be. It's one of the great unspoiled sailing destinations.

CHART DATUM

Included on every chart is the "datum," which tells you when it was last updated by a hydrological survey. As survey technology improves, charts get better and better. In some of the more remote regions of the world, you will occasionally see dates from more than 100 years ago, meaning that the data was collected painstakingly by hand, using sounding lines to determine the depth and astrological data to determine location. This older data is generally less reliable than that provided by modern ships using sonar and GPS positioning. In Madagascar, pay particular attention to the chart datum.

A BOY TENDS TO HIS HERD OF ZEBU AT LOW TIDE ON NOSY BE (ABOVE, LEFT). A GROUP OF FISHERMAN SAILING THEIR DHOW (ABOVE, RIGHT). ONE OF MADAGASCAR'S MAGNIFICENT ROCK FORMATIONS (BELOW, LEFT). LOCALLY FARMED PRODUCE AT THE MARKET (BELOW, RIGHT).

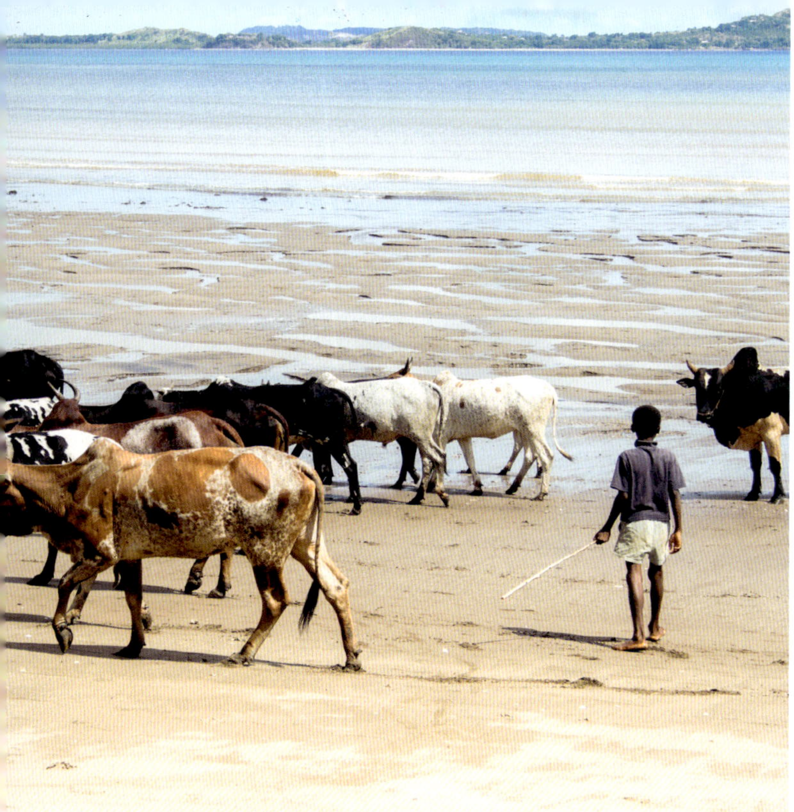

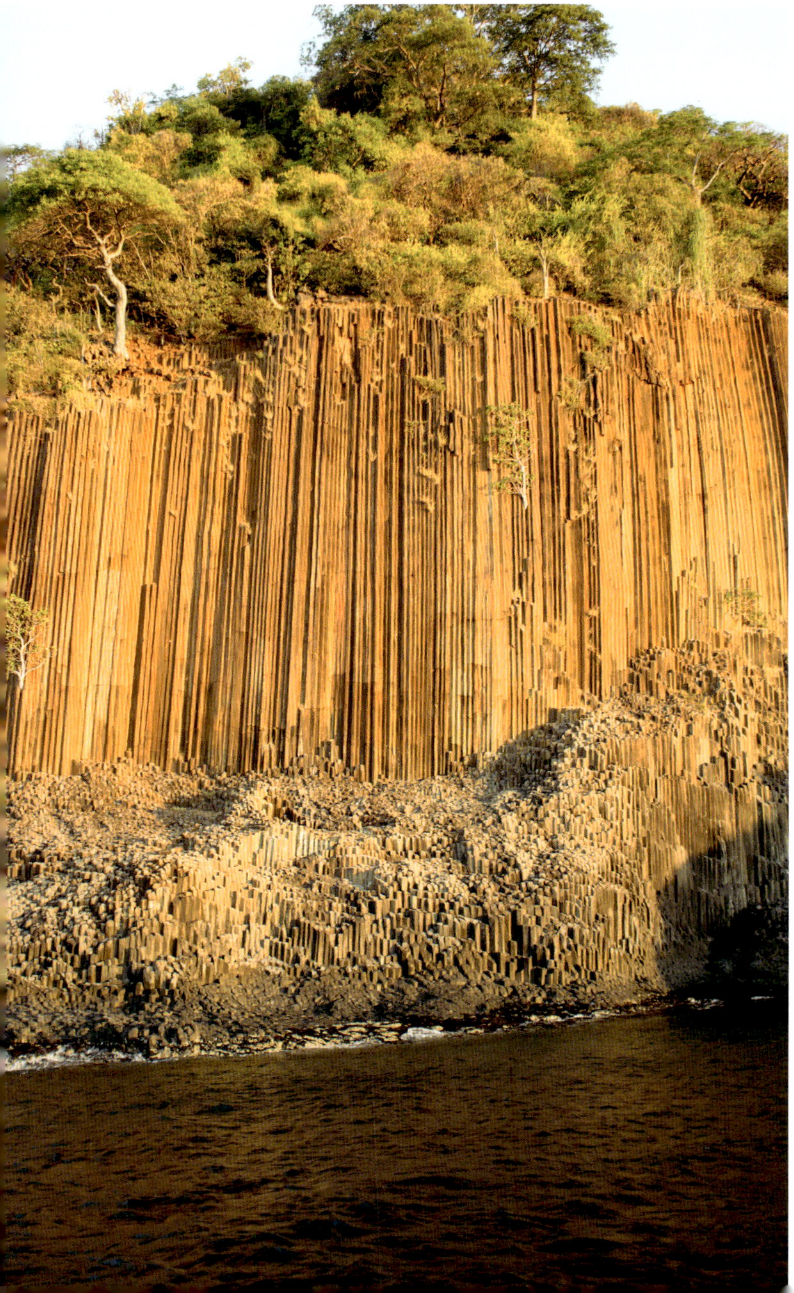

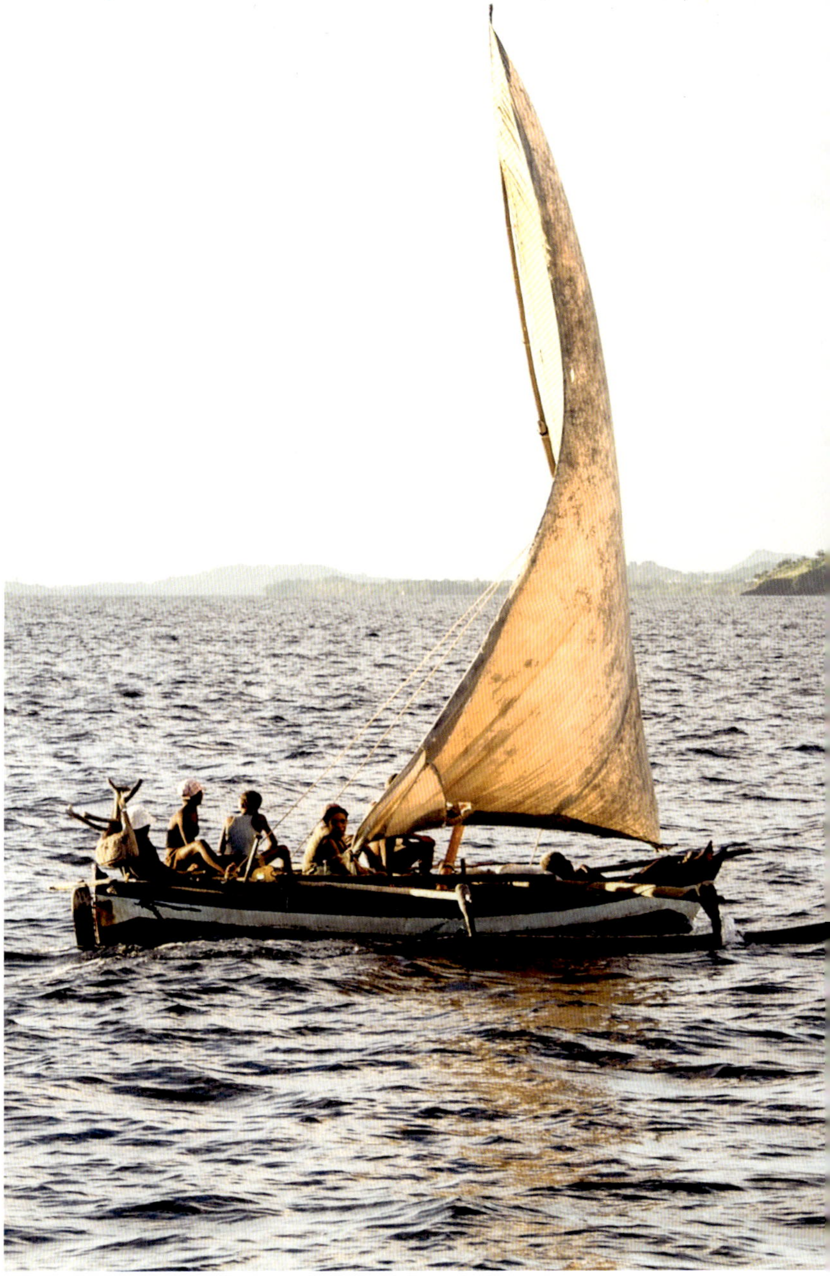

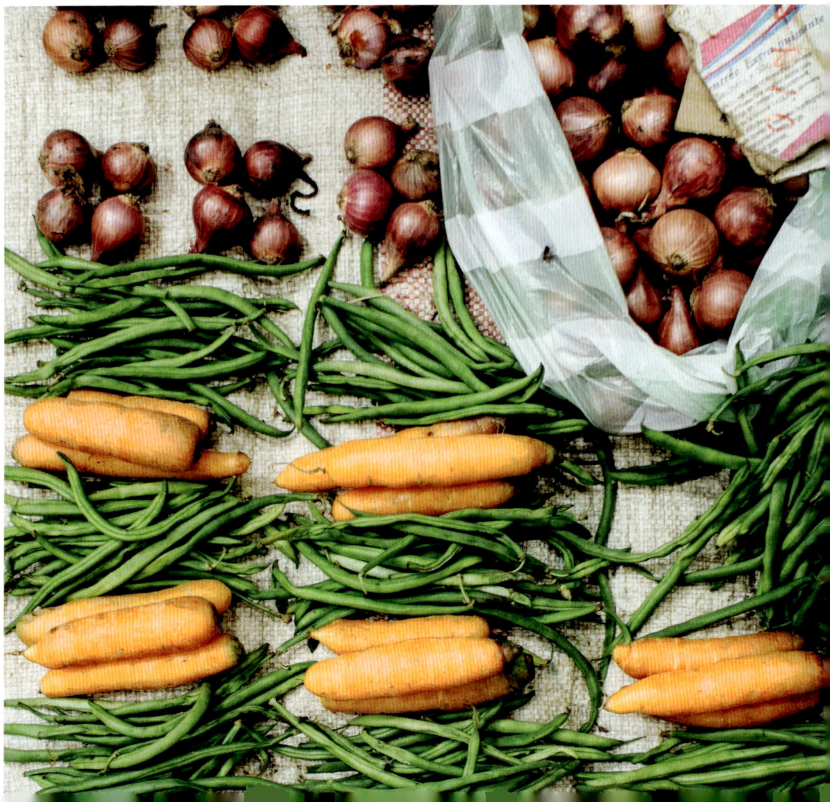

CAPTAIN'S NOTES *NOSY BE*

RECOMMENDED ITINERARY

Crater Bay, Nosy Be
13° 23′30″S, 48° 13′19″E
The main yacht harbor sits just down the road from Hell-Ville on the well-protected southern side of Nosy Be. Limited yacht services are available, but this is your best option in the region for repairs. This bay has both laid moorings and room for anchoring in the center of the mooring field. The moorings have a stern-bow tie system with two mooring blocks, designed for mooring lines to be tied on both the bow and stern of your boat; this prevents all the yachts in the harbor from swinging during the tidal switch.

Russian Bay
13° 32′45″S, 48° 00′30″E
This large bay is made up of three inner inlets, each one a bay in its own right. Baie d'Andassy to the west is the first one you will see on entering and has good holding near an inhabited beach. The bay has deep water in the center and anchorages along the shoreline. Anchor in 5 fathoms on the west side of the bay and explore the village on shore.

Nosy Mitsio
12° 51′22″S, 48° 35′29″E
Anchor off the sandy beach in the nook of the south side of the bay, inside the protection of Nosy Ankarea. This island has no piers, jetties, or yacht services of any kind. Five villages are located along the western bay, living off of the electrical and communication system, but water can be brought from the local well in jugs if you have the labor on hand. Sail to the island of Tsarabanjina, south of Nosy Mitsio, for an afternoon anchorage. A luxury resort is located on the south beach. Anchor in 4 fathoms but not overnight, as the wind switches from a sea breeze to a land breeze, causing the anchorage to be rolly.

Nosy Iranja
13° 37′40″S, 47° 48′23″E
Two islands, connected by a dramatically gorgeous sand spit, can only be visited in fair winds and settled seas. Anchor in sand and be careful not to drop in the beds of seagrass, where holding is poor—your anchor will also damage an important food source for turtles.

Nosy Sakatia
13° 19′09″S, 48° 09′38″E
An anchorage on the south side gives you access to a well-appointed resort with a restaurant. A dive operation based out of Sakatia lodge offers incredibly knowledgeable guides, who will happily educate you about the astounding biodiversity found in these waters.

RECOMMENDED ANCHORAGES

Tsarabanjina
Nosy Tanikely

ITINERARY DURATION

9+ days recommended

PREVAILING WIND

From October to July you will experience an easterly sea breeze off the mainland in the mornings and a westerly wind in the afternoons. The easterly is known locally as a *Varatraz* and the westerly is referred to as the *Talo*. From August to September, the *Varatraz* wind dominates and is strongest during the afternoon, when it can reach as high as force 9.

SEASON

The best sailing is between January and March.

FOOD

Vanilla
Madagascar is the largest producer of vanilla in the world, with much of the produce coming directly from Nosy Be. Across the globe, it has become a coveted (and expensive) ingredient for chefs, but here it's readily available and affordable.

GOOD TO KNOW

Tidal variation
A normal semidiurnal tide has a variation of anywhere from 30 centimeters to 4.5 meters between high tide and low tide. In mainland bays and river mouths with large freshwater inflow, the tidal variation can become unpredictable.

Remote voyaging
Voyaging in remote stretches of the world means being away from many yachting resources that we grow accustomed to in areas with marinas and boatyards. On these islands, everything is more complicated because of the isolation. Something as simple as topping off the boat's water tanks can quickly turn into a lesson in the scarcity of resources. The common practice here is to keep four 20-liter water jugs on hand for topping off. These jugs are brought ashore on the dinghy, hiked up to the local water source, and carried back to be poured into the boat's tanks. Between the captain, chef and a few heavy lifters from a nearvy village, this can easily take a few hours in the hot sun. What is true of filling the water tanks is also true of every little detail that it takes to keep a boat running smoothly.

Magnetic variance
Magnetic Declination: -15° (WEST)

N W E S

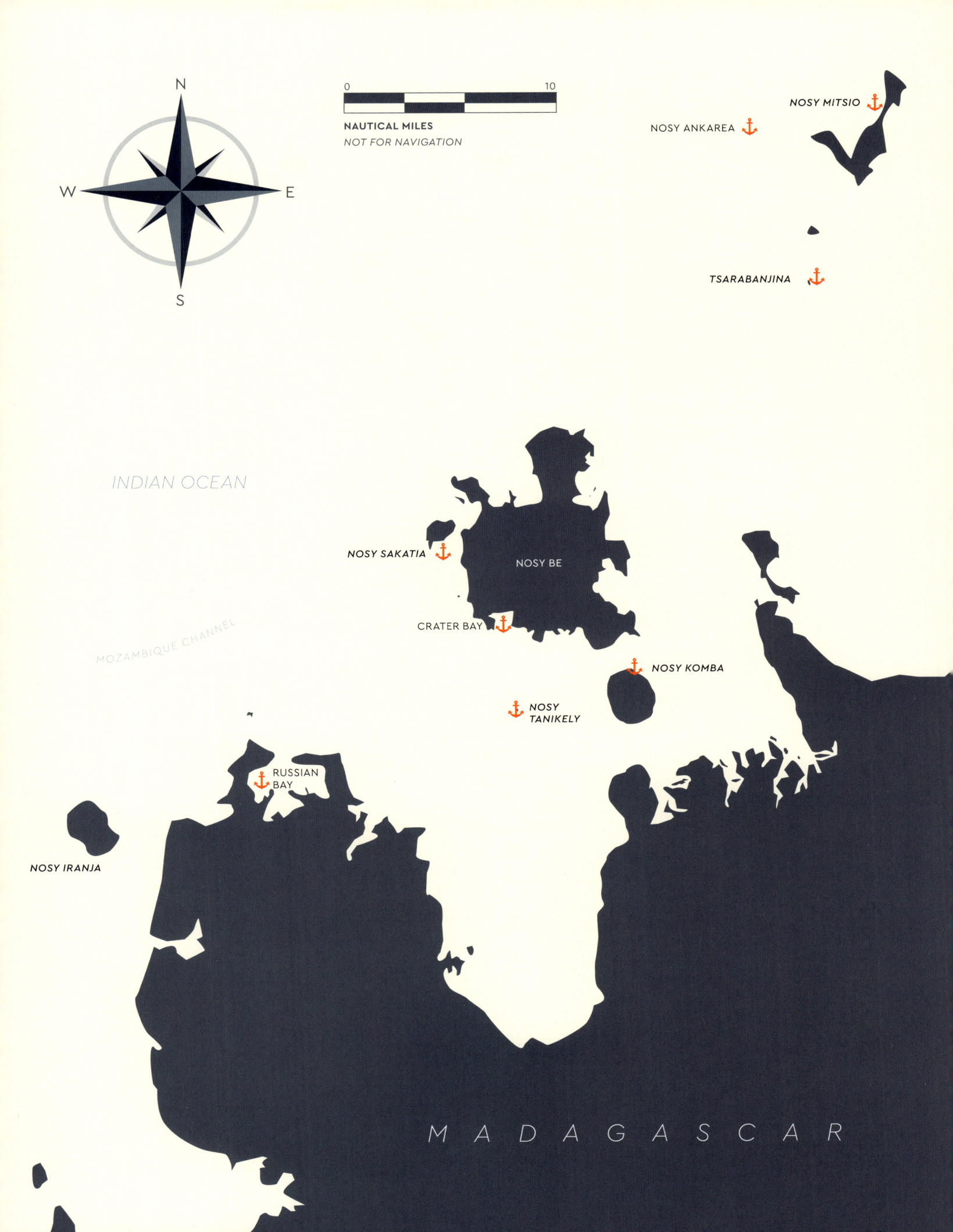

0 — 10
NAUTICAL MILES
NOT FOR NAVIGATION

NOSY MITSIO ⚓

NOSY ANKAREA ⚓

TSARABANJINA ⚓

INDIAN OCEAN

NOSY SAKATIA ⚓

NOSY BE

CRATER BAY ⚓

MOZAMBIQUE CHANNEL

⚓ NOSY KOMBA

⚓ NOSY TANIKELY

⚓ RUSSIAN BAY

NOSY IRANJA

M A D A G A S C A R

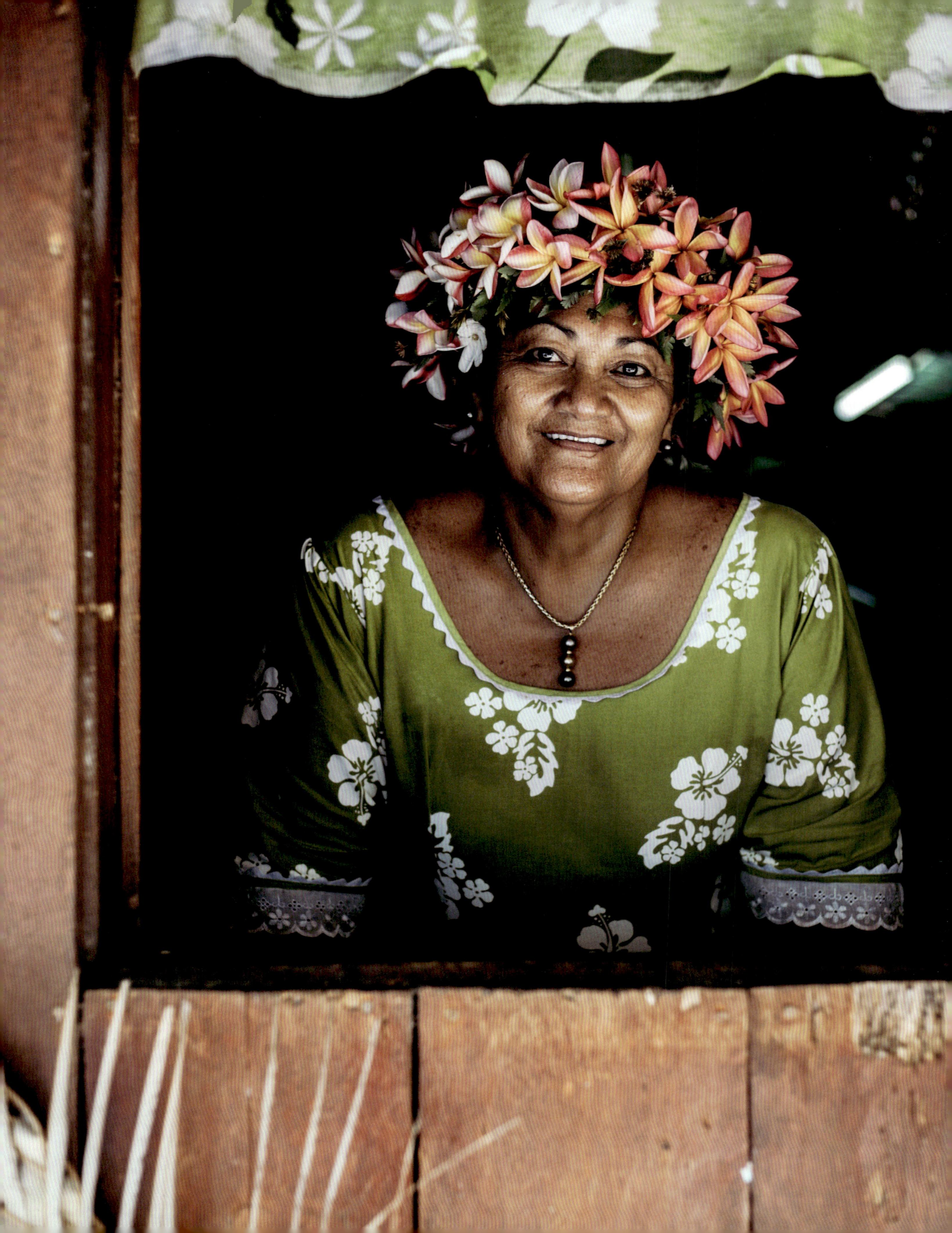

THE CORAL LAGOONS OF FRENCH POLYNESIA

HALFWAY BETWEEN THE AMERICAS AND ASIA, FRENCH POLYNESIA IS AS FAR AWAY AS YOU CAN POSSIBLY SAIL. THESE HUNDREDS OF TINY ISLANDS DOTTED THROUGHOUT THE PACIFIC OCEAN ARE A TROPICAL PARADISE SURROUNDED BY A DEEP BLUE SEA.

At first glance, the South Pacific appears to be the largest stretch of unbroken ocean on the planet. A closer look and you'll notice strings of unlikely islands sitting in depths of water where land seems improbable. Upon further inspection, some of these islands are fringed by perfect coral lagoons allowing for boats to sit safely in their harbors while the vast ocean throws gigantic waves barreling onto reefs. You have stumbled on French Polynesia, a cluster of some 118 dispersed islands and atolls that spans over 1,200 miles and that is part of the larger constellation of islands stretching from Hawaii to New Zealand that makeup Polynesia as a whole. You could spend a lifetime exploring this region and there would still be more to see. If time is limited, consider narrowing your sailing itinerary to the Leeward Islands, and, more specifically, to Raiatea, Taha'a, Huahine, Bora Bora, and Maupiti.

Geography and culture come together in the Leeward Islands to create a remarkably wonderful sailing destination. These dramatic mountainous islands are blessed with very pleasant anchorages along pristine reefs, and the majesty of this place continues well beyond the ancient volcanic and coral geography that created them. Historically, the people who live here are part of one of the planet's most advanced seafaring cultures, spread across thousands of miles of ocean but sharing a mother language that proves that the art of navigation here was far beyond what Europeans had conceived of.

Most of the Leeward Islands consist of tall formerly volcanic peaks that have eroded enough that the coral that once grew on the outer banks of the island now makes up a ring around an inner lagoon. There are small low-lying islands called *motus* where the reef supports a sandy landmass. Some of the *motus* are large enough to be inhabited and, in the case of both Maupiti and Bora Bora, the island's airport is actually out on a *motu* where some of the only land flat enough to land a plane is. Most of the nice beaches are on *motus* rather than the islands proper, and the good snorkeling and diving along the reef tends to be closer to the *motus* than the main islands.

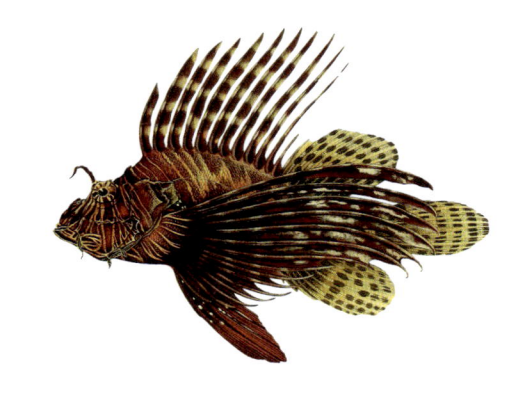

Boat access is an important part of traveling to many of the beautiful places since they are dispersed between *motus* and islands all around.

The relationship to tourism and outside influence is a storied one and manifests uniquely in the culture of each individual island. The over-the-water bungalow resorts of Bora Bora for instance simply don't exist on Maupiti, making for a very different economy and a different way of life without honeymooners wading in the shallows around every corner. The mood on the *motus* of Bora Bora is protective, with locals enforcing the right to limit trespassers on the land that they have managed to hold onto. Foreign investments here are not always to the profit of everyone and there is a strong independence movement to leave the French Republic.

Because boat travel is so important to the way of life, paddling the traditional outrigger canoe called a *Va'a* is a beloved sport and races are popular and festive events. It is not unusual to have a local teenager in a one-man *Va'a* pull in close behind your boat and paddle hard to surf your stern wake as you make your way to your anchorage only to peel off when they see another boat headed back the way they came.

RAIATEA

Home to most of the region's charter bases, Raiatea is a likely starting point. This is an appropriate place for any journey to begin because, in accordance with the oral histories of Polynesian culture, all of humanity's voyage began right here. Even the Maori—as far away as New Zealand is—have this island as part of their origin story. The second-largest island in the Leeward Islands, Raiatea is mountainous and lush with plenty of agriculture to make for a plentiful farmers market in Uturoa each day. The lagoon that surrounds it is almost entirely navigable except for a few impassable sections where yachts must exit a pass in the reef and enter another to continue.

Raiatea is a great place to schedule a visit to a pearl farm or to find a guide to take you into the mountains in search of one of the rarest plants in the world. The Tiare Apetahi flower has never been successfully cultivated off the island and can only be found near the peak of the island in a forest that requires around four hours of hiking.

TAHA'A

Amidst the Leeward Islands is one of the archipelago's more picturesque islands, Taha'a. Located just north of Raiatea. Sailing between Huahine and Bora Bora, Taha'a is an ideal midpoint to break up the passage and spend a few days discovering all the island's deepwater coves along the shore and sandy anchorages along the reef. Besides heading north from Raiatea, there are two entry points where boats can access the lagoon—to the east lies Passe Toahotu and along the west lies Passe Paipai. Sailing from Huahine and entering through the eastern passage, you will sail between two small *motus*, the northern one is open to the public for a small fee and has a little beach club with a bar and showers under towering coconut palms.

SPORT

The Va'a canoes are typically built for either one or six people and they move about the lagoons at incredible speed under the power of the competitive paddlers.
The annual Hawaiki Nui Va'a race in six man canoes between Huahine and Bora Bora over the course of three days is the nation's largest sporting event and people come from over 100 islands as well as countries across oceans to compete. It is worth finding the dates of this race, which is usually held in late October, as you plan your travels because of the large influx of racers and spectators: everything requires much more advanced planning if you plan to attend.

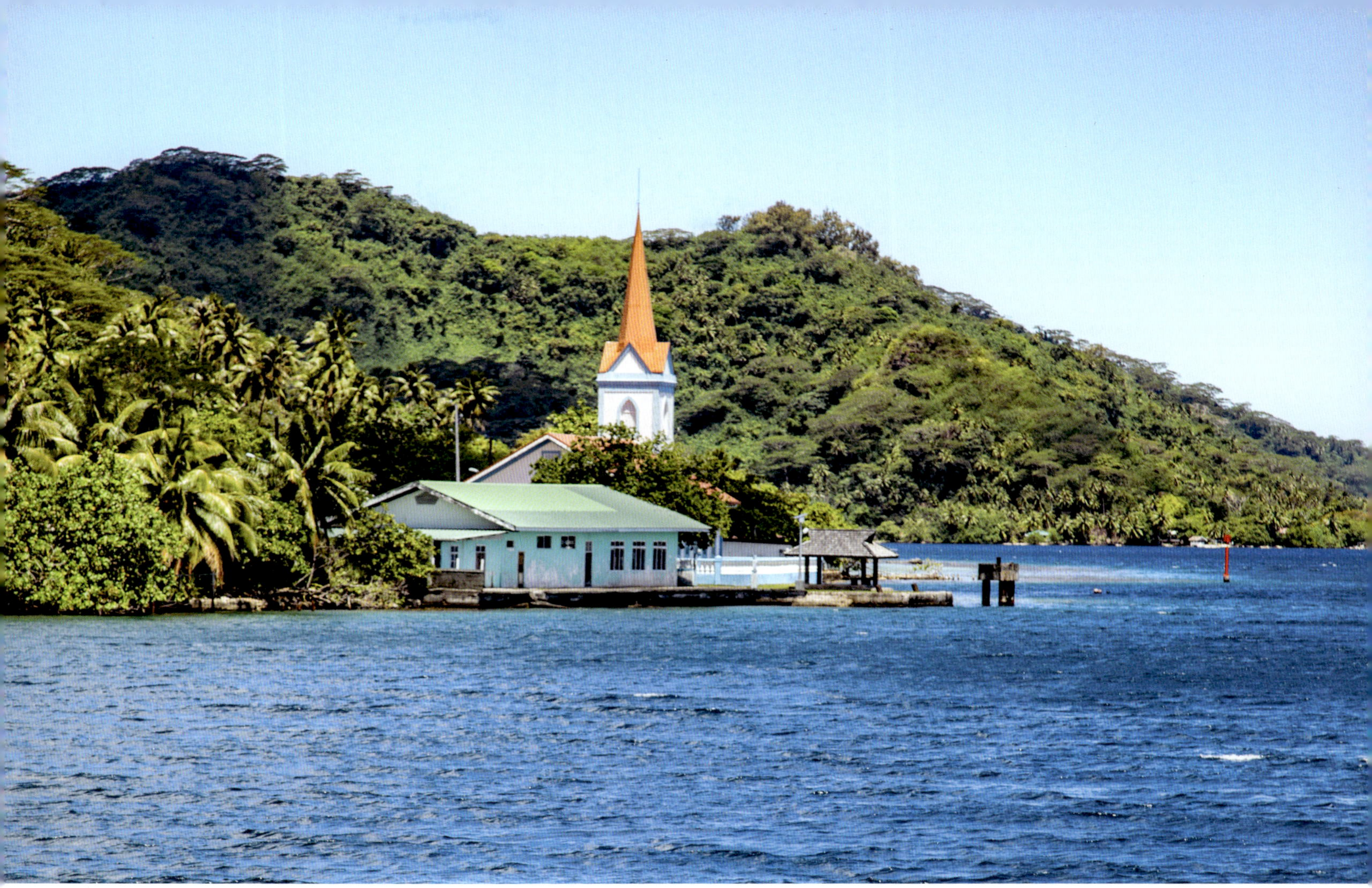

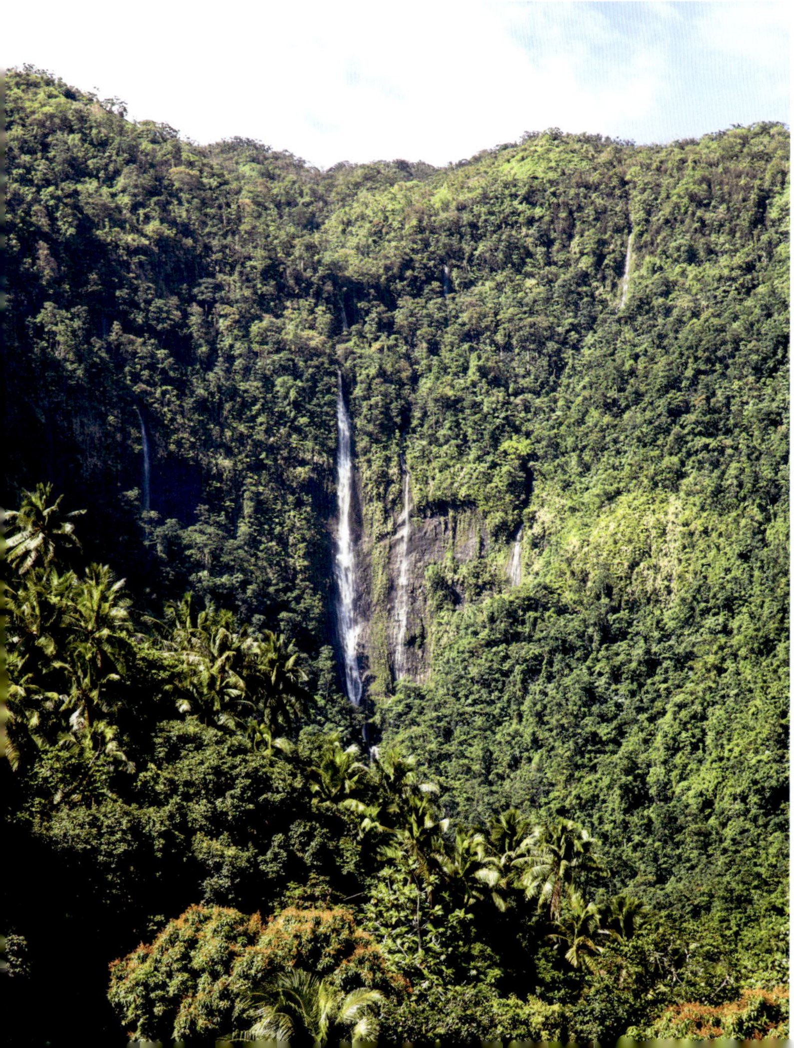

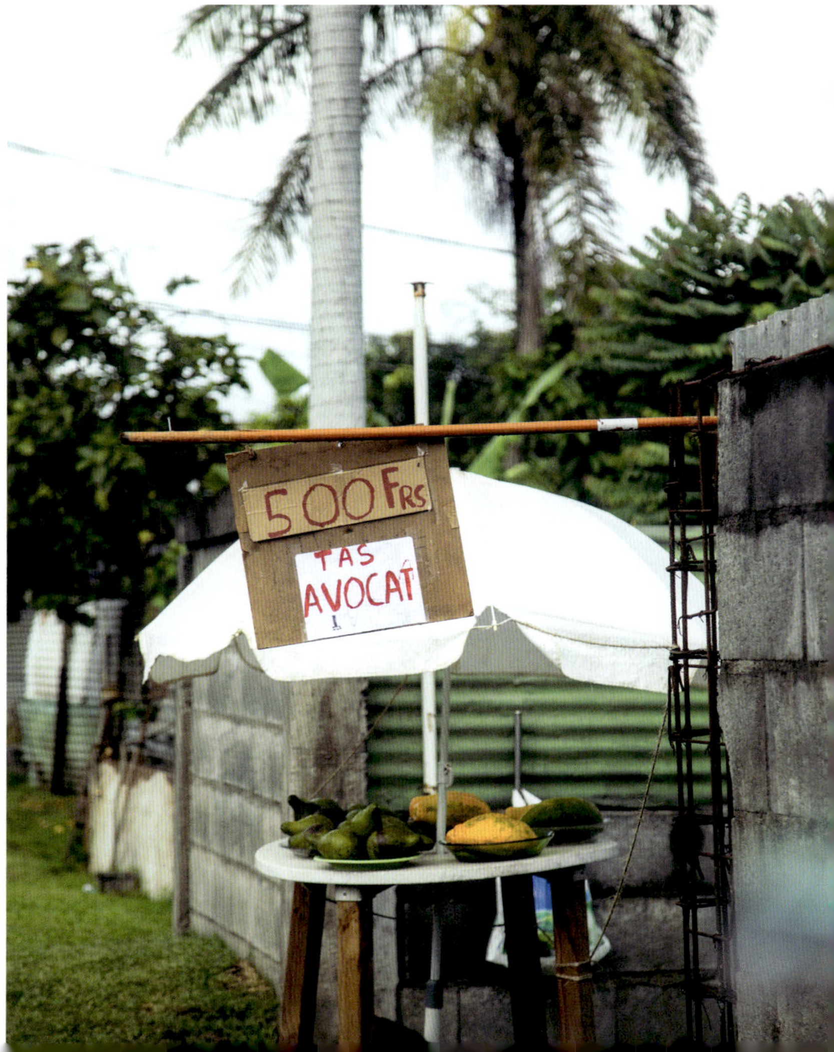
500 Frs
TAS
AVOCAT

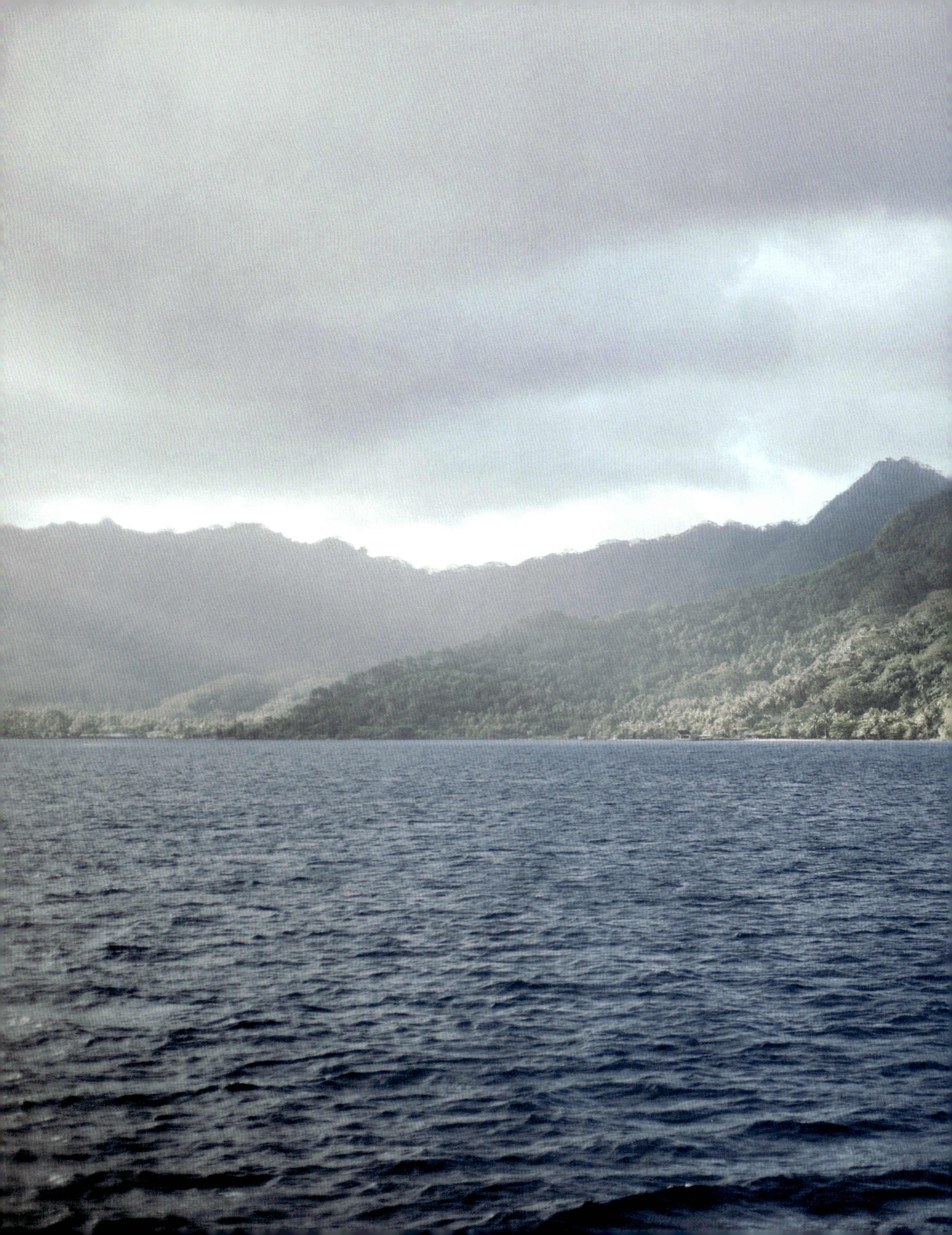

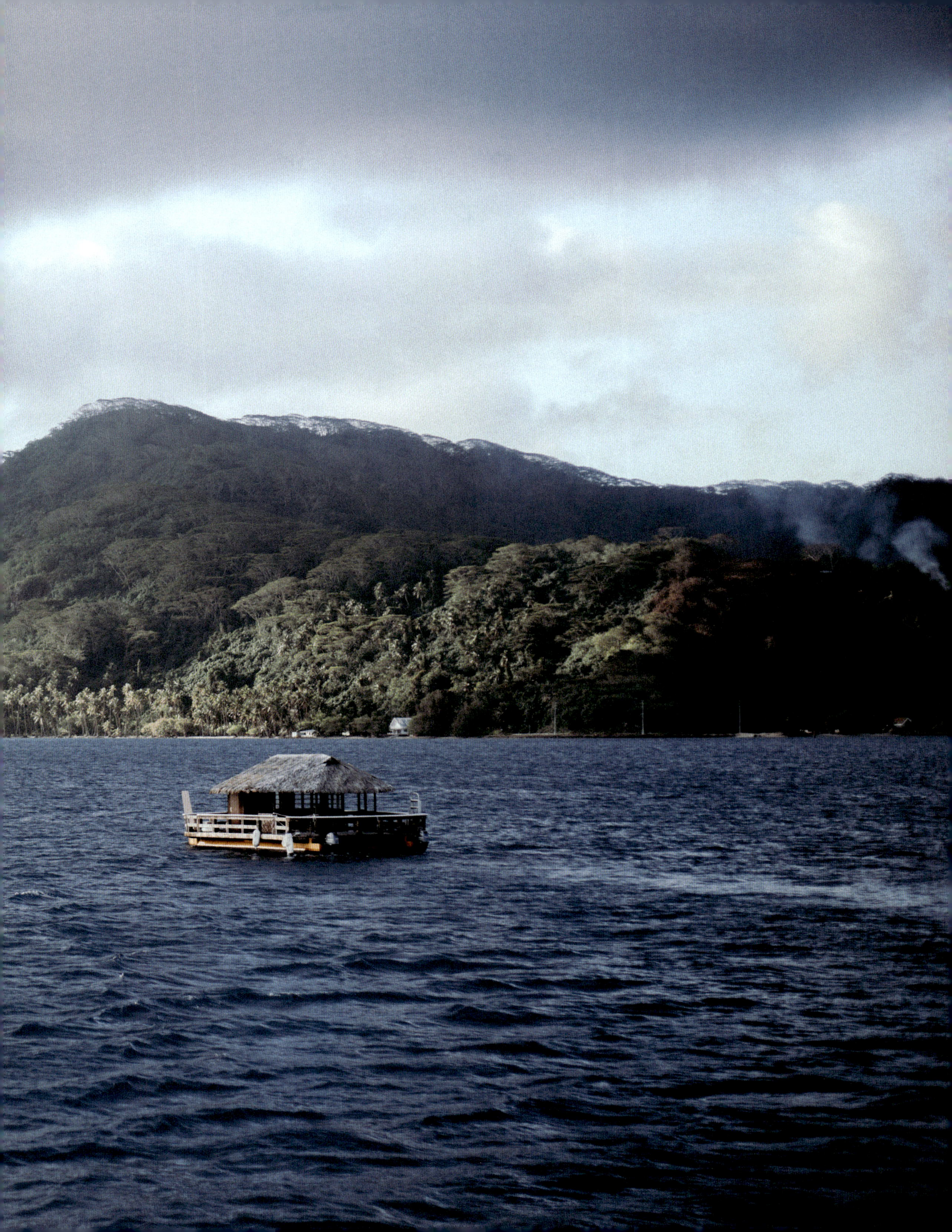

Taha'a is home to wonderful snorkeling locations, too many to list, with lively corals and tropical fish swimming unhurriedly past. If you enter at Passe Paipai you can head north inside the reef to a nice anchorage near three *motus*: Tautau, Maharare, and Motuaivi. The largest is home to Taha'a hotel with bungalows that sit above the sandy shallows on stilts. Between the two smaller *motus* lives one of the most exotic and fascinating natural aquariums. Here, the ocean current that runs through the two islands and pushes swimmers along a channel of colorful corals. Walk on Motu Maharare to the outer reef and let the saltwater river take you downstream back towards your boat. If you want more time in the drift, simply hike back upstream and do it again.

HUAHINE

Two islands connected by a low bridge, Huanine Nui (the big island) and Huahine Iti (the smaller) share a lagoon that has limited passes navigable in a sailboat. This is the most easterly island in the Leewards. The experience of sailing to this island will stay with you long after you depart this unique destination, it has a certain magical ambiance. All of the nearby islands are lush, however, Huahine is even greener with a sprawling jungle that envelopes the twin peaks. Hidden in the thick brush are marae, ancient temples, and these mountains are home to more of these archaeological sites than anywhere in French Polynesia. During an excursion ashore, you can find yourself on hiking trails or a rental bike on your way to the historic landmarks with mythical intrigue.

There are 15 suitable anchorages mostly located in the western lagoon. At the main town of Fare, mariners can dinghy ashore to reprovision and buy freshly caught tuna and vanilla that is grown on the island's farms. Further south located near Hotel Le Mahana on the southwest point of Huahine Iti you will find Chez Tara, a local restaurant situated along a white sand beach offering a traditional meal served only on Sunday at lunch called *Ma'a Tahiti*: fish, meats, and vegetables cooked overnight in the ground and served buffet-style while a band plays traditional local music. The bay in front has plenty of room to anchor with good holding. During the calving season when humpback whales come to warmer waters to have their babies lucky sailors might witness them swimming inside the lagoon. Listen carefully in the still of the night as you sit at anchor, if a whale is close you will hear it taking enormous breaths at the surface.

BORA BORA

The pearl of the Pacific—the very name Bora Bora is synonymous with exotic adventures at the end of the world, but none of the lore and legend prepares you for the feeling of sailing through the impossibly blue waters of the lagoon in the shadow of a sheer cliff face. Bora Bora is so odd in its formation that it takes on radically different shapes and personalities as you sail around it. Viewing the famous spire is like looking for shapes in clouds, ever-changing before your eyes. From the southwest the peak is a jagged tooth, from the east it's a mainsail on a heeled-over ship, from the southeast it is clearly the tail of a

---

BLACK PEARLS

One of the most important local industries is pearl farming and there are many local pearl farms that will happily show you around and sell you the gorgeous dark specimens that are made here. Sail to the Anapa Pearl Farm on the west coast of Raiatea for a tour, it stands out as a unique experience for its location. A friendly former-professional surfer named Summer will greet you at your boat and shuttle you in her speedboat to a bungalow on stilts over the reef where you can see the complicated process of seeding oysters and the underwater operation with your own eyes.

THE CORAL RIVER ON TAHA'A (ABOVE, LEFT).
FRENCH POLYNESIA IS FAMED FOR PEARLS WITH A UNIQUE METALLIC COLOR (BELOW, RIGHT).
PREDOMINANT RELIGION TODAY (ABOVE).

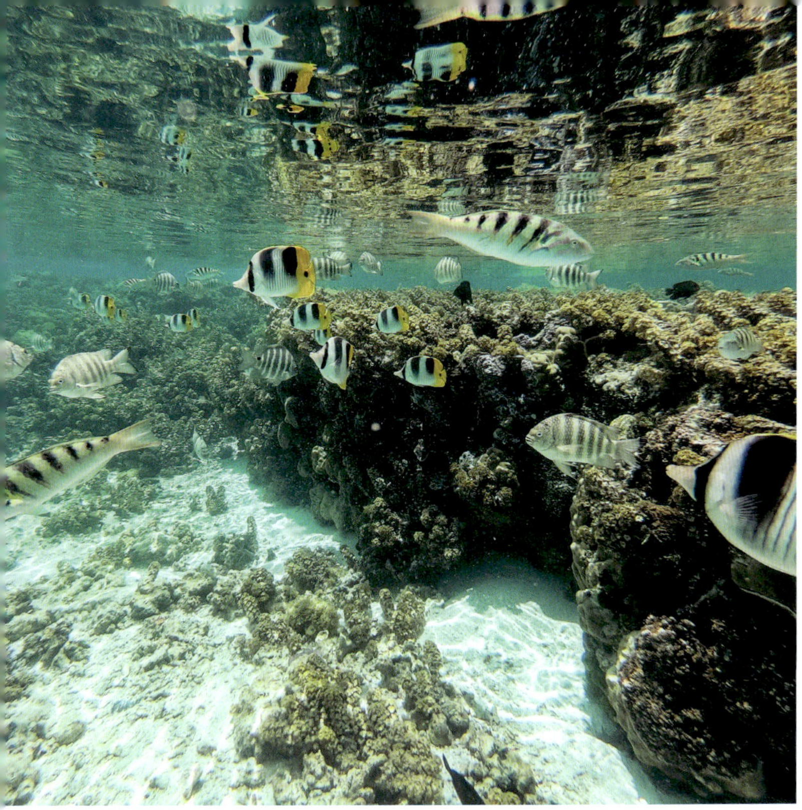

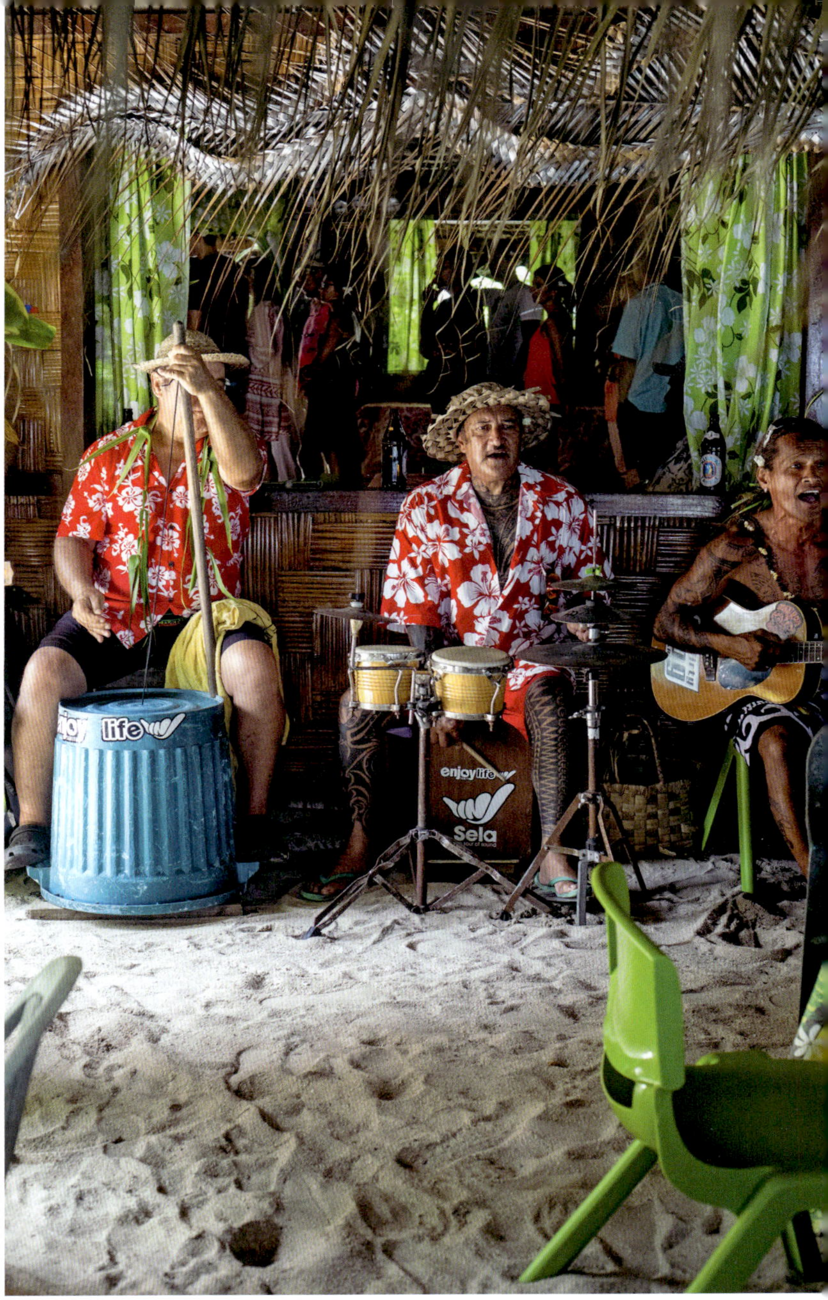
life
enjoy life
Sela

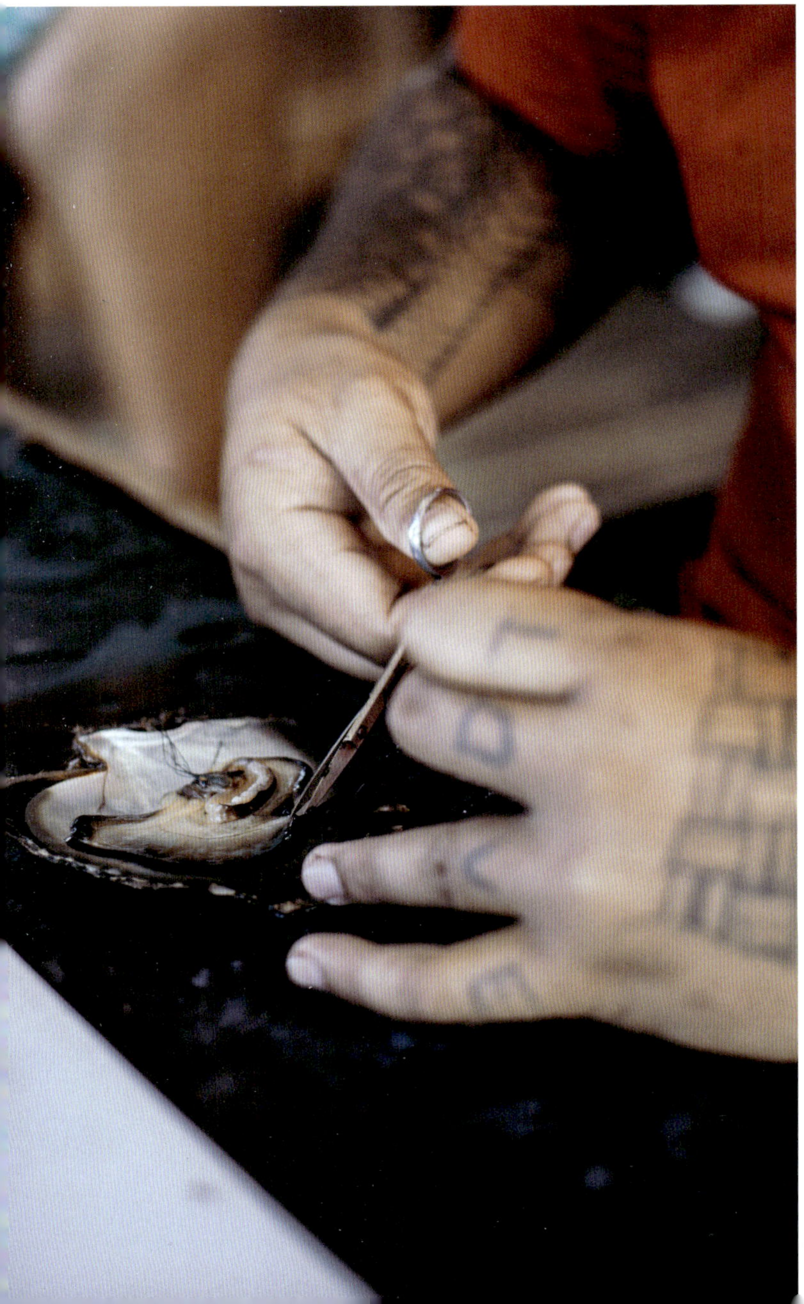

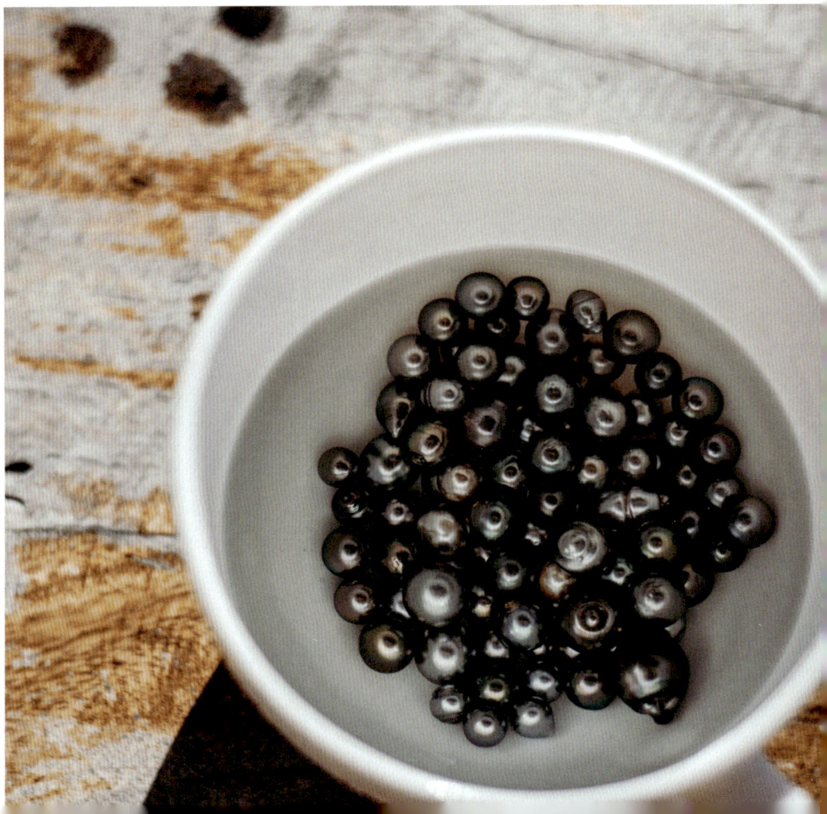

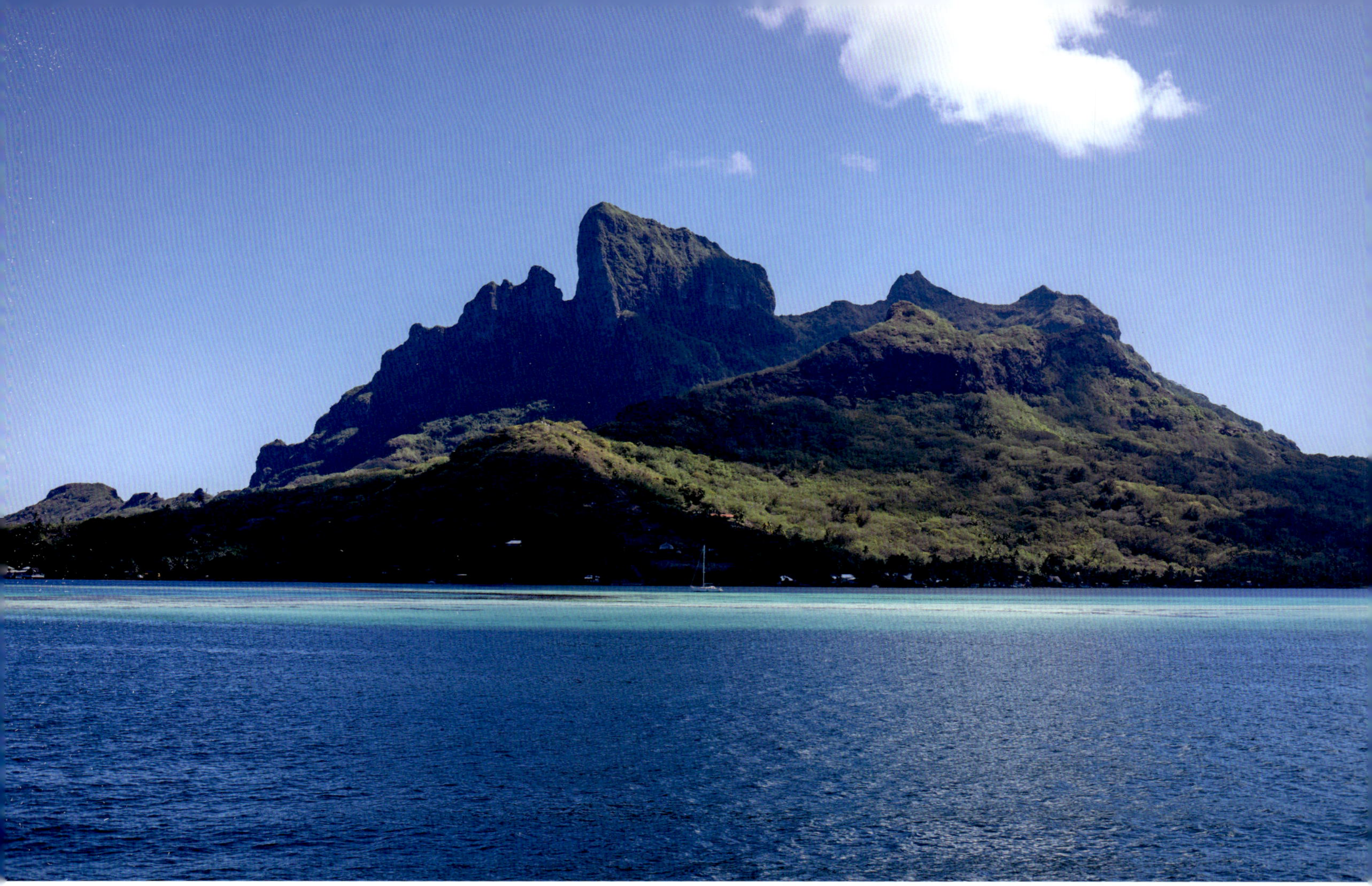
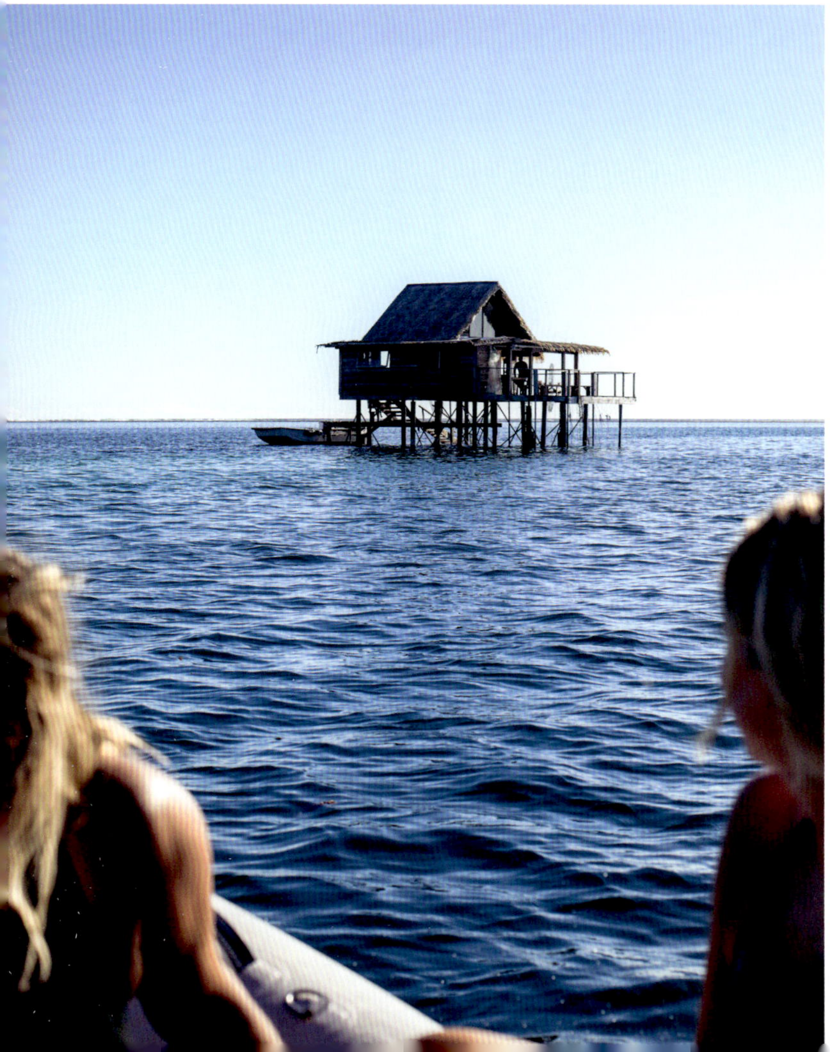
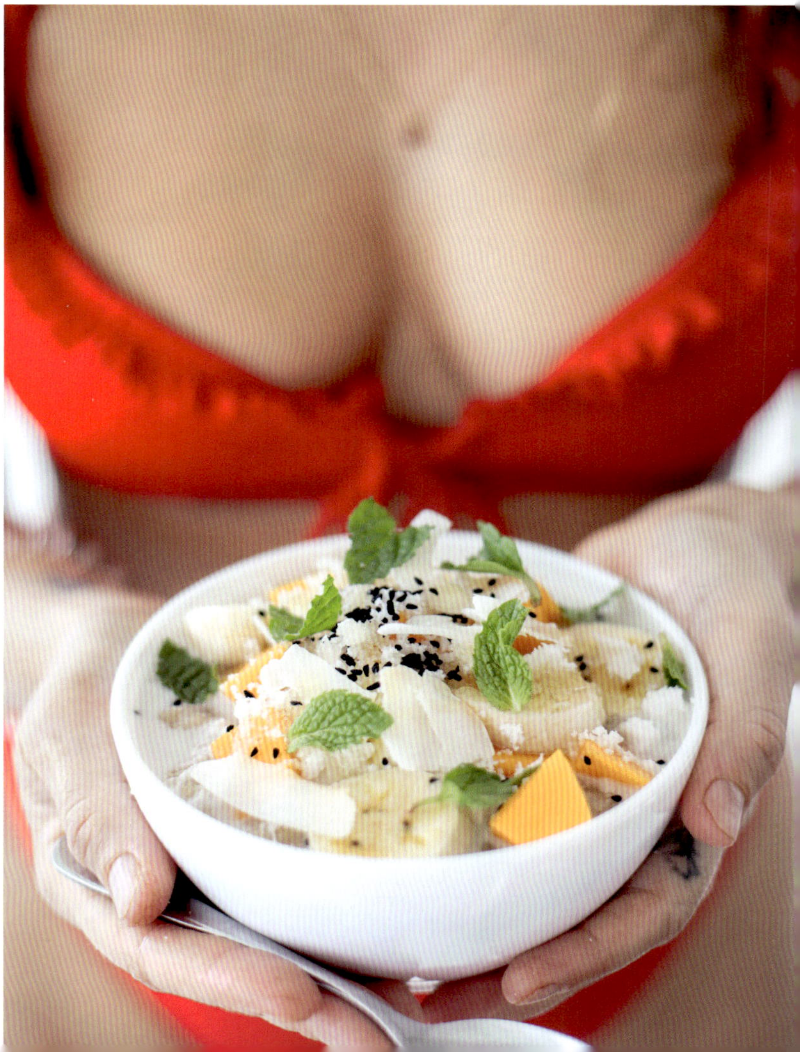

dragon where the knife-edge ridge leads to a stone plateau.

The legendary lagoon of Bora Bora is blue in every imaginable shade, it varies in depth between hundreds of feet and just a few inches deep and has a corresponding color for every gradient. The water is serenely calm and perfect for wading in the shallows or snorkeling on the well-preserved reefs. If you are lucky you may spot a manta ray in the deeper waters as you swim. These enormous rays are filter feeders and have no particular interest in humans but they do come to the reef so that fish can help clean their thick skin. Spotting a manta ray at one of these "cleaning stations" is a rare opportunity to see one of these majestic animals stick around long enough to be properly observed.

With fancy hotels comes fancy dining and sailors can take advantage of the superb culinary offerings at some of the more famous establishments on the island: Four Seasons has Arii Moana, the Conrad has Iriatai, and the InterContinental has Le Corail. Also on the island are pleasant establishments outside the hotel developments: visit Bloody Mary's or the charming Bora Bora Yacht Club for Bora island vibes. At Bloody Mary's you will be serenaded by local musicians nightly and have an incredible selection of fish and meats prepared on the grill right by the bar. Their drink special is obviously a Bloody Mary but don't let the predictability of it deter you, it's really delicious.

MAUPITI

Sitting 28 nautical miles west of Bora Bora is the island of Maupiti, often referred to as 'little Bora Bora' for its geographic similarities, but culturally the two islands sit an ocean apart. Maupiti has none of the luxurious hotels that ring the lagoon at Bora Bora and the culture of the island is a little more relaxed because of it. Maupiti has only one passage into the protected lagoon, which must be navigated with care—the channel is narrow and can become unnavigable during rough seas when large swells block the entrance.

Once safe at anchor inside the lagoon, dinghy ashore to explore. The best way to get around Maupiti is by bicycle, which can be rented from the garage with the woodworking tools just a little south of the red steepled church along the main road. The one road that circles the island is only a one hour ride and a perfect activity to get to know Maupiti. At Terei'a Beach, Chez Mimi offers grilled fish that is served to you on picnic tables. The swimming nearby is more like floating in shallow water, just deep enough to cool off. It stays shallow all the way across and you can walk through from this beach across the lagoon to Motu Auira. There are trails around the *motu* to the far beach on the outer reef, or head towards the hilltop for a sweeping view of Maupiti peak and the shallow lagoon that you crossed to get here.

There is also a hiking trail from town that takes you to the top of the peak on Maupiti. From the trailhead near the municipal market and post office, you will follow switchbacks

---

LITERATURE

Jack London wrote extensively about his time here in The Cruise of the Snark. *He built a 45 foot sailboat in California to travel the world and made the difficult crossing from Hawaii in 1906 with no working engine. He describes a harrowing moment sailing inside the lagoon between Raiatea and Taha'a in a local boat returning to his Snark after a memorable reception visiting a village on Taha'a. His story highlights both the wonder of sailing in these incredible lagoons and the potential dangers that lay waiting in a sudden squall and lee reef. Not just this chapter but the entire book leading up to it is worth a read for any sailor that plans to voyage here, it gives a good perspective on just how remote these islands are.*

up the steep hillside until the trail devolves into a scramble with fixed ropes to help you up the rocks. The view from the top is legendary and a great location to view the beauty and protection of the lagoon with its dendritic patterns of coral branching between the mainland and the *motus*. Looking out, you see the Pacific Ocean disappear unbroken on every horizon.

~

Sailing the Leeward Islands provides once-in-a-lifetime moments every day. Between the wildlife, culture, and geography, there is hardly time to take it all in. Sail here and you will make the time, each day will feel like a week's worth of experiences and each week will feel like it flew by in an instant. One moment you'll be in the water with stingrays, the next on a mountain peak looking down at your boat, and before you know it sailing through a coral pass and headed for the next island across the unfathomable depths of the South Pacific.

The pearl of the Pacific— the very name of Bora Bora is synonymous with exotic adventures at the end of the world.

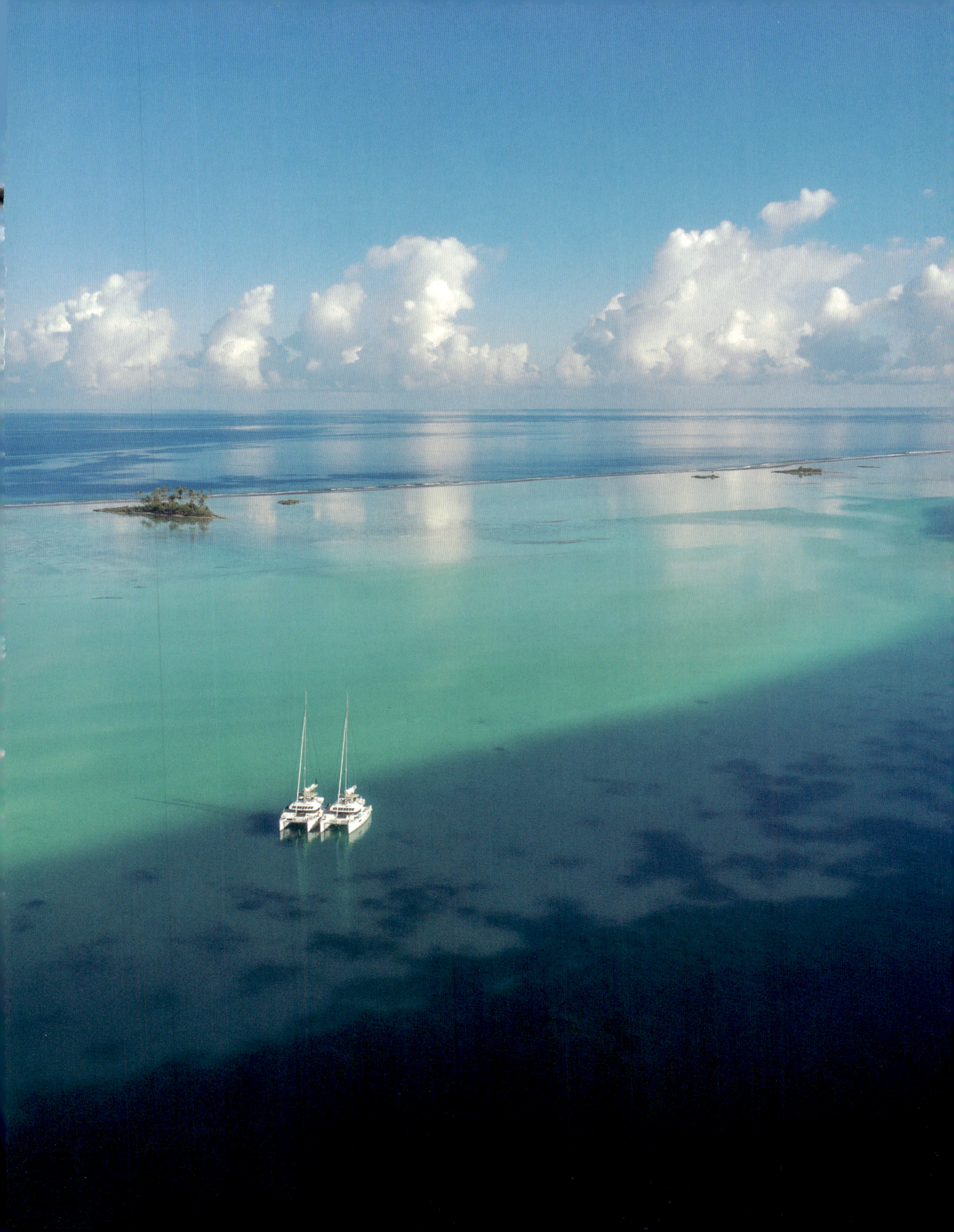

CAPTAIN'S NOTES *LEEWARD ISLANDS*

RECOMMENDED ITINERARY

Uturoa, Raiatea
6° 43' 18" S, 151° 26' 50" W
The main town on Raiatea has good provisioning and a few marinas, with berths available and repair facilities for sailboats. The pier is available for public use if you need to quickly stop into the market just across the street. Moorings are available northeast of the town along the reef.

Motu Mahaea, Taha'a
16° 38' 22" S, 151° 25' 41" W
This large, open anchorage has depths for any size boat but is particularly well protected for shoal-draft boats, which can tuck up onto the sand shelf.

Coral River, Motu Tautau, Taha'a
16° 36' 15" S, 151° 33' 28" W
Anchor north of the resort on the second step of the sand shelf in 2 fathoms of water. Do not anchor directly off the resort, where an undersea power cable runs from Taha'a.

Taurere, Bora Bora
16° 31' 49" S, 151° 42' 24" W
Moor in a large field of well-protected moorings for exquisite views of Bora Bora from within its legendary lagoon. A steep sandbank leaves very shallow water close to the motu, which makes for nice swimming in the warm ocean water.

Maupiti
16° 26' 49" S, 152° 14' 40" W
Entering Maupiti should be attempted only when conditions are favorable. Swell over 2 meters can completely close out the only channel and make passage untenable. Once inside, there are nice options for anchoring in the sand around the lagoon and a well-marked channel connecting the anchorages. Anchor just north of the town and you can leave your dinghy on the floating pier that is north of the red-roofed church when you go to explore.

Fare, Huahine Nui
16° 42' 47" S, 151° 02' 20" W
The town of Fare has some of the best provisioning around. A large supermarket across the street from the dock is well stocked and often surrounded by local vendors selling fish and fresh produce. Moorings are available here, or make use of sandy anchorage areas near town. The yacht club sells giant bags of ice and has a dinghy dock.

RECOMMENDED ANCHORAGES

To'opua, Bora Bora
Anapa Pearl Farm
Motu Vaiorea, Huahini Ita

ITINERARY DURATION

7 to 14 days recommended

PREVAILING WIND

The Leeward Islands' prevailing winds are east-southeast, with an average force of 4 to 5 on the Beaufort scale. With these conditions, the sea can be choppy, with a swell of 1–1.5 meters. A significantly stronger southeast wind, known locally as the *Maraamu*, tends to blow only in winter, between June and August. The *Maaramu* brings larger swells in open water.

SEASON

The rainy and warm season runs from November to April, and the dry and cool(er) season from May to October, with stronger winds. The best weather for sailing comes in the fall, in April and May, and the spring in September and October.

GOOD TO KNOW

Wildlife
While locals will be quick to tell you that the sharks are all friendly in the Leeward Islands—and shark attacks are rare, with falling coconuts far more deadly—it is still worth considering that these are large predators that have very sharp teeth! You will very likely see sharks while snorkeling, so be mentally prepared and know how to behave around them. If you are lucky enough to come across whales while sailing, never approach closer than 50 meters and always from behind if possible, to give them the opportunity to swim away easily or dive. If they approach your boat on their own, be sure to keep your engines off, and if they approach you while you are swimming be courteous, hold your position, and never swim between a young calf and its mother.

Anchoring in lagoons
The amazing protection of the lagoons around the Leeward Islands can also make for tricky anchoring. Much of the lagoon on each island is far too deep for most boats to anchor, and rises steeply to the island and the reef, leaving no suitable zone for spending the night. Most of the good anchorages are against the outer reef, on sand shelves that can also be spotted with dangerous coral heads.

Magnetic variance
Magnetic Declination: +12° (EAST)

MAUPITI

N W E S

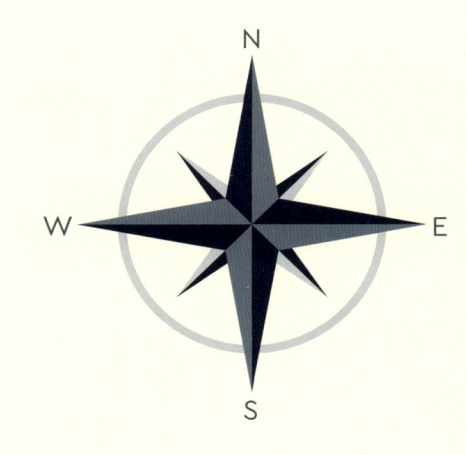

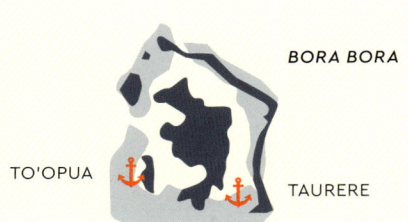

TUPAI

SOUTH PACIFIC OCEAN

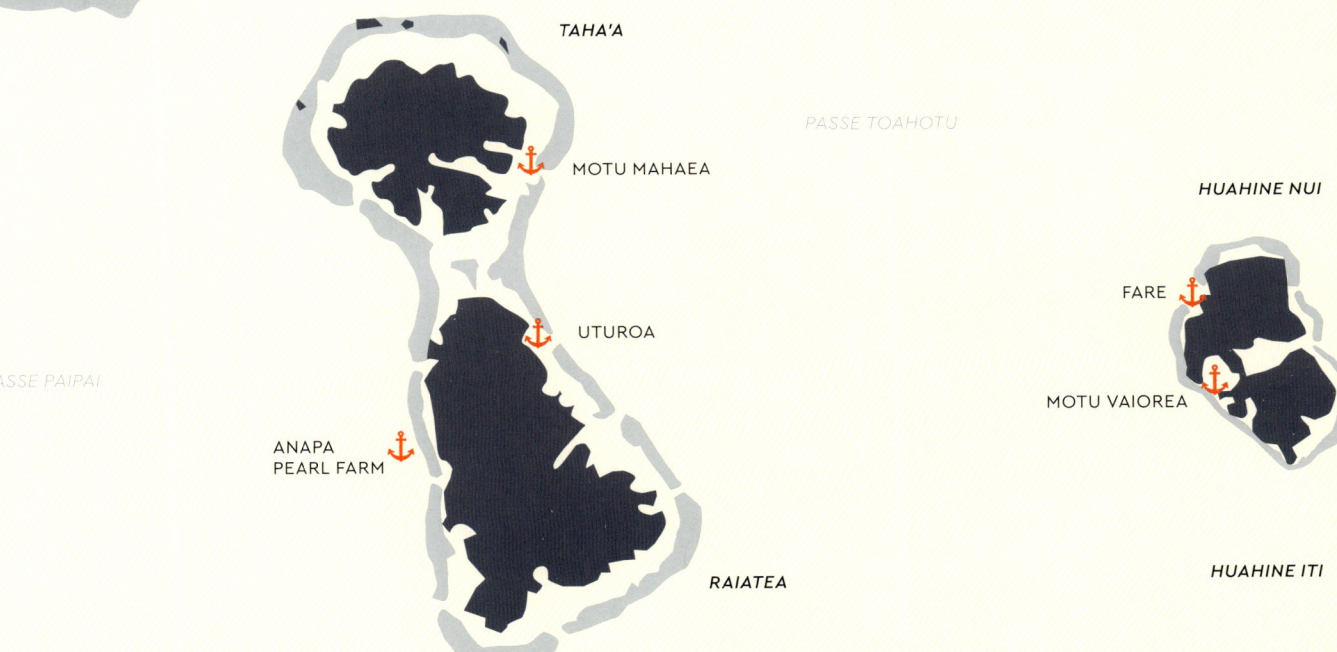

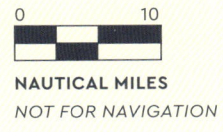

BORA BORA

TO'OPUA TAURERE

TAHA'A

MOTU MAHAEA

PASSE TOAHOTU

HUAHINE NUI

FARE

UTUROA

MOTU VAIOREA

PASSE PAIPAI

ANAPA
PEARL FARM

RAIATEA

HUAHINE ITI

0 — 10
NAUTICAL MILES
NOT FOR NAVIGATION

SAILING THE SEAS
A VOYAGER'S GUIDE TO OCEANIC GETAWAYS

This book was conceived, edited, and designed by gestalten.

Edited by Robert Klanten and Lincoln Dexter
Contributing Editor: Sailing Collective

Text and preface by Dayyan Armstrong and Ross Beane

Images by Dayyan Armstrong

Additional Images by Ross Beane, Sidney Bensimon, Eva Mrak-Blumberg, Ashley Camper, Matt Glueckert, Bronwyn Knight, Phillip Mahoney, Ingrid Sophie Schram, Stefan Wigand, and Philipp Zechner / Alamy Stock Photo (pp. 24–25), Suzy Bennett / Alamy Stock Photo (p. 204), Reinhard Dirscherl / Alamy Stock Photo (p. 211 top)

Special Thanks: Sarah Rowland for copy editing assistance, the Sailing Collective crew for their leadership in creating innovative travel, and most of all, the travelers who have trusted in us to lead their voyages throughout the world.
For more information visit www.sailingcollective.com
Instagram: @thesailingcollective

Design, layout and cover by Sophie Charlotte Andresen
Map design by Sophie Charlotte Andresen

Typefaces: Narziss Regular von Hubert Jocham, Bell MT Pro by Monotype Design Studio and Richard Austin, and Cera Pro by Jakob Runge

Photo editor: Madeline Dudley-Yates

Illustrations by Natalka Dmitrova

Printed by Schleunungdruck GmbH, Marktheidenfeld
Made in Germany
Published by gestalten, Berlin 2020
ISBN 978-3-89955-997-2

5th printing, 2024

© Die Gestalten Verlag GmbH & Co. KG, Berlin 2020

All rights reserved. No part of this publication may be reproduced or transmitted in any form or by any means, electronic or mechanical, including photocopy or any storage and retrieval system, without permission in writing from the publisher.

Respect copyrights, encourage creativity!

For more information, and to order books, please visit www.gestalten.com

Bibliographic information published by the Deutsche Nationalbibliothek. The Deutsche Nationalbibliothek lists this publication in the Deutsche Nationalbibliografie; detailed bibliographic data is available online at www.dnb.de

This book was printed on paper certified according to the standards of the FSC®.

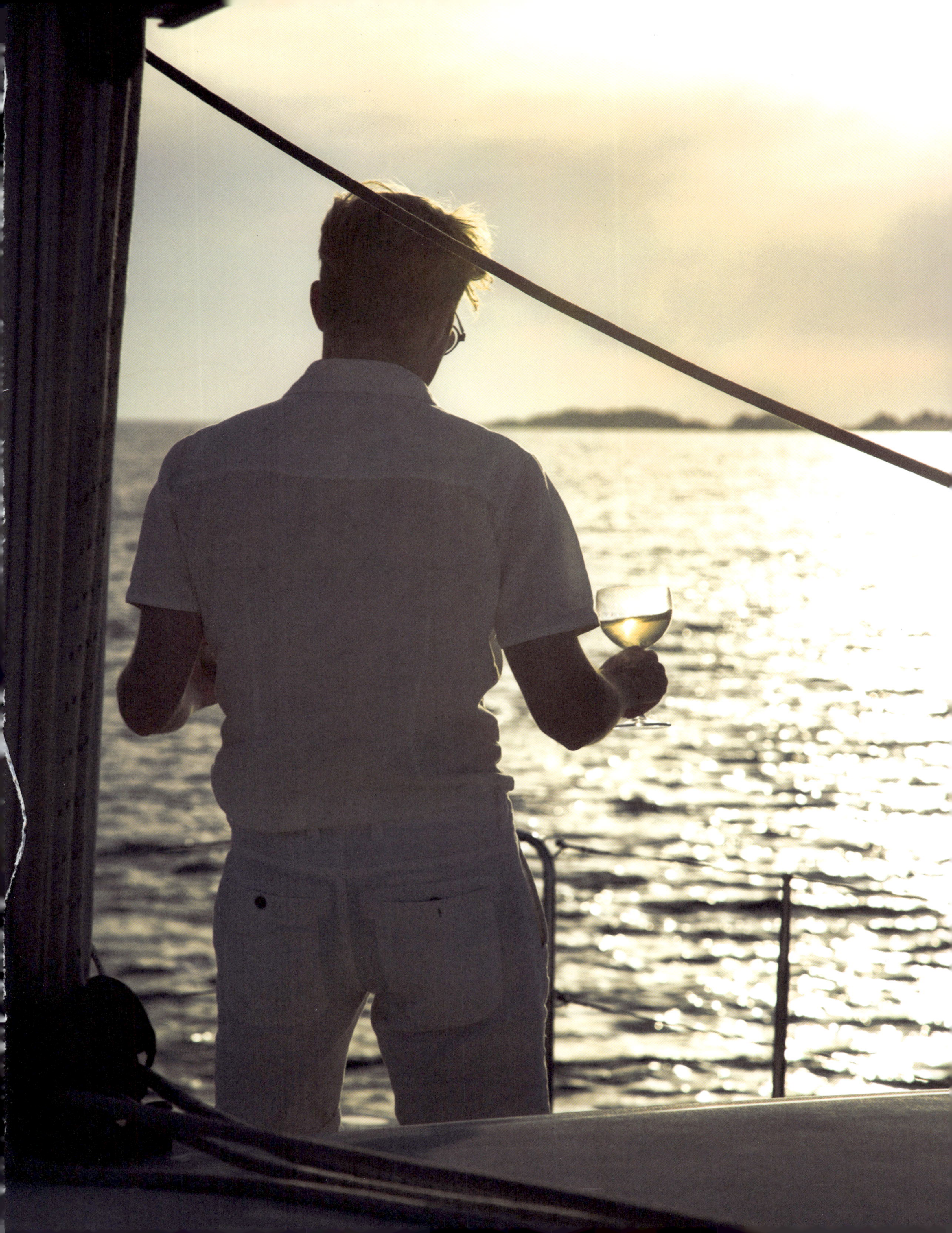

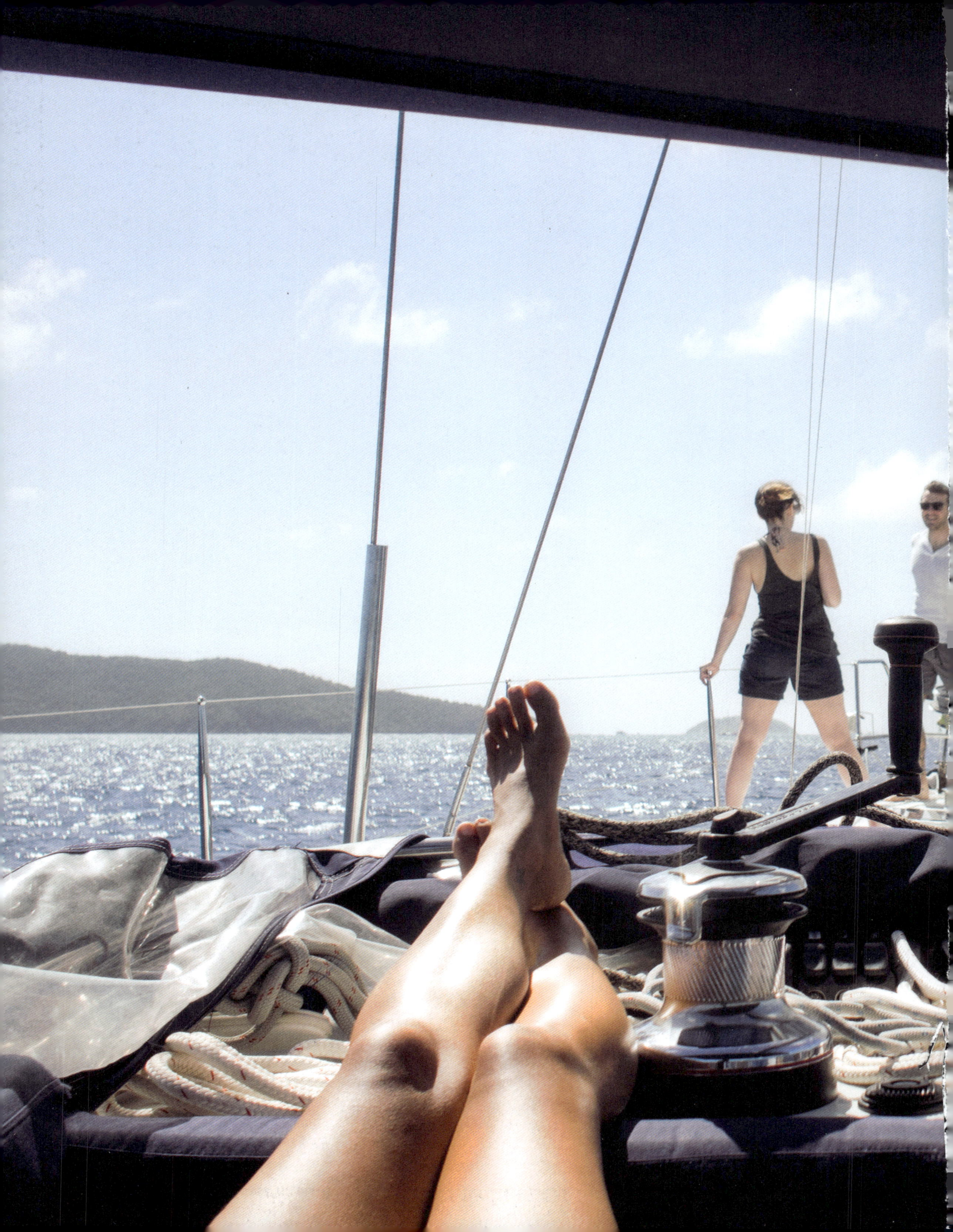